WEBSTER'S NEW WORLD™

DICTIONARY

— of —

COMPUTER TERMS

SIXTH EDITION

By Bryan Pfaffenberger, Ph.D.

Webster's New World™

Dictionary of Computer Terms, 6th Edition

Macmillan General Reference
A Simon & Schuster Macmillan Company
1633 Broadway
New York, NY 10019-6785

Macmillan Publishing books may be purchased for business or
sales promotional use. For information please write: Special
Markets Department, Macmillan Publishing USA,
1633 Broadway, New York, NY 10019.

A Webster's New World™ Book

Library of Congress Catalog Card Number: 97-80220

ISBN: 0-02-861890-4

Manufactured in the United States of America

    3 4 5 6 7   8 99 00 1 02

Dedication

To my family

About the Author

Bryan Pfaffenberger, the author of more than 50 books on personal computing and the Internet, teaches technical writing and the sociology of technology at the University of Virginia's pioneering Division of Technology, Culture, and Communication. When he's not doing such serious things, he enjoys backpacking, wine tasting, anime, and driving his white Probe GT. He lives with his family in the country near Charlottesville, Virginia.

Introduction

We live in a computerized society—and, increasingly, knowledge of computer terminology paves the way to personal and professional advancement.

- Commerce on the Internet, currently valued at less than US$1 billion annually, is projected to grow to as much as $5 to $10 billion by the year 2000. If you want to be part of this, you'll need to know why *strong authentication* is necessary, how to tell the difference between a *digital signature* and a *certificate*, and why *cookies* are needed to implement virtual *shopping carts.*

- Computer knowledge and expertise bring big payoffs in the job market. The biggest pay increases in 1996, according to a *Money Magazine* survey, went to computer workers at all levels. In today's job market, though, yesterday's computer skills won't pay off. You'll be wise to know the difference between *Java* and *Javascript*, why *virtual private networks (VPN)* are replacing *leased lines*, and whether *ActiveX* or *JavaBeans* represents the best choice for adding active content to a Web page.

- Currently, the Internet is used by an estimated 40 to 45 million people in the U.S. alone; these numbers are projected to grow to 100 million by 1998. A major impetus is electronic mail, which is increasingly a favorite method of staying in touch. Unless you want to be left in the dark, you'll be wise to know what people are talking about when they begin that litany of acronyms: *S/MIME, POP, IMAP, X.509, LDAP*, and many more.

- Already, nearly 40 percent of U.S. homes have a personal computer and that number is growing at a 10 to 15 percent annual clip. If you're thinking about purchasing a computer, or upgrading an existing one, you'll need to choose between such obscure things as *EDO RAM* and *SDRAM,* a *Pentium Pro* and *Pentium II*, and—if you want a *SCSI* device—whether you need *Fast SCSI, Wide SCSI,* or *Ultra Wide SCSI.* If your head's spinning, welcome to the club.

This book can help. Offering thousands of definitions in every area of computer and Internet technology, this book defines terms in clear, plain English. What's more, it goes beyond merely defining the terms; you'll find additional background information that will prove invaluable in understanding *why* a particular term is important and *how* it relates to others. For example, the *ActiveX* definition explains what ActiveX is—and *also* explains how ActiveX relates to *Java*, and more broadly, to competitive trends in the Internet market.

You can use this book as a learning tool by following the extensive cross-references. For example, take a look at the definition of *Unix,* where you'll learn why some people think that this *operating system* has a future. Follow the cross-reference to *Rhapsody,* and you'll learn about the recent troubles at Apple Computer—in particular, the failure of *MacOS* to implement a vital feature called *preemptive multitasking.* Follow that link, and you'll learn a great deal more about why *Microsoft Windows 95* and *Microsoft Windows NT* are so successful.

Special features help make this book easier to use. Some words have more than one sense; if so, they're numbered. Where it's not obvious, you'll find abbreviations that indicate whether a word's a noun (n.) or verb (v.).

Just by exploring cross-references in this way, you can round out your knowledge in a wide variety of computer- and Internet-related subjects. Learn about artificial intelligence, object-oriented programming (OOP), application programming interfaces (API), control structures, computer security, computer network architectures, public-key cryptography—this book will take you where you want to go.

Bryan Pfaffenberger
Charlottesville, Virginia

Acknowledgements

No work of this scope could have been undertaken without a great deal of help, and this book is no exception. If readers find excellence here, credit goes to Marie Butler-Knight's vision and guidance. I would like to give special thanks to Faithe Wempen, development editor, whose painstaking critique of the manuscript was founded on her dedication to the reader's needs as well as her impressive technical expertise. It was a special joy, too, to work with editors Sydney Jones and Judy Brunetti whose eye for detail matches their love for the English language. Layout technicians Holly Wittenberg and Dana Davis, and proofreaders Linda Quigley, Angel Perez, and Natalie Hollifield worked long, tedious hours to make sure that this book is as accurate as we can make it. Ultimately, though, the responsibility for any errors or omissions you might find is mine and mine alone, so please address your ire to me (bp@virginia.edu); you may very well find your contribution reflected in the next edition of this work!

Symbols

@ In an e-mail address, a symbol used to separate the user name from the name of the computer on which the user's mailbox is stored (for example, frodo@bagend.org). Pronounced "at."

@ function Pronounced "at function." See *built-in function.*

^ See *caret.*

0.25 micron technology An advanced submicron technology that is capable of reducing the distance between gates (switching devices) to one-fourth of a *micron.* This technology is needed for today's fastest *microprocessors,* which can operate at speeds of 300 *MHz* and higher, perhaps as high as 700 MHz.

0.35 micron technology A submicron technology that reduces the distance between gates (switching devices) to approximately one-third of a *micron.* This technology can produce *microprocessors* capable of running at 233 *MHz* or 266 MHz, but *0.25 micron technology* is needed for speeds of *300* MHz and higher.

0.5-micron technology A standard submicron technology that places switching devices within as little as 0.5 micron of each other, producing *microprocessors* capable of running at speeds of up to 200 *MHz.*

100% column graph A *column graph* that resembles a pie graph in that each "slice" of the column displays the relative percentage of that data item compared to the total. See *stacked column graph.*

100% Pure Java A certification from *JavaSoft,* the *Sun Microsystems* venture founded to promote the Java programming language, that a given *Java* product conforms to the current *cross-platform* Java specification, contained in the current *Java development kit (JDK),* and will therefore execute on any platform for which a Java *interpreter* has been developed. The 100% Pure Java program is intended to protect Java's "write-once, run anywhere" philosophy against proprietary versions of the language, which could contain extensions that would restrict Java programs to execution on a single platform.

100 Base-T   An *Ethernet* local area network (LAN) capable of transmitting 100 megabits of data per second via *twisted-pair* cable. Synonymous with *Fast Ethernet*.

101-key keyboard   See *extended keyboard*.

104-key keyboard   A keyboard that contains three additional keys besides the ones on the *extended keyboard*. The additional keys vary by manufacturer. The Microsoft Natural keyboard, for example, contains extra keys that perform special functions in *Windows 95*. Gateway 2000, a leading computer manufacturer, also has a 104-key keyboard, with the additional keys used for programming keyboard *macros*.

10 Base–2   An *Ethernet local area network (LAN)* capable of transmitting 10 megabits of data per second via thin *coaxial cables,* to a maximum length of 200 meters.

10 Base–5   An *Ethernet local area network (LAN)* capable of transmitting 10 megabits of data per second via thick *coaxial cables,* to a maximum length of 500 meters.

10 Base–T   An *Ethernet local area network (LAN)* capable of transmitting 10 megabits of data per second via *twisted-pair* cabling.

10x   In *CD-ROM drives,* a drive that can transfer data at up to approximately 1500 kilobytes per second, roughly ten times as fast as the first CD-ROM drives.

128-bit video adapter   A *video adapter* with an *internal data bus* 128 bits wide, making it the fastest kind of video adapter available for personal computer *monitors* today. A 128-bit video adapter can significantly speed up *graphics*-intensive tasks such as *computer-aided design (CAD)* and animation.

12x   In *CD-ROM drives,* a drive that can transfer data at up to approximately 1800 kilobytes per second, roughly 12 times as fast as the first CD-ROM drives.

12x minimum/16x maximum CD-ROM drive   A *CD-ROM drive* marketed with an honest description of its processing capabilities; such a drive employs *constant angular velocity (CAV),* in which the disk spins at a constant speed, so that data is read more quickly from the inner tracks than the outer tracks. Many CAV drives that are ostensibly *16x* drives are outperformed by *12x* drives that employ *constant linear velocity (CLV),* in which the drive increases the rotational speed of the disc as the read head moves to the disc's outer edge.

14-inch monitor   A *monitor* with an overall diagonal *display* measurement of an ostensible 14 inches. In reality, the edges of the display are hidden by the monitor housing, and the area of the screen actually used measures 12.8 to 13.5 inches diagonally. 14-inch monitors are too small for the high *resolutions* and large screen areas that *Graphical User Interfaces (GUIs)* demand.

15-inch monitor   A *monitor* with an overall diagonal *display* measurement of 15 inches and an area measuring 13.3 to 14 inches diagonally actually available for display tasks. Though 15-inch monitors are better than *14-inch monitors, 17-inch monitors* are much preferred over both.

16450   The *Universal Asynchronous Receiver/Transmitter (UART)* chip found on IBM Personal Computer AT machines and compatibles. The 16450 can handle faster *modems* than its predecessor in the *8250,* but is technically inferior to the *16550A* because of its tendency to cause *overrun errors* under fast data-transfer conditions. The *16550A* UART is needed for today's high-speed modems.

16550A   The *Universal Asynchronous Receiver/Transmitter (UART)* chip found on fast, modern computer systems. As the state-of-the-art UART, the 16550A has a much larger storage buffer than the obsolete *8250* and *16450,* making it less prone to *overrun errors.*

16-bit application   In Microsoft Windows, an application that is designed to use the 16-bit processing mode of Intel microprocessors. Most 16-bit Windows applications are designed to run with the popular *Microsoft Windows 3.1* operating system. *Microsoft Windows 95,* the newest consumer version of Windows, is a hybrid 16/32 bit operating system that is capable of running 16-bit applications as well as newer *32-bit applications,* which take full advantage of Intel's *32-bit microprocessors.*

16-bit color   A *color depth* of 16 *bits,* which enables the display of up to 65,536 colors. See *8-bit color* and *24-bit color.*

16-bit microprocessor   A *microprocessor* that can handle two *bytes* of data at a time, making it significantly faster than an *8-bit microprocessor.* The *Intel 8086* and *Intel 80286* are 16-bit microprocessors. See *external data bus, internal data bus,* and *register.*

16-bit operating system   An *operating system* that employs a *microprocessor's* 16-bit processing mode, in which two *bytes* of data can be processed simultaneously. *Microsoft Windows 3.1* is a 16-bit operating system. See *32-bit operating system*.

16-bit sound board   A *sound board* capable of processing and reproducing sounds and music recorded with 16-bit *resolution*— the resolution of the *Compact Disc-Digital Audio (CD-DA)* standard. Most 16-bit sound boards can process sounds recorded at resolutions lower than 16 bits, too.

16x   In *CD-ROM drives,* a drive that can transfer data at up to approximately 2400 kilobytes per second, roughly 16 times as fast as the first CD-ROM drives. 16x drives that use *constant angular velocity (CAV)* may be slower than *12x* drives that use *constant linear velocity (CLV)*.

17-inch monitor   A *monitor* with an overall diagonal *display* measurement of 17 inches and an area measuring 15.4 to 16.6 inches diagonally actually available for display tasks. 17-inch monitors are becoming the standard for *desktop computers,* since they allow high *resolutions* and make it easy to see two or more windows at the same time.

2$^1/_2$-inch disk   A defunct *floppy disk* standard once used on a few Zenith *portable computers*. Many *hard disks* for *portable computers* are 2$^1/_2$ inches in diameter, though.

20-inch monitor   A *monitor* with an overall diagonal *display* measurement of 20 inches and an area measuring approximately 19 inches diagonally actually available for display tasks. 20-inch monitors are somewhat less expensive than *21-inch monitors* but can still display two pages of a document simultaneously, making them appropriate for *desktop publishing (DTP)* applications.

21-inch monitor   A *monitor* with an overall diagonal *display* measurement of 21 inches and an area measuring 20 inches diagonally actually available for display tasks. 21-inch monitors are ideal for *desktop publishing (DTP)* and document imaging applications, in which a two-page layout needs to be viewed.

24-bit color   A *color depth* of 24 bits, which enables the display of more than 16 million colors simultaneously. With a *video adapter* and *monitor* capable of processing and displaying 24-bit color, users can view beautiful, photographic-quality images at high *resolutions*. Displaying 24-bit color in *resolutions* higher than standard *VGA* (650 x 480) requires 2M or more of *video memory.*

2X   See *double-speed drive.*

3¹/₂-inch disk   A *floppy disk,* originally developed by Sony Corporation, used for magnetically storing data. The disk is enclosed in a hard plastic case with a sliding metal access door. High-density 3¹/₂-inch disks, capable of storing 1.44M, are most common. Older, double-density disks hold 720K, while new, somewhat rare 3¹/₂-inch disks store 2.88M. *Macintosh* 3¹/₂-inch disks hold either 800K (*double density*) or 1.4M (*high density*).

30-pin SIMM   A small rectangular circuit board containing memory chips that is designed to press into a *30-pin SIMM slot.* SIMM is an acronym for *single in-line memory module (SIMM),* a memory upgrade system that represents a major improvement over its predecessor (inserting individual memory chips into individual sockets). Although obsolete, these chips can still be used by purchasing a 30-to-72-pin SIMM converter, an accessory that modifies the 30-pin SIMM socket.

30-pin SIMM slot   A socket, usually on the *motherboard,* for 30-pin *single in-line memory modules (SIMMs).* Such SIMMs are obsolete and have been replaced with 72-pin versions. See *72-pin SIMM slot.*

32-bit application   A program designed to take full advantage of the processing capabilities of *32-bit microprocessors,* which can handle four *bytes* of data at a time. *Microsoft Windows 3.1* is a *16-bit operating system (OS)* and cannot handle 32-bit programs without modification. *Microsoft Windows 95* and *Microsoft Windows NT* can handle 32-bit applications.

32-bit computer   A computer that is capable of processing 32 bits of information (four bytes) at a time, thanks to a data bus that is 32 bits wide.

32-bit microprocessor   A *microprocessor* that can handle four *bytes* of data at a time, making it much faster than *16-bit microprocessors.* 32-bit microprocessors like the *Intel 486* and *Intel 386DX* have *internal data buses* 32 bits wide that connect to 32-bit *external data buses,* while the *Intel 386SX,* another 32-bit microprocessor, is a compromise design that connects to a less expensive 16-bit external data bus.

32-bit operating system   An *operating system* that takes full advantage of the *32-bit microprocessors,* which can perform operations on 32 bits of information at a time. Among the many advantages of 32-bit operating systems are their ability to set up a *flat address space,* in which the operating system can map out the available memory without restrictions imposed by segmentation (see *segmented memory architecture*). *Microsoft Windows NT* and *Unix* are true 32-bit operating systems; *Microsoft Windows 95* is a hybrid, retaining some 16-bit code so that users can continue to run their Windows 3.1 applications.

32-bit video adapter   An obsolete type of *video adapter* with a *graphics co-processor* that is capable of processing 32 bits of data at a time. 32-bit video adapters cannot handle the high resolutions that make *Microsoft Windows 95* easy to use, and are too slow for most modern *graphics* tasks. *64-bit video adapters* and *128-bit video adapters* have replaced 32-bit video adapters.

3-D graph   See *three-dimensional graph.*

4X   See *quad-speed drive.*

5^1/$_4$-inch disk   A *floppy disk* enclosed in a flexible plastic *shell.* The most widely used floppy disk before 1987, 5^1/$_4$-inch disks have been almost entirely replaced by *3^1/$_2$-inch disks.*

64-bit microprocessor   A *microprocessor* that can handle eight *bytes* of data at the same time, and the fastest microprocessor ever mass-produced for personal computer use—much faster than *8-, 16-,* or *32-bit microprocessors.* The *Pentium* is a 64-bit microprocessor whose 64-bit *internal data bus* connects to a 32-bit *external data bus.* The difference in bus width at the 64-bit level does not cause a significant performance decrease.

64-bit operating system   An *operating system* that is capable of taking full advantage of a *64-bit microprocessor's* data-processing capabilities. A full 64-bit microprocessor features a 64-bit *external data bus,* bringing impressive gains in *input/output (I/O)* performance. Relatively little software is currently available for 64-bit operating systems, which are mainly used for engineering and science applications, but it is likely that 64-bit Web servers will become more common as *Internet* usage increases.

64-bit video adapter   A *video adapter* with a *graphics coprocessor* that is capable of processing 32 bits of data at a time. Though *128-bit video adapters* are faster, 64-bit video adapters represent the best balance between cost and performance for *personal computers* today.

680x0   The generic designation of the *Motorola* microprocessor architecture that is *binary compatible* with Macintosh software. See *Motorola 68000, Motorola 68020, Motorola 68030,* and *Motorola 68040.*

6845   A *video controller* chip that has appeared on or been simulated on all *video adapters* since IBM's early 1980s *MDA* standard. *Video drivers* can program the 6845's *registers* and define the characteristics of the video signal the 6845 sends to the screen.

6X   In *CD-ROM drives,* a drive that can transfer data at up to 600K per second, six times as fast as the first CD-ROM drives.

72-pin SIMM   A small rectangular *circuit board* containing *memory* chips that is designed to press into a 72-*pin SIMM slot.* SIMM is an acronym for *single in-line memory module (SIMM),* a memory upgrade system that represents a major improvement over its predecessor (inserting individual memory chips into individual sockets). 72-pin SIMMS are the standard for today's computers. For use with *Pentium* microprocessors, SIMMs must be upgraded two at a time because each SIMM makes available only half of the required 64-bit memory path. See *DIMM.*

72-pin SIMM slot   A socket, usually on the *motherboard,* for 72-pin *single in-line memory modules (SIMMs).* These slots enable users to upgrade memory capacity by inserting *72-pin SIMMs;* the chip is inserted at an angle and then snapped into place.

765   A *chip* that controls the flow of *data* and instructions between the *central processing unit (CPU)* and the *floppy disk drive.* The 765, because it is easily programmed with *BIOS* instructions, has been used in personal computers for many years.

8.3 filename   A filename corresponding to the standard *MS-DOS* file-naming conventions, which restrict *file names* to 8 characters and optional *extensions* to 3 characters.

80x8   The generic designation of early *Intel* microprocessors. See *Intel 8086* and *Intel 8088.*

80x86   The generic designation of the following family of *Intel* microprocessors: *Intel 80286, Intel 80386,* and the several types of *Intel 486.*

8250   The *Universal Asynchronous Receiver/Transmitter (UART)* chip found on the original IBM Personal Computer, the IBM Personal Computer XT, and compatible machines. The 8250, now obsolete, will experience *overrun errors* if used with modern machines, since it cannot handle the fast data transfers they demand.

83-key keyboard   The type of *keyboard* found on the original IBM Personal Computer. The 83-key keyboard was panned because of its odd key layout. It was replaced by the *AT keyboard*.

84-key keyboard   See *AT keyboard*.

8514/A   An IBM *video standard* for 1024 *pixel* by 768 line *resolution*. Largely because it was designed for the doomed *Micro Channel Architecture (MCA)*, 8514/A is obsolete.

8-bit color   A *color depth* of 8 *bits*, which enables the display of up to 256 colors. See *16-bit color, 24-bit color*.

8-bit microprocessor   A *microprocessor* that can handle only one *byte* of data at a time. The *Intel 8088*, used in the first IBM personal computers, is an 8-bit microprocessor and has an *internal data bus* 8 bits wide.

8-bit sound board   An type of inexpensive *sound board* that can process and generate sounds recorded with 8-bit resolution. 8-bit boards do a good job with voice and simple *MIDI* music files (such as those found in games), but *16-bit sound boards* and 32-bit sound boards provide much better sound quality.

8-bit video adapter   A color *video adapter* that can display 256 colors simultaneously.

micron technology   The most advanced submicron technology in use at this writing; it is capable of miniaturizing the basic switching components of processing chips (called gates) to one-fourth of a *micron* (one millionth of a meter). The smaller the distance between gates, the faster the semiconductor can operate. Using 0.18 micron technology, a single chip can contain as many as 125 million transistors, roughly the number found in an entire PC (including 16MB of memory, supporting chips on the motherboard, disk controllers, modem, and sound card).

AAMOF   Abbreviation for "as a matter of fact." Commonly used *abbreviation* on *Internet Relay Chat (IRC), e-mail,* and *Usenet.*

abandon   To clear a *document, spreadsheet,* or other work from the screen—and therefore from memory—without saving it to a *floppy* or *hard disk.* The work is irretrievably lost.

abbreviation   Commonly used shorthand in *Internet Relay Chat (IRC), chat rooms, e-mail,* and *Usenet.*

Common Abbreviations on Internet Relay Chat (IRC) and Usenet

Abbreviation	Meaning
AAMOF	As a matter of fact
AFAIK	As far as I know
AFK	Away from keyboard
BBIAF	Be back in a few (minutes)
BBL	Be back later
BRB	Be right back
CUL8R	See you later
DIIK	Damned if I know
EG	Evil grin
FYI	For your information
GMTA	Great minds think alike
IMHO	In my humble opinion
K	Okay
LOL	Laughing out loud
OIC	Oh, I see
PPL	People
RE	Regards
ROFL	Rolling on the floor laughing
RUMOF	Are you male or female

continues

Common Abbreviations on Internet
Relay Chat (IRC) and Usenet (cont.)

Abbreviation	Meaning
TIA	Thanks in advance
TTYL	Talk to you later
WB	Welcome back
YMMV	Your mileage may vary

abort   To cancel a *program, command,* or procedure while it's in progress. You can often abort a procedure manually, or a procedure may abort by itself because of a *bug* in the program, power failure, or other unexpected cause.

A-B roll editing   In *multimedia,* a method for creating a master edited video sequence by directing selected portions of video signals from two video sources (VCRs or camcorders) to a destination recording device, usually a VCR.

absolute address   In a *program,* specifying a location in *random-access memory (RAM)* by its address instead of using an expression to calculate the address.

absolute cell reference   A *spreadsheet cell* reference that doesn't adjust when you *copy* or move a *formula.* An absolute cell reference includes a symbol (such as $) before both the *column* letter and the *row* number (A6). Use absolute cell references when you refer to cells containing *key variables,* such as the inflation rate or a standard discount. See *relative cell reference.*

absolute link   In an *HTML* document, a *hyperlink* that fully and precisely specifies the file location of the referenced remote document. An absolute link specifies the *protocol* (such as http:// or ftp://), as well as the name of the computer and the location of the referenced file within the computer's directory structure. See *relative URL (RELURL).*

absolute path   In a *hierarchical file system,* such as MS-DOS or Unix, a *path* specification that includes all the information necessary to locate the file relative to the *root directory.* See *relative path.*

absolute value   The positive value of a number, regardless of its sign (positive or negative). The absolute value of −357, for example, is 357. In *Microsoft Excel* and many other *spreadsheet* programs, the @ABS *built-in function* returns the absolute value of a number.

Abstract Syntax Notation One (ASN.1)   An international standard that specifies how varying types of data can be coded so that applications can recognize which type of data they are dealing with. The rules that express how this coding should be done are called *Basic Encoding Rules (BER)*. Examples of data types include telephone numbers and bibliographic citations. The standard is a key part of the *OSI Protocol Suite* but has had relatively little impact on other networking standards, with the exception of e-mail protocols such as *X.400* and *X.500*.

ACAP   See *Application Configuration Access Protocol.*

Accelerated Graphics Port (AGP)   A *port* specification developed by Intel Corporation to support high-speed, high-resolution graphics, including 3-D graphics.

accelerator board   A circuit board designed to speed up some function of your computer. A *graphics accelerator board,* for example, contains a *microprocessor* that relieves the *central processing unit (CPU)* of many video chores, enabling it to get to other work sooner.

accent   A mark that forms one of the special characters of many languages. Some examples include:

ç   Cedilla

`   Grave

¯   Macron

˜   Tilde

Accented characters are included in most *font* sets, and some application programs include commands or keystrokes that insert accented characters for you. See *compose sequence* and *extended character set.*

Acceptable Use Policy (AUP)   An *Internet service provider (ISP)* policy that indicates which types of uses are permissible. Epitomized by the *AUP* of *NSFnet,* the backbone network formerly funded by the U.S. *National Science Foundation (NSF),* the AUPs of publicly funded *networks* sharply restrict commercial use. Independent ISPs often forbid abusive network behavior, such as *spamming.*

acceptance test   A final demonstration of a new *software* or *hardware* product that illustrates the product's capabilities and special features. When companies or other entities hire systems analysts or other computer consultants to do work for them, the acceptance test serves to show that the consultants have satisfied their contract obligations.

access   1. The right or ability to gain entry to a computer system and make use of its resources. 2. On a computer system, to open or retrieve any kind of data or document. 3. To retrieve *data* or *program* instructions from a *hard* or *floppy disk drive* or another computer connected to your computer by a *network* or a *modem*.

Access   See *Microsoft Access*.

access arm   See *head arm*.

access code   An identification number or *password* you use to gain access to a computer system.

access control   In a *network*, a means of ensuring the system's *security* by demanding that users supply a *login name* and *password*.

access control list (ACL)   In a *network*, a *database* that lists the valid users of the systems and the level of network access that they have been granted.

access hole   See *head access aperture*.

access privileges   On a *network*, the extent of a user's capability to use and modify *directories, files,* and *programs* located on other computers in the network. See *local area network (LAN)*.

access time   The amount of time that lapses between a request for information from *memory* and the delivery of the information. Access times apply to disks and to *random-access memory (RAM)*. RAM access times are much shorter than disk access times, so adding extra RAM can dramatically improve a computer's overall performance.

accessory slot   Synonymous with *expansion slot*.

account   In a *network*, a contractual agreement between the user and the service provider. In return for network access, the user agrees to abide by the service provider's regulations and, in some cases, pay a fee.

accounting package   A *program* or group of programs intended to help a small-business owner automate a firm's accounting procedures. Though accounting packages have grown easier to use recently, they still often require a level of accounting expertise that small-time entrepreneurs usually lack and require tedious *data* entry. See *integrated accounting package* and *modular accounting package*.

accumulator   A *register* in a *central processing unit (CPU)* that holds values to be used later in a computation. Computer multiplication, for example, frequently is done by a series of additions; an accumulator holds the intermediate values until the process is completed.

accuracy   A statement of how correct a measurement is. Accuracy is different from *precision,* which describes the number of decimal places to which a measurement is computed.

ACK   1. Commonly used abbreviation for the acknowledge character (*ASCII* code 6) in the standard ASCII character set. 2. Commonly used abbreviation for the acknowledgment message used in *handshaking* operations between two communication devices, such as *modems*.

ACL   See *access control list*.

ACM   See *Association for Computer Machinery*.

acoustic coupler   A *modem* with cups that fit around the earpiece and mouthpiece of a standard (not cellular) telephone receiver. The cups contain a *microphone* and a speaker that convert the computer's digital signals into sound, and vice versa. With the almost-universal use of *modular jacks, direct-connect modems* have supplanted acoustic modems in general use.

acoustical sound enclosure   An insulated cabinet for noisy *impact printers* that reduces the noise such *printers* make.

acronym   A new word made from the first or other important letters in a descriptive phrase; used to help people remember technical phrases. For example, *RAM* is an acronym for *random-access memory*. To pronounce acronyms, spell out the letters unless the acronym contains enough vowels to make it pronounceable as a word *(BASIC, SIMM)*.

ACT!   A *contact management program* from *Symantec* that enables businesses to create customer and client databases. Available for

Windows systems, the program contains an integrated calendar that tracks calls and alerts the user to scheduled meetings.

active area   In a *spreadsheet* document, such as a *Lotus 1-2-3* or *Microsoft Excel* worksheet, the area bounded by *cell* A1 and the lowest rightmost cell containing *data*.

active cell   In a *spreadsheet,* the *cell* in which the *cell pointer* is located. Synonymous with *current cell.*

active configuration   The way you configure a *modem,* usually with an *initialization string,* at the beginning of a communications session. The active configuration supersedes the *factory configuration* and remains in effect until you turn off the modem or *reboot* the computer.

active database   In *database management,* the *database* file in use and present in *random-access memory (RAM).*

active file   The document that appears on-screen when you're working with an application program.

active index   In *database management systems (DBMSs),* the *index* file being used to determine the order in which *data records* are displayed.

active matrix display   A full-color *liquid-crystal display (LCD)* in which each of the screen's *pixels* is controlled by its own transistor. Active matrix displays offer higher *resolution, contrast,* and *vertical refresh rate* than cheaper *passive matrix displays.* Although active matrix displays are most commonly found on laptops, the technology has matured sufficiently that larger active matrix displays have now appeared for desktop systems.

active sensing   In *multimedia,* a *Musical Instrument Digital Interface (MIDI)* message that tells a device to monitor its channels to determine whether messages occur on the channels within a predetermined time frame (called a time window).

active termination   Like *passive termination* and *forced perfect termination,* a means of ending a chain of *Small Computer System Interface (SCSI)* devices. Active termination is noted for its ability to reduce electrical interference in a long string of SCSI devices.

active window   In a *program* or *operating system* that displays multiple *windows,* the window in which the *cursor* is located and where text appears if you start typing. See *windowing environment.*

ActiveX The newest version of Microsoft Corporation's object linking and embedding *(OLE)* technology, which enables applications to communicate with each other by means of messages passed with the aid of the computer's *operating system (OS)* (see *interprocess communication [IPC]*). The previous version was called *Component Object Model (COM)*. ActiveX adds features designed to enable the distribution of executable programs, called *controls,* via the Internet. To use these controls, a computer must be running an operating system that supports OLE, such as *Microsoft Windows 3.1, Microsoft Windows 95, Microsoft Windows NT,* or *MacOS.* Unlike *Java applets,* which run in a *sandbox* that protects the computer's file system, ActiveX controls can directly affect files. For this reason, ActiveX controls are packaged with *digitally designed certificates,* which prove that the program emanates from a respectable software publisher (and will therefore presumably not do nasty things to one's computer). See *Java.*

ActiveX control An executable program that is designed to be distributed in Microsoft's *ActiveX* packaging, which includes *digitally signed certificates.* To execute ActiveX controls, the user must be running a *Web browser* that supports ActiveX, as well as an operating system that supports Microsoft's Object Linking and Embedding *(OLE)* technology for *interprocess communication (IPC)*—and in practice, that means Microsoft Windows and the *MacOS.*

activity light On the front panel of a computer's *case,* a small colored light that flickers when a *hard* or *floppy disk drive* is reading or writing data.

actuator See *head actuator.*

Ada A *high-level programming language* developed by the U.S. Department of Defense and required by the DoD for all military programming applications. Ada uses the principles of *structured programming,* including the use of program *modules* that can be compiled separately. Ada programs are designed to be highly readable so they're easy to maintain. Recent versions include ADA++, an object-oriented version of Ada, and ADA 95, the most recent version. See *compiler, high-level programming language, Modula-2, object-oriented programming (OOP) language, Pascal* and *structured programming.*

adapter 1. A *circuit board* that plugs into an *expansion slot* in a computer, giving the computer additional capabilities. Synonymous with card. Popular adapters for personal computers include *video adapters* that produce video output, memory expansion boards, internal *modems,* and *sound boards.* 2. A transformer that enables a computer or peripheral to work with line voltage that differs from its electrical requirements.

adapter segment   See *upper memory area.*

adaptive answering   In *modems,* a feature that enables a *fax modem* to determine whether an incoming call contains a fax or computer data.

Adaptive Differential Pulse Code Modulation (ADPCM) In *multimedia,* a method of digital waveform compression where the difference between successive samples (rather than their actual values) is encoded. Using ADPCM, the quantity of audio information that can be stored on a single *CD-ROM* increases from 1 hour to about 16 hours, while maintaining or improving fidelity. ADPCM is the storage technique used by *CD-ROM/XA, certificate authority (CA),* and *Compact Disc-Interactive (CD-I)* disks. See *pulse code modulation (PCM).*

ADB   See *Apple Desktop Bus.*

A/D converter   See *analog-to-digital converter.*

ADCPM   See *Adaptive Differential Pulse Code Modulation.*

add–in program   An accessory or *utility program* designed to work with and extend the capabilities of an *application* program. Add–in programs can be created by other software developers, such as Allways by Funk Software, or included with the application, such as the auditors, file viewers, and "what-if" programs included in many *spreadsheet* programs. This term is often used synonymously with *plug-in* programs, which take advantage of built–in program *hooks* to add new commands to an application's menus. Two popular programs that have such hooks are *Adobe Photoshop* and *Netscape Navigator.*

address   1. The precise location of some type of resource (such as a file, a Web site, or storage space) in a computer system or network (see *memory address*). 2. In *e-mail,* an *e-mail address.* 3. In the *Internet,* the location of a *host* on the network. See *IP address.*

addressability   A measure of *monitor* performance. Address-ability describes the number of positions on the display at which a monitor's *electron guns* can be pointed. *Dot pitch, resolution,* and *refresh rate* are more important specifications of monitor performance.

address book   In an *e-mail* program, a utility that enables users to store and retrieve *e-mail addresses* and other contact information.

address bus   An internal electronic channel from the *microprocessor* to *random-access memory (RAM),* along which the addresses of memory storage locations are transmitted. Like a post office box, each memory location has a distinct number or address; the address bus provides the means by which the *central processing unit (CPU)* can *access* the contents of every location in memory.

addressing   In *microprocessor architecture,* the method used to determine how the *operand* of an instruction is stored temporarily for processing purposes. For example, a common method is to store operands in a *register.*

address mask   See *subnet mask.*

address resolution   In a *local area network (LAN)* that is connected to the *Internet,* the automated process by which the LAN address of each workstation is converted into an *IP address.* The translation is needed because the Internet and LANs handle workstation addresses in different ways. Programs based on the *Address Resolution Protocol (ARP)* handle the translation.

Address Resolution Protocol (ARP)   An *Internet* standard that provides *IP addresses* to *workstations* on a *local area network (LAN).*

ADI   See *Apple Desktop Interface.*

adjacency operator   In *database* searching, an *operator* (typically abbreviated ADJ) that enables the searcher to specify that records should not be retrieved unless the terms linked by the operator are next to each other. For example, the *query* "Hale ADJ Bopp" rejects a record unless these two terms are adjacent to one another. See *proximity operator.*

Adobe Acrobat   A *cross-platform* document distribution program created by *Adobe Systems.* With Adobe Acrobat, a document publisher can create a file in Adobe's *PDF (Portable Document Format)* format. This file can be read on any computer system that can run an Adobe Acrobat *reader*. Versions of the reader are available for most popular computing formats, including Windows, Macintosh, and Unix.

Adobe FrameMaker   A *desktop publishing* program created by *Adobe Systems* that is designed to handle very large (book-length) manuscripts. The program includes word processing capabilities as well as a full suite of desktop publishing tools and is available in versions for Windows, Macintosh, and Unix.

Adobe Illustrator   A full-featured *vector graphics* program that is suitable for professional graphics design applications. Created by *Adobe Systems,* the program is available in Windows and Macintosh versions.

Adobe PageMaker   A *desktop publishing* program created by Aldus, Inc., and later acquired by *Adobe Systems,* that is designed for professional-quality production of short- to medium-length documents, including newsletters, brochures, and flyers. The program is available in Windows and Macintosh versions. See *Adobe FrameMaker*.

Adobe PageMill   A Web publishing program created by *Adobe Systems*. PageMill is a *WYSIWYG* editor, which enables Web authors to create Web pages without knowing any *HTML*. The program is available in Windows and Macintosh versions.

Adobe Photoshop   A complex, full-featured illustration and photo retouching program developed by *Adobe Systems*. Photoshop is widely used by professional designers and Web publishers and is available for both Windows and Macintosh systems.

Adobe PostScript   See *PostScript*.

Adobe Systems   A software publisher, headquartered in San Jose, Calif., that focuses on desktop publishing software (see *Adobe FrameMaker* and *Adobe PageMaker)* and related technologies, such as portable document formats (see *Adobe Acrobat),* graphics imaging and illustration (see *Adobe Illustrator* and *Adobe Photoshop), World Wide Web* publishing software *(Adobe PageMill),* printer description languages (see *PostScript),* and display technologies (see *Display Postscript).*

Adobe Type Manager (ATM)   A *font utility* that enables Windows and Macintosh users to display *PostScript* Type 1 fonts on-screen. The program is available in Windows and Macintosh versions. See *TrueType*.

ADPCM   See *Adaptive Differential Pulse Code Modulation*.

ADSL   Acronym for Asymmetric Digital Subscriber Line. A digital telephone standard, available only in a few selected markets, that enables download speeds of up to 6 *Mbps*. The standard is asymmetric because upload speeds are markedly slower, reflecting the notion—common among commercial content providers—that most residential Internet users wish to consume rather than to originate content.

Advanced Interactive eXecutive (AIX)   An *IBM* version of the *Unix* operating system. AIX runs on PS/2 computers equipped with the *Intel 80386* microprocessor, IBM *workstations, minicomputers,* and *mainframes.*

Advanced Micro Devices (AMD)   A manufacturer of *microprocessors* and other *integrated circuits (ICs)*. Based in Sunnyvale, California, AMD is the fifth-largest U.S. chipmaker and is known for the *Am386,* the *Am486,* and the *AMD K5.*

Advanced Power Management (APM)   In *portable computers,* a power-saving display feature that shuts off the display power after a predetermined period of inactivity.

Advanced Research Projects Agency (ARPA)   An agency of the U.S. Department of Defense (DoD), now called Defense Advanced Research Projects Agency (DARPA), and a major source of funding for important computer innovations. In the late 1960s and early 1970s, ARPA funded the development of the *ARPANET,* the *Internet's* predecessor, and the *TCP/IP* protocols, which have since provided the foundation for the emergence of a *wide-area network (WAN)* of global proportions.

Advanced Run–Length Limited (ARLL)   A method of storing and retrieving information on a *hard disk* that increases the density of *Run-Length Limited (RLL)* storage by more than 25 percent and offers a faster data-transfer rate (9 megabits per second). See *data-encoding scheme.*

Advanced SCSI Programming Interface (ASPI)   A standard that states how *Small Computer System Interface (SCSI)* devices work with each other and the rest of the computer system.

advanced setup options   Options in the BIOS setup program that let you choose PCI interrupts, port addresses, and *hard disk* setup options.

Advanced Technology Attachment Packet Interface (ATAPI)   A standard that makes it very easy to connect a *CD-ROM drive* to an *Enhanced IDE* host adapter.

AFAIK   Abbreviation for "as far as I know." Commonly used *abbreviation* on *Internet Relay Chat (IRC), chat rooms, e-mail,* and *Usenet.*

AFK   Abbreviation for "away from keyboard." Commonly used on *Internet Relay Chat (IRC) and chat rooms.*

aftermarket   The market for *software* and *peripherals* created by the sale of large numbers of a specific brand of computer or software. See *add-in program.*

agate   A 5.5-*point* type size often used in newspaper classified advertisements and financial tables.

agent   1. A program specifically designed to interact with a *server* and access data on the user's behalf; synonymous with *client.* 2. An automatic *program* that is designed to operate on the user's behalf, performing a specific function in the background. When the agent has achieved its goal, it reports to the user. In the future, agents may roam the world's computer networks, looking for information and reporting only when the information has been retrieved.

aggregate function   In *database management* programs, a command that performs arithmetic operations on the values in a specific *field* in all the *records* within a *database,* or in one *view* of the database.

aggregate operator   In a *database management* program, a command that tells the program to perform an *aggregate function.*

AGP   See *Accelerated Graphics Port.*

AI   See *artificial intelligence.*

AIFF   An 8-bit *monaural sound file format* developed by *Apple Computer* for storing digitized *wave sounds.* The format is also widely found on Silicon Graphics *workstations* and is often encountered on the *Internet.*

AIX   See *Advanced Interactive eXecutive (AIX)*.

alert box   In a *graphical user interface (GUI)*, a *dialog box* that appears on-screen to warn you that the *command* you've given may result in lost work or other errors, or that explains why an action can't be completed. Alert boxes remain on-screen until you take some action—usually clicking an OK button—to remove the box or cancel the operation.

ALGOL   An early programming language, little used today, that was designed for scientific computation.

algorithm   A mathematical or logical procedure for solving a problem. An algorithm is a recipe for finding the right answer to a difficult problem by breaking down the problem into simple steps. Algorithms also are used to improve the performance of your computer. Algorithms are used, for example, in *caches* to determine what *data,* if any, should be replaced by incoming data.

alias   1. A secondary or symbolic name for a *file,* a collection of *data,* a computer user, or a computer device. 2. In a *spreadsheet,* a *range* name, such as Income, is an alias for a range, such as A3..K3. 3. In *networks,* group aliases provide a handy way to send *e-mail* to two or more people simultaneously.

aliasing   In *graphics,* the undesirable jagged or stair-stepped appearance of diagonal lines in computer-generated images. A low-resolution monitor causes aliasing. Bit-mapped characters, especially when they are enlarged, have aliasing. Synonymous with the jaggies. See *anti-aliasing.*

alignment   The placement of hard and floppy disk drives *read/write heads* over the disk *tracks* they must read and write. In *desktop publishing,* synonymous with *justification.*

allocate   To reserve sufficient *memory* for a *program's* operation.

all points addressable (APA) graphic   See *bit-mapped graphic.*

AltaVista   A *search engine* for *keyword* searches on the *World Wide Web (WWW)* created by Digital Electronics Corp. (DEC) and considered by many to be the most powerful available. Combining a huge database of Web resources with a flexible and very fast search program, AltaVista enables users to perform a

A
B
C

simple search using *natural language,* or an advanced search using *Boolean operators.* One drawback of AltaVista is that untrained searchers may retrieve too many irrelevant documents *(false drops).* Better results can be obtained by using AltaVista's search-restriction features, including *case-sensitive* searching, *field-based searches,* and *phrase searches.* See *HotBot, Lycos.*

alt hierarchy   In *Usenet,* one of several top-level classifications (hierarchies) of *newsgroups.* Alt (short for alternative) newsgroups can be created by anyone who knows the appropriate news-group origination commands, thus by-passing the voting proce-dures required to originate newsgroups in the *standard newsgroup* hierarchies (such as *comp, soc,* and *talk*). However, Usenet admin-istrators are not compelled to carry alt newsgroups, and they are not available at all Usenet sites.

Alt key   On *IBM PC-compatible keyboards,* a key used in combi-nation with other keys to select commands from the menu or as shortcut keys to execute commands. In *WordPerfect,* for example, pressing Alt+F2 begins a search-and-replace operation. See *Control key (Ctrl)* and *Shift key.*

alphanumeric characters   Characters available on a *keyboard,* including upper- and lowercase letters A through Z, numbers 0 through 9, punctuation marks, and special keyboard symbols. See *data type.*

alpha software   An early version of a program that is generally so buggy that it is tested in-house prior to more widespread *beta tests.* See *alpha test.*

alpha test   The first stage in the testing of computer products before they are released for public use. Alpha tests are usually conducted by the *hardware* manufacturer or *software* publisher. Later tests, called *beta tests,* are conducted by selected users. See *alpha software* and *beta software.*

ALU   See *arithmetic-logic unit.*

Am386   A *microprocessor* manufactured by *Advanced Micro Devices (AMD)* that is *binary compatible* and *pin compatible* with the *Intel 80386.*

Am486   A *microprocessor* manufactured by *Advanced Micro Devices (AMD)* that is *binary compatible* and *pin compatible* with the *Intel 80486.* See *Am486DX2* and *Am486DX4.*

Am486DX2   A *clock-doubled* version of the *Am486* that competes with the *Intel 486DX2*. The fastest Am486DX2 runs at 80 *megahertz (MHz)*.

Am486DX4   A *clock tripled* version of the *Am486* that competes with the *Intel 486DX4*. The fastest Am486DX4 runs at 100 *megahertz (MHz)*.

Am5x86   A *microprocessor*, manufactured by *Advanced Micro Devices (AMD)*, that is *binary compatible* and *pin compatible* with the Intel *Pentium* P75 microprocessor.

AMD   See *Advanced Micro Devices*.

AMD K5   A family of microprocessors, created by *Advanced Micro Devices (AMD)*, that is *binary compatible* with the *Pentium*. Unlike the Pentium, which can begin processing two instructions simultaneously, the K5 is a *quad-issue microprocessor*, capable of initiating four instructions at one time. By employing *reduced instruction-set computer (RISC)* design and a *register renaming* scheme that allows 40 *registers*, the K5 performs at speeds equal to or better than Pentiums of comparable *clock speeds*.

AMD K6   An advanced *microprocessor* manufactured by *Advanced Micro Devices (AMD)* that rivals the performance of the *Pentium Pro* microprocessor running at 200 MHz but costing approximately 25 percent less and offering *MMX* graphics processing capabilities. The chip contains the equivalent of 8.8 million transistors.

American National Standards Institute (ANSI)   A nonprofit organization devoted to the development of voluntary standards designed to improve the productivity and international competitiveness of American industrial enterprises. ANSI committees have developed recommendations for computer languages such as *COBOL, C,* and *FORTRAN* and the DOS *device driver ANSI.SYS*. ANSI is the U.S. representative of the *International Organization for Standardization (ISO)*.

American Standard Code for Information Interchange
See *ASCII*.

America Online (AOL)   The largest *online information service* (with 2.5 million subscribers), headquartered in Vienna, Virginia. The firm's 1996 revenues exceeded US$1 billion. Offering a mix of news, sports, *chat rooms, e-mail,* computer support, *Internet* access, and fee-based services, AOL targets new computer users. AOL's major competitors include *CompuServe* and the *Microsoft Network*.

Amiga   A computer system developed by Commodore International, based on the *Motorola 68000 microprocessor.* Though the Amiga is no longer manufactured, it has a rabid following among graphic artists and musicians, who laud its strong graphics and sound capabilities. The Amiga, with *aftermarket* Video Toaster hardware, is used extensively in television production. See *MIDI*.

Ami Pro   See *Lotus Word Pro*.

ampersand   A character (&) sometimes used in place of the English word "and." The ampersand was originally a *ligature* of et, which is Latin for "and." The ampersand is used as an operator in *spreadsheet programs* to include text in a *formula*.

analog   Based on continuously varying values or voltages. A speedometer is an analog device that shows changes in speed using a needle indicator that can move over an infinite range of speeds up to the maximum limit of the vehicle. Analog techniques also are used for the reproduction of music in standard LP records and audio cassettes. See *digital*.

analog computer   A computer used to measure conditions that change constantly, such as temperature, heartbeat, or atmospheric pressure. Analog computation is used widely in laboratory settings to monitor ongoing, continuous changes and to record these changes in *charts* or *graphs*. See *digital computer*.

analog device   A *peripheral* that handles information in continuously variable quantities instead of digitizing the information into discrete, *digital* representations. An *analog monitor,* for example, can display millions of colors with smooth, continuous gradations.

analogical reasoning   A form of *analysis* in which the dynamics of something in the real world—such as the aerodynamics of a proposed airplane—are understood by building a model and exploring its behavior. One of the computer's greatest contributions has been to lower the cost (and increase the convenience) of analogical reasoning. See *model*.

analog modem   The most common kind of *modem* available today. Analog modems, unlike *digital modems,* are designed to communicate over *Plain Old Telephone Service (POTS)* lines. An analog modem converts a computer's digital data to an analog sound and sends it over the phone lines to another modem, which in turn converts the data back to digital form.

A
B
C

analog monitor A *monitor* that accepts a continuously varied video signal and consequently can display a continuous range of colors, limited only by the *color depth* (the number of bits) used to encode the *palette* of colors. With a color depth of 24 bits, for example, an analog monitor can display 16.7 million colors. In contrast, a *digital monitor* can display only a finite number of colors. Most analog monitors are designed to accept input signals at a precise frequency; however, higher frequencies are required to carry higher-resolution images to the monitor. For this reason, *multiscanning monitors* have been developed that automatically adjust themselves to the incoming frequency. *Video Graphics Array (VGA)* monitors are analog monitors.

analog-to-digital converter (A/D converter) An adapter that allows a *digital computer* to accept *analog* input, such as that from laboratory instruments. Analog-to-digital converters are frequently used when monitoring temperature, movement, and other conditions that vary continuously.

analog transmission A communications scheme that uses a continuous signal varied by amplification. See *broadband* and *digital transmission*.

analysis A method of discovery in which a situation is broken down to its component parts, and the parts are studied to try to understand how they affect one another. In personal computing, a common form of analysis is sensitivity testing, or "what-if" analysis, using a *spreadsheet* program. In sensitivity testing, you alter the variables in a formula to see how changing each variable affects the outcome of the calculation.

analytical graphics The preparation of *charts* and *graphs* to help in the understanding and interpretation of *data*. The graphs available with spreadsheet programs fall into this category because they're useful for clarifying trends in worksheet numbers, but *presentation graphics* packages still have the edge in creating stunning charts.

anchor In *hypertext,* a word, phrase, or image—usually demarcated by color, underlining, or both—that provides the gateway (called a *link* or *hyperlink*) to another document.

anchor cell   In a *spreadsheet program,* the *cell* in a *range* in which the *cell pointer* is located.

anchored graphic   A *graph* or picture fixed in an absolute position on the page rather than attached to specific text. See *floating graphic* and *wrap-around type.*

AND   1. In *Boolean logic,* an *operator* that specifies that a statement is true only if both of its arguments are true. 2. In computer database searching, a query operator that retrieves a record only if the record contains both of the terms linked with AND (for example, the query "computers AND internet" retrieves a term only if a record contains both of these terms). Boolean operators are capitalized by convention; they are not acronyms. See *NOT* and *OR.*

angle bracket   The less-than (<) or greater-than (>) characters found on the standard *ASCII* keyboard, when used in place of parentheses to enclose a string of characters, for example, <NAME>.

animated GIF   A *GIF* file that contains multiple images, enabling graphic designers to create simple, effective animations that require little storage space. When an application displays the multiple images in a looping sequence, the result is an animation, albeit a rather jerky one. Because most Web browsers can download GIF animations quickly and display the enclosed files in a sequence without requiring *helper applications* or *plug-ins,* the use of GIF animations has become widespread in Web publishing. GIF animations require software that supports the *GIF89a* standard.

animation   Creating the illusion of movement by saving a series of images that show slight changes in the position of the displayed objects, and then displaying these images back fast enough that the eye perceives smooth movement. The illusion is convincing only if the *frame rate* (number of frames displayed per second) is sufficiently fast to trick the eye into seeing continuous motion. See *cell animation.*

annotation   An explanatory note or comment inserted into a *document.* With some *application programs,* you can insert an annotation as an *icon* that, when clicked by the person who reads the *document,* opens a separate *window* containing the note. Users of personal computers equipped with *sound boards* and *microphones* can add voice annotations to their documents.

anonymous   Originating from a concealed or unknown source. In *Usenet* and *e-mail,* anonymity cannot be assured by simply omitting one's signature or typing a phony name; the article's or message's *header* information shows where the message originated. Anonymity can be guaranteed only by sending the message through an *anonymous remailer.*

A
B
C

anonymous FTP   In systems linked to the *Internet,* the use of a file-transfer program to contact a distant computer system to which you have no access rights, log on to its public *directories,* and transfer files from that computer to your own. When logging on to an anonymous FTP server, you should type anonymous as your name and your *e-mail* address as your password. For help in finding files to access via anonymous FTP, you can use *Archie, Gopher,* a *Wide Area Information Server (WAIS),* or the *World Wide Web (WWW).*

anonymous post   In *Usenet,* an article that has been posted through an *anonymous remailer* so that the identity of the person posting the article is impossible to determine.

anonymous remailer   An *Internet* mailing service that strips an *e-mail* message of its originating *header* information, so that its origin cannot be easily determined. True anonymous remailers retain absolutely no information regarding the messages they relay; they should be distinguished from *pseudoanonymous remailers,* which retain origin information in order to facilitate replies to the message's originator.

ANSI   See *American National Standards Institute.*

ANSI graphics   A set of *cursor*-control codes, developed by the *American National Standards Institute (ANSI),* that enables the display of *graphics* and colors on a remote computer's *monitor.*

ANSI/ISO C++   A standardized version of the *C++* programming language, developed by a committee affiliated with the *American National Standards Institute (ANSI)* and the *International Organization for Standardization (ISO).* The standard is widely perceived to be needed in order to eliminate incompatibilities introduced by publishers of proprietary *C++* compilers.

ANSI screen control   A set of standards developed by the *American National Standards Institute (ANSI)* to control the display of information on computer screens and enable *ANSI graphics.* See *ANSI.SYS.*

ANSI.SYS   In *MS-DOS,* a configuration file containing instructions needed to display *ANSI graphics* and to control *cursor* location, line wrapping, and the behavior of the *keyboard,* following the recommendations of *the American National Standards Institute (ANSI).* Some programs require that you include the instruction DEVICE=ANSI.SYS in the *CONFIG.SYS* file so the program displays properly.

answer mode   See *auto-dial/auto-answer modem.*

answer/originate   In *modems,* the capability of a communications device to receive (answer) and send *(originate)* messages.

anti–aliasing   The automatic removal or reduction of stair-step distortions *(aliasing)* in a computer-generated *graphic* image. This is accomplished by filling the jagged edges with gray or color to make the *aliasing* less noticeable. Unfortunately, the result is often a fuzzy display.

anticipatory paging   In *virtual memory,* a method of increasing the speed of virtual memory operations in which the *operating system* attempts to predict which memory pages will be needed in advance of their actual demand from applications. See *demand paging.*

anti–glare   Any procedure or treatment used to reduce the reflection of outside light sources on a *monitor,* ranging from repositioning the monitor in relation to windows to coating the *display* with a light-damping chemical. Chemical anti–glare treatments can reduce the *brightness* of a display.

Antistatic mat   A mat or pad placed on or near a computer device. The mat absorbs static electricity, which can damage *semiconductor* devices if the devices aren't properly grounded.

antivirus program   A utility designed to check for and remove computer *viruses* from *memory* and disks. An antivirus program detects a virus by searching code recognized as that of one of the thousands of viruses known to afflict computer systems. See *Trojan horse, vaccine* and *worm.*

AOL   See *America Online.*

APA graphic   See *bit-mapped graphic.*

aperture grille   The equivalent of a *shadow mask* in Sony *Trinitron monitors* and *monitors* of similar design. Aperture grilles use vertical wires to direct electron beams to *phosphors* of a particular color. *Slot pitch* and *screen pitch* are the Trinitron equivalent of *dot pitch,* so compare monitors on those specifications.

API   See *application program interface.*

APL (A Programming Language)   A *high-level programming language* well-suited for scientific and mathematical applications. APL uses Greek letters and requires a *display* device that can display these letters. Previously used only on IBM *mainframes,* the language is now available for IBM PC-compatible computers.

APM   See *Advanced Power Management.*

app   Common slang expression for *application* or *applet.*

append   To add *data* at the end of a *file* or a *database.* In *database management,* for example, to append a record is to add a new record after all existing records.

Apple Computer   A Cupertino, California–based company best-known for manufacturing the *Macintosh* line of computers, with 1996 revenues of US$9.8 billion. Unlike *International Business Machines (IBM),* its main competitor, Apple kept the *architecture* of its computers *proprietary*—a move that many analysts say cost it market share in the business computing community. Regardless, Apple established a strong following among graphics designers, for whose purposes Macintoshes are especially well-suited. As *IBM PC-compatible* computers improved, though, Apple's market share eroded. Apple recently licensed a handful of other companies to make Macintosh *clones,* which may boost the Macintosh's market share—but not necessarily Apple's finances. Among Apple's recent setbacks include its failure to complete the *Copland* operating system; falling behind technologically, the firm acquired NeXT, Inc., and plans to adapt the sophisticated NeXT system software for a next-generation Macintosh (see *Rhapsody*).

Apple Desktop Bus (ADB)   An interface for connecting keyboards, *mice, trackballs,* and other input devices to *Macintosh* computers. These computers come with an ADB *serial port* capable of a maximum *data transfer rate* of 4.5 *kilobits* per second. You can connect up to 16 devices to one ADB port, with each additional device daisy-chained to the previous device. See *asynchronous communication.*

Apple Desktop Interface (ADI)   A set of *user interface* guide-lines, developed by *Apple Computer* and published by Addison-Wesley, intended to ensure that the appearance and operation of all *Macintosh* applications are similar.

Apple File Exchange   A *utility program* provided with each Macintosh computer that allows Macs equipped with suitable *floppy disk drives* to exchange *data* with IBM PC-compatible computers.

AppleShare   A file server utility for *AppleTalk* networks. AppleShare transforms any Macintosh on the network into a *dedicated* file server; the server's hard disk icon appears on every network user's desktop.

applet   1. A small- to medium-sized computer program that provides a specific function, such as emulating a calculator. 2. In *Java*, a mini-program embedded in a Web document that, when downloaded, is executed by the browser. Both of the leading browsers (Netscape Communicator and Microsoft Internet Explorer) can execute Java applets. See *Java applet* and *Java application*.

AppleTalk   A *local area network (LAN)* standard developed by *Apple Computer*. AppleTalk can link as many as 32 *Macintosh* computers, *IBM PC-compatible* computers, and *peripherals* such as *laser printers*. Every Macintosh computer has an AppleTalk port; the only hardware required for an AppleTalk network is a set of *LocalTalk* connectors and ordinary telephone wire for cables (called *twisted-pair* cable). AppleTalk networks are simple and inexpensive but quite slow—capable of transmitting only up to 230 *kilobits* per second compared to *EtherTalk,* which is capable of speeds of up to 10 million *bits per second (bps)*.

application   A program that enables you to do something use-ful with the computer, such as writing or accounting (as opposed to *utilities,* programs that help you maintain the computer).

Application Configuration Access Protocol (ACAP)   A proposed *Internet* standard that transfers crucial user configuration settings (including *address books, bookmarks,* and options choices) to an Internet-accessible file. Because these settings are stored on the network instead of the user's computer, they are accessible no matter which computer is being used. ACAP will greatly benefit anyone who accesses the Internet from more than one computer.

application control menu   See *control menu.*

application development system   A coordinated set of
program development tools, typically including a *full-screen editor;*
a *programming language* with a *compiler,* linker, and *debugger;* and
an extensive library of ready-to-use program modules. The use
of an application development system lets experienced users
develop a stand-alone application more easily than writing a
program using a language such as *C++* or *COBOL.*

application heap   In a *Macintosh,* the area of memory set aside
for user *programs.* Synonymous with *base memory.*

application icon   In *Microsoft Windows 95,* an on-screen
graphic representation of a minimized program. The *icon* appears
on the *taskbar* to remind you that the application is still present
in memory. *Double-click* the application icon to switch to that
program.

application layer   In the *OSI Reference Model* of computer
network architecture, the first or top-most of seven *layers,* in
which the data is presented to the user. At this layer, protocols are
needed to ensure that products made by different manufacturers
can work together. For example, every *e-mail* program should use
the same protocols for sending and receiving e-mail. When the
data is ready to be sent to the network, it is passed "down" the
protocol stack to the next layer, the presentation layer.

application program   See *application.*

application program interface (API)   1. A set of standards
or conventions by which programs can *call* specific *operating system* or network services. 2. In *Web servers,* the standards or conventions that enable a *hyperlink* to originate a call to a program
that is external to the server. See *CGI, ISAPI* and *NSAPI.*

application shortcut key   In *Microsoft Windows 95,* a *short-cut
key* you assign to launch or bring an application to the foreground. Application shortcut keys are also available in applications such as DESQview and PC Tools Desktop to launch and
switch among programs.

application software   *Programs* that perform specific tasks,
such as *word processing* or *database management,* in contrast to
system software, which runs the computer system, and utilities,
which help you maintain and organize the system.

application window   In a *graphical user interface (GUI)*, an application's main window, containing a *title bar*, the application's *menu bar*, and a work area. The work area can contain one or more document windows.

Approach   See *Lotus Approach*.

A Programming Language   See *APL*.

Archie   An *Internet* tool for finding specific files that are available in publicly accessible *File Transfer Protocol (FTP)* archives. A major drawback of Archie is that you must know the precise spelling of some or all of the file names in order to retrieve the file. See *anonymous FTP*.

Archie gateway   In the *World Wide Web (WWW)*, a Web page that provides an easy-to-use interface to the *Archie* search service.

architecture   The overall conceptual design of a *hardware* device or computer network that specifies how its various components interact.

archival backup   A *backup* procedure in which a *backup utility* backs up all files on the *hard disk* by copying them to *floppy disks*, *tape*, or some other backup medium. See *incremental backup*.

archive   1. An infrequently accessed but comprehensive collection of data. 2. A compressed *file* designed for space-efficient storage or distribution that contains two or more original (uncompressed) files. In *Unix*, the most popular archive program is tar, which lacks compression capabilities. In *Microsoft Windows*, WinZip is the most popular archiving and compression program, while StuffIt holds this place among *Macintosh* users.

archive attribute   In *MS-DOS* and *Microsoft Windows* file systems, a hidden *code*, stored with a *file's* directory entry, that indicates whether the file has been changed since it was last copied using XCOPY or a *backup utility*.

archive site   An *Internet*-accessible computer that serves as a repository for a large or complete collection of data, such as all the messages exchanged on a mailing list or *newsgroup*. Synonymous with FTP site because archive sites are frequently accessed by FTP programs.

ARCnet   See *Attached Resource Computer Network*.

area graph   In *presentation graphics,* a *line graph* in which the area below the line is filled in to emphasize the change in volume from one time period to the next. The *x-axis* (categories axis) is the horizontal axis, and the *y-axis* (values axis) is the vertical axis.

A
B
C

areal density   The tightness with which data can be packed onto a *hard disk* or *floppy disk.* Both the smoothness of the disk surface and the nature of the recording medium affect areal density, which is expressed in megabits per square inch (Mb/in²). Areal densities of between 100 and 200 Mb/in² are typical for modern hard disks.

argument   In a programming *statement* that calls a *routine,* a value or option that provides data for the routine to process or tells the routine which option to use when processing this data. For example, if the statement calls a routine that rounds numbers, the argument tells the routine how many decimal places to use. This term is often used synonymously with *parameter,* but in some usages the term parameter is used to refer to nonoptional values that are subject to change. 2. In *command-line interfaces* and *applications,* such as *spreadsheets,* that employ typed *commands,* a value or option that modifies how the command is carried out. See *parameter* and *switch.*

argument separator   In *spreadsheet* programs and *programming languages,* a comma or other punctuation mark that sets off one *argument* from another in a *command.*

arithmetic–logic unit (ALU)   The portion of the *central processing unit (CPU)* that makes all the decisions for the microprocessor, based on the mathematical computations and logic functions it performs.

arithmetic operator   A symbol that tells a *program* the arithmetic operation to perform, such as addition, subtraction, multiplication, and division. In most computer programs, addition is represented by a plus sign (+), subtraction by a hyphen or minus sign (−), multiplication by an asterisk (*), division by a slash (/), and exponent by a caret (^). See *Boolean operator* and *relational operator.*

ARLL   See *Advanced Run-Length Limited.*

ARP   See *Address Resolution Protocol.*

ARPA   See *Advanced Research Projects Agency.*

ARPANET A *wide area network (WAN),* created in 1969 with funding from the *Advanced Research Projects Agency (ARPA).* Undergoing constant research and development in the early to mid-1970s, ARPANET served as the testbed for the development of *TCP/IP* (the protocols that make the *Internet* possible). Initially, the ARPANET was available only to government research institutes and to universities holding Department of Defense (DoD) research contracts. In 1983, ARPANET was divided into a high-security military network (Milnet) and an ARPANET that was recast as a research and development network, supervised by the *National Science Foundation (NSF).* NSF constructed a new TCP/IP-based network *backbone* called *NSFnet* and decommissioned the remnants of ARPANET in 1990.

array 1. In *programming,* a fundamental data structure consisting of a single or multidimensional table that the program treats as one data item. Any information in the array can be referenced by naming the array and the location of the item in the array. 2. In hard disks, a collection of hard drives that have been linked together to provide a large amount of auxiliary storage.

arrow keys See *cursor-movement keys.*

article In *Usenet,* a contribution that an individual has written and posted to one or more *newsgroups.* There are two kinds of articles: original articles on new subject, and *follow-up posts.* By means of *cross-posting,* an article can appear in more than one newsgroup.

article selector In *Usenet,* a *newsreader* feature in which the newsreader groups and displays the *articles* that are currently available for reading. *Threaded newsreaders* automatically sort the articles in such a way that you can see the *thread* of discussion; an article is followed immediately by all of its follow-up articles.

artificial intelligence (AI) A computer science field that tries to improve computers by endowing them with some of the characteristics associated with human intelligence, such as the capability to understand *natural language* and to reason under conditions of uncertainty. See *expert system.*

artificial life A scientific research area devoted to the creation and study of computer simulations of living organisms. Computer *viruses* have forced a renewal of the debate on the definition of life. Besides forcing us to re-examine our definition of life, artificial life research may create more effective technology.

By applying artificial life concepts to real-life problems, we can program computer-generated solutions to compete for survival based on their capability to perform a desired task well.

AS See *autonomous system*.

ascender In typography, the portion of the lowercase letters b, d, f, h, k, l, and t that rises above the height of the letter x. The height of the ascender varies in different *typefaces*. See *descender*.

ascending order A *sort* in which items are arranged from smallest to largest (1, 2, 3) or from first to last (a, b, c). Ascending order is the default sort order for virtually all applications that perform sorting operations. Compare to *descending sort*.

ASCII (Pronounced as-kee) Acronym for American Standard Code for Information Interchange. See *ASCII character set* and *extended character set*.

ASCII art Low-brow art in a high-tech medium, using only the *ASCII character set*. *Smileys*, sideways faces, such as a :-) happy face and :-(frowning face, provide emotional and social context for *e-mail* messages and provide yet another genre for ASCII art. See *emoticon*.

ASCII character set A standard character set consisting of 96 upper- and lowercase letters, plus 32 nonprinting *control characters*, each of which is numbered to achieve uniformity among different computer devices. Based on a 7-bit coding scheme, the ASCII character set dates from the 1960s and is incapable of representing the *character sets* of most non-English languages. Most modern computers use an *extended character set* containing accented, technical, and illustrative characters. However, these character sets are proprietary and partially incompatible with each other; for example, the IBM PC's extended character set differs from the one employed by the Macintosh. To avoid these problems on the Internet, Web *browsers* use the *ISO Latin-1* character set encoding.

ASCII file A *file* that contains only characters drawn from the *ASCII character set*. No special *formatting* (such as boldface or underlining) is in an ASCII file. See *binary file*.

ASCII sort order A *sort order* determined by the sequence used to number the standard *ASCII character set*. Words or lines that begin with spaces or punctuation come first, followed by those beginning with numbers. Next sorted are words or lines that begin with uppercase letters, followed by those that begin with lowercase letters. Note that this sort order violates most publication style guidelines. (Compare to *dictionary sort*.)

ASCII transfer   A *file transfer protocol* that employs no *error-correction protocol* or *flow control*. ASCII transfers are less efficient than *binary* protocols like *XMODEM,* but they are the only type of transfer some older computers, particularly *mainframes,* support.

A-sized paper   As defined by the *American National Standards Institute (ANSI),* a page that is 8.5 by 11 inches (210 by 297 millimeters) in size.

ASM   1. See *Association for Systems Management (ASM).* 2. The *MS-DOS file name extension* usually attached to a *file* containing *assembly language source code.*

ASN   See *autonomous system number.*

ASN.1   See *Abstract Syntax Notation One.*

aspect ratio   In *graphics,* the ratio of the width of an image to its height. When changing the size of a graphic, maintaining the width-to-height ratio is important to avoid distortions.

ASPI   See *Advanced SCSI Programming Interface.*

assembler   A *program* that transforms an *assembly language* program into *machine language* so the computer can execute the program.

assembly language   A *low-level programming language* in which each *program* statement corresponds to an instruction that the *microprocessor* can carry out. Assembly languages are *procedural languages.* They tell the computer what to do in precise detail, requiring as many as two dozen lines of code to add two numbers. Assembly language programs are difficult and tedious to write. On the other hand, assembly language code is compact, operates quickly, and, when assembled, is more efficient than a *compiled program* written in a *high-level language.* See *BASIC, C, compiler,* and *Pascal.*

assign   To give a *value* to a named *variable.*

assigned number   In the *Internet,* a value associated with a specific *protocol* that is controlled by the *Internet Assigned Numbers* Authority *(IANA).* An example of an assigned number is the *port number* assigned to a specific network service, such as *Usenet* or *Internet Relay Chat (IRC).*

assignment   The process of storing a value in a named variable.

assignment operator   In *programming,* a symbol that enables the programmer to assign a *value* to a *variable.* This is usually an equals sign (=).

assignment statement   In *programming,* a program statement that places a *value* into a *variable.* In *BASIC,* for example, the statement LET A=10 places the value 10 into the variable A.

associated document   A *file* linked at the system level with the *application* that created it or knows how to read its data type. In the *MacOS,* association is automatic because applications record their identity in a new file's *resource fork.* In Windows, association is based on three-letter *file extensions*; for example, .doc files can be associated with Microsoft Word. Users or *setup programs* can change the association between an application and an extension.

Association for Computer Machinery (ACM)   The oldest professional society for computer experts. ACM was founded in 1948 and sponsors conferences, journals, book publishing, and student groups at colleges and universities. The ACM is known for its annual Computer Science Conference and its ethical code, to which all members are expected to adhere. A popular feature of the organization is its numerous Special Interest Groups (SIGS), which facilitate communication among ACM members with shared interests.

Association for Systems Management (ASM)   A professional society for systems analysts and other computer professionals. The ASM has chapters in most cities and offers many short courses in systems analysis and other information-systems topics. The ASM was formerly known as the Systems and Procedures Association (SPA).

Association for Women in Computing (AWC)   A professional society dedicated to the advancement of women in computer-related fields. The organization strives to promote professional growth through networking and the society's professional programs, which include career awareness workshops. Founded in 1978, AWC is currently headquartered in San Francisco, Calif., and has numerous state and local chapters.

Association of Shareware Professionals   A professional society for authors and marketers of user-supported software *(shareware)* that is devoted to strengthening the future of shareware as an alternative to commercial software. The organization's members subscribe to a respected code of ethics. Founded in 1987, the organization is currently headquartered in Muskegan, MN.

AST Research, Inc.   An Irvine, CA.–based manufacturer of personal computers, and one of the world's 10 largest computer makers. With 1996 revenues of US$2.1 billion, the firm manufacturers desktop, notebook, and hand-held computers, as well as color monitors, graphics, and memory enhancement products.

asterisk   In DOS, the wild-card symbol (*) that stands for one or more characters; contrast this with the *question mark* (?) wild card, which stands for only one character. An asterisk is also the arithmetic symbol for multiplication. See *arithmetic operator*.

Asymmetric Digital Subscriber Line   See *ADSL*.

asynchronous   Not kept in time (synchrony) by the pulses of a *system clock* or some other timing device. See *asynchronous communication*.

asynchronous communication   A method of *data communication* in which the transmission of bits of data isn't synchronized by a clock signal but is accomplished by sending the bits one after another, with a *start bit* and a *stop bit* to mark the beginning and end, respectively, of each data unit. Telephone lines can be used for asynchronous communication. See *baud rate, modem, synchronous communication,* and *Universal Asynchronous Receiver/ Transmitter (UART)*.

ATA   See *Integrated Drive Electronics (IDE)*.

ATA-2   See *Enhanced IDE (EIDE)*.

ATA-3   An experimental standard for attaching many different recording media, such as *disk drives* and *tape drives,* to a PC. ATA-3 is capable of transferring data at a rate of 30 megabits *(Mb)* per second.

ATAPI   See *Advanced Technology Attachment Packet Interface.*

ATA packet interface (ATAPI)   See *Advanced Technology Attachment Packet Interface.*

AT Attachment (ATA)   See *Integrated Drive Electronics (IDE).*

AT bus   The 16-bit *expansion bus* used in the IBM Personal Computer AT, as distinguished from the 8-bit bus of the original IBM Personal Computer and the 32-bit bus of computers using the *Intel 80386* and *Intel 486* microprocessors. Most 80386 and 486 machines contain AT-compatible *expansion slots* for *backward compatibility.* See *local bus* and *Micro Channel Bus.*

AT command set   See *Hayes command set.*

AT keyboard   An 84-key *keyboard* introduced with the IBM Personal Computer AT in response to complaints about the original IBM Personal Computer keyboard, which used a layout different from that of office typewriters. The AT keyboard is considered a minimal standard today; most IBM and IBM-compatible computers come equipped with a 101-key *enhanced keyboard.* See *keyboard layout.*

ATM   1. See *Adobe Type Manager (ATM).* 2. Acronym for Asynchronous Transfer Mode. A network architecture that divides messages into fixed-size units (called *cells*) of small size (53 bytes) and establishes a switched connection between the originating and receiving stations. Network speed, determined partly by the speed of the switching devices, is as high as 622 megabits per second *(Mbps).* The advantage of breaking all transmissions into small-sized cells is that the network can transmit voice, audio, and computer data over a single line without any single type of data dominating the transmission. ATM's *connection-oriented* design differs from the Internet's *connectionless* design; unlike the *Internet,* ATM enables service providers to bill by network usage, and is capable of very high transmission speeds. For these reasons, ATM is often touted as a potential architecture for the *Information Superhighway.*

at sign   The symbol (@) used to distinguish between the mailbox name and computer name in *e-mail addresses.* An address such as frodo@bagend.com is read "Frodo at bagend dot com."

AT-size case   A type of *desktop* (that is, flat-lying) case that matches the design of the case IBM used for its Personal

Computer AT in 1984. AT-size cases, with their horizontally mounted *motherboards,* provide lots of room for *adapters* and other components but as a result have very large *footprints.* See *Baby AT case, mini-AT-size case, mini-tower case,* and *tower case.*

Attached Resource Computer Network (ARCnet)

A popular *local area network (LAN)* originally developed by Datapoint Corporation for *IBM PC-compatible* computers and now available from several vendors. ARCnet interface cards are inexpensive and easily installed. ARCnet networks use a *star network* a *token-passing* protocol, and *coaxial* or *twisted-pair* cables. The network can transmit data at speeds of 2.5*M* per second. See *network interface card* and *network topology.*

attachment   In *e-mail,* a *binary file,* such as a program or a compressed word processing document, that has been attached to an e-mail message. The contents of the file do not appear within the e-mail message itself. Instead, on the *Internet,* they are encoded following the specifications of the *MIME* standard or older encoding standards called *BinHex* or *uuencode.* To include an attached document with an e-mail message, both the sender and receiver must have e-mail programs that are capable of working with the same encoding format. MIME is the most widely used format.

attachment encoding   The encoding format used to attach a *binary file* to an *e-mail* message. See *BinHex, MIME,* and *uuencode.*

attenuation   The loss of signal strength when cables exceed the maximum length stated in the network's specifications. Attenuation prevents successful data communications. You can use a device called a *repeater* to extend a network's cable range.

attribute   1. In many *word processing* and *graphics programs,* a character emphasis, such as *boldface* and *italic,* and other characteristics, such as *typeface* and *type size.* 2. In *MS-DOS* and *Microsoft Windows 95,* information about a file that indicates whether the file is a *read-only* file a *hidden file,* or a *system file.* See *archive attribute* and *file attribute.*

ATX   A *motherboard* design created by chipmaker *Intel* that provides better accessibility to motherboard components, better cooling, more full-size expansion slots, and a more convenient layout for system upgrades. The ATX design replaces the previous AT layout, which is but a small modification from the 1981 IBM *Personal Computer (PC)* motherboard layout.

AU 1. An 8-bit monaural sound file format that is widely used on *Unix workstations,* including Sun and NeXT machines for storing digitized *wave sounds.* The format employs an advanced storage technique that enables 14-bit sounds to be stored in only 8 bits of data, with minimal loss. 2. In the Internet's *domain name system (DNS),* an abbreviation for Australia.

audible feedback The capacity of a *keyboard* to generate sounds each time a key is pressed. Audible feedback makes it easier for some people to determine when a key has been depressed sufficiently for a character to be generated on-screen. See *tactile feedback.*

Audio file In computers and computer-based reproduction systems, such as audio compact discs, sound described by taking many thousands of samples of the sound each second, and recording the sound's waveform as a discrete value.

audio monitor Any speaker, but especially a speaker mounted on a *modem* that lets you hear what is happening on the telephone line. It lets you hear a busy signal, or the hissing sound of two modems establishing a carrier.

audit trail In an *accounting package,* any program feature that automatically keeps a record of transactions so you can backtrack to find the origin of specific figures that appear on reports.

AUP See *Acceptable Use Policy.*

authenticate To establish the identity of a person accessing a computer network. See *authentication* and *strong authentication.*

authentication In a *network,* the process by which the system attempts to ensure that the person logging on is the same person to whom the *account* was issued. The sole means of authentication in most networks is the demand for a *password,* even though password-based authentication is known to have several serious security flaws.

authoring In *multimedia,* the process of preparing a presentation. This involves not only writing the text, but also preparing the sound, graphic, and video components.

authoring language A *computer-assisted instruction (CAI)* application that provides tools for creating instructional or presentation *software.* A popular authoring language for *Macintosh* computers is *HyperCard,* provided free with every Macintosh

A
B
C

computer. Using HyperCard, educators can develop instructional programs quickly and easily.

auto–answer mode   See *auto-dial/auto-answer modem.*

AutoCad   A *computer-assisted design (CAD)* program, created by AutoDesk, that is widely used in professional engineering and architectural settings.

auto–dial/auto–answer modem   A *modem* that can generate tones to dial the receiving computer and can answer a ringing telephone to establish a connection when a call is received.

auto–dial mode   See *auto-dial/auto-answer modem.*

AUTOEXEC.BAT   In *MS-DOS,* a *batch file* containing instructions that DOS executes when you start the system. AUTOEXEC.BAT files commonly include *Path* statements that tell DOS where to find *application programs* and the commands to install a *mouse* or operate your *printer.* All this information must be provided at the start of every operating session; AUTOEXEC.BAT does the task for you. See *CONFIG.SYS, path,* and *path statement.*

auto–logon   A feature of *communications programs* that lets you automate the process of logging on to a *BBS* or *online information service.*

automatic backup   An *application program* feature that saves a *document* automatically at a period the user specifies, such as every 5 or 10 minutes. After a power outage or system *crash,* you can retrieve the last automatic backup file when you restart the application. This feature can help you avoid catastrophic work losses.

Automatic Data Processing, Inc.   The largest data processing firm in the U.S., with revenues of US$3.6 billion (1996 sales year). Headquartered in Roseland, New Jersey, the firm specializes in tax filing, accounting systems, and inventory management.

automatic emulation switching   In *printers,* the ability to change *printer control languages* without human intervention. Printers with automatic emulation switching sense the language, such as *PostScript* or *PCL5,* used by incoming documents and adjust automatically.

automatic font downloading   The transfer of *downloadable fonts* from the *hard disk* to the *printer* by a *utility program* as the *fonts* are needed to complete a printing job.

automatic head parking   A *hard disk* feature that moves the *read/write head* over the *landing zone*—preventing a *head crash*—whenever power is shut off.

automatic hyphenation   See *hyphenation.*

automatic mode switching   In *video adapters,* the automatic detection and adjustment of a video adapter's internal circuitry to the video output of a *program* on an IBM PC–compatible computer. Most *Video Graphics Array (VGA)* adapters, for example, switch to adjust to *Color Graphics Adapter (CGA), Monochrome Display Adapter (MDA), eXtended Graphics Array (EGA),* or VGA output from applications.

automatic name recognition   In *databases* and Web *search engines,* a feature that automatically detects that a supplied *keyword* is a person's name and restricts the search to capitalized names.

automatic network switching   A feature of departmental *laser printers* and *workgroup* printers that allows them to serve several different kinds of computers and several different kinds of *networks.* A printer equipped with automatic network switching can receive data from *Ethernet, AppleTalk,* or *TCP/IP* networks and print it without human attention. See *automatic emulation switching.*

automatic recalculation   In a *spreadsheet,* a mode in which *cell* values are recalculated every time any cell changes in the worksheet. Automatic recalculation can be switched to *manual recalculation* while you're entering data into a large spreadsheet if recalculation takes a long time. See *background recalculation.*

automatic speed sensing   A *modem* feature that lets the modem automatically determine the maximum speed at which a connection can be made. Performed during the *handshaking* period at the beginning of a call, modems with automatic speed sensing will *fall back* to the fastest speed the two connected modems, and line conditions, can support.

automation   The replacement of human skill by automatic machine operations. *Word processing* software is an example of the potential of automation. These programs automate tasks as simple as centering text and as complex as sorting a mailing list into ZIP code order.

autonomous system (AS)   In *Internet* network *topology,* a collection of *routers* that is under the control of a single administrative authority. Within an autonomous system, an administrator can create and name new *subdomains* and assign *IP addresses* and *domain names* to workstations on the network.

autonomous system number (ASN) In an *autonomous system,* an *IP address* that has been assigned by an automatic protocol to one of the workstations on the network.

AutoPlay   A *Microsoft*-initiated standard for *CD-ROMs.* When an AutoPlay disc is inserted into a CD-ROM drive, *Microsoft Windows 95* searches for an AutoRun file, which it begins executing automatically.

autorepeat key   A *key* that repeatedly enters a character as long as you hold it down.

autosave   See *automatic backup.*

autosizing   A *monitor* feature that allows a monitor to size an image to fit the *display,* regardless of its *resolution.* Autosizing monitors maintain the *aspect ratio* of an image, but enlarge or reduce it to fit in the space available.

autostart routine   A set of *instructions* contained in *read-only memory (ROM)* that tells the computer how to proceed when you switch on the power. See *BIOS* and *Power-On Self-Test (POST).*

autotrace   In a *graphics* program, such as *Adobe Illustrator,* a *command* that transforms an imported *bit-mapped graphic* into an *object-oriented graphic.* Object-oriented graphics print at the printer's maximum resolution (up to 300 dots per inch for *laser printers*). Using the autotrace tool, you can transform low-resolution graphics into art that prints at a higher *resolution.*

A/UX   *Apple Computer's* version of the *Unix operating system.* To use A/UX, you need a Macintosh with a *Motorola 68020* or *68030 microprocessor* and 4M of *random-access memory (RAM).*

AUX   In *MS-DOS,* an abbreviation for the auxiliary *port,* the communications *(COM)* port DOS uses by default (usually COM1).

auxiliary battery In a *portable computer,* a small, built-in battery that can power the computer for a few minutes while you insert a freshly charged *battery pack.*

auxiliary speakers Two or more stereo speakers that connect to the *sound board* and allow you to hear its output. Auxiliary speakers replace a computer's *on-board speaker* and are usually magnetically shielded to prevent interference with the monitor.

auxiliary storage See *secondary storage.*

avatar A graphical representation of a person that appears on the computer screen in an interactive game or communication system. The avatar's appearance, actions, and words are controlled by the person whom the avatar represents.

average access time See *access time.*

average latency See *latency.*

average seek time See *seek time.*

AVI Acronym for Audio Video Interleave. A *file format* for storing audio and video information developed by Microsoft Corporation and specifically designed for recording and playback on *Microsoft Windows* systems. The AVI format can produce near-CD quality stereo, as well as videos with an associated sound track, but AVI files consume large amounts of file space relative to other audio and video file formats.

AWC See *Association for Women in Computing.*

axis See *x-axis, y-axis* and *z-axis.*

b   Abbreviation for *byte* (8 *bits*).

B   An experimental programming language created at AT&T's Bell Laboratories in 1970, also a predecessor to *C*.

baby AT case   A computer case and power supply unit that will accommodate a *baby AT motherboard*.

baby AT motherboard   A *motherboard*, 9 by 10 inches in size, that superceded the motherboard size of the original IBM PC. The baby AT standard was in turn superceded by *ATX*.

backbone   In a *wide area network (WAN)*, such as the *Internet*, a high-speed, high-capacity medium that is designed to transfer data over hundreds or thousands of miles. A variety of physical media are used for backbone services, including microwave relay, satellites, and dedicated telephone lines.

backbone cabal   In *Usenet's* telephone-based *store-and-forward network* (see *UUCP*), the informal consortium of key Usenet system administrators who attempted to control the official list of newsgroups. The ability of these administrators to exercise such control collapsed with the migration of Usenet to the Internet. See *backbone site*.

backbone site   In *Usenet's* telephone-based *store-and-forward network* (see *UUCP*), a site that is centrally located on the article distribution network, such that the site administrator's decisions about which newsgroups to carry can affect the newsgroup selection available at dozens or even hundreds of downstream sites (see *backbone cabal*). The ability of these administrators to control and censor the newsgroup list collapsed with the migration of Usenet to the Internet via the *NNTP* protocol.

backdoor   An undocumented way to gain access to a *program*, some *data*, or an entire *computer system*, often known only to the *programmer* who created it. Backdoors can be handy when the standard way of getting at information is unavailable, but usually they constitute a security risk.

back end   The portion of a *program* that accomplishes the processing tasks that the program is designed to perform, but in such a way that it is not apparent to the user. In a *local area* *network (LAN)* with *client/server* architecture, the back-end application may be stored on the *file server,* while *front-end* programs handle the *user interface* on each workstation.

back end processor   A processing unit (such as a *microprocessor*) that is dedicated to perform a back-end task, such as processing complex graphics images.

background   In computers that can do more than one task at a time, the environment in which tasks (such as printing a *document* or *downloading a file*) are carried out while the user works with an *application* in the *foreground*. In computers that lack *multitasking* capabilities, background tasks are carried out during brief pauses in the execution of the system's primary (foreground) tasks.

background communication   Data communication, such as downloading a file from an online information service, that takes place in the background while the user concentrates on another application in the foreground. See *multitasking*.

background noise   See *noise*.

background pagination   See *pagination*.

background printing   The printing of a *document* in the *background* while a *program* is active in the *foreground*. Background printing is particularly useful if you frequently print long documents or use a slow printer. With background printing, you can continue to work while the document prints. See *multitasking, print queue,* and *print spooler*.

background recalculation   In *spreadsheet programs,* an option that causes the program to perform recalculations in the *background* while you continue to work in the spreadsheet.

background tasks   In a *multitasking* operating system, the operations occurring in the *background* (such as printing, sorting a large collection of *data,* or searching a *database*) while you work in another *program* in the *foreground*.

backlighting   A *display* design that involves shining light at a *liquid crystal display (LCD)* from behind, increasing the contrast between light and dark *pixels*. Though backlighting increases power consumption, it makes LCDs much more readable in bright-light conditions, such as those outdoors.

backlit display   A *display* design that incorporates *backlighting*.

backoff   The time delay (often selected randomly) initiated by a network *workstation* when the computer attempts to send data to the network, but experiences a *collision*. At the conclusion of the backoff period, the computer attempts to retransmit the data. A random backoff ensures that the colliding workstations will not attempt to retransmit simultaneously.

Back Office   See *Microsoft BackOffice*.

backplane   A *motherboard*. Originally, the term described a main *circuit board* mounted vertically at the rear of the *case*.

back quote   The left single quote character on the standard ASCII keyboard (`); also called grave accent.

backslash   The backwards–slanting slash character on the standard ASCII keyboard (\); also known as reverse slash.

backspace   A *key* used to delete the character to the left of the *cursor's* position, or the act of moving one space to the left by using the backspace or *cursor-movement keys*.

backup   1. A copy of installed *application software* or of *data files* you've created. Also, the act of copying files to another *disk*. Regular *backup procedures* are required for successful use of a *hard disk* system. See *archival backup, full backup,* and *incremental backup*. 2. To make a backup copy.

backup procedure   A regular maintenance procedure that copies all new or altered *files* to a *backup* storage medium, such as a *floppy disk* or a *tape drive*.

backup utility   A *utility program* designed to back up program and data files from a *hard disk* to a backup medium such as a *floppy disk* or a *tape drive*. Backup utility programs include *commands* to schedule regular *backups*, to back up only selected directories or files and to restore all or only a few files from a backup set.

Backus–Naur Form (BNF)   A set of rules for describing the organization of a *program* without actually writing instructions in any particular *programming language*. BNF is useful for teaching programming concepts and for comparing procedures written in different languages.

backward chaining In *expert systems,* a commonly used method of drawing inferences from IF/THEN rules. A backward chaining system starts with a question such as "How much is this property worth?" and searches through the system's rules to determine which ones allow the system to solve the problem and what additional data you must provide. A backward-chaining expert system asks questions of the user, engaging him or her in a dialogue. See *forward chaining* and *knowledge base.*

backward compatible Compatible with earlier versions of a *program* or earlier models of a computer. *Microsoft Windows 95,* for example, is backward compatible with *application programs* designed to run on Windows 3.1 but won't run on IBM PCs and PC compatibles equipped with the *Intel 8088* microprocessor, even though millions of those machines exist.

backward search In a *database, spreadsheet,* or word processor document, a search that begins at the *cursor's* location and proceeds backward toward the beginning of a database or *document* (rather than searching forward to the end).

bad break An improperly *hyphenated* line break.

bad page break In a *document* or *spreadsheet,* a *soft page break* that divides text at an inappropriate location. Headings can be left dangling at the bottom of pages *(orphans); data tables* can be split; and a single line of text *(widows)* can be left at the top of a page. A common flaw in documents produced on computers, bad page breaks can be caught by a final, careful review of the document using the program's print preview command or with widow/ orphan protection features in some software. See *block protection.*

bad sector An area of a *floppy* or *hard disk* that won't reliably record *data.* Almost all hard disks have some bad sectors as a result of manufacturing defects. The *operating system* locks these *sectors* out of reading and writing operations so you can use the disk as though the bad sectors don't exist. In addition, bad sectors may develop as the disk is being used, requiring the use of a disk *utility program* to identify these sectors and lock them out of storage operations. See *bad track table.*

bad track A *hard disk* or *floppy disk track* that contains a *bad sector.* Marked as unusable in the *file allocation table (FAT),* bad tracks are harmless unless Track 0 is bad, in which case the disk must be replaced.

bad track table   A document attached to or packaged with a *hard disk* that lists the *bad sectors* of the disk. Almost every hard disk comes off the assembly line with some defects. During the *low-level format,* these defective areas of the disk are locked out so system software can't use them.

BAK   The *MS-DOS file-name* extension usually attached to a *file* containing *backup* data. Many *application programs* assign the .BAK extension to the old version of a file any time you change the file's name.

ball bat   In *Unix,* a common slang term for an exclamation point (!). Also called a bang character or an astonisher. See *bang path.*

balloon help   In the *MacOS,* an optional help feature that displays cartoon balloons containing an explanation of an on-screen feature (such as an icon or part of a window) when the user positions the mouse over it.

band   In a *database management* program's *report* function, an area set aside for a certain type of information, such as a header area or *data* from *fields.* Also, the track on which a *band-stepper actuator* travels.

band–stepper actuator   A mechanism, incorporating a *stepping motor* and a track (a band), that positions the *read/write head* of a *hard disk* over a *track.* Band-stepper actuators are not as common as *servo-voice coil actuators* on today's hard disks.

bandwidth   The amount of data that can be transmitted via a given communications channel (such as a computer network) in a given unit of time (generally one second). For *digital* devices, bandwidth is measured in *bits per second (bps).* The bandwidth of *analog* devices is measured in cycles per second *(cps).*

bang   1. In programming, a common slang term for an exclamation point (!). 2. In HTML, a common slang term for a forward slash (/), especially when telling someone a *URL* ("Go to www–dot–Microsoft–dot–com–bang–search–dot–html").

bang path   In *Unix-to-Unix Copy Program (UUCP),* an *e-mail* address that specifies the location of a specific computer on a UUCP-based *network.* The address is called a bang path because the various units of the address are separated by exclamation points (*bang* characters).

bank switching   A way of expanding memory beyond an *operating system's* or *microprocessor's* address limitations by switching rapidly between two banks of memory. See *Expanded Memory Specification (EMS).*

bar code   A printed pattern of wide and narrow vertical bars used to represent numerical codes in machine-readable form. Computers equipped with *bar code readers* and special software can interpret bar codes. Supermarkets use bar codes conforming to the Universal Product Code (UPS) to identify products and ring up prices, while the U.S. Postal Service uses POSTNET bar codes to make ZIP codes machine-readable. The latest versions of word processing programs, such as *WordPerfect* and *Microsoft Word,* include options to print POSTNET bar codes on envelopes.

bar code reader   An input device that scans *bar codes* and, with special *software,* converts the bar code into readable data.

bar graph   In *presentation graphics,* a *graph* with horizontal bars commonly used to show the values of unrelated items. The *x-axis* (categories axis) is the vertical axis, and the *y-axis* (values axis) is the horizontal axis. Often confused with a *column graph,* which uses vertical bars, a bar graph is best for conveying quantities while a column graph is best for conveying changes over time. See *line graph* and *paired bar graph.*

base64   A data encoding method that converts a *binary file* into plain ASCII text, which can be transmitted via the *Internet* and other computer networks. This encoding method is used in *MIME.*

baseband   In *local area networks (LANs),* a communications method in which the information-bearing signal is placed directly on the cable in *digital* form without *modulation.* Because many baseband networks can use *twisted-pair* (ordinary tele-phone) *cables,* they're cheaper to install than broadband networks that require *coaxial* cable. However, a baseband system is limited in its geographic extent and provides only one channel of communication at a time. Most personal computer local area networks are baseband networks. See *broadband.*

base font   The default *font* that is used throughout a docu-ment. Changes, such as *italics* or **bold** and larger or smaller sizes, are variations of the base font. You can change to a different *type-face* at any point in the document, but if you change the base font while working in a document, the font change is applied for the entire document. In most *word processing* programs, you can choose a default base font for all documents or for just the document you're editing.

base–level synthesizer   In *multimedia,* the minimum capabilities of a music synthesizer required by *Microsoft Windows 95* and its Multimedia Personal Computer (MPC) specifications. A base-level synthesizer must be capable of playing at least six simultaneous notes on three melodic instruments and three simultaneous notes on three percussion instruments. See *extended-level synthesizer* and *MIDI.*

baseline   In *typography,* the lowest point that characters reach (excluding *descenders*). For example, the baseline of a line of text is the bottom of letters such as a and x, excluding the lowest points of p and q, which have descenders.

base memory   See *conventional memory.*

BASIC   Acronym for Beginner's All-Purpose Symbolic Instruction Code. An easy-to-use *high-level programming language* developed in 1964 for instructional purposes. Initially, BASIC was criticized for encouraging poor program structure due to the use of *goto* statements and the lack of *control structures.* Newer versions, such as Microsoft's *Visual BASIC,* incorporate the principles of *structured programming* and some of the features of *object-oriented programming (OOP).* See *spaghetti code.*

BASICA   An *interpreter* for the Microsoft *BASIC* programming language that was supplied on the *MS-DOS* disk provided with IBM-manufactured personal computers.

Basic Encoding Rules (BER)   The set of standardized rules for encoding data according to the *Abstract Syntax Notation One (ASN.1)* protocol. The purpose of these rules is to encode all data in such a way that BER–compatible applications can immediately recognize which type of data the encoding contains. BER is not widely used.

basic input/output system   See *BIOS.*

Basic Rate Interface (BRI)   In the *Integrated Services Digital Network (ISDN)* specification, the basic digital telephone and data service that is designed for residences. BRI offers two 64,000 *bit per second (bps)* channels for voice, graphics, and data, plus one 16,000 bit per second channel for signaling purposes. See *Primary Rate Interface (PRI)*.

BAT   The *MS-DOS file-name extension* attached to a *batch file*. See *AUTOEXEC.BAT.*

batch file   A *file* containing a series of MS-DOS *commands* executed one after the other, as though you had typed them. The mandatory .BAT file extension causes *COMMAND.COM* to process the file one line at a time. Batch files are useful when you need to type the same series of MS-DOS commands repeatedly. Almost all *hard disk* users have an *AUTOEXEC.BAT* file, a batch file that MS-DOS loads at the start of every operating session.

batch processing   A *mode* of computer operation in which program instructions are executed one after the other without user intervention. Batch processing efficiently uses computer resources but is less convenient than *interactive processing,* in which you see the results of your commands on-screen so you can correct errors and make necessary adjustments before completing the operation.

battery pack   A rechargeable battery that supplies power to a computer, usually a *portable computer,* when external (main) power isn't available. Most battery packs use nickel-cadmium *(NiCad)* batteries, which have two significant drawbacks: They're prone to becoming incapable of accepting a full charge, and, because of their cadmium content, are extremely toxic. Increasing in popularity are nickel metal hydride *(3NiMH)* and *lithium-ion* battery packs, which provide increased capacity without either drawback. See *auxiliary battery.*

baud   A variation or change in a signal in a communications channel. See *baud rate* and *bits per second (bps).*

baud rate   The maximum number of changes that can occur per second in the electrical state of a communications circuit. Under *RS-232C communications protocols,* 300 *baud* is likely to equal 300 *bits per second (bps),* but at higher baud rates, the number of bits per second transmitted is usually twice the baud rate because two bits of data can be sent with each change. Therefore, the transfer rate of modems, for example, is usually stated in *bps.* See *asynchronous communication, modem, serial port, serial printer,* and *telecommunications.*

bay   See *drive bay.*

BBS   Acronym for Bulletin Board Service. A small-scale online information service, usually set up by a personal computer hobbyist for the enjoyment of other hobbyists, and based on a single personal computer that is accessed by means of direct-dial modem links. A typical BBS includes topically oriented discussion groups, file downloading, and games. The Internet's explosive popularity has eroded the popularity of BBSs, many of which have responded by making their resources accessible by means of direct Internet connections.

BCD   See *binary coded decimal.*

bed   In *multimedia,* the instrumental or choral music that provides the enveloping background for a presentation.

Bell 103A   In the United States, a *modulation* protocol for computer *modems* governing sending and receiving data at a speed of 300 *bits per second (bps).* See *ITU-TSS* protocol.

Bell 212A   In the United States, a *modulation* protocol for computer *modems* governing sending and receiving data at a speed of 1200 *bits per second (bps).* See *ITU-TSS* protocol.

bells and whistles   Advanced features that make a program more useful for specialized purposes, such as a *mail merging* utility in a word processing program.

benchmark   A standard measurement, determined by a *benchmark program,* that is used to test the performance of different brands of equipment.

benchmark program   A *utility program* used to measure a computer's processing speed and component performance so that its overall performance can be compared to that of other computers running the same program. See *cache memory* and *throughput.*

BeOS   An operating system for *Macintosh* computers and clones created by Be, Inc., which is led by ex-Apple executive Jean-Louis Gassée. Designed from the ground up as an entirely new operating system, BeOS does not interface with applications by means of time-consuming procedural calls, but rather by means of an elegantly designed *object-oriented* interface. The operating system is highly *multithreaded* and supports *parallel processors.*

BeOS is targeted to high-end multimedia developers, who need these features in order to create compelling, high-resolution multimedia presentations.

BER   See *Basic Encoding Rules.*

Berkeley Software Distribution (BSD)   A version of the *Unix* operating system that was developed and formerly maintained by the University of California, Berkeley. BSD helped to establish the *Internet* in colleges and universities because the distributed software included *TCP/IP.*

Berkeley Unix   A version of the *Unix* operating system, developed at the University of California at Berkeley, that takes full advantage of the *virtual memory* capabilities of Digital Equipment Corporation (DEC) *minicomputers.*

Bernoulli box   An innovative removable *secondary storage* device developed by Iomega Corporation for IBM PC-compatible and Macintosh computers. Bernoulli boxes have removable cartridges containing flexible disks that can hold up to 230M of *data.* Bernoulli boxes are extremely resistant to *head crashes,* but *removable hard disks* have stolen considerable market share from Iomegas one-time flagship product.

beta   Common abbreviation of *beta software.*

beta site   The company, university department, or individual authorized to *beta test* software. When developing a program or a version of an existing program, a company chooses out-of-house beta sites where the program is subjected to demanding, heavy-duty usage. This process reveals the program's remaining *bugs* and shortcomings.

beta software   In *software* testing, a preliminary version of a *program* that's widely distributed before commercial release to users who test the program by operating it under realistic conditions. See *alpha software, alpha test, beta site,* and *beta test.*

beta test   The second stage in the testing of computer software, after *alpha test,* but before commercial release. Beta tests are at *beta sites.* Also used as a verb, as in, the software is ready to be beta-tested.

Bézier curve   (Pronounced beh-zee-ay) A mathematically generated line that can take the form of non-uniform curves.

In a Bézier curve, the locations of two midpoints—called control *handles*—are used to describe the overall shape of an irregular curve. In *graphics* applications, by dragging the control handles (shown as small boxes on-screen), you manipulate the complexity and shape of the curve.

bibliographic retrieval service   An *online information service* that specializes in maintaining huge computerized indexes to scholarly, scientific, medical, and technical literature. The two leading information firms are BRS Information Technologies (Latham, NY) and DIALOG Information Services (Menlo Park, CA). Serving mainly corporate and institutional customers, these companies' fees average more than $1 per minute. Personal computer users can access, at substantially lower rates, special menu-driven night and weekend versions of these services, BRS/After Dark and Knowledge Index.

bidirectional communication   A quality of new *parallel port* designs that enables a computer and a peripheral device to exchange messages through a parallel cable. Both the *enhanced parallel port (EPP)* and the *extended capabilities port (ECP)* offer bidirectional communication.

bidirectional parallel port   A *parallel port,* capable of both sending and receiving detailed messages, that can transfer data much faster than a standard parallel port. In its standard *IEEE 1284,* the Institute of Electrical and Electronics Engineers (IEEE) established the technical rules governing bidirectional parallel ports. Both the *enhanced parallel port (EPP)* and the *extended capabilities port (ECP)* conform to IEEE 1284, and one of the two standards—probably the ECP, experts say—will replace the standard parallel port in the next few years.

bidirectional printing   Printing by means of a *bidirectional parallel port,* which enables *bidirectional communication* between the printer and the operating system. With bidirectional printing, you see detailed error messages when the printer malfunctions.

Big Blue   Slang for International Business Machines (IBM) Corporation, which uses blue as its corporate color.

big-endian   A philosophical orientation towards computer system and network design that favors putting the most significant (largest) digit first in numerical encoding schemes. The contrasting orientation, *little-endian,* favors putting the most significant digit last. Because it cannot be proven that either orientation is more efficient, the dispute between big-endians and little-endians classically exemplifies the pointless *holy war,* in which the various positions taken are based on irreducible pseudo-religious principles rather than reason. The terms derive from Jonathan Swift's *Gulliver's Travels,* which depicts Lilliputian wars concerning whether boiled eggs should be opened at the big end or the little end.

bin   Common abbreviation for *binary file.*

binaries   Two or more *binary files.*

binary coded decimal (BCD)   A method of coding long decimal numbers so that they can be processed with great *precision* in a computer. Each decimal digit is encoded using a four-bit binary number.

binary compatible   In *microprocessors,* capable of running software designed for another company's *central processing unit* (CPU). In *software,* a program will run on any *microprocessor* with which it is binary compatible.

binary file   A *file* containing data or program instructions in a computer-readable format. Using the *MS-DOS* TYPE command or a *word processing* program, you can't display the actual contents—ones and zeroes—of a binary file in a useful form. The opposite of a binary file is an *ASCII file.*

binary newsgroup   In *Usenet,* a *newsgroup* in which the articles contain (or are supposed to contain) binary files, such as sounds, *graphics,* or movies. These files have been encoded with *uuencode,* a program that transforms a *binary file* into coded ASCII characters so it can be transferred via the *Internet.* In order to use these files, it is first necessary to decode them (using a program called uudecode, or a *newsreader* that has built-in uudecoding capability).

binary numbers   A number system with a base (radix) of 2, unlike the number systems most of us use, which have bases of 10 (decimal numbers), 12 (measurement in feet and inches), and 60 (time). Binary numbers are preferred for computers for *precision* and economy. Building an electronic circuit that can detect the difference between two states (high current and low current, or 0 and 1) is easy and inexpensive; building a circuit that detects the difference among 10 states (0 through 9) is much more difficult and expensive. In fact, the word *bit* derives from the phrase BInary digiT.

binary search   A search *algorithm* that avoids a slow search through hundreds or thousands of *records* by starting in the middle of a sorted *database* and determining whether the desired record is above or below the midpoint. Having reduced the number of records to be searched by 50 percent, the search proceeds to the middle of the remaining records, and so on, until the desired record is found.

binary transfer   1. In data communications generally, *file transfer protocol (FTP)* that allows users to transfer *binary files* to and from a remote computer using *terminal emulation* software. 2. In *FTP*, a file download or upload that preserves binary files intact (unlike an ASCII transfer).

Binary Tree Predictive Coding (BTPC)   A compression method for still graphics that performs both *lossless compression* and *lossy compression* and is particularly effective for the computer transmission and presentation of photographs.

binder   Before the invention of *thin-film magnetic media,* the adhesive that held a recording medium on the surface of a *hard disk.* Binder was mixed with the medium (and sometimes a lubricant, too) and applied to the *substrate,* by *sputtering* or some other means.

binding offset   In *word processing* and *desktop publishing (DTP),* a gap left on one side of a printed page to allow room for binding the *document.* Binding offset is used only for documents printed or reproduced on both sides of the page *(duplex printing);* the text is shifted to the left on *verso* (left, even-numbered) pages and to the right on *recto* (right, odd-numbered) pages.

BinHex   A method of encoding *binary files* so that the coded file contains nothing but the standard *American Standard Code for Information Interchange (ASCII)* characters and can, therefore, be transferred to other computers via the *Internet.* The receiving computer must decode the file using BinHex-capable decoding software. BinHex is popular among *Macintosh* users. Note that BinHex is not a compression technique and that a BinHexed file may actually be longer than the source file. For this reason, BinHexed files are generally compressed after they are encoded using the Macintosh standard compression program, StuffIt.

BIOS   A set of *programs* encoded in *read-only memory (ROM)* on IBM PC-compatible computers. These programs handle startup operations such as the *power-on self-test (POST)* and low-level control for hardware, such as *disk drives, keyboard,* and *monitor.* The BIOS programs of IBM personal computers are copyrighted, so manufacturers of IBM PC-compatible computers must create BIOSs that emulate the IBM BIOS or buy an emulation from companies, such as Phoenix Technologies and American Megatrends, Inc. Some system components have a separate BIOS. The BIOS on a *hard disk controller,* for example, stores a table of *tracks* and *sectors* on the drive.

B-ISDN   See *Broadband ISDN.*

bit   The basic unit of information in a binary numbering system (BInary digiT). The electronic circuitry in computers detects the difference between two states (high current and low current) and represents these states as one of the two numbers in a binary system: 1 or 0. These basic high/low, either/or, yes/no units of information are called bits. Because building a reliable circuit that tells the difference between a 1 and a 0 is easy and inexpensive, computers are accurate in their internal processing capabilities, typically making fewer than one internal error in every 100 billion processing operations. Eight bits comprise an *octet,* sometimes called a *byte.*

bitmap   The representation of a video image stored in a computer's memory as a set of *bits.* Each picture element *(pixel),* corresponding to a tiny dot on-screen, is controlled by an on or off code stored as a bit (1 for on or 0 for off) for black-and-white displays. Color and shades of gray require more information. The bitmap is a grid of rows and columns of the 1s and 0s that the computer translates into pixels to display on-screen. See *bit-mapped graphic* and *block graphics.*

bit-mapped font   A *screen* or *printer font* in which each character is composed of a pattern of dots. To display or print bit-mapped fonts, the computer or *printer* must keep a full representation of each character in memory. When referring to bit-mapped fonts, the term font should be taken literally as a complete set of characters of a given *typeface, weight, posture,* and *type size.* If you want to use Palatino (Roman) 12 and Palatino Italic 14, for example, you must load two complete sets of characters into memory. You can't scale bit-mapped fonts up or down without introducing grotesque staircase distortions, called *aliasing*. See *anti-aliasing*.

bit-mapped graphic   A *graphic* image formed by a pattern of *pixels* and limited in *resolution* to the maximum resolution of the *display* or *printer* on which it is displayed. Bit-mapped graphics are produced by *paint programs*. Considered inferior to *vector graphics* for most applications, bit-mapped graphics may have *aliasing* caused by the square shape of pixels. See *Encapsulated PostScript (EPS) file and object-oriented graphic*.

BITNET   A *wide area network (WAN)* that links *mainframe* computer systems at approximately 2,500 universities and research institutions in North America, Europe, and Japan. BIT-NET (an acronym for Because It's Time Network) does not use the *TCP/IP* protocols but can exchange *e-mail* with the *Internet*. BITNET is operated by the Corporation for Research and Educational Networking (CREN), with headquarters in Washington, D.C. To become a member of the *network,* an organization must pay for a *leased line* that connects to the nearest existing BITNET site, and it must also agree to let another institution connect with this line in the future. Faced with competition from the Internet, BITNET is slowly dying.

bits per inch (bpi)   In magnetic media, such as backup *tape drives* or *disk drives,* a measurement of the medium's recording density.

bits per second (bps)   In *asynchronous communications,* a measurement of *data* transmission speed. In *personal computing,* bps rates frequently are used to measure the performance of *modems* and *serial ports.* The bps rates are enumerated incrementally: 110 bps, 150 bps, 300 bps, 600 bps, 1200 bps, 2400 bps, 4800 bps, 9600 bps, 14,400 bps, 19,200 bps, 38,400 bps, 57,600 bps, and 115,200 bps. See *baud rate.*

black letter   In *typography,* a family of *typefaces* derived from German handwriting of the medieval era. Black letter typefaces often are called Fraktur (after the Latin word fractus, meaning broken) because the medieval scribes who created this design lifted their pens from the line to form the next character—fracturing the continuous flow of handwriting.

black-write technique   See *print engine.*

blank cell In a *spreadsheet program,* a *cell* that contains no *values, labels,* or *formatting* different from the worksheet's *global formats.*

bleed In *desktop publishing,* a photograph, text box, or other page-design element that extends to the edge of the page, such as the thumb tab index at the edge of this page. This usually isn't possible if you're printing with a *laser printer,* which can't print in a $1/8$-inch strip around the page's perimeter.

bleed capability The ability of a *printer* to print *bleeds.*

blessed folder On the Macintosh, the System Folder, which is automatically searched by programs that are looking for needed files. This folder contains the configuration files (called Preferences), as well as other support files, that are needed by installed applications.

blind carbon copy (BCC) In *e-mail,* a copy of a message that is sent to one or more persons without the knowledge of the recipient. Also called blind courtesy copy (BCC).

bloat The unwarranted and inefficient multiplication of software features, which are added in an attempt to make a program more marketable. See *creeping featurism.*

bloatware See *fatware.*

block 1. A unit of information that's processed or transferred. The unit may vary in size. 2. In *modems,* a unit of information passed from one computer to another is a block. If, for example, you use *XMODEM,* a file transfer protocol *(FTP),* 128 bytes are considered a block. Under *MS-DOS,* a block transferred to or from a *disk drive* is 512 bytes in size. 3. In *word processing,* a unit of text that you mark so you can use a *block operation* to move, copy, or otherwise affect that text.

block definition See *selection.*

block graphics On IBM PC-compatible computers, *graphics* formed on-screen by *graphics characters* in the *ASCII extended character set.* The graphics characters in the ASCII extended character set are suitable for creating and shading rectangles but not for fine detail. Because the block graphics characters are handled the same way as ordinary characters, the computer can display block graphics considerably faster than *bit-mapped graphics.*

block move   A fundamental editing technique in *word processing* in which a marked *block* of text is cut from one location and inserted in another. Synonymous with *cut* and *paste*.

block operation   The act of transferring a *block* of information from one area to another. In *word processing,* an editing or formatting operation, such as copying, deleting, moving, or underlining, performed on a marked block of text. See *block move.*

block protection   In *word processing* and *page layout programs,* a *command* that prevents the insertion of a *soft page break* in a specific block of text, preventing a *bad page break.*

block size   The size of an individual piece of data transmitted by a file transfer protocol or *error-correction protocol* over a *modem. XMODEM* uses a block size of 128 *bytes,* for example.

Blue Book   1. The first of the four official references for the *PostScript* display language. 2. Commonly used name for one of three official references on the *SmallTalk* programming language. 3. The standards issued by the International Telecommunications Union (ITU) in 1988 describing a number of important e-mail and fax protocols. See *X.400.*

blurb   In *desktop publishing,* a brief explanatory subheading that's set below or next to a headline.

BMP   In *Microsoft Windows 95,* an extension indicating that the file contains a Windows-compatible *bit-mapped graphic.*

BNC connector   In an *Ethernet,* a male connector mounted at each end of a length of *coaxial cable.*

BNF   See *Backus-Naur Form.*

board   An electronic *printed circuit board.* Boards that are designed to press into *expansion slots* are also called *adapters* or *cards.*

body type   The *font* (usually 8- to 12-*point*) used to set paragraphs of text, distinguished from the font used to set headings, captions, and other typographical elements. *Serif typefaces,* such as Century, Garamond, and Times Roman, are preferred over *sans serif* typefaces for body type because they're more legible. See *display type.*

bogus newsgroup   In *Usenet*, a *newsgroup* that does not corre-spond to the site's list of approved newsgroups. Most *newsreaders* are programmed to detect such newsgroups and delete them automatically. Bogus newsgroups may originate from program-ming errors or somebody's effort to create the group by skirting the normal newsgroup creation process.

boilerplate   A block of text used over and over in letters, memos, or reports. See *template*.

boldface   A character *emphasis* visibly darker and heavier in *weight* than normal type. Each entry word in this dictionary is in boldface type.

bomb   1. To *crash*. 2. To impede someone's *e-mail* access by fill-ing their *inbox* with hundreds or even thousands of unwanted messages. 3. In the *Macintosh*, a most unwelcome icon that informs you that the computer has crashed. 4. Abbreviation for *logic bomb*.

Bookmark   1. To record the location of a desired Web page or passage in a word processing document so that the user can easily return to it later. 2. In word processing, a code inserted at a particular point in a *document* so that point can easily be found later. You might insert a bookmark in a part of a novel you're writing that needs to be revised, for example. 3. In *Netscape* or other *Web browser,* one of the user's favorite places on the *World Wide Web (WWW),* someplace you'd like to visit again. Synonymous with *favorite* (the term used by *Microsoft Internet Explorer*) and *hotlist item (Mosaic).*

book weight   A *typeface* that's darker and heavier than most typefaces, but not so dark and heavy as *boldface*. Book weight *fonts* are used to set lengthy sections of text so that they're easy to read and produce a pleasing gray tone on the page. See *weight*.

Boolean logic   A branch of mathematics, founded by nineteenth-century English logician George Boole (1815-1864), in which all operations produce one of two alternative values: true or false. Boole's work remained obscure until the rise of digital computing based on *binary numbers,* which have just two values: 1 and 0. Boolean logic is used to design computing cir-cuits. It provides the conceptual foundation for computer searches using *Boolean operators.*

Boolean operator   A word, generally typed in capital letters, that indicates how search terms should be combined in a *Boolean search*. Synonymous with logical operator.

Boolean Operators

If you link two search terms with:	The search retrieves:
AND ("Chardonnay AND Zinfandel")	Only those records or documents that contain both of these terms
OR ("Chardonnay OR Zinfandel")	Any record or document that contains either of these terms
NOT ("Chardonnay NOT Zinfandel")	Any record or document that contains "Chardonnay," except those that also contain "Zinfandel"

Boolean search   A search that involves the use of Boolean operators (AND, OR, and NOT). In a Boolean search, you can use these operators to refine the scope of your search.

boot   1. To initiate an automatic routine that clears the memory, loads the *operating system (OS),* and prepares the computer for use. Included in the computer's *read-only memory (ROM)* is the *Power-On Self-Test (POST),* which executes when the power is switched on (a *cold boot*). After a system *crash* or lockup occurs, you usually must boot the computer again, or reboot, by pressing the Reset button or a key combination such as Ctrl+Alt+Del (IBM PCs and compatibles) or Ctrl+Command+Start (Macintoshes) (a *warm boot*). The term is derived from the expression "pulling oneself up by the bootstraps." 2. The process of starting the computer (cold boot) or restarting (warm boot).

BOOTP   Acronym for Bootstrap Protocol, an *Internet* protocol that enables workstations on a *local area network (LAN)* to find their *IP address* dynamically.

boot sector   The first track on an *IBM PC-compatible hard* or *floppy disk* (track 0). During the *boot* process, *read-only memory (ROM)* tells the computer to read the first block of data on this track and load whatever *program* is found there. If *system files* are found, they direct the computer to load *MS-DOS*.

boot sector virus See *boot virus.*

boot sequence The order in which a computer's *basic input-output system (BIOS)* searches *disk drives* for *operating system* files. Unless programmed otherwise, most personal computers look for the operating system on drive A first and then search drive C.

boot virus A computer *virus* that infects the crucial *boot sector* of a disk, so that it is loaded into the computer's memory at the beginning of every operating session. A boot virus will subsequently infect any additional disks that are inserted into the system.

Border Gateway Protocol An *Internet* protocol that defines the routing of Internet data between an *Autonomous System (AS)* and the wider Internet. This protocol replaces the older *Exterior Gateway Protocol.*

Borland C++ A *development suite* for the C++ programming language created by Borland. The package includes a *compiler, debugger,* version management utilities, and installation utilities. The compiler conforms to *ANSI/ISO C++.*

Borland International, Inc. A Scotts Valley, CA.–based software publisher that focuses on providing database systems and programming languages for developers. Current products include *Delphi,* a programming environment similar to *Microsoft Visual BASIC,* and *Borland C++.*

bot 1. In Multi-User Dungeons *(MUDs)* and *Internet Relay Chat (IRC),* a character whose on-screen actions stem from a *program* rather than a real person. The term is a contraction of robot. The most famous of all bots, Julia, inhabits a MUD called LambdaMoo and has tricked thousands into thinking that she is a real human being. Bots are frequently used for pranks or antisocial actions and are not welcome on most IRC servers. See *MOO.* On IRC, bots are often used for mischievous purposes and are not allowed on many servers. 2. In *Internet* searching, an automated search agent that explores the Internet autonomously, and reports back to the user when the search conditions have been successfully fulfilled.

bounce In *e-mail,* to come back marked as undeliverable (see *bounce message*).

bounce message   An *e-mail* message informing the user that an e-mail message could not be delivered to its intended recipient. The failure may be due to an incorrectly typed e-mail address or to a network problem.

Bourne shell   An early user interface *(shell)* for the *Unix* operating system, as developed by S.R. Bourne at Bell Laboratories in 1978. The Bourne shell is a *command-line operating system* that requires users to remember command syntax. The Bourne shell has been largely supplanted by more recent Unix shells, such as *csh.*

bowl   In *typography,* the curved strokes that enclose or partially enclose a blank space, called the *counter,* that's part of a letter, such as the blank space in the letter a or c.

box   1. Common slang term for a computer of a particular type (a "Wintel box" or a "Unix box"). 2. Abbreviation of *dialog box.* 3. A border around a paragraph or graphic in a *word processing* or *desktop publishing* document.

bpi   See *bits per inch.*

bps   Acronym for *bits per second (bps),* a fundamental measurement of transmission speed of digital data in a communications channel. Rapid gains in transmission speed necessitate the following: *Kbps* (kilobits per second), *Mbps* (megabits per second), and *Gbps* (gigabits per second).

brace   The left { or right } curved bracket character on the standard keyboard. Synonymous with *curly brace.* Compare to *angle bracket* and *bracket.*

bracket   The left ([) or right (]) bracket character on the standard keyboard. See *angle bracket, brace* and *curly brace.*

branch   1. In a *tree structure,* a subordinate line off the tree that leads to a leaf. 2. In *MS-DOS,* one or more *subdirectories* located within a *directory.* In *Microsoft Windows 95 Explorer* and other graphical *file* manager utilities, directory branches can be displayed or hidden, depending on your needs. 3. In programming, to route program execution to a *subroutine.*

branch control structure   In *programming,* a *control structure* that tells a *program* to branch to a *subroutine* only if a specified condition is met. If a program detects that a vital data file has been irretrievably corrupted, for example, the program branches to display a message that says something like, "The file you want to open is corrupted." Synonymous with *selection*. See *IF/THEN/ELSE*.

branch prediction   An educated guessing method employed by *microprocessors* that use *superscalar architecture.* By looking at a *program* and predicting how a true/false test will turn out, a microprocessor that employs branch prediction can get ready to execute the code that follows a certain test outcome. The *Pentium* microprocessor employs branch prediction and guesses correctly 90 percent of the time.

break   A user-initiated signal that interrupts processing or receiving *data.* See *Control+Break.*

break-out box   A testing device inserted into a communications cable or between a *serial port* and a serial cable that allows each signal to be tested separately.

breakpoint   A location in a *program* where it pauses to let the user decide what to do next.

BRI   See *Basic Rate Interface.*

bridge   In *local area networks (LANs),* a device that allows two *networks* (even ones dissimilar in *topology,* wiring, or *communications protocols*) to exchange *data.*

brightness   A *monitor* control that regulates the strength of electron beams striking the rear of a *cathode ray tube (CRT)* display. A high brightness setting increases the strength of the beams and makes the on-screen image brighter, while a low brightness setting weakens the beams and dims the image. *LCD* and other types of displays have similar controls that have the same effects.

broadband   In *local area networks (LANs),* an *analog* communications method characterized by high *bandwidth.* The signal usually is split, or *multiplexed,* to provide multiple communications channels. Because a computer's signals are *digital* signals, they must be transformed by a process called *modulation* before they can be conveyed over an analog signal network. A *modem* at each end of a *network* cable performs this task. Broadband communications can extend over great distances and operate at extremely high speeds. See *baseband.*

Broadband ISDN (B-ISDN)   A high-*bandwidth* digital telephone standard for transmitting up to 1.5 *Mbps* over *fiber-optic cables*. See *Basic Rate Interface (BRI)* and *ISDN.*

broadcast message   In a *network,* a message to all system users that appears when you *log on* to the system. For example, broadcast messages are used to inform users when the system will be shut down for maintenance.

brownout   A period of low-voltage electrical power caused by unusually heavy demand, such as that created by summertime air conditioner use. Brownouts can cause computers to operate erratically or to *crash,* either of which can result in *data* loss. If brownouts frequently cause your computer to crash, you may need to buy a *line-interactive UPS* to work with your machine.

browse   1. To look for information by manually looking through a series of storage locations. 2. To look for information on the *World Wide Web (WWW)* by jumping from hyperlink to hyperlink.

browse mode   In a *database management program,* a mode in which *data records* are displayed in columns for quick, on-screen review. Generally, you cannot modify data while in the browse mode. Synonymous with list view or table view in some programs. See *edit mode.*

browser   A program that enables the user to navigate the *World Wide Web (WWW).* The two leading browsers are *Netscape Navigator,* part of Netscape Communication's *Netscape Communicator* package, and *Microsoft Internet Explorer.* A browser serves as the *client* for Web and other types of Internet *servers.* Synonymous with *Web browser.* Increasingly, browsers are becoming the interface of choice for all the various types of data accessible by means of networks based on Internet technology. See *light client.*

browsing   In a *hypertext,* an information-seeking method that involves manually searching through linked documents. In the *World Wide Web (WWW),* browsing is rarely effective for finding information on a specific topic (it's much better to use subject trees and search engines), but it's lots of fun. Browsing, for no particular reason, is called *surfing.* See *search engine* and *subject tree.*

brush script   In *typography,* a typeface design that simulates script drawn with a brush or broad-pointed pen.

brute force In *programming,* a crude technique for solving a difficult problem by repeating a simple procedure many times. Computer spell-checkers use a brute-force technique. They don't really "check spelling"; they merely compare all the words in a *document* to a dictionary of correctly spelled words.

BSD Unix See *Berkeley Unix.*

B-size paper A page that measures 11×17 inches, as specified by the American National Standards Institute (ANSI). Compare to *A-size paper,* which is 8.5×11 inches.

B-size printer A printer capable of printing on *B-size* (11×17 inch) and smaller paper.

BTW In *online* conferences, an *acronym* for By The Way.

bubble-jet printer A variation on the *inkjet printer* concept that uses heating elements instead of piezoelectric crystals to shoot ink from nozzles.

bubble memory A type of *memory* that employs materials that can be magnetized in only one direction. When a magnetic field is applied at right angles to the plane of magnetization, the materials form a tiny circle (a "bubble"). The resulting differences between the properly magnetized and bubbled areas can be used to represent digital data. Bubble memory is nonvolatile and is sometimes used in portable computers to store data between operating sessions. However, it is considerably slower than competing *non-volatile memory* technologies, such as *EEPROM,* and *Flash Erasable Programmable Read-Only Memory (Flash EPROM).*

buckyball toner In computer printers, a *toner* made of large molecules of a synthetic carbon called buckminsterfullerene. Buckyball toner, named after engineer Buckminster Fuller, is easier to control than toner made of other types of carbon and is frequently used in today's printers.

buffer A unit of memory given the task of holding information temporarily, especially while waiting for slower components to catch up.

buffer overflow A system error that results from a faulty program, which writes more data to a *buffer* than the memory unit can accommodate.

bug   A *programming* error that causes a *program* or a computer system to perform erratically, produce incorrect results, or *crash.* The term bug was coined when a real insect was discovered to have fouled up one of the circuits of the first electronic *digital* computer, the ENIAC. A *hardware* problem is called a *glitch.*

bug fix release   A *maintenance release* of a computer program that is intended to repair a *bug.* Instead of a bug fix release, a publisher may release a *patch,* which modifies the original program's code to eliminate the bug.

built-in   Included in the most basic functions of a computer program or programming language.

built-in font   A *printer* font encoded permanently in the printer's *read-only memory (ROM).* All *printers* offer at least one built-in font. Also called a resident font. See *cartridge font, downloadable font,* and *screen font.*

built-in function   In a *spreadsheet program,* a ready-to-use formula, also called an @ function, that performs mathematical, statistical, trigonometric, financial, and other calculations. A built-in *function* begins with a special symbol (usually @ or =), followed by a *keyword,* such as AVG or SUM, that describes the formula's purpose. Most built-in functions require one or more *arguments* enclosed in parentheses and separated by commas *(argument separators).*

built-in pointing device   In *portable computers,* a *trackball* or *pointing stick* that's built into the computer's *case* in a fixed position. See *clip-on pointing device, freestanding pointing device, mouse,* and *snap-on pointing device.*

bulk storage   *Magnetic media* that can store *data.* Synonymous with mass storage. See *secondary storage.*

bullet   Originally, a hollow or solid circle about the height of a lowercase letter, used to set off items in a list. Today, squares, triangles, pointing fingers, and a variety of other *graphic* characters are used as bullets. Often combined with indentation, bullets are used when listing items whose content is roughly equal in emphasis or significance. See *hanging indent.*

bulleted list chart   In *presentation graphics,* a text *chart* that lists a series of ideas or items of equal weight.

bulletin board system (BBS)   See *BBS*.

bulletproof   Capable, because of high *fault tolerance,* of resisting external interference, and recovering from situations that would crash other programs. A bulletproof program is said to be *robust.*

bundled software   *Software* included with a *computer system* as part of the system's total price. Also, several programs that are packaged and sold together, now frequently called *software suites.*

burn-in   Operating a newly assembled *computer system* to screen for failures. *Semiconductor* components, such as memory chips and *microprocessors,* tend to fail either in the first few hours of operation or late in their lives. Responsible computer retailers, therefore, run systems continuously for 24 to 48 hours before releasing the systems to customers. Sometimes used incorrectly to refer to permanently burning, or etching, the screen phosphors of a *display* when the same image is constantly on-screen. This phenomenon is actually called *ghosting.*

burst   A temporary, high-speed data transfer mode that, under certain or ideal conditions, can transfer data at significantly higher *data transfer rates* than the rate normally achieved with a non-burst technology. For example, memory chips can be designed so that, under certain circumstances, a processor can write quickly to a matrix of memory locations, without having to address each of these locations individually.

burst EDO RAM   A high-speed version of Extended Data Out random access memory (*EDO RAM*) that improves read and write times significantly by eliminating *wait states,* or computer *clock cycles* that are wasted while memory operations take place. Although burst EDO RAM is faster than EDO RAM, it is being replaced by *SDRAM,* the fastest memory technology that is currently available in the mass PC market. See *DRAM, FPM* and *random-access memory (RAM).*

bus   An internal electrical pathway along which signals are sent from one part of the computer to another. Personal computers have a processor bus design with three pathways: The *data bus* sends data back and forth between the memory and the *microprocessor* divided into an *external data bus* and an *internal data bus;* the *address bus* identifies which memory location will come into play; and the *control bus* carries the control unit's signals. An extension of the data bus, called the *expansion bus,* connects the computer's expansion slots to the processor. The data, address, and expansion buses are wired in parallel rows so that all the bits being sent can travel simultaneously, like cars side by side on a 16- or 32-lane freeway.

bus architecture　The overall design of a bus, especially as it affects the compatibility of expansion boards. See *EISA, Industry Standard Architecture (ISA)* and *Micro Channel Architecture (MCA).*

business audio　A category of sound hardware that supports sounds useful in business applications, such as putting background music into presentations, adding voice annotations to *word processing* documents, and voice-checking *spreadsheets. 12-bit sound boards* are generally considered acceptable for business audio, but higher-quality *16-bit sound boards* are not much more expensive.

Business Software Alliance (BSA)　A consortium of software publishers, founded in 1988, that seeks to reduce *software piracy.* The BSA does so by means of public education, lobbying to increase protection for intellectual property, and lawsuits against copyright infringers.

bus mouse　A *mouse* connected to the computer by a dedicated mouse *adapter* inserted into an available expansion slot. Compare to *serial mouse.*

bus network　In *local area networks (LANs),* a decentralized *network topology* used by *AppleTalk* and *Ethernet,* for example, in which a single connecting line, the bus, is shared by a number of *nodes,* including workstations, shared *peripherals,* and *file servers.* In a bus network, a workstation sends every message to all other workstations. Each node in the network has a unique address, and its reception circuitry monitors the bus for messages being sent to the node, ignoring all other messages.

button　In *graphical user interfaces (GUIs),* a *dialog box* option used to execute a command, choose an option, or open another dialog box. See *Cancel button, default button, OK button, pushbutton,* and *radio button.*

button bar　See *icon bar* and *toolbar.*

byline　In *desktop publishing,* the author's name (often including organizational affiliation and address) positioned directly after the article's title.

byte   Eight contiguous *bits,* the fundamental data unit of personal computers. Storing the equivalent of one character, the byte is also the basic unit of measurement for computer storage. Because computer *architecture* is based (for the most part) on *binary* numbers, bytes are counted in powers of two. Many members of the *Internet* community prefer to call groups of eight bits *octets.* The terms kilo (in *kilobyte,* abbreviated as K) and mega (in *megabyte,* abbreviated as M) are used to count bytes but are misleading; they derive from decimal (base 10) numbers. A kilobyte actually is 1024 bytes, and a megabyte is 1,048,576 bytes. Many computer scientists criticize these terms, but the terms give those who think in decimal numbers a convenient handle on the measurement of memory.

bytecode   In *Java,* a compiled Java program, with the extension .class, that can be executed by a *Java virtual machine.* Unlike ordinary compiled languages, which produce *machine language* suitable for execution on a particular brand of computer, Java compilers produce an intermediary format, called bytecode, which can be executed on any computer capable of running a bytecode interpreter (such as a Java-compatible *browser*). However, because bytecode is interpreted, Java applications execute more slowly than programs designed specifically for a given type of computer (though not so slowly as true *interpreted code*).

bytecode compiler   A *compiler* that outputs a program in *bytecode* rather than *machine code.*

A
B
C

C

C   A *high-level programming language* widely used for professional *programming* and preferred by most major software publishers. A general-purpose *procedural language,* C combines the virtues of high-level programming languages with the efficiency of an *assembly language.* Most big-name programs are written in C or *C++,* while many *shareware* programs are written in other languages, such as *Visual BASIC.* Because the programmer can embed instructions that directly reach the *bit*-by-bit representation of data inside the *central processing unit (CPU),* compiled C programs run significantly faster than programs written in other high-level programming languages. C programs are highly *portable,* being easily and quickly rewritten to run on a new computer as long as the target environment has a C *compiler.*

C: In *IBM PC-compatible* personal computers, the *default* letter assigned to the first *hard disk.*

C++   A *high-level programming language* developed by Bjarne Stroustrup at AT&T's Bell Laboratories. Combining all the advantages of the *C* language with those of *object-oriented programming (OOP) languages,* C++ has been adopted as the standard house programming language by several major software vendors, such as *Apple Computer.*

ca   In the Internet *domain name system (DNS),* the country code for Canada.

cache   (Pronounced "cash.") 1. A storage area that keeps frequently accessed *data* or *program* instructions readily available so that the computer does not retrieve them repeatedly from slow storage. Caches improve performance by storing data or instructions in faster sections of memory and by using efficient design to increase the likelihood that the data needed next is in the cache. See *cache memory.* 2. In a *browser,* a section of the hard drive that is set aside for storing recently accessed Web pages. When you revisit one of these pages, the browser retrieves the page from the cache rather than the network, bringing about a considerable improvement in apparent retrieval speed.

cache controller   A *chip,* such as the *Intel 82385,* that manages the retrieval, storage, and delivery of *data* to and from *cache memory* or a *hard disk.* When data or instructions are requested

by the *central processing unit (CPU)*, the cache controller intercepts the request and handles the delivery from *random-access
memory (RAM)*. The cache controller then determines where in
the cache to store a copy of the just-delivered data, when to
fetch data or code from adjacent addresses in RAM in case it's
needed next, where in the cache to store this new data, and
which data to discard if the cache is full. The cache controller
also keeps an up-to-date table of the addresses of everything it's
holding. Despite the magnitude of these duties and the small
amount of memory actually used (32K to 256K), a well-
designed cache controller can predict and have stored in the
cache what the CPU needs next with an accuracy greater than
95 percent.

cache hit   A successful request for data from *cache memory;* the
data is present in the cache and does not have to be retrieved
from the considerably slower main memory circuits. See *cache
miss* and *hit rate.*

cache memory   A small unit (typically ranging in size from
a few kilobytes to 256K or 512K) of ultra-fast memory that is
used to store recently accessed or frequently accessed data, so
that the microprocessor does not have to retrieve this data from
slower memory circuits. Cache memory that is built directly
into the *microprocessor's* circuits is called *primary cache* or *L1 cache.*
Cache memory contained on an external circuit is called
secondary cache or *L2 cache.*

cache miss   An unsuccessful request for data from *cache memory;* the data is not present in the cache and must be retrieved
from the considerably slower main memory circuits. See *hit rate.*

cache settings   Options in the *setup program* that enable or disable a motherboard's *secondary cache.* Sometimes disabling the
secondary cache will make a game designed for a slow computer
easier to play on a computer that would otherwise run it so fast
as to make it unplayable.

CAD   See *computer-aided design.*

CAD/CAM   Acronym for computer-assisted design/
computer-assisted manufacturing. The direct linkage of *computer-
assisted design (CAD)* output with computer-controlled manufacturing tools, so that the actual production of a component can
begin almost immediately after the design has been completed.

CADD See *computer-aided design and drafting.*

caddy A tray, usually plastic, into which a *CD-ROM* is inserted before it is placed in certain *CD-ROM drives.* Caddies prevent fingerprints from getting on the disk surface, but it can be a hassle to load and unload caddies every time you want to change CD-ROMs.

Café See *Visual Café.*

CAI See *computer-assisted instruction.*

calculated field In a *database management* program, a *data field* that contains the results of calculations performed on other fields. Current balance and total score are examples of calculated fields. Synonymous with derived field.

call In *programming,* a statement that transfers *program* execution to a *subroutine* or procedure. When the subroutine or procedure is complete, program execution returns to the command following the call statement. Also, a statement that invokes a *library routine.*

callback A user *authentication* method used by some dial-up computer services. When you log on, the system notes your user ID and password, and hangs up. The system then calls you back at a pre-authorized number and enables you to connect to the service. This protects the system against somebody who obtains a user ID and password and attempts unauthorized access from an unauthorized telephone number but can be a problem for traveling salespeople and field engineers who are often on the road and use a variety of telephone numbers.

caller ID A premium telephone company service that, with compatible equipment, displays the caller's number and name when the phone rings. Increasingly, voice-capable modems incorporate caller ID features.

Call for Votes (CFV) In the standard *Usenet newsgroups,* a voting procedure that controls the creation of new newsgroups. Following a period of discussion, the call for votes is posted to the newsgroup news.announce.newgroups. During the voting period, 21 to 31 days in length, any Usenet participant may vote for or against the new newsgroup's creation by sending *e-mail* to an independent tabulator (a volunteer). To pass, a newsgroup must receive at least 100 more Yes votes than No votes, and the number of Yes votes must be at least two-thirds of the total. If the newsgroup passes the vote, the newsgroup creation commands are issued and Usenet administrators are expected to carry the newsgroup, but there is no mechanism to force them to do so. The voting procedure does not apply to newsgroups outside the *standard newsgroup hierarchy,* such as the *alternative newsgroup hierarchy.*

callout   In *desktop publishing (DTP),* items of text that name parts of an illustration, usually with a line or arrow pointing to the part of the illustration the text describes.

call waiting   A service provided by the telephone company that lets you put one call on hold while you answer another. This feature can play havoc with *modem* communications, so many users disable call waiting before dialing a number with the modem. (Entering *70 and a comma before the number in your *communications program* is a common method of disabling call waiting.)

camera-ready copy   A finished, printed manuscript or illustration ready to be photographed by a printing company for reproduction.

campus-wide information system (CWIS)   An information system that provides students, faculty, staff, and the public with all the information pertinent to a large college or university, including registration information, events, faculty and staff telephone numbers, and access to the library catalog. The need to create user-friendly navigation software for a CWIS led to the development of *Gopher* at the University of Minnesota. Increasingly, colleges and universities are abandoning Gopher in favor of systems based on the *World Wide Web (WWW).*

cancelbot   In Usenet, a program that can hunt down a given individual's posts and remove them from the network. Cancelbots, such as the one used by the storied *Cancelmoose,* are frequently wielded against *spammers,* those who post unwanted messages to dozens or even hundreds of newsgroups, but they have also been used to try to silence unwanted opinion.

Cancel button   An option in a *graphical user interface (GUI)* dialog box that you use to cancel a command and return to the active document. Equivalent to pressing *Esc.*

Cancelmoose   In *Usenet,* an individual, whose identity remains unknown, who takes upon himself the task of canceling articles that are inappropriately posted to a large number of *newsgroups* (this is called *spamming*). Although Usenet software ordinarily permits only the author of an article to cancel it (remove it from *Usenet*), Cancelmoose has devised ingenious software (called a *cancelbot*) that gets around this restriction, allowing him or her to cancel any person's articles. Although the Cancelmoose's actions are controversial, many *Usenet* participants believe that his or her actions are fully justified.

canonical form   In mathematics and *programming,* an expression that conforms to established principles learned only through practice, apprenticeship, and interaction with experts. It's possible to write a programming expression that's entirely functional but not in canonical form, thus preventing social acceptance in learned mathematical and computer science societies. Most people, however, are concerned with getting the right answer.

canonical name   In the *Internet*, the official name of an Internet *host*, as opposed to its aliases.

cap height   In a *typeface,* the height of capital letters, measured in *points,* from the *baseline*.

Caps Lock key   A *toggle key* that locks the *keyboard* so that you can enter uppercase letters without pressing the *Shift key.* When you're in uppercase mode, most keyboards have a light that illuminates; many programs also display a message, such as CAPS LOCK or CAPS. The Caps Lock key has no effect on the number and punctuation keys.

caption   In *desktop publishing (DTP),* a descriptive phrase that identifies a figure, such as a photograph, illustration, or graph.

capture   1. In *modem* communications, to record what happens on the *monitor* and store it in a *file* that can be viewed later. Capturing data is useful if you're paying a per-minute connection charge. 2. In computer graphics, to copy all or part of an image on-screen and convert it to a *graphics file format* to insert in a *document* or save on a disk.

Carbon Copy   A *remote control program* that enables Windows users to operate a computer from a remote location via a dialup modem connection or an Internet connection.

card   A *circuit board* or *expansion board*.

cardinal number   A number used in counting to show the total number of units in an assembly of something. See *ordinal number*.

caret   A symbol (^) commonly found over the 6 key on computer *keyboards*. In *spreadsheet* programs, the caret is the symbol for exponent, or "to the power of." Caret also can be used to stand for the *Ctrl* key in computer documentation, as in "Press ^ C."

carpal tunnel syndrome   A type of *repetitive strain injury (RSI)* caused by repeated compression of the medial nerve within the carpal tunnel, an opening into the hand formed by the bones of the wrist and certain hand ligaments. The nerves of the wrist. Symptoms begin with numbness in the medial nerve's distribution area (the palm, the thumb, and the first three digits, but not the little finger), such that it might feel like one's whole hand is asleep. This may be followed by severe pain that travels up the arm and could result in severe incapacitation, including an inability to bring the thumb into opposition with the hand. Therapy may include the improved workstation *ergonomics,* the use of a brace, cortisone injections, vitamin B6 therapy, or surgery.

carpet bomb   See *spam*.

carriage return   A signal that tells the *printer* to move to the left margin. Some printers also perform a *line feed* when executing a carriage return; such distinctions are handled by *printer drivers*. See *Enter/Return*.

carrier detect signal   A signal sent from the *modem* to the rest of the computer to indicate that a connection has been made and the carrier tone has been established. The carrier detect (CD) light on *external modems* will illuminate when the carrier detect signal is sent.

Carrier Sense Multiple Access with Collision Detection
See *CSMA/CD*.

carrier signal   In data communications, a continuous signal that can be modulated (altered or varied) to convey data. In amplitude modulation (AM), the volume (amplitude) of the carrier signal is varied to correspond with the input signal; in frequency modulation (FM), the frequency of the carrier signal is varied to accomplish the same result.

Cartesian coordinate system   A method, created by 17th-century French mathematician René Descartes, of locating a point in a two-dimensional space by defining a vertical axis and a horizontal axis. A *mouse* uses the Cartesian coordinate system to locate the *pointer* on-screen. In some *graphics applications,* you can display the coordinates so the pointer can be located precisely.

cartridge   A removable module containing data *storage media* such as magnetic tape or disks. In *printers,* a removable module that expands the printer's memory or contains *fonts,* called *cartridge fonts.*

cartridge font   A *printer font* supplied in the form of a *read-only memory (ROM) cartridge* that plugs into a receptacle on Hewlett-Packard LaserJet *laser printers* and *clones.* Unlike *down-loadable fonts,* a cartridge font is immediately available to the printer and doesn't consume space in the printer's *random-access memory (RAM),* which can be used up quickly when printing documents loaded with *graphics.* The popular cartridges contain multiple fonts, often more than 100. Most laser printers now use *built-in fonts* or software-generated fonts.

cascade   In follow-up messages posted to *Usenet,* the accretion of quotation markers in messages that have been repeatedly quoted. Each time a message is quoted in a follow-up message, a newsreader adds quotation markers, as in the following:

> >>>>>>Let's stop this thread.
> >>>>>I agree.
> >>>>Me too.
> >>>You shouldn't post just to say, "Me too."
> >>I agree.
> >Me too.
> Aargh!

cascading menu   A *menu* system where selecting a command on a *pull-down menu* causes another menu to appear, or cascade, next to the selected command. The presence of a cascading menu is usually indicated by a triangle at the right edge of the menu. Synonymous with submenu.

cascading style sheet (CSS)   In *HTML,* a specification of document formats in which specific formatting attributes (such as alignment, text style, font, and font size) are assigned to specific HTML *tags*, so that all subsequent uses of the tag in the same page take on the same formats. Like a *style sheet* in a word processing document, CSS enables a Web designer to make a single change that affects all the text marked with the same tag. Previously, it was necessary to go through the page and make each change manually, a laborious process with a large document. The Level 1 definition of cascading style sheets is defined by the World Wide Web Consortium *(W3C),* but competing definitions are being pushed by Netscape (see *JavaScript style sheets [JSS])* and Microsoft.

cascading windows   In a *graphical user interface (GUI),* two or more *windows* displayed so they overlap. This mode is convenient because you still can see the *title bar* and an edge of all the other windows you've opened. See *overlaid windows* and *tiled windows.*

case   The metal cabinet that contains the *motherboard, adapters,* and any internal components, such as *disk drives.* There are several types of cases, but the most basic distinction is between *desktop cases,* which lie flat, and *tower cases,* which stand vertically. Cases typically are sold with a *power supply* installed. See *AT-size case* and *mini-AT-size case.*

case-insensitive   In a search, ignoring the difference between upper- and lowercase letters.

case-insensitive search   A search in which a program ignores the pattern of upper- and lowercase letters. A case-insensitive search for Carter would match any of the following: cArter, CARTER, carter, and carTER.

case-sensitive   Distinguishing the difference between upper- and lowercase letters.

case-sensitive search   A search in which a program tries to match the exact pattern of upper- and lowercase letters. A case-sensitive search for Porter, for example, matches Porter but not PORTER, porter, or porTer.

Castanet   A *push* medium developed by Marimba that enables computer users to "tune" to *Java* software delivery channels. When updated versions of a program become available, the software is automatically downloaded and installed without the user's involvement. Castanet has been incorporated into

Netscape Communicator's Netcaster module, which also delivers content to the desktop.

cast-based animation   In *multimedia,* an animation method in which each object in a production is treated as an individual *graphic* image (a cast member). You can manipulate each cast member individually by means of a *script.*

catalog   In *database management,* a list of related database files you've grouped together so you can easily distinguish them from others. All *relational database management systems (RDBMS)* can work with more than one file at a time. Frequently, the results of relational operations (such as a *join*) produce a new file. Also, you create several *indexes* and other files that support the application. A *catalog* helps you track all these related files in a unit.

catatonic   Unable to respond. A catatonic computer has probably *crashed*; a catatonic network connection may eventually produce a *timed out* message.

catch up   In *Usenet,* a command commonly implemented in *newsreaders* that marks all the current *articles* in a *newsgroup* as read, even if you have not actually read them. When you access the newsgroup again, you will see only the articles that have come in since the last time you accessed the newsgroup.

catenet   An obsolete term for an *internet; a wide area network (WAN)* composed of physically distinct *local area networks (LANs),* which are connected by means of *routers.* The term is a contraction of "concatenated network." The *Internet* (note the capital "I") is a world-wide catenet based on the *TCP/IP* protocols.

cathode ray tube (CRT)   In a *monitor,* a vacuum tube that uses an *electron gun* (cathode) to emit a beam of electrons that illuminates *phosphors* on-screen as the beam sweeps across the screen repeatedly. The monitor is often called a CRT. The same technology is used in television sets.

CAV   See *constant angular velocity.*

CBT   See *computer-based training.*

CC   See *courtesy copy.*

CCITT   Acronym for Comité Consultatif International Téléphonique et Télégraphique, a defunct international organization that designed standards for *analog* and *digital* communications involving *modems,* computer *networks,* and *fax* machines. For computer users, CCITT's most important role lay in the establishment of international standards for modem connectivity, the famous "V–dot" standards (such as *V.32bis* and *V.34*). The CCITT has been replaced by the *International Telecommunications Union-Telecommunications Standards Section (ITU-TSS).*

A
B
C

CCITT protocol   A standard for the transmission of data using a computer *modem, serial port,* or a *network.* The following protocols are in the V series: *V.17, V.21, V.22, V.22bis, V.27ter, V.29, V.32, V.32bis, V.34, V.42,* and V. *42bis.*

CCP   See *Certified Computer Programmer.*

CD   See *compact disc.*

CD-DA   See *Compact Disc-Digital Audio.*

CDEV   See *control panel device.*

CD-I   See *Compact Disc-Interactive.*

CDP   See *Certified Data Processor.*

CD-R   A recordable *CD-ROM.* CD-R technology is useful to law offices and other business that must permanently *archive* large amounts of information, and it enables individuals to manufacture salable CD-ROMs. Unlike most other storage media, though, CD-R disks can be recorded upon only once.

CD-ROM   Acronym for compact disc–read only memory, a read-only *optical storage* technology that uses compact discs. CD-ROMs can store up to 630M of data in the most commonly used format. CD-ROM technology was originally used for encyclopedias, dictionaries, and software libraries, but now they often are used in *multimedia* applications and for software distribution. To access the data on a CD-ROM, you need a *CD-ROM drive.*

CD-ROM changer   A machine that will robotically load any of up to 100 *CD-ROMs* into a *CD-ROM drive.* Synonymous with jukebox, a CD-ROM changer usually requires about five seconds to locate and load a requested disk.

CD-ROM drive   A read-only disk drive designed to read the data encoded on *CD-ROMs* and to transfer this data to a computer. Unlike audio compact disc players, CD-ROM drives contain circuitry optimized to locate *data* at high speeds; audio CD players need to locate only the beginning of audio tracks, which they play sequentially. CD-ROM drives retrieve data much more slowly than computer disk drives. The speed of CD-ROM drives is typically expressed as a multiple of the original CD-ROM specification, which called for a *data transfer rate* of 150K per second; typical drives today function at *10x*, *12x*, or even *16x* (10, 12, or 16 times faster than the original specification).

CD-ROM interface　A feature of a *sound board* that lets you connect a *CD-ROM drive* directly to the sound board, thereby easing installation and enabling you to send audio from a *CD-ROM* directly to the sound circuitry, without taxing the rest of the computer.

CD-ROM player　See *CD-ROM drive*.

CD-ROM/SD　See *CD-ROM/Super Density*.

CD-ROM/Super Density (CD-ROM/SD)　A little-used standard for packing up to 9.6G onto a *CD-ROM*. The CD-ROM/SD standard uses both sides of disks and is not compatible with any mass-produced *CD-ROM drives*. See *MMCD*.

CD-ROM/XA　A *CD-ROM drive* that conforms to the CD-ROM/eXtended Architecture standard, created by a consortium of media and computer firms (including Microsoft, Sony, and Phillips). This standard enables CD-ROMs to combine music and data.

CD-RW　A recordable *CD-ROM* technology that enables unlimited write operations (unlike CD-R, which restricts you to one write only).

cell　1. In a *spreadsheet* or table, a rectangle formed by the intersection of a row and column in which you enter information in the form of text *(a label)* or numbers *(a value)*. 2. In *Asynchronous Transfer Mode (ATM)* networking, a small unit of data that has been broken up for efficient transmission (synonymous with *packet*).

cell address　In a *spreadsheet*, a letter and number combination that identifies a cell's location on the worksheet by column and row (A3, B9, C2, and so on). If you refer to a cell in a formula, the cell address is called the *cell reference*.

**A
B
C**

cell animation   An *animation* technique in which a background painting is held in place while a series of transparent sheets of celluloid containing objects are placed over the background painting, producing the illusion of movement. Cell animation is much easier than drawing a new background for every frame in the animation sequence. A *Macintosh* animation program that uses a computerized version of cell animation is Macromedia Director.

cell definition   The actual contents of a *cell* in a *spreadsheet,* as displayed on the *entry line.* If you place a *formula* in a cell, the program displays the result of the calculation rather than the formula itself.

cell format   In a *spreadsheet,* the way the *program* displays the contents of *cells. Label* formats include aligning the text on the left, right, or center. *Numeric formats* include currency, percent, including commas, setting a number of decimal places, and date and time display. You can change the *font* and *font size,* and make *values* and labels *bold* and *italic.* See *current cell, global format, graphics spreadsheet, label alignment,* and *range format.*

cell pointer   In *spreadsheet* programs, the rectangular highlight that indicates the *current cell.* When you enter *data* in the spreadsheet, it's recorded in the current cell.

cell protection   In a *spreadsheet* program, a *format* applied to a cell, a *range* of *cells,* or an entire *file* that prevents you from altering the contents of protected cells.

cell reference   In a *spreadsheet* formula, the address of the *cell* that contains a value needed to solve the formula. When used in a formula, a cell reference tells the program to go to the named cell (such as B1) and use the value in that cell to perform the calculation. A cell reference can refer to a cell containing a formula, which may contain its own cell references to other cells, which can themselves contain formulas. A change made to any constant in such a worksheet affects intermediate values and, ultimately, the bottom line. See *recalculation method.*

Center for Innovative Computer Applications (CICA)
An Indiana University–based research center that fosters innovative research in computer visualization and artificial intelligence. For *Internet* users, CICA is better known as the home of a massive Windows *shareware* archive, accessible by means of *File Transfer Protocol (FTP)* and the *Virtual Software Library (VSL).*

central mass storage   See *file server.*

central processing unit (CPU)   A computer's internal storage, processing, and control circuitry, including the *arithmetic-logic unit (ALU)*, the *control unit, read-only memory (ROM)*, and *random-access memory (RAM)*. The ALU and control unit are wholly contained on a chip called the *microprocessor;* the memory is elsewhere on the *motherboard* or an adapter on the *expansion bus.*

Centre Universitaire d'Informatique (CUI)   A unit of the University of Geneva, located in Geneva, Switzerland, that has played a leading role in the development of the *World Wide Web (WWW).*

Centronics interface   The original *parallel port* of IBM PC-compatible computers, named after the company that designed a predecessor to this interface standard.

Centronics port   See *parallel port.*

CERN   Acronym for Conseil European pour la Recherche Nucleaire (European Laboratory for Particle Physics). A Geneva, Switzerland-based research center for advanced physics research. CERN is the birthplace of the *World Wide Web (WWW)*, which the center's computer staff began in 1989 as a collaborative network for high-energy physicists.

CERT   Acronym for Computer Emergency Response Team. An *Internet* security task force that is designed to detect and respond rapidly to Internet security threats. Formed by the *Defense Advanced Research Project Agency (DARPA)* in 1988 in response to the infamous *Internet Worm*, CERT monitors Internet security and alerts system administrators concerning the activities of computer *crackers* and *computer virus* authors.

certificate   An encrypted and digitally signed attachment to an *e-mail* message or downloaded file that attests that the received data really comes from its claimed source and has not been altered while it was en route. A certificate is virtually impossible to fake. To be considered valid, however, the certificate should be digitally signed by a *certificate authority (CA)*, an independent agency that uses some type of identity-checking procedure (such as viewing a driver's license) prior to signing the certificate. Synonymous with digital ID. See *personal certificate* and *public-key cryptography.*

certificate authority (CA)   A company that verifies the identity of individuals and issues *certificates* attesting to the veracity of this identity. To obtain a certificate, an individual may be asked to show identification, such as a driver's license.

certified   Guaranteed by the manufacturer to accurately hold a certain quantity of data. For example, a disk might be certified for 1.44*M* of data.

Certified Computer Programmer (CCP)   A person who has earned a Certificate in Computer Programming from the *Institute for Certification of Computer Professionals (ICCP)*. CCPs must pass an examination in *programming* rules and concepts. CCP certification is considered equivalent to Certified Public Accountant status for accountants, though it is rarely an employment requirement.

Certified Data Processor (CDP)   A person who has earned a Certificate in Data Processing from the *Institute for Certification of Computer Professionals (ICCP)*. CDPs must pass an examination in *hardware, software, programming,* and *systems analysis.* CDP certification is equivalent to Certified Public Accountant status for accountants, though it is rarely an employment requirement.

CGA   See *Color Graphics Adapter.*

CGI   See *Common Gateway Interface.*

CGM   See *Computer Graphics Metafile.*

chain printing   The printing of separate *files* as a unit by placing commands at the end of the first file to direct the program to continue printing the second file, and so on. Full-featured *word processing* programs, such as *Microsoft Word,* allow chained printing with continuous pagination and, in some cases, the generation of a complete table of contents and index for the linked files. See *master document.*

chaining   A relaying operation in which e-mail messages are routed through several *anonymous remailers* to destroy any possibility of back-tracking the message's path.

Challenge-Handshake Authentication Protocol (CHAP)
In *Internet* dial-up services that use the Point-to-Point Protocol *(PPP),* a standard that prevents hackers from intercepting passwords. CHAP is used to verify the identity of the person

logging on by using a three-way handshake. After the link is established, the service provider's computer sends a "challenge" message to the user's computer, which must then consult a "secret" stored on the user's computer, as well as on the service provider's computer, but is never sent over the network. The user's computer then performs a calculation using the challenge as well as the secret. If the result does not match the service provider's calculation, the connection is terminated. This *authentication* method provides a very high degree of protection against previous password-based authentication measures and is more secure than its predecessor, the *Password Authentication Protocol (PAP)*.

chamfer   In *desktop publishing (DTP)* and *presentation graphics,* a beveled edge between two intersecting lines.

channel   1. On *Internet Relay Chat (IRC),* a named, topically focused forum where you can *chat* in *real time* with other computers. Synonymous with *chat room.* 2. In *push media,* a named link to a network-based *transmitter* to which a user can "tune." For example, you can tune to Corel's channel to receive automatic updates to the company's Java version of its Corel Suite software.

channel access   In *local area networks (LANs),* the method used to gain access to the data communication channel that links the computers. Three common methods are contention, *polling,* and *token passing.*

channel op (CHOP)   On *Internet Relay Chat (IRC),* a person who possesses *op* (operator) privileges, including the right to kick unruly users out of the channel.

character   Any letter, number, punctuation mark, or symbol that you can produce on-screen by pressing a *key* on the *keyboard,* or (for certain little-used characters) a key combination. A character uses one *byte* of memory.

character-based program   A *program* that relies on the *ASCII* and *extended ASCII character sets* that includes *block graphics* to create its screens and display the text you enter.

character graphics   See *block graphics.*

character-mapped display   A method of displaying characters in which a special section of *memory* is set aside to represent the displayed image; programs generate a display by inserting characters into the memory-based representation of the screen. Therefore, the whole screen—not just one line—remains active, and the user or the program can modify characters anywhere on-screen. See *teletype (TTY) display.*

A B C

character mode In *IBM PC-compatible* computers, a *display* mode in which the computer displays only those characters contained in its built-in *character set.* Synonymous with text mode. See *character view* and *graphics mode.*

character set The fixed set of *keyboard* codes that a particular computer system uses. See *ASCII character set, code page,* and *extended character set.*

characters per inch (cpi) The number of *characters* that fit in an inch of type of a given *font.* Standard sizes drawn from typewriting are pica (10 cpi) and elite (12 cpi). Non-typewriter fonts are measured in *points.*

characters per second (cps) A measurement of the speed of a *modem* (though modem speed is most often measured in *bits per second [bps]*), an *impact printer,* or an *inkjet printer.*

character string Any series of *characters* (including spaces) that a *program* treats as a group. In *programming* and *database management,* you distinguish character strings from reserved words (command names) by enclosing strings in quotation marks; as a result, the characters in the string give no instructions to the computer. In a database management query language, for example, the expression FIND "Wyoming" causes the computer to search for the first record that exactly matches the character string Wyoming. Synonymous with string.

character view In some *MS-DOS application programs,* a mode in which the program switches the *display adapter* circuitry to character mode; also called draft mode by some programs. In character mode, the computer can display only those characters contained in the computer's built-in *character set.* See *character mode* and *graphics view.*

charge-coupled device (CCD) A device used in a *scanner* or *digital camera* to convert light into electrical signals readable by the computer. A scanner's horizontal resolution is determined by the number of CCDs it packs into a row—usually 300, but in some high-endscanners, 600.

chart   A representation of data in pictorial form. Charts make it easier to discern the significance of data and identify trends.

chat   In an *online information service, BBS, or Internet Relay Chat (IRC),* to converse with other computer users by exchanging typed lines of text in a *real-time* conversation.

chat room   In a *BBS* or *online information service,* a named, topically-focused forum or conference for online, *real-time* chatting. See *chat* and *channel.*

check box   In a *Graphical User Interface (GUI)* dialog box, a square box that you choose to *toggle* an option on or off. When the option is turned on, an X or a checkmark appears in the check box. A check box can appear alone or with other check boxes in a list of items. Unlike *radio buttons,* you can choose more than one check box.

checksum   An acronym for SUMmation CHECK. In *data* communications, an *error-checking* technique in which the number of *bits* in a unit of data is summed, transmitted along with the data, and checked by the receiving computer. If the sum differs, an error probably occurred in transmission and the transmission is repeated. A commonly used personal computer communications protocol called *XMODEM* uses the checksum technique. In *virus* scanning software, such as Central Point Anti-Virus, checksums are calculated for every file in a directory and the results saved in a file stored in the directory. When the program is scanning, it compares the checksum information stored in the directory with the current checksum for each scanned file. A difference in the sum may indicate that the file has been infected by a virus that doesn't leave a recognized signature.

Chiclet keyboard   A *keyboard,* frequently found on calculators, that uses small rectangular keys the size of Chiclet chewing gum. Chiclet keys are difficult to use because the keys are too small and offer little *tactile feedback.* A Chiclet keyboard was featured on one of *IBM's* most notorious marketing failures, the PC Jr. home computer.

child   A subcategory. In a hierarchical file system, a subdirectory is a child of the *parent* directory.

child process   In *Unix,* a utility program or *subroutine* that executes under the control of a controlling program, called a *parent process.*

chip   A miniaturized electronic circuit mass-produced on a tiny wafer of silicon. Chips are made out of semiconducting materials and duplicate the function of several transistors and other electronic components. The first *integrated circuits (ICs)* contained only a few components, but the same manufacturing techniques can now generate 16 million components on a chip smaller than a fingertip. Today's *Pentium*, for example, sells for less than $500, but is the electronic equivalent of a *mainframe* computer priced at several million dollars just 20 years ago. The achievement of chip-manufacturing technology has spread the use of computer technology throughout society.

chip set   The collection of *chips* that work together to perform a function, such as helping a *microprocessor* access memory or update a *display*. The chips that comprise a chip set must be designed to work together and typically come from a single manufacturer. Sometimes spelled as a single word: chipset.

choose   In a program that uses *menus* and *dialog boxes,* the process of picking an option that begins an action.

Chooser   A Macintosh *desk accessory (DA)* supplied by *Apple Computer* with the Mac's *operating system*—the *System.* The Chooser governs the selection of *printer* and *network drivers,* the programs that control communication with the *printer* and *local area network (LAN).* The Chooser displays the *icons* of the printer and network drivers installed in the *System Folder.*

chord   In *desktop publishing* and *presentation graphics,* a straight line that connects the end points of an arc.

chrominance   In *multimedia*, the portion of a composite video signal that contains color information.

CICA   See *Center for Innovative Computer Applications.*

ciphertext   In *cryptography,* a message that's encrypted so it can be read only by the intended recipient, who has the *key* needed to decode the message. See *cleartext, encryption, public-key cryptography.*

circuit board   A flat plastic board on which electrically conductive circuits are laminated. Synonymous with printed circuit board. See *adapter, card* and *motherboard.*

circuit switching network   A type of *wide area network (WAN),* epitomized by the world telephone system, in which the originating and receiving stations are linked by a single, physical circuit, created by complex switching mechanisms. The connection is maintained until the communication is finished. Compare to *packet-switching network.*

circular reference   In a *spreadsheet,* an error condition caused by two or more *formulas* that refer to one another. A circular reference occurs, for example, when the formula +B5 is placed in *cell* A1, and the formula +A1 is placed in cell B5. Spreadsheet programs usually have a *command* that displays a screen that includes a list of the cells containing circular references. Circular references don't always result in errors. They can be used deliberately, for example, to create an iterative function in a worksheet: Each recalculation increases the values of the two formulas.

CISC   See *complex instruction set computer.*

clari   In *Usenet,* an *alternative newsgroup hierarchy* that includes dozens of read-only *newsgroups* containing wire service articles—the same ones that will appear in today's newspapers. These wire services include United Press International (UPI), Newsbytes, and TechWire. The Clari hierarchy is available only at those Usenet sites that have paid a fee to ClariNet, the organization that collates the wire service articles and posts them to the dozens of clari newsgroups. The articles posted to the clari newsgroups are copyrighted and cannot be redistributed without ClariNet's written approval.

Claris Corporation   A major publisher of easy-to-use software for Windows and Macintosh computers, including *Claris FileMaker Pro, Claris Home Page,* and *ClarisWorks.* The company is subsidiary of *Apple Computer.*

Claris FileMaker Pro   An easy-to-use *relational database* program for Windows and Macintosh, created by Claris. Ready-to-use templates enable quick creation of popular applications, including purchase orders and cash receipts. FileMaker Pro Server transforms the program into a multi-user database application capable of serving up to 100 simultaneous users on an *IPX/SPX* or *TCP/IP* network.

Claris Home Page   An easy-to-use *WYSIWYG* editor for Web publishing created by Claris, and available for Macintosh and Windows systems. The program enables Web authors to create Web pages without knowing *HTML* and comes with over

1,000 royalty-free clip art images. The program can create *frames* and tables in a "what-you-see-is-what-you-get" environment.

ClarisWorks   An easy-to-use *integrated program* that combines word processing, spreadsheet, database, and graphics functions. The Internet Edition of this program includes Internet access software, the *Netscape Navigator* browser, and *Claris Home Page*.

class   In *object-oriented programming (OOP),* a category of *objects* that perform a certain function. The class defines the *properties* of an object, including definitions of the object's variables and the procedures that need to be followed to get the object to do something. In *Java, applets* and *Java applications* receive the *extension* .class, indicating that they contain all the necessary information to implement the functionality that the program contains.

Class 1   A standard for *fax modems* that describes the way in which the *Hayes command set* is modified to send faxes. Class 1 fax modems, unlike *Class 2* fax modems, leave most of the tasks relating to digitizing images and preparing faxes for transmission to software, which is perfectly fine in most computers.

Class 2   A standard for *fax modems* that describes the way in which the *Hayes command set* is modified to send faxes. Class 2 fax modems handle most of the fax-preparation tasks that *Class 1* fax modems leave to software, which makes Class 2 modems very expensive. Class 2 isn't even a true industry standard, so you're better off buying a Class 1 fax modem.

Class A certification   A Federal Communications Commission (FCC) certification that a given make and model of computer meets the FCC's Class A limits for *radio frequency interference (RFI),* which are designed for commercial and industrial environments.

Class A network   On the *Internet,* a participating *network* that is allocated up to 16,777,215 distinct Internet addresses (called *IP addresses*). Current Internet addressing limitations define a maximum of 128 Class A networks.

Class B certification   A Federal Communications Commission (FCC) certification that a given make and model of computer meets the FCC's Class B limits for *radio frequency interference (RFI),* which are designed for homes and home offices. Class B standards are tougher than Class A and are designed to protect radio and television reception in residential neighborhoods from excessive RFI generated by computer usage. Class B computers are also shielded more heavily from external interference.

Class B network   On the *Internet,* a participating *network* that is allocated up to 65,535 distinct Internet addresses (called *IP addresses*). Current Internet addressing limitations define a maximum of 16,384 Class B networks.

Class C network   On the *Internet*, a participating *network* that is allocated up to 256 distinct Internet addresses (called *IP addresses*). Current Internet addressing limitations define a maximum of 2,097,152 Class C networks.

clear   To remove *data* from a *document*. In the *Microsoft Windows 95* and *Macintosh* environments, the Clear command (Edit *menu*) completely wipes out the selection, as opposed to Cut, which removes the selection to the *Clipboard* (from which you can retrieve the selection, if you later discover that you deleted it by mistake). Synonymous with delete.

cleartext   In *cryptography,* a message that is transmitted without any encryption, so that it can be easily intercepted and read while it is en route. A major security drawback of the Internet is that, with most *password authentication* schemes, passwords are transmitted in cleartext. See *ciphertext.*

Clear to Send/Ready to Send   See *CTS/RTS.*

click   To press and quickly release a *mouse* button. You frequently see this term in instructions such as "Click the Bold check box in the Fonts dialog box." For users of computers that are *IBM-PC compatible,* this instruction means, "Move the mouse pointer so its tip touches the Bold check box and then click the left mouse button." See *double-click* and *Shift+click.*

client   1. In a *client/server* network, a program that is designed to request information from a *server.* See *client/server, heavy client, light client.* 2. In Object Linking and Embedding *(OLE),* an *application* that includes data in another application, called the *server application.* See *client application.*

client application   In Object Linking and Embedding *(OLE),* an *application* in which you can create a linked object or embed an object.

client/server A design model for *applications* running on a *network,* in which the bulk of the *back-end* processing, such as performing a physical search of a *database,* takes place on a *server.* The *front-end* processing, which involves communicating with the user, is handled by smaller programs (called *clients*) that are distributed to the client workstations. See *light client, heavy client, local area network (LAN),* and *wide area network (WAN).*

A
B
C

clip art A collection of *graphics,* stored on disk and available for use in a *desktop publishing* or *presentation graphics program.* The term clip art is derived from a graphics design tradition in which packages of printed clip art are sold in books and actually clipped out by layout artists to enhance newsletters, brochures, and presentation graphics. Most page layout or presentation graphics programs can read *graphics file formats* used by clip art collections available on disk.

Clipboard In a *windowing environment,* such as *Microsoft Windows 95* or the *Macintosh Finder,* a temporary storage area in memory where material cut or copied from a document is stored until you paste the material elsewhere.

clip-on pointing device A *trackball* that clips on the side or front of a *portable computer.* See *built-in pointing device, freestanding pointing device, mouse, pointing stick,* and *snap-on pointing device.*

Clipper A *compiler* developed by Nantucket Systems, Inc., for the *dBASE* software command language. Many application developers consider Clipper superior to the compiler offered by dBASE's publisher.

Clipper Chip A U.S. government–backed encryption technology, housed on a semiconductor that would have been manufactured in massive quantities, that would provide private individuals with the means to encrypt their messages. However, the Clipper Chip includes a *back door* that would enable law enforcement agencies to eavesdrop on the message. In order to do so, law enforcement personnel would have to obtain a warrant, which is now required to eavesdrop on telephone communications. Privacy advocates fear that the government would abuse its power, eavesdropping on conversations without having obtained the proper certification, while law enforcement personnel fear that encryption technologies will prevent the detection of terrorist and drug–dealing activity. The Clipper Chip proposal was seriously derailed after a researcher proved that its encryption scheme was not reliable, but U.S. government security agencies continue making similar proposals.

clock   Synonymous with system clock. An electronic circuit that generates evenly spaced pulses at speeds of millions of *hertz (Hz)*. The pulses are used to synchronize the flow of information through the computer's internal communication channels. Most computers also contain a separate circuit that tracks the time of day, but this has nothing to do with the system clock's function. See *clock/calendar board* and *clock speed*.

clock/calendar board   An *adapter* that includes a battery-powered clock for tracking the time and date and is used in computers that lack such facilities on their *motherboards*.

clock cycle   The time between two ticks of a computer's *system clock*. A typical personal computer goes through millions or even billions of clock cycles each second.

clock–doubled   Operating twice as fast as the *system clock,* a 50 *MHz* 486DX2 operates on a *motherboard* with a 25 MHz system clock, for example, and completes internal *microprocessor* operations faster than a 25 MHz 486DX on the same motherboard. A clock-doubled chip, though, does nothing to speed up operations outside the microprocessor. See *clock-tripled, clock-quadrupled*.

clock–quadrupled   Operating close to four times as fast as the *system clock*, a 133 MHz 486 processor operates on a *motherboard* with a 33 MHz system clock. See *clock-doubled* and *clock-tripled*.

clock speed   The speed of the internal clock of a *microprocessor* that sets the pace—measured in *megahertz (MHz)*—at which operations proceed within the computer's internal processing circuitry. Higher clock speeds bring noticeable gains in micro-processor-intensive tasks, such as recalculating a *spreadsheet,* but isn't the only feature that determines performance. Disk-intensive operations proceed slowly, regardless of clock speed, if *hard* and *floppy disks* are sluggish. When comparing clock speeds, compare only computers that use the same microprocessor, such as the *Pentium* 90, which runs at 90Mhz and the *Pentium* 120, which runs at 120MHz.

clock–tripled   Operating three times as fast as the *system clock*. Clock tripled microprocessors perform internal *microprocessor* functions faster than *clock-doubled* or standard microprocessors but do nothing to speed up the rest of the system. See *clock-doubled* and *clock-quadrupled*.

A · B · C

clone   A functional copy of a *hardware* device, such as a *personal computer,* that runs the *software* and uses all the peripherals intended for the IBM Personal Computer. Also, a functional copy of a *program,* such as a *spreadsheet* program, that reads *Lotus 1-2-3* files and can recognize most or all Lotus commands. See *IBM PC-compatible.*

close   In a *program* that can display more than one document window, to exit a file and remove its window from the *display.*

close box   In a *Graphical User Interface (GUI),* a box on the *title bar* of a *window* that is used to close the window.

closed bus system   A design in which the computer's *data bus* doesn't contain receptacles and isn't easily upgraded by users. See *open bus system.*

closed-loop actuator   A mechanism that moves the *read/write head* of a *hard disk* and then sends messages to the *hard disk controller* confirming its location. Closed-loop actuators, because the read/write head can be positioned with greater accuracy over the recording medium, improve *areal density.*

cluster   On a *floppy* or *hard disk*, the basic unit of *data* storage. A cluster includes two or more *sectors.*

CLV   See *constant linear velocity.*

CMOS   See *Complementary Metal-Oxide Semiconductor.*

CMOS reset jumper   A *jumper* on the *motherboard* that, when moved, clears the *advanced setup options.* The CMOS reset jumper is useful if poor setup-option choices render your computer unable to start.

CMYK   A *color model* that makes all colors from combinations of cyan, magenta, yellow, and black. The CMYK model supports device-independent color better than the *RGB* and *HSB* models.

coated paper   Specially treated paper that enhances the output of *color printers. Thermal wax-transfer printers* require coated paper, which is much more expensive than standard *printer* paper. See *consumables.*

coaxial cable   In *local area networks (LANs),* a high-*bandwidth* connecting cable in which an insulated wire runs through the middle of the cable. Surrounding the insulated wire is a second wire made of solid or woven metal. Coaxial cable is much more expensive than *twisted-pair cable* (ordinary telephone wire) but can carry more *data.* Coaxial cables are required for high-bandwidth *broadband* systems and for fast *baseband* systems, such as *Ethernet.*

COBOL   A *high-level programming language* specially designed for business applications. Short for COmmon Business Oriented Language, COBOL is a compiled language that was released in 1964 and was the first language to use the *data record* as a principal data structure. Because COBOL is designed to store, retrieve, and process corporate accounting information and to automate functions, such as inventory control, billing, and payroll, the language quickly became the language of choice in businesses. COBOL is the most widely used programming language in corporate mainframe environments. Versions of COBOL are available for personal computers, but business applications for personal computers are more frequently created and maintained in *C* or *Xbase.* See *high-level programming language.*

CODASYL   See *conference on data-systems languages.*

code   1. Instructions written in a computer *programming language.* See *object code* and *source code.* 2. To express a problem-solving *algorithm* in a *programming language.* Also a synonym of *source code.*

codec   In *multimedia,* a program that compresses audio, video, or graphics files for efficient storage or transmission, and decompresses them for playback purposes. Codec is an abbreviation of compression/decompression. See *lossless compression* and *lossy compression.*

code page   In *MS-DOS,* a table of 256 codes for an IBM PC-compatible computer's *character set.* The two kinds of code pages are classed as follows:

- Hardware code page. The character set built into the computer's ROM.

- Prepared code page. A disk-based character set you can use to override the hardware code page.

codes See *hidden codes.*

code snippet One or more lines of *source code* embedded in a user-defined *menu* option or *button.* The instructions define what the button or option does.

coercivity A measure (in Oersteds) of the strength of the magnetic field required to alter the direction of magnetization in magnetic tape or disks.

CoffeeCup A non-WYSIWYG *HTML editor* that includes many resources for creating eye-catching Web pages quickly, including *animated GIFs, JavaScripts,* and *ActiveX controls.* The *shareware* program is available for Windows.

cold boot Starting a computer by turning on the system's power switch. See *boot* and *warm boot.*

cold link A method of copying information from one *document* (the source document) to another (the target document) so that a link is created. To update the link, choose a command that opens the source document, reads the information, and recopies the information if it has changed. See *Dynamic Data Exchange (DDE), hot link,* and *Inter-Application Communication (IAC).*

collaboratory In scientific networking, (a shared workspace, including shared scientific *databases*) facilities for teleconferencing, and network-accessible facilities for collaborative experimentation. See *federated database* and *Grand Challenge.*

Collabra In *Netscape Communicator,* a module that enables users to access *Usenet* newsgroups or private newsgroups set up with Netscape's Collabra server.

collapse When creating an outline or viewing a *directory tree* (such as in the *Windows Explorer*), the process of hiding all the outline levels or *subdirectories* below the selected outline heading or directory.

collate To organize the pages of a printout when more than one copy is printed. With collation, one complete copy of a document is printed before the next copy begins, and so on.

collision In *local area networks (LANs),* a garbled transmission that results when two or more workstations transmit to the same network cable at exactly the same time. Networks have means of preventing collisions.

color In *typography,* the quality of the printed portion of the page, which should be perceived by the eye as an even shade of gray. Defects, such as *rivers, bad breaks,* poor character spacing, or uneven line spacing, disrupt this even appearance. To maintain good color, use consistent word spacing, avoid *widows* and *orphans,* use *kerning* as necessary (especially for display type), and avoid *hyphen ladders.*

color depth In *monitors,* the number of colors a *video adapter* can display at one time. The *Video Graphics Array (VGA)* standard, for example, allows a color depth of 256. In scanners, the number of data bits with which a *scanner* records each *pixel* of a scanned image. The greater its color depth, the more colors or shades of gray a scanner can distinguish. A 24-bit scanner can depict 16.7 million colors and 256 shades of gray. A 30-bit scanner can record more than a billion colors and 1,024 levels of gray.

Color Graphics Adapter (CGA) A *bit-mapped graphics* display adapter for *IBM PC-compatible* computers. The CGA *adapter* displays four colors simultaneously with a resolution of 200 *pixels* horizontally and 320 *lines* vertically, or displays one color with a resolution of 640 pixels horizontally and 200 lines vertically.

color inkjet printer An *inkjet printer* generating color output. Some color inkjet printers create all colors from cyan, magenta, and yellow inks, but better ones use black ink, too, to fully conform with the *CMYK* model.

color laser printer A *laser printer* generating output that includes color, but that (for now, anyway) cannot match the output quality of *thermal wax transfer, dye sublimation,* or *thermal dye sublimation* printers. Color laser printers are less expensive, faster, and have lower *consumables* costs than other color–capable printers, but are more expensive than *monochrome* laser printers.

color model The way in which colors are described and altered. Three popular color models exist: the *HSB* model, the *RGB* model (used in *monitors*), and the *CMYK* model, which can support *device-independent color* systems such as the *Pantone matching system (PMS).*

color monitor A *display* device that can display an image in multiple colors, unlike a *monochrome monitor* that displays one color on a black or white background.

color scanner   A *scanner* that records colors as well as shades of gray. Color scanners are distinguished from one another mainly by their *color depth*.

color separation   The separation of a multicolor *graphic* into several layers of color, with each layer corresponding to one of the colors that will be printed when a professional printer reproduces the graphic. See *Pantone Matching System (PMS)*.

column   1. In character-based video displays, a vertical one-character-wide line down the screen. 2. In a *spreadsheet,* a vertical block of *cells* usually identified by a unique alphabetical letter. 3. In a *database management* program, the terms column and *field* are sometimes used synonymously. 4. In word processing and desktop publishing, a rectangle of text that is arranged vertically on the page along with one or more additional columns.

column graph   In analytical and *presentation graphics,* a *graph* with vertical columns. Column graphs are commonly used to show the values of items as they vary at precise intervals over a period of time. The *x-axis* (category axis) is the horizontal axis, and the *y-axis* (value axis) is the vertical axis. Such graphs are often called *bar graphs,* but technically speaking, bar graphs have horizontal bars.

column indicator   In *word processing programs,* such as *Microsoft Word*, a message in the *status bar* that shows the current horizontal position of the *cursor* on the screen.

column text chart   In *presentation graphics*, a chart showing related items as side-by-side columns of text.

column-wise recalculation   In *spreadsheet programs,* a *recalculation order* that calculates all the values in column A before moving to column B, and so on.

COM   1. In *MS-DOS*, a device name that refers to the *serial ports* available in your computer. Your computer can have up to four COM ports, designated as COM1, COM2, COM3, and COM4. 2. See *Component Object Model*.

com   On the *Internet*, a top-level domain name that is assigned to a corporation or business. Top-level domain names come last in a given Internet computer's domain name (such as www.apple.com).

combinatorial explosion   A barrier to the solution of a problem that occurs when the possibilities that must be computed are too numerous. See *artificial intelligence.*

COMDEX   Acronym for Computer Dealers Exhibition. A huge computer-industry trade show at which hardware manufacturers and software publishers display their wares for customers, the computer press, and each other. Held twice annually (in the spring in Atlanta and in the fall in Las Vegas).

Comité Consultatif International Téléphonique et Télégraphique   See *CCITT.*

comma-delimited file   A *data file,* usually in *ASCII* format, in which a user or *program* separates the data items by commas to facilitate the transfer of data to another program. See *tab-delimited file.*

command   A user-initiated signal given to a *program* that initiates, terminates, or otherwise controls the execution of a specific operation. In *command-driven programs,* you type the command statement and its associated syntax and press Enter. In a *menu-driven program,* you choose a command from an on-screen *menu.*

command button   In *Graphical User Interfaces (GUIs)* such as *Microsoft Windows 95* or the Macintosh *Finder,* a *pushbutton* in a *dialog box* that initiates an action, such as carrying out a command with the options chosen, canceling a command, or displaying another dialog box. You can quickly choose the default button just by pressing Return (for Macintoshes) or Enter (for Windows systems).

COMMAND.COM   In *MS-DOS,* a *file* that contains the *command interpreter.* This file must be present on the startup disk for MS-DOS to run.

command-driven program   A *system, utility,* or *application program* that requires you to type *command* statements, with the correct *syntax* and nomenclature, to use the program's features. See *Graphical User Interface (GUI)* and *menu-driven program.*

Command key   On *Macintosh keyboards,* a key marked with ⌘ that's frequently used in combination with alphabetical keys to provide keyboard shortcuts for *menu* options. Apple standardized these shortcuts so all Macintosh *applications* support them.

command language   See *software command language.*

command-line interface   In a *command-line operating system,* an interface that requires the user to type commands one line at a time. Synonymous with Teletype interface.

command-line operating system   A *command-driven* operating system, such as *MS-DOS,* that requires you to type commands using the *keyboard.* Compare to *Graphical User Interface (GUI).*

command mode   A *modem* mode in which it takes instructions from other parts of the computer, such as the *keyboard,* instead of transmitting everything over the phone line. For example, in command mode you could issue an instruction for the modem to lower the volume of its speaker or dial a number. *Communications programs* usually handle the distinction between command mode and *communications mode.*

command processor   The part of an *operating system* that accepts input from the user and displays prompts and messages, such as confirmation and error messages. Also referred to as the command interpreter. See *COMMAND.COM* and *command-line operating system.*

comment   See *remark.*

comment out   In *programming,* to place a symbol (such as a semicolon) or a command at the beginning of a line that marks the line as documentation. The *compiler* or *interpreter* ignores any lines preceded with this symbol.

Common Gateway Interface (CGI)   A standard that describes how *HTTPD*-compatible *World Wide Web (WWW)* servers should access external programs, so this data is returned to the user in the form of an automatically generated Web page. CGI programs, called scripts, come into play when a Web user fills out an on-screen form; the form generates output that is handled by the script, which brings other programs into play as necessary. These may include a database search engine or a mailer program. Common applications of CGI include providing a means for users to type and mail feedback, enabling database searches, and creating *gateways* to other Internet services that are not directly accessible through the Web.

Common Object Request Broker Architecture (CORBA)
A *middleware* standard that enables *objects* to communicate with each other in a computer network, even if the network connects

physically dissimilar computers and if the objects are written in varying programming languages. Netscape Communications has endorsed CORBA as part of its Open Network Environment (ONE) platform. Microsoft proposes a competing standard, called *DCOM*.

Common User Access (CUA)   An IBM-developed standard for user interfaces that draws on many of the ideas underlying *Graphical User Interfaces (GUI)*, including drop-down menus and dialog boxes. However, CUA can be implemented on text-only displays.

communications mode   A *modem* mode in which everything sent to the modem, such as text from the *keyboard*, is put onto the telephone line. See *command mode*.

communications parameters   In *telecommunications* and serial printing, the settings (parameters) that customize serial communications for the *hardware* you're contacting. See *baud rate, communications protocol, full duplex, half duplex, parameter, parity bit* and *stop bit*.

communications program   An *application* that turns your computer into a *terminal* for transmitting data to and receiving data from distant computers through the telephone system.

communications protocol   The standards that govern the transfer of information among computers on a *network* or using *telecommunications*. The computers involved in the communication must have the same settings and follow the same standards to avoid errors.

communications settings   See *communications parameters* and *communications protocol*.

comp   Abbreviation for composite. In *desktop publishing (DTP)*, a complete mock-up of a page layout design, showing what the final printed page will look like.

compact disc (CD)   A plastic disc, 4.75 inches in diameter, that uses optical storage techniques to store up to 72 minutes of music or 650*M* of digitally encoded computer data. CDs originally provided read-only data storage. The computer can read information from the disk, but you can't change this information or write new information to the disk. Therefore, this storage medium accurately is termed *compact disc-read only memory*

(CD-ROM). Erasable optical disk drives are now available and are expected to have a major impact on secondary storage techniques in the next decade. See *erasable optical disk drive, optical disk* and *secondary storage.*

Compact Disc–Digital Audio (CD-DA)   The sort of *CD-ROM* you can buy in a record store. Based on an early-1980s standard for recording sounds on compact discs, CD-DA is one of the most popular music-recording media around.

Compact Disc–Interactive (CD-I)   A *compact disc (CD)* standard designed for interactive viewing of audiovisual recordings with a television set and a CD-I player. Designed for education, training, and entertainment, CD-I has been slow to find a market.

comparison operator   See *relational operator.*

compatibility   The capability of a device, *program,* or *adapter* to function with or substitute for another make and model of computer, device, or program. Also, the capability of one computer to run the *software* written to run on another computer. To be truly compatible, a program or device should operate on a given system without changes; all features should operate as intended and run, without changes, all the software the other computer can run. See *clone.*

comp hierarchy   In *Usenet,* one of the seven standard newsgroup hierarchies; the comp.* newsgroups deal with every conceivable aspect of computing, including *artificial intelligence, computer-aided design (CAD), database* systems, digital telephony, *graphics,* the *Internet,* professional organizations, *programming languages, networks, operating systems,* specific *computer systems,* and theory. The comp.binaries.* newsgroups contain *freeware* and *shareware* programs.

compiled program   A program that has been transformed into machine-readable *object code* by a *compiler.* Compiled programs run significantly faster than *interpreted programs* because the program interacts directly with the *microprocessor* and doesn't need to share memory space with the *interpreter.* See *machine code language.*

compiler   A program that reads the statements written in a human-readable *programming language,* such as *Pascal* or *Modula-2,* and translates the statements into a machine-readable executable program.

Complementary Metal-Oxide Semiconductor (CMOS)
An energy-saving chip made to duplicate the functions of other chips, such as memory chips or *microprocessors.* CMOS chips are used in battery-powered *portable computers* and in other applications where reduced electrical consumption is desired. CMOS also refers to a special CMOS chip that operates the real-time clock included on a motherboard and stores the basic *system configuration,* including the *floppy* and *hard disk* types, amount of installed memory, and *wait state* settings. These settings are retained while the computer is off with only nominal battery support.

complex instruction set computer (CISC)   A type of *central processing unit (CPU)* that can recognize as many as 100 or more instructions, enough to carry out most computations directly. Most microprocessors are CISC chips. The use of reduced instruction set computer *(RISC)* technology, however, is becoming increasingly common in professional workstations. Apple's Power Macintosh computers use a compromise RISC/CISC processor.

component   1. A part or *module* of a program or *package.* For example, Netscape Messenger is a component of Netscape Communicator. 2. An *object* (see *object-oriented programming [OOP]*).

Component Object Model (COM)   A standard developed by Microsoft Corporation that enables properly prepared *objects* to exchange data with each other, even if the objects have been created with varying programming languages. COM requires that the computer's operating system be equipped with *OLE,* which is fully implemented (at present) only on Microsoft Windows systems. See *ActiveX* and *OLE.*

compose sequence   A series of *keystrokes* that lets you enter a *character* not found on the computer's keyboard.

composite   See *comp.*

composite color monitor   A *monitor* that accepts a standard video signal that mixes red, green, and blue signals to produce the color image. Display quality is inferior to that of *RGB monitors.* See *composite video.*

composite video   A method for broadcasting video signals in which the red, green, and blue components, as well as horizontal and vertical synchronization signals, are mixed together. Composite video, regulated by the U.S. *National Television Standards Committee (NTSC)*, is used for television. Some computers have composite video outputs that use a standard RCA phono plug and cable, such as on the backplane of a hi-fi or stereo system. See *composite color monitor* and *RGB monitor.*

A
B
C

compound device   In *multimedia,* a device, such as a *Musical Instrument Digital Interface (MIDI) sequencer,* that reproduces sound or other output that you recorded in a specific media file.

compound document   In Object Linking and Embedding *(OLE),* a single *file* created by two or more applications. When you use OLE to embed a *Microsoft Excel* chart into a *Microsoft Word* document, for example, the resulting file contains the Word text as well as the Excel *object.* The object contains all the information Excel needs to open the chart for editing. This information results in file sizes considerably larger than normal. See *OpenDoc.*

compress   1. A *Unix compression* utility that creates files with the *.Z extension. A copyrighted program, compress cannot be freely redistributed, so many Unix users prefer to use the Open Software Foundation's gunzip, which creates compressed files with the *.gz extension. 2. To reduce the size of a file by running a *compression* program on it.

compressed file   A *file* converted by a *file compression utility* to a special format that minimizes the disk storage space that is required.

compressed SLIP (CSLIP)   An optimized version of the *Serial Line Interface Protocol (SLIP),* commonly used to connect PCs to the *Internet* by means of dial-up connections, that includes compression and produces improved throughput. Because of its security shortcomings, *Internet service providers (ISPs)* prefer to implement dial-up access using the Point-to-Point Protocol *(PPP).*

compression   The reduction of a *file's* size by means of a compression program. The technique used to reduce the file's size (and to restore the data when the file is decompressed) is called the *compression algorithm.*

compression algorithm   The method used to *compress* a file and to restore the data when the file is decompressed for use.

The two types of compression algorithms are *lossless compression* and *lossy compression*. In lossless compression, the compression process allows for the subsequent decompression of the file with no loss of the original data. Lossless compression is used for program and data files. Lossy compression, in which the compression processes remove some of the data in a way that is not obvious to a person using the data. Lossy compression is used for sounds, graphics, animations, and videos. Many modems offer on-the-fly compression, and often use the *MNP5* or *V.42bis* protocols.

CompuServe   The second-largest *online information service,* which offers many of the same services as *America Online,* including file *downloading, e-mail,* news, up-to-the-minute stock quotes, an online encyclopedia, chat rooms, *Internet* access, and conferences on a wide variety of topics.

computation   The successful execution of an *algorithm,* which can be a textual search or *sort,* as well as a calculation.

computationally infeasible   Not capable of being solved due to practical constraints, even though a known algorithm exists. With some *encryption* algorithms, such as *DES,* it is theoretically possible to crack the code without possessing the *key*, but doing so would require such an enormous expenditure of computing resources, money, and time that the algorithm is considered secure.

computer   A machine that can follow instructions to alter *data* in a desirable way and to perform at least some operations without human intervention. Computers represent and manipulate text, *graphics,* symbols, and music, as well as numbers. See *analog computer* and *digital computer.*

computer addiction   See *computer dependency.*

computer-aided design (CAD)   The use of the *computer* and a CAD program to design a wide range of industrial products, ranging from machine parts to homes. CAD has become a mainstay in a variety of design-related fields, such as architecture, civil engineering, electrical engineering, mechanical engineering, and interior design. CAD applications are *graphics-* and calculation-intensive, requiring fast *microprocessors* and high-*resolution* video *displays.*

computer-aided design and drafting (CADD)   The use of a *computer system* for industrial design and technical drawing.

CADD software closely resembles *computer-aided design (CAD)* software, but has additional features that enable the artist to produce drawings conforming to engineering conventions.

computer-assisted design/computer assisted manufacturing See *CAD/CAM.*

computer-assisted instruction (CAI) The use of programs to perform instructional tasks, such as drill and practice, tutorials, and tests. Unlike human teachers, a CAI program works patiently with bright and slow students alike. Ideally, CAI can use sound, graphics, and on-screen rewards to engage a student in learning with huge payoffs.

computer-assisted manufacturing See *CAD/CAM.*

computer-based training (CBT) The use of *computer-aided instruction (CAI)* techniques to train for specific skills, such as operating a numerically controlled lathe.

Computer Dealers Exhibition See *COMDEX.*

computer dependency A psychological disorder characterized by compulsive and prolonged computer usage. For example, medical authorities in Denmark reported the case of an 18-year-old who spent up to 16 hours a day with his computer. Doctors found that he was talking to himself in a *programming language.*

Computer Emergency Response Team See *CERT.*

computer ethics A branch of ethics that is specifically concerned with the ethical use of computer resources. Areas of concern include *unauthorized access,* computer *viruses,* unethical behavior towards others on a computer network (see *netiquette*), and *software piracy.*

Computer Fraud and Abuse Act of 1984 A U.S. federal law that criminalizes the abuse of U.S. government computers or *networks* that cross state boundaries. Fines and/or prison sentences are spelled out for *unauthorized access,* theft of credit data, and spying with the intent to aid a foreign government.

Computer Graphics Metafile (CGM) An international graphics file format that stores *object-oriented graphics* in device-independent form so you can exchange CGM files among users of different computer systems (and different *programs*). A CGM file contains the graphic image as well as the instructions required for another program to create a file. Personal computer programs that can read and write to CGM file formats include Harvard Graphics and Ventura Publisher. It's the standard format used by *Lotus 1-2-3*. See *Windows Metafile Format (WMF)*.

computer–mediated communication (CMC)   Any communication between or among people that employs computers as a medium. Examples of CMC include *chat, e-mail, MUDs,* and *Usenet*.

Computer Professionals for Social Responsibility (CPSR)
A nonprofit, public advocacy organization, based in Palo Alto, California, that brings together computer scientists, computer educators, and interested citizens who are broadly concerned about the impact of computer technology on human welfare. Issues of CPSR concern include worker health and safety, the impact of computer technology on modern warfare, and civil liberties in the electronic age. The group's activities include education, conferences, publications, lobbying, and litigation.

computer system   A complete computer installation— including *peripherals,* such as *hard* and *floppy disk drives, monitor, mouse, operating system, software,* and *printer*—in which all the components are designed to work with each other.

CON   In *MS-DOS,* the device name for *console,* which refers to the *keyboard* and *monitor.*

concatenation   To link together two or more units of information, such as *strings* or *files*, so they form one unit. In *spreadsheet* programs, concatenation is used to combine text in a formula by placing an ampersand between the formula and text.

concordance file   A *file* containing the words you want a *word processing* program to include in the index that the program constructs.

concurrency control   In a *local area network (LAN)* version of an *application program,* the features built into the program that govern what happens when two or more people try to access the same program feature or *data file.* Many programs not designed for networks can run on a network and allow more than one person to access a *document,* but it may result in one person accidentally destroying another person's work. Concurrency control addresses this problem by enabling multiple access, where such access can occur without losing data, and by restricting multiple access, where access could result in destroyed work. See *file locking, LAN-aware program,* and *LAN-ignorant program.*

concurrency management See *concurrency control.*

concurrent processing See *multitasking.*

condensed type Type narrowed in width so more characters can fit into a linear inch. In *dot-matrix printers,* condensed type usually is set to print 17 *characters per inch (cpi).*

conference on data–systems languages (CODASYL) A professional organization dedicated to improving and standard-izing *COBOL.*

confidentiality In network security, the protection of any type of message from being intercepted or read by anyone other than its intended recipient.

CONFIG.SYS In *MS-DOS,* an *ASCII* text *file* in the *root directory* that contains *configuration* commands. MS-DOS consults this file at system startup.

configuration The choices made in setting up a *computer system* or an *application program* so it meets the user's needs. Properly configuring your system or program is one of the more onerous tasks of personal computing and, unfortunately, hasn't been eliminated by the arrival of *windowing environments.* In *Microsoft Windows 95,* for example, you must perform some manual configuration to obtain maximum performance from Windows and to take full advantage of the memory available on your system. When established, the configuration is saved to a *configuration file,* such as *WIN.INI* or *AUTOEXEC.BAT.*

configuration file A *file* created by an *application program* that stores the choices you make when you install the program so they're available the next time you start the program. In *Microsoft Word,* for example, the file MW.INI stores the choices you make from the Options menu.

configuration manager In *Microsoft Windows 95,* the utility program that keeps track of the software drivers associated with hardware devices. See *hardware tree.*

confirmation message An on-screen message asking you to confirm a potentially destructive action, such as closing a *window* without saving your work. See *alert box.*

connectionless   Not requiring a direct electronic connection in order to exchange data. See *connection-oriented, packet-switching network*.

connectionless protocol   In *wide area networks (WANs)*, a standard that enables the transmission of data from one computer to another even though no effort is made to determine whether the receiving computer is online or able to receive the information. This is the underlying protocol in any *packet-switching network*, such as the *Internet*, in which a unit of data is broken down into small-sized packets, each with a header containing the address of the data's intended destination. In the Internet, the connectionless protocol is the *Internet Protocol (IP)*. IP is concerned only with breaking data down into packets for transmission and reassembling the packets after they have been received. A *connection-oriented protocol* (on the Internet, TCP) works at another level to assure that all the packets are received. Research on computer networks has disclosed this design is highly efficient. See *Transmission Control Protocol (TCP)*.

connection-oriented   Requiring a direct electronic connection, by means of switching circuits, in order to exchange data. See *connectionless, connectionless protocol* and *packet-switching network*.

connection-oriented protocol   In *wide area networks (WANs)*, a standard that establishes a procedure by which two of the computers on the *network* can establish a physical connection that lasts until they have successfully exchanged data. This is accomplished by means of *handshaking*, in which the two computers exchange messages that say, in effect, "OK, I'm ready," "I didn't get that; please re-send," and "Got it, bye." In the *Internet*, the *Transmission Control Protocol (TCP)* is a connection-oriented protocol; it provides the means by which two Internet-connected computers can enter into communication with each other to ensure the successful transmission of data. In contrast, *the Internet Protocol (IP)* is a *connectionless protocol*, which enables the transmission of data without requiring handshaking.

connectivity   The extent to which a given computer or *program* can function in a *network* setting.

connectivity platform   A *program* or *utility* designed to enhance another program's capability to exchange *data* with other programs through a local area network (LAN). Oracle for the *Macintosh*, for example, provides *HyperCard* with the connectivity required to search for and retrieve information from large corporate *databases.*

connector conspiracy   A computer manufacturer's plot to force its customers to buy its products, which contain bizarre connectors that work only with peripherals made by the same company. Vastly unpopular with users, connector conspiracies nevertheless spring up eternally, fueled by greed. A recent version, the proprietary *CD-ROM* connectors on *sound cards,* forces you to buy a *CD-ROM drive* made by the same manufacturer (unless you're willing to live with reduced functionality).

connect speed   The data-transmission rate at which a *modem,* after performing a *handshaking* sequence with another modem and determining the amount of *line noise,* establishes a connection. The connect speed may be lower than the modem's top speed.

console   A *terminal,* consisting of a *monitor* and *keyboard.* In *multi-user systems,* console is synonymous with *terminal,* but console also is used in *personal computer* operating systems to refer to the keyboard and display. See *CON.*

constant   In a *spreadsheet program,* a number you type directly into a *cell* or place in a *formula.* See *cell definition* and *key variable.*

constant angular velocity (CAV)   In *data storage media* such as *hard* and *floppy disk drives,* a playback technique in which the disk rotates at a constant speed. This technique results in faster data retrieval times as the *read/write head* nears the *spindle;* retrieval times slow as the read/write head moves toward the perimeter of the disk. See *constant linear velocity (CLV).*

constant linear velocity (CLV)   In *CD-ROM drives,* a playback technique that speeds or slows the rotation of the disk to ensure that the velocity of the disk is always constant at the point where the disk is being read. To achieve constant linear velocity, the disk must spin more slowly when reading or writing closer to the *spindle.* See *constant angular velocity (CAV).*

consumables   The supplies a *printer* uses up as it operates. Consumables expenses, such as those for ink cartridges and paper, can add up quickly. Consumables costs are usually expressed as a *cost per page,* which for some high-end color-capable printers can exceed $3.00.

contact head   In a *hard disk,* a *read/write head* that skates on the surface of a *platter* instead of flying over it. Contact heads offer resistance to *head crashes* and improved *areal density.*

contact management program   An application program that enables business people to create directories of their business contacts and to set up contact schedules. See *ACT!* and *personal information manager (PIM).*

container   See *compound document.*

contention   In *local area networks (LANs),* a channel access method in which access to the communication channel is based on a first-come, first-served policy. See *CSMA/CD* and *device contention.*

context-sensitive help   In an *application program,* a user-assistance mode that displays documentation relevant to the *command, mode,* or action you are now performing. Context-sensitive help reduces the time and keystrokes needed to get on-screen help.

context switching   Changing from one *program* to another without exiting either program. See *multiple program loading.*

contiguous   Adjacent; placed one next to or after the other. A *range* of *cells* in a *spreadsheet* is often, but not always, made up of contiguous cells.

continuous paper   Paper manufactured in one long strip, with perforations separating the pages, so you can feed the paper into a *printer* with a *tractor-feed* mechanism. Synonymous with continuous-feed paper.

continuous-tone image   *Printer* output in which colors and shades of gray blend smoothly together, as they would in a chemically printed photograph.

continuous-tone printer   A *printer* that can generate *photorealistic output,* with smooth gradations between colors or shades of gray.

contrast   In *monitors,* the degree of distinction between dark and light *pixels.* Most monitors have a contrast control that you can adjust to regulate contrast.

control   1. In a *Microsoft Windows 95* program, a *dialog box* feature (such as a *check box, radio button,* or *list box*) that allows the user to choose options. 2. In *ActiveX*, a downloaded mini-program that adds functionality to a Web page.

Control+Break　In *MS-DOS*, a *keyboard command* that cancels the execution of a *program* or command at the next available *breakpoint*.

control bus　A data pathway that has been set aside to carry control instructions from the computer's *central processing unit (CPU)*.

control character　See *control code*.

control code　In *American Standard Code for Information Interchange (ASCII)*, a code reserved for *hardware*-control purposes, such as advancing a page on the printer. ASCII has 32 control codes.

Control key (Ctrl)　In *IBM PC-compatible* computing, a *key* frequently pressed in combination with other keys to issue *program* commands. In *Microsoft Word*, for example, pressing Ctrl+F calls up the Find *dialog box*.

controlled vocabulary　In database searching, a fixed set of predetermined subject terms that can be used to describe a *data record's* content unambiguously. The use of controlled vocabulary dramatically increases the *precision* of information retrieval operations, but coding records with the controlled terms is time-consuming. See *free text search*.

controller　See *hard disk controller* and *floppy disk controller*.

controller card　An *adapter* that connects *hard* and *floppy disk drives* to the computer. Most personal computer controller cards contain circuitry to connect one or more *floppy disks* and a *hard disk*.

control menu　In *Microsoft Windows 95*, a *pull-down menu*, found in all *windows* and *dialog boxes*, that contains options for managing the *active window*. The control menu icon, a button containing a bar shaped like a hyphen, is on the left end of the *title bar*. The contents of the menu vary, but the menu usually includes commands to move, size, *maximize*, and *minimize* windows, as well as to close the current window or switch to another application window or the next document window.

control panel   In the *Macintosh* and *Microsoft Windows 95* operating environments, the control panel is a utility window that lists options for *hardware* devices, such as the *mouse, monitor,* and *keyboard.*

control panel device (CDEV)   Any *Macintosh* utility program placed in the *System Folder* that appears as an option in the *control panel.*

control structure   A logical organization for an *algorithm* that governs the sequence in which *program* statements are executed. Control statements govern the flow of control in a program by specifying the sequence in which the steps in a program or *macro* are carried out. Control structures include branch structures that cause a special set of instructions to be executed if a specified situation is encountered; loop structures that execute over and over until a condition is fulfilled; and procedure/function structures that set aside distinct program functions or procedures into separate modules, which are invoked from the main program.

control unit   A component of the *central processing unit (CPU)* that obtains program instructions and emits signals to carry them out. See *arithmetic-logic unit (ALU).*

convenience copier   A *printer/scanner* combination or a *fax* machine that can be used to make small numbers of photocopies.

conventional memory   In any IBM PC-compatible computer, the first 640K of *random-access memory (RAM)*. The *Intel 8086* and *Intel 8088 microprocessors,* which were available when the IBM Personal Computer (PC) was designed, could directly use 1*M* of *random-access memory (RAM)*. The PC's designers decided to make 640*K* of RAM accessible to programs, reserving the rest of the 1M memory space for internal system functions. *Microsoft Windows 95* gives programs direct access to all of a system's RAM.

conventional programming   The use of a *procedural programming language,* such as *BASIC, FORTRAN,* or *assembly language,* to code an *algorithm* in machine-readable form. In conventional programming, the programmer must be concerned with the sequence in which events occur within the computer. Nonprocedural programming languages let the programmer focus on the problem without worrying about the precise procedure the computer must follow to solve the problem. See *declarative language*.

convergence   1. In *monitors*, the alignment of the red, blue, and green *electron guns* to create colors on-screen. If they aren't perfectly aligned, poor convergence results, causing a decrease in image sharpness and *resolution*. White areas also tend to show colors around their edges. 2. In a *packet-switching network*, an automatic process of network mapping that occurs after a router is switched on. A *router* is a device, usually a dedicated computer, that "reads" each incoming packet and determines where to send it next. In order to do its job correctly, the router needs an accurate map of the networks to which it is directly connected. If this map had to be updated manually, organizations would have to devote a considerable amount of time and human resources to the job. Convergence software enables the router to detect changes to the network, such as the addition or removal of workstations, and to adjust its map automatically. The process is called convergence because it takes a few minutes for the router's map to "converge" to reality (the current state of the network).

conversion utility   A program that transforms the *file format* in which data is stored. For example, Microsoft Word comes with several conversion utilities that can read files created by other word processing programs and rewrite them using Word's proprietary file format.

cookie   1. In Unix, a one- or two-line quotation that can be automatically appended to an outgoing e-mail message. 2. In the *World Wide Web (WWW)*, a small text file that the *server* writes to the user's hard disk without the user's knowledge or permission. The data in the cookie file enables one Web page to pass information to other pages, thus directly addressing a major shortcoming of the underlying Web protocol, *HTTP*. Many cookie applications benefit the user, for example, the *shopping basket* used by many online "shopping malls" would not function without cookies. However, direct marketing firms are using cookies to compile information about user's browsing habits in ways that have raised grave concerns among privacy advocates. *Netscape Communicator* enables users to switch cookies off.

cooperative multitasking   In an *operating system*, a means of running more than one *program* at a time. In cooperative multitasking, one *application program* cannot force another to do something. An application yields to another voluntarily but only after checking the electronic equivalent of a message box to see if any other applications have made a request. If the application is involved in a lengthy processing operation, however, it may not check the message box until the operation is completed. See *preemptive multitasking.*

cooperative network   A *wide-area network (WAN),* such as *BITNET* or *UUCP,* in which the costs of participating are borne by the linked organizations. See *research network.*

Copland   Code name for a grandiose and unsuccessful revision of the Macintosh's *System 7* operating system, which would have brought to the *MacOS* features that have already been successfully implemented in *Microsoft Windows 95* and *Microsoft Windows NT,* including *multithreaded processing, symmetric multiprocessing, preemptive multitasking,* and *protected memory.* In conceding the failure of the Copland product, Apple announced that the next version of MacOS, *version 8,* will offer improved multitasking, but that the future Macintosh operating system will be based on *Rhapsody,* a version of the *NeXT* operating system acquired from NeXT, Inc.

copper pair   Standard telephone cable that cannot handle high-speed *digital* communications services, such as the *Integrated Services Digital Network (ISDN).* The copper pair wire that pervades American residences and businesses will have to be replaced before high-speed digital communication can become commonplace. See *twisted-pair.*

coprocessor   A *microprocessor* support *chip* that takes over a specific processing operation, such as handling mathematical computations or displaying images on the video display. See *numeric coprocessor.*

copy   1. The material, including text, *graphic* images, pictures, and artwork, to be assembled for printing. To reproduce part of a *document* at another location in the document or in another document.

copy fitting   In *desktop publishing (DTP),* a method used to determine the amount of copy (text), in a specified *font,* that can fit into a given area on a page or in a publication.

copyleft   A type of copyright promoted by the Free Software Foundation that is intended to promote the free distribution of copyrighted software for noncommercial purposes.

copy protection Hidden instructions included in a *program* intended to prevent you from making unauthorized copies of *software.* Because most copy-protection schemes impose penalties on legitimate owners of programs, such as forcing them to insert a specially encoded "key disk" before using a program, most business software publishers have given up using these schemes. Copy protection is still common, however, in recreational and educational software.

CORBA See *Common Object Request Brokerage Architecture.*

core dump In *mainframe* computing, a *debugging* technique that involves printing out the entire contents of the computer's core, or memory. In slang, the term refers to a person who, when asked a simple question, recites everything he or she remembers about a subject. See *dump.*

Corel Corporation A major publisher of consumer and business software, including *CorelDRAW!, Corel Office Pro,* and *Corel WordPerfect Suite.* The company is based in Ottawa, Ontario, Canada.

CorelDRAW! A *vector graphics* program that includes a wide variety of special effects and utilities, including 3-D *rendering* and *animation,* photo editing, and *presentation graphics.* The program is *Internet*-ready in that it saves graphics to Internet color palettes and *file formats.*

Corel Office Pro An *office suite* for Windows systems that includes word processing (Corel WordPerfect), spreadsheet (Corel QuattroPro), presentation graphics (Corel Presentations), database software (Paradox), and utilities (including Sidekick, Dashboard, and clip art images). The suite closely resembles *Corel WordPerfect Suite,* except that the Office Pro suite includes database software.

core-logic chip set A collection of integrated circuits that allows a *central processing unit (CPU)* to work with an *external cache, random-access memory (RAM),* and an *expansion bus.*

Corel Quattro Pro A full-featured *spreadsheet program* for Windows computers that incorporates Internet connectivity and publishing features, as well as an unusually large number of functions (more than 500) and chart styles (more than 50). This program competes with *Lotus 1-2-3* and *Microsoft Excel.*

Corel WordPerfect Suite　An *office suite* that features word processing (Corel WordPerfect), spreadsheet (Corel QuattroPro), presentation graphics (Corel Presentations), several additional utilities, and more than 10,000 *clip art* images. The suite is essentially the same as the *Corel Office Pro* suite, except that it lacks database software. It is available for Windows systems only; Corel WordPerfect is available for the Macintosh.

core set of modulation protocols　The methods for transmitting data that are built into *modems.* The core set of modulation protocols in modern modems typically includes *Bell 103A, Bell 212A, V.22, V.22bis, V.32,* and *V.32bis,* and enables virtually any pair of modems to communicate successfully.

corona wire　In *laser printers,* a wire that applies electrostatic charge to paper.

corrupted file　A *file* that contains scrambled and unrecoverable data. Files can become corrupted due to bad *sectors* (surface flaws on the disk), *hard* or *floppy disk drive controller* failures, or *software* errors.

cost-benefit analysis　A projection of the costs and benefits of buying certain equipment or taking certain action.

cost per page　In *printers,* an estimate of the cost of *consumables* for each page of output generated. Because consumables can ultimately cost more than the printer, pay attention to cost per page figures when shopping for printers. Some high-end color-capable printers have costs per page of $3.00 or more.

Cougar　Code name for the next version of *HTML,* currently under review by the *World Wide Web Consortium (W3C).* Building on the achievements of HTML 3.2, Cougar will incorporate a better mechanism for representing information about the document (such as authenticating the author's name by means of digital signatures), support locally executable scripting languages such as *JavaScript,* formally specify frames tags, extend forms (with particular attention to providing access for people with disabilities), specify the means for including *objects* (such as *Java applets*), and additional improvements to support the international usage of HTML.

counter　In *typography,* the space fully or partially enclosed by a *bowl,* the strokes that form a letter, such as the blank space inside the letter a or o.

Courier   A *monospace typeface,* commonly included as a *built-in font* in *laser printers,* that simulates the output of office typewriters. For example, This is Courier type.

courseware   Software developed for computer-assisted instruction (CAI) or computer-based training (CBT) applications.

courtesy copy (CC)   In *e-mail,* a copy of an e-mail message that is sent to one or more addresses. These addresses are included in the header information that the message's recipient sees. In a *blind courtesy copy (BCC),* the recipient does not know who, if anyone, has received copies of the message.

cpi   See *characters per inch.*

CP/M (Control Program for Microprocessors)   An early *operating system* for personal computers that used the 8-bit Intel *8080* and Zilog Z-80 *microprocessors.* CP/M was created in the late 1970s as *floppy disk drives* became available for early personal computers.

CPM   See *critical path method.*

cps   See *characters per second.*

CPU   See *central processing unit.*

CPU fan   A fan that mounts directly on top of the microprocessor *chip* to keep it cool. Newer *microprocessors,* such as the *Pentium,* get extremely hot and can malfunction if allowed to overheat.

cracker   A computer hobbyist who gets kicks from gaining unauthorized access to computer systems. Cracking is a silly, egotistical game in which the object is to defeat even the most secure computer systems. Although many crackers do little more than leave a "calling card" to prove their victory, some attempt to steal credit card information or destroy data. Whether or not they commit a crime, all crackers injure legitimate computer users by consuming the time of system administrators and making computer resources more difficult to access. In the press, the term "cracker" is used synonymously with "*hacker,*" but hacking has a completely different meaning and plays a valuable role in computing. See *hacker ethic* and *security.*

crash   An abnormal termination of *program* execution, usually (but not always) resulting in a frozen *keyboard* or an unstable state. In most cases, you must *reboot* the computer to recover from a crash.

CRC   See *cyclic redundancy check.*

creator type   In the *Macintosh*, a four-letter code that identifies the program used to create a *document*. The code associates the document with the application so you can start the application by opening the document. See *associated document.*

creeping featurism   An unfortunate tendency in *programming* where *software* developers add more and more *features* in an attempt to keep up with the competition. The result is a program that's hopelessly complex, sluggish, and hogs disk space.

crippled version   A freely distributed version of a *program* that lacks one or more crucial features, such as printing, that have been deliberately disabled in an attempt to introduce the user to the program in the hope that the user will buy the full version. Synonymous with working model. See *demo.*

criteria range   In a *spreadsheet program* that includes *database* functions, the *range* of *cells* that contains the conditions, or criteria, you specify to govern how a search is conducted or an *aggregate function* is calculated.

critical path method (CPM)   In *project management,* a technique for planning and timing the execution of tasks where you identify a critical path—a series of tasks that must be completed in a timely fashion if the entire project is to be completed on time. Project management *software* helps project managers identify critical paths.

cropping   A *graphics* editing operation in which you trim the edges from a graphic to make it fit into a given space or to remove unnecessary parts of the image.

cross-hatching   A pattern of parallel and crossed lines added to solid areas in a graph to distinguish one data range from another.

cross-linked files   In *Microsoft Windows 95,* a file-storage error that occurs when the *file allocation table (FAT)* indicates that two *files* claim the same disk cluster. Like *lost clusters,* cross-linked files occur when the computer is interrupted (by a *crash* or a power outage) while it's writing a file. To repair cross-linked files, run

ScanDisk frequently. Repairing files quickly can minimize the extent of data loss.

cross-platform   Able to operate on a network in which the workstations are of dissimilar make (for example, Macintoshes, Windows systems, and Unix computers). *Netscape Communicator* is a cross-platform browser because there are versions of the program for all three major computing formats, and the program conforms to *cross-platform standards*, which do not lock users into *proprietary standards.*

cross-platform standard   A communication standard or *protocol* that does not require the use of a *proprietary* operating system or proprietary hardware in order to function. Microsoft's *ActiveX* standard could become a cross-platform standard if versions of the underlying *OLE* technology are developed for Unix computers (and if the level of OLE support for the Macintosh were improved), but at present ActiveX obliges the user to access ActiveX *controls* by means of a Windows-based system.

cross-post   In *Usenet,* to *post* a contribution to two or more *newsgroups* simultaneously. Cross-posting is rarely warranted and is a favorite tactic of *spammers* who post unsolicited, unwanted, and off-topic advertisements to hundreds or even thousands of newsgroups at a time.

cross-reference   In *word processing programs,* a code name used to refer to material discussed elsewhere in a *document.* Cross-references, such as "See the discussion of burnishing methods on page 19," are helpful to the reader, but they can become a nightmare if you add or delete text. The best word processing programs (such as *WordPerfect* and *Microsoft Word*) contain cross-reference features, enabling you to mark the original text and assign a code name to the marked text, such as BURNISH. Then you type the code name (not the page number) when you want to cross-reference the original text. When you print your document, the program substitutes the correct page number for the code name. If you add or delete text later and print again, the cross-references are updated to reflect the new page numbers.

crosstalk   The interference generated by cables too close to one another. You sometimes hear crosstalk on the telephone. When speaking long-distance, hearing other voices or entire conversations in the background of your conversation isn't uncommon. Crosstalk often prevents error-free transmission of *data.*

CRT   See *cathode ray tube.*

cryptanalysis   The science of breaking encrypted messages, both to determine the strength of encryption techniques and to provide the nation with a military advantage.

cryptography   The science of coding messages so they cannot be read by any person other than the intended recipient. Cryptography dates back to ancient Rome, but it has always been plagued by the messenger problem: If you want to send an encrypted message to somebody, then you must also somehow send the key that is needed to decode the message. There is always the threat that the key could be intercepted en route without your knowing, thus defeating the purpose of encryption. Possibly the most significant event in the history of cryptography is the recent invention of *public-key cryptography,* which completely eliminates the need to send a key via a separate, secure channel, and enables two people who have never before communicated to exchange virtually unbreakable messages. See *cryptanalysis.*

csh   A *shell* (user interface) for the *Unix* operating system that enables programmers to write *shell scripts* using a scripting language closely resembling *C* (csh is an acronym for C Shell). See *Bourne shell.*

CSMA/CD   Acronym for Carrier Sense Multiple Access with Collision Detection. In *local area networks (LANs),* a method used by *Ethernet, AppleTalk,* and other *network protocols* for controlling a computer's access to the communication channel. With CSMA/CD, each component of the *network* (called a *node*) has an equal right to access the communication channel. If two computers try to access the network at the same time, the network uses a random number to decide which computer gets to use the network first. This channel access method works well with relatively small- to medium-sized networks (two or three dozen nodes). Large networks use alternative channel access methods, such as *polling* and *token passing* to prevent overloading or locking up the system.

CSO name server   An *Internet*-accessible white pages directory that an organization makes available. Listing the names, telephones, and *e-mail* addresses of all the organization's employees, a CSO name server provides an alternative to the telephone directory. The acronym CSO stands for Computing Service Office

(CSO), a unit of the University of Illinois, where the original name server software was developed.

Ctrl See *Control key (Ctrl)*.

Ctrl+Break See *Control+Break*.

CTS/RTS Also called hardware *handshaking,* a method of flow control used between the *modem* and the computer in which it is installed. When ready to send data, the computer will send a Request To Send (RTS) signal, to which the modem will reply with a Clear To Send (CTS) signal when it is ready to receive data. CTS/RTS prevents the computer from sending more data than the modem can handle.

CUA See *Common User Access*.

cumulative trauma disorder See *repetitive strain injury (RSI)*.

Curie temperature A distinct temperature at which a material's *coercivity* changes drastically. *Magneto-optical (MO) drives* take advantage of the Curie temperature by recording data at high temperatures but storing and reading it at low temperatures, ensuring a long shelf life for the data.

curly brace The brace characters ({ and }) on the standard keyboard. Synonymous with *brace*. See *angle bracket, bracket*.

current cell In a *spreadsheet* program, such as *Excel,* the *cell* in which the *cell pointer* is positioned. Synonymous with active cell.

current cell indicator In *a spreadsheet* program, such as *Excel,* a message in the upper-left corner that displays the *address* of the *cell* in which the *cell pointer* is positioned.

current directory The *directory* that *MS-DOS* or an *application program* uses by default to store and retrieve *files*. Synonymous with default directory.

current drive The *hard* or *floppy disk* the *operating system* uses for an operation unless you specify otherwise. Synonymous with default drive.

cursor An on-screen blinking *character* that shows where the next character will appear. See *pointer*.

cursor-movement keys   The *keys* that move the *cursor* on-screen. Synonymous with arrow keys.

CU-SeeMe   An *Internet* conferencing program, created by White Pine Software, that enables users of systems equipped with *digital cameras* (such as QuickCam or Apple AV) to engage in real-time *video conferences* with up to eight people at a time.

cut   To delete selected text, a graphic, or some other object from a document. The cut object is stored temporarily in the *Clipboard*, from which it can be pasted elsewhere, or discarded.

cut and paste   See *block move.*

cut-sheet feeder   A paper-feed mechanism that feeds separate sheets of paper into the printer, where a friction-feed mechanism draws the paper through the printer.

CWIS   See *campus-wide information system.*

cyberphobia   An exaggerated and irrational fear of computers. Noted by the psychotherapist Craig Brod and others, cyberphobia stems from the stress individuals encounter as they try to cope with an increasingly computer-driven society. Alert employers that offer training to employees new to computers can help ease employee transition to a computerized work environment.

cyberpunk   A genre of science fiction that depicts a dystopian future dominated by worldwide computer *networks,* battling *artificial intelligences,* monopoly capitalism, and a world culture as ethnically eclectic as it is politically apathetic and alienated. On this stage are chronicled the exploits of *hackers* who use hallucinogenic drugs, cyborg implants, and trance states to carry out criminal and heroic missions within the networks' fabulous realms of *virtual reality.* The originator of the genre is William Gibson in his 1982 book *Neuromancer,* which coined the term *cyberspace.* Curiously, Gibson knew little about computing when he wrote the book—on a typewriter.

cybersex   A form of long-distance eroticism made possible by a *real-time* computer *chat room;* synonymous with compusex. To stimulate your virtual partner, you relay a favorite sexual fantasy or describe in vivid terms what you would be doing if the person were actually present.

cyberspace   The virtual space created by *computer systems.* One definition of space is "a boundless three-dimensional extent in which objects and events occur and have relative position and direction." In the 20th century, computer systems are creating a new kind of space that fits the previous definition, called cyberspace. (The prefix "cyber" refers to computers.) Cyberspace can take the form of elaborate *virtual reality* worlds or relatively simple *e-mail.* E-mail advocates will readily testify that the ability to communicate with other users, located all over the world, breaks down social and spatial boundaries in an exhilarating way. See *cyberpunk, Internet,* and *virtual reality.*

cyclic redundancy check (CRC)   An automatic error-checking method used by *MS-DOS* when writing data to a *hard* or *floppy disk.* When MS-DOS later reads data from the disk, the same error-check is conducted, and the results of the two checks are compared to make sure that the data hasn't changed. If you see an error message such as CRC ERROR READING DRIVE C, it signals serious problems with the disk. A similar CRC checking procedure also is commonly used by file compression utilities (such as PKZIP) and when transferring files using *data communications.* See *XMODEM/CRC.*

cylinder   In *hard* and *floppy disk drives,* a unit of storage consisting of the set of *tracks* that occupy the same position on opposite sides of the *platter.* On a double-sided disk, a cylinder includes track 1 of the top and the bottom sides. On hard disks in which several disks are stacked on top of one another, a cylinder consists of track 1 on both sides of all the disks.

Cypherpunk   A *programmer* who strongly believes that private citizens possess the right to send a secure, encrypted message to anyone they please and that *encryption* technology should not be regulated.

Cyrix   A manufacturer of computer chips.

Cyrix 486DLC   A *microprocessor* that is *binary compatible* with *software* written for *x86* computers and *pin compatible* with the *Intel 386DX,* making the 486DLC an option for 386DX owners who want to upgrade their machines. Unlike the Intel 486DX, the 486DLC, which runs at clock speeds up to 33 *megahertz (MHz),* does not have a *numeric coprocessor,* so to upgrade fully, computer owners have to install a Cyrix 83D87 chip as well. Internet reports say the 486DLC will not work with the *NeXTStep* operating system. See *Cyrix CX486DX2.*

Cyrix 486DX2   A *microprocessor* that is both *binary compatible* with *x86 software* and *pin-compatible* with the *Intel 486DX2* microprocessor. Though it is *clock-doubled* like the Intel 486DX2, the *Cyrix* part has a smaller *internal cache* and is therefore slower.

Cyrix 486SLC   A *microprocessor* that is *binary compatible* with software written for x86 computers and *pin-compatible* with the *Intel 386SX* chip and is designed to upgrade 386SX systems to near-486 performance levels. The 486SLC is available in 16 *megahertz (MHz)* and 25 MHz versions.

Cyrix 6x86   A *Pentium*-compatible *microprocessor* designed to compete with Intel's highly successful offering. With its *super-scalar architecture,* the 6x86 is generally similar in design to the Pentium, and the two *chips* are supposed to be *binary compatible,* but the 6x86 offers several advantages over the Pentium, including *superpipelining,* multibranch prediction, *speculative execution, register renaming,* and fewer *issue restrictions. Cyrix* claims that the 6x86 outperforms comparable Pentium chips, but the 6x86 does not support *MMX* graphics processing.

Cyrix 6x86MX   A Pentium-compatible *microprocessor* that is designed to compete with Intel's *Pentium II* processor. Called M2 during its development, the chip is a high-speed *Cyrix 6x86* that supports the *MMX* graphics extensions.

Cyrix CX486DRu2   A clock-doubled version of the Cyrix 486DLC microprocessor, designed to run at a clock speed of 66 *megahertz (MHz)*.

DA   See *desk accessory.*

DAC   Acronym for digital to analog converter. Synonymous with *analog-to-digital converter (A/D converter).*

daemon   A program, usually on a computer running *Unix,* that serves some obscure function (such as routing *e-mail* to its recipients) and usually has a very limited user interface. There's some debate about the origins of the word, but most say it derives from the devilish spirits of Greek mythology.

daisy chain   A method of connecting together several devices along a *bus* and managing the signals for each device. Devices that use a *Small Computer System Interface (SCSI),* such as a *CD-ROM,* hard disk, and scanner, can be daisy-chained to one *SCSI port.*

daisy chaining   In displays, the act of linking several *monitors* together so they all show the same thing. Daisy chaining is convenient when large numbers of people must see the output of a computer simultaneously, such as at a convention or trade show.

daisywheel printer   An obsolete *impact printer* that simulates the typescript produced by a typewriter. The term daisywheel refers to the metal or plastic disk consisting of characters mounted on spokes connected to a hub, resembling a daisy. To produce a character, the printer spins the wheel until that character is in front of a hammer that strikes the character against an inked ribbon, transferring the image to paper. Daisywheel printers can print many typefaces, but changing fonts within a document is tedious, because you must change the daisywheel manually.

DAP   See *Directory Access Protocol.*

DARPA   See *Defense Advanced Research Project Agency.*

DASD   See *Direct Access Storage Device.*

DAT   Acronym for Digital Audio Tape. A digital magnetic tape format originally developed for CD-quality audio recording and now used for computer backup tapes. The latest DAT storage format, *DDS,* specifies storage capacities of up to 24G.

data   Factual information (such as text, numbers, sounds, and images) in a form that can be processed by a computer. Although data is the plural of the Latin word datum, the term "data" is commonly used to represent both singular and plural. In formal contexts (such as university computer science and engineering departments), the plural (data) and the singular (datum) are sometimes distinguished.

database   A collection of related *information* about a subject organized in a useful manner that provides a base or foundation for procedures, such as retrieving information, drawing conclusions, and making decisions. Any collection of information that serves these purposes qualifies as a database, even if the information isn't stored on a computer. In fact, important predecessors of today's sophisticated business database systems were files kept on index cards and stored in file cabinets. Information usually is divided into *data records*, each with one or more *data fields*.

database design   The choice and arrangement of *data fields* in a *database* so that fundamental errors (such as *data redundancy* and *repeating fields*) are avoided or minimized.

database driver   A program that enables a spreadsheet program to exchange *data* with other *database* programs, such as *dBASE*.

database management   Tasks related to creating, maintaining, organizing, and retrieving information from a *database*. See *data manipulation*.

database management program   An *application program* that provides the tools for *data retrieval,* modification, deletion, and insertion. Such programs also can create a *database* and produce meaningful output on a *printer* or on-screen. In *personal computing,* three kinds of *database management programs* exist: *flat-file, relational,* and text-oriented. See *band* and *relational database management system*.

database management system (DBMS)   A program that organizes *data* in a *database,* providing information storage, organization, and retrieval capacities, sometimes including simultaneous access to multiple databases through a shared field *(relational database management)*. See *flat-file database management program*.

database structure   In *database management,* a definition of the *data records* in which information is stored, including the number of *data fields;* a set of field definitions that specify the type, length, and other characteristics of the data that can be entered in each *field;* and a list of *field names.* See *data type.*

data bits   The number of *bits* a computer uses to represent a character of data. When two computers communicate by *modem,* they must use the same number of data bits—usually 8, but sometimes 7. See *parity* and *stop bit.*

data bus   An internal electronic pathway that enables the *microprocessor* to exchange data with *random-access memory (RAM).* The width of the data *bus,* usually *16* or *32 bits,* determines how much data can be sent at one time.

D
E
F

data communication   The transfer of information from one computer to another. The transfer can occur via direct cable connections, as in *local area networks (LANs),* or over telephone lines using *modems.* See *telecommunications.*

Data Communications Equipment (DCE)   The term used by the specification that defines the standard *serial port* to describe the electronics that connect the computer to a *modem* or *fax modem.*

data compression   See *compression.*

data-compression protocol   In *modems,* a standard for automatically *compressing* data when it's sent and *decompressing* data when it's received. With data compression, you can realize gains of up to 400 percent in effective transmission speed. The two most common data-compression protocols are *V.42bis* and *MNP-5.* See *CCITT protocol.*

data deletion   In a *database management program,* an operation that deletes records according to specified criteria. Many *database* programs don't actually delete the *records* in such operations; they merely mark the records so that they aren't included in *data retrieval operations.* Therefore, you usually can restore the deleted records if you make a mistake.

data dependency   A situation in which *a central processing unit (CPU)* using *superscalar architecture* and multiple *pipelines* must have the result of one calculation before beginning another. See *false dependency.*

data dictionary   In a *database management program,* a list of all the *database* files, indexes, views, and other *files* relevant to a database application. A data dictionary also can include data structures and any information pertinent to the maintenance of a database.

data-encoding scheme   The technique a *disk drive controller* uses to record bits of data on the magnetic surface of a floppy disk or hard disk. Disk drives are categorized by the data-encoding scheme the drive uses. See *Advanced Run-Length Limited (ARLL), disk drive controller, Modified Frequency Modulation (MFM),* and *Run-Length Limited (RLL).*

data encrypting key   In *SSL* and other security protocols that begin a secure connection with *public key encryption*, a *symmetric encryption* key that is used to encrypt the transmitted data after a secure *key exchange* has taken place.

Data Encryption Standard (DES)   A controversial IBM-developed *encryption* technique that was adopted by the U.S. government for non-classified information and widely used by financial institutions to transfer large sums of money electronically. Critics charge that DES technology was deliberately weakened so the government would be able to break DES-encoded messages when it chose to do so.

data-entry form   In a *database management program,* an on-screen form that makes entering and editing *data* easier by displaying only one *data record* at a time.

data field   In a *database management program,* a space reserved for a specified piece of information in a *data record.* In a *relational database management program,* in which all *retrieval operations* produce a table with rows and columns, data fields are displayed as vertical columns.

data file   A *file* containing the work you create with a program; unlike a *program file* that contains instructions for the computer.

data fork   In the *Macintosh file system,* the file component that contains the data stored in the file, such as a *spreadsheet* or word processing document. The other component is the *resource fork.*

datagram   The preferred *Internet* term for a data packet. See *packet* and *packet switching network.*

data independence   In *database management,* the storage of data in a way that enables you to access that *data* without knowing exactly where it's located or how it's stored. Newer *database management programs* include command languages, called *query languages,* that let you phrase questions based on content rather than the data's physical location. See *SQL.*

data insertion   In a *database management program,* an operation that adds new records to the database. Unlike appending records, however, insertion lets you add records anywhere in the database. See *append.*

data integrity   The accuracy, completeness, and internal consistency of the information stored in a *database.* A good *database management program* ensures data integrity by making it difficult (or impossible) to accidentally erase or alter data. *Relational database management programs* help to ensure data integrity by eliminating *data redundancy.*

data interchange format (DIF) file   In *spreadsheet programs* and some *database programs,* a *standard file format* that simplifies importing and exporting data between different spreadsheet programs. Originally developed by Software Arts—the creators of VisiCalc—DIF is supported by *Lotus 1-2-3, Microsoft Excel, Quattro Pro,* and most other spreadsheet programs.

data link layer   In the *OSI Reference Model* of computer network architecture, the sixth of seven *layers,* in which the addressed packets are transformed so they can be physically conveyed at the physical layer. At this layer, protocols govern the detection and resolution of transmission errors, the conversion of data into a form appropriate for the *physical layer* that is being used, and the regulation of data to avoid bottlenecks. When the data is ready to be sent out over the network, it is transferred to the physical layer, where the data is encapsulated by physical layer protocols.

data manipulation   In database management, the use of the basic database manipulation operations—*data deletion, data insertion, data modification,* and *data retrieval*—to change data records.

data mask   See *field template.*

data mining   In a *data warehouse,* a discovery method applied to very large collections of data. In contrast to traditional database queries, which phrase search questions using a *query language,* such as *SQL,* data mining proceeds by classifying and clustering data, often from a variety of different and even mutually incompatible databases, and then looking for associations.

data modem   A *modem* that can send and receive *data*, but not faxes. Compare to *fax modem*.

data modification   In *database management*, an operation that updates one or more records according to specified criteria. You use a *query language* to specify the criteria for the update. For example, the following statement, written in a simplified form of Structured Query Language *(SQL)*, tells the program to find records in which the supplier field contains CC and then increases the value in the price data field by 15 percent:

```
UPDATE inventory
SET price = price * 1.15
WHERE supplier = "CC"
```

datapac   A type of *packet-switching network*. Datapac networks use the *TCP/IP network* protocol.

data privacy   In *local area networks (LANs)*, limiting access to a file so that other users in the network can't display the contents of that file. See *encryption, field privilege, file privilege,* and *password protection*.

data processing   Preparing, storing, or manipulating *information*.

Data Processing Management Association (DPMA)   A professional society, specializing in business computing issues, for *programmers, systems analysts,* and managers. DPMA established the *Certified Data Processor (CDP)* recognition process in the 1960s but later turned the responsibility for certification over to the *Institute for Certification of Computer Professionals (ICCP)*.

data record   In a *database management program,* a complete unit of related *data* items stored in *named data fields*. In a *database,* data record is synonymous with *row*. A data record contains all the information related to the item the database is tracking. Most programs display data records in two ways: as *data-entry forms* and as *data tables*. In a *relational database management program,* the data records are displayed as horizontal rows and each data field is a column.

data redundancy   In *database management,* the repetition of the same data in two or more *data records*. Generally, users should never enter the same data in two different places within a database; if someone mistypes just one character, the error destroys accurate retrieval because the computer does not know that the two entries are supposed to be the same. Data integrity is a serious issue for any database management system, and careful system design can help reduce redundancy-related problems.

data retrieval   In *database management programs,* an operation that retrieves information from the database according to the criteria specified in a *query.* A database management program is most useful when you want to access only a few records: all the customers in Florida or those who haven't been contacted in the last 90 days. By using queries, you can tell the program to sort the data, perhaps by customer last name, or to select only certain records, such as customers in Atlanta. In some programs, the query can specify which *fields* to display after the matching records are selected.

data series   In business and *presentation graphics*, a collection of *values* that all pertain to a single subject, such as the third-quarter sales of three products. In *spreadsheet* programs, a *column, row,* or block of values that increases or decreases a fixed amount. When creating a data series, you indicate a beginning value, the amount to increase or decrease the value, and an ending value.

data storage media   Collectively, the technologies used for *auxiliary storage* of computer data, such as disk drives and magnetic tapes.

data stream   In data communications, a flow of undifferentiated data that is transmitted byte after byte.

data striping   An important method employed by *Redundant Arrays of Independent Disks (RAID)* in which a single unit of data is distributed across several *hard disks,* increasing resistance to a failure of one of the drives.

data table   In a *database management program,* an on-screen view of information in a columnar (two-dimensional) format, with the field names at the top. Most database management programs display data tables as the result of sorting or querying operations. See *data-entry form.* In spreadsheet programs, a form of what-if analysis where a formula is calculated many times using different values for one or two of the arguments in the formula. The results are displayed in a table.

D
E
F

Data Terminal Equipment (DTE)   The term used by the specification that defines the standard *serial port* to describe the computer that is connected to a *modem* or *fax modem*.

data transfer rate   In *modems*, the speed, expressed in *bits per second (bps)*, at which a *modem* can transfer, or is transferring, data over a telephone line. See *connect speed*. In *hard disks*, the theoretical speed at which a hard disk can transfer data to the rest of the computer. Data transfer rate is established by laboratory tests; *throughput* is a better indication of how well a hard disk performs.

data type   In a *database management program*, a classification you give to a *data field* that governs the kind of data you can enter. See *field template*. In popular database management programs, for example, you can choose among the following data types:

- Character field (or text field). Stores any character you can type at the keyboard, including numbers. The program can't, however, perform computations on character fields. A character field can contain approximately one line of text.

- Numeric field. Stores numbers in such a way that the program can perform calculations on them.

- Logical field. Stores information in a true/false, yes/no format.

- Date field. Stores dates so that the program can recognize and compare them.

- Object field. Contains an *object*, such as a picture or sound.

data warehouse   A collection of related *databases* that have been collected and stored together so that the maximum value can be extracted from them. The basic idea of data warehousing is to gather as much data as possible, in the hope that somehow a meaningful picture will emerge. *Data mining* techniques enable programmers to collate and extract meaningful data from the warehouse; by means of a technique, called *drill down*, the data mining software enables data warehouse users to see as much detail or summarization as they need to support decision-making.

daughterboard   A *printed circuit board* that is designed to attach to another, larger circuit board, such as a *motherboard* or an *adapter*.

dBASE A *relational database management system (RDBMS)* for personal computers that was developed with the assistance of U.S. government funding in the 1970s and subsequently marketed by Ashton-Tate, which was subsequently acquired by *Borland International*. The dBASE data, query, and file formats have become a *de facto standard*, known as *xBASE,* and is implemented in other commercial database packages, such as Microsoft's FoxPro and Computer Associates' CA-dbFAST.

DBMS See *database management system*.

DCE See *Data Communications Equipment* or *Distributed Computing Environment*.

DCE speed The speed, measured in *bits per second (bps)* at which *Data Communications Equipment (DCE)* devices can communicate over a telephone line.

DCOM Acronym for Distributed Component Object Model. A *middleware* standard developed by Microsoft that extends the company's *OLE*-based *Component Object Model (COM)* to the network *level*. DCOM is Microsoft's answer to *CORBA*.

DDE See *Dynamic Data Exchange*.

DDS Acronym for Digital Data Storage, a *tape backup* format for digital audio tape (*DAT*) cartridges.

DeBabelizer A graphic processing program created by Equilibrium. Scripting capabilities enable graphic artists to perform graphics processing operations on thousands of graphic images or video frames, including translating images into more than 90 graphics file formats. This program is suited to professional production tasks in multimedia authoring, Web publishing, and desktop video studios.

debug In programming, to detect or locate, and subsequently to fix, errors in the program's *source code*.

debugger A *utility program*, often included in *compilers* or *interpreters,* that helps programmers find and fix *syntax errors* and other errors in *source code*.

debugging The process of locating and correcting errors in a *program*.

D
E
F

decimal   The numbering system in use throughout the indus-trialized world, with a base or radix of 10. See *binary numbers, hexadecimal,* and *octal.*

decimal tab   In a *word processing* or *page layout program,* a *tab stop* configured so that values align at the decimal point.

declaration   In programming, a statement that binds a given value with a constant or links a variable to a specific memory location or data type.

declarative language   A *programming language* that frees the *pro-grammer* from specifying the exact procedure the computer needs to follow to accomplish a task. Programmers use the language to describe a set of facts and relationships so that the user may then query the system to get a specific result. For example, Structured Query Language *(SQL)* allows you to perform a search by asking to see a list of records showing specific information instead of by telling the computer to search all records for those with the appropriate entries in specified fields. See *data independence, expert system, declarative markup language (DML),* and *procedural language.*

declarative markup language (DML)   In text processing, a markup language—a system of codes for marking the format of a unit of text—that indicates only that a particular unit of text is a certain part of the document, such as an abstract, a title, or an author's name and affiliation. The actual formatting of the docu-ment part is left up to another program, called a parser, which displays the marked document and gives each document part a distinctive format (fonts, spacing, etc.). An international standard DML is the *Standard Generalized Markup Language (SGML),* which was little known until a subset of SGML, the HyperText Markup Language *(HTML),* came into widespread use on the *World Wide Web (WWW).* HTML is a declarative markup lan-guage, and the Web browsers in use by millions today are parsers for HTML.

decompress   To restore compressed data to its original state.

decrement   To decrease a value. See *increment.*

decryption   In *cryptography,* the decoding of an encrypted message by means of a *key.* See *encryption.*

dedicated file server   In a *local area network (LAN),* a computer dedicated exclusively to providing services to the users of the network and running the *network operating system (NOS).* Some *file servers* can be used for other purposes. In *peer-to-peer networks,* for example, all the networked computers are potential file servers, although they're being used for stand–alone applications.

dedicated line   A telephone line, devoted to data communications, that has been specially conditioned and permanently connected. Dedicated lines are often *leased lines* from regional telephone companies or *public data networks (PDN).*

D
E
F

de facto standard   A software or hardware standard, or a communications *protocol,* that has come into very widespread use, not because any international standards body has ratified it, but rather because the company that makes products using this standard has overwhelmingly dominated the market in a particular sector. In the late 1980s, for example, keyboard commands used by the most popular word processing program, WordStar, were emulated by most other programs.

default   Automatically configured; set up with a certain predefined value or option, usually because such a setting is likely to be preferred by most users.

default button   In *graphical user interfaces,* such as *Microsoft Windows 95,* the highlighted button automatically selected as your most likely choice in a dialog box. You can press Enter to choose this button quickly. See *pushbutton.*

default directory   See *current directory.*

default editor   In a *Unix* system, the text editor (such as *emacs* or *vi*) that the system automatically starts when the services of a text editor are needed.

default extension   The three-letter extension an *application program* uses to save and retrieve *files* unless you override the default by specifying another extension. Using the default extension makes retrieving files easier. During retrieval operations, programs that use a default *extension* display a list of only the files that use their default extension. If you give a file a different extension, you still can retrieve the file, but you must remember the file's name or change the *file-name* entry to *.* so that all files are listed.

default font   The font that the printer uses unless you tell it otherwise. Synonymous with *initial base font.*

default home page   In a *Web browser,* the *World Wide Web (WWW)* document that appears when you start the program or click the Home button. Most Web browsers are set up to display the browser publisher's *home page,* but you can easily change this setting so the browser displays a more useful default home page.

default numeric format   In a *spreadsheet* program, the *numeric format* that the program uses for all *cells* unless you choose a different one.

default printer   The *printer* a *program* automatically uses when you tell it to print. If you change printers for a single *print job,* some programs return to the printer designated as the default when the document is closed. Others treat the currently selected printer as the default printer until you select another printer.

default setting   The settings that a program uses unless you specify another setting. For example, a word processing program has a *default font,* and a spreadsheet has a default column width.

default value   A value that a *program* uses when you don't specify one. For example, you might set up a currency field in a database that has a default value of $.00 unless you enter a different number.

Defense Advanced Research Projects Agency (DARPA)
A unit of the U.S. Department of Defense (DoD), the successor to the *Advanced Research Projects Agency (ARPA)* that played a key role in the development of the *ARPANET,* the *Internet's* predecessor. DARPA is one of several U.S. agencies that participates in the *High Performance Computing and Communications Program (HPCC).*

deflection yoke   See *yoke.*

defragmentation   A procedure in which all the *files* on a *hard disk* are rewritten on disk so that all parts of each file are written to contiguous *sectors.* The result is an improvement of up to 75 percent in the disk's speed during retrieval operations. During normal operations, the files on a hard disk eventually become fragmented so that parts of a file are written all over the disk, slowing down retrieval operations.

degaussing   In a *monitor,* the process of balancing the monitor's internal magnetic field so that it compensates for the earth's magnetic field. An internal magnetic field that has not been balanced by degaussing may produce unwanted color distortions. Degaussing is sometimes needed after moving a monitor.

Delete key (Del)   A *key* that erases the character to the right of the cursor. Use the *backspace* and Delete keys to correct mistakes as you type.

delimiter   A code, such as a space, tab, or comma, that marks the end of one section of a *command* and the beginning of another section. Delimiters also are used to separate data into fields and records when you want to export or import data using a *database* format. For example, using delimiters makes it easy to *export* a merge file created using a *word processing program* or to *import* data into a *spreadsheet program* and have lines of *data* divided logically into columns.

D
E
F

Delphi   An easy-to-learn programming language created by Borland International, Inc., to compete with *Microsoft Visual BASIC*. Delphi is an *object-oriented programming (OOP)* language that is based on an object-oriented version of *Pascal*. Delphi *development suites* equip the programmer with libraries of reusable *objects* as well as a *compiler* that produces executable programs.

delurk   In *Usenet,* to post a message in which you reveal your identity and confess that you have been reading the newsgroup for a long time without contributing anything. See *lurk.*

demand paging   In *virtual memory,* a method of moving data from the disk to memory that waits until the required data is needed. See *anticipatory paging.*

demo   An animated presentation or a preview version of a *program* distributed without charge in an attempt to acquaint potential customers with a program's features. Synonymous with demoware. See *crippled version.*

demodulation   In *telecommunications,* the process of receiving and transforming an analog signal into its digital equivalent so that a computer can use the information. See *modulation.*

demount   To remove a *disk* from a *disk drive.* See *mount.*

density   See *areal density.*

departmental laser printer   A high-end *laser printer* designed to serve large groups of people and print 12,000 pages or more each month. Departmental laser printers often feature *automatic* *emulation switching, automatic network switching, bi-directional communication, duplex printing,* and *remote management.*

dependent worksheet   In *Microsoft Excel,* a worksheet that contains a link, or reference formula, to data in another Excel worksheet, called the source worksheet, on which it depends for the data. More than one worksheet can depend on a single source worksheet. In other spreadsheet programs, such as Lotus 1-2-3 and Quattro Pro, a worksheet containing a link is called a target worksheet. See *external reference formula* and *source worksheet.*

derived field   See *calculated field.*

DES   See *Data Encryption Standard.*

descender   The portion of a lowercase letter that hangs below the baseline. Five letters of the English alphabet have descenders: g, j, p, q, and y. See *ascender.*

descending sort   A *sort* that reverses the normal *ascending sort* order. Rather than sort A, B, C, D and 1, 2, 3, 4, for example, a descending sort lists D, C, B, A and 4, 3, 2, 1.

descriptor   In *database management,* a word used to classify a data record so that all records containing the word can be retrieved as a group. In a video store's database, for example, the descriptors Adventure, Comedy, Crime, Horror, Mystery, or Science Fiction can be entered in a field called CATEGORY to indicate where the film is shelved in the store. See *identifier* and *keyword.*

desk accessory (DA)   In a *graphical user interface (GUI),* a set of *utility programs* that assists with day-to-day tasks, such as jotting down notes, performing calculations on an on-screen calculator, maintaining a list of names and phone numbers, and displaying an on-screen calendar. See *Font/DA Mover.*

desktop   In a *graphical user interface (GUI),* a representation of your day-to-day work, as though you were looking at an actual desk with folders full of work to do. In *Microsoft Windows 95,* this term refers specifically to the background of the screen on which *windows, icons,* and *dialog boxes* appear.

desktop computer   A *personal computer* or professional *workstation* designed to fit on a standard-sized office desk that's equipped with sufficient memory and disk storage to perform business computing tasks. See *portable computer.*

Desktop Management Interface (DMI)   A system for *printers* developed by the *Desktop Management Task Force (DMTF)* that warns users when printers need attention, such as when *toner* runs low, paper jams occur, or paper is exhausted. DMI is expected to supersede the *Simple Network Management Protocol (SNMP)*.

Desktop Management Task Force (DMTF)   A consortium of computer-equipment manufacturers that has established standards for the *Desktop Management Interface (DMI)* and *Plug and Print*.

desktop pattern   In *graphical user interfaces* like *Microsoft Windows*, a graphical pattern—called wallpaper—displayed on the *desktop* (the background "beneath" *windows*, *icons*, and *dialog boxes*).

desktop presentation   The use of a *slide show* feature available in a *presentation graphics* program (and some spreadsheet programs) to create a display of *charts* or other illustrations that can be run on a desktop *computer*. You can tell the program to run the presentation automatically or to give you a menu of options. See *presentation graphics*.

desktop publishing (DTP)   The use of a personal computer as an inexpensive production system for creating typeset-quality text and *graphics*. Desktop publishers often merge text and graphics on the same page and print pages on a *high resolution laser printer* or typesetting machine. Desktop publishing software lets one person produce typeset-quality text and graphics with a personal computer, enabling an organization to reduce publication costs by as much as 75 percent.

desktop video   A *multimedia application* that displays a *full-motion video adapter* on the computer's display. Without special processing circuitry (a *video adapter* with special support for decompressing and playing videos at high speed), the result may be a postage-stamp–sized video playing with jerky motion.

destination   The record, file, document, or disk to which information is copied or moved, as opposed to the *source*.

destination document   In Object Linking and Embedding *(OLE)*, the document in which you insert or embed an object. When you embed a *Microsoft Excel* object (such as a chart) into a

Microsoft Word file, for example, the Word document is the destination document. See *source document*.

destination file   In many DOS commands, the file into which data or program instructions are copied. See *source file*.

development suite   A package of utilities that enable programmers to create programs as quickly and effortlessly as possible. Typically included are a *compiler, debugger,* a *text editor, libraries* of useful *routines,* and tools for such tasks as connecting to *databases*.

device   Any *hardware component* or *peripheral,* such as a *printer, modem, monitor,* or *mouse,* that can receive and/or send data. Some devices require special software, called *device drivers.*

device contention   The technique that *Microsoft Windows 95* uses to handle simultaneous requests from multitasked *programs* to access devices.

device dependent   Unable to operate successfully on a certain type of computer system or on a computer that is not equipped with a certain type or brand of peripheral, such as a sound card or modem.

device–dependent color   A printer or monitor's *color palette* that does not conform to any established color scheme, but instead results from the device's unique characteristics. Because most printers and monitors generate device-dependent color, it is often difficult to accurately match a color generated by one device with a color generated by another. *Device-independent color* overcomes this deficiency.

device driver   A program that provides the *operating system* with the information needed for it to work with a specific device, such as a *printer.*

device independence   The capability of a *program, operating system,* or *programming language* to work on a variety of computers or *peripherals,* despite their electronic variation. *Unix,* an operating system for multi-user computer systems, is designed to run on a wide variety of computers, from *personal computers* to *mainframes. PostScript,* a *page description language (PLD)* or high-quality printing, is used by many printer manufacturers.

device-independent   Able to work correctly on a variety of computers or on computers equipped with a variety of different peripherals.

device-independent color   A method of describing colors in a standard way, such as with the *Pantone matching system (PMS)*, then modifying output devices, such as *printers* and *monitors,* to conform to the standard. Though rare and expensive, device-independent color is far superior to *device-dependent color* and is essential if you're in the publishing business.

D
E
F

device name   In *DOS,* a three-letter abbreviation that refers to a peripheral device. See *AUX, COM, CON,* and *LPT.*

device node   In *Microsoft Windows 95,* an *object* in the *hardware tree* that represents a piece of *hardware.* Synonymous with *Plug and Play (PnP)* object.

diagnostic program   A *utility program* that tests computer hardware and software to determine whether they're operating properly.

dialer program   In *SLIP* and *PPP,* a program that dials an *Internet* service provider's number and establishes the connection. A dialer program is unlike a *communications program,* which transforms your computer into a *terminal* of a *remote computer.* Instead, the dialer program establishes the connection that fully integrates your computer into the Internet. Many service providers distribute preconfigured dialer programs that enable users to connect to their service without configuring or programming the dialer; if you cannot obtain a *preconfigured dialer,* you may have to write your own *login script,* which can be tedious for people who lack *programming* experience.

dialog   Synonymous with *dialog box*.

dialog box   In a *graphical user interface (GUI),* an on-screen message box that conveys or requests information from the user.

dialup access   A means of connecting to another computer, or a network like the *Internet,* with a *modem*-equipped computer. There are two major types of dialup access. The cheapest is to dial into a Unix system using a telecommunications program, but you're restricted to text-only applications, such as e-mail and text-only Web browsing. In *dialup IP*, your computer becomes part of the Internet, and you can use graphical tools, such as browsers. See *Internet service provider (ISP)*.

dialup IP   A *dialup access* method that gives you full access to the Internet. By means of dialup IP (in conjunction with Point to Point Protocol [PPP] or Serial Line Internet Protocol [SLIP]), you can use graphical programs like *Netscape Navigator* to browse the *World Wide Web (WWW)* and collect *e-mail*. See *Internet service provider (ISP)*.

dialup modem   In contrast to a *modem* designed for use with a *leased line*, a modem that can dial a telephone number, establish a connection, and close the connection when it is no longer needed. Most *personal computer* modems are dialup modems.

dictionary flame   In *Usenet,* a *follow-up post* that initiates or prolongs a controversy over the meaning of a word or phrase, such as "Second Amendment" or "right to life."

dictionary sort   A *sort order* that ignores the case of characters as data is rearranged. See *sort*.

DIF   See *data interchange format (DIF) file*.

Diffie-Hellman public key encryption algorithm   A *public key encryption algorithm* that was created by the inventors of public key encryption and subsequently named after them. Diffie-Hellman has not seen widespread use in comparison to *RSA public key encryption algorithm,* but is expected to come into much wider use because the inventor's patent is about to expire.

digest   In *Usenet,* an article that appears in a moderated *newsgroup* summarizing the posts received by the newsgroup's *moderator*.

digital   A form of representation in which distinct objects, or digits, are used to stand for something in the real world—temperature or time—so that counting and other operations can be performed precisely. *Data* represented digitally can be manipulated to produce a calculation, a *sort,* or some other *computation*. In digital electronic computers, two electrical states correspond to the 1s and 0s of *binary numbers*, which are manipulated by computer programs. See *algorithm, analog,* and *program*.

Digital Audio Tape   See *DAT*.

digital camera A portable camera, incorporating one or more *charge-coupled devices (CCDs),* that records images in a machine-readable format. Though digital cameras are expensive and generate output of far lesser quality than that of film-based cameras, they eliminate the potentially expensive and time-consuming film-processing and photo-scanning steps involved in getting photos into computer-readable form. Digital cameras are sometimes used to manufacture security badges quickly.

digital cash A proposed method of ensuring personal privacy in a world in which electronic commerce becomes common. In digital cash commerce, a person who maintains an electronic bank account could make online purchases, which would be debited automatically and transferred to the payee. The transactions would be secure for all three parties concerned—the bank, the payer, and the payee—yet none of these parties, nor any outside investigator, would be able to determine just what has been done with the money. Relying on *public key cryptography,* this technology alarms government and law enforcement officials, who see it as an open invitation to tax cheats and drug dealers. Lacking U.S. Department of Commerce certification, digital cash schemes are currently in an experimental stage; one *World Wide Web (WWW)* accessible service allows you to obtain $5 of pretend money that you can "spend" at participating Web pages. Synonymous with e-cash.

D E F

digital computer A computer that uses digits 0 and 1 to represent *data* and then uses partly automatic procedures to perform computations on this information. A digital computer doesn't have to be electronic; an abacus is a digital computer because it represents information by means of separable units *(digits),* and because the user can follow a procedural recipe to solve problems. Most of today's computers are digital, although analog computers are still used for certain specialized applications (such as real-time data analysis). See *analog computer.*

digital controls *Monitor* controls that, instead of knobs or dials, consist of pushbuttons. Digital controls, like analog controls, can adjust *brightness, contrast,* and image size.

Digital Data Storage See *DDS.*

digitally signed In *e-mail,* signed with a *certificate* that confirms that the person sending the message is actually who he or she claims to be. See *digital signature.*

digitally signed certificate   A *certificate* to which someone's or some organization's *digital signature* has been affixed as a further corroboration of its authenticity.

digital modem   A communications *adapter* designed to connect one computer to another digitally. *Digital* modems are not really modems at all, since *modulation* and *demodulation* are necessary only for *analog* connections. Digital modems, such as IBM's WaveRunner, work with digital telephone systems such as the *Integrated Services Digital Network (ISDN),* and therefore have not achieved widespread use.

digital monitor   A *monitor* that accepts digital output from the display adapter and converts the digital signal to an analog signal. Digital monitors can't accept input unless the input conforms to a digital standard, such as the IBM *Monochrome Display Adapter (MDA), Color Graphics Adapter (CGA),* or *Enhanced Graphics Adapter (EGA)* standards. All these adapters produce digital output, but, unlike *Video Graphics Array (VGA)* and other *analog monitors*, can display a limited number of colors.

digital signal processor (DSP)   A programmable sound-processing circuit, used in both *modems* and *sound boards*. Sound boards use DSPs to handle a variety of sound *resolutions,* formats, and sound–altering filters without requiring separate circuits for each one, while modems use DSPs to handle several *modulation protocols.*

digital signature   An encrypted, tamper-proof attestation, usually attached to an encrypted *e-mail* message or a *certificate,* that the person or authority signing the certificate is confident that the message's originator is actually the person he or she claims to be. See *certificate authority (CA).*

Digital Simultaneous Voice Video   See *DSVD.*

digital transmission   A *data communications* technique that passes information encoded as discrete on–off pulses. Digital transmission doesn't require digital-to-analog converters at each end of the transmission; however, *analog transmission* is faster and can carry more than one channel at a time.

digitize   The process of transforming *analog* data into *digital* form. A *scanner* converts *continuous-tone images* into *bit-mapped graphics. CD-ROMs* contain many digital measurements of the pitch and volume of sound. See *digitizing tablet.*

digitizing tablet   In *computer-aided design (CAD),* a *peripheral* device, usually measuring 12×12 or 12×18 inches and $1/2$ inch thick, that is used with a pointing device called a cursor to convert graphics, such as pictures and drawings, into digital data that a computer can process. The location of the cursor on the tablet is sensed magnetically in relation to a wire grid embedded within the tablet, and the position is tracked on-screen. Synonymous with *graphics tablet*. See *Cartesian coordinate system.*

DIMM   Acronym for dual in-line memory module. A rectangular *circuit board* that contains memory chips and fits into a receptacle with a 64-bit data bus. Unlike *SIMMs* (single inline memory modules), which fit into 32-bit receptables and have to be paired in order to function, DIMMs enable users to upgrade by inserting one module at a time.

dimmed   The display of a *menu* command, *icon*, or *dialog box* option in a different color or shade of gray to indicate that the selection isn't available. Sometimes called grayed out.

dingbats   Ornamental characters, such as *bullets*, stars, pointing hands, scissors, and flowers, used to illustrate text. Dingbats originally were used between columns or, more commonly, between paragraphs, to provide separation. See *Zapf Dingbats.*

DIP   Can stand for either *document image processing* or *dual in-line package.*

DIP switch   One or more toggle switches enclosed in a small plastic housing, called a *dual in-line package (DIP)*. This housing is designed with downward-facing pins so it can be inserted into a socket on a *circuit board* or soldered directly to the circuit board. DIP switches are often used to provide user-accessible configuration settings for computers, *printers*, and other electronic devices.

Direct3D   An *application programming interface (API)* developed by Microsoft Corporation to support computer games programming in the Windows environment. Direct3D enables programmers to write generic instructions to hardware devices, such as video cards, without their having to know exactly how these devices are wired and configured.

Direct Access Storage Device (DASD)   Any storage device, such as a *hard disk,* that offers *random access* or direct access to the stored data; in contrast to a *sequential access* device (such as a tape drive).

D
E
F

direct–connect modem   A *modem* equipped with a jack like the standard jack found in a telephone wall outlet, both of which accept an *RJ-11* plug. The modem can be connected directly to the telephone line using ordinary telephone wire, unlike an *acoustic coupler* modem designed to cradle a telephone headset.

DirectDraw   A interface standard, developed by Intel and subsequently by Microsoft, that enables applications to send video instructions directly to the video adapter, bypassing the CPU.

direct–map cache   A means of organizing *cache memory* by linking it to locations in *random-access memory (RAM)*. Although direct–map caches are simpler than other types of caches and easier to build, they are not as fast as other cache designs. See *full-associative cache* and *set-associative cache*.

direct memory access   See *DMA*.

direct memory access conflict   See *DMA conflict*.

direct memory access controller   See *DMA controller*.

Director   See *Macromedia Director*.

directory   A *logical* storage unit that enables computer users to group files in named, hierarchically organized folders and subfolders. See *current directory, directory markers, hierarchical file system, parent directory, path name,* and *subdirectory*.

Directory Access Protocol (DAP)   A mail standard (part of the X.500 protocol suite) that defines a complex client program for accessing white page directories (containing names, addresses, phone numbers, e-mail addresses, and additional contact information). Due to its complexity, DAP has proven difficult to implement and is being replaced by the Lightweight Directory Access Protocol (LDAP).

directory markers   In DOS, symbols displayed in a directory table that represent the *current directory* (.) and the *parent directory* (..). See *directory* and *subdirectory*.

directory of servers   In *Wide Area Information Servers (WAIS)*, a *database* of WAIS database names, consisting of the names of current WAIS-accessible public databases and a short description of their contents. The first step in searching WAIS is to access the directory of servers, several copies of which are available by means of the *Internet*. There is also a *WAIS gateway* accessible by means of the *World Wide Web (WWW)*. You begin your search by using very general topical key words, such as "education" or "child psychology." The directory of servers then lists the databases that contain information pertinent to your topic.

directory sorting   The organized display of the *files* in a *directory*, sorted by name, *extension*, or date and time of creation. The Windows Explorer can sort the contents of directories in several ways.

directory title   In *Gopher,* an item on a Gopher menu that, when accessed, reveals another menu (rather than a *document, graphic,* or other item).

directory tree   A graphical representation of a disk's contents that shows the branching structure of *directories* and *subdirectories. The Microsoft Windows 95 Windows Explorer*, for example, displays a directory tree.

direct-to-drum imaging   Hewlett-Packard's design for *color laser printers.* The *print drum* in HP Color LaserJets turns four times—once each for cyan, magenta, yellow, and black—and once more to fuse the various toners to the page. With this method, as many as five pages can be printed each minute. See *CMYK.*

DirectX   An *application programming interface (API)* developed by Microsoft Corporation that enables programmers to write multimedia instructions for Windows devices, even if they do not know precisely what kind of device is installed.

dirty   1. Full of extraneous signals or noise. A dirty telephone line causes problems when you try to log on with a *modem* to a distant computer system or *BBS.* You'll know if the line's dirty; you'll see many *garbage characters* on the screen. Log off, hang up, and dial again. 2. A *file* that has been changed but hasn't yet been saved.

dirty power   An AC power line that is subject to voltage fluctuations, surges, or other anomalies sufficient to cause problems with computing equipment.

disable   To temporarily disconnect a *hardware* device or *program* feature; to make it unavailable for use.

discrete speech recognition   The prevailing type of computer speech recognition, in which users must speak each word separately and distinctly (with a pause between each) so the system can accurately transcribe spoken language. Discrete speech recognition is unpleasant and unnatural to use. Continuous speech recognition programs, which transcribe normal (non-discrete) speech, have been available for certain highly specialized applications in medicine and other professional fields, but only recently have consumer products appeared that make continuous speech recognition more widely available.

disk   See *floppy disk* and *hard disk*.

disk array   See *drive arrays*.

disk buffer   See *cache controller*.

disk cache   1. In a *Web browser*, a portion of your hard disk that has been set aside to store the *World Wide Web (WWW)* documents you have accessed recently. When you re-access these pages, the browser first checks with the server to find out whether the document has been changed; if not, the browser retrieves the document from the disk cache rather than the network, resulting in significantly faster retrieval. Synonymous with *cache*. 2. In general personal computing, a portion of *random-access memory (RAM)* set aside to hold data recently retrieved from a disk. Disk caches can significantly speed up a system's performance.

disk capacity   The storage capacity of a *floppy disk* or *hard disk*, measured in *kilobytes (K)* or *megabytes direct memory access (DMA)* A channel that's used to transfer *data* from *memory* to *peripheral* devices, such as *hard disk controllers, network adapters,* and *tape backup* equipment. Requests for data are handled by a special chip called a *Direct Memory Access (DMA) controller*, which operates at one-half the *microprocessor's* speed. When data is transferred using DMA channels, the microprocessor is bypassed completely, leaving it free to process other requests. The capacity of a floppy disk depends on the size of the disk and the *areal density* of the magnetic particles on its surface. The two most popular disk sizes are $5^1/_4$ inch and $3^1/_2$ inch. *Single-sided disks* were once common but are obsolete now; *double-sided disks* are the norm. Also standard today are *high-density disks. Extra-high-density disks* are available, but aren't common. The remaining variables are the *operating system* you use to *format* the disk and the capabilities of the disk drive you're using. The following table shows the relationship of the variables and the resulting capacity:

Size	Density	System	Drive	Capacity
$3^1/_2$"	DD	MS-DOS	Standard	720K
$3^1/_2$"	DD	Mac	Standard	800K
$3^1/_2$"	HD	Mac	Superdrive	1.4M
$3^1/_2$"	HD	MS-DOS	High density	1.44M
$3^1/_2$"	HD	MS-DOS	Extra-high density	2.88M
$5^1/_4$"	DD	MS-DOS	Standard	360K
$5^1/_4$"	HD	MS-DOS	High–density	1.2M

disk compression utility   A *compression utility* that operates on all or most of the files of an entire drive, making the drive appear to have as much as two to three times its normal storage capacity. Compression and decompression is performed on the fly, which means some loss of performance due to the *overhead* produced by these operations.

disk drive   A *secondary storage* device, such as a *floppy disk drive* or a *hard disk*. This term usually refers to floppy disk drives. A *floppy disk* drive is an economical *secondary storage* medium that uses a removable magnetic disk that can be recorded, erased, and reused over and over. Floppy disk drives are too slow to serve as the main data storage for today's *personal computers* but are needed to copy software and disk-based data onto the system and for backup operations. See *random access, read/write head,* and *secondary storage.*

disk drive controller   The circuitry that controls the physical operations of the floppy disks and/or hard disks connected to the computer. With the advent of the *Integrated Drive Electronics (IDE)* standard, which transfers much of the controller circuitry to the drive itself, disk drive controller circuitry is often included on the *motherboard* instead of on a plug-in card. The disk drive controller circuitry performs two functions: it uses an interface standard (such as *ST-506/ST-412, Enhanced Small Device Interface [ESDI],* or *Small Computer System Interface [SCSI])* to establish communication with the drive's electronics, as well as a data encoding scheme (such as *modified frequency modulation [MFM]*, *run-length limited [RLL]*, or advanced run-length limited *[ARLL]*) to encode information on the magnetic surface of the disk.

diskette   See *floppy disk.*

diskless workstation   In a *local area network (LAN)*, a *workstation* that has a central processing unit (CPU) and random-access memory (RAM) but lacks its own disk drives. Diskless workstations ensure that everyone in an organization produces compatible data and helps reduce security risks. However, diskless workstations cause serious loss of speed, flexibility, and originality and with greater vulnerability to the effects of a disk or system *crash*. See *distributed processing system* and *personal computer.*

disk operating system   See *operating system.*

disk optimizer   See *defragmentation.*

display   See *monitor.*

display adapter   See *video adapter.*

display card   See *video adapter.*

display memory   See *video memory.*

display power management signaling (DPMS)   A system in which a specially equipped *video adapter* sends instructions to a compatible *monitor* telling it to conserve electricity. The video adapter can tell the monitor to assume any of three levels of power conservation.

display type   A *typeface*, usually 14 *points* or larger and differing in style from the *body type*, used for headings and subheadings. Synonymous with display font.

distributed bulletin board   A collection of computer conferences, called *newsgroups*, automatically distributed throughout a wide area network (WAN) so that individual postings are available to every user. The conferences are organized by topic, embracing such areas as ecology, politics, current events, music, specific computers and computer programs, and human sexuality. See *follow-up post, Internet, moderated newsgroup, post, thread, unmoderated newsgroup,* and *Usenet.*

Distributed Computing Environment (DCE)   A set of middleware standards developed by the Open Software Foundation (OSF) that defines the method of communication between clients and servers in a cross-platform computing environment. By following the DCE guidelines, a client program can initiate a request that can be processed by a program that is written in a different computer language and housed on a computer platform that differs from one running the client. Unlike object-oriented middleware systems such as CORBA, however, DCE is rooted in traditional programming concepts—but that may prove advantageous if organizations continue. See *Common Object Request Broker Architecture (CORBA)*.

D
E
F

distributed object architecture   In computer networks, a design in which programs called *object request brokers (ORB)* can detect the presence of other *objects* on the network. An object is a unit of computer code that contains data as well as the procedures, called *methods*, for performing specific tasks with this data. When a new object is detected, its methods become available for use by other objects, perhaps in ways that were not anticipated by the objects' programmers. See *Common Object Request Broker Architecture (CORBA)* and *Internet Inter-ORB Protocol (IIOP)*.

distributed processing system   A *computer system* designed for multiple users that provides each user with a fully functional computer. In personal computing, distributed processing takes the form of *local area networks (LANs),* in which the *personal computers* of the members of a department or organization are linked by high-speed cable connections. Distributed processing offers some advantages over *multi-user systems.* If the *network* fails, you can still work. You also can select software tailored to your needs. You can start a distributed processing system with a modest initial investment because you need only two or three workstations and, if desired, a central *file server.*

distribution   In *Usenet*, the geographic area throughout which you want your *post* to be distributed. With most systems, you can choose from world distribution (the default in most systems), your country, your state, your local area, or your organization. Choose a distribution that is appropriate for your message, unless you really want your "Dinette Set for Sale in New Jersey" post to be read in Wollongong, Australia.

dithering   In color or *grayscale* printing and *displays*, the mingling of dots of several colors to produce what appears to be a new color. With dithering, you can combine 256 colors to produce what appears to be a continuously variable color palette, but at the cost of sacrificing *resolution*; the several colors of dots tend to be mingled in patterns rather than blended well.

DLL   The *MS-DOS file-name extension* attached to a collection of *library routines.*

DMA   Acronym for *Direct Memory Access (DMS)*. A method of improving the computer's performance by enabling peripherals to access the computer's main memory directly, instead of requiring all connections to be made with the processor's help. See *DMA channel* and *DMA conflict.*

DMA channel   A circuit that enables a peripheral device to access the computer's memory directly instead of going through the processor. Each peripheral must be assigned its own, unique DMA channel in order to avoid a *DMA conflict.*

DMA conflict   A problem that results when two *peripherals* try to use the same *DMA channel*. A DMA conflict usually causes a system *crash*, and can be solved by assigning one of the conflicting peripherals a new DMA channel. See *Plug and Play (PnP).*

DMA controller   A *chip* that controls the flow of *data* through the *DMA channels*. By handling the work of regulating data flow through the channels, the DMA controller frees the *microprocessor* to do other work.

DMI   See *Desktop Management Interface.*

DMTF   See *Desktop Management Task Force.*

DNS   See *Domain Name Service.*

docking station   A cabinet containing *disk drives,* video circuits, and special receptacles designed to house a portable computer. When the portable is inserted into the docking station, the portable can use devices attached to the docking station.

document   A file containing work you've created, such as a business report, a memo, or a worksheet. The term strongly connotes the authority of an original—that is, fixed text—with a clearly named author. However, with today's *network* technology, a document can become text in flux, constantly accessed and modified by many people and with *dynamic data exchange (DDE),* even by the computer itself, as it detects changes in supporting documents and updates dynamic links automatically. See *groupware* and *word processing.*

documentation   The instructions, tutorials, and reference information that provide the information needed to use a *program* or *computer system* effectively. Documentation can appear in printed form or in online help systems.

document comparison utility   A *utility program* or *word processing* command that compares two *documents* created with word processing programs. If the two documents aren't identical, the program displays the differences between them, line by line.

document file icon   In *Microsoft Windows 95*, the *icon* of a *document* associated with an application program. You can open the document and launch the application simultaneously just by double-clicking a document file icon.

document format   In a *word processing program,* a set of formatting choices that control the page layout of the entire document. Examples of document formats include margins, headers, footers, page numbers, and columns.

document image processing (DIP)   A system for the imaging, storage, and retrieval of text-based documents that includes scanning documents, storing the files on optical or magnetic media, and viewing when needed using a *monitor, printer,* or *fax.* The goal of a document image processing system is a "*paperless office,*" but the goal probably will not be realized until *optical character recognition (OCR)* technology improves.

document processing   The use of computer technology during every stage of the production of *documents,* such as instruction manuals, handbooks, reports, and proposals. A complete document processing system includes all the *software* and *hardware* needed to create, organize, edit, and print such documents, including generating indexes and tables of contents. See *desktop publishing (DTP)* and *word processing program.*

document type definition (DTD)   In *SGML,* a complete definition of a *markup language* that defines the *elements* of the document as well as the *tags* used to identify them. HTML is defined by a standard DTD maintained by the *World Wide Web Consortium (W3C).*

D
E
F

domain   On the *Internet*, the highest subdivision, usually a country. However, in the United States, the subdivision is by type of organization, such as commercial (.com), educational (.edu), or government (.gov and .mil).

domain name   In the system of domain names used to identify individual *Internet* computers, a single word or abbreviation that makes up part of a computer's unique name (such as watt.seas.virginia.edu). Reading from left to right, the parts of a domain name go from specific to general; for example, "watt" is a specific computer, one of several RS-6000 *minicomputers* in service at the School of Engineering and Applied Science (seas) at the University of Virginia (virginia). At the end of the series of domain names is the top-level domain (here, edu), which includes hundreds of colleges and universities throughout the U.S. See *Domain Name Service (DNS)*.

Domain Name Service (DNS)   A program that runs on an *Internet*—connected *computer system* (called a DNS server) and provides an automatic translation between domain names (such as watt.seas.virginia.edu) and *IP addresses* (128.143.7.186) The purpose of this translation process, called *resolution,* is to enable Internet users to continue using a familiar name (such as www.yahoo.com) even though the service's IP address may change.

domain name system (DNS)   In the *Internet*, the conceptual system, standards, and names that make up the hierarchical organization of the Internet into named *domains.*

dongle   A small piece of *hardware* that plugs into a *port* and serves some purpose. Some very expensive programs use dongles as *copy-protection* devices—if you don't have the dongle plugged in, the program won't work. Other dongles provide infrared data transfer or *network* connectivity.

Doom   A pioneering and violent three-dimensional game, created by ID Software, in which a player guides an action figure through a space station taken over by demonic forces. The three-dimensional imaging gives the illusion of traveling through an enormously complex maze of underground tunnels and rooms, filled with perils and rewards. Doom pioneered a new genre of computer games and has been widely imitated.

doping   In semiconductor manufacturing, the process of deliberately introducing impurities in order to create variations in the electrical conductivity of the materials.

DOS   See *MS-DOS* and *operating system.*

Doskey   A personal utility provided with *MS-DOS* (5.0 and later) that enables you to type more than one DOS command on a line, store and retrieve previously used DOS commands, create stored macros, and customize all DOS commands.

DOS prompt   In *MS-DOS*, a letter representing the current *disk drive* followed by the greater-than symbol (>), which together inform you that the *operating system* is ready to receive a command. See *prompt.*

dot address   See *IP address.*

dot file   In *Unix*, a *file* that has a name preceded by a dot. Such a file normally isn't displayed by Unix file-listing *utility programs.* Dot files are frequently used for user configuration files, such as a file that lists the *newsgroups* the user regularly consults.

dot-matrix printer   An impact printer that forms text and graphic images by hammering the ends of pins against a ribbon in a pattern (a matrix) of dots. Dot-matrix printers are relatively fast, but their output is generally poor quality because characters aren't well-formed. These printers also can be extremely noisy. See *font, near-letter quality (NLQ),* and *non-impact printer.*

dot pitch   The size of the smallest dot a *monitor* can display. Dot pitch determines a monitor's maximum *resolution. High-resolution* monitors use dot pitches of approximately 0.31 mm or less; the best monitors use dot pitches of 0.28 mm or less.

dot prompt   In *dBASE*, the prompt, a lone period on an otherwise empty screen, for the command-driven interface of the program.

dots per inch (dpi)   A measure of *resolution* that states the number of dots that the device can print, scan, or display in a linear inch.

double-click   To click a *mouse* button twice in rapid succession.

double density   A widely used recording technique that packs twice as much data on a *floppy* or *hard disk* as on the earlier, single density standard. See *high density, Modified Frequency Modulation (MFM), Run-Length Limited (RLL),* and *single density.*

double-layer supertwise nematic   See *DSTN.*

D
E
F

double-scanned passive matrix   See *dual-scan.*

double-sided floppy disk   A *floppy disk* that can store data on both its surfaces. Most floppy disks are double-sided, although a few obsolete floppy disks record data on only one side.

double-speed drive   A *CD-ROM drive* that can transfer data at up to 300*K* per second. Though the maximum *data transfer rate* of double-speed disk drives is twice that of the first CD-ROM drives, the *access times* of the two are about equal.

DO/WHILE loop   In *programming,* a *loop* control structure that continues to carry out its function until a condition is satisfied. A DO/WHILE control structure establishes a condition that, if true, causes the program to wait until the test is false and then move on to the next instruction. See *loop, sequence control structure,* and *syntax.*

Dow Jones News/Retrieval Service   An *online information service* from Dow Jones, the publishers of *The Wall Street Journal* and *Barron's,* that offers a computer-searchable index to financial and business publications and to up-to-date financial information, such as stock quotes.

download   To transfer a *file* from another computer to your computer by means of a *modem* and a telephone line. See *upload.*

downloadable font   A *printer font* that's transferred from the *hard disk* to the printer's *memory* at the time of printing. Often called soft fonts, downloadable fonts are the least convenient of the three types of printer fonts you can use. Downloading can consume from 5 to 10 minutes at the start of every operating session. See *bit-mapped font, built-in font, cartridge font, downloading utility, font, font family, outline font, page description language (PDL),* and *PostScript.*

downloading   Transferring a copy of a *file* from a distant computer to a disk in your computer using data communication links. See *FTP* and *modem.*

downloading utility   A *utility program* that transfers *downloadable fonts* from your computer or printer *hard disk* to the printer's *random-access memory (RAM).* Downloading utilities usually are included with the downloadable fonts you buy. You may not need the utility if the *word processing* or *page layout program* you're using has downloading capabilities built in, as do *WordPerfect,*

Microsoft Word, Ventura Publisher, and *PageMaker. Microsoft Windows 95* downloads needed fonts automatically.

downward compatibility   *Hardware* or *software* that runs without modification when using earlier computer components or files created with earlier software versions. *Video Graphics Array (VGA) monitors,* for example, are downward compatible with the original IBM PC if you use an 8-bit VGA *video adapter* that fits in the PC's 8-bit *expansion bus.*

dpi   See *dots per inch.*

DPMA   See *Data Processing Management Association.*

DPMS   See *display power management signaling.*

drag   To move the *mouse* pointer while holding down a mouse button.

drag-and-drop   In *Microsoft Windows 95* and *Macintosh* programs running under *System* 7.5, a technique that enables you to perform operations on objects by *dragging* them with the mouse. You can open a document by dragging its *icon* to an *application icon,* or install icons in folders by dragging icons to them. Many *word processing programs* feature *drag-and-drop editing,* which speeds re-arrangement of text.

drag-and-drop editing   An editing feature that enables you to perform a *block move* or copy by *highlighting* a block of text and then using the *mouse* to *drag* the block to its new location. When you release the mouse button, the text appears in the new location. Some DOS programs, such as WordPerfect 6.0, allow drag-and-drop editing.

DRAM   Acronym for dynamic random-access memory (DRAM). A type of *random-access memory (RAM)* that represents information by using capacitors to store varying levels of electrical charges. Because the capacitors eventually lose their charge, DRAM chips must refresh regularly (hence dynamic). DRAM chips are often used on inexpensive *video adapter* cards to store video information. See *SRAM.*

draw program   A *graphics program* that uses *vector graphics* to produce *line art.* A draw program stores the components of a drawing, such as lines, circles, and curves, as mathematical formulas rather than as a configuration of bits on-screen, as *paint* *programs* do. Unlike images created with paint programs, line art created with a draw program can be sized and scaled without introducing distortions. Draw programs produce output that prints at a printer's maximum *resolution*.

draw tool   In any program that includes graphics capabilities, a command that transforms the cursor into a "pen" for creating *object-oriented (vector) graphics*. Draw tools typically include options for creating lines, circles, ovals, polylines, rectangles, and *Bézier curves*.

drill down   In *data mining*, a method of data exploration and analysis that involves more detailed examination of the data that produced a summary value or aggregate.

drive   See *disk drive*.

drive activity light   A small signal light, often mounted so it shows through the computer's *case*, that indicates when a *disk drive* is in use.

drive arrays   Groups of *hard disks* organized, often as a *Redundant Array Of Inexpensive Disks (RAID)*, to improve speed and provide protection against data loss. Drive arrays may incorporate *data striping* schemes.

drive bay   A receptacle or opening into which you can install a *hard* or *floppy disk drive*. Half-height drive bays are common in today's IBM and IBM-compatible personal computers. See *half-height drive*.

drive designator   In *DOS*, an argument that specifies the drive to be affected by the command. The command FORMAT B:, for example, tells DOS to format the disk in drive B. B: is the drive designator.

driver   A *file* that contains information needed by a *program* to operate a *peripheral* such as a *monitor* or *printer*. See *device driver*.

DriveSpace   A disk compression program included with *Microsoft Windows 95* and DOS 6.22.

drop cap   An initial letter of a chapter or paragraph, enlarged and positioned so that the top of the character is even with the top of the first line, and the rest of the character descends into the second and subsequent lines. See *initial*.

drop-down list box   In *industry-standard interface* and *graphical user interface (GUI),* a list of command options that displays as a single-item text box until you select the command, which causes a list of options to drop down (or pop up). After you "drop down" the list, you can choose one of its options. The drop-down list box lets a *programmer* provide many options without taking up much space on-screen.

dropouts   Characters lost in data transmission for some reason. On slower systems, for example, a fast typist may find that some typed characters don't make it into a *word processing* program's *data file*; this is caused by an interruption of user input when the program must access the disk for some reason. The user soon learns to pause when the *drive activity light* comes on.

dropout type   In typography, white characters printed on a black background.

drop shadow   A shadow placed behind an image, slightly offset horizontally and vertically, creating the illusion that the topmost image has been lifted off the surface of the page.

drunk mouse   A *mouse* whose *pointer* seems to jump wildly and irritatingly just as you're about to select something. Many users suspect that this malady is caused by a *virus,* but its most common cause is simply dirt in the mouse's inner mechanism.

DS/DD   A *double-sided disk* that uses *double-density* formatting.

DS/HD   A *double-sided disk* that uses *high-density (HD)* formatting.

D-shell connector   The connector that plugs into the *video adapter* end of the cable between the video adapter and the *monitor. Video Graphics Array (VGA)* and *Super VGA* video adapters use 15-pin D-shell connectors; older *video standards* use 9-pin D-shell plugs.

DSMR   See *dual-stripe magneto-resistive (DSMR) head.*

DSP   See *digital signal processor.*

DSTN   Acronym for double-layer supertwise nematic. A *passive matrix* display, used mainly in *notebook computers,* that uses two superimposed *liquid-crystal display (LCD)* layers to improve color rendition. Synonymous with *dual-scan.*

DSVD   Acronym for Digital Simultaneous Voice Video. A *protocol* for high-speed modems that enables users of two DSVD modems to converse via *real-time* voice communication while they exchange data. This feature is particularly attractive to computer game players.

DTE   See *Data Terminal Equipment*.

DTE speed   The rate, measured in *bits per second (bps)*, at which a *Data Terminal Equipment (DTE)* device, such as a personal computer, can send data to a *Data Communication Equipment (DCE)* device like a *modem*.

DTMF   See *Desktop Management Task Force*.

DTP   See *desktop publishing*.

dual–actuator hard disk   A *hard disk* design that incorporates two *read/write heads*. Dual-actuator hard disks have better *access times* than standard hard disks, because they have half the *latency*: a needed bit of data is always less than half a revolution away from one of the heads, instead of a full revolution away in a standard hard disk.

dual in–line package (DIP)   A standard packaging and mounting device for *integrated circuits*. DIP is the favored packaging for *dynamic random-access memory (DRAM)* chips, for example. The package, made of hard plastic material, encloses the circuit; the circuit's leads are connected to downward-pointing pins that stick in two parallel rows. The pins are designed to fit securely into a socket; you also can solder them directly to a circuit board. See *single in-line package (SIP)*.

dual–issue processor   A type of *central processing unit (CPU)* that can process two instructions simultaneously, each in its own *pipeline*. See *superscalar architecture*.

dual–scan   An improved *passive matrix LCD* design in which the *display* is *refreshed* twice as fast as standard passive matrix *liquid-crystal displays (LCDs)*. Though dual-scanned passive matrix displays have better *brightness* and *contrast* than standard *passive matrix displays*, they are generally inferior to *active matrix displays*.

dual–stripe magneto–resistive (DSMR) head   A new *read/write head* design for *hard disks* that reduces their sensitivity to interference from the outside environment. DSMR heads have separate portions for reading and writing, and pack data tightly onto disks.

dual-tone multifrequency (DTMF) tones   The tones generated by a touch-tone telephone during dialing. Most *dialup modems* generate DTMF tones, as well.

dual y-axis graph   In presentation and analytical graphics, a *line* or *column graph* that uses two y-axes (values axes) when comparing two sets of data measured differently.

dumb terminal   See *terminal*.

dump   To transfer the contents of *memory* to a *printer* or disk storage. *Programmers* use memory dumps while debugging programs to see exactly what the computer is doing when the dump occurs. In graphics, a *screen dump* prints or saves what is currently displayed on-screen. See *core dump* and *Print Screen (PrtScr)*.

duplex   See *full duplex* and *half duplex*.

duplex printing   Printing or reproducing a document on both sides of the page so the *verso* (left) and *recto* (right) pages face each other after the document is bound. See *binding offset*.

duplication station   A *printer/scanner* combination that can serve as a light-duty photocopier.

DVD   Acronym for Digital Versatile Disk. A *CD-ROM* format capable of storing up to a maximum of 17G of data (enough for a full-length feature movie). This format is expected to replace current CD-ROM drives in computers, as well as VHS video tapes and laser disks, in the years to come. Initially available in read-only 4.7G single-sided disk drives, DVD players will subsequently offer *write-once* recording and, later, full read/write capabilities. DVD players will be *downward compatible* with existing CD-ROMs.

Dvorak keyboard   An alternative *keyboard* layout in which 70% of the keystrokes take place on the home row (compared to 32% with the standard *QWERTY* layout). A Dvorak keyboard is easier to learn and faster to use. However, every time you return to a *QWERTY* keyboard, you must go back to the hunt-and-peck method.

dye sublimation   A high-quality color printing process in which tiny heating elements are used to evaporate pigments from a plastic film and fuse them to the paper. The result is a photographic-quality image with brilliant color and good definition. Dye sublimation printers are expensive, and so is the pigment-bearing film.

dynamic astigmatism control   See *dynamic beam forming.*

dynamic bandwidth allocation (DBA)   In *ISDN,* a method of allocating bandwidth on the fly so that the line can handle data and voice communications simultaneously. DBA works with the *Multilink Point-to-Point Protocol (MPPP)* and enables an ISDN user to accept a call on one of the lines even if both are being used to download or upload data. See *Basic Rate Interface (BRI).*

dynamic beam forming   A *monitor* design that ensures that electron beams are perfectly round when they strike the *display,* no matter where on-screen the *yoke* steers them. Without dynamic beam forming, electron beams would be elliptical at the edges of the display—like a flashlight beam striking the ground at an angle—and poor focus would result.

Dynamic Data Exchange (DDE)   In *Microsoft Windows 95* and *Macintosh* System 7, an *interprocess communication channel (IPC)* based on the *client-server* model through which programs can exchange data and control other applications. To be capable of DDE, *programs* must conform to Microsoft Corporation's specifications. DDE enables simultaneously running programs to exchange data as the information changes. Through the use of Object Linking and Embedding *(OLE),* which makes using DDE easier, a DDE-capable *spreadsheet* program can receive real-time data from an *online information service,* record changes in the price of key stocks and bonds, and recalculate the entire worksheet as the change occurs. See *client application, dynamic link,* and *server application.*

dynamic link   A method of linking *data* so it's shared by two programs. When data is changed in one program, the data is also changed in the other when you use an update command. See *hot link.*

dynamic object   A *document* or portion of a document pasted or inserted into a destination document using Object Linking and Embedding *(OLE)* techniques. A linked object is automatically updated if you make changes to the *source document.* An embedded object includes information to enable you to open the application used to create the object and edit the object.

dynamic random-access memory   See *DRAM.*

dynamic range   The range of colors a *scanner* can detect, and, along with *color depth* one of the main indicators of a scanner's quality. Though any 24-*bit* scanner can record 16.7 million colors and 265 levels of gray, a 24-bit scanner with a narrow dynamic range could not detect both pale shades of yellow and very dark indigo hues.

D
E
F

Easter egg   A message or animation buried within a *program* and accessible only through an undocumented procedure. These are inserted by programmers as a joke. Buried in the *Macintosh* System, for example, is the message "Help! Help! We're being held prisoner in a system software factory!"

EBCDIC   Pronounced "ebb-see-dick." Acronym for Extended Binary Coded Decimal Interchange Code. A *character set* coding scheme that represents 256 standard characters. IBM *mainframes* use EBCDIC coding; *personal computers* use *ASCII* coding. *Networks* that link personal computers to IBM mainframes must include a translating device to mediate between the two systems.

echoplex   A *communications protocol* in which the receiving station acknowledges and confirms the reception by echoing the message back to the transmitting station. See *full duplex* and *half duplex*.

ECP   See *extended capabilities port*.

edge connector   The part of an *adapter* that plugs into an *expansion slot*.

edgelighting   A scheme for shining light at a *liquid crystal display (LCD)* to improve readability in bright light conditions. Unlike *backlighting*, which shines light from behind the LCD, edgelighting relies on shining lights around the borders of an LCD. Edgelighting is considered less effective than backlighting.

EDI   See *Electronic Data Interchange*.

edit mode   A *program* mode that makes correcting text and data easier. In *Lotus 1-2-3*, for example, you press F2 to display the contents of a cell in the second line of the control panel, where you can use editing keys to correct errors or add characters. Few programs have special edit modes anymore because they allow editing in their normal modes.

editor   See *text editor*.

EDO RAM   Acronym for Extended Data Output random access memory. A type of *dynamic random-access memory (DRAM)*, the main memory of the computer, that is significantly faster than conventional DRAM. Experts expect the even faster *SDRAM* to replace EDO RAM in high-end machines.

edu   A *domain name* denoting a U.S. college or university.

edutainment   *Application programs* designed to tell the user about a subject but presented in the form of a game that is sufficiently entertaining or challenging to hold the user's interest. A longtime best-selling example of edutainment is the Microsoft Flight Simulator, which many people buy to play as a game but which many flight schools use as a prelude to flight instruction in the air. Almost as well known is the Carmen Sandiego series of games, including "Where in the World Is Carmen Sandiego?" and "Where in Europe Is Carmen Sandiego?"

D
E
F

EEMS   See *Enhanced Expanded Memory Specification.*

EEPROM   Acronym for Electrical Erasable Programmable Read-Only Memory. A type of *read-only memory (ROM)* that can be erased and reprogrammed by applying an electrical current to the memory chips and then writing new instructions to them. See *EPROM* and *Flash Erasable Programmable Read-Only Memory.*

effective resolution   The *resolution* of a *printer's* output on which *resolution enhancement* has been performed. Some *laser printers* claim effective resolutions of 1200 *dots per inch (dpi)*, but their output is of lower quality than that of printers that can achieve 1200 dpi without resolution enhancement.

effective transmission rate   The rate at which a *modem* that uses *on-the-fly data compression* communicates *data* to another modem. Data compression ensures that a given amount of data can be communicated at a given speed in a shorter amount of time than uncompressed data, so modems that use on-the-fly compression have higher *throughput* than modems that do not.

EGA   See *Enhanced Graphics Adapter.*

EIDE   See *Enhanced IDE.*

EInet Galaxy   In the *World Wide Web (WWW)*, a *subject tree* maintained by Enterprise Integration Network (EINet), a division of Microelectronics and Computer Technology Corporation. Like all *subject trees*, EINet Galaxy's coverage is limited by the ability of the staff responsible for maintaining it to find and classify useful new Web pages. The service also includes a *search* *engine* that helps users find the entries that the subject tree contains.

EISA   A 32-bit *expansion bus* design introduced by a consortium of *IBM PC-compatible* computer makers to counter IBM's proprietary *Micro Channel Bus.* Unlike the Micro Channel Bus, the EISA bus is downwardly compatible with existing 16-bit peripherals, such as disk drives and display adapters. Once the state-of-the-art in personal computing, EISA machines have been eclipsed by the *Peripheral Component Interconnect (PCI) expansion bus.*

EISA-2   An improved version of the *EISA* expansion bus that can transfer *data* at 132M per second. The earlier EISA standard could transfer data at only 33M per second. Like EISA, EISA-2 has been mostly replaced by the *Peripheral Component Interconnect (PCI)* standard, but it remains in some high-end *Ethernet* servers.

electrocutaneous feedback   A primitive method of providing *tactile feedback* in *virtual reality* systems by administering a low-voltage shock to the user's skin. The user feels a mild buzz. Varying the voltage and frequency of the current produces variations in the buzz that the user can learn to discriminate.

electron gun   A cathode (electron emitter) in the back of a *cathode ray tube (CRT)* that releases a stream of electrons toward the *display.* Steered by the *yoke,* the electrons "paint" an image on the display. *Color monitors* have three electron guns—one for each primary color—while *monochrome monitors* have only one.

Electronic Communications Privacy Act (ECPA)   A U.S. federal law, enacted in 1986, that prevents U.S. investigative agencies from intercepting *e-mail* messages, or reading such messages that are temporarily stored in interim storage devices (up to 180 days) without first obtaining a warrant. In a major omission that might stem from the legislators' lack of technical knowledge, the act does not prevent such agencies from obtaining and reading copies of e-mail permanently stored in *archives.* Investigators used this loophole to obtain Oliver North's e-mail messages to other White House officials involved in the Iran-Contra scandal. The act does not prevent any other persons or agencies from intercepting or reading e-mail. See *confidentiality.*

Electronic Data Interchange (EDI)   A standard for the electronic exchange of business documents, such as invoices and purchase orders. The Data Interchange Standards Association (DISA) developed the standard. Using field codes, such as BT for Bill To or ST for Ship To, EDI specifies the format in which data is being transmitted electronically. By ensuring that all EDI-based communications have the same data in the same place, this protocol enables companies to exchange purchase orders and other documents electronically.

Electronic Frontier Foundation (EFF)   A nonprofit public advocacy organization dedicated to ensuring the survival of privacy and civil liberties in the computer age. Spurred by an ill-conceived but heavy-handed Secret Service program that resulted in the seizure of *hackers' computer systems* throughout the United States, the organization's founders, Mitchell Kapor and John Perry Barlowe, initially contributed to hackers' legal defense funds and have since developed an extensive public education and lobbying program.

electronic mail   see *e-mail*.

electrostatic printer   A *printer* that relies on the attraction between oppositely charged particles to draw *toner* to paper. *Laser printers* and *LED printers* are electrostatic printers.

element   In *HTML,* a distinctive component of a document's structure, such as a title, heading, or list. HTML divides elements into two categories: head elements (such as the document's title) and body elements (headings, paragraphs, links, and text).

elevator seeking   In *hard disks,* a way to sort *data* requests to minimize jumping between *tracks.* In an elevator-seeking scheme, the drive handles data requests in track order; that is, it gets needed data from inner tracks first and then from the outer tracks. Elevator seeking minimizes *access time.*

elite   A typeface (usually on a typewriter) that prints 12 *characters per inch (cpi).* See *pitch*.

em   A distance equal to the width of the capital letter M in a given *typeface.*

emacs   A *Unix*-based *text editor* that is sometimes configured as the default editor on Unix systems. Programmed in *LISP,* emacs is an excellent *hacker's* tool, but can be difficult for users accustomed to *user-friendly word processing programs.*

e-mail   The use of a *network* to send and receive messages. Also called *electronic mail*. Some e-mail systems are strictly local, providing communication services for users of a *local area network (LAN)*. But the emerging *lingua franca* of electronic communication is *Internet* e-mail, which creates billions of potential connections that cross national boundaries. With an *e-mail client*, users can compose messages and transmit them in seconds to anyone of an estimated 50-60 million users worldwide.

e-mail address   A series of characters that precisely identifies the location of a person's electronic mailbox. On the *Internet*, e-mail addresses consist of a mailbox name (such as rebecca) followed by an at sign (@) and the computer's domain name (as in rebecca@hummer.virginia.edu).

e-mail client   A program or program module that provides *e-mail* services for computer users, including receiving mail into a locally stored inbox, sending e-mail to other network users, replying to received messages, and storing received messages. The better programs include *address books, mail filters,* and the ability to compose and read messages coded in *HTML*. Synonymous with user agent.

embed   In Object Linking and Embedding *(OLE),* to place an object in a document. See *embedded object.*

embedded chart   In *Microsoft Excel,* a chart created within a *worksheet* rather than as a separate chart document.

embedded formatting command   A text formatting command placed directly in the text to be formatted. In some *programs,* the command doesn't affect the text's on-screen appearance, which can make the program more difficult to use. In other programs, such as *WordPerfect,* only a few embedded commands—full *justification* or a *font* change—do not change the screen display. *Microsoft Windows 95* applications include a graphical display that immediately displays formatting. Synonymous with *off-screen formatting.* See *hidden codes, on-screen formatting* and *what-you-see-is-what-you-get (WYSIWYG).*

embedded object   In Object Linking and Embedding *(OLE),* an object wholly inserted, or embedded, into a *destination document* created by an application other than that which created the destination document. The object can be text, a chart, a *graphic,* or sound. See *linked object.*

em dash In typography a lengthy dash (equal to the width of the capital letter M in a given typeface) that is used to introduce parenthetical remarks. The following sentence contains em dashes: The butler—or someone who knows what the butler knows—must have done it.

em fraction A single-character fraction that occupies one *em* of space and uses a diagonal stroke ($^1/_4$) rather than a piece fraction made from three or more characters (1/4). See *en fraction.*

EMM See *expanded memory manager.*

EMM386.EXE In MS-DOS running on a computer with an *80386* or higher *microprocessor* and *extended memory,* an *expanded memory emulator* that enables DOS applications to use the extended memory as though it were *expanded memory (EMS).* EMM386.EXE also enables the user to load *device drivers* and programs into the *upper memory area.*

emoticon In *e-mail* and *newsgroups,* a sideways face made of *ASCII characters* that puts a message into context and compensates for the lack of verbal inflections and body language that plagues electronic communication. Also see *ASCII art.* Synonymous with smileys. The following are some commonly used emoticons:

:-)	Smile (don't take the last thing I said too seriously).
:-D	Big (stupid) grin.
:-★	Kiss.
:-O	Yawn; this thing is so boring.
;-)	Wink
:-(	Frown
:-<	Big frown
>:-(	Angry
:'-(	Crying

emphasis The use of a non-Roman *type style*—such as underlining, italic, bold, or small caps typefaces—to highlight a word or phrase.

EMS Acronym for Expanded Memory Specification. An *expanded memory* standard that allows the programs that recognize the standard to work with more than 640K RAM under DOS. The LIM EMS Version 4.0 standard, introduced in 1987,

D
E
F

supports up to 32*M* of expanded memory and lets programs run in expanded memory.

emulation   The duplication within a device of another device's functional capability, or a device designed to work exactly like another. In *telecommunications,* for example, a *personal computer* emulates a dumb *terminal*—a terminal without its own microprocessor—for online communication with a distant computer. With printers, lesser-known brands will emulate popular models like Hewlett-Packard's LaserJet line.

emulation sensing   See *automatic emulation switching* and *automatic network switching.*

emulation switching   See *automatic emulation switching.*

en   In typesetting, a unit of measurement that equals half the width of an *em* space, which is the width of the capital letter M in a typeface. En dashes are used in place of the English words to or through, as in January 9–January 23 or pp. 63–68. They also are used as minus signs, as in −30 degrees Fahrenheit. See *em dash.*

Encapsulated PostScript (EPS) file   A *high-resolution graphic* image stored in the *PostScript* page description language. The EPS standard enables users to transfer high-resolution graphics images between applications. You can size EPS images without sacrificing image quality. A major drawback of EPS graphics is that to print them, you usually need a PostScript-compatible *laser printer.* A second drawback is that with most application programs, you cannot view the image on-screen unless you attach a screen image to it. To provide an alternative to expensive PostScript printers, developers have created programs, such as LaserGo, Inc.'s GoScript, that interpret and print EPS files on standard *dot-matrix printers* or non-PostScript laser printers.

encapsulation   In *wide-area networks,* the process by which transmitted data is altered as it moves down the computer's *protocol stack.* As each *layer's* protocols alter the data, it is translated into a form that can be sent out over the network. At the receiving computer, this process is reversed so that the data is restored, in such a form that it can be passed to an application and made intelligible to the user.

encryption In *cryptography,* the process of converting a message into a *ciphertext* (an encrypted message) by using a *key,* so the message appears to be nothing but gibberish. However, the intended recipient can apply the key to decrypt and read the message. See *decryption, public key cryptography,* and *rot-13.*

End key A key on *IBM PC-compatible keyboards,* with functions that vary from program to program. Frequently, pressing the End key moves the cursor to the end of the line or the bottom of the screen, but the assignment of this key is up to the *programmer.*

endless loop A fundamental programming error in which the computer is made to cycle in a repeating loop, which cannot be broken without shutting down the computer.

endnote A footnote positioned at the end of a *document* or section rather than the bottom of a page. Many *word processing programs* let the user choose between footnotes and endnotes.

end of line (EOL) A *control character* that demarcates the end of a line of text in a text file.

end user The person who uses a *computer system* and its *application programs* at home or at work to perform tasks and produce results.

Energy Star A U.S. Environmental Protection Agency (EPA) program that seeks to reduce energy waste by encouraging *monitor* and *printer* manufacturers to reduce the amount of electricity that their devices require. Energy Star devices typically have a *sleep mode* that reduces their power consumption when they are not being used. Energy Star devices, identifiable by a blue and green EPA sticker, can save their owners hundreds of dollars in electrical costs each year.

en fraction A single-character fraction that occupies one *en* of space and uses a horizontal stroke, like this: $\frac{1}{4}$. Contrast to *em fractions,* which are built with regular-width characters, like this: $^1/_2$. See *em fraction.*

enhanced 101-key keyboard See *enhanced keyboard.*

Enhanced ATA See *ATA-2.*

Enhanced CD A standard created by *Microsoft Corporation* for audio compact discs. This standard enables audio CD publishers to include digital information on compact discs; for example, a jazz disk could include information on each track's performers. The information about the performers could be read on a specially equipped CD player.

Enhanced Expanded Memory Specification (EEMS)   A version of the original *Lotus-Intel-Microsoft Expanded Memory Specification (LIM EMS)* that is enhanced to enable DOS applications to use more than 640K of memory. See *bank switching* and *expanded memory.*

Enhanced Graphics Adapter (EGA)   A color, bit-mapped, graphics *video adapter* standard for *IBM PC-compatible* computers. The EGA adapter can display as many as 16 colors simultaneously with a resolution of 640 *pixels* horizontally by 350 lines vertically. You select the 16 colors from the EGA color palette, which contains 64 colors (including black and shades of gray). See *Color Graphics Adapter (CGA), Super VGA,* and *Video Graphics Array (VGA).*

Enhanced Graphics Display   A color *digital monitor* designed to work only with the IBM *Enhanced Graphics Adapter (EGA).*

Enhanced IDE (EIDE)   An improved version of the *integrated drive electronics (IDE)* disk–interface standard that dictates how *hard disks* and *CD-ROM drives* connect to the rest of the computer. The EIDE standard allows hard disk drives as large as 8.4G, while IDE supports hard disks no larger than 528M. Also, the EIDE standard enables you to connect four hard disks to your computer rather than two.

enhanced keyboard   The modern *keyboard* standard. An enhanced keyboard has 104 *keys,* including a *numeric keypad,* 12 *function keys,* and several navigation keys.

enhanced parallel port (EPP)   An improvement on the *parallel port,* which enables two–way communication. Using an EPP, for example, a *printer* can tell a *microprocessor* how much paper or toner remains in its bins. The *extended capabilities port (ECP)* might eventually replace the EPP, but for now, many *motherboards* support both standards.

enhanced serial port (ESP)   A speedy *serial port* that uses dedicated *random-access memory (RAM)* to move data quickly.

Enhanced System Device Interface (ESDI) An *interface standard* for hard disk drives. Drives that use the ESDI standard transfer at 10 to 15 *megabits of data per second (Mbps),* which is two to three times as fast as the earlier *ST-506/ST-412* interface standard. Faster, more flexible *Integrated Drive Electronics (IDE)* drives have almost totally replaced ESDI drives.

Enter/Return A *key* that confirms a command, sending the command to the *central processing unit (CPU);* synonymous with *carriage return.* In *word processing,* the Enter/Return key starts a new paragraph. Early IBM PC keyboards labeled this key with a hooked left arrow. On more recent AT and enhanced keyboards, the word *Enter* is printed on the key. (The word *Return* appears on *Macintosh* keyboards.) Most *IBM PC-compatible* keyboards have an Enter key to the right of the typing area and a second one in the numeric keypad's lower-right corner. These two keys have identical functions in most but not all programs.

entity In the *HyperText Markup Language (HTML),* a code that represents a non-ASCII character, such as an accented character from a foreign language.

entry-level system A *computer system* considered to be the minimal system for using serious computer *application programs,* such as *spreadsheet* programs or *word processing software.* The definition of an entry-level system changes rapidly. Ten years ago, an entry-level system—incapable of running the latest versions of today's most popular software—had at least one 360K *floppy disk drive,* a *monochrome* text monitor, and 256K of *random-access memory (RAM).* Modern entry-level systems have *Pentium microprocessors, VGA monitors,* and at least 16M of RAM.

entry line In a *spreadsheet* program, a text entry area where the user can type a value or formula. The program does not insert the characters into the current cell until the user presses Enter. The entry line also facilitates editing, since formulas do not appear in cells. Synonymous with formula bar.

envelope printer A *printer* designed specifically to print names, addresses, and U.S. Postal Service POSTNET *bar codes* on business envelopes. Businesses that use the bar codes receive an attractive discount on postal rates and receive faster and more accurate delivery of their business correspondence. Many *laser* and *inkjet printers* can print POSTNET codes. Envelope printers, however, do a better job of handling high-volume printing jobs.

D
E
F

environment   The *hardware* and *operating system* for *application programs,* such as the *Macintosh* environment. In *MS-DOS,* the environment also is a space in memory reserved for storing variables that applications running on your system can use. See *environment variable.*

environment variable   An instruction stored in the *MS-DOS environment* that controls, for example, how to display the DOS *prompt,* where to store any temporary files, and the *path* of directories that DOS searches to find commands. The PATH, COMSPEC, PROMPT, and SET commands in the AUTOEXEC.BAT file all define environment variables.

EOF   Abbreviation for end of file.

EOL   Abbreviation for *end of line.*

e-pistle   See *e-mail.*

EPP   See *enhanced parallel port.*

EPP/ECP port   An improved version of the *parallel port* that supports both the *enhanced parallel port (EPP)* and *extended capabilities port (ECP)* standards. EPP/ECP ports can transmit data very fast—as fast as an *Ethernet network interface card.*

EPROM   A *read-only memory (ROM)* chip that can be programmed and reprogrammed with a special electronic device. EPROM chips are packaged in a clear plastic case so the contents can be erased using ultraviolet light. The erasability of EPROM chips matters to computer manufacturers, who often find that they need to reprogram ROM chips containing bugs. *Programmable read-only memory (PROM)* chips, which can't be reprogrammed, must be discarded when a programming error is discovered.

EPS   See *Encapsulated PostScript (EPS) file.*

equation typesetting   Codes in a *word processing* document that cause the program to print multi-line equations, including mathematical symbols such as integrals and summation signs. The best word processing programs, such as *WordPerfect* and *Microsoft Word,* offer *what-you-see-is-what-you-get (WYSIWYG)* on-screen equation editors, which let you see the equation as you build it.

erasable optical disk drive A *read/write* data storage medium that uses a laser and reflected light to store and retrieve data on an *optical disk*. Unlike *CD-ROM drives* and *write-once, read-many (WORM)* drives, erasable *optical disk* drives can be used like *hard disks*. You can write and erase data repeatedly. Storage capacities are sizable; current drives store up to 650*M* of information. They're expensive and much slower than hard disks, however. See *secondary storage.*

erasable programmable read–only memory See *EPROM.*

e rate See *vertical refresh rate.*

ergonomic keyboard A *keyboard* designed to reduce strain on the wrists, which can result in *repetitive stress injury (RSI)*. Some ergonomic keyboards, such as the Microsoft Natural Keyboard, angle keys away from the center, while others put keys in pits into which a naturally curved hand can fit.

ergonomics The science of designing machines, tools, computers, and physical work areas so that people find them easy and healthful to use.

error-correction protocol In *modems,* a method for filtering out *line noise* and repeating transmissions automatically if an error occurs. Error correction requires the use of sending and receiving modems that conform to the same error-correction protocols. When error correction is in use, a *reliable link* is established. Two widely used error-correcting protocols are *MNP-4* and *V.42.* See *CCITT protocol.*

error handling The way that a *program* copes with errors, such as the failure to access data on a disk or a user's failure to press the right key. A poorly written program might fail to handle errors at all, leading to a system *crash.* The best *programmers* anticipate possible errors and provide information that helps the user solve the problem. See *error trapping.*

error message In *application programs,* an on-screen message informing you that the program can't carry out a requested operation. Early computing systems assumed users were technically sophisticated and frequently presented cryptic error messages. Applications for general use should display more helpful error messages that include suggestions about how to solve the problem, such as the following:

```
You are about to lose work you have not saved.
Choose OK if you want to abandon this work.
Choose Cancel to return to your document.
```

error trapping   An application's capability to recognize an error and perform a predetermined action in response to that error.

Esc   A key that *application programs* can implement in various ways. In most applications, pressing Esc cancels a command or an operation.

escape character   In *Telnet,* a command (often Ctrl+[) that enables you to interrupt the link with the Telnet server so you can communicate directly with your Telnet client. The escape character comes in handy when the Telnet server isn't responding.

escape code   A series of characters, combining Esc (ASCII value 27) with one or more *ASCII characters,* that you can use to change screen colors, control the *cursor,* create special *prompts,* reassign *keys* on the *keyboard,* and change your printer's settings (to compressed type or bold, for example). Also, the series of characters that engages a modem's *command mode.* In the *Hayes command set,* the escape sequence consists of three plus signs (+++). Synonymous with *escape sequence.*

escape sequence   See *escape code.*

ESDI   See *Enhanced System Device Interface.*

ESP   See *enhanced serial port.*

Ethernet   A *local area network (LAN)* hardware, communication, and cabling standard, originally developed by Xerox Corporation, that can link up to 1,024 nodes in a *bus network.* A high-speed standard using a *baseband* (single-channel) communication technique, Ethernet provides for a raw data transfer rate of 10 *megabits per second (Mbps),* with actual *throughput* in the range of 2 to 3 megabits per second. Ethernet uses *carrier sense multiple access with collision detection (CSMA/CD)* techniques to prevent network failures when two devices try to access the network at the same time. See *AppleTalk.*

EtherTalk   An implementation of *Ethernet local area network (LAN)* hardware, jointly developed by Apple and 3Com, and designed to work with the *AppleShare* network operating system. EtherTalk transmits data through *coaxial cables* at the Ethernet rate of 10 megabits per second, in contrast to *AppleTalk's* rate of 230 kilobits per second.

ETX/ACK handshaking   See *handshaking*.

Eudora   A pioneering *e-mail* program, now available for Windows and Macintosh computers, currently published by Qualcomm. The program includes *mail filtering* and other advanced utilities that simplify e-mail management.

European Laboratory for Particle Physics See *CERN*.

D E F

even parity   In *asynchronous communications,* an error-checking technique that sets an extra *bit* (called a *parity bit*) to 1 if the number of 1 bits in a one-byte data item adds up to an even number. The parity bit is set to 0 if the number of 1 bits adds up to an odd number. See *odd parity* and *parity checking.*

event   In an *event-driven environment,* an action, such as moving the *mouse* or clicking a mouse button, that generates a message. See *event handler.*

event-driven environment   A *program* or *operating system* that normally functions in an idle *loop,* waiting for events, such as a *mouse click, keyboard* input, or a message from a device, to occur. When an event occurs, the program exits the idle loop and executes the program code designed to handle the specific event. This code is called an *event handler.* After handling the event, the program returns to the idle loop. *Microsoft Windows 95* and *Macintosh* System software are event-driven environments.

event-driven language   A *programming language* that creates *programs* that respond to events, such as input, incoming data, or signals received from other applications. Such programs keep the computer in an idle *loop* until an event occurs, at which time they execute code that is relevant to the event. *HyperTalk,* the language included with the *HyperCard* application packaged with every *Macintosh,* is an event-driven language. See *object-oriented programming (OOP) language.*

event-driven program   See *event-driven environment*.

event handler   In an *event-driven environment*, a block of *program* code designed to handle the messages generated when a specific kind of event occurs, such as a *mouse click*.

Excel   See *Microsoft Excel*.

EXE   In *MS-DOS*, a file-name extension that indicates that the file is an executable *program*. To run the program with DOS, simply type the file name (but not the extension) and press Enter.

executable file   See *executable program*.

executable program   A *program* that is ready to run on a given computer. For a program to be executable, it first must be translated, usually by a *compiler*, into the *machine language* of a particular computer.

execute   To carry out the instructions in an *algorithm* or *program*.

expand   1. In an *outlining utility* or a graphical file management utility (such as the *Windows Explorer*), to reveal all the subordinate entries below the selected outline heading or *directory*. In Explorer, for example, you can expand a directory quickly by double-clicking the directory *icon*—a folder. 2. In file compression, synonymous with *decompress*.

expandability   The capability of a *computer system* to accommodate more *memory*, additional *disk drives*, or *adapters*. Computers vary in their expandability. When shopping for a computer, consider systems configured the way that you want but with space for growth. Look for one or two empty *drive bays*, three to five empty *expansion slots*, and room for at least four times as much *random access memory (RAM)* as comes installed.

expanded memory   In older IBM PCs and compatibles running MS-DOS, a method of using more than 640KB of *random-access memory (RAM)*. Expanded memory works by paging blocks of data into and out of a fixed location within *conventional memory*, creating the appearance of a larger memory (but at the sacrifice of *overhead* due to the processing operations).

expanded memory board   An adapter that adds *expanded memory* to an *IBM PC-compatible* computer.

expanded memory emulator   A *utility program* for Intel 80386 and *Intel 486* computers that uses *extended memory* to simulate *expanded memory* to accommodate older programs and the many games that require it. See *EMM386.EXE*.

expanded memory manager (EMM)   A *utility program* that manages *expanded memory* in an *IBM PC-compatible* computer equipped with an *expanded memory board*. See *EMM386.EXE*.

Expanded Memory Specification (EMS)   See *Lotus-Intel-Microsoft Expanded Memory Specification (LIM EMS)*.

expanded type   A *typeface* that places characters farther apart or makes the characters wider so there are fewer *characters per inch (cpi)*.

expansion board   See *adapter*.

expansion bus   An extension of the computer's *data bus* and *address bus* that includes several *expansion slots* for *adapters*. *Peripheral Component Interconnect (PCI)* and *Industry Standard Architecture (ISA)* are the most popular expansion bus designs available today. See *Micro Channel bus, VESA local bus,* and *motherboard*.

expansion bus bottleneck   A phenomenon that occurs when the *microprocessor* performs far better than the *expansion bus* and which results in poor overall *computer system* performance. The expansion bus bottleneck problem has been solved by fast expansion bus standards like the *Peripheral Component Interconnect (PCI)* standard.

expansion card   See *adapter*.

expansion slot   A receptacle connected to the computer's *expansion bus,* designed to accept *adapters*.

expect statement   In a *communication program's* login *script,* a statement that tells the dialer to wait for the service provider's computer to send certain characters (such as "Please type your password").

expert system A *program* that contains much of the knowledge used by an expert in a specific field and that assists non-experts as they try to solve problems. Expert systems contain a *knowledge base* expressed in a series of IF/THEN rules and an engine capable of drawing inferences from this knowledge base. The system prompts you to supply information needed to assess the situation and come to a conclusion. Most expert systems express conclusions with a confidence factor, ranging from speculation to educated guess to firm conclusion. See *artificial intelligence (AI), backward chaining, forward chaining* and *PROLOG.*

expiration date In *Usenet,* the date at which a *post* is set to expire. The expiration date can be set in two ways: by the article's author and by Usenet system administrators. Although an article's author usually can choose to set an expiration date, not all *newsreaders* support this capability; if the author doesn't set a date, the expiration date field (part of the article's header) remains blank. Usenet system administrators can also choose to set default expiration dates for all the articles in a given newsgroup, such as two weeks from the date of delivery. On the expiration date, the article is deleted to conserve disk space for incoming articles. See *expired article.*

expired article In *Usenet,* an article that is still listed in the article selector, even though the Usenet system software has deleted the article because it has expired. You cannot read an expired article. See *expiration date.*

exploded pie graph A pie chart in which one or more of the slices is offset slightly (exploded) from the others to emphasize the data represented by the exploded slice. See *pie graph.*

export To save *data* in a *format* that another *program* can *read.* Most programs can export a document in *ASCII* format, which almost any program can read and use. When saving a *document* with a recent versions of a *word processing program,* you can choose a format from a list of dozens. See *import.*

Extended Binary Coded Decimal Interchange Code See *EBCDIC.*

extended capabilities port (ECP) An improvement on the *parallel port* that supports two-way communication between the computer and a *peripheral* device. Using an ECP, for example, a *scanner* can tell the *central processing unit (CPU)* that it has a paper jam and needs attention. The ECP may eventually displace the competing *enhanced parallel port (EPP)* standard, although many *motherboards* currently support both standards.

extended character set   In *IBM PC-compatible* computing, a 256-character *character set* stored in a computer's *read-only memory (ROM)* that includes, in addition to the 128 *ASCII* character codes, a collection of foreign language, technical, and block graphics characters. The characters with numbers above ASCII code 128 sometimes are referred to as higher-order characters.

eXtended Graphics Array (XGA)   A *video standard* intended to replace the *8514/A* standard and to bring 1024-*pixel* by 768-line *resolution* to IBM and *IBM PC-compatible displays.* An XGA board equipped with sufficient memory (1*M* or more) can display 65,536 colors at its low-resolution mode (640×480) and 256 colors at its high-resolution mode (1024×768). For *downward compatibility* with *software* that supports earlier standards, XGA boards also support the *Video Graphics Array (VGA)* standard. The XGA standard faces stiff competition from makers of extended VGA (high-resolution *Super VGA) video adapters.*

Extended Industry Standard Architecture   See *EISA.*

extended keyboard   The 101-key keyboard distributed with the original *IBM PC AT,* which includes a numeric keypad, additional function keys, and cursor-control keys.

extended-level synthesizer   In the *Microsoft Windows 95* Multimedia Personal Computer *(MPC)* specification, a synthesizer that can play a minimum of 16 simultaneous notes on nine melodic instruments and 16 simultaneous notes on eight percussive instruments. See *base-level synthesizer.*

extended memory   In *Intel 80286* or later *IBM PC-compatible* computers, the *random-access memory (RAM),* if any, above 1*M* (megabyte) that usually is installed directly on the *motherboard* and is directly accessible to the microprocessor. *Operating System/2 (OS/2)* and *Microsoft Windows 95* do not make distinctions among various portions of RAM.

extended memory manager   A *utility program* that lets certain *MS-DOS* programs access *extended memory.* The programs must be written to conform to the *eXtended Memory Specification (XMS)* standard. See *conventional memory* and *HIMEM.SYS*.

eXtended Memory Specification (XMS)   A set of standards and an operating environment that enables all programs to access *extended memory*. XMS requires a *utility program* known as an *extended memory manager,* such as *HIMEM.SYS* (which is provided with DOS 5.0).

extended VGA   See *Super VGA*.

extensible   Capable of accepting new, user-defined commands.

extension   A three-letter suffix (such as *.BMP, .RTF,* or *.ASM*) added to an *MS-DOS file name* that describes the file's contents. The extension is optional and is separated from the file name by a period.

Exterior Gateway Protocol (EGP)   An *Internet* protocol that defines the routing of Internet data between an *Autonomous System (AS)* and the wider Internet. This protocol has been superceded by the *Border Gateway Protocol*.

external cache   See *secondary cache*.

external command   An *MS-DOS* command that executes a *program*. The program file must be present in the current *drive, directory,* or *path*. FORMAT and DISKCOPY are examples of external commands. See *internal command*.

eXternal CoMmanD (XCMD)   In *HyperTalk* programming, a user-defined command (written in a language such as *Pascal* or *C*) that uses built-in *Macintosh library routines* to perform tasks not normally available within *HyperCard*. A popular XCMD is ResCopy, which is widely available in *public domain* or *shareware* stack-writing *utility programs*. ResCopy enables a HyperTalk programmer to copy external commands and external resources from one program or stack to another. See *external function (XCFN)* and *ResEdit*.

external data bus   A set of communications channels that facilitates communication between a *central processing unit (CPU)* and other components on the *motherboard,* including *random-access memory (RAM)*.

external function (XCFN)   In *HyperTalk programming,* a *program* function (written in a language such as Pascal or C) that is external to HyperTalk but returns values to the program that can be used within the HyperTalk program. For example, Resources, an XCFN widely available in *public domain* or *shareware* stack-writing utilities, returns a list of all named resources in a file of a specified type. See *eXternal CoMmanD (XCMD)*.

external hard disk   A *hard disk* equipped with its own case, cables, and power supply. External hard disks usually cost more than *internal hard disks* of comparable speed and capacity.

external modem   A *modem* with its own case, cables, and power supply, designed to plug into a *serial port*. See *internal modem*.

external reference formula   In *Microsoft Excel* and other *dynamic data exchange (DDE)*–capable *spreadsheet programs*, a *formula* placed in a cell that creates a link to another spreadsheet.

external table   In *Lotus 1-2-3*, a *database* created with a *database management program* (such as *dBASE*) that 1-2-3 can access directly.

extraction   The process of decompressing or decoding a compressed or encoded file. For example, extraction refers to the process of using *uudecode* to decode a *file* encoded for *network* transmission by *uuencode*, a *Unix utility program*.

extra-high density floppy disk   A type of *floppy disk* that requires a special *floppy disk drive* (equipped with two heads rather than the usual one) and can hold 2.88*M* when formatted for *MS-DOS*.

extranet   An *intranet* (internal TCP/IP network) that has been selectively opened to a firm's suppliers, customers, and strategic allies.

extremely low-frequency (ELF) emission   A magnetic field generated by commonly used electrical appliances such as *monitors,* electric blankets, hair dryers, and food mixers, and extending one to two meters from the source. ELF fields have caused tissue changes and fetal abnormalities in laboratory test animals and might be related to reproductive anomalies and cancers among frequent users of computers. Despite repeated assurances that computer displays are safe, evidence continues to accumulate of reproductive disorders and miscarriages among pregnant computer users.

F2F In *e-mail*, a common abbreviation that means "face to face"—a real-life meeting.

fabless Without large-scale fabrication facilities. A fabless *chip* maker, such as *Advanced Micro Devices (AMD)*, must farm out chip-manufacturing jobs to other companies.

facing pages The two pages of a bound document that face each other when the document is open. See *recto* and *verso*.

facsimile machine See *fax machine.*

factory configuration The set of operating parameters built in to a hardware device. The configuration can be overridden by the user.

fall back In *modems,* to decrease the *data transfer rate* to accommodate communication with an older modem or across a *dirty* line. Some modems also *fall forward* if *line noise* conditions improve.

fall forward In *modems,* to increase the *data transfer rate* if the quality of a connection improves. Some modems that *fall back* due to *line noise* can fall forward again if noise abates.

false dependency In *microprocessors* that use *superscalar architecture,* a condition in which the results of two calculations are written to the same *register* if separate *pipelines* perform the calculations simultaneously. The more registers a microprocessor has, the fewer false dependencies are likely to occur. See *data dependency* and *register renaming.*

false drop In a *database* search, a retrieved record that has nothing to do with the searcher's interests. False drops are an unintended consequence of *free text searching,* in which users type keywords in an attempt to retrieve relevant documents. For example, a search for the computer game Quake may retrieve documents relating to a recent earthquake in Japan. See *precision* and *recall.*

FAQ See *Frequently Asked Questions.*

Fast ATA See *Enhanced IDE (EIDE).*

Fast Ethernet   A new *Ethernet* specification that enables data transmission rates of 100 Mbps. Fast Ethernet networks use the same *media access control* method that 10Base-T Ethernet networks use (see *CSMA/CD*), but achieve 10 times the data transmission speed. Fast Ethernets use *twisted-pair* wiring or *fiber-optic cable.* Synonymous with *100Base-T.*

Fast Page Mode   See *FPM.*

Fast SCSI   A *SCSI* standard that uses an 8–bit data bus and supports *data transfer rates* of up to 10 *Mbps.* See *Ultra SCSI, Fast Wide SCSI* and *Ultra Wide SCSI.*

D
E
F

Fast Wide SCSI   A *SCSI* standard that uses a 16–bit data bus and supports *data transfer rates* of up to 20 *Mbps.* See *Fast SCSI, Ultra SCSI* and *Ultra Wide SCSI.*

FAT   See *file allocation table.*

FAT16   In *Microsoft Windows 95,* a *file allocation table (FAT)* that restricts the maximum size of a hard drive to 2.6GB; this limitation stems from the use of a 16–bit *cluster* addressing method. In addition, FAT16 utilizes disk space inefficiently (the smallest allocation unit is a cluster, as large as 32KB on a 1.2BG drive), so that a 1–byte file requires an entire cluster. See *FAT32.*

FAT32   In *Microsoft Windows 95,* a *file allocation table (FAT)* made available in Service Release 2 (OSR2). FAT32 removes the previous 2.1GB limit on hard disk size by employing a 32–bit *cluster* addressing method; FAT32 can use disks as large as 2 *terabytes.* In addition, FAT32 improves storage efficiency by using 4KB clusters as the smallest allocation unit. See *FAT16.*

fatal error   An error in a program that, at best, causes the program to *abort,* and, at worst, causes a *crash* with loss of data. *Bulletproof* programs are supposed to be immune to fatal errors, but they usually are not.

fat binary   A Macintosh program that can run on the original *Motorola 680x0* or the new *PowerPC* processors.

fat client   In *client/server* networks, a *proprietary* client application program that consumes a great deal of local and network processing time and forces data to be captured in proprietary file formats. See *light client.*

fatware   *Software* that is so laden with *features,* or is designed so inefficiently, that it monopolizes huge chunks of *hard disk* space, *random-access memory (RAM),* and *microprocessor* power. Fatware is one of the undesirable results of *creeping featurism.*

fault tolerance   The capability of a *computer system* to cope with internal *hardware* problems without interrupting the system's performance, often by automatically bringing backup systems online when the system detects a failure. Fault tolerance is indispensable whenever computers are assigned critical functions, such as guiding an aircraft to a safe landing or ensuring a steady flow of medicines to a patient. Fault tolerance also is beneficial for non-critical, everyday applications. See *bulletproof* and *Microsoft Windows NT.*

fault tree analysis   In testing, a method of discovering potential faults by tracking down every conceivable option in the way the program or hardware can be used.

favorite   In *Microsoft Internet Explorer,* a saved *hyperlink* to which the user plans to return. Synonymous with bookmark and hotlist item.

fax   To send and receive printed pages between two locations using a telephone line. Fax is short for facsimile. See *fax machine.*

fax machine   A stand-alone device that can send and receive images of pages through a phone line. A fax machine scans a sheet of paper and creates an image in a coded form that the machine can then transmit. A fax machine on the other end receives and translates the code and then prints a replica of the original page. See *fax modem.*

fax modem   A *circuit board* that fits into an *expansion slot* in a computer, providing many of the features of a *fax machine* at a lower cost, as well as crisper output and convenience, as well as providing the features of a high-speed modem. If you are traveling, or at a remote location, you can use a *portable computer* with a fax board to *fax* materials to and from any place with a phone. Fax boards send a coded image of a *document* and receive that image in the form of a file that you can then print. Before using a fax board to send printed or handwritten material, you must use special video equipment to scan or record the material. See *modem.*

fax program   An *application* that enables you to use a *fax modem*. Usually, a fax program enables you to compose, send, receive, and print faxes, and complete one of a variety of fax cover pages included with the program. When you receive documents that include text, the newest fax programs use *optical character recognition (OCR)* to convert the faxed image back into text so you can edit the document by using any of the popular word processing programs.

fax server   A computer or dedicated device that provides fax capabilities to all the *workstations* in a *local area network (LAN)*. See *fax modem*.

fax switch   A device that routes incoming telephone calls to the telephone, the *modem,* or the *fax machine,* whichever is appropriate. A fax switch can save the cost of extra telephone lines.

D
E
F

FCC certification   An attestation, formerly made by the U.S. Federal Communications Commission (FCC), that a given brand and model of a computer meets the agency's limits for radio frequency emissions. There are two certification levels: *Class A certification,* for computers to be used in industrial and commercial locations (specifically, mainframes and minicomputers), and *Class B certification,* for computers to be used in home locations, including home offices. All personal computers are explicitly defined as Class B equipment. See *radio frequency interference (RFI)*.

FDD   An acronym for *floppy disk drive* sometimes used in advertisements.

FDDI   See *Fiber Distributed Data Interface*.

FDHD   An acronym for *floppy drive high density*. See *high density*.

feathering   Adding an equal amount of space between each line on a page or column to force *vertical justification*.

feature   A capability of a *program*. Occasionally, programs contain undocumented features. Of recent concern is *creeping featurism* where, in an attempt to remain competitive, manufacturers load their programs with extra features that slow a program's operation and clutter the interface.

federated database   In scientific networking, a collaborative database (part of a *collaboratory*) in which scientists pool their knowledge and discoveries. Federated databases are one proposed solution to the *Grand Challenges*—problems that are so complex that they far outstrip the capabilities of individual scientists, or even individual research institutions, to tackle them independently.

female connector   A cable terminator and connection device with receptacles designed to accept the pins of a *male connector.*

femto-   A prefix indicating one quadrillionth, or a millionth of a billionth (10^{15}).

Fetch   A popular *FTP client* for Macintosh computers developed by Dartmouth College. The program is *freeware.*

Fiber Distributed Data Interface (FDDI)   A standard for creating high-speed computer networks that employ *fiber-optic cable.* The FDDI specification calls for networks up to 250km long that can transfer data at speeds of 100 million bits per second *(Mbps).*

fiber-optic cable   A high-speed physical medium that can be used for transmitting *data.* Constructed from thin fibers of glass, fiber-optic cable guides the light of transmitting lasers without significant loss, despite twists and turns along the way. At the receiving end, optical detectors transform the light into electrical impulses. Fiber optics enables very high-speed networking (the *Fiber Distributed Data Interface [FDDI]* specification calls for data transfer at speeds of 100 Mbps) but is expensive and difficult to work with.

fiber optics   A data transmission technology that uses *fiber-optic cable* to convey information.

Fidonet   A set of data exchange standards and procedures that permit privately operated computer *bulletin board systems (BBSs)* to exchange data, files, and *e-mail* internationally, using the world telephone system. At an agreed-on time when telephone rates are low, subscribing BBSs send e-mail messages and files to a regional host, which in turn distributes them to other bulletin boards. Responses, or *echoes,* eventually find their way back to the host bulletin board. A popular Fidonet feature is EchoMail, a set of moderated conferences that cover a variety of popular subjects, such as *Star Trek,* model aircraft, and political issues. See *Internet* and *wide area network (WAN).*

field See *data field.*

field-based search In a *database* or a Web *search engine,* a search that is restricted to a given field in the database. This is one of several methods that can be used to improve the *recall* and *precision.* The following table shows examples of the *syntax* used to perform field-based searches in *AltaVista:*

Field	Example
applet	applet:HoppingBunny
domain	domain:ca
from	from:"me@anywhere.com" (Usenet searches only)
host	host:"microsoft.com"
image	image:"Hale-Bopp"
keywords	keywords:GPS
link	link:http://www.pages.com/mypage.html
newsgroup	newsgroup:rec.boats.cruising (Usenet searches only)
site	site:www.microsoft.com
subject	subject:"keyboard shortcuts for Netscape" (Usenet searches only)
title	title:"Carpal Tunnel Syndrome"

field definition In a *database management program,* a list of the attributes that define the type of information that you can enter into a *data field.* The field definition also determines how the field's contents appear on-screen.

field name In a *database management program,* a unique name given to a *data field.* The name should help users identify the field's contents.

field privilege In a *database management program,* a database definition that establishes what you can do with the contents of a *data field* in a protected database.

field template   In *database management* programs, a
field definition that specifies the kind of data that you
can type in the *data field*. If you try to type some data into
a field that doesn't match the field template, the program
displays an error message. Synonymous with *data mask*. Use
field templates as often as possible. They help prevent users
from adding inappropriate information to the database.
See *data type*.

file   A *document* or other collection of information stored on a
disk and identified as a unit by a unique name. When you save a
file, the disk may scatter the data among dozens or even hundreds
of noncontiguous *clusters*. The *file allocation table (FAT)* is an index
of the order in which those clusters are linked to equal a file. To
the user, however, files appear as units on disk *directories* and are
retrieved and copied as units. See *secondary storage*.

file allocation table (FAT)   A hidden table of every *cluster* on
a *floppy* or *hard disk*. The FAT records how files are stored in distinct—and not necessarily contiguous—clusters. A file allocation
table uses a simple method, much like a scavenger hunt, to keep
track of data. The directory file stores the address of the file's first
cluster. In the FAT entry for the first cluster is the address of the
second cluster used to store the file. In the entry for the second
cluster is the address of the third cluster, and so on, until the last
cluster entry, which contains an end-of-file code. Because this
table provides the only means for finding data on a disk, DOS
creates and maintains two copies of the FAT in case one is damaged. See *file fragmentation*.

file attribute   A *hidden code,* stored with a file's directory, that
contains the file's read-only or archive status and whether the
file is a system, hidden, or directory file. See *archive attribute,
hidden file, locked file* and *read-only attribute*.

file compression utility   A *utility program,* such as PKZIP,
StuffIt or DriveSpace, that compresses and decompresses infrequently used files so that they take up 40 to 90 percent less
room on a hard disk. You use another utility to decompress a
file. Specialty file compression utilities that compress only certain
types of files, such as *downloadable font* files, are also available.
These programs usually load a special driver that remains in
memory to decompress and recompress the files as needed.
See *archive, bulletin board system (BBS), disk compression utility,*
and *compressed file*.

file conversion utility   A *utility program* that converts text or graphics files created with one program to the file format used by another program. The best application programs now include a conversion utility that can handle a dozen or more file formats.

file defragmentation   See *defragmentation*.

file deletion   The process of rendering a *file* unusable. There are two types of file deletion: physical and logical. Logical deletion makes a file disappear but ensures that it is recoverable. Dragging a file to the *Macintosh* Trash Can icon or the *Microsoft Windows 95* Recycling Bin logically deletes it.

file extension   See *extension*.

file format   The patterns and standards that a program uses to store data on disk. Few programs store data in *ASCII format*. Most use a *proprietary file format* that other programs cannot read, ensuring that customers continue to use the company's program and enabling programmers to include special features that standard formats might not allow. See *file conversion utility* and *native file format*.

file fragmentation   The allocation of a file in noncontiguous sectors on a *floppy* or *hard disk*. Fragmentation occurs because of multiple file deletions and write operations. File fragmentation can seriously reduce disk efficiency because a disk drive's read/write head must travel longer distances to retrieve a file that's scattered all over the disk. Defragmenting can improve disk efficiency by as much as 50 percent by rewriting files so that they are placed in contiguous clusters. See *defragmentation*.

file locking   On a *network,* a method of *concurrency control* that ensures the integrity of data. File locking prevents more than one user from accessing and altering a file at the same time. See *local area network (LAN)*.

file management program   A *program* that enables you to manage *files, directories,* and disks by displaying a disk's directory structure and listing existing files. Commands available on the program's menus are used to move and copy files, create directories, and perform other housekeeping tasks that help improve disk performance and protect your data. The *Windows Explorer* and XTree Gold are popular file management programs.

File Manager   In *Microsoft Windows 3.1,* a utility, included with the operating system, that enables users to perform basic file maintenance and organization tasks. See *Windows Explorer.*

file name   A unique name assigned to a *file* when the file is written on a disk. In *MS-DOS* and early versions of *Operating System/2 (OS/2),* file names have two parts: the file name and the *extension.* These names must conform to the following rules:

- Length. You can use as many as eight characters for the file name and as many as three characters for the extension. The extension is optional.

- Delimiter. If you use the extension, you must separate the file name and extension with a period.

- Legal characters. You can use any letter or number on the keyboard for file names and extensions, but not spaces. You also can use the following punctuation symbols:

  ` ~ ! @ # $ ^ & ( ) _ { }

In *MacOS,* you can use as many as 32 characters for file names, and file names can contain any character (including spaces) except the colon (:). In *Microsoft Windows 95,* you can use up to 255 characters, including spaces, but the name cannot contain any of the following characters:\ / : * ? " < > | .

file privilege   In *dBASE,* an attribute that determines what you can do with a protected *database* on a *network.* The options are DELETE, EXTEND, READ, and UPDATE. See *field privilege.*

file recovery   Restoring an erased disk *file.* See *undelete utility.*

file server   In a *local area network (LAN),* a computer that stores on its *hard disk* the *application programs* and *data files* for all the *workstations* in the *network.* In a *peer-to-peer network,* all workstations act as file servers because each workstation can provide files to other workstations. In the more common *client/server* architecture, a single, high-powered machine with a huge hard disk is set aside to function as the file server for all the workstations (clients) in the network. See *network operating system (NOS).*

filespec   In *MS-DOS,* a complete statement of a file's location, including a drive letter, *path name, file name,* and *extension,* such as C:\REPORTS\REPORT1.WK1. Synonymous with path name.

file transfer protocol (ftp) In *asynchronous communications,* a standard that ensures the error-free transmission of program and data files through the telephone system. When written in lower-case, ftp refers to any protocol, such as *XMODEM, Kermit,* or *ZMODEM.* Compare to the Internet standard, *FTP.*

File Transfer Protocol See *FTP.*

file transfer utility A *utility program* that transfers files between different *hardware* platforms, such as the IBM Personal Computer and the *Macintosh,* or between a *desktop* and a *laptop* computer. Popular file transfer utilities include MacLink Plus, which links PCs and Macs through their serial ports, and Brooklyn Bridge, which links desktop IBM computers with *IBM PC-compatible* laptops.

fill To enter the same text or *value* (numbers, dates, times, or formulas), or a sequence of values, in a *spreadsheet* programs *work-sheet.* In *Lotus 1-2-3,* for example, you use the Data Fill command to fill a *range* with values, indicating the value in the first cell, the amount to increase or decrease each number placed in the range, and the number where Lotus should stop filling.

filter Any software feature or program that functions automatically to screen data. In *e-mail,* you can use a filter to delete unwanted messages automatically or move certain types of messages to folders you have created.

filter command In MS-DOS, a command that takes input from a device or file, changes the input by passing it through a filter, and then sends the result to the screen or printer. The DOS *filters* are MORE (which scrolls long output screen by screen), FIND (which searches for text), and SORT (which sorts in order of *ASCII* characters).

Finder A file management program provided by *Apple Computer* for *Macintosh* computers. The Finder provides a file management *shell* for the Macintosh operating system *(MacOS).*

FinePrint A *resolution enhancement technology* that produces an *effective resolution* of 600 by 600 *dots per inch (dpi)* in Apple *laser printers.* Normally, the resolution is 300 dpi. See *PhotoGrade.*

finger An *Internet* utility that enables you to obtain information about a user who has an *e-mail* address. Normally, this information is limited to the person's full name, job title, and address. However, the user can set up finger to retrieve one or more text files that contain information (such as a resume) that the user wants to make public.

firewall A *security* procedure that places a specially programmed computer system between an organization's *local area network (LAN)* and the *Internet*. The firewall computer prevents *crackers* from accessing the internal network. Unfortunately, it also prevents the organization's computer users from gaining direct access to the Internet. The access that the firewall provides is indirect and mediated by programs called *proxy servers.*

FireWire A standard established by the *Institute of Electrical and Electronic Engineers (IEEE)* that lays out specifications for a very fast *port* that may someday replace the *serial port*. FireWire ports have not yet appeared on any commercially available *computer systems*.

firmware Broadly, the *system* software stored in a computer's *read-only memory (ROM)* or elsewhere in the computer's circuitry, such as the *basic input-output system (BIOS)* chips in *IBM PC-compatible* computers.

FIRST See *Forum of Incident Response and Security Teams.*

first generation computer The earliest phase of electronic digital computer technology, dating from the mid-1940s to the late 1950s. Huge, power-hungry, and expensive, these computers used vacuum tubes for switching devices. Significant achievements during this period were: the stored program concept, the notion that the program instructions as well as the data could be stored in the computer's memory; the use of binary instead of decimal numbers for processing purposes; and the development of auxiliary storage using magnetic tape drives.

first generation programming language The earliest programming language, which involved writing instructions in *machine language.*

fixed disk Synonymous with *hard disk.*

fixed-frequency monitor An *analog monitor* designed to receive input signals at only one frequency. In contrast, a *multiscanning monitor* automatically adjusts to match the incoming signal. Most of the *Video Graphics Array (VGA)* monitors sold with inexpensive entry-level 486-class systems are fixed-frequency monitors.

fixed-length field   In a *database management program,* a field whose length is set and cannot vary, as opposed to a variable-length field, which can adjust to accommodate entries of different lengths.

fixed numeric format   In *spreadsheet* programs, a *numeric format* that rounds values to the number of decimal places that you specify.

Fkey   1. A *Macintosh* utility program that you execute by pressing the Command (⌘) and Shift keys with a number key from 0 to 9—the keys that simulate the function keys on *IBM PC-compatible* keyboards. The *Macintosh System* software includes four Fkey utilities, *shareware* and commercial sources offer additional Fkey utilities (and *software* for managing them).

F key   See *function key*.

flag   1. A variable that serves as an indicator about the status of a *program,* a *file,* or some data. A flag in a *database record* might be true if the other fields in the record show that a videotape is overdue, for example. 2. Synonymous with *file attribute*.

flame   1. In *Usenet* and e-mail, a message that contains abusive, threatening, obscene, or inflammatory language. In e-mail, a slang term meaning to lose your self-control by writing a message that uses derogatory, obscene, or inappropriate language. See *flame bait, flame war, moderated newsgroup,* and *rave*. 2. To write an abusive, threatening, obscene, or inflammatory *e-mail* message or *Usenet* post out of anger.

flame bait   In an *unmoderated newsgroup,* a posting that contains opinions that prompt *flames*—abusive remarks and personal attacks—and may ultimately launch a *flame war*. Flame-bait topics include abortion, homosexuality, and the desirability of using *Microsoft Windows 95*. True flame bait unintentionally elicits such responses; when these postings are made intentionally, the post is more properly called a *troll*. See *moderated newsgroup*.

flame war   In *newsgroups, LISTSERVs,* and *mailing lists,* an unproductive and long-running debate marked by high emotion and little information. See *flame, flame bait,* and *unmoderated newsgroup.*

flash BIOS　A *read-only memory (ROM)* chip storing the computer's *basic input-output system (BIOS)* that you can reprogram with software, instead of having to remove the BIOS chip, reprogram it in a special machine, and then replace the *chip.* With flash BIOS, a computer manufacturer can easily update BIOS chips simply by sending to users a properly encoded *floppy disk.* Flash BIOS is made possible by *Flash Erasable Programmable Read-Only Memory (Flash EPROM).*

Flash Erasable Programmable Read-Only Memory (Flash EPROM)　A type of *read-only memory (ROM)* that can be erased by an electrical current and then reprogrammed with new instructions at very high speeds. After the reprogramming occurs, the circuits retain these instructions even if the power is switched off. Flash EPROM is used in *Flash BIOS* as well as *modems* that are set up so you can download and install support for new communications *protocols* as they become available.

flat　Lacking elaborate structure. A file system without *subdirectories* in which you can group files is said to be flat. Such systems have not been used since the earliest days of personal computing.

flat address space　A method of organizing a computer's memory so the *operating system* can allocate portions of the *memory* without restriction. The opposite of a flat address space is the *segmented memory architecture* of *MS-DOS* and Microsoft Windows 3.1, which divides memory into 64K sections (called segments). A flat memory space design is more efficient because the processor does not have to map each memory address to a specific 64K segment, but such a design requires the use of 32-bit memory addresses. *Microsoft Windows 95,* which employs 32-bit memory addresses, creates a flat address space for your applications.

flatbed scanner　A *scanner* with a flat scanning area large enough to accommodate a letter-sized page ($8^{1}/_{2}$ by 11 inches) or more of material. A sheet feeder to automate scanning multiple-page documents is an available option. See *digitize.*

flat-file database management program　A *database management program* that stores, organizes, and retrieves information from one file at a time. Such programs lack *relational database management* features. See *data integrity*.

flat–panel display   A thin display screen that uses one of several display technologies, such as electroluminescence, *gas plasma display, liquid crystal display (LCD)*, or thin film transistor (TFT). A backlit display makes the display easier to read. Generally used in portable computers, flat-panel displays are starting to make their appearance on the desktop.

flat–square monitor   A *monitor* that is more gently curved than most but really neither flat nor square. Although such monitors have less distortion than most displays, they are not free of spherical distortion, as *flat tension-mask monitors* are.

flat tension–mask monitor   A *monitor* design that includes an absolutely flat—and therefore distortion-free—*display*. Flat tension-mask monitors are the only truly distortion-free monitors available but are too expensive for most computer users. See *flat-square monitor* and *vertically flat*.

flicker   A visible distortion that occurs when you scroll the screen of a *monitor* that uses a low *refresh* rate. Also, a visible distortion apparent in light areas on an interlaced monitor. See *interlacing*.

floating graphic   A graph or picture that hasn't been fixed in an absolute position on the page, so it moves up or down on the page as you delete or insert text above it.

floating point   A method for storing and calculating numbers so that the location of the decimal isn't fixed but floating (the decimal moves around as needed so the calculation takes into account significant digits). Numeric coprocessors or software can implement floating-point calculation to improve the accuracy of computer calculations.

floating-point unit (FPU)   A portion of a *microprocessor* that handles operations in which the decimal point moves left and right to allow for very high precision when dealing with very large or very small numbers. An FPU usually makes a microprocessor much faster.

floppy disk   A removable and widely used data storage medium that uses a magnetically coated flexible disk of Mylar enclosed in a plastic envelope or case. Software publishers

D E F

sometimes distribute their applications on floppy disks. At one time, they also were the only medium for data storage for *personal computers,* but the availability of inexpensive *hard disks* has relegated floppy disks to the sidelines. See *double density, head access aperture, high density, read/write head, single-sided disk* and *write-protect notch.*

floppy disk controller   The circuitry responsible for operating a *floppy disk drive.* Usually based on the *765* controller *chip,* the floppy disk controller moves the *read/write head* and operates the *spindle motor* under directions from the *host adapter.*

floppy disk drive   A mechanism that enables a computer to read and write information on *floppy disks.* Floppy disk drives come in two sizes—*$3^1/_2$ inch* and *$5^1/_4$ inch*—and several *densities,* to handle a variety of floppy disks. A *high-density* floppy disk drive can work with both high-density and *double-density* floppy disks, but a double-density floppy disk drive can use only double-density disks.

floptical disk   A removable *optical disk* the size of a *$3^1/_2$-inch floppy disk* but with a capacity of 20M to 25M.

floptical drive   A data storage device that uses laser technology to illuminate optical tracts on a *floptical disk.* The reflected light is sensed by a photodetector, which generates a signal that allows precise positioning of the *read/write heads.* The pattern of *tracks,* created when the disk is manufactured, is extremely compact, making it possible to create $3^1/_2$-inch floptical disks the same size as the familiar *$3^1/_2$-inch floppy disks* but capable of storing 21M of information. Floptical drives manufactured by such companies as Iomega can read and write on standard $3^1/_2$-inch floppy disks.

flow   A feature that allows text in a page layout to wrap around graphics and to move automatically from column to column (called *newspaper columns* or snaking columns). *Page layout programs* and better word processing programs can format text this way.

flow chart   A chart that contains symbols referring to computer operations, describing how the program performs. Sometimes written as one word: flowchart.

flow control   A method of ensuring that the data device, such as a *modem* or a *computer system,* does not overwhelm the receiving device, such as a modem. *Software handshaking* (also called

XON/XOFF handshaking) regulates communications between two modems. *Hardware handshaking (CTS/RTS)* regulates data flow between the computer and the modem.

flush   To clear or empty. Flushing a printer's *random-access memory (RAM)* by turning it off for a few seconds and then turning it on again may correct certain problems.

flush left   In *word processing,* the alignment of text along the left margin, leaving a ragged right margin. See *justification.*

flush right   In *word processing,* aligning text along the right margin, leaving a ragged left margin. Flush–right alignment is seldom used except to create decorative effects or cover pages. See *justification.*

D
E
F

FMD   See *frequency division multiplexing.*

FM synthesis   In *sound boards* that use the *Musical Instrument Digital Interface (MIDI)* standard, a method of simulating musical instruments that is less costly than *wave-table synthesis* but also of much lower quality.

folder   In the Macintosh *Finder* and *Microsoft Windows 95* desktop, an on-screen representation of a file folder on the desktop and into which you can organize *files.* Folders are called *directories* in MS-DOS.

follow–up post   In an online *newsgroup,* a contribution posted in response to a previous posting. Unlike a reply, a follow–up post is public and can be read by everyone in the newsgroup. Follow-up posts form a *thread* of discussion. See *distributed bulletin board, netiquette* and *Usenet.*

font   One complete collection of letters, punctuation marks, numbers, and special characters with a consistent and identifiable *typeface, weight* (roman or bold), *posture* (upright or italic), and *type size.* The term often is used incorrectly in reference to a typeface or *font family.* Two kinds of fonts exist: *bit-mapped fonts* and *outline fonts.* Each comes in two versions: *screen fonts* and *printer fonts.* See *book weight.*

font cartridge   A plug-in *read-only memory (ROM)* cartridge—designed to fit into a receptacle on a *printer*—that contains one or more *fonts* and expands the printer's font capabilities. See *cartridge font.*

Font/DA Mover   A *utility program,* provided with *Macintosh* System software, that adds *fonts* and *desk accessories (DA)* to the *System Folder* of the computer's *startup disk.*

font downloader   See *downloading utility.*

font family   A set of *fonts* in several sizes and weights that share the same typeface. A font family can sometimes include several similar typefaces. Arial Helvetica, and MS Sans Serif are all considered part of the Swiss font family, for example.

font ID conflict   In the *Macintosh* environment, a system error caused by conflicts between the identification numbers assigned to the screen fonts stored in the *System Folder.* The Macintosh System and many Mac *application programs* recognize and retrieve fonts by the identification number, not by name. The original Mac operating system let you assign only 128 unique numbers, so you could inadvertently assemble a repertoire of screen fonts with conflicting numbers, causing printing errors. Beginning with System 6, Macintosh introduced a New Font Numbering Table (NFNT) scheme that lets you assign 16,000 unique numbers, reducing—but not eliminating—the potential for font ID conflicts.

font metric   The width and height information for each character in a *font.* The font metric is stored in a width table.

font smoothing   In high-resolution *laser printers,* the reduction of *aliasing* and other distortions when text or *graphics* are printed.

font substitution   Substituting an *outline font* in place of a *bit-mapped screen font* for printing purposes. In the *Macintosh* environment, the Apple LaserWriter printer driver substitutes the outline fonts *Helvetica,* Times Roman, and Courier for the screen fonts Geneva, New York, and Monaco.

font utility   A *utility program,* used with early laser printers, that downloaded fonts to the printer's memory so they could be used to print a document. The functions of font utilities are now built into current operating systems, such as *Microsoft Windows 95.*

footer   In a *word processing* or *page layout* program, repetitive material printed at the bottom of the documents pages. See *header.*

footnote In a *word processing* or *page layout program,* a reference or note positioned at the bottom of the page. Most word processing programs number footnotes automatically and renumber them if you insert or delete a note. The best programs can float lengthy footnotes to the next page so that they take up no more than half the page. See *endnote.*

footprint The amount of space occupied by a computer, printer, monitor, or other piece of equipment on a desk, shelf, or floor.

forced page break A *page break* inserted by the user; the page always breaks at this location. Synonymous with *hard page break.*

forced perfect termination Like *active termination* and *passive termination,* a way of ending a *Small Computer System Interface (SCSI) daisy chain.* Terminating the chain of SCSI devices presents a problem because the terminator may reflect signals, causing errors. Forced perfect termination actively monitors the electrical characteristics of the bus to make sure that no reflection occurs.

forecasting In a *spreadsheet* program, a method of analysis that projects past trends into the future.

foreground task In a computer capable of *multitasking,* the *job* that the computer is performing in the *active window.* In *networks* and *MS-DOS,* a *foreground task* is a job that receives priority status before *background tasks* are executed. *Background printing* or calculation, for example, takes place in brief pauses while the foreground task executes.

forgery In *Usenet,* mailing lists, or *e-mail,* a message written by someone other than the apparent author. *Internet* software enables any person with a modicum of technical knowledge to forge messages. An old Usenet custom is a host of April Fool's Day forgeries, which are harmless enough, but many forgeries are intended to embarrass and harass. A famous 1995 forgery faked a press release announcing that Microsoft Corporation had purchased the Roman Catholic Church. Microsoft had to issue a statement denying the forgery's allegations.

form 1. In *database* programs, an on-screen form that enables users to supply data in the provide data entry areas. 2. In *Hyper-Text Markup Language (HTML)* and *World Wide Web (WWW)* documents, a set of document features (including fill-in text areas, drop-down list boxes, check boxes, and option buttons) that enable you to interact with a Web page. Not all *Web browsers* can interact with forms. See *forms-capable browser.*

format   The organization of information for storage, printing, or displaying. The format of *floppy disks* and *hard disks* is the magnetic pattern laid down by the formatting utility. In a document, the format includes margins; the *font* and *alignment* used for text, headers, footers, and page numbering; and the way that numbers are displayed. In a *database management program;* the format is the physical arrangement of field names and data fields in an on-screen data-entry form.

formatting   An operation that establishes a pattern for the display, storage, or printing of data. In operating systems, an operation that prepares a floppy disk for use in a particular computer system by laying down a magnetic pattern. See *format, high-level format* and *low-level format.*

form factor   The physical size (usually just height) of a *hard disk* or *floppy disk drive.* Most modern hard and floppy disks fit into *half-height* drive bays, but a few high-capacity hard disks require *full-height* bays.

form feed   A command that forces the printer to eject the current page and start a new page.

forms-capable browser   A *Web browser* that can deal with *HyperText Markup Language (HTML) tags* that create on-screen, interactive *forms,* including fill-in text boxes, option buttons, and drop-down list boxes. Some early *Web browsers* could not interact with forms; the leading programs, such as *Microsoft Internet Explorer* and *Netscape Navigator,* have no trouble with these features.

formula   In a *spreadsheet* program, a *cell definition* that defines the relationship between two or more *values.* In a database management program, an expression that tells the program to perform calculations on numeric data contained in one or more data fields. See *calculated field* and *precedence.*

formula bar   In *Microsoft Excel,* the bar, located below the *toolbar,* in which you enter or edit *formulas* and which displays the address of the *current cell.*

FOR/NEXT loop In *programming,* a *loop* control structure that carries out a procedure a specified number of times. Suppose that you have a list of 10 items. A FOR/NEXT loop to change each item might read "Set the count to 1. Select to the end of the line. Apply formatting. Move down one line. Then set the count to the previous count plus 1. Keep doing this until the count is equal to 10." See *macro.*

FORTH A *high-level programming language* that offers direct control over hardware devices. Astronomer Charles Moore developed FORTH in 1970 to help him control the equipment at the Kitt Peak National Radio Observatory. FORTH (short for *fourth-generation programming language*) has been slow to gain acceptance as a general-purpose programming language. Because FORTH accepts user-defined commands, one FORTH programmer's code might be unintelligible to another programmer. FORTH sometimes is preferred for laboratory data acquisition, robotics, machine control, arcade games, automation, patient monitoring, and interfaces with musical devices.

D E F

FORTRAN The first compiled *high-level programming language.* FORTRAN (short for *formula translator*), which strongly resembles *BASIC,* enables programmers to describe and solve complex mathematical calculations. Still highly suited to mathematical applications, FORTRAN is widely used in scientific, academic, and technical settings. See *modular programming, Pascal* and *structured programming.*

forum See *newsgroup.*

Forum of Incident Response and Security Teams (FIRST) A unit of the *Internet Society* that coordinates the activities of several *Computer Emergency Response Teams (CERTs)* worldwide. FIRSTs purpose is to bring these teams together to foster cooperation and coordination when security-related incidents occur and to promote the sharing of information concerning the security perils facing the Internet.

forward chaining In *expert systems,* an inference technique that requires the user to state all the relevant data before processing begins. A forward chaining system starts with the data and works forward through its rules to determine whether additional data is required and how to draw the inference. See *backward chaining* and *knowledge base.*

foundation classes In an *object-oriented programming (OOP) language,* a *library* of basic *routines* that programmers can use to handle essential program functions, such as responding to user input, displaying windows on the screen, and interacting with peripherals.

fourth-generation computer An electronic digital computer created using *Very Large Scale Integration (VLSI)* technology, including *microprocessors.* VLSI technology, with origins in the late 1970s, enables computer manufacturers to publish complicated computer circuits in huge quantities; this has led to the phenomenon of ubiquitous computing, in which computers penetrate deeply into virtually every facet of our lives.

fourth-generation programming language A *programming language* that is designed to work with an application, producing dramatic effects with a minimum of programming effort. An example is a *database* program's report-generation language.

four-way set-associative cache The *set-associative cache* design that strikes the best balance between speed and cost control. Four-way set-associative caches are faster than *two-way set-associative caches* and *direct-map caches* but are also more expensive.

FPM Acronym for Fast Page Mode. A type of *dynamic random-access memory (DRAM)* that divides the memory into pages, which can be directly accessed by the microprocessor and transferred in an entire block (see *page mode RAM*). FPM is not sufficiently fast for today's microprocessors and has been superceded by *EDO RAM* and, more recently, *SDRAM.*

fps See *frames per second.*

FPU See *floating-point unit.*

fragmentation See *file fragmentation.*

frame 1. In data communications, a unit *(packet)* of data that is transmitted via the network. 2. In *desktop publishing (DTP)* and *word processing,* a rectangular area absolutely positioned on the page. The frame can contain text, graphics, or both. 3. In the *World Wide Web (WWW),* a section of the window that has been partitioned off to display a separate document. This is done with frame *tags.* 4. In *animation* and video, one of the still images that, when played at a rapid speed (see *frame rate*), produces the illusion of continuous movement.

frame buffer   1. A portion of *video memory* that stores the information used to generate an image on-screen. Usually, the *central processing unit (CPU)* writes data to the frame buffer; then the *video controller* reads it, but dual-ported *video RAM (VRAM)* allows simultaneous reads and writes. A frame buffer that can handle more information than the display might be used for *hardware panning*. 2. In *Lotus 1-2-3,* the shaded border across the top of the spreadsheet containing the column letters and down the left of the *spreadsheet* containing the row numbers.

FrameMaker   See *Adobe FrameMaker.*

frame rate   In *animation* and video, the number of still images that are presented per second. The frame rate is measured in *frames per second (fps).*

frames per second (fps)   The number of still images (frames) that are presented per second in an *animation* or video. To produce the illusion of continuous movement, an animation or video should display at least 15 fps; roughly 30 fps is required to produce a convincing illusion of smooth motion.

free-form text chart   In *presentation graphics,* a text chart used to handle information difficult to express in lists, such as lengthy explanations, directions, invitations, and certificates.

Freehand   See *Macromedia Freehand.*

freenet   A community-based *bulletin board system (BBS),* usually based in a public library, that attempts to make useful resources available to the local citizenry. Such resources include transcripts of city council meetings, access to the local library's card catalog, the names and addresses of community organizations, and, increasingly, access to the *Internet.* In keeping with the freenet's public-service orientation, access is free or very inexpensive.

Free Software Foundation (FSF)   A nonprofit organization, based in Massachusetts, that is devoted to the ideal of the free sharing of useful software for noncommercial purposes. To promote this goal, FSF supports a *Unix*-compatible *operating system* (called GNU) and system utilities, which are freely redistributable under FSF's General Public License (GPL). See *copyleft.*

freestanding pointing device   A pointing device, such as a *mouse* or *trackball,* connected to the computer through the serial or mouse port that isn't otherwise attached to the computer. See *built-in pointing device* and *clip-on pointing device.*

free text search   In a *database,* a search that begins by supplying one or more *keywords,* which the search software attempts to match against an *inverted file* (an index of all the words that appear in all the *data records).* Although free text searching is easy to do, the results are often unsatisfactory because the list of retrieved items is likely to contain many *false drops* (records that do not pertain to the actual search subject). In addition, free text searches generally achieve poor *recall* (a measure of the percentage of records that are actually in the database that were retrieved by the search). To improve the results of a free text search, search restrictions may be needed, including *case-sensitive searches, controlled vocabulary, field-based searches,* and *phrase searches.*

freeware   Copyrighted *programs* that have been made available without charge for public use. The programs cannot be resold for profit. See *public domain program* and *shareware.*

freeze   1. To stop software development at a point at which the developer judges that the software is sufficiently stable for release. 2. To stop functioning (synonymous with *crash).*

frequency division multiplexing (FDM)   In *local area networks (LANs),* a technique for transmitting two or more signals over one cable by assigning each to its own frequency. *Broadband* (analog) networks use this technique. See *multiplexing.*

frequency modulation (FM) recording   An early, low-density method of recording digital signals on recording media, such as *tapes* and disks. Synonymous with *single-density* recording. See *Modified Frequency Modulation (MFM).*

frequency shift keying (FSK)   In *modems,* an obsolete way of communicating data by changing the frequency of the *carrier.* The *Bell 103A* protocol employs FSK, but newer data transmission protocols use *group coding* or *trellis-code modulation (TCM).*

Frequently Asked Questions (FAQ)   In *Usenet,* a document automatically posted to a *newsgroup* at regular intervals and designed to assist new users. A FAQ contains a list of the questions that are commonly posted to the newsgroup, together with the answers that have emerged from the newsgroup participants collective experience. FAQs are well worth reading, for two reasons: First, they can save you the embarrassment of posting a common question, and second, many FAQs are exceptionally well developed and may contain some of the best information that you will find anywhere on a subject.

friction feed A *printer* paper-feed mechanism that draws individual sheets of paper through the printer by using a platen to exert pressure on the paper. See *cut-sheet feeder* and *tractor feed*.

fried Burned out; short-circuited.

front end The portion of a *program* that interacts directly with the user. A front end can also be a separate program that acts as a user-friendly *interface* for a more difficult environment; for example, HyperText Markup Language (HTML) has been called a front end for the Internet. A *local area network (LAN)* might distribute the front end to each workstation so that the user can interact with the *back-end* application on the *file server.* See *client/server.*

FrontPage See *Microsoft FrontPage.*

FTP Acronym for File Transfer Protocol. An *Internet* standard for the exchange of files. FTP (Uppercase letters) is a specific set of rules that comprise a *file transfer protocol (ftp,* note the lowercase letters). To use FTP, you start an FTP client, an *application program* that enables you to contact another computer on the Internet and exchange files with it. To gain access to the other computer, you normally must supply a login name and password, after which you are given access to the computer's file *directory* system, and you can send (upload) and receive (download) files. An exception is *anonymous FTP,* which makes a file archive publicly accessible to any Internet user who possesses an FTP client; in response to the authentication prompts, you enter anonymous rather than a login name and, as a courtesy, supply your *e-mail* address as a password. Many *Web browsers* can function as FTP clients to download files from anonymous FTP file archives.

FTP client A program that is able to assist the user in uploading or downloading files from an *FTP site.* There are many stand-alone FTP clients, and FTP downloading capabilities are built into *Web browsers* such as *Netscape Navigator.*

FTP server In the *Internet,* a *server* program that enables external users to *download* or *upload* files from a specified directory or group of directories. In *anonymous FTP,* the server accepts all external requests for downloads, but uploading or other file operations are generally prohibited.

FTP site   In the *Internet,* an Internet *host,* running an FTP server, that makes a large number of files available for downloading. See *anonymous FTP.*

full–associative cache   A *secondary cache* design that is superior to the *direct-map cache* design but inferior to the *set-associative cache* design. Full-associative caches require the *central processing unit (CPU)* to search the entire *cache* for a needed piece of information. See *four-way set-associative cache.*

full backup   A *hard disk* backup of every file on the entire hard disk. Synonymous with *global backup.* Although extremely tedious if you're backing up to floppy disks, the procedure is necessary for secure computing. If your full *backup procedure* takes too long, consider adding a tape drive to your system. See *incremental backup.*

full bleed   Text or graphics extending from one edge of a page to the other. See *bleed capability.*

full duplex   An *asynchronous communications* protocol that allows the communications channel to send and receive signals at the same time. See *communications protocol, echoplex,* and *half duplex.*

full–height drive bay   A mounting space in the computer's *case* for a component 3.38 inches tall. Designed to accept an old IBM *hard disk,* a single full–height drive bay can accept two modern hard disks. See *half-height drive* and *half-height drive bay.*

full justification   See *justification.*

full–motion video adapter   A video adapter that can display moving video images—prerecorded or live—in a *window* that appears on the display. To display video images, you connect the adapter to a videocassette recorder, laser disk player, or a camcorder. Most full-motion video adapters come with software that enables users to develop a *multimedia* presentation, complete with wipes, washes, fades, animation, and sound. Full-motion video applications are expected to play a growing role in corporate and professional presentations and training applications.

full-page display   A *monitor* that can display a full page of text at a time. Such monitors are used most frequently with *computer systems* dedicated to *desktop publishing (DTP)*. With a full-page display, you can view and edit an entire page of text, figures, or graphics at a time, providing a better overview of your documents structure and organization. If you're thinking about equipping your DOS system with a full-page display, be aware that not all the programs that you're using can take advantage of it. Check your programs' documentation. The *Macintosh Finder* and *Microsoft Windows 95* support full-page displays.

D
E
F

full-screen editor   A *word processing* utility, often included with *application development systems,* designed specifically for creating and editing *programs*. Such utilities include special features for indenting lines of program code, searching for non-standard characters, and interfacing with program interpreters or compilers. See *line editor* and *programming environment*.

full-travel keyboard   A *keyboard* on which the *keys* can be depressed at least ⅛ inch. Full-travel keyboards provide good *tactile feedback* and enable professional typists to work quickly.

fully formed character printer   A *printer,* such as a *daisy-wheel printer,* that prints one character at a time.

function   In *programming languages* and *spreadsheet programs,* a named and stored procedure that returns one value. In spreadsheets, synonymous with *built-in function*.

function key   A programmable *key*—conventionally numbered F1, F2, and so on—that provides special functions, depending on the *software* that you're using. See *Fkey*.

fuser wand   In *laser printers,* a heated roller that melts *toner* onto the page. Dirty fuser wands sometimes cause unwanted vertical stripes on output.

G

G   Abbreviation for *gigabyte.*

game port   A socket that lets you connect a *joystick,* control yoke (a device that simulates an aircraft's control devices), or other game device to your computer. Without a game port, which may be included on your *sound board,* you'll find it's much harder to defeat the Empire of Galactic Doom.

gamut   In *graphics,* the range of colors that a color *monitor* can display.

garage   A special bracket in *inkjet printers* in which an unused ink cartridge may be stored without the ink drying out. Also, the place the *print head* goes when it is not in use.

garbage characters   In *modems,* meaningless characters caused by *line noise.* In *printers,* meaningless characters caused by line noise, a faulty *printer driver,* or some other communication problem.

garbage collection   A process by which a program goes through *random-access memory (RAM),* decides which information stored there is no longer needed, and prepares the addresses housing the unneeded data for re-use. Garbage collection prevents programs from filling RAM with useless data and causing a *crash.*

gas plasma display   See *plasma display.*

gateway   1. A means by which users of one computer service or network can access certain kinds of information on a different service or network. This may be achieved by means of hardware devices called *bridges,* by computer programs that perform the necessary translation, or both. For example, *Internet* e-mail users can exchange mail with *CompuServe* users by means of a gateway. Similarly, people using *Web browsers* can access the Archie service by means of a Web page that functions as an Archie gateway. 2. In *networks,* a device that connects two dissimilar *local area networks (LANs)* or connects a local area network to a *wide area network (WAN),* a *minicomputer,* or a *mainframe.* A gateway has its own microprocessor and memory and may perform *network protocol* conversion and *bandwidth* conversion. See *bridge.*

Gbps   See *bits per second.*

GDI   See *Graphical Device Interface.*

GDI printer   See *Graphical Device Interface (GDI) printer.*

general format   In most *spreadsheet programs,* the default *numeric format* in which all the numbers on either side of the decimal point (up to the furthest number that isn't a zero) are displayed but without commas or currency signs. When a number is too large to display with the current column width, scientific notation is used.

General MIDI (GM)   In *multimedia,* a standard controlled by the *MIDI Manufacturers' Association (MMA)* that defines a set of 96 standard voices corresponding to traditional musical instruments and an additional set of voices corresponding to nonmelodic percussion instruments. When you use the standard code numbers from these sets to create a *MIDI* (Musical Instrument Digital Interface) *file,* any GM-compatible synthesizer will reproduce the sounds in the file the way you intended them.

G H I

general protection fault (GPF)   In *Microsoft Windows 3.1,* a computer *crash* that is caused by one program invading another's memory space. GPF-related crashes are common in Windows 3.1 and any other operating system that implements *cooperative multitasking,* in which programs must be expertly designed to coexist in the computer's memory. More recent operating systems, such as *Microsoft Windows 95,* offer *preemptive multitasking,* in which the operating system intervenes in memory-space squabbles; these operating systems offer significantly more reliable operation. See *protected mode.*

General Public License (GPL)   A *freeware* software license, devised by the Open Software Foundation (OSF), which stipulates that a given program can be used without payment or permission as long as the use is non-commercial.

general-purpose computer   In contrast to a computer that is *dedicated* to a specific purpose, such as collecting the results of a laboratory experiment, a general-purpose computer is one that is designed to run a variety of applications. The function of a general purpose computer depends on the specific applications that it runs, rather than the configuration of its hardware.

generate   To produce something by setting in motion an automatic procedure. For example, after marking the entries and indicating the table, list, and index locations, you can generate a table of contents, lists of figures, and an index in a *word processing program* when you choose the generate command.

GEnie   Developed by General Electric, an *online information service* that, like *CompuServe,* offers many of the attractions of a *bulletin board system (BBS)* and up-to-date stock quotes, conferences, *Internet e-mail,* home shopping, and news updates.

geometry   The physical layout of a *hard disk's* surface, including number of *tracks,* number of *sectors,* tracks per sector and *landing zone* location. Disk geometry specifications are part of a disk's *setup parameters.*

ghost   The effect of an image being displayed continuously on-screen. Such images "burn" into the screen *phosphors,* resulting in a ghost image. See *screen saver.*

GIF   (pronounced "jiff" or "giff") A *graphics* file originally developed by *CompuServe* and widely used to encode and exchange graphics files on the *Internet.* The *bit-mapped* GIF format employs a patented *lossless compression* technique (called *LZW*) that reduces the size of the graphics file. Although GIF graphics are in widespread use, the *JPEG* format (which uses *lossy compression*) reduces graphics files to a size roughly one-third the size of a corresponding GIF file, leading to speedier *Internet* transmission. However, GIF graphics are more efficient than JPEGs if the depicted image contains many areas of solid color. Because GIF graphics rely on a patented compression algorithm, efforts are underway to replace GIFs with *PNG* graphics, which use public-domain algorithms. See *animated GIF* and *GIF89a.*

GIF89a   A revised version of the CompuServe *GIF* graphics format, which enables animation, transparent backgrounds, and interleaving. See *animated GIF.*

giga-   A prefix indicating one billion (10^9).

gigabit   A unit of measurement approximately equal to 1 billion bits (1,073,741,824). Usually used when indicating the amount of data that can be transferred or transmitted per second.

gigabyte A unit of measurement approximately equal to 1 billion bytes (1,073,741,824). Used when stating an amount of memory or disk capacity. One gigabyte equals 1,000M (megabytes).

GIGO Acronym for "garbage in, garbage out," which is usually said in response to fouled-up output that's attributable to erroneous input (such as a mistyped command).

glare Light reflected off the *display* from an outside source, such as a lamp or a window, and into your eyes. Glare makes the display hard to read and may cause eyestrain or headaches. Several *anti-glare* techniques exist but the simplest one is to reposition the *monitor*.

glitch A momentary power interruption or some other unexpected fluctuation in electronic circuits, such as those caused by power *surges* or dirty connections, that causes computer systems to generate garbage output or, in the extreme, to crash. A glitch is a *hardware* problem; a *software* problem is called a *bug*.

G
H
I

global backup See *full backup*.

global format In a *spreadsheet program*, a *numeric format* or *label alignment* choice that applies to all *cells* in the worksheet. With most programs, you can override the global format by defining a format for certain cells.

global heap In *Microsoft Windows 3.1*, the total amount of memory available for user programs, including the 640K *conventional memory* and all the *extended memory* installed in the computer. This *heap* isn't truly global, though: A drawback of Windows 3.1 is that required *dynamic link libraries (DLLs)* must be stored in cramped space of conventional memory—and that is why Windows 3.1 often runs out of memory for applications even though there are several megabytes of free extended memory available.

global kill file In a *Usenet* newsreader program, a file containing words, phrases, names, or *network* addresses that you have identified as signals of an unwanted message (such as "Make Money Fast!"). The program screens incoming articles for these signals and automatically deletes the articles before you even see them. A global kill file performs this function in all newsgroups, while a *newsgroup kill file* deletes unwanted messages only in specific newsgroups.

glossary   In a *word processing program,* a feature used to store frequently used phrases and *boilerplate* text for later insertion into documents when needed.

glossy finish   A quality of paper that reflects light harshly. Glossy finish paper is less popular for laser printer use than *matte finish* paper.

GM   See *General MIDI.*

Gopher   In Unix-based systems linked to the *Internet,* a menu-based program that helps you find files, programs, definitions, and other resources on topics you specify. Gopher was originally developed at the University of Minnesota and named after the school mascot. Unlike *FTP* and *Archie,* Gopher doesn't require you to know and use the details of host, directory, and file names. Instead, you browse through menus and press Enter when you find something interesting. You usually see another menu, with more options, until finally you select an option that displays information. You can then read the information or save it to your disk storage area after retrieving it with *anonymous FTP.* The *World Wide Web (WWW)* has made Gopher and other text-based Internet search tools obsolete, although some Gopher servers are still operating.

gopherspace   In *Gopher,* the enormous computer-based "space" that is created by the global dissemination of Gopher-accessible resources. A search tool called *Veronica* enables you to search Gopherspace for *directory titles* and resources that match keywords you supply.

gov   A *domain name* denoting a government office or agency.

grabber hand   In *graphics programs* and *HyperCard,* an on-screen image of a hand that you can position with the *mouse* to move selected units of text or graphics from place to place on-screen.

grab handle   In a graphics program, the small black boxes on the periphery of an object. By dragging on these handles, the user can move, size, or crop the object.

Grand Challenge   An unsolved scientific or engineering problem of such fabulous complexity that no individual researcher, nor even an individual research institute, can hope to tackle it alone. Examples include mapping the human genome or understanding the astrophysics of the Milky Way. Advanced computer *networks* may help researchers tackle the Grand Challenges by fostering *collaboratory* research and resource sharing by means of *federated databases.*

granularity of allocation   The smallest unit of storage space available. The granularity of *hard* and *floppy disks* is determined by the size of their *clusters;* if a disk has a cluster size of 100*K*, even files smaller than 100K will be assigned an entire cluster.

Graphical Device Interface (GDI)   A programming resource—part of a graphical user interface—that enables programmers to generate dialog boxes and other graphical elements in a consistent style. GDIs handle the detail work of drawing such elements on-screen; the programmer need only tell the GDI what to draw and where to draw it.

Graphical Device Interface (GDI) printer   Synonymous with Windows printer, a *printer* that has no *raster image processor (RIP)* and leaves much of the task of preparing a page for printing to *software.* GDI printers can be used only with *Microsoft Windows.* GDI printers tax the often already-burdened *central processing unit (CPU)* and may not be supported by future versions of Windows, so they're probably not a good buy.

Graphical User Interface (GUI)   A design for the part of a program that interacts with the user and uses *icons* to represent program features. The Apple Macintosh and Microsoft Windows operating environments are popular GUIs. Having found that people recognize graphic representations faster than they read words or phrases, a Xerox research team designed a user interface with graphic images called *icons.* GUIs typically work with *mousable interfaces* with *pull-down menus, dialog boxes, check boxes, radio buttons, drop-down list boxes, scroll bars, scroll boxes,* and the like. Programs with a GUI require a computer with sufficient speed, power, and memory to display a high-resolution, bit-mapped display.

graphical Web browser   See *Web browser.*

graphics   In personal computing, the creation, modification, and printing pictures, as opposed to text. The two basic types of computer-produced graphics are *object-oriented graphics*, also called vector graphics, and *bit-mapped graphics,* often called raster graphics. *Vector graphics* programs, usually called *draw programs,* store

G H I

graphic images in the form of mathematical representations that can be sized and scaled without distortion. Object-oriented graphics programs are well suited for architecture, computer-aided design, interior design, and other applications in which precision and scaling capability are more important than artistic effects. *Bit-mapped graphics* programs, often called *paint programs*, store graphic images in the form of patterns of screen pixels. Unlike draw programs, paint programs can create delicate patterns of shading that convey an artistic touch, but any attempt to resize or scale the graphic may result in unacceptable distortion.

graphics accelerator   See *graphics accelerator board*.

graphics accelerator board   A *video adapter* that includes a *graphics coprocessor* and all the other circuitry normally found on a *video adapter*. The graphics accelerator handles the graphics processing, freeing the *central processing unit (CPU)* for other important tasks and thereby dramatically improving your system's capability to run *Microsoft Windows* and other graphical applications.

graphics adapter   See *video adapter*.

graphics board   See *video adapter*.

graphics card   See *video adapter*.

graphics character   In a computer's built-in *character set*, a character composed of lines, shaded rectangles, or other shapes. You can combine graphics characters to form *block graphics:* simple images, illustrations, and borders. Some programs, called *character-based programs,* use no graphics other than those made up of graphics characters.

graphics coprocessor   A *microprocessor* specially designed to speed the processing and display of *high-resolution* video images. A *graphics accelerator board* that includes a graphics coprocessor can speed the display of programs, such as Microsoft Windows, that use *graphical user interfaces (GUIs)*. Popular graphics coprocessors include the Weitek W5086 and W5186 and S3 Inc.'s 86C911.

graphics file format   In a *graphics program,* the way in which the information needed to display a graphic is arranged and stored on *disk*.

Graphics Interchange Format   See *GIF*.

graphics mode   In video adapters, a display mode in which everything on-screen, including text and graphics, is drawn using *pixels* instead of characters from the *character set*. Many adapters also offer a *character mode*, which runs more quickly because it uses the computer's built-in, ready-made characters instead of composing them individually. Some programs enable you to switch between a *graphics view*, which uses graphics mode and accurately shows what printed output will look like, and character view, which is faster than graphics view.

graphics primitive   In an *object-oriented graphics program*, the most basic unit of graphic expression, such as a line, arc, circle, rectangle, or oval.

graphics scanner   A *graphics* input device that transforms a picture into an image that can be displayed on-screen.

graphics spreadsheet   A *spreadsheet program* that displays the worksheet by using *bit-mapped graphics* instead of relying on the computer's built-in *character set*. Graphics spreadsheets, such as *Microsoft Excel* and *Lotus 1-2-3* for Windows, include *desktop publishing* tools, such as multiple *typefaces,* type sizes, *rules,* and screens (grayed areas). Also, printouts can combine spreadsheets and business graphs on one page.

G
H
I

graphics tablet   An input device that lets you draw with an electronic pen on an electronically sensitive table. The pen's movements are relayed to the screen. See *pen computer.*

graphics view   In some DOS applications, a mode in which the program switches the display circuitry to its *graphics mode.* In graphics mode, the computer can display bit-mapped graphics. On all except the fastest computers, graphics mode is significantly slower than *character mode.* Some programs have a fast *character view* that does not offer the *what-you-see-is-what-you-get (WYSIWYG)* features of graphics view.

grayscale   In computer graphics, a series of shades from white to black.

grayscale monitor   A *monitor* (and compatible *display adapter*) that can display a full range of shades from white to black, but no colors.

grayscale scanner   A *scanner* that generates *monochrome* output in levels of gray. The best grayscale scanners can produce output that resembles the tonal range of black-and-white photographs.

greeking   Displaying a simulated version of a page on-screen, showing lines or bars instead of text so that the overall page layout design is apparent. Some word processing and page layout programs use a print preview feature that's similar to greeking.

Greek text   A block of simulated text or lines used to represent the positioning and point size of text in a designer's composition of a page, used so that the aesthetics of the page design can be assessed.

Green Book   A Philips standard for packing text, sound, and video onto a *CD-ROM* that is best known as *CD-I (Compact Disc-Interactive)*.

green PC   A computer system designed to operate in an energy-efficient manner. Powerful green PCs typically draw from 90 to 130 watts, while standard systems draw 130 to 160 watts. Green PCs also include power-saving modes that dim *monitors* and stop *hard-disk* rotation when they are not in use. In *sleep mode*, green PCs draw between 28 and 36 watts. Electrical efficiency can quickly translate to big monetary savings in offices equipped with hundreds of machines. See *Energy Star*.

Group 1   An obsolete, very slow standard for *fax* machines.

Group 2   An obsolete, very slow standard for *fax* machines.

Group 3   The most common standard for *fax* machines and *fax modems*, published by the *ITU-TSS*. The Group 3 specification dictates methods by which a page-long fax can be sent in a minute or less. Several other standards support Group 3, including the *V.27ter, V.29*, and *V.17* standards.

Group 4   A standard for *fax* transmission designed to work with digital transmission networks such as *Integrated Services Digital Network (ISDN)*. Group 3 will continue to reign until *digital communications* find their way into more homes and offices.

group coding   Like *frequency shift keying (FSK),* a means used by a *modem* to transmit data by altering the character of the *carrier*. Unlike FSK, though, group coding enables the modem to convey more than one *bit* per change in the carrier. Group coding, which is used in most modern modems, uses *quadrature modulation* and other *modulation* techniques to modify the carrier.

groupware   Programs that increase the cooperation and joint productivity of small groups of co-workers. An example of groupware is ForComment (by Broderbund Software), designed to make collaborative writing easier. The program enables each member of the group to insert comments and make changes to the text, subject to the other members' approval. Some industry observers thought that groupware was just a marketing gimmick after it was reported that Broderbund didn't use ForComment for internal collaborative writing. The success of *Lotus Notes*, a groupware program designed for *minicomputer* and *mainframe* computer systems as well as *local-area networks (LANs)* and *wide area networks (WANs)*, may suggest otherwise.

guest   In a *local area network (LAN)*, an access privilege that enables you to access another computer on the network without having to provide a *password*.

GUI   See *Graphical User Interface*.

guide   In a page layout program, a nonprinting line that appears as a dotted line on-screen, showing the current location of margins, gutters, and other page layout design elements.

guru   In computing, an expert who can talk about highly technical subjects in an intelligible way (a rare quality) and doesn't mind doing so (even rarer).

gutter   See *binding offset*.

gzip   A *Unix* compression program, created by the Open Software Foundation (OSF) and free from patent restrictions, that is widely used to compress files on the *Internet*. Files compressed with gzip have the extension .gz.

G
H
I

hack 1. A clever and original rearrangement of the existing system or network resources that results, as if by magic, in a stunning improvement in system performance (or an equally stunning prank). A hacker is one who uses computers to perform hacks and is not necessarily a computer criminal. See *cracking, hacker ethic* and *phreaking*. 2. A "quick and dirty" job that produces results, but without following any logical or orderly procedure.

hacker 1. A computer enthusiast who enjoys learning everything about a computer system or network and through clever *programming*, pushing the system to its highest possible level of performance. 2. In the press, synonymous with *cracker*. 3. An adept programmer.

hacker ethic A set of moral principles that were common to the first-generation *hacker* community (roughly 1965–1982), described by Steven Levy in *Hackers* (1984). According to the hacker ethic, all technical information should, in principle, be freely available to all. Therefore, gaining entry to a system to explore data and increase knowledge is never unethical. However, destroying, altering, or moving data in such a way that could cause injury or expense to others is always unethical. In increasingly more states, unauthorized computer access is against the law. See *cracker, cyberpunk, cyberspace, hack* and *phreaking*.

half duplex An *asynchronous communications* protocol in which the communications channel can handle only one signal at a time. The two stations alternate their transmissions. Synonymous with *local echo*. See *communications protocol, echoplex* and *full duplex*.

half-height drive A disk drive half the size of the three-inch-high drives in the original IBM Personal Computer. *Half-height drive bays* and drives are standard in today's PCs.

half-height drive bay A mounting space for half-height devices, such as *half-height drives,* in a computer's *case.* A half-height drive bay is 1.625 inches tall. See *full-height drive bay.*

halftone 1. In computer graphics, a continuous tone image, such as a photograph, that has been digitized by means of *dithering*, in which patterns of black and white dots are used to simulate shades of gray. 2. In printing, a photograph prepared for printing by breaking down the continuous gradations of tones into a series of dots with a special screen or a *scanner*. Dense patterns of thick dots produce dark shades, and less dense patterns of smaller dots produce lighter shades. See *Tagged Image File Format (TIFF)*.

hand–held scanner   A *scanner* that you hold and move over the material that you are scanning. Hand-held scanners are somewhat less expensive than *flatbed scanners* but often require more than one pass to scan page-size documents. Avoid hand-held scanners unless you plan to scan narrow material, such as *newspaper columns.* See *sheet-fed scanner.*

handle   1. In a computer *chat room* or *Internet Relay Chat (IRC),* an alias or pseudonym. 2. In programming, a unique number that can be used to access a *peripheral* device or an *object* such as a window or file. When programs request access to a resource from the *operating system,* they receive a handle, which they can then use to access the needed resource. For example, in *Microsoft Windows,* when a program requests extended memory, *HIMEM.SYS* gives the program a handle to an extended memory block. The parameter /NUMHANDLES=num informs HIMEM.SYS how many handles it must manage. 3. In a graphics application, the small, black squares around a selected object. You use these squares to drag, size, or scale the object. Synonymous with grab handles. See *draw program* and *vector graphics.*

handler   A driver, *utility program,* or subroutine that takes care of a task. The A20 handler, for example, is a routine that controls access to *extended memory.* If *HIMEM.SYS* cannot gain control of the A20 address line, you use the /MACHINE:code parameter to tell HIMEM.SYS what type of computer you are using, which usually solves the problem. Handlers can also be a set of programming instructions attached to a *push button.* The instructions control what happens when the user selects a button. See *event-driven environment* and *object-oriented programming (OOP) language.*

handshaking   A method for controlling the flow of serial communication between two devices so that one device transmits data only when the other device is ready. In *hardware handshaking,* a separate wire sends a signal when the receiving device is ready to receive the signal; *software handshaking* uses special control characters. Devices such as *serial printers* use *hardware* handshaking because they are close to one another and can use a special cable. Because the telephone system doesn't have an extra wire available, the telephone connections that *modems* use require software handshaking. The two software handshaking techniques are *ETX/ACK,* which uses the *ASCII* character Ctrl+C to pause data transmission, and *XON/XOFF,* which uses Ctrl+S to pause and Ctrl+Q to resume transmission.

hang A type of computer *crash* in which a program initiates an operation but cannot complete it for some reason. The program does not and cannot respond, and it may be necessary to restart the system in order to continue processing.

hanging indent A paragraph indentation in which the first line is flush with the left margin, but subsequent lines (called *turnover lines*) are indented.

hard Permanent, physically defined, permanently wired, or fixed, as opposed to soft (changeable or subject to redefinition). The printed document is hard because changing the printed document is difficult. A document in the computer's memory is soft because you can still make changes to it. See *hard copy, hard hyphen, hard return, hard space* and *hard-wired.*

hard boot A system restart initiated by means of pressing the *hardware reset switch,* or on computers lacking such a switch, by switching the power off and then back on again. A hard boot may be necessary after a *crash* so severe that the controls used for the normal restarting procedure (a *soft boot*) do not work.

hard card A *hard disk* and *disk drive controller* that are contained on a single plug-in *adapter.* By using a hard card, you can easily add a hard disk to a system; you simply press the adapter into the *expansion slot* just as you would any other adapter.

hard copy Printed output, distinguished from data stored on disk or in memory.

hard disk A *secondary storage* medium that uses several rigid disks coated with a magnetically sensitive material and housed, together with the recording heads, in a hermetically sealed mechanism. Typical storage capacities range from 1 to 4 *gigabytes (G).* Hard drive performance is measured in terms of *access time, seek time,* rotational speed (measured in revolutions per minute), and *data transfer rate.* Hard drive *interface standards*—the means by which hard drives transmit their contents to other parts of a computer—include *ST506/ST-412, Integrated Drive Electronics (IDE), Enhanced System Device Interface (ESDI),* and *Small Computer System Interface (SCSI),* and *Wide SCSI.* IDE and SCSI are most common today.

hard disk backup program   A *utility program* that backs up *hard disk* data and programs onto *floppy disks.* See *backup utility.*

hard disk controller   The circuitry, usually mounted on the *hard disk* itself, that controls the *spindle motor* and the *head actuator* of a hard disk. Under instructions from the *host adapter,* the hard disk controller searches for needed information and communicates it to the rest of the computer. *Integrated Drive Electronics (IDE)* hard disk controllers must be configured in different ways, depending on whether they are *master* or *slave* drives.

hard disk drive   See *hard disk.*

hard disk interface   An electronic standard for connecting a *hard disk* to the computer. See *Enhanced System Device Interface (ESDI), Integrated Drive Electronics (IDE)* and *Small Computer System Interface (SCSI).*

hard drive   See *hard disk.*

hard hyphen   In *word processing programs,* a special hyphen that acts as a regular character so that text can't word wrap at this hyphen. Synonymous with *nonbreaking hyphen.* See *soft hyphen.*

hard page break   A *page break,* inserted by the user, that remains in effect even after the user later adds or deletes text above the break. In contrast, the *soft page break* inserted by the program moves automatically as you add and delete text. Synonymous with *forced page break.*

hard return   In *word processing programs,* a *line break* created by pressing the Enter key, as opposed to a *soft return,* which a program creates automatically at the end of a line. Unlike a soft return, a hard return stays in place when you insert and delete text.

hard space   In *word processing programs,* a space specially formatted as a regular character so that the text can't start a new line, breaking the phrase, at the space's location. Hard spaces often are used to keep two-word proper nouns or month and date together on the same line, such as **Key Biscayne,**[hard space] **West Point,** and **January**[hard space]**25.**

hardware   The electronic components, boards, peripherals, and equipment that make up your computer system; distinguished from the programs (*software*) that tell these components what to do.

hardware cache   A *buffer* on a *disk drive controller* or a *disk drive.* The buffer stores frequently accessed program instructions and data, as well as additional *tracks* of data that a program might need next. A computer can access required data much more quickly from the hardware cache than from the disk. The data is then delivered as fast as the *expansion bus* can carry it. Both 32-bit and 16-bit cached disk controller cards are available. See *disk drive controller.*

hardware error control   Physical modem circuits that implement an error-correction *protocol,* such as *MNP4* or *V.42.* The alternative (found in less expensive modems) is software error control, which requires the computer's *central processing unit (CPU)* to monitor the *data stream* for errors.

hardware handshaking   In a serial data communications device such as a *modem,* a method of synchronizing two devices in a communications channel by means of separate physical circuits, which are used to send signals indicating that a device is ready to receive data. Compare *software handshaking,* in which this task is performed by inserting information into the data stream. See *CTS/RTS.*

hardware panning   A *video adapter* feature that enables it to simulate a *display* larger than the one to which the video adapter is connected. By having extra *video memory* and being capable of changing the portion of video memory designated as the *frame buffer,* a video adapter enables you to drag the *mouse* to the edge of the screen and scroll into other parts of a large "virtual" display.

hardware platform   A *hardware* standard, such as *IBM PC-compatible* or *Macintosh.* Devices or programs created for one platform cannot run on others. See *device independence* and *platform independent.*

hardware reset   Restarting the system by pushing the computer's *hardware reset switch.* A hardware reset might be necessary after a system *crash* so severe that you can't use the keyboard restart command (in DOS, Ctrl+Alt+Del) to restart the computer. See *hard boot, soft boot* and *warm boot.*

hardware reset switch   A switch or button, generally located on the front of the computer's case, that initiates a *hardware reset* (synonymous with *hard boot*).

hardware sprite   A *video adapter* feature that enables the video adapter to draw a *cursor* or mouse *pointer* on the *display* without having to redraw the entire screen. Hardware sprites, included in all video standards since the late-1980s *eXtended Graphics Array (XGA)* adapter, make *programming* easier because programs can move the cursor or pointer with very simple commands.

hardware tree   In Microsoft Windows 95, a graphical representation of the various devices and adapters installed in a computer. It's visible in the System dialog box (from the Control Panel).

hardware windowing   A method of improving video performance, employed by most *graphics accelerator boards.* A hardware windowing design is particularly well suited to *multitasking* environments, such as *Microsoft Windows 95* or *IBM's Operating System/2 (OS/2),* because it keeps track of the screen area (or window) in which each program runs. Besides freeing the *central processing unit (CPU)* from managing windows, hardware windowing systems enable the graphics accelerator board to work faster because it has to alter only the window in which a change occurs, not the whole screen.

hard-wired   Built into the computer's electronic circuits instead of facilitated by *program* instructions. To improve computer performance, computer designers include circuits that perform specific functions, such as multiplication or division, at higher speeds. These functions are hard-wired. The term hard-wired also refers to the program instructions contained in the computer's *read-only memory (ROM)* or *firmware.*

hash   1. An identifying value produced by performing a numerical operation called a *hash function* on a data item. The value uniquely identifies the data item but requires far less storage space. For this reason, the computer can search for hash values more quickly than it can search for the longer data items themselves. A *hash table* associates each hash value with a unique data item. 2. An identifying value that is used to verify the *data integrity* of messages transmitted over a computer network. Using a secret algorithm, the sending computer computes the hash value for the message. This value constitutes, in effect, a digital fingerprint for the message, since the hash value is uniquely a product of the message's content. In addition, the hashing algorithm cannot be derived from the message content or the hash value (see *one-way hash function*). The message and the hash value are then transmitted. The receiving computer, which also knows the secret hash algorithm, performs the same computation on the message. If the resulting hash value does not agree with the value received from the sending computer, then it is proved that the message was altered en route and it is discarded.

hash function   In *databases,* a calculation performed on the *key* of a *data record* that produces a value, called a *hash* value, which uniquely identifies the record. The hash function records the hash value, as well as a *pointer* to the record's physical location, in a *hash table*.

hash mark   See *hash sign*.

hash sign   Common slang expression for the pound symbol (#). Synonymous with hash mark.

hash table   In *databases,* a table of *hash* values that provides rapid access to *data records*. The hash values are generated by running a *hash function* on the *keys* of each record, such as a person's last name. The hash function uniquely identifies each record, and the hash table includes *pointers* to each record.

hat   Common slang expression for the *caret* symbol (^).

Hayes command set   A standardized set of instructions used to control *modems,* introduced by Hayes, a pioneering modem manufacturer. Common Hayes commands include the following:

AT	Attention (used to start all commands)
ATDT	Attention, dial-in tone mode
ATDP	Attention, dial-in pulse mode
+++	Enter the command mode during the communication session
ATH	Attention, hang up

Hayes-compatible modem   A *modem* that recognizes the *Hayes command set*.

HDD An acronym for *hard disk drive* frequently used in advertisements.

head See *read/write head*.

head access aperture The opening in a *floppy disk's shell* that enables the *read/write head* to work with the recording medium. In *3¹/₂-inch floppy disks*, a sliding metal shutter covers the head access aperture, but *5¹/₄-inch disks* expose the head access aperture whenever the disk is out of its protective sleeve.

head actuator In a *disk drive*, a mechanism that moves the assembly containing the *read/write heads* across the surface of the disk to the location where data is to be written or read. See *random access* and *sequential access.*

head arm In a *disk drive,* a rigid mechanical rod with a *read/write head* flexibly connected at one end and attached to a single moving assembly on the other end. Several head arms, one for each side of each platter in a hard disk, are attached to the same assembly so they can move as a unit.

G
H
I

head crash In a hard disk, the collision of a *read/write head* with the surface of the disk, generally caused by a sharp jolt to the computer's case, and resulting in damage to the disk surface and possibly to the head.

header 1. In word processing, repeated text, such as a page number and a short version of a document's title, that appears at the top of the pages in a document. 2. In computer networking, the portion of a data *packet* that precedes the data and provides information about the packet's source and destination. 3. In *e-mail* or a *Usenet* news *article,* the beginning of a message. The header contains important information about the sender's address, the subject of the message, and other information. 4. In programming, a preceding line that states the purpose of a program, function, or subroutine.

head–mounted display (HMD) A stereoscopic set of head-mounted goggles that produce a sensation of three-dimensional space. Head-mounted displays are an integral part of *virtual reality* systems, in which users feel as though they're exploring a real world that has actually been created within the computer system. See *stereoscopy.*

head parking Positioning the *read/write head* over the *landing zone* to prevent a *head crash,* in which the head strikes and usually damages the disk surface. Older hard disks required you to issue a command to park the head; newer hard disks feature *automatic head parking.*

head seek time   See *access time.*

head slot   See *head access aperture.*

heap   1. A section of memory that an operating system or application sets aside for storing a certain type of data. 2. In programming, a list of data that is sorted only partially, but enough so that a given value can be located more quickly than would be the case for a completely unsorted list.

heat sink   A finned metal assembly that sits on top of a hot component, such as a *microprocessor,* and draws heat out of it, preventing it from overheating. *Pentium* microprocessors get very hot and often need a heat sink—and sometimes a CPU fan—to keep cool.

heavy client   In a *client/server* network, a complex *client* program that is difficult to learn, expensive to maintain, and restricted in its flexibility. See *light client.*

helper program   In a *Web browser,* a supplementary program that enables the browser to handle *multimedia* files, such as animations, videos, and sounds. When the browser encounters a file it cannot read, it examines the file's *extension.* The browser then consults a lookup table that tells it which helper program to start. Users must configure this lookup table manually and make sure that the necessary helper programs are installed. When the helper program starts, it runs as a separate program, unlike *plugins*, which extend the capabilities of the browser and can often display the multimedia data within the browser window.

Helvetica   A *sans serif typeface* frequently used for *display type* and occasionally for *body type.* One of the world's most widely used *fonts,* Helvetica is included in many *laser printers* as a *built-in font.* The following are examples of Helvetica type:

ABCDEFGHIJKLMNOPQRSTUVWXYZ
abcdefghijklmnopqrstuvwxyz1234567890

Hercules Graphics Adapter   A *monochrome display adapter* for *IBM PC-compatible* computers. The Hercules Graphics Adapter displays text and graphics on a monochrome *monitor* with a resolution of 720 *pixels* horizontally and 320 lines vertically. Hercules adapters are obsolete but were prized in their heyday for the fine graphics resolution they made possible on monochrome monitors. See *Monochrome Display Adapter (MDA)*.

hertz (Hz)   A unit of measurement of electrical vibrations; one Hz is equal to one cycle per second. See *megahertz (MHz)*.

heterogeneous network   A computer network that includes computers and devices from several manufacturers and transmits data using more than one communications *protocol*.

heuristic   A method of solving a problem by using rules of thumb acquired from experience. Unlike an *algorithm,* a heuristic cannot guarantee a solution, but it may provide the only way to approach a complex problem. See *expert system* and *knowledge base.*

Hewlett–Packard Graphics Language (HPGL)   A *page description language (PDL)* and *file format* for graphics printing with the HP LaserJet line of printers, HP *plotters,* and high-end *inkjet printers,* now widely emulated by HP-compatible laser printers. See *Hewlett-Packard Printer Control Language (HPPCL).*

Hewlett–Packard Printer Control Language (HPPCL)
The proprietary *printer control language (PCL)* that Hewlett-Packard introduced in 1984 with the company's first LaserJet printer. Like the *Hayes command set* in the *modem* world, HPPCL has become a standard.

hex   See *hexadecimal.*

hexadecimal   A numbering system that uses a base (radix) of 16. Unlike decimal numbers (base 10), hexadecimal numbers include 16 digits: 0, 1, 2, 3, 4, 5, 6, 7, 8, 9, A, B, C, D, E, and F. Although *binary* numbers are ideally suited to the devices used in computers, they are inconvenient and hard to read. Binary numbers grow long quickly; for example, 16 is 1000 in binary and 10 in hexadecimal format. Therefore, *programmers* use hexadecimal numbers as a convenient way to represent binary numbers. A *byte* is conveniently represented as two consecutive hexadecimal numbers.

G
H
I

Hexadecimal	Decimal	Binary
0	0	0000
1	1	0001
2	2	0010
3	3	0011
4	4	0100
5	5	0101
6	6	0110
7	7	0111
8	8	1000
9	9	1001
A	10	1010
B	11	1011
C	12	1100
D	13	1101
E	14	1110
F	15	1111

hidden character   In word processing, a character formatted with a special style that makes it invisible when printed.

hidden codes   The hidden text formatting codes embedded in a document by a word processing program. In the main, these codes are proprietary, which explains why the files created by one word processing program cannot be read by another unless a *conversion utility* is used.

hidden file   A *file* with the hidden attribute set so that when users view a directory by using the DIR command, the file name isn't displayed. You can't erase or copy hidden files.

hierarchical file system   In an *operating system,* a method of organizing files in a *tree structure.* The top-most level, called the *root directory,* contains leaves, called *subdirectories,* which can in turn contain further subdirectories. When uppercase, refers to a Macintosh; see *Hierarchical File System (HFS).*

Hierarchical File System (HFS)   A *Macintosh* disk storage system, designed for use with *hard disks*, that stores files within folders so only a short list of files appears in *dialog boxes*.

hierarchy   1. A method of organizing data so that the most general category is at the top of the list; beneath this category are second-level subcategories, each of which may contain additional subcategories. See *hierarchical file system*. 2. In *Usenet,* a category of *newsgroups*. Within the standard newsgroups, for example, seven hierarchies exist: *comp, misc, news, rec, sci, soc,* and *talk*. The term *hierarchies* suggests the way that newsgroups are internally categorized. For example, the rec.★ hierarchy includes many newsgroups pertaining to hobbies and recreation; the rec.comics.★ hierarchy contains several newsgroups for comic collectors; and the rec.comics.elfquest newsgroup focuses on Wendy and Richard Pini's Elfquest comics. See *alt hierarchy, local newsgroup hierarchies,* and *standard newsgroup hierarchies*.

G
H
I

high bit   In a *binary number,* the *most significant bit (msb)*. This is the left-most digit in a standard binary number.

high density   A *floppy disk* storage technique that uses extremely fine-grained magnetic particles. High-density disks are more expensive to manufacture than *double-density* disks but can store $1M$ or more of information on one $5^{1}/_{4}$- or $3^{1}/_{2}$-inch disk. Synonymous with *quad density*.

high-density disk   See *floppy disk*.

High-Density Multimedia CD (HDMMCD)   See *MMCD*.

high end   An expensive product at the top of a firm's offerings that includes features or capabilities likely to be needed only by the most discriminating users or professionals. See *low end*.

higher-order characters   See *extended character set*.

high-level format   A formatting operation that creates the *boot record, file allocation table (FAT),* and *root directory* on a bootable disk.

high-level programming language   A *programming language* such as *BASIC* or *Pascal* that provides a level of abstraction above *assembly language*, so that programmers can write using more readable instructions (such as FOR NEXT or PRINT). High-level programming languages enable programmers to create programs more quickly and easily than assembly language, but the program must be translated into assembly language by an *interpreter* or *compiler,* resulting in varying losses of efficiency.

highlight   A character, word, text block, or command displayed in *reverse video,* indicating the current *selection.*

highlighting   The process of marking characters or command names in *reverse video* on–screen. Synonymous with selecting.

high/low/close/open (HLCO) graph   In *presentation graphics,* a *line graph* in which a stock's high value, low value, closing price, and *open price* are displayed. The graph aligns the x-axis (categories) horizontally and the y-axis (values) vertically. Another application for a high/low/open/close graph is a record of daily minimum, maximum, and average temperatures. Synonymous with *HLCO chart.* See *column graph* and *line graph.*

high memory   See *high memory area.*

high memory area (HMA)   In a DOS computer, the first 64K of *extended memory* above 1M. Programs that conform to the *eXtended Memory Specification (XMS)* can use HMA as a direct extension of *conventional memory.* In *MS-DOS* versions 5.0 and higher, most of the portions of DOS that you formerly had to load into conventional memory can be loaded into the high memory area by placing the command DOS=HIGH in the *CONFIG.SYS* file.

High Performance Computing Act of 1991   A U.S. federal legislative act that is intended to promote the development of gigabit networking (*wide area networks (WANs)* capable of transferring a billion or more bits of information per second). The act calls for the construction of the *National Research and Education Network (NREN),* the purpose of which is to link several supercomputer research centers. The act created the High Performance Computing and Communications (HPCC) program, which brings together several federal agencies in support of high-performance computing.

high resolution   In computer systems, using a sufficient number of *pixels* in *monitors* or *dots per inch (dpi)* when printing to produce well-defined text characters as well as smoothly defined curves in graphic images. The standards for what constitutes high resolution change as technology advances. Currently, a high-resolution video adapter and monitor can display 1,024 pixels horizontally by 768 lines vertically; a high-resolution printer can print at least 300 dpi. See *low resolution*.

high-rez   Slang for *high resolution*.

High Sierra   An obsolete standard for encoding data onto *CD-ROMs*. Although based on to High Sierra, the widely used *ISO 9660* standard is incompatible with it.

high-speed modem   A *modem* that transfers data at or near the highest possible speed enabled by current *modulation protocols*. The standard for what constitutes high speed changes as technology advances. At this writing, the term is used for modems capable of transferring data at speeds of at least 28,800 *bps*.

High Speed Technology (HST)   A *proprietary* data transmission standard developed by U.S. Robotics for *modems*. HST allows for data transmission at 14,400 *bits per second (bps)* in the direction in which the most data is moving and 450 bps in the other direction. The universally accepted *V.32bis* protocol has replaced HST, which is obsolete.

HIMEM.SYS   An *MS-DOS device driver* that configures *extended memory* and the *high memory area (HMA)* so that programs conforming to the *eXtended Memory Standard (XMS)* can access it. See *CONFIG.SYS, eXtended Memory Specification (XMS)* and *upper memory area*.

hint   In *X Windows*, a request for the modification of an object's properties (such as window size), that the window management software will try to fulfill, if possible.

hinting   In digital *typography*, reducing the weight (thickness) of a *typeface* so that small-sized *fonts* print without blurring or losing detail on 300-*dots per inch (dpi)* printers.

histogram   A *stacked column graph* in which you place the columns close together to emphasize differences in the data items within each stack. By stacking data in a column, you emphasize the contribution that each data item makes to the whole (as in a *pie graph*). By placing the columns next to each other, you lead the viewer to compare the relative proportions of one data item as it varies from column to column.

history list   In a Web browser, a window that shows all the Web sites that the browser has accessed during a given period, such as the last 30 days.

hit   1. In database searching, a *data record* that matches the search criteria. 2. In the *World Wide Web (WWW),* an externally originated request for a specific file, such as a graphic or *HTML* page, by means of the *HyperText Transfer Protocol (HTTP).* Servers record the number of hits a Web site receives, but this is not identical to the number of unique individuals who have accessed the site; because many pages contain graphics, *Java* applets, sounds, and other resources, retrieving one page may require as many as a dozen or more hits. 3. See *cache hit.*

hit rate   In a *cache memory*, the percentage of data requests that result in provision of the requested data. If the data has expired from the cache, it must be retrieved from a slower memory unit, such as a disk drive.

HLCO graph   See *high/low/close/open (HLCO) graph.*

HMA   See *high memory area.*

holy war   A protracted and often incendiary debate within the computing community regarding the merits of a particular computer, operating system, or programming style. The term nicely captures the inflexible and often dogmatic positions that the various participants take in the debate. Famous holy wars include the debate between those who feel that the most significant bit in a unit of represented data should come first (*little-endian*) or last (*big-endian*). Holy wars tend to strike outsiders as ridiculous.

home computer   A *personal computer* specifically designed and marketed for home applications, such as educating children, playing games, balancing a checkbook, paying bills, and controlling lights or appliances.

home directory   In *Unix,* a *directory* that is assigned to a user to store the user's files, including configuration files. Normally, this is the same as the *login directory.*

Home key   A key on computer *keyboards* that, in most programs, moves the cursor to the beginning of the line or the top of the screen. However, the assignment of this key is up to the *programmer.*

home page   1. In any *hypertext* system, including the *World Wide Web (WWW),* a document intended to serve as an initial point of entry to a *web* of related documents. Also called a welcome page, a home page contains general introductory information, as well as *hyperlinks* to related resources. A well-designed home page contains internal *navigation buttons,* which help users find their way among the various documents that the home page makes available.   2. A central information repository for a given subject ("this is the home page for owners of Catalina 27 sailing craft").   3. The *start page* that is automatically displayed when you start a *Web browser* or click the program's Home button.   4. A personal page listing an individual's contact information, and favorite links, and (generally) some information—ranging from cryptic to voluminous—about the individual's perspective on life.

G
H
I

home server   In *Gopher,* the server that the Gopher client program is configured to display automatically when you start the program.

homophone error   A type of spelling error that involves using an incorrect word that sounds the same as the correct word (as in "Two Bee, Oar Knot Too Be"). Although many application programs' spell checking features fail to find homophone errors, grammar checking programs usually do find them.

hook   A feature included in a *software* or *hardware* product to enable hobbyists and *programmers* to add their own custom features. For example, *Microsoft Word* is loaded with hooks that enable experts to create custom *dialog boxes,* which greatly extends the program's functionality for specific applications. In hardware, an *open architecture* system might make it easy to design specialized monitoring tools or improved sound capabilities.

hop   In a *wide area network (WAN),* the path data travels from one *router* to the next. So that the data can reach its destination, several hops may be necessary. This requires processing time, resulting in network *latency.*

horizontal application   A program of such general utility that it can be applied in a wide variety of settings. An example of a horizontal application is a *spreadsheet program* or a *word processing program*. See *vertical application*.

horizontal frequency   A measure (usually in *kilohertz [KHz]*) of how fast a *monitor* draws horizontal lines on its *display*. Unlike *vertical frequency*, horizontal frequency does not vary significantly from one monitor to another. Synonymous with horizontal scan rate and line rate.

horizontal retrace   The process of the electron beam in a *cathode ray tube (CRT)* being directed by the *yoke* from the end of one horizontal scan line to the beginning of the next. *Video adapters* must allow time for horizontal retrace in preparing the video signal.

horizontal scan rate   See *horizontal frequency*.

horizontal scroll bar   See *scroll bar/scroll box*.

host   1. In the *Internet*, any computer that can function as the beginning and end point of data transfers. An Internet host has a unique Internet address (called an *IP address*) and a unique *domain name*. 2. In *networks* and telecommunications generally, a *server* that performs centralized functions, such as making program or data files available to other computers.

host adapter   The *adapter* that transfers data and instructions back and forth between a *hard* or *floppy disk drive controller* and the *central processing unit (CPU)*. Usually an adapter that plugs into the *expansion bus*, the host adapter complies with a specification such as *Integrated Drive Electronics (IDE)*, *Enhanced IDE (EIDE)*, or *Small Computer System Interface (SCSI)*.

HotBot   A *search engine* for *keyword* searches on the *World Wide Web (WWW)*, created by *Wired* magazine, that produces markedly better results when used for *free text searching* than competing search engines. HotBot retrieval lists are generally shorter and contain more *relevant* items than the longer lists produced by *AltaVista* and *Lycos*. To restrict the search further, searches can use *case-sensitive* searching and *phrase searches*.

HotDog   An *HTML editor* published by Sausage Software that offers a number of features attractive to authors of complex sites, including a project manager that automatically opens all the files of a site and uploads them via *FTP* in a manner that preserves their location within the server's directory structure.

hot key   A keyboard shortcut that accesses a menu command. A *shortcut key,* in contrast, gives you direct access to a dialog box or other feature.

hot link   In Object Linking and Embedding *(OLE),* a method of copying information from one document (the *source document*) to another (the *destination document)* so that the target document's information is updated automatically when the source document's information changes.

hotlist   In a *Web browser,* a list of favorite *World Wide Web (WWW) sites* that a user saves for future use while browsing. To retrieve hotlist items, you select the item that you want in a menu or dialog box and then choose the Go To command or its equivalent. In *Netscape Navigator,* the hotlist items are called *bookmarks,* and the hotlist is called the bookmark list. In *Microsoft Internet Explorer,* the preferred term is *favorites* list.

G
H
I

hotlist item   In a *Web browser's hotlist,* a stored *URL* that enables the user to quickly return to the URL just by choosing the item from a menu. Synonymous with *favorite* and *bookmark.*

HoTMetaL   A stand-alone *HTML editor,* created by SoftQuad Systems, for *Microsoft Windows 95* systems. Widely distributed as *shareware,* HoTMetaL is also available in a professional version called HoTMetaL Pro.

housekeeping   Computer maintenance, including organizing files and directories in a logical manner; running utility programs such as *defragmentation* utilities and *virus checkers;* and deleting unneeded files to free up disk space.

HP-compatible printer   A printer that responds to the *Hewlett-Packard printer control language (HPPCL),* which has become the standard for laser printing in the IBM and IBM-compatible computing world.

HPGL   See *Hewlett-Packard Graphics Language.*

HPPC   See *High Performance Computing Act of 1991.*

HPPCL   See *Hewlett-Packer Printer Control Language.*

HTML Acronym for *HyperText Markup Language*. A *declarative language* for marking the portions of a document (called *elements*) so that, when accessed by a program called a *Web browser*, each portion appears with a distinctive format. HTML is the markup language behind the appearance of documents on the *World Wide Web (WWW)*. HTML is standardized by means of a *document type definition (DTD)* composed in the *Standard Generalized Markup Language (SGML)*. HTML includes capabilities that enable authors to insert *hyperlinks*, which when clicked display another HTML document. The agency responsible for standardizing HTML is the *World Wide Web Consortium (W3C)*.

HTML 1.0 The original *HTML* specification, drafted in 1990. Because it contains certain *tags* that are no longer used, this specification is considered obsolete. The *HTML 3.2* specification is now considered authoritative. Also known as HTML Level 1.

HTML 2.0 A now-obsolete *HTML* specification that described HTML practice, as of mid-1994, and formalizes these practices as an *Internet Draft*. The major updates from *HTML 1.0* are the inclusion of forms and the removal of certain little-used *tags*. The HTML 2.0 specification does not include many practices, such as tables and the *Netscape extensions*, that have arisen since its release.

HTML 3.0 A proposed *HTML* specification that would have greatly extended HTML relative to the 2.0 standard. However, this specification did not line up well enough with prevailing Web practice and has been superseded by the current recommended standard, 3.2.

HTML 3.2 The HTML specification that is (at this writing) recommended by the *World Wide Web Consortium (W3C)*, the organization responsible for standardizing Web practices. HTML incorporates many widely used and called-for features, including tables, subscript and superscript characters, text flow around images, *Java* applets, and *style sheets*. See *Cougar*.

HTML editor A program that provides assistance in preparing documents for the *World Wide Web (WWW)* using the *HTML*. The simplest HTML editor is a word processing program that enables you to type text and add HTML *tags* manually. Standalone HTML editors provide automated assistance with HTML coding and display some formats on-screen. See *HoTMetaL* and *HotDog*.

HTTP   The *Internet* standard that supports the exchange of information on the *World Wide Web (WWW)*. By defining *Universal Resource Locators (URLs)* and how they can be used to retrieve resources (including not only Web documents but also *File Transport Protocol [FTP]*-accessible files, *Usenet newsgroups,* and *Gopher* menus) anywhere on the Internet, HTTP enables Web authors to embed *hyperlinks* in Web documents. HTTP defines the process by which a Web client, called a *browser*, originates a request for information and sends it to a *Web server,* a program designed to respond to HTTP requests and provide the desired information. HTTP 1.0, in widespread use, has many shortcomings, including an inefficient design and slow performance. A new specification, HTTP 1.1, directly addresses these issues and will result in improved network performance, but *servers* will have to be updated.

HTTPS   1. A variation on the HTTP protocol that provides *SSL* security for online transactions using the *World Wide Web (WWW)*. 2. A *Web server* for *Microsoft Windows NT* created and maintained by the European Microsoft Windows NT Academic Centre (EMWAC) project, at the University of Edinburgh. The server is available through *anonymous FTP* and incorporates several unique features, such as the capability to search *Wide Area Information Server (WAIS) databases* in response to browser queries.

hub   In a *local area network (LAN),* a device used to create a small-scale network by connecting several computers together.

hub ring   The ring of Teflon or plastic in the center of a $5^1/_2$-*inch floppy disk*. The hub ring, which not all disks have, protects the disk from wear caused by contact with the *spindle*.

Huffman encoding   A *data compression* technique that takes advantage of the fact that computer data contains many repeated patterns. In place of a pattern, an encoding symbol is created that is much shorter than the lengthier pattern. The shortest encoding symbols are used for the longest patterns of data. This is a *lossless compression* technique because, when the user decompresses the data, it is fully restored to its exact state prior to compression.

human-computer interaction (HCI)   An organized field of study that focuses on how people actually use computers and formulates guidelines for user-friendly system design.

hung   Not responding to input. See *crash, hang* and *hung system*.

hung system   A computer that has experienced a system failure and is no longer processing data, even though the cursor might still be blinking on-screen. The only option in most cases is to restart the system, which means losing any unsaved work.

HyperCard   A software product, available with the Apple Macintosh computer, for developing information systems based on *hypertext*. See *HyperTalk*.

hyperlink   In a *hypertext* system, an underlined or otherwise emphasized word or phrase that, when clicked with the *mouse,* displays another document.

hypermedia   A *hypertext* system that employs multimedia resources (graphics, videos, animations, and sounds). The best hypermedia systems employ various media in ways that are more than just "window dressing," but materially support the presentation's objective.

HyperTalk   A *scripting* language provided with *HyperCard,* an accessory program shipped with every Macintosh. HyperTalk is an *event-driven language.* To create a HyperTalk program, you first use HyperCard to create screen objects (cards with text fields, *push buttons,* and other features). You then write short, English-like programs, called *scripts*, that tell HyperCard what to do when the program's user manipulates one of the screen objects. HyperTalk programming is fun and introduces a programming novice to the fundamental principles of the *object-oriented programming (OOP) language.* The language is too slow, however, for professional program development, for which it was never intended. See *SmallTalk*.

hypertext   A method of preparing and publishing text, ideally suited to the computer, in which readers can choose their own paths through the material. To prepare hypertext, you first "chunk" the information into small, manageable units, such as single pages of text. These units are called *nodes.* You then embed *hyperlinks* (also called anchors) in the text. When the reader clicks on a hyperlink, the hypertext software displays a different node. The process of navigating among the nodes linked in this way is called *browsing.* A collection of nodes that are interconnected by hyperlinks is called a *web.* The *World Wide Web (WWW)* is a hypertext system on a global scale. Hypertext applications are particularly useful for working with massive amounts of text, such as encyclopedias and multivolume case law reporters.

HyperText Markup Language   See *HTML*.

HyperText Transfer Protocol   See *HTTP.*

HyperText Transfer Protocol Daemon (httpd)   A *Web server* originally developed at the Swiss *Center for Particle Research (CERN)* and originally called CERN httpd. Subsequently, httpd was developed independently at the *National Center for Super-computing Applications (NCSA)* for Unix systems. An important innovation in the history of Web servers, NASA httpd introduced *forms,* clickable *image maps, authentication,* and *keyword searches.* Most of these features are now taken for granted in other Web servers. An adaptation of the program for *Microsoft Windows 95,* called *Windows httpd,* is available.

hyphenation   In *word processing* and *page layout programs,* an automatic operation that hyphenates words at the end of lines as needed. If you use it carefully and manually confirm each hyphen, a hyphenation utility can improve a document's appearance, especially when you are using *newspaper columns* or large margins. See *hard hyphen, hyphen ladder* and *soft hyphen*.

hyphen ladder   A formatting flaw caused by the repetition of hyphens at the end of two or more lines in a row. Hyphen ladders distract the eye and disrupt the text's readability. If you use automatic hyphenation, proofread the results carefully for hyphen ladders. Adjust word spacing and hyphenation manually, if necessary. Synonymous with *hyphen stack*.

Hytelnet   A *hypertext*-based guide to the *Telnet*-based resources accessible on the Internet, including libraries, *freenets, bulletin board systems (BBS),* and other information sites. A *World Wide Web (WWW)* gateway version is available.

G
H
I

IAB   See *Internet Architecture Board*.

IAC   See *Inter-Application Communication*.

IANA   See *Internet Assigned Numbers Authority*.

I-beam pointer   In Macintosh and *Microsoft Windows* applications, an I-shaped *mouse* pointer that appears when the pointer is moved over a screen area when you can edit text. The I-beam pointer is thin enough that you can position the pointer between characters with precision.

IBM 486SLC2   An energy-saving *microprocessor*, designed by IBM for use in *portable computers*, that is *pin-compatible* with *Intel 486* chips. The 486SLC2 boasts performance on par with the *Intel 486SX*.

IBM 8514   A *video adapter* for IBM Personal System/2 computers that, with the on-board *Video Graphics Array (VGA)* circuitry, produces a resolution of 1024 *pixels* horizontally and 768 lines vertically. The adapter also contains its own processing circuitry that reduces demand on the *central processing unit (CPU)*. The 8514 replaces the 8514/A and MCGA adapters, which have been discontinued. See *Super VGA*.

IBM Blue Lightning   A 32-bit *microprocessor*, introduced in 1993, that is functionally identical to the *Intel 486DX4*.

IBM PC-compatible   Able to run all or almost all the software developed for the IBM Personal Computer, and accepts the IBM computer's cards, adapters, and peripheral devices.

ICCP   See *Institute for Certification of Computer Professionals*.

icon   In a graphical user interface (GUI), an on-screen symbol that represents a *program*, data *file*, or some other computer entity or function. Several icons might appear together on an icon bar, an on-screen row of *buttons*, usually placed just above the document *window*, that enables the user to choose frequently accessed menu options without having to use the *menus*. On each button is an icon that shows the button's function. For example, the Print button might display a tiny picture of a printer.

icon bar   In an application a row of buttons that can be pressed to initiate commands. Synonymous with *toolbar.*

IDE   See *Integrated Drive Electronics.*

IDEA   See *International Data Encryption Algorithm.*

IDE drive   A hard disk that contains most of the control circuitry within the drive itself. Synonymous with AT Attachment drives, IDE drives combine the speed of *Enhanced System Device Interface (ESDI)* drives with the integration of the *Small Computer System Interface (SCSI)* hard drive interface. This performance is offered at a price lower than most ESDI and SCSI drives. See *Integrated Drive Electronics (IDE).*

identifier   In *database management,* a *descriptor* used to specify the uniqueness of the information contained in the data record. For example, in a database of travel films, the descriptor "Norway" might appear in a data record for the only travel films that depict scenery from that country.

**G
H
I**

IEEE 802   A series of telecommunications standards governing *local area networks (LANs).* Established by the *Institute of Electrical and Electronic Engineers (IEEE),* the standards include 10Base2 and 10Base-T cabling, network bridges, and *topologies.* See *bridge, bus network, Ethernet, fiber optics,* and *star network.*

IEEE 1284   A standard developed by the *Institute of Electrical and Electronics Engineers (IEEE)* that governs the design of *bidirectional parallel ports.* Both the *enhanced parallel port (EPP)* and the *extended capabilities port (ECP)* conform to IEEE 1284.

IEEE Computer Society   See *Institute of Electrical and Electronic Engineers Computer Society.*

IESG   See *Internet Engineering Steering Group.*

IETF   See *Internet Engineering Task Force.*

IF/THEN/ELSE   In programming, a structure that conducts a test to see whether a condition is true. If the condition is true, then the program branches to one option; if the condition is false, the program branches to another option. IF/THEN/ELSE structures, with slight variations in the language, are used when writing *macros,* as merge codes, as functions in *spreadsheet* software, and as part of all *high-level programming languages.*

IIOP   See *Internet Inter-ORB Protocol.*

ill-behaved   Poorly designed, inefficient, wasteful of system resources due to fundamental design errors.

illegal character   A character that can't be used according to the syntax rules of command-driven programs and *programming languages.* Such characters usually are reserved for a specific program function. With DOS, for example, you can't assign a *file name* to a *file* if the name includes an asterisk (★). The asterisk is reserved for use as a *wild-card* symbol. Commas, spaces, slashes, and several other punctuation characters also are illegal characters for file names.

Illustrator   See *Adobe Illustrator.*

image compression   The use of a compression technique to reduce the size of *graphics* files, which usually consume inordinate amounts of disk space. A single 100K *grayscale Tagged Image File Format (TIFF)* file can be reduced by as much as 96 percent to 4K or 5K for *telecommunications* or storage purposes. Some graphics programs compress images automatically.

image map   In *HTML,* a graphic that has been coded so that specific regions of the graphic are associated with specific *URLs.* When the user clicks one of these regions, the browser initiates a *hyperlink* jump to the associated document or resource. See *image map utility.*

image map utility   In *HTML,* a program that enables Web publishers to create an image map easily by drawing rectangles, circles, and polygons on the image map graphic and then associating the marked region with a *URL.*

image processing   In *graphics,* the use of a computer to enhance, embellish, or refine a graphic image. Typical processing operations include enhancing or reducing contrast, altering colors so that the image is more easily analyzed, correcting underexposure or overexposure, and outlining objects so they can be identified.

imagesetter   A professional typesetting machine that generates very high-resolution output on photographic paper or film.

imaging model   The method of representing output on-screen. In a *graphical user interface (GUI)*, for example, the imaging model is for the *screen font* to closely resemble the way the text is printed.

IMAP   See *Internet Message Access Protocol.*

IMAP4   Acronym for Internet Message Access Protocol version 4.

IMHO   In a *chat room* or *Usenet,* an *acronym* for In My Humble Opinion.

impact printer   A *printer* that generates output like type-writers, by actually striking the page with something solid. *Daisywheel* and *dot-matrix printers* are impact printers. Impact printers are slow and noisy, but they are inexpensive by printer standards and are necessary for filling out multi-part forms.

G
H
I

import   To load a file created by one program into a different program. See *export.*

include   1. To quote someone's *e-mail* or *Usenet* message within one's own message. 2. To incorporate another file into the current file.

increment   To increase a value. See *decrement.*

incremental backup   A *backup* procedure in which a hard disk *backup utility* backs up only the *files* changed since the last backup procedure. See *archival backup.*

incremental update   See *maintenance release.*

indent style   In a programming language, the conventions used to govern the indentation of lines of code. These indentations make it easier to read the code.

indentation   The *alignment* of a paragraph to the right or left of the document margins.

index   1. In *database management* programs, a file containing information about the physical location of records in a database file. When searching or sorting the database, the program uses the index rather than the full database. Such operations are faster than sorts or searches performed on the actual database. Synonymous with *inverted index*. 2. In *word processing* programs, an appendix to your document you can generate that lists important words, names, and concepts in alphabetical order, and the page numbers where the terms appear. With most word processing programs, you must mark terms to be included in the index the program constructs. See *active index, concordance file, sort,* and *sort order.* 3. On the *World Wide Web (WWW),* a Web page that gathers together the leading or best hyperlinks in a particular topical area.

indexed sequential access method (ISAM) In *hard disks,* a method for accessing data on a hard disk that combines sequential access with indexing, resulting in high access speeds overall. Data that is stored sequentially can be directly accessed without consulting the index.

index hole In a *floppy disk,* a hole that's electro-optically detected by the drive to locate the beginning of the first *sector* on the disk. Few disk drives use the index hole anymore.

indexing The method a *floppy disk drive* uses to locate the *track* on which needed information is located. Indexing involves moving the *read/write head* to the outermost track on a disk and moving inward, one track at a time, until the needed track is reached.

Industry Standard Architecture (ISA) The *expansion bus* design of IBM's AT (Advanced Technology) computer, which uses a 16-bit bus with several 8-bit slots for downward compatibility. The *AT bus* added more than a simple doubling of the width of the data bus. The *address bus* was increased to 24 lines, enough to address 16M of memory. Downward compatibility was assured by adding a supplemental connector to the original 8-bit, 62-pin connector. Several new *interrupt request (IRQ)* lines and *direct memory access (DMA)* control lines were added. See *channel, Extended Industry Standard Architecture, local bus* and *Micro Channel Architecture (MCA).*

Industry Standard Architecture (ISA) expansion bus A generally outmoded 16-bit *expansion bus* design developed in the early 1980s. The ISA expansion bus can transfer data at 8M per second and was adequate for connecting adapters to the *central* *processing unit (CPU)* until, in the early 1990s, microprocessor performance created an *expansion bus bottleneck* with the ISA standard.

industry standard interface   A *user interface* that includes the windowing features made popular by the Apple Macintosh, including sizable windows, pull-down or click-down menus, dialog boxes, and the use of the mouse for interface control.

infection   The presence of a *virus* within a computer system or on a disk. The infection may not be obvious to the user; many viruses, for example, remain in the background until a specific time and date, when they display prank messages or erase data. See *Trojan horse* and *worm*.

infinite loop   In *programming,* a *loop* whose condition for terminating is never fulfilled. For example, a loop designed to add 5 to an integer variable until the variable equaled 133.2 would never end—at least not until a *crash* occurred or the computer was *rebooted.*

G
H
I

infix notation   In computer programming languages, a *syntax* preference in which functions or operators are placed between *operands* (such as a + b). See *prefix notion* and *Reverse Polish Notation (RPN).*

Infobahn   A term preferred by some for the so-called *Information Superhighway,* a high-speed information system that would link homes, schools, and offices with high-bandwidth local delivery systems and backbone systems capable of gigabit-per-second speeds.

information   Data—whether in the form of numbers, graphics, or words—that has been organized, systematized, and presented so that the underlying patterns become clear. The temperature, humidity, and wind reports from hundreds of weather stations are data; a computer simulation that shows how this data predicts a strong possibility of tornadoes is information.

information kiosk   See *kiosk.*

information service   See *bibliographic retrieval service, BBS* and *online information service.*

Information Superhighway   An envisioned information infrastructure that will bring high-speed computer networking within the reach of homes, schools, and offices. The term is misleading in that the freeways, high-speed backbone networks, already exist; what is lacking is a good system of local roads. The current telephone system does not have the bandwidth to deliver high-speed digital services to the home; a capital investment on the order of $325 billion would be necessary to replace the existing telephone lines with high-speed fiber optic cables. The replacement will occur, but we will be decades into the 21st century before it is complete.

Infoseek A *search engine* for *keyword* searches on the *World Wide Web (WWW)*, created by Infoseek Corporation. Searchers can choose from Ultraseek, an unusually capable Web search engine, or Ultrasmart, which displays links to subject categories that are possibly relevant to the supplied search keywords. The search engine is capable of *case-sensitive* searches, *automatic name recognition, field-based searches, phrase searching,* and automatic detection of word variants.

infrared port A port that enables a PC to exchange data with infrared-capable *portable computers* or *peripheral* devices, without using cables. Usually created by attaching a *dongle* to a *serial port,* infrared ports can move data at more than 115,000 *bits per second (bps).*

inheritance In *object-oriented programming,* the ability of newly created *objects* to take on the *properties* of existing objects.

INIT In the Macintosh environment, a *utility program* that executes during a system start or restart, such as SuperClock, which displays the current system date and time in the *menu bar,* and Adobe Type Manager, which uses outline-font technology to display Adobe *screen fonts.*

initial In *typography,* an enlarged letter at the beginning of a chapter or paragraph. Initials set down within the copy are *drop caps,* and initials raised above the top line of the text are stickup initials.

initial base font The *font* used by *word processing programs* for all documents unless you instruct otherwise. The initial base font is part of the *printer* definition. Whenever you select a different printer, the initial base font may change.

initialization 1. In *modems,* the establishment of an *active configuration* that, in whole or in part, supersedes the *factory* *configuration.* By using an *initialization string,* you can configure the modem to work well with your *communications program.*

2. In disks, the process of *formatting* a hard disk and floppy disks so that they are ready for use.

initialization string   In *modems,* a group of *AT commands,* issued to the modem by a *communications program* at the beginning of a communication session, that establishes an *active configuration.* Initialization strings enable communications programs to work smoothly with a variety of modems, and often you can choose an initialization string appropriate for your modem from a list provided in your communications program. See *initialization.*

initialize   To prepare *hardware* or *software* to perform a task. A *serial port* is initialized using the MODE command to set the *baud, parity, data,* and *stop bit* values, for example. In some programs, initializing can be setting a counter or *variable* to zero before running a procedure.

inkjet printer   A *non-impact printer* that forms an image by spraying ink from a matrix of tiny jets.

inline   In typography, placed within or directly adjacent to lines of text. See *in-line image.*

in-line image   A graphic that has been placed so that it appears on the same line with text. In *HTML,* in-line images are defined by the IMG tag, which specifies the source of the graphic, its alignment (top, middle, or bottom), and the text to display if the document is accessed by a text-only browser.

in-order execution   In a *reduced instruction set computer (RISC)* architecture, a method of providing programs with a means of ensuring that specific instructions are carried out in a specified order.

in-place activation   In Object Linking and Embedding *(OLE)* in *Microsoft Windows 95,* the use of a *server application's* functions within the *client application,* without the need to switch to a *window* containing the server application.

input   Any *information* entered into a computer.

input device   Any *peripheral* that assists you in getting data into a computer, such as a *keyboard, mouse, trackball, voice recognition* system, *graphics tablet,* or *modem.*

input/output (I/O) redirection   In DOS and *Unix,* the routing of a program's *output* to a *file* or device, or the routing of a program's input from a file rather than the *keyboard.* Most DOS commands (such as DIR) send output to the screen, but you can easily redirect a command's output by using the greater–than sign (>). To redirect the output of DIR to the LPT1 (printer) port, for example, you type DIR > lpt1 and press Enter. To redirect the command's output to a file, type DIR > dir.txt and press Enter. In DOS, input redirection is frequently used with filters. See *filter* and *MS-DOS.*

input/output (I/O) system   One of the chief components of a computer system's architecture, the link between the *microprocessor* and its surrounding components.

Insert (Ins) key   On IBM PC–compatible *keyboards,* a programmable key frequently (but not always) used to toggle between *insert mode* and *overtype mode* when entering text.

insertion point   In Macintosh and *Microsoft Windows* applications, the blinking vertical bar that shows the point at which text will appear when you start typing. The insertion point is similar to the *cursor* in DOS applications.

insert mode   In *word processing programs,* a program mode in which inserted text pushes existing text to the right and down. The Insert key is used to toggle between insert and *overtype modes.*

installation program   A *utility program* provided with an *application* that helps you install the program on a *hard disk* and configure the program so you can use it.

instantiate   To create an *instantiation.*

instantiation   In *object-oriented programming (OOP) language,* to produce a completed *object* by filling in values in place of variables in a *class* template.

Institute for Certification of Computer Professionals (ICCP)   An organization that sanctions examinations that establish professional competence in various computer fields. The ICCP awards data processing and computer programming certification, making people who pass its examinations *Certified Data Processors (CDPs)* and *Certified Computer Programmers (CCPs).*

Though ICCP certification is recognized as a professional achievement, it is rarely required for employment or for the awarding of a contract.

Institute of Electrical and Electronic Engineers (IEEE) A membership organization of engineers, scientists, and students; the largest technical society in the world, with more than 300,000 members worldwide. IEEE has also declared standards for computers and communications. Of particular interest is the *IEEE 802* standard for local area networks, although the IEEE drew up a complete set of specifications for the *AT bus,* also called the ISA bus. See *Industry Standard Architecture (ISA).*

Institute of Electrical and Electronic Engineers Computer Society (IEEE Computer Society) A part of the *Institute of Electrical and Electronic Engineers (IEEE)* that specializes in computer issues. The IEEE Computer Society holds conferences and sponsors publications on computer-related topics.

instruction In *programming,* a program statement interpreted or compiled into *machine language.* See *interpreter* and *compiler.*

instruction cycle The time it takes a *central processing unit (CPU)* to carry out one instruction and move on to the next.

instruction mnemonic In *assembly language,* an abbreviation that represents a machine instructions, such as ADD or MOVE.

instruction set A list of keywords describing all the actions or operations that a *central processing unit (CPU)* can perform. See *complex instruction set computer (CISC)* and *reduced instruction set computer (RISC).*

integer A whole number. If a number contains decimal places, the numbers to the left of the decimal point are the integer portion of the number.

integrated accounting package An *accounting package* that includes all the major accounting functions: general ledger, accounts payable, accounts receivable, payroll, and inventory. Integrated programs update the general ledger every time an accounts payable or accounts receivable transaction occurs.

integrated circuit (IC) A *semiconductor* that contains more than one electronic component. Synonymous with chip. An

G
H
I

integrated circuit is fabricated on a wafer of silicon. To produce the resistance differentials that produce the effect of separate electronic components, such as transistors, areas of the wafer are differentially mixed, in a procedure called *doping,* with other elements. The first ICs offered the equivalent of a few transistors, but improvements in IC design and manufacturing have brought about spectacular improvements in circuit density (today's *microprocessors* contain as many as ten million transistors). See *Small Scale Integration (SSI), large-scale integration (LSI),* and *very large scale integration (VLSI).*

Integrated Drive Electronics (IDE)   A *hard disk interface* standard for 80286, 80386, 80486, and Pentium computers that offers high performance at low cost. The IDE standard transfers most of the controller electronics to the hard disk assembly. For this reason, the IDE interface can be contained on the computer's motherboard; no *controller card* or expansion slot is necessary. See *IDE drive.*

integrated program   A *program* that combines two or more software functions, such as *word processing* and *database management.* Microsoft Works and ClarisWorks are examples of integrated programs.

Integrated Services Digital Network (ISDN)   See *ISDN.*

Intel   The world's largest manufacturer of *microprocessors* and other *semiconductors,* based in Santa Clara, California. About three-fourths of the world's *microcomputers* have Intel *central processing units (CPUs).* Intel faces competition from several companies, including *Advanced Micro Devices (AMD), Cyrix,* and *NexGen.*

Intel 386DX   See *Intel 80386.*

Intel 386SL   A power-conserving variation of the *Intel 386SX* designed with *power management* features for use in *portable computers.* The 386SL includes a *sleep mode* that preserves work, while using very little electricity, during periods of disuse.

Intel 386SX   A slower but less expensive version of the *Intel 80386 microprocessor.* The 386SX uses a 16-bit *external data bus,* compared with the 386DX's 32-bit data pathway. The 386SX can address only 20M of *random-access memory (RAM),* compared to the 386DX's ability to handle 4G of RAM.

Intel 4004   The first microprocessor, a 4-bit processor released in 1971, and containing the equivalent of 2,300 transistors.

Intel 486DX   A *32-bit microprocessor* that dominated the PC market prior to the introduction of the *Pentium*. Introduced in 1989, the 486DX offers a significant speed improvement over the Intel *386DX,* its predecessor. By using *pipelining* and an on-board *numeric coprocessor,* the 486DX can manage 4*G* of *random-access memory (RAM)* and 64*T* of *virtual memory.* The two versions of the 486DX operate at *clock speeds* of 25 *megahertz (MHz)* and 33 MHz, though *clock-doubled* and *clock-tripled* versions operate at higher clock speeds. See *Intel 486DX2, Intel 486DX4* and *Intel 486SX.*

Intel 486DX2   An improved version of the *Intel 486DX* that uses *clock-doubling* techniques to achieve *clock speeds* inside the *microprocessor* of 50 *megahertz (MHz)* or 66 MHz, while the microprocessor is installed on a *motherboard* running at half the chip's clock speed (25 MHz or 33 MHz, respectively). Though the performance of the microprocessor far outstrips the perfor-mance of the motherboard, good *external cache* design can mini-mize the time a clock-doubled microprocessor spends waiting for the motherboard to catch up with it.

Intel 486DX4   An improved version of the *Intel 486DX micro-processor* that, by means of *clock tripling,* operates at *clock speeds* of 75 *megahertz (MHz)* or 100 MHz. The 486DX4 boasts a larger *internal cache* than other 486s, and operates at 3.3 volts instead of 5 volts.

Intel 486SL   A power-saving version of the *Intel 486DX micro-processor.* Designed for *portable computers,* the 486SL includes a *sleep mode* that lets you stop working and start again later with-out having to *reboot.*

Intel 486SX   A 32-bit *microprocessor* based on the *Intel 486DX,* but without the 486DX's *numeric coprocessor.* Designed to be a slower but more affordable alternative to the 486DX, the two versions of the 486SX run at *clock speeds* of 20 *megahertz (MHz)* and 25 MHz.

Intel 8080   The *8-bit microprocessor* found in the Altair, a popu-lar 1970s *microcomputer.* The Intel 8080, which runs at a *clock speed* of 2 *MHz,* has a 16-bit address bus and can handle one-half million instructions per second. Introduced in 1974, Intel 8080 was obsolete by the early 1980s; however, its odd and

error-prone memory addressing architecture continues to influ-
ence Intel microprocessor design to this day because Intel is
committed to ensuring that their newer microprocessors are
downwardly compatible with previous ones

Intel 8086   A *16-bit microprocessor,* introduced in 1978, that was
based on the architecture of the *Intel 8080* and retained downward compatibility with code designed for that chip. Because the
8086 can process two bytes of data at a time, in contrast to 8-bit
processors (which can process only one byte of data at a time), it
was considerably faster than previous Intel chips. However, the
8086 did not find widespread use due to the high cost and low
availability of 16-bit peripherals in the early 1980s. See *Intel
8088.*

Intel 8088   Essentially an *Intel 8086* with an 8-bit data bus, the
4.77 megahertz (MHz) Intel 8088 was the engine in the earliest
IBM personal computers. Though it was a 16-bit *microprocessor,*
the 8088's 8-bit data bus enabled computer manufacturers to use
inexpensive, off-the-shelf 8-bit *peripherals.* Introduced in 1979,
the 8088 powered the hugely successful IBM PC, introduced in
1981.

Intel 80186   A *32-bit microprocessor,* operating at 6 MHz and
introduced in 1981, that is functionally very similar to the *Intel
8086* (both chips employ a 16-bit internal and external data
bus), but includes additional functions that previously had to be
parceled out to expensive support chips, such as timers, *DMA*
channels, and interrupt controllers. Motherboards created with
the 80186 could use up to 22 fewer support chips than 8086
motherboards. Because the technically superior *Intel 80286*
microprocessor appeared shortly after the 80186's introduction,
it saw very little use.

Intel 80286   The now obsolete *16-bit microprocessor* that was
used in the IBM Personal Computer AT, unveiled in 1984, and
compatible computers. Introduced in 1982, the 80286 operates
at *clock speeds* as fast as 20 *MHz.* The 80286 represents an attempt
to overcome the memory-addressing limitations of the previous
80x6 architecture, which was limited to a maximum of 1MB of
RAM. By switching from the 80x6-compatible *real mode* into
a new mode, called the *protected mode,* the chip could use up to
16MB of *random-access memory (RAM).* Unfortunately, the 80286
cannot switch between these two modes without *rebooting*—a

serious design flaw that led to the 80286's replacement by the Intel 80386.

Intel 80386   A *32-bit microprocessor* that helped to launch the Windows era. Thanks to its incorporation of advanced memory management circuitry, the Intel 80386 enables programs to switch from *real mode* to *protected mode* without *rebooting;* in short, the Intel 80386 made protected-mode operating systems and applications possible for the first time. The chip's 32-bit *address bus* lets it manage as much as 4G of *random-access memory (RAM)* and 64T of *virtual memory.* Various versions of the 80386 run at *clock speeds* of 16 *megahertz (MHz),* 20 MHz, 25 MHz, and 33 MHz. Introduced in 1985, the 80386 was renamed the Intel 386DX when the *Intel 386SX* (a cheaper version of the microprocessor, with a 16-bit data bus) was introduced.

Intel 80486   A *32-bit microprocessor,* released in 1989 and down-wardly compatible with the *Intel 80386,* that incorporates certain design improvements, such as a larger *primary cache* and a built-in *math co-processor.* After Intel found that it could not protect the 80x86 numbering system from use by other semiconductor manufacturers, the company switched to a different numbering scheme; the original 80486 was renamed *Intel 846DX.* Synonymous with i486 and iAPX 80486.

Intel 80x86   Generic name for the family of *Intel* CISC *(complex instruction set computer)* microprocessors that dominates the personal computer marketplace. See *Intel 80186, Intel 80286, Intel 80386, Intel 80486, Pentium, Pentium Pro* and *Pentium II.*

intellectual property   Ideas, as well as the tangible expression of those ideas, that uniquely derive from an individual's painstaking intellectual efforts. Society cannot expect creative individuals, such as artists and inventors, to create intellectual property without some means of protecting the fruits of their efforts; this protection is given by copyrights and patents. In areas of high technology such as computing, however, the authorities responsible for granting patents may make errors in distinguishing between genuine intellectual property and well-established ideas that must remain in the *public domain* if technological progress is to continue.

Intel Pentium   See *Pentium, Pentium Pro* and *Pentium II.*

interactive   Able to engage in a dialogue with the user, generally by means of a text-based interface.

interactive processing   A method displaying the computer's operations on a monitor so the user can catch and correct errors before the processing operation is completed.

interactive videodisk   A *computer-assisted instruction (CAI)* technology that uses a computer to provide access to up to two hours of video information stored on a videodisk. Like *CD-ROM,* videodisks are *read-only* optical storage media, but are designed for the storage and *random-access* retrieval of images, including stills and continuous video. You need a *front-end* program to access the videodisk information. With a videodisk of paintings in the National Gallery of Art, the user can demand, "Show me all the Renaissance paintings that depict flowers or gardens," and be led through a series of vivid instructional experiences while retaining complete control.

Inter–Application Communication (IAC)   In the Macintosh *System 7,* a specification for creating *hot links* and *cold links* between applications.

interface   1. The connection between two *hardware* devices, between two *applications,* or between different sections of a computer *network.* 2. The portion of a program that interacts with the user.

interface standard   A set of specifications for the connection between the two *hardware* devices, such as the drive controller and the drive electronics in a hard disk. Common hard disk interface standards in personal computing include ST506, *Enhanced System Device Interface (ESDI),* and *Small Computer System Interface (SCSI).* Other standards exist for connections with serial and parallel ports, such as the *Centronics interface.* See *ST-506/ST-412.*

Interior Gateway Protocol   An *Internet* standard (*protocol*) that governs the routing of data within an *autonomous system (AS)*—a network or group of networks that is under a single administrator's control.

interlaced   See *interlacing.*

interlaced GIF   A *GIF* graphic saved to a special file format (defined by the GIF 89a standard) that enables a graphics program or Web browser to display a rough, out-of-focus version of the graphic immediately. Other page elements, such as text, can appear while the graphic's details are being filled in.

interlacing   1. A method of displaying or transferring information so that the rough contours are sketched out immediately; subsequently, the details are sketched in. See *interlaced GIF.* 2. A *monitor* technology that uses the monitor's electron gun to paint every other line of the screen with the first pass and the remaining lines on the second pass. When most of the screen display is a solid, light-color background, the eye perceives the alternating painted and fading lines as a slight flicker or shimmer. This technique provides higher resolution but at the price of visual comfort.

interleaved memory   A method of speeding the retrieval of data from *dynamic random-access memory (DRAM)* chips by dividing all the RAM into two or four large banks; sequential bits of data are stored in alternating banks. The microprocessor reads one bank while the other is being refreshed. Naturally, this memory arrangement doesn't improve speed when the central processing unit (CPU) requests nonsequential bits of data. See *random-access memory (RAM).*

interleave factor   The ratio of physical disk *sectors* on a hard disk that are skipped for every sector actually used for write operations. With an interleave factor of 6:1, a disk writes to a sector, skips six sectors, writes to a sector, and so on. The computer figures out what it needs next and sends the request to the hard drive while the disk is skipping sectors. 80386SX and higher computers operate faster than hard disks, so a 1:1 interleave is standard today. The interleave factor is set by the hard disk manufacturer but can be changed by software capable of performing a *low-level format.* Synonymous with sector interleave.

interleaving   A method of intentionally slowing down the reading of data from a *hard disk* to prevent the hard disk from outrunning other parts of the computer system. By placing sectors in nonsequential order, the read/write head has to jump around while collecting data. The *interleave factor* describes the amount of interleaving employed on a hard disk.

internal cache   A very high-speed *cache memory* that is built directly into the electronic circuits of a microprocessor, in contrast to an *external cache* or *L2 cache,* which require a separate circuit. Synonymous with primary cache.

G
H
I

internal command   In DOS, a command, such as DIR or COPY, that's part of COMMAND.COM, and therefore is in memory and available whenever the DOS prompt is visible on-screen. See *external command.*

internal data bus   The circuitry on which data moves inside a *microprocessor.* Internal data bus size is measured in *bits,* the more bits a bus can handle (the wider it is), the faster it can move data. The internal data bus is independent of the *external data bus,* which is often half as wide as the internal data bus.

internal font   See *printer font.*

internal hard disk   A *hard disk* designed to fit within a computer's or printer's case and use electricity from the device's *power supply.*

internal modem   A *modem* designed to fit into the *expansion bus* of a personal computer. See *external modem.*

internal navigation aid   In a series of related *World Wide Web (WWW)* documents, the hyperlinks or clickable buttons that provide users with a way of navigating through the documents without getting lost. If you see a Home button on one of the pages in a web, for example, you can click it to return to the web's *welcome page.* This is different from clicking the browser's Home button, which displays the browser's default home page. See *home page.*

International Data Encryption Algorithm (IDEA)   An *encryption* technique that employs a 128-bit *key* and is considered by most cryptanalysts to be the most secure encryption algorithm available today.

International Organization for Standardization (ISO)
A nonprofit organization, headquartered in Geneva, Switzerland, that seeks technological and scientific advancement by establishing nonproprietary standards. An umbrella organization for the standards bodies of more than 90 nations, the ISO is responsible for the development of the Open System Interconnection (OSI) Reference Model, a means of conceptualizing computer networks that has proven extremely influential. In the U.S., the ISO is represented by the *American National Standards Institute (ANSI).*

International Telecommunications Union-Telecommunications Standards Section (ITU-TSS) An organization, sponsored by the United Nations, that sets standards for communications technology. In computers, ITU-TSS standards, such as the widely used *V.32bis* protocol that governs some *high-speed modem* communications, enable *modems* from different manufacturers to communicate with one another. The ITU-TSS is the successor the Comité Consultatif International Téléphonique et Télégraphique (CCITT).

International Traffic in Arms Regulation See *ITAR.*

internet A group of local area networks (LANs) that have been connected by means of a common communications protocol and *packet* redirection devices called *routers,* so that, from the user's perspective, this group of networks seems as if it is one large network. Note the small "i"—many internets exist besides the *Internet,* including many *TCP/IP-* based networks that are not linked to the Internet (the Defense Data Network is a case in point).

Internet An enormous and rapidly growing system of linked computer networks, world-wide in scope, that facilitates data communication services such as remote login, file transfer, electronic mail, the World Wide Web, and newsgroups. Relying on *TCP/IP,* also called the *Internet Protocol* (IP) suite, the Internet assigns every connected computer a unique *Internet address,* also called an *IP address,* so that any two connected computers can locate each other on the network and exchange data. Although there are Internet connections in virtually every country in the world, the network is still predominantly English-speaking and most users live in English-speaking countries. Within English-speaking countries, the Internet is best seen as a new public communications medium, potentially on a par with the telephone system or television in ubiquity and impact. The Internet is the largest example in existence of an *internet.*

Internet access provider (IAP) A company or consortium that provides high-speed access to the Internet to businesses, universities, nonprofit organizations, and Internet service providers (ISPs), who in turn provide Internet access to individuals. Some IAPs are also ISPs.

Internet Activities Board (IAB) An organization, founded in 1983, that was charged with the development of TCP/IP; its activities have been taken over by the *Internet Architecture Board (IAB)*.

Internet address   The unique, 32-bit address assigned to a computer that is connected to the Internet, represented in dotted decimal notation (for example, 128.117.38.5). Synonymous with *IP address*.

Internet Architecture Board (IAB)   A unit of the *Internet Society (ISOC)* (Athat provides broad-level oversight over the *Internet's* technical development and adjudicates technical disputes that occur in the standards-setting process. Among the units that the organization oversees are *Internet Engineering Task Force (IETF), Internet Research Task Force (IRTF),* and *Internet Assigned Numbers Authority (IANA)*.

Internet Assigned Numbers Authority (IANA)   A unit of the *Internet Architecture Board (IAB)* that supervises the allocation of IP addresses, port addresses, and other numerical standards on the *Internet*.

Internet Control Message Protocol (ICMP)   An extension to the original *Internet Protocol (IP)* that provides much-needed error and congestion control. Using ICMP, for example, routers can "tell" other routers that a given branch of the network is congested or not responding. ICMP provides an echo function that enables *ping* applications to determine whether a given *host* is reachable.

Internet Draft   A working document of the *Internet Engineering Task Force (IETF),* a unit of the *Internet Architecture Board (IAB)*. Internet Drafts are unofficial discussion documents, meant to be circulated on the *Internet,* that are not intended to delineate new standards.

Internet Engineering and Planning Group (IEPG)   A unit of the *Internet Society (ISOC)* that promotes the technical coordination of day-to-day *Internet* operations. IEPG is composed of Internet backbone service providers and is not concerned with the development of new standards.

Internet Engineering Steering Group (IESG)   A unit of the *Internet Society* that reviews proposed standards created by the *Internet Engineering Task Force (IETF),* in consultation with the *Internet Architecture Board (IAB)*; standards are published in the form of *Requests for Comments (RFC)*.

Internet Engineering Task Force (IETF) A unit of the *Internet Architecture Board (IAB)* that is concerned with the immediate technical challenges facing the *Internet*. The IETF's technical work is done in a number of working groups, which are organized by topics, such as security, routing, and network management. Managed by the *Internet Engineering Steering Group (IESG),* the IETF convenes several meetings per year and publishes its proceedings.

Internet Experiment Notes (IEN) An obsolete publication series that was formerly used to report the results of research on the *TCP/IP* protocols.

Internet Explorer See *Microsoft Internet Explorer (MSIE).*

Internet Inter-ORB Protocol (IIOP) An Internet standard (*protocol*) that enables *interoperability* between Internet clients and CORBA servers, on the one hand, and between CORBA clients and Internet servers on the other. CORBA, an acronym for *Common Object Request Broker Architecture (CORBA),* is a *middleware* standard for large-scale, multi-platform *local area networks (LANs).* In a CORBA-based network, programmers create an object (a mini-program with a well-defined function) just once and make this available throughout the network. Using CORBA standards, programs can request functionality from an object; for example, if a program needs to perform a statistical analysis, it can request a copy of the object that makes this possible, and this functionality becomes available seamlessly. IIOP extends this functionality throughout the Internet.

Internet Message Access Protocol (IMAP) In Internet *e-mail,* one of two fundamental protocols (the other is *POP-3*) that governs how and where users store their incoming mail messages. IMAP stores messages on the mail server rather than facilitating downloading to the user's computer, as does the *POP3* standard. For many users, this standard may prove more convenient than POP3 because all of one's mail is kept in one central location, where it can be organized, archived, and made available from remote locations. IMAP4 is supported by *Netscape Messenger,* the mail package in *Netscape Communicator,* and by other leading e-mail programs.

Internet Monthly Report (IMR) A monthly publication of the *Internet Architecture Board (IAB)* that summarizes the current status of the Internet. The report includes statistical summaries of

G
H
I

usage, descriptions of technical challenges and the steps being taken to meet them, and the reports of various technical committees.

Internet PCA Registration Authority (IPRA)   A unit of the *Internet Society (ISOC)* that is devoted to the global implementation of *public key crytography* applications on the *Internet,* both for the purposes of *authentication* and *privacy.*

Internet Protocol (IP)   In *TCP/IP,* the standard that describes how an Internet-connected computer should break data down into packets for transmission across the network, and how those packets should be addressed so that they arrive at their destination. IP is the connectionless part of the TCP/IP protocols; the *Transmission Control Protocol (TCP)* specifies how two Internet computers can establish a reliable data link by means of *handshaking.* See *connectionless protocol* and *packet-switching network.*

Internet Relay Chat (IRC)   A real-time, Internet-based chat service, in which one can find "live" participants from the world over. Created by Jarkko Oikarinen of Finland in 1988, IRC requires the use of an IRC client program, which displays a list of the current IRC channels. The names of each channel, created by participants with the requisite technical knowledge to create and name them, sometimes indicate the channel's interest area, such as Elfquest comics. After joining a channel, you can see what other participants are typing on-screen, and you can type your own repartee. There is often a frustrating delay, however, before others see your message and respond.

Internet Research Task Force (IRTF)   A unit of the *Internet Architecture Board (IAB)* that deals with the long-range challenges facing the Internet, such as the lack of sufficient IP addresses.

Internet service provider (ISP)   A company that provides Internet accounts and connections to individuals and businesses. Most ISPs offer a range of connection options, ranging from dial-up modem connections to high-speed *ISDN.* Also provided is *e-mail, Usenet,* assistance with publishing material on the *World Wide Web (WWW).* See *Internet access provider (IAP).*

Internet Society (ISOC)   An international, not-for-profit organization, headquartered in Reston, Virginia, that seeks to maintain and broaden the *Internet's* availability. Created in 1992, ISOC is governed by an elected board of trustees. Members include individuals and organizations (including service providers, product providers, Internet enterprise operators, educational institutions, computer professional organizations, international treaty organizations, and government agencies). The organization sponsors annual conferences and has numerous publication programs. Spearheading the Internet's technical operation and development, the Internet Society coordinates the activities of the *Internet Architecture Board (IAB),* the *Internet Engineering Task Force (IETF),* the *Internet Engineering Steering Group (IESG),* the *Internet Engineering and Planning Group (IEPG),* the *Internet Assigned Numbers Authority (IANA),* and the *Internet PCA Registration Authority (IPRA).*

Internet Worm   A rogue program, ostensibly designed as a harmless experiment, that propagated throughout the Internet in 1988, overloading and shutting down thousands of computer systems worldwide. Robert Morris, Jr., the author of the program and at the time a graduate student in computer science at Cornell University, was convicted under the *Computer Fraud and Abuse Act of 1986.* He was sentenced to 3 years of probation, 400 hours of community service, and a $10,000 fine.

G
H
I

InterNIC   A consortium of two organizations that provide networking information services to the *Internet* community, under contract to the *National Science Foundation (NSF)* Currently, AT&T provides directory and database services, while Network Solutions, Inc., provides registration services for new *domain names* and *IP addresses.*

interoperability   The ability of one computer system to control another, even though the two systems are made by different manufacturers. Interoperability is one of the chief technical achievements of the *TCP/IP* protocols; using *File Transfer Protocol (FTP),* for instance, you can use a Macintosh to log on to a *Sun* workstation and direct that workstation to send a file to you via the Internet. In another example, a U.S. Robotics *modem* can exchange data with a Zoom modem, as long as both conform to a common standard such as *v.32bis.*

interpolated resolution   A means of improving the output of a *scanner* by means of a software *algorithm.* Instead of relying solely on closely spaced *charge-coupled devices (CCDs),* scanners that use interpolated resolution average the readings of each pair of adjacent CCDs and insert an extra pixel between them. Though a given interpolated resolution is not as good as the same *optical resolution,* it can cost effectively improve scan quality.

interpreted   Executed line-by-line from *source code* rather than from *object code* created by a *compiler.* See *interpreted code, interpreter.*

interpreted code   Program code that requires an *interpreter* to execute, in contrast to *compiled* programs, which are *executable.*

interpreter   A *translator* for a *high-level programming language* that translates and runs the program at the same time. Interpreters are excellent for learning how to program because, if an error occurs, the interpreter shows you the likely place (and sometimes even the cause) of the error. You can correct the problem immediately and execute the program again, learning interactively how to create a successful program. However, interpreted programs run much more slowly than compiled programs. See *compiler.*

interprocess communication (IPC)   In a *multitasking* computing environment, such as *Microsoft Windows* running in the *386 Enhanced mode,* the communication of data or commands from one program to another while both are running, made possible by *dynamic data exchange (DDE)* specifications. In *Microsoft Excel,* for example, you can write a DDE command that accesses changing data, such as stock prices, that's being received online in a communications program.

interrupt   A signal to the *microprocessor* indicating that an event has occurred that requires its attention. Processing is halted momentarily so that input/output or other operations can take place. When the operation is finished, processing resumes.

interrupt controller   Part of the *motherboard's chip set* that distributes hardware *interrupt request (IRQ) lines.* The interrupt controller prevents more than one *peripheral* device from communicating with the *microprocessor* at one time.

interrupt handler   A program that executes when an *interrupt* occurs. Such programs deal with events that are far below the threshold of user perception; for example, they deal with matters as minute as the reception of characters from the keyboard input.

interrupt request (IRQ)   In *microprocessors,* an input line through which *peripherals* (such as printers or modems) can get the attention of the microprocessor when the device is ready to send or receive data.

InterSLIP   A *freeware* program, created by InterCon Systems Corp., that provides Serial Line Internet Protocol *(SLIP)* connectivity, including a dialer program, for Macintosh computers. InterSLIP requires *MacTCP.*

intranet   A computer network designed to meet the internal needs of a single organization or company that is based on *Internet* technology *(TCP/IP).* Not necessarily open to the external Internet and almost certainly not accessible from the outside, an intranet enables organizations to make internal resources available using familiar Internet *clients,* such as *Web browsers, newsreaders,* and *e-mail.* Simply by publishing information, such as employee manuals or telephone directories on the Web rather than printed media, companies can realize significant *returns on investment (ROI)* by creating intranets. An intranet that has been selectively opened to strategic allies (including suppliers, customers, research labs, and other external allies) is called an *extranet.*

inverted file   See *inverted index.*

inverted index   In *databases,* a file containing *keys* and *pointers.* Each key uniquely describes a *data record,* while the pointers tell the program precisely where the record can be physically located in the database. The index is inverted in the sense that it is sorted by the keys, not the pointers. This removes the need to sort the records themselves, which remain (in most systems) in the order they were sequentially added to the database.

invisible file   See *hidden file.*

I/O   Common abbreviation for *input/output,* the portion of a computer's architecture that deals with the reception and transmission of signals to the computer's *peripherals.* See *input/output (I/O) system.*

I/O adapter   An *adapter* that plugs into your computer's *expansion bus* and provides several ports to which peripheral devices may attach. Typically, an I/O adapter provides a *bidirectional parallel port,* a *serial port* with a *16550A Universal Asynchronous Receiver/Transmitter (UART),* and a *game port.* Often, ports are built into the *motherboard* and an I/O adapter is not needed.

I/O buffering   A feature of *high-end network printers* that enables them to print one document while receiving information about another, which is to be printed next.

Iomega Corporation   The leading manufacturer of *removable hard disks,* including the *Jaz drive* and *Zip drive.* Headquartered in Roy, Utah, Iomega was founded in 1980.

IP address   A 32-bit *binary number* that uniquely and precisely identifies the location of a particular computer on the *Internet.* Every computer that is directly connected to the Internet must have an IP address. Because binary numbers are so hard to read, IP addresses are given in four-part decimal numbers, each part representing 8 bits of the 32-bit address (for example, 128.143.7.226). On networks and *SLIP/PPP* connections that dynamically assign IP numbers when you log on, this number may change from session to session.

IPC   See *interprocess communication.*

IPng   See *IPv6.*

IP number   See *Internet address.*

IPv6   The Next Generation Internet Protocol, also known as IPng, an evolutionary extension of the current *Internet Protocol (IP)* suite that is under development by the *Internet Engineering Task Force (IETF).* Ipv6 was originally intended to deal with the coming exhaustion of *IP addresses,* a serious problem caused by the Internet's rapid growth. However, the development effort has broadened to address a number of deficiencies in the current versions of the fundamental Internet protocols, including security, the lack of support for *mobile computing,* the need for automatic configuration of network devices, the lack of support for allocating bandwidth to high-priority data transfers, and other shortcomings of the current protocols. An unresolved question is whether the working committee will be able to persuade network equipment suppliers to upgrade to the new protocols.

IPX/SPX   The *transport protocol* used in *Novell NetWare* networks.

IRC   See *Internet Relay Chat.*

IRPA   See *Internet PCA Registration Authority.*

IRQ   See *interrupt request.*

IRQ conflict   A problem that results when two *peripheral* devices have been assigned the same *interrupt request (IRQ) line* and try to communicate with the *microprocessor* simultaneously. Assigning a new peripheral an unused IRQ line in order to prevent an IRQ conflict is usually done by trial and error, but the *Plug-and-Play* standard is supposed to eliminate guesswork in installing new *adapters.*

IRTF   See *Internet Research Task Force.*

ISA   See *Industry Standard Architecture.*

ISAPI   Acronym for *Internet Server Application Programming Interface.* An *application programming interface (API)* that enables programmers to include links to computer programs, such as database searches, in Web pages. ISAPI is designed to work with *Microsoft Information Server.* ISAPI provides the same functionality as *Common Gateway Interface (CGI),* but with markedly improved functionality and reduced *overhead;* ISAPI requests make full use of the Windows programming environment, and the called programs remain resident in memory in case they will be needed again.

ISA slot   A receptacle on the *motherboard* that accepts *peripherals* designed to conform to the *Industry Standard Architecture (ISA)* standard. ISA slots are not as fast as *VESA local bus slots* or *Peripheral Component Interconnect (PCI) bus slots,* but they continue to appear alongside those faster slots on the expansion buses of modern computers. See *expansion bus.*

ISDN   A world-wide standard for the delivery of digital telephone and data services to homes, schools, and offices. ISDN services fall into to three categories: *Basic Rate Interface (BRI), Primary Rate Interface (PRI),* and *Broadband ISDN (B-ISDN).* Designed as the basic option for consumers, Basic Rate Interface offers two 64,000 bit per second channels for voice, graphics, and data, plus one 16,000 bit per second channel for signaling purposes. Primary Rate ISDN provides 23 channels with 64,000 bits per second capacity. Broadband ISDN, still under development, would supply up to 150 million bits per second of data transmission capacity.

G
H
I

ISO   See *International Organization for Standardization.*

ISO 9660   The current standard for encoding data onto *CD-ROMs*. Practically all *CD-ROM drives* embrace the ISO 9660 standard, though a few cling to the obsolete, incompatible *High Sierra* standard on which ISO 9660 is based.

ISO Latin 1   A character set defined by the *International Standards Organization (ISO)*. ISO Latin 1 contains the characters needed for most Western European languages and also contains a nonbreaking space, a soft hyphen indicator, 93 *graphics characters,* and 25 control characters. With certain exceptions, ISO Latin 1 is the default character set used in *HyperText Markup Language (HTML)*.

ISP   See *Internet service provider.*

issue restrictions   In a *microprocessor* with *superscalar architecture* and multiple *pipelines,* the set of rules that determines whether two instructions may be processed simultaneously. Generally, the fewer issue restrictions a microprocessor has, the faster it processes instructions. See *data dependency* and *false dependency*.

italic   A *typeface* characteristic, commonly used for emphasis, in which the characters slant to the right. Two words in the following sentence are in italic. See *oblique* and *Roman*.

ITAR   Acronym for International Traffic in Arms Regulations (ITAR). A section of U.S. government regulations enacted under the Export Control Act of 1994 that forbid U.S. individuals or companies from exporting encryption software or utilities that cannot be broken by means of *cryptanalysis.* The restrictions stem from the concerns of defense experts who are well aware that encryption technologies have played a decisive role in 20th century warfare. However, the restricted algorithms are already widely available outside the U.S., so that—according to computer industry critics of ITAR—the only function of the regulations is to prevent U.S. companies from competing in a lucrative international market for secure business communication.

iteration   The repetition of a command or program statement. See *loop.*

ITU–TSS   See *International Telecommunications Union-Telecommunications Standards Section.*

J++ A *programming environment* for *Java* programming created by Microsoft Corporation. The package includes all the tools needed to create *Java applets* and *Java applications* efficiently, including a *compiler* and *debugger*. Microsoft's implementation of this programming environment has come under some criticism because it includes many hooks to Microsoft's version of the *Java virtual machine (VM)*, a version that is optimized to run efficiently under Microsoft Windows. Programs written using these features may not execute properly on other platforms, thereby contradicting the "write-once, run anywhere" benefit of Java programming. However, it is possible to use J++ to write applets or applications that will execute properly in a cross-platform environment.

jaggies See *aliasing*.

Java A *cross-platform* programming language created by Sun Microsystems that enables programmers to write a program that will execute on any computer capable of running a Java interpreter (which is built into today's leading *Web browsers*). Java is an *object-oriented programming (OOP) language* that is very similar to C++, except that it eliminates some features of C++ that programmers found to be tedious and time-consuming. Java programs are compiled into *applets* (small programs designed to be executed by a browser) or *applications* (larger, stand-alone programs that require a Java *interpreter* to be present on the user's computer), but the compiled code contains no *machine code*. Instead, the output of the compiler is *bytecode,* an intermediary between *source code* and machine code that can be transmitted via computer networks, including the Internet.

When the bytecode is received, it is interpreted, which means that Java programs run more slowly than programs that are designed with a specific processor in mind. However, Java programs run more quickly than "pure" interpreted languages, such as BASIC, in which the code is not compiled into any intermediary form. By means of a Java *JIT compiler,* the bytecode can also be compiled on the fly into machine code, resulting in improved performance. To prevent rogue programs from destroying data on the user's computer, Java applets execute in a *virtual machine* (also known as a *sandbox*), where they have no access to the file system of the computer on which they are executing.

However, this limitation restricts Java applets to a relatively trivial level of functionality. Java applets gain increased functionality, and the user's system security is protected by means of *certificates* that attest to the applet's authenticity.

Java applet   A small program *(applet)* that is desigoned for distribution on the *World Wide Web (WWW)* and for interpretation by a Java-capable *Web browser,* such as *Microsoft Internet Explorer* or *Netscape Navigator.* Java applets execute within the browser window and seamlessly add functionality to Web pages. However, their functionality is restricted due to security restrictions, which prevent applets from gaining access to the computer's file system. See *Java application.*

Java application   A Java program that, unlike a *Java applet,* executes in its own window and possesses full access to the computer's file system. To run a Java application, the user's computer must be equipped with a stand-alone Java interpreter, such as the one included with the *Java Development Kit (JDK).* If Java applications are written in conformity to Sun's *100% Pure Java* specifications, they will run on any computer that is capable of running a Java interpreter.

JavaBean   A *reusable object,* created with *Java* and in conformity to Sun's *100% Pure Java* specifications, that is packaged according to the JavaBeans specifications. A JavaBean differs from a Java applet in that it has *persistence* (it remains on the user's system after execution). Additionally, Beans are capable of communicating and exchanging data with other JavaBeans by means of *interprocess communication.* In this sense a JavaBean is similar to an *ActiveX control,* but with a very important exception: unlike ActiveX controls, which execute only on computers that support Object Linking and Embedding *(OLE)* at the *operating system* level, a JavaBean will execute on any computer platform that is capable of running a Java interpreter. Users will find that Beans seamlessly add functionality to Beans-aware applications, while developers can quickly create applications by combining Bean components.

JavaBeans   A *component architecture* for *Java applets* and *Java applications* that enables Java programmers to package Java programs in a container, similar to *ActiveX,* for increased interoperability with other *objects* and improved security. Java development environments that conform to the JavaBeans specification enable programmers to create Beans, which are reusable Java-based components that are capable of exchanging data with other components.

Java Development Kit (JDK)   A package of Java utilities and development tools, created by Sun Microsystems and distributed free of charge, that represents the *de facto standard* for the *Java* programming language. The package contains an *interpreter* that enables users to run *Java applications*.

JavaScript   A *scripting language* for Web publishing, developed by *Netscape Communications,* that enables Web authors to embed simple *Java*-like programming instructions within the *HTML* text of their Web pages. Originally called LiveScript, JavaScript was made more Java-like after Netscape Communications realized that Java would succeed, but JavaScript lacks the powerful *inheritance* capabilities of Java and is, at best, a simple scripting language. JavaScript is an interpreted language that executes much more slowly than Java, which is a hybrid compiled/interpreted language, and it requires its own interpreter, which is built into popular Web browsers. However, JavaScript is not effectively standardized yet; Microsoft has developed a competing version called *Jscript* for implementation in *Microsoft Internet Explorer,* and this version reportedly differs sufficiently from JavaScript that Jscript programs may not execute properly with other browsers. Until recently a *de facto standard,* JavaScript has been submitted to the European Computer Manufacturing Association (ECMA) for standardization.

JavaScript style sheet (JSS)   A proprietary *extension* to the *World Wide Web Consortium (W3C)* standards for *Cascading Style Sheets (CSS).* JSS is designed to enable *JavaScript* programmers to create dynamic effects by including JavaScript instructions in the various style definitions. See *style sheet.*

JavaSoft   A subsidiary of *Sun Microsystems* that is responsible for developing and promoting the *Java* programming language and related products.

Java Virtual Machine (VM)   A Java *interpreter* and runtime *environment* for *Java applets* and *Java applications.* This environment is called a virtual machine because, no matter what kind of computer it is running on, it creates a simulated computer that provides the correct platform for executing Java programs. In addition, this approach insulates the computer's file system from rogue applications. Java VMs are available for most computers.

J
K
L

Jaz drive A popular removable *disk drive*, made by Iomega Corporation, that offers up to 1 gigabyte of storage.

JDBC Acronym for Java Database Connectivity. A *JavaSoft*-developed *application program interface (API)* that enables Java programs to interact with any database program that complies with the *SQL* query language.

JDK See *Java Development Kit*.

JIT compiler Abbreviation for Just in Time compiler. A *compiler* that receives the *bytecode* from a *Java* application or *applet*, and compiles the bytecode into *machine code* on the fly. Code compiled with a JIT executes much faster than code executed by a Java *interpreter*, such as the ones built into popular *Web browsers*.

jitter In a *network*, an annoying and perceptible variation in the time it takes various workstations to respond to messages—some respond quickly, while some respond slowly, and some do not respond at all. Jitter is to be expected when the network cannot ensure fixed latency, the amount of time required for a message to travel from point A to point B in a network.

job A task for a computer. The word derives from the days when people had to take their *programs* to a computing department to be run on a *mainframe* and thereby assign a job to the computing department.

job control language (JCL) In *mainframe* computing, a programming language that enables programmers to specify *batch processing* instructions, which the computer then carries out. The abbreviation JCL refers to the job control language used in IBM mainframes.

job queue A series of tasks automatically executed, one after the other, by the computer. In *mainframe* data processing during the 1950s and 1960s, the job queue was literally a queue, or line of people waiting to have their programs run. With interactive, multi-user computing and personal computing, you usually don't need to line up to get your work done (although jobs can still back up at a busy *printer*).

join In a *relational database management program,* a data retrieval operation in which a new *data table* is built from data in two or more existing data tables. To understand how a join works and why join operations are desirable in database applications, suppose that for your video store you create a database table called RENTALS that lists the rented tapes with the phone number of the person renting the tape and the due date. You create another database table, called CUSTOMERS, in which you list the phone number, name, and credit card number of all your customers. To find out whether any customers are more than two weeks late returning a tape, you need to join information from the two databases. Suppose that you want to know the title and due date of the movie and the phone number and name of the customer. The following *Structured Query Language (SQL)* command retrieves the information:

```
SELECT TITLE, DUE_DATE, PHONE_NO, L_NAME, F_NAME
FROM RENTALS, CUSTOMERS
WHERE DUE_DATE=<05/07/92
```

This command tells the program to display the information contained in the data fields TITLE, DUE_DATE, PHONE_NO, L_NAME, and F_NAME, but only for those records in which the data field DUE_DATE contains a date equal to or earlier than May 7, 1992. The result is the following display:

TITLE	DUE_DATE	PHONE_NO	L_NAME	F_NAME
Alien Beings	05/07/92	499-1234	Jones	Terry
Almost Home	05/05/92	499-7890	Smith	Jake

See *join condition*.

join condition   In a *relational database management* program, a statement of how two *databases* are to be joined together to form a single table. The statement usually specifies a field common to both databases as the condition for joining records. See *join*.

Joint Photographic Experts Group (JPEG)   A committee of computer graphics experts, jointly sponsored by the *International Standards Organization (ISO)* and the *Comité Consultif International de Télégraphique et Téléphonique (CCITT)*, that developed the *JPEG* graphics standard.

joystick   A control device widely used, as an alternative to the keyboard, for computer games and some professional applications, such as computer-aided design.

JPEG   A graphics format that is ideal for complex pictures of natural, real-world scenes, including photographs, realistic artwork, and paintings. (The format is not well suited to line drawings, text, or simple cartoons.) Developed by the *Joint Photographic Experts Group (JPEG),* a committee created by two international standards bodies, the JPEG graphic format employs *lossy compression.* Exploiting a known property of human vision, namely that small color changes are less noticeable than changes in brightness, JPEG compression is not noticeable unless very high compression ratios are chosen. Typically, JPEG can achieve compression ratios of 10:1 or 20:1 without noticeable degradation in picture quality—a much better compression ratio than that of the *Graphics Interchange Format (GIF).*

JPEGView   A popular graphics manager for Macintosh computers that can open and display images in *JPEG, PICT, GIF, TIFF, BMP, MacPaint,* or *startup screen* formats.

Jscript   Microsoft's version of *JavaScript;* it is not completely compatible with JavaScript, however, and for this reason is not widely used.

Jughead   In *Gopher,* a search service that enables you to search all of *Gopherspace* for key words appearing in directory titles (not menu items). To search both directory titles and menu items, use *Veronica.*

jukebox   A *peripheral* that allows access to a group of disks. See *CD-ROM changer.*

jumper   An electrical connector that enables the user to select a particular configuration on a *circuit board.* The jumper is a small rectangle of plastic with two or three receptacles. You install a jumper by pushing it down on two or more pins from a selection of many that are sticking up from the circuit board's surface. The placement of the jumper completes the circuit for the configuration you want to use.

jumper settings   The configuration of movable conductors on an *adapter.* Jumper settings dictate how an adapter interacts with the rest of a system by determining its *interrupt request (IRQ)* channel, for example.

jump line   A message at the end of part of an article in a newsletter, magazine, or newspaper, indicating the page on which the article is continued. *Desktop publishing (DTP)* programs include features that make using jump lines for newsletters easier.

justification   The alignment of multiple lines of text along the left margin, the right margin, or both margins. The term justification often is used to refer to full justification, or the alignment of text along both margins. See *color.*

J
K
L

K   Abbreviation for *kilobyte* (1024 bytes).

K56plus   One of two competing *modulation protocols* for 56 Kbps *modems*. The K56plus standard is backed by Lucent and Rockwell; the competing x.2 standard is backed by U.S. Robotics. The two standards do not work together. A decision concerning the 56 Kbps modem standard will be made by the *ITU-TSS*.

Kb   Abbreviation for *kilobit* (1024 bits).

Kbps   See *bits per second (bps)*.

Kerberos   An *authentication* system for computer networks developed at the Massachusetts Institute of Technology (MIT). Unlike server-based authentication systems, which provide only a single point of entry to the network, Kerberos enables administration and management of authentication at the network level. Passwords are encrypted to prevent interception en route.

Kermit   An *asynchronous communications* protocol that makes the error-free transmission of program files via the telephone system easier. Developed by Columbia University and placed in the public domain, Kermit is used by academic institutions because, unlike *XMODEM,* Kermit can be implemented on mainframe systems that transmit 7 bits per byte. See *communications protocol*.

kernel   In an *operating system,* the core portions of the program that reside in memory and perform the most essential operating system tasks, such as handling disk input and output operations and managing the internal memory.

kerning   The adjustment of space between certain pairs of characters, so that the characters print in an aesthetically pleasing manner.

Kerr effect   The tendency of polarized light to shift its orientation slightly when reflected from a magnetized surface. *Magneto-optical (MO) drives* rely on the Kerr effect to read and write data.

key   1. In *cryptography,* the procedure that is used to encipher the message so that it appears to be just so much nonsense. The key also is required for *decryption*. In *public key* cryptography, there are two keys, a *private key* and a *public key*. A user makes the public key known to others, who use it to encrypt messages; these messages can be decrypted only by the intended recipient of a message, who use the private key to do so. 2. In databases, a unique value that is used to identify a *data record*. Synonymous with *primary key*.

key assignments   The functions given to specific keys by a computer program. Most of the keys on a personal computer *keyboard* are fully programmable, meaning that a programmer can use them in different ways. The best programs, however, stick to an *industry standard interface*.

keyboard   The most frequently used *input device*. The keyboard provides a set of alphabetic, numeric, punctuation, symbol, and control keys. When a character key is pressed, a coded input signal is sent to the computer, which echoes the signal by displaying a character on-screen. See *autorepeat key, keyboard layout,* and *toggle key*.

keyboard buffer   See *keystroke buffer*.

keyboard layout   The arrangement of keys on the computer's *keyboard*. A PC's keyboard layout uses the standard *QWERTY* layout that typewriters have used for a century. However, three different standards are used for arranging special computer keys such as Control and Alt: the original 83-key IBM PC keyboard, the 84-key IBM PC AT keyboard, and the current standard, the 101key enhanced keyboard.

keyboard template   A plastic card or strip with an adhesive backing that you can attach to the *keyboard* to explain the way a program configures the keyboard. Many applications provide keyboard templates, which are helpful when you're learning to use new programs.

key disk   A computer software protection scheme that requires the user to insert a specially encoded *floppy disk* before the program will start. This is intended to prevent the recipients of illegal copies of the program from running the program on their machines. Protection schemes that involve key disks are a hassle and are becoming rare. See *software piracy*.

key escrow   A scheme, strongly promoted by government security agencies, that would enable investigators to obtain valid court authorization to decrypt scrambled messages. In order for this to work, *encryption* tools would have to be redesigned so that a *decryption* key could be held in escrow by an appropriate independent agency. The U.S. government's failed *Clipper Chip* proposal would have accomplished this end, but it was shown to introduce vulnerabilities that made Clipper-encrypted messages subject to interception by unauthorized parties.

key status indicator An on-screen status message displayed by many application programs that informs you which, if any, *toggle keys* are active on the *keyboard*.

keystroke The physical action of pressing down a key on the *keyboard* so that a character is entered or a command is initiated.

keystroke buffer A holding area in memory that's used to save your current *keystrokes* if you type something while the *microprocessor* is busy with something else. If, for example, you begin typing while a file is being saved, the characters you type are placed in the keystroke buffer. When it's full (usually the buffer holds 20 characters), you'll hear a beep each time you press another key, indicating that your input isn't being accepted. When the microprocessor completes its task, the characters in the buffer are sent to the screen.

key variable In a *spreadsheet* program, a constant placed in a *cell* and referenced throughout the spreadsheet using *absolute cell references*.

keyword 1. In *programming languages* (including *software command languages*), a word describing an action or operation that the computer can recognize and execute. A *database query* might include several keywords. 2. In a document summary, one or more words that succinctly describe a document's contents. In the document summary of a letter inquiring about *green PCs,* a keyword might be electricity.

keyword search In a *database* system, a search that begins by supplying the computer with one or more words that describe the topic of your search. To retrieve items on North Carolina's Outer Banks, for example, you could type "outer" and "banks." With most systems, you can use *Boolean operators* to focus or broaden the search. For example, if you type outer and banks, the system will retrieve only those documents in which both of these words appear.

kick   In *Internet Relay Chat (IRC),* an action undertaken by a *channel operator* to expel an unwanted user from the channel. Ostensibly, this is to be done only when the user has grossly violated IRC etiquette, but it is sometimes done quite arbitrarily, or for the channel operator's amusement.

kill   To stop an ongoing process. In the better Usenet *newsreaders,* to delete an article containing a certain word, name, or origin site so that articles containing this information do not appear subsequently in the article selector. See *article selector, global kill file,* and *kill file.*

kill file   In a *Usenet* newsreader, a file that contains a list of subjects or names that you don't want to appear on the list of messages available for you to read. If you no longer want to read messages from Edward P. Jerk, you can add Ed's name to your *newsreaders* kill file, and his contributions will be discarded automatically before they reach your screen.

kilo-   A prefix indicating one thousand (10^3).

kilobit (Kb)   1024 bits of information.

kilobyte (K)   The basic unit of measurement for computer memory and disk capacity, equal to 1024 bytes. The prefix kilo- suggests 1000, but the computer world is based on twos, not tens: $2^{10} = 1024$. Because one byte is the same as one character in personal computing, 1K of data can contain 1024 characters (letters, numbers, or punctuation marks).

kiosk   A publicly accessible computer system that has been set up to allow interactive information browsing. In a kiosk, the computer's operating system has been hidden from view and the program runs in a full-screen mode, which provides a few simple tools for navigation. See *kiosk mode.*

kiosk mode   In a *Web browser,* a mode that zooms the program to full screen, permitting its use as an information navigation tool in a *kiosk.*

kluge   Pronounced "klooge." An improvised, technically inelegant solution to a problem. Also spelled kludge.

knowbot   See *agent.*

knowledge   In contrast to *data* or *information,* a set of propositions about something that is capable of generating additional propositions by means of deduction. For example, one may infer from the following propositions that Sri Lanka is a South Asian country: (1) Sri Lanka is adjacent to India. (2) Sri Lanka is a country. (3) All the countries adjacent to India are in South Asia.

knowledge acquisition　In *expert system* programming, the process of acquiring and systematizing knowledge from experts. A major limitation of current expert system technology is that *knowledge engineers* must acquire knowledge in a slow and painstaking process, called *knowledge representation,* that is designed to express the knowledge in terms of computer-readable rules.

knowledge base　In an *expert system,* the portion of the program that includes an expert's knowledge, often in IF/THEN rules. (Such as "If the tank pressure exceeds 600 pounds per square inch, then sound a warning".)

knowledge domain　In *artificial intelligence (AI),* an area of problem-solving expertise. Current artificial intelligence technology works well only in sharply limited knowledge domains, such as the configuration of one manufacturer's computer systems, the repair of a specific robotic system, or investment analysis for a limited collection of securities.

knowledge engineer　In *expert system* programming, a specialist who obtains the knowledge possessed by experts on a subject and expresses this knowledge in a form that an expert system can use. See *knowledge domain.*

knowledge representation　In *expert system* programming, the method used to encode and store the knowledge in a *knowledge base.* Although several alternative knowledge representation schemes are used, most commercially available expert systems use the production system approach in which knowledge is represented in the form of production rules, which have the following form:

```
IF {condition} THEN {action}
```

A given rule may have multiple conditions as in the following example:

```
IF {a person's intraocular pressure is raised}
AND {the person has pain in the left quadratic region}
THEN {immediate hospitalization is indicated}
```

Korn Shell   A popular *shell* (user interface) for the *Unix* operating system. Sometimes abbreviated ksh. A *command-line* interface that is difficult to learn for computer neophytes, the Korn Shell is nevertheless greatly esteemed by experienced computer users due to its programmability and many time-saving shortcuts.

ksh   See *Korn Shell*.

J
K
L

L1 cache   See *primary cache*.

L2 cache   See *secondary cache*.

label   1. In a spreadsheet program, text entered in a cell. A number entered in a cell, by contrast, is a *value*. 2. In DOS batch files, a string of characters preceded by a colon that marks the destination of a GOTO command.

label alignment   In a *spreadsheet* program, the way *labels* are aligned in a cell (flush left, centered, flush right, or repeating across the cell). Unless you specify otherwise, labels are aligned on the left of the cell. See *label prefix*.

label prefix   In most *spreadsheet* programs, a punctuation mark at the beginning of a cell entry that tells the program that the entry is a label and specifies how the program should align the label within the cell. Programs that use prefixes enter the default label prefix—usually an apostrophe (')—when the cell entry begins with a letter. In such programs, you can control the alignment of a label as you type it by beginning the label with one of these prefixes:

Label Prefix	Alignment
'	Flush left
^	Centered
"	Flush right
\	Repeating across the cell

This system has fallen into disuse as more and more programs offer alignment commands on their toolbars and menus that are easier to use than these prefixes.

label printer   A *printer* designed specifically to print names and addresses on continuous-feed labels.

LAN   See *local area network*.

LAN-aware program   A version of an *application program* specifically modified so that the program can function in a *local* *area network (LAN)* environment. Network versions of *transactional application* programs—database management programs—create and maintain shared files. An invoice-processing program, for example, has access to a database of accounts receivable. The network versions of *non-transactional programs,* such as word processing programs, include file security features to prevent unauthorized users from gaining access to your documents. LAN-aware programs boast features, such as *concurrency control,* which manages multiple copies of files, and *file locking* and prevents unauthorized users from accessing certain files. LAN-aware programs usually are stored on a *file server.*

LAN backup program   A program designed specifically to back up the programs and data stored on a *local area network's (LAN's)* file server. The best LAN backup programs automatically back up the file server at scheduled times, without user intervention.

landing zone   Ideally, the only area of a *hard disk's* surface that actually touches the *read/write head.* Through a process called *head parking,* the read/write head moves over the landing zone before the computer is shut off and drifts to rest there. The landing zone, on which no data is encoded, is designed to prevent the read/write head from damaging portions of the disk used to store data.

landscape font   A *font* in which the characters are oriented toward the long edge of the page. See *portrait font.*

landscape orientation   A page layout in which text and/or graphics are printed across the long edge of the paper. Contrast with *portrait orientation.*

landscape printing   Printing so *graphics* and characters are oriented toward the long edge of the page. In landscape printing, the 11-inch sides of *A-sized paper* are the top and bottom of the page.

LAN-ignorant program   An *application program* designed for use only as a stand-alone program and that contains no provisions for use on a network, such as *file locking* and *concurrency control.*

LAN memory management program   A *utility program* designed specifically to free *conventional memory* so that you can run large applications on a network workstation. Every workstation must run local area network (LAN) software, which can consume as much as 100K of *conventional memory*. As a result, workstations may not be capable of running certain memory-hungry applications. *Local area network (LAN)* memory managers move the network software, as well as *device drivers, terminate-and-stay-resident (TSR)* programs, and other utilities—into the upper memory area, *extended memory,* or *expanded memory.* A popular and well-rated LAN management program is NetRoom by Helix Software. See *network operating system (NOS).*

LAN server See *file server* and *print server.*

LAPM See *Link Access Protocol for Modems.*

laptop computer A small, portable computer that's light and small enough to hold on your lap. Small laptop computers, which weigh less than 6 pounds and can fit in a briefcase, are called *notebook computers.* The smallest portable computers, weighing about 5 pounds, are called subnotebook computers.

large-scale integration (LSI) In integrated circuit technology, placing up to 100,000 transistors on a single chip. See *very large scale integration (VLSI).*

laser font See *outline font.*

laser printer A high-resolution printer that uses a version of the electrostatic reproduction technology of copying machines to fuse text and graphic images to paper. To print a page, the printer's controller circuitry receives the printing instructions from the computer and builds a bitmap of every dot on a page. The controller ensures that the *print engine's* laser transfers a precise replica of this bitmap to a photostatically sensitive drum or belt. Switching on and off rapidly, the beam travels across the drum, and as the beam moves, the drum charges the areas exposed to the beam. The charged areas attract toner (electrically charged ink) as the drum rotates past the toner cartridge. An electrically charged wire pulls the toner from the drum onto the paper, and heat rollers fuse the toner to the paper. A second electrically charged wire neutralizes the drum's electrical charge. See *light-emitting diode (LED) printer* and *resolution.*

latency 1. In a computer network, the amount of time required for a message to travel from the sending to the receiving computer. This is far from instantaneous in a *packet-switching* network, given the fact that the message must be read and passed on by several *routers* before it reaches its destination and results in *jitter*. 2. In disk drives, the time required for the portion of the disk containing needed information to rotate under the *read/write head*. The faster a disk drive spins, the lower its latency.

LaTeX A *page description language (PDL)* that enables a programmer to prepare a page for typesetting. It is not widely used.

launch To start a program.

layer 1. In some illustration and page-layout applications, an on-screen sheet on which you can place text or graphics so that they're independent of any text or graphics on other sheets. The layer can be opaque or transparent. 2. In a computer network, a portion of the total network architecture that is differentiated from other portions because it has a distinctive function, such as preparing data to be transmitted over the network's physical media. Network design is aided by functionally differentiating layers and assigning standards, or *protocols,* to each. See *OSI Reference Model* and *protocol stack*.

layout In *desktop publishing* and *word processing,* the process of arranging text and graphics on a page. In database management systems, the arrangement of report elements, such as headers and fields, on a printed page.

LBA See *Logical Block Addressing.*

LCD See *liquid crystal display.*

LCD printer See *liquid crystal display (LCD) printer.*

LCS printer See *liquid crystal shutter (LCS) printer.*

LDAP See *Lightweight Directory Access Protocol.*

leader In *word processing,* a row of dots or dashes that provides a path for the eye to follow across the page. Leaders often are used in tables of contents to lead the reader's eye from the entry to the page number. Most word processing programs let you define tab stops that insert leaders when you press the Tab key.

leading The space between lines of type, measured from *baseline* to baseline. Synonymous with line spacing. The term originated from letterpress-printing technology, in which lead strips were inserted between lines of type to add spacing between lines.

leading zero   The zeros added in front of numeric values so that a number fills up all required spaces in a data field. For example, three leading zeros are in the number 00098.54.

leased line   A permanently connected and conditioned telephone line that provides *wide area network (WAN)* connectivity to an organization or business. Most leased lines transfer digital data at 56 *Kbps.*

least significant bit (LSB)   In a *binary number,* the last or rightmost bit that conveys the least amount of information, given its low place value.

LED   See *light-emitting diode.*

LED indicator   See *drive activity light.*

LED printer   See *light-emitting diode (LED) printer.*

left justification   Synonymous with ragged-right alignment. See *justification.*

legacy application   A computer program that was specifically designed for *legacy hardware* and continues to be used, despite inefficiencies, a poor user interface, or other shortcomings, because the system is too expensive to replace.

legacy hardware   Older computers or computer *peripherals* that do not conform to the standards or performance levels found in newer equipment. For example, an adapter that does not conform to the *Plug and Play* standard is legacy hardware. In networking, this term strongly connotes hardware that is designed to work with *proprietary* communication protocols rather than *open standards.*

legacy system   A computer system, consisting of outdated applications and hardware, that was developed to solve a specific business problem. Many legacy systems are still in use because they solve the problem well and replacing them would be too expensive. See *legacy application* and *legacy hardware.*

legend   An area of a chart or graph that explains what data is being represented by the colors or patterns used in the chart.

Lempel–Ziv compression   Also known as LZW. A compression method that looks for recurring (lengthy) patterns in data to be compressed and assigns a shorter key to each pattern. The resulting compressed file is significantly smaller than the original, but it can be decompressed so that the resulting output file is an exact copy of the original. Unisys holds a patent for LZW compression.

letter-quality printer   A printer that offers fully formed text characters as good as those produced by a high-quality office typewriter.

library   A collection of programs kept with a computer system and made available for processing purposes. The term often refers to a collection of *library routines* written in a given programming language such as C or Pascal.

library routine   In *programming,* a well-tested subroutine, procedure, or function in a given programming language. The library routine handles tasks that all or most programs need, such as reading data from disks. The programmer can draw on this library to develop programs quickly.

ligature   In *typography,* two or more characters designed and cast as a distinct unit for aesthetic reasons, such as æ.

light client   Synonymous with *Web browser.* In the *client/server* model of network architecture, traditional client programs were proprietary, complex, and expensive to maintain. By using familiar Web browsers as a universal client for all kinds of servers, network designers can substantially reduce the cost of client maintenance and user training, while at the same time ensuring that the users of differing types of computers will be able to access important data. See *heavy client.*

light-emitting diode (LED)   A small electronic device made from semiconductor materials. An LED emits light when current flows through it. LEDs are used for small indi-cator lights, but because they draw more power than *liquid crystal displays (LCD),* they rarely are used for computer displays.

J
K
L

light-emitting diode (LED) printer   A high-quality printer that closely resembles the *laser printer* in that it electrostatically fuses toner to paper; however, the light source is a matrix of light-emitting diodes rather than a laser. To create the image, the diodes flash on and off over the rotating print drum. See *liquid crystal display (LCD) printer.*

light pen   An *input device* that uses a light-sensitive stylus so that you can draw on-screen, draw on a graphics tablet, or select items from menus.

Lightweight Directory Access Protocol (LDAP)   An *Internet* standard *(protocol)* that enables users of *Web browsers* to access and search directory databases (for example, a corporate telephone directory).

LIM EMS   See *Lotus-Intel-Microsoft Expanded Memory Specification.*

line   In *programming,* one program statement. In data communications, a circuit that directly connects two or more electronic devices.

line adapter   In data communications, an electronic device that converts signals from one form to another so you can transmit the signals. A *modem* is a line adapter that converts the computer's digital signals to analog equivalents so they can be transmitted using standard telephone lines.

line art   In *graphics,* a drawing that doesn't contain *halftones* (shading). Line art can be accurately reproduced by low- to medium-*resolution* printers that have limited or no halftone printing capability.

line chart   See *line graph.*

line editor   A primitive *word processing* utility that's often provided with an operating system as part of its programming environment. Unlike with a *full-screen editor,* you can write or edit only one line of program code at a time. See *programming environment.*

line feed   A signal that tells the printer when to start a new line. See *carriage return* and *Enter/Return.*

line graph   In presentation and analytical graphics, a graph that uses lines to show the variations of data over time or to show the relationship between two numeric variables. In general, the *x-axis* (categories) is aligned horizontally, and the *y-axis* (values) is aligned vertically. A line graph, however, may have two y-axes. See *bar graph* and *presentation graphics*.

line interactive UPS　A type of *uninterruptible power supply (UPS)* that provides protection from brownouts as well as power failures. A line interactive UPS monitors electrical current from a wall outlet and provides full operating power if the line voltage drops or disappears. See *standby UPS*.

line mode terminal　A terminal that is designed to communicate with the user with one line of text at a time, like an old-fashioned teletype machine (in fact, such terminals are often abbreviated TTY, which stands for "teletype"). You type a one-line command, and the *terminal* responds with a one-line conformation or error message. See *network virtual terminal (NVT)* and *Telnet*.

line noise　Interference in a telephone line caused by current fluctuations, poor connections in telephone equipment, cross-talk from adjacent lines, or environmental conditions such as lightning. Line noise may reduce the *data transfer rate* a *modem* can sustain, or may introduce *garbage characters* into the data stream.

liner　The cloth envelope that fits between the recording medium of a *floppy disk* and its *shell*. The liner reduces friction and keeps dust off the recording medium.

line rate　See *horizontal frequency*.

line spacing　See *leading*.

link　To establish a connection between two files or data items so that a change in one is reflected by a change in the second. A *cold link* requires user intervention and action, such as opening both files and using an updating command, to make sure that the change has occurred. A *warm link* occurs automatically. See *hot link* and *OLE*.

Link Access Protocol for Modems (LAPM)　An *error-correction protocol* included in the *V.42* standard. V.42 tries to establish a connection with LAPM but will try *MNP4* if it fails. Like other error-correction protocols, LAPM exists to ensure that data is transmitted accurately and *garbage characters* are eliminated.

J
K
L

linked list   See *list*.

linked object   In Object Linking and Embedding *(OLE),* a document or portion of a document (an object) created with one application that's inserted in a document created with another application. Linking places a copy of the object, with hidden information about the source of the object, into the *destination document.* If you change the source document while the destination document is open, the object in the destination document is automatically updated. If the destination document isn't open, the object is updated the next time you open it. Object linking and embedding is possible only when you're using OLE-compatible applications on a *Microsoft Windows* system or on a Macintosh system running System 7. See *embedded object.*

linked pie/column chart   See *linked pie/column graph.*

linked pie/column graph   In *presentation graphics,* a pie graph paired with a column graph so that the column graph displays the internal distribution of data items in one slice of the pie.

link rot   In the *World Wide Web (WWW),* a slang expression for the tendency of *hyperlinks* to go *stale* (cease to function) when the page targeted by a hyperlink is moved or disappears entirely.

Linux   A version of the *Unix* operating system developed for *Intel* microprocessors. Linux is available as *freeware,* under the terms of the Free Software Foundation's *General Public License (gpu).*

liquid crystal display (LCD)   Low-power *display* technology used in *laptop computers* and small, battery-powered electronic devices such as meters, testing equipment, and digital watches. The display device uses rod-shaped crystal molecules that change their orientation when an electrical current flows through them. Some LCD designs use *backlit* screens to improve readability but at the cost of drawing more power.

liquid crystal display (LCD) printer   A high-quality *printer* that closely resembles the *laser printer* in that it electrostatically fuses toner to paper; however, the light source is a matrix of liquid crystal shutters. The shutters open and close to create the pattern of light that falls on the print drum. See *light-emitting diode (LED) printer.*

liquid crystal shutter (LCS) printer   A *printer* that uses a light source and a series of shutters and lenses, instead of a laser beam, to create an electrostatic charge on a page. LCS printers may have longer lives than *laser printers* because they have fewer moving parts.

LISP   A *high-level programming language,* often used for *artificial intelligence* research, that makes no distinction between the program and the data. This language is considered ideal for manipulating text. One of the oldest programming languages still in use, LISP is a *declarative language;* the programmer composes lists that declare the relationships among symbolic values. Lists are the fundamental data structure of LISP, and the program performs computations on the symbolic values expressed in those lists. Like other public domain programming languages, however, a number of mutually unintelligible versions of LISP exist. A standardized, fully configured, and widely accepted version is Common LISP. See *interpreter.*

list   In *programming,* a data structure that lists and links each data item with a pointer showing the item's physical location in a database. Using a list, a programmer can organize data in various ways without changing the physical location of the data. For example, the programmer can display a database so that it appears to be sorted in alphabetical order, even though the actual physical data records still are stored in the order in which they were entered.

LISTSERV   A commercial mailing list manager, originally developed in 1986 for BITNET mailing lists, that has since been ported to *Unix, Microsoft Windows,* and *Windows 95.* LISTSERV is marketed by L-Soft International. See *Majordomo.*

literal   In programming, a constant, as opposed to a *variable.*

lithium–ion battery   In *portable computers,* a rechargeable battery technology that offers as much as twice the charge capacity of competing technologies (NiCad and NiMH batteries) with significantly less environmental risk. Lithium ion batteries currently cost more, but the price differential is expected to decrease as battery factories increase production.

little–endian   In computer architecture, a design philosophy which prefers placing the *least significant bit* at the beginning of a *data word.*

J
K
L

live copy/paste   See *hot link*.

load   To transfer program instructions or data from a disk into the computer's *random-access memory (RAM)*.

local area network (LAN)   Personal and other computers within a limited area that are linked by high-performance cables so users can exchange information, share peripherals, and draw on programs and data stored in a dedicated computer called a file server. Ranging tremendously in size and complexity, LANs may link only a few personal computers to an expensive, shared peripheral, such as a *laser printer*. More complex systems use central computers *(file servers)* and allow users to communicate with each other via *e-mail* to share multi-user programs and to access shared databases. See *AppleTalk, baseband, broadband, bus network, Ethernet, multi-user system, NetWare, network operating system (NOS), peer-to-peer network, ring network,* and *star network*.

local bus   A high-speed bus architecture for IBM-compatible computers that directly links the computer's *central processing unit (CPU)* with one or more slots on the *expansion bus*. This direct link means the signals from an adapter (video or hard disk controller, for example) don't have to travel through the computer's expansion bus, which is significantly slower. Local bus designs enjoyed some prominence in the mid-1990s, but new systems use the *Peripheral Component Interconnect (PCI) bus,* which offers even better performance. See *VESA local bus*.

local drive   In a *local area network (LAN),* a disk drive that is part of the *workstation* you are now using, as distinguished from a network drive (a drive made available to you through the *network*).

locale   In *Microsoft Windows 95,* the geographical location of a computer. The locale determines the language in which messages appear; the formats for time, date, and money expressions; and the time of day.

local echo   See *half duplex*.

local loop   The *copper pair* wire that connects a home or business to a telephone company switching station. Local loop wires have very low *bandwidth,* and need to be replaced before high-speed *digital* telecommunications, such as those provided by the *Integrated Services Digital Network (ISDN),* can be implemented.

local printer   In a *local area network (LAN),* a *printer* directly connected to the *workstation* you're using, as distinguished from a network printer (a printer made available to you through the *network*).

LocalTalk   The physical connectors and cables manufactured by Apple Computer for use in *AppleTalk* networks.

local Usenet hierarchy   In *Usenet,* a category of *newsgroups* that is set up for local distribution only, for example, within the confines of a company or university. Local *newsgroups* are not ordinarily accessible outside the organization.

locked file   In a *local area network (LAN),* a file attribute that prevents applications or the user from updating or deleting the file.

log   A record. In *communications programs,* a log feature can record everything that appears on the *monitor* for later review, which can save you money if you're paying a per-minute connection fee.

logarithmic chart   See *logarithmic graph.*

logarithmic graph   In *analytical* and *presentation graphics,* a graph displayed with a *y-axis* (values) that increases exponentially in powers of 10. On an ordinary y-axis, the 10 is followed by 20, 30, 40, and so on. On a logarithmic scale, however, 10 is followed by 100, 1,000, 10,000, and so on. This makes a logarithmic graph useful when great differences exist in the values of the data being graphed. In an ordinary graph, you can hardly see a data series or data item with small values; on a logarithmic chart, however, the small values show up much better.

logical   Having the appearance of, and treated as, a real thing, even though it does not exist. See *logical drives* and *physical drive.*

Logical Block Addressing (LBA)   Part of the *Enhanced IDE* standard, LBA permits *hard disks* to store up to 8.4*G* of data.

logical drives   Sections of a *hard drive* that are formatted and assigned a drive letter, each of which is presented to the user as though it were a separate drive. Another way logical drives are created is by substituting a drive letter for a directory. Also, *networks* typically map directories to drive letters, resulting in logical drives. See *logical, partition,* and *physical drive.*

J
K
L

logical format   See *high-level format.*

logical network   A *network* as it appears to the user. In fact, the network could be composed of two or more physical networks, or portions of these, which are linked and coordinated in such a way that they appear to be a unit. One of the most remarkable facts about the *Internet* is that, even though it links tens of thousands of physically heterogeneous networks, they nevertheless appear to the user to comprise a single, immense network of global proportions.

logical operator   See *Boolean operator.*

logic board   See *motherboard.*

logic bomb   In *programming,* a form of sabotage in which a programmer inserts code that causes the program to perform a destructive action when some triggering event occurs, such as terminating the programmer's employment.

logic gate   An automatic switch, incorporated into *microprocessors* and other *chips,* that tests for certain conditions and takes certain actions if those conditions are satisfied. Logic gates are at the center of a computer's ability to carry out instructions and solve problems. See *arithmetic-logic unit.*

login   In a computer network, the *authentication* process in which a user supplies a *login name* and *password.* Also spelled logon.

login ID   See *login name.*

login name   In a *network,* a unique name assigned to you by the system administrator that is used as a means of initial identification. You must type this name and also your *password* to gain access to the system.

login script   In *dialup access,* a list of instructions that guides the *dialer program* through the process of dialing the service provider's number, supplying the user's login name and password, and establishing the connection.

login security   An *authentication* process that requires you to type a *password* before gaining access to a system.

Logo   A *high-level programming language* well-suited to teaching fundamental programming concepts to children. A special version of *LISP,* Logo was designed as an educational language to illustrate the concepts of recursion, extensibility, and other concepts of computing, without requiring math skills. The language also provides an environment in which children can develop their reasoning and problem-solving skills and includes turtle graphics—a teaching aid that involves telling an on-screen "turtle" how to draw pictures.

log off   The process of terminating a connection with a computer system or *peripheral* device in an orderly way.

log on   The process of establishing a connection with, or gaining access to, a computer system or *peripheral* device. In MS-DOS, logging on refers to the process of changing to another drive by typing the drive letter and a colon and then pressing Enter. In *networks,* you may be required to type a *password* to log on.

logon file   In a *local area network (LAN),* a batch file or configuration file that starts the network software and establishes the connection with the network when you turn on the *workstation.*

lookup function   A procedure in which a *program* consults stored data listed in a table or *file.*

lookup table   In a *spreadsheet* program, data entered in a *range* of *cells* and organized so that a lookup function can use the data, for example, to determine the correct tax rate based on annual income.

loop   In *programming,* a *control structure* in which a block of instructions repeats until a condition is fulfilled. See *DO/WHILE loop* and *FOR/NEXT loop.*

loopback plug   In *serial communications,* a diagnostic plug that connects serial inputs to serial outputs so that each circuit in the port can be tested.

lossless compression   A *data compression* technique that reduces the size of a file without sacrificing any original data, used by file compression programs to reduce the size of all the program and document files on a *hard disk.* In lossless compression, the expanded or restored file is an exact replica of the original file before it was compressed, while in *lossy compression,* data is lost in a way imperceptible to humans. Lossless compression is suitable for text and computer code, while lossy compression is good mainly for shrinking audio and graphics files.

lossy compression A *data compression* technique in which some data is deliberately discarded to achieve massive reductions in the size of the compressed file. Lossy compression techniques can reduce a file to $1/50$ of its former size (or less), compared to the average of one-third achieved by lossless compression techniques. Lossy compression is used for graphics files in which the loss of data, such as information about some of the graphic's several million colors, isn't noticeable. An example is the *JPEG* compression technique. See *lossless compression*.

lost chain In *MS-DOS,* a group of clusters that are connected to each other in the *file allocation table (FAT)* but are no longer connected to a specific *file*.

lost cluster A *cluster* that remains on the disk, even though the *file allocation table (FAT)* contains no record of its link to a file. Lost clusters can occur when the computer is turned off (or the power fails) or tries to perform other operations while a file is being written.

Lotus 1-2-3 A full-featured *spreadsheet program* known for its ability to work with *Lotus Notes* and *e-mail* programs. Lotus 1-2-3 competes with *Microsoft Excel* and *Quattro Pro.* Though praised for its strength in managing multiple *what-if analysis* and its ability to link spreadsheet information to maps, 1-2-3 is considered to be third in the pack of three major spreadsheet programs.

Lotus Approach A *database management program* for *Microsoft Windows* that has the distinction of being both easy to use and capable of handling complex operations. A competitor of *Microsoft Access* and *dBASE* for Windows, Lotus Approach makes it possible to analyze *data* in a variety of forms (including dBASE, Microsoft Access, *Microsoft Excel,* and Borland Paradox) without performing any programming.

Lotus Domino An *Internet*-based server for Lotus's proprietary *Lotus Notes* software, which brings *groupware* functions (including *e-mail,* collaboration and scheduling) to enterprise networks. Domino competes with *Microsoft Exchange server.* Unlike the Microsoft offering, which is best used where the decision has been made to standardize on Windows workstations and servers, Domino is a *cross-platform* product that includes support for *Unix* and *OS/2.*

Lotus-Intel-Microsoft Expanded Memory Specification (LIM EMS) An *expanded memory* standard that allows the programs that recognize the standard to work with more than 640K RAM under DOS. The LIM Version 4.0 standard, introduced in 1987, supports up to 32*M* of expanded memory and lets programs run in expanded memory.

Lotus Notes A proprietary *groupware application* that brings *features* such as discussion tracking, *e-mail,* group scheduling and calendaring, and database sharing to large and small workgroups. First released in 1988, Lotus Notes is the most popular groupware application available. Lotus Notes comes with an elaborate application-development language that enables it to be tailored to the needs of a particular workgroup. Lotus Notes faces competition from *Microsoft Exchange.* An *Internet*-capable version of Notes, *Lotus Domino,* brings Notes functions to *TCP/IP*-based networks.

Lotus Organizer A *personal-information manager (PIM)* included with *Lotus SmartSuite* and designed to work well with *Lotus Notes.* With Lotus Organizer, the time of an appointment you enter is visible to other Notes users as a time you're not available, so they know not to try setting up meetings with you then.

Lotus SmartSuite A *suite* of *application programs,* published by Lotus, that includes *Lotus Word Pro, Lotus 1-2-3, Lotus Approach,* and *Lotus Organizer.* Lotus SmartSuite competes with *Corel WordPerfect Suite* and *Microsoft Office Professional.*

J K L

Lotus Word Pro Formerly called Ami Pro, a *word processing program* created by Lotus Corporation for Windows systems. In keeping with Lotus' commitment to groupware, Word Pro emphasizes collaborative writing (including review and editing of shared documents), while also offering a full suite of the writing and editing features found in other leading word processing programs (such as *Microsoft Word*).

low end An inexpensive product at the bottom or near the bottom of a firm's offerings. Low-end products include only a few of the features available in more expensive products and may rely on obsolete or near-obsolete technology to keep costs down.

low-level format Defining the physical location of magnetic *tracks* and *sectors* on a disk. This operation, sometimes called a physical format, is different from the *high-level format* that establishes the sections where DOS system files are stored and that records the free and in-use areas of the disk.

low-level programming language   In *programming,* a language, such as *machine language* or *assembly language,* that describes exactly the procedures to be carried out by the computer's central processing unit (CPU). See *high-level programming language.*

low-power microprocessor   A *microprocessor* that runs on 3.3 volts of electricity or less. Low-power microprocessors are often used in *portable computers* to conserve battery power. See *0.5-micron technology* and *Complementary Metal-Oxide Semiconductor (CMOS).*

low resolution   In *monitors* and *printers,* a visual definition that results in characters and graphics with jagged edges. The IBM *Color Graphics Adapter (CGA)* and monitor, for example, can display 640 pixels horizontally, but only 200 lines vertically, resulting in poor visual definition. *High resolution* monitors and printers produce well-defined characters or smoothly defined curves in graphic images.

low-rez   Slang for a technically unsavvy person. Usage: "Our boss is nice enough, but he's kind of low-rez." See *high resolution.*

LPT   In DOS, a device name that refers to a parallel port to which you can connect parallel printers.

LSB   See *least significant bit.*

LSI   See *large-scale integration.*

lurk   To read a newsgroup or mailing list without ever posting a message. See *delurk.*

LViewPro   A *shareware* graphics viewer program for Microsoft Windows, created by Leonardo H. Loureiro and widely available on the Internet. Often used as a *helper program* for Web browsers, the program can read JPEG, TIFF, Targa, GIF, PCX, Windows bitmap, OS/2 bitmap, PBM, PGM, and PPM files. A feature of LViewPro of interest to Web developers is the program's ability to create *transparent GIFs.*

Lycos A *search engine* for locating *World Wide Web* documents. Lycos, named after a particularly energetic night-hunting spider, relies on an automated search routine (called a *spider*) that prowls the Web, discovering new Web, *FTP*, and *Gopher* documents (about 5,000 per day). The additions become part of Lycos' huge database. For each document, Lycos indexes words in the title, headings, subheadings, all of the document's hyperlinks, the 100 most important words in the document, and the words in the first 20 lines of text. A searcher wishing to locate documents containing words buried more deeply in a page should use *AltaVista,* which indexes the entire document text. A significant drawback of the Lycos search engine is its failure to include needed provisions for reducing the scope of a search, including *case-sensitive* searches, *field-based searches,* and *phrase searches.* See *Infoseek.*

LYNX A full-screen, text-only *Web browser* for *Unix* computers, created by Lou Montoulli of the University of Kansas. LYNX is a full-featured Web browser but it cannot display *in-line images.*

LZW Acronym for Lempel-Zif-Welsh. A *data compression* technique that is widely used for a number of applications (including *GIF* graphics, *PostScript* printing, *V.42bis* compression, and *Adobe Acrobat* files). The patent for LZW compression is held by Unisys Corporation, which levies a licensing fee on every software publisher that creates programs using the LZW algorithm. The *Portable Network Graphics (PNG)* specification is an open graphics standard that does not employ any patented algorithms.

J
K
L

M Abbreviation for megabyte (1,048,576 *bytes*).

Mac See *Macintosh.*

MAC See *media access control.*

MacBinary A *file transfer protocol (ftp)* for *Macintosh* computers that enables you to store Macintosh files on non–Macintosh computers without losing important information in the *resource fork* of Macintosh files, including *icons,* graphics, and information about the file (such as the creation date). Most Macintosh *communication programs* send and receive files in MacBinary.

machine code The program instructions that are actually read and acted on by the computer's processing circuitry. Machine code is phrased in *binary numbers* and is virtually impossible for humans to read; for this reason, programmers use *assembly language* or a *high-level programming language* to write programs, which are then *compiled* into machine code. In some processors (especially *RISC* processors), machine code instructions directly generate control signals that tell the processor which tasks to perform, but a more common design uses *microcode,* an intermediary, built-in control language, to interpret the machine code instructions. Because machine code takes advantage of the unique characteristics of a given processor, a compiled program written for one processor (or processor family) will not execute on a different processor design; in order to develop programs for more than one system, then, it is necessary to use *compilers* that generate the code needed for each type of processor. Synonymous with machine language.

machine cycle One complete, four-step process that the computer's processing unit performs for each *machine code* instruction, in which an instruction is fetched from memory, decoded so that the processor can generate the correct control signals, and executed by generating the control signals. The results are stored in memory.

machine dependent The inability of a given computer program to run on any computer other than the one for which it was designed. See *device dependent.*

machine language   See *machine code.*

machine learning   The capacity of a computer program or system to improve its efficiency, speed, or some other aspect of performance based on conclusions drawn from previous experience.

MacHTTP   A popular, easy-to-use *Web server* for *Macintosh* computers that can handle up to 10 simultaneous connections. A more powerful commercial version is called WebStar.

Macintosh   A line of *personal computers* created by *Apple Computer,* released in 1984. The Macintosh pioneered the *graphical user interface (GUI),* which was first developed, but never successfully marketed, by Xerox Corporation. The Macintosh also pioneered the concept of *Plug and Play (PnP)* peripherals, built-in *Small Computer System Interface (SCSI)* device support, and built-in local area networking. Early Macs were based on the Motorola 680x0 series of microprocessors; today's *Power Macintoshes* use Motorola's *PowerPC* microprocessor, a *RISC* chip. Since the introduction of Microsoft Windows, Apple has seen its technological lead steadily erode; this has been complicated by the firm's inability to develop a new operating system for the Macintosh that is capable of *preemptive multitasking.* Measures recently taken to halt the Macintosh's decline include licensing the Macintosh operating system, *MacOS,* to *clone* manufacturers (a step Apple's critics claim should have been made in the late 1980s), and purchasing NeXT, Inc., principally for its innovative operating system (see *Rhapsody*).

Macintosh file system   The file storage architecture of the *Macintosh* computer, in which every file has two components, called forks. The *data fork* stores data, such as a spreadsheet or word processing document; this component corresponds to the sole contents of files on other computer systems. Unique to the Macintosh is the second component, the *resource fork,* which contains program icons and information about the program, such as the name of the application that created it. See *MacBinary.*

M
N
O

MacOS   The *operating system* of *Macintosh* computers. Offering a *graphical user interface (GUI)* and limited *multitasking* capabilities, the MacOS began to lag behind competing operating systems (such as *Microsoft Windows 95* and *Microsoft Windows NT*) in mid-1990s, chiefly because of Apple's failure to introduce features crucial to running several programs at the same time in a stable OS environment. (These features include *multithreaded processing, symmetric multiprocessing, preemptive multitasking,* and *protected memory.*) The failure of the much–delayed *Copland* project, which would have brought these and many more features to System 8 (the successor to the current System 7), led Apple to go shopping for an operating system upgrade. After considering *BeOS,* Apple acquired *NextStep,* the operating system of NeXT computers, and *OpenStep,* the NeXT-developed object-oriented *application programming interface (API)* that enables rapid and inexpensive application development. These will be given a Macintosh user interface and released as Apple's next-generation system software (currently code-named *Rhapsody*). However, this new operating system is not currently planned to be *downward compatible* with current Macintoshes or Macintosh applications. For this reason, Apple has introduced a two-pronged OS strategy, which will include support for the current MacOS for three or four more years. *MacOS 8,* not yet released at this writing, offers an upgrade path for current Macintosh users; the revision should bring long-overdue OS stability to users of Macintosh systems.

MacPaint   The original *paint program,* developed for the earliest (1984) Macintosh.

macro   A *program* consisting of recorded *keystrokes* and an application's *command language* that, when run within the application, executes the keystrokes and commands to accomplish a task. Macros can automate tedious and often-repeated tasks, such as saving and backing up a file to a floppy, or create special *menus* to speed data entry.

Macromedia Director   A leading *animation* and multimedia *authoring* program for Windows and Macintosh systems, created by Macromedia. The company's *Shockwave* software enables multimedia authors to embed animations into Web pages; to play these animations, the browser must be equipped with the Shockwave *plug-in.*

Macromedia Freehand   A leading *vector graphics* program for Macintosh and Windows systems, created by Macromedia, that is optimized for Web publishing as well as professional design and illustration. See *Adobe Illustrator.*

MacTCP   A *Macintosh utility program,* developed by *Apple Computer* and included with *System* 7.5, that provides the

TCP/IP support needed to connect Macintoshes to the Internet. A separate *communications program* is needed to connect via Serial Line Internet Protocol *(SLIP)* or Point-to-Point Protocol *(PPP)*.

magic cookie   Older *Unix* term for a small unit of data that is passed from one program to another so that the receiving program can perform an operation. Synonymous with *cookie*.

magnetic disk   In data storage, a *random-access* storage medium that is the most popular method for storing and retrieving computer programs and data files. In personal computing, common magnetic disks include *5¹/₄-inch floppy disks, 3¹/₂-inch floppy disks,* and *hard disks* of various sizes. The disk is coated with a magnetically sensitive material. Magnetic *read/write heads* move across the surface of the spinning disk under the disk drive's automatic control to the location of desired information. The information stored on a magnetic disk can be repeatedly erased and rewritten, like any other magnetic storage medium.

magnetic medium   A *secondary storage* medium that uses magnetic techniques to store and retrieve data on disks or *tapes* coated with magnetically sensitive materials. Like iron filings on a sheet of waxed paper, these materials are reoriented when a magnetic field passes over them. During write operations, the *read/write head* emits a magnetic field that orients the magnetic materials on the disk or tape to represent encoded data. During read operations, the read/write head senses the encoded data on the medium.

magnetic tape   See *tape* and *tape drive*.

magneto-optical (MO) cartridge   The removable storage device used in a *magneto-optical (MO) drive*. MO cartridges are either 5¹/₄ inches across (with capacities up to 1300*M*) or 3¹/₂ inches across (with capacities up to 230M). The data on a magneto-optical cartridge is highly stable, unlike the data on *floppy* and *hard disks,* which tends to self-erase if the data isn't rewritten regularly.

**M
N
O**

magneto-optical (MO) drive   A data storage device that uses laser technology to heat an extremely small spot on a *magneto-optical (MO) cartridge* so that the magnetic medium used in the MO disk becomes capable of having its magnetic orientation changed by the *read/write head*. Though magneto-optical drives are slow (average *seek time* of 30 *ms,* compared to about 15 ms for hard drives) and expensive, they are highly suitable for backup storage and for storing large programs or data that is accessed infrequently.

magneto–resistive (MR) head　A technologically advanced kind of *read/write head* that uses a special metal alloy to improve *areal density* by packing *tracks* more tightly and increases *throughput* by having separate reading and writing portions. MR heads are often used in *hard disks* that employ *PRML read channel technology.*

mail bombing　A form of harassment that involves sending numerous large *e-mail* messages to a person's electronic mailbox.

mailbox　In *e-mail,* the storage space that has been set aside to store an individual's e-mail messages.

mailbox name　In an *Internet e-mail* address, one of the two basic parts of a person's address: the part to the left of the *at sign* (@), which specifies the name of the person's *mailbox.* To the right of the @ sign is the *domain name* of the computer that houses the mailbox. A person's mailbox name often is the same as his or her *login name.*

mail bridge　A *gateway* that enables users of one *network* or *online information service* to exchange *e-mail* with users of other networks or services. For example, *CompuServe* users can exchange mail with *Internet* users by means of a gateway.

mail client　See *e-mail client.*

mail exploder　See *mailing list manager.*

mail filter　A *filter* program or utility within an *e-mail* program that screens incoming mail, and then sorts the mail into folders or directories based on content found in one or more of the message's fields. For example, incoming mail from a mailing list can be directed to a separate folder for later reading, so that these messages do not obscure the more important personal mail in the user's inbox.

mail gateway　A computer that enables two mutually incompatible computer networks to exchange *e-mail.* America Online users, for example, can exchange e-mail with *Internet* users by means of a gateway. In some cases, gateways cannot handle *attachments.*

Mailing List Manager   A program that enables a mailing list moderator to manage an e-mail–based mailing list. The leading mailing list managers, such as Majordomo, provide tools for subscribing and unsubscribing users, distributing information about the list, and redistributing incoming messages so that everyone on the list receives a copy. Also called mail exploder.

mail merge   In *word processing programs,* a utility that draws information from a *database*—usually a mailing list—and incorporates it into a form document to create multiple copies of the document. Each copy of the document includes information from one record from the database. The most common application of mail merge utilities is to personalize form letters. Instead of generating "Dear Applicant" letters, you can use a mail-merge utility to generate letters that start, "Dear Mr. Bergman."

mail reflector   See *LISTSERV* and *mailing list manager.*

mail server   A *program* that responds automatically to *e-mail* messages. Mail server programs exist that enter or remove subscriptions to mailing lists and send information in response to a request.

mailto   In *HTML,* an *attribute* that enables Web authors to create a link to a person's *e-mail* address. When the user clicks the mailto link, the browser displays a window for composing an e-mail message to this address.

mail user agent   See *e-mail client.*

mainframe   A multi-user computer designed to meet the computing needs of a large organization. Originally, the term mainframe referred to the metal cabinet that housed the *central processing unit (CPU)* of early computers. The term came to be used generally to refer to the large central computers developed in the late 1950s and 1960s to meet the accounting and information-management needs of large organizations. The largest mainframes can handle thousands of *dumb terminals* and use terabytes of *secondary storage.* See *minicomputer, personal computer (PC),* and *workstation.*

M
N
O

main loop   In an *event-driven program,* the topmost level in the program's *control structure.* Typically, the main loop waits for user input in the form of a mouse click or a keystroke.

main memory   See *random-access memory (RAM)*.

main program   In *programming,* the part of a *program* containing the master sequence of instructions, unlike the *subroutines,* procedures, and functions that the main program calls.

main storage   See *random-access memory (RAM)*.

maintenance programming   Altering *programs* after they have been in use for a while. Maintenance programming may be performed to add *features,* correct *bugs* that escaped detection during testing, or update key variables (such as the inflation rate) that change over time.

maintenance release   A program revision that corrects a minor *bug* or makes a minor new feature available, such as a new *printer driver*. Maintenance releases are usually numbered in tenths (3.2) or hundredths (2.01), to distinguish them from major program revisions. Synonymous with interim update.

Majordomo   A popular *freeware* mailing list manager for *Unix computer systems*. See *LISTSERV* and *mailing list manager*.

male connector   In cables, a cable terminator and connection device in which the pins protrude from the connector's surface. Male connectors plug into *female connectors*.

mall   On the *World Wide Web (WWW)*, a shopping service that provides Web publishing space for business *storefronts* (Web pages that describe retail or service offerings). Malls typically offer credit-card ordering by means of secure servers and *shopping baskets,* which enable users to select purchases and pay for them all when they are finished shopping.

management information base   In a computer network, a database of the various network devices, such as *routers,* that enables network administrators to detect malfunctions and optimize network performance. See *Simple Network Management Protocol (SNMP)*.

management information system (MIS)   A *computer system,* based on a *mainframe, minicomputer,* local area network (LAN), or wide area network (WAN), designed to provide business managers with up-to-date information on the organization's performance.

man page In *Unix*, a page of online documentation concerning a given command.

manual recalculation In a *spreadsheet program*, a recalculation method that suspends the recalculation of values until you issue a command that forces recalculation to take place.

map A representation of *data* stored in memory. See *bitmap*.

MAPI See *Messaging Application Program Interface*.

mapping 1. The process of converting *data* encoded in one *format* to another format. In *database management*, for example, the database index provides a way of mapping the actual *data records* (which are stored on disk in a fixed order) to the display screen in useful ways. 2. In a *local area network (LAN)*, mapping refers to assigning *drive* letters to specific volumes and directories.

marquee 1. In Web pages, a scrolling banner containing information or advertising. 2. In *Microsoft Excel*, a moving dotted line that surrounds a cell or a range of cells that you've cut or copied. 3. In programs, an initial screen or banner that gives the program and publisher's names.

mask 1. A pattern of symbols or characters that, when imposed on a *data field*, limits the kinds of characters that you can type into the field. In a *database management program*, for example, the mask AZ lets you type any alphabetical character, uppercase or lowercase, but not numbers or other symbols. Synonymous with input mask. 2. In computer graphics, a pattern that enables a graphic designer to eliminate detail or isolate an image from its background.

massively parallel processing A type of *parallel processing* architecture that employs more than 1,000 inexpensive but fast *microprocessors* to tackle an unusually complex scientific or engineering problem.

mass storage See *secondary storage*.

master The first disk in a string of two attached to an *integrated drive electronics (IDE) host adapter*. Though the master disk does not control the *slave* disk, it interprets commands from the host adapter for it.

M
N
O

master document   In *word processing,* a *document* that contains commands that tell the program to print additional documents at the commands' locations. The program prints all the documents as though they were one, with consistent running headers/footers and page numbering. See *chain printing.*

masthead   In *desktop publishing (DTP),* the section of a newsletter or magazine that gives the details of its staff, ownership, advertising, subscription prices, etc.

math coprocessor   A secondary *microprocessor* that frees the *central processing unit (CPU)* from tedious, calculation-intensive chores. Math coprocessors can significantly speed up *computer-aided design (CAD)* drawing and *spreadsheet* calculation, but won't significantly improve *Microsoft Windows 95's* performance. Some CPUs, such as the *Intel 486DX* and *Pentium,* have math coprocessors built in. See *numeric coprocessor.*

Mathematica   A state-of-the-art environment for technical computing, created by Wolfram Research, that can solve equations and produce scientific graphs. Widely used in science and engineering for data visualization and problem solving, it is also widely used as an instructional tool.

matte finish   A quality of paper that does not reflect light as harshly as a *glossy finish.* Most users prefer matte finish paper to glossy finish paper, because it matches the light-absorbent qualities of *laser printer* text.

maximize   To zoom or enlarge a window so it fills the screen. See *minimize.*

maximize button   In *Microsoft Windows 3.1* and other *graphical user interfaces,* a button that enables the user to *maximize* a window so it fills the screen.

maximum RAM   The amount of *random-access memory (RAM)* that could possibly be installed on a particular *motherboard.* Maximum RAM specifications usually are expressed as "expandable-to" statements in advertisements, as in, "The motherboard has 8*M* RAM, expandable to 128M."

maximum transmission unit (MTU)   The largest *packet* that may be transmitted over a *packet-switching network.*

MB   Alternative abbreviation for megabyte (1,048,576 bytes).

Mbone   An experimental method of distributing data packets on the Internet in which a server broadcasts data to two or more servers simultaneously. This technique, also called *IP multicasting*, moves data packets to their multiple destinations in streams rather than packets, and is therefore more suitable for real–time audio and video than the standard TCP/IP network. Special routers are required.

Mbps   See *bits per second (bps)*.

MCA   See *Micro Channel Architecture*.

MCD   See *magneto-optical (MO) drive*.

MCGA   Acronym for MultiColor Graphics Array (MCGA). A *video standard* of IBM's Personal System/2. MCGA adds 64 *grayscale* shades to the *Color Graphics Adapter (CGA)* standard and provides the *Enhanced Graphics Adapter (EGA)* standard *resolution* of 640 *pixels* by 350 lines with 16 possible colors.

MCI   See *Media Control Interface*.

MDA   See *Monochrome Display Adapter*.

MDI   See *multiple document interface*.

mean time between failures (MTBF)   The statistical average operating time between the start of a component's life and the time of its first electronic or mechanical failure.

mechanical mouse   Unlike an *optical mouse,* a mechanical *mouse* relies on metal rollers, which are turned by the mouse's rubberized ball, to communicate its movements to the *central processing unit (CPU)*. Though mechanical mice may be used almost anywhere, their internal mechanisms tend to get dirty and require cleaning.

M
N
O

mechanicals   In *desktop publishing (DTP)*, the final pages or boards with pasted–up galleys of type and *line art,* sometimes with acetate or tissue overlays for *color separations* and notes, which you send to the offset printer. See *camera-ready copy*.

media   The plural of medium. See *secondary storage*.

media access control (MAC)   In a computer *network*, the *layer* that controls under what circumstances a *workstation* can get access to the physical media in order to originate a message to another workstation. A *protocol* is needed to prevent data *collisions,* which occur when two workstations begin broadcasting simultaneously. *Ethernet* networks use the *CSMA/CD* access protocol.

Media Control Interface (MCI)   In *Microsoft Windows 95,* the *multimedia extensions* that greatly simplify the task of *programming* multimedia device functions such as Stop, Play, and Record.

Media Player   An accessory provided with *Microsoft Windows 95* that provides a control center for *multimedia* devices, such as *CD-ROM drives.* The buttons resemble the familiar controls of a cassette tape player.

medium   See *storage medium.*

meg   Common abbreviation for *megabyte.*

mega–   Prefix indicating 1 million.

megabyte (M)   A measurement of storage capacity equal to approximately 1 million *bytes* (1,048,576 bytes).

megaflop   A *benchmark* used to rate *professional workstations, mainframes,* and *minicomputers.* A megaflop is equal to 1 million floating-point operations per second.

megahertz (MHz)   A unit of measurement, equal to 1 million electrical vibrations or cycles per second, commonly used to compare the *clock speeds* of computers.

membrane keyboard   A flat and inexpensive *keyboard* covered with a dust- and dirt-proof plastic sheet on which only the two-dimensional outline of computer keys appears. The user presses the plastic sheet and engages a switch hidden beneath. Accurately typing on a membrane keyboard is more difficult, but such keyboards are needed in restaurant kitchens or other locations where users may not have clean hands.

memory   The computer's *primary storage,* such as *random-access memory (RAM),* as distinguished from its *secondary storage,* such as *disk drives.*

memory address   A code number that specifies a specific location in a computer's *random-access memory (RAM).*

memory cache   See *cache memory.*

memory check   Part of the *power-on self-test (POST)* that verifies that the computer's *random-access memory (RAM)* is properly plugged in and is functioning well. As the computer goes through its *boot* routine, you can often see the progress of the memory check on the *display*. If there is a problem in memory, be sure to record the *memory address* of the error and give it to a computer repair technician.

memory controller gate array   Alternative term for Multicolor Graphics Array (*MCGA*), a *video standard* once used in the *low-end* models of IBM's Personal System/2 computers.

memory leak   A programming flaw that causes a program to use new portions of memory instead of rewriting previously used portions. A program with a memory leak (a common flaw of *beta software*) will consume additional memory as it is used; in the worst case, the program will consume all of the available memory and eventually cause the computer to stop operating.

memory management   Collective term for a variety of strategies for ensuring that programs have sufficient available memory to function correctly. See *memory-management program* and *virtual memory*.

memory management unit (MMU)   In a computer equipped with *virtual memory*, a chip (*integrated circuit*) that enables the computer to use a portion of the hard disk as if it were an extension of the computer's *random-access memory (RAM)*. See *virtual memory*.

memory-management program   A *utility program* that increases the apparent size of *random-access memory (RAM)* by making *expanded memory*, *extended memory*, or virtual memory available for the execution of programs. See *EMM386.EXE*, *expanded memory emulator*, and *HIMEM.SYS*.

M
N
O

memory map   An arbitrary allocation of portions of a computer's *random-access memory (RAM)*, defining which areas the computer can use for specific purposes.

memory protection   See *protected memory*.

memory-resident program   See *terminate-and-stay-resident (TSR) program*.

memory word   See *word*.

menu   An on-screen display that lists available command choices. See *menu bar* and *pull-down menu*.

menu bar   In a *graphical user interface (GUI)*, a bar stretching across the top of the screen (or the top of a *window*) that contains the names of available *pull-down menus*. See *industry standard interface*.

menu-driven program   A *program* that provides you with menus for choosing program options so you don't need to memorize commands. Contrast with *command-driven program*.

merge printing   See *mail merge*.

message queue   In Microsoft Windows, a special space in the memory that is set aside to list the messages that applications send each other. In Microsoft Windows 3.1, there is only one message queue. If an application hangs and prevents other applications from checking the queue, the entire system is frozen beyond recovery. In *Microsoft Windows 95,* each *32-bit application* has its own message queue. If one application *aborts,* the others are not affected.

message transfer agent (MTA)   In *e-mail,* a program that sends e-mail messages to another message transfer agent. On the *Internet,* the most widely used MTA is *sendmail*.

Messaging Application Program Interface (MAPI)   The Microsoft implementation of an *application program interface* that provides access to messaging services for developers. MAPI Version 3.2 provides resources to programmers for cross-platform messaging that is independent of the operating system and underlying hardware and makes applications mail-aware. MAPI can send messages to and from *Vendor Independent Messaging (VIM) programs*.

metal-oxide semiconductor (MOS)   A *chip* based on the conductive and insulative properties of silicon dioxide, aluminum oxide, and other oxidized metals. MOS chips are electrically efficient but must be handled carefully because static electricity can destroy them. See *Complementary Metal-Oxide Semiconductor (CMOS)* and *semiconductor*.

metal–oxide varistor (MOV)   A device used to protect the computer from abnormally high line voltages. A MOV conducts electrical current only when it exceeds a certain voltage. A MOV in a *surge protector* conducts electrical current in excess of 350 volts away from the computer. See *surge*.

MFM   See *Modified Frequency Modulation*.

MHz   Abbreviation for *megahertz*.

MIB/MI   See *Plug and Print*.

mice   See *mouse*.

micro-   Prefix for small. Also a prefix indicating one millionth and an abbreviation (increasingly rare) for microcomputer.

Micro Channel Architecture (MCA)   The design speci-fications of IBM's proprietary *Micro Channel Bus*. An MCA-compatible peripheral is designed to plug directly into a *Micro Channel Bus* but won't work with other bus architectures.

Micro Channel Bus   A proprietary (and now obsolete) 32-bit *expansion bus* introduced by IBM for its PS/2 computers.

microcode   Program instructions embedded in the internal circuitry of a *microprocessor*. Microcode makes *software* program-mers' jobs easier because they can remain a step removed from the nitty-gritty details of what physically happens inside a microprocessor. It makes the task of *chip* designers harder. Because chips equipped with microcodes need extra internal components to translate external instructions into physical actions, they need to be bigger, slower, and more complex than they might otherwise be. See *complex instruction set computer (CISC)* and *reduced instruction set computer (RISC)*.

Microcom Networking Protocol (MNP)   Any of 10 error-correction and *data-compression protocols* used by *modems*. MNP 1 is obsolete; MNP-2, MNP-3, and *MNP-4* are error-correction protocols used in the *V.42* international standard. *MNP-5* is an on-the-fly data-compression protocol used by most modern modems, and MNP-6 through MNP 10 are *proprietary* commu-nications standards.

microcomputer   Any computer with its *arithmetic-logic unit (ALU)* and *control unit* contained on one *integrated circuit,* called a *microprocessor*. In the 1980s, microcomputers could be effectively contrasted with *minicomputers* and *mainframes* and typified as inexpensive, single–user systems. However, this is no longer true because minicomputers and even mainframes employ micro-processors. See *personal computer (PC)* and *professional workstation*.

microfine toner   Special *toner* for *laser* and *liquid crystal shutter (LCS) printers* that consists of finer particles than standard toner, enabling it to render text and *graphics* with finer detail.

micron   One millionth of a meter (about 0.0000394 inch).

microphone   A device that converts sounds into electrical sig-nals that can be processed by a computer. Commonly found on *Macintosh* computers but less often seen on *IBM PC-compatible* computers, microphones can be used to record new system sounds or to add voice annotations to *documents*.

microprocessor   An *integrated circuit* that contains the *arith-metic-logic unit (ALU), control unit* and sometimes the *floating-point unit (FPU)* of a computer's *central processing unit (CPU)*. Many microprocessors have been, are, or will be available, including the *Am386,* the *Am486,* the *Am486DX2,* the *Am486DX4,* the *AMD K5,* the *Cyrix 486DLC,* the *Cyrix 486DX2,* the *Cyrix 486SLC,* the *Cyrix CX486DRu2,* the *Cyrix 6x6MX,* the *IBM Blue Lightning,* the *Intel 80386,* the *Intel 386SL,* the *Intel 386SX,* the *Intel 80486,* the *Intel 486DX/2,* the *Intel 486DX/4,* the *Intel 486SL,* the *Intel 486SX,* the *Pentium Pro,* the *Motorola 68000,* the *Motorola 68020,* the *Motorola 68030,* and the *Pentium*.

microprocessor architecture   The overall design concept of a *microprocessor*. The two top–level architectural options are *complex instruction set computer (CISC)* and *reduced instruction set computer (RISC)*.

Microsoft   The world's largest and most successful publisher of *operating systems* and *application programs* for personal computers, headquartered in Redmond, WA, with 1996 annual sales of US $8.7 billion. Key products include *Microsoft Windows 95, Microsoft Windows NT, Microsoft Access, Microsoft Office, Microsoft Internet Explorer,* and *Microsoft Exchange*. Formerly perceived by many corporations as primarily a provider of single-user operating sys-tems and applications, Microsoft is now penetrating the enter-prise *client/server* market, thanks to the increasingly popular pairing of *Microsoft Windows NT* and powerful *Intel*-based *servers.*

Microsoft Access   A *relational database management system (RDBMS)* that features *wizards,* automated assistants that help organize and locate data, and Visual BASIC, an *application programming language.*

Microsoft at Work   A *Microsoft*-originated architecture for connecting *Microsoft Windows 3.1* computers with a variety of office peripherals, including fax and copy machines. The standards have been incorporated into *Microsoft Windows 95.*

Microsoft BackOffice   A package of *Web server* programs and utilities, from Microsoft Corporation, and designed for *Windows NT*-based networks. The package includes *Microsoft Windows NT Server, Microsoft Internet Information Server, Microsoft FrontPage,* and a series of utilities, including Microsoft Exchange Server (enterprise-wide *e-mail*), Microsoft SQL Server (database searching), Microsoft Proxy Server (enables external Internet access from behind a *firewall*), Microsoft Systems Management Server (provides centralized management tools for network administrators), and Microsoft SNA Server (integrates existing *legacy systems* with *intranets*).

Microsoft BASIC   A version of the BASIC programming language, designed for beginners in computing, that was originally developed by Microsoft co-founder Bill Gates for the Altair, the first commercially available microcomputer. *Microsoft Visual BASIC* has supplanted Microsoft BASIC.

Microsoft Bookshelf   A *CD-ROM*–based *application* that makes *The Original Roget's Thesaurus, The American Heritage Dictionary, The Columbia Dictionary of Quotations, The Hammond Intermediate World Atlas,* and *The World Almanac and Book of Facts* available on your computer. Considered a valuable resource for writers and other experts who need immediate access to reference data, Microsoft Bookshelf saves the time required to look up information in a bound volume.

M
N
O

Microsoft Excel   The market-dominating *spreadsheet program,* created by Microsoft Corporation, for Windows and Macintosh computers and sold separately or as part of the company's *Microsoft Office* suite. Microsoft Excel boasts extensive *formatting* tools and some extremely powerful *built-in functions* for many disciplines, including finance, engineering, and statistics. Microsoft Excel competes with *Quattro Pro* and *Lotus 1-2-3.*

Microsoft Exchange   A message-management program capable of managing faxes and several types of *e-mail* on a *local area network.* Microsoft Exchange Server provides enterprise–wide e-mail and groupware support for enterprises. Because many businesses are constructing *extranets* that require data exchange beyond the boundaries of the corporate LAN, Microsoft is migrating Exchange to an *Internet* protocol base; Exchange 5.0 supports *NNTP* news, *POP3* and *IMAP* mail, and other Internet protocols.

Microsoft FrontPage   A *WYSIWYG* editor for *HTML,* created by Microsoft, that combines advanced Web publishing with graphical site management. Some of the advanced features do not work unless your *Internet service provider (ISP)* is running the Microsoft FrontPage extensions for *Microsoft Internet Information Server.* The program is available for Windows and Macintosh systems.

Microsoft Intellimouse   An innovative *mouse* that includes a scrolling wheel positioned between the two mouse buttons. In compatible applications, the wheel can be used to zoom and scroll windows.

Microsoft Internet Assistant   An *HTML editor* and *Web browser* add–on for *Microsoft Word for Windows 6.0.* Distributed free of charge, Microsoft Internet Assistant transforms Microsoft Word into a *what-you-see-is-what-you-get (WYSIWYG)* HTML editor, in which you see the results of the HTML *tags* rather than the tags themselves.

Microsoft Internet Explorer (MSIE)   A popular *Web browser* for *Microsoft Windows* and *Macintosh* computers. Competing effectively with the most popular browser package, *Netscape Communicator,* the Internet Explorer suite includes e-mail and newsgroups via *Microsoft Outlook Express, push media* support with *Webcaster, WYSIWYG* HTML composing with a stripped-down version of *Microsoft FrontPage* called *FrontPad,* Internet telephony and videoconferencing with *Microsoft NetMeeting,* and streaming audio and video with *Microsoft NetShow.*

Microsoft Internet Information Server   A *Web server,* created by Microsoft Corporation for *Microsoft Windows NT* systems, that offers excellent performance on a much less expensive hardware platform than competing *Unix* servers. Included is a built-in search engine for searching documents, management tools, *Microsoft FrontPage,* and *ODBC* support for searching external *databases.* Tightly integrated with Windows NT (and requiring Windows NT Server), this server is a good choice for companies that have adopted Windows widely and that have Windows technical expertise; *Netscape Enterprise Server* is better suited to *cross-platform* networks that include *Unix* systems.

Microsoft Mail   A *proprietary* enterprise *e-mail* standard introduced by *Microsoft* with its enterprise messaging application, *Microsoft Exchange.* Microsoft is currently migrating mail formats to *Internet* protocols.

Microsoft Money   A home finance management program, similar to *Quicken,* that enables home computer users to balance their checkbooks, keep track of credit card accounts, and create budgets for household expenditures.

Microsoft Mouse   A *mouse* and associated software for IBM and *IBM PC-compatible* personal computers, including IBM's PS/1 and PS/2 computers. Available in serial and bus versions, the Microsoft Mouse uses the *mechanical mouse* technology that most mouse users favor.

Microsoft Natural Keyboard   An *ergonomic* keyboard developed by Microsoft Corporation that divides the keys into two split panels, which are angled outward so users' wrists are not bent at an angle when the keyboard is used. This arrangement is believed to reduce the incidence of painful *repetitive strain injuries (RSI)* such as *carpal tunnel syndrome (CTS).*

Microsoft NetMeeting   An Internet telephony and video-conferencing application for *Microsoft Windows 95* and *Microsoft Windows NT* that enables users to place free long-distance telephone calls via the Internet. Once connected, conference participants can engage in videoconferencing, text chatting, use a shared whiteboard, and—if both are running Microsoft Windows 95 or NT—share Windows applications so both users can make modifications to a shared on-screen window.

Microsoft NetShow   A *streaming audio* and *streaming video* application for *Microsoft Windows 95* and *Microsoft Windows NT.* Supplied with *Microsoft Internet Explorer,* NetShow can enable high-speed, television-quality broadcasting in real time over corporate LANs as well as deliver prerecorded audio and video of acceptable quality over 28.8 Kbps modem connections. NetShow broadcasting requires the NetShow server, included with *Microsoft Internet Information Server (IIS)*.

Microsoft Office Professional   A *suite* of *application programs,* published by *Microsoft Corporation,* that includes *Microsoft Access* in addition to the programs in *Microsoft Office Standard*. Microsoft Office Professional competes with *Lotus SmartSuite* and *Corel Office Pro*.

Microsoft Office Standard   A *suite* of *application programs,* published by *Microsoft Corporation,* that includes *Microsoft Word, Microsoft Excel, Microsoft PowerPoint,* and *Microsoft Mail*. Microsoft Office Standard competes with *Corel WordPerfect Suite* and *Lotus SmartSuite*. See *Microsoft Office Professional*.

Microsoft Outlook   A *personal information manager (PIM),* created by Microsoft Corporation, that combines *e-mail,* scheduling and calendar functions, a *contact management program,* simple *project management,* and favorite *World Wide Web (WWW)* sites and documents. For Windows computers, Outlook is available separately or as part of the *Microsoft Office* package.

Microsoft Outlook Express   An easy-to-use *e-mail* program, distributed with Internet Explorer, that includes advanced features such as *filters* and *S-MIME* encryption.

Microsoft PowerPoint   A *presentation graphics* program that enables you to incorporate information from *spreadsheets* and *word processors* (especially *Microsoft Excel* and *Microsoft Word,* with which Microsoft PowerPoint coexists in the *Microsoft Office Standard* and *Microsoft Office Professional suites*) into attractive, persuasive presentations. Microsoft PowerPoint makes it easy to jazz up dull numbers and lists with color, graphical elements, and *clip art*.

Microsoft Project   A *project management program* for Windows and Macintosh computers, created by Microsoft Corporation, that enables project planners and managers to plan tasks and allocate resources in a graphical environment.

Microsoft Publisher   An inexpensive *desktop publishing (DTP)* program targeted toward the home and small business user. It lacks the sophisticated features of programs like QuarkXPress and *Adobe PageMaker*, but it provides many pre-designed templates and is very easy to use.

Microsoft Visual BASIC A version of the *BASIC* programming language that enables programmers to develop functioning Windows applications quickly. Tightly integrated with Microsoft Windows, Visual BASIC obviates the need to create the user interface; programmers use built-in tools to create the user interface visually and then attach code to the various on-screen objects. The Professional Edition includes a *compiler* that creates executable programs that do not require an *interpreter*. A host of Microsoft and third-party utilities enable programmers to quickly add components, such as database searching or Internet connectivity.

Microsoft Windows Generic name for the various *operating systems* in the Microsoft Windows family, including *Microsoft Windows CE, Microsoft Windows 3.1, Microsoft Windows 95,* and *Microsoft Windows NT.*

Microsoft Windows 3.1 A *16-bit operating system* for Intel *microprocessors* that enables users of MS-DOS computers to use programs with a graphical user interface (GUI). Essentially an *MS-DOS* program that switches the microprocessor into its *protected mode*, Windows enables users to run *Windows 3.1 applications*, but without providing protections that would prohibit programs from invading each other's memory space when run simultaneously (see *protected memory*). *Multitasking* is slow because Windows 3.1 does not implement *multithreading*. Despite these flaws, Windows 3.1 is still in use on millions of computers worldwide (including a reported 74% of corporate PCs), and many users see no reason to upgrade to Microsoft's current offerings (Windows 95 and Windows NT).

M N O

Microsoft Windows 95 A *32-bit operating system* for Intel *microprocessors* that takes full advantage of the processing capabilities of *Intel 80486* and *Pentium* microprocessors, while retaining downward compatibility with Windows 3.1 programs. Compared to *Microsoft Windows 3.1,* Windows 95 offers a redesigned *Graphical User Interface (GUI)* that enhances ease of learning as well as day-to-day usability. Additional innovations include long *file names*, 32-bit disk and file systems, *preemptive multitasking, multithreading*, improved handling of *system resource* problems, *general* *protection faults (GPF),* and built-in support for the *Microsoft Network* and the *Internet.* It also combines 16-bit and 32-bit *source code* to ensure reliable operation of existing 16-bit applications. Windows 95 is not a true 32-bit operating system (like *OS/2 Warp* or Microsoft's own *Microsoft Windows NT*); nevertheless, users appreciate not having to upgrade their applications. For corporate environments, Windows 95 includes built-in network support, offering a consistent interface for accessing network resources on a variety of physical media. To aid in the often arduous task of installing new hardware components, Windows 95 incorporates *Plug and Play (PnP)* capabilities, which allow nearly automatic installation and configuration of compatible accessories (such as sound cards and CD-ROM drives).

Microsoft Windows CE   A 32-bit *operating system* for handheld portable computers. Closely resembling the familiar Windows 95 but with reduced functionality, Windows CE comes with similarly miniaturized ("pocket") versions of *Microsoft Word, Microsoft Excel,* and *Microsoft Internet Explorer,* and is an important factor in the market success of *palmtop computers.*

Microsoft Windows NT   A *32-bit operating system* for Intel *micrprocessors.* The official name of the product is *Microsoft Windows NT Workstation,* to distinguish the client-level program from *Windows NT Server,* but it is usually referred to as Windows NT. On high-end *Pentium* systems, Windows NT provides the performance of *Unix workstations* that cost far more money— and without sacrificing compatibility with personal productivity applications. Windows NT is designed for engineers, scientists, statisticians, and other professional or technical workers who carry out processor-intensive tasks. In addition to high-performance Intel processors, Windows NT runs on workstations based on the Alpha and MIPS processors. From version 4.0, Windows NT boasts a user interface that is identical to the one used on *Microsoft Windows 95.*

Microsoft Windows NT Server   A Windows NT-based *server* for networks in which the workstations are running *Microsoft Windows NT* or other versions of Windows. Using powerful *Intel*-based PCs that are capable of matching the performance of many *mainframe* computer systems, enterprises can create *client/server* systems using Windows NT at a fraction of the cost of previous solutions. *Internet* and *intranet* capabilities are added with *Microsoft Internet Information Server,* which requires Windows NT Server.

Microsoft Word A full-featured *word processor*. Microsoft Word competes mainly with *WordPerfect* but also with *Lotus Word Pro*. Word has surpassed longtime favorite WordPerfect in terms of *feature*-richness and usability, not to mention market share. One of Microsoft Word's most useful advanced features is Auto-Correct, which automatically fixes spelling errors you make frequently (such as the common substitution of "teh" for "the"). *Wizards,* automated helpers that assist with such things as *mail merges* and *formatting,* and support for object linking and embedding *(OLE),* are also included in Microsoft Word. Microsoft Word is highly customizable: *toolbars* and *menu bars* can be altered to suit individual tastes, and a very powerful *macro* language, based on Visual BASIC, is included.

micro-to-mainframe The linkage of *personal computers* to *mainframe* or *minicomputer networks.*

middleware In a *cross-platform network,* programs that serve as intermediaries between *clients* requesting information and *server* programs that provide requested data, even though the clients and servers may be running on different computing platforms and were not originally designed to work with each other. A simple example of middleware is a *Web server* script written according to *Common Gateway Interface (CGI)* guidelines; the script enables external Web browsers to communicate with programs that can provide such functions as database searching. See *Common Object Request Brokerage Architecture.*

MIDI Acronym for Musical Instrument Digital Interface. A standard *communications protocol* for the exchange of information between computers and music synthesizers. MIDI provides tools that many composers and musicians say are becoming almost indispensable. With a synthesizer and a computer equipped with the necessary software and a MIDI port, a musician can transcribe a composition into musical notation by playing the composition at the *keyboard.* After the music is placed into computer-represented form, virtually every aspect of the digitized sound—pitch, attack, delay time, tempo, and more—can be edited and altered. On the *Internet,* a major advantage of MIDI is that the exchanged files are text-based and very small. When playing MIDI sounds, best results are obtained with a *wave-table synthesis* sound card.

**M
N
O**

MIDI cueing In *multimedia,* a set of *MIDI* messages that determines the occurrence of events other than musical notes (such as recording, playing back, or turning on lighting devices).

MIDI file A file containing musical data encoded according to *MIDI* specifications. In *Microsoft Windows 95,* MIDI files use the extension .MID.

MIDI interface See *MIDI port.*

MIDI port A receptacle that enables you to connect a personal computer directly to a musical synthesizer. See *MIDI.*

migration A change from an older *hardware* platform, *operating system,* or *software* version to a newer one. For example, industry observers expect corporations to migrate from Microsoft Windows 3.1 to *Microsoft Windows 95.*

milli– Prefix indicating one thousandth.

million instructions per second See *MIPS.*

millisecond (ms) A unit of measurement, equal to one-thousandth of a second, commonly used to specify the *access time* of hard disk drives.

MIME Acronym for Multipurpose Internet Mail Extensions. An *Internet* standard that specifies how tools, such as *e-mail* programs and *Web browsers,* can transfer *multimedia* files (including sounds, graphics, and video) via the Internet. Prior to the development of MIME, all data transferred via the Internet had to be coded in *ASCII text.* See *uuencode* and *uudecode.*

MIME encoding In an *e-mail* message, a method of encoding *binary files* in conformance with the Multipurpose Internet Mail Extension *(MIME)* standard. In order to receive the Mail message, the user must be running an *e-mail client* that is capable of decoding this format. Another commonly used encoding format is *uuencode.*

MIME type In Multipurpose Internet Mail Extensions *(MIME),* a code that specifies the content type of a multimedia file. The *Internet Assigned Numbers Authority (IANA)* controls the naming of MIME types. A Web browser detects MIME types by examining the file's extension; for example, a file with the extension *.mpg or *.mpeg contains an MPEG video.

mini–AT-size case A desktop (horizontal) case that mounts the *motherboard* in the same way as the *AT-size case* but takes up less space and has fewer *expansion slots.* See *tower case.*

minicomputer A multi-user computer designed to meet the needs of a small company or a department. A minicomputer is more powerful than a personal computer but not as powerful as a *mainframe.* Typically, about 4 to 100 people use a minicomputer simultaneously.

mini-driver In *Microsoft Windows 95,* the portion of a *driver* that relates directly to *hardware,* such as a *printer* or *modem.* Mini-drivers take up less disk space than old-style drivers because they share more resources with the *operating system.*

minimize In a *graphical user interface (GUI),* to shrink a window so that it collapses to an *icon* on the *desktop.* You minimize a window by clicking the minimize button (the left button in the upper-right corner) or by choosing Minimize from the *Control menu.* When you minimize an application in *Microsoft Windows 95,* the application appears as an icon on the *taskbar.*

mini-tower case A vertical case designed to fit into a smaller space than a full-sized *tower case.* Though they have less space for *disk drives* and other devices than tower cases, mini-tower cases can have as many *expansion slots* as desktop cases, even with their smaller *footprint.* See *AT-size case* and *mini-AT-size case.*

MIPS Acronym for million instructions per second (MIPS). A *benchmark* method for measuring the rate at which a computer executes *microprocessor* instructions. A computer capable of 0.5 MIPS, for example, can execute 500,000 instructions per second.

mirror To copy automatically to another storage location.

mirror site An *FTP* site that keeps an exact copy of another FTP site available for the convenience of users in a specific country or region of a country or to relieve the traffic load on a very popular site.

M
N
O

MIS See *management information system.*

misc hierarchy In *Usenet,* one of the *standard newsgroup hierarchies,* containing newsgroups that do not fit in the other categories (comp, sci, news, rec, soc, and talk). Examples of misc newsgroups include misc.consumers, misc.kids.computers, and misc.writing.

mixed cell reference In a *spreadsheet program,* a cell reference in which the column reference is absolute but the row reference is relative ($A9), or in which the row reference is absolute but the column reference is relative (A$9). See *absolute cell reference, cell reference,* and *relative cell reference.*

mixed column/line graph In presentation and analytical graphics, a graph that displays one *data series* using columns and another data series using lines. You use a line graph to suggest a trend over time; a column graph groups data items so that you can compare one to another.

MMCD Acronym for Multimedia Compact Disc. A proprietary multimedia *CD-ROM* standard developed by Sony Corporation that can store up to (3.7G) of multimedia data on a single disc. This proposed standard has been abandoned in favor of industry-wide consensus of the *DVD* (Digital Video Disc) standard.

MMU See *memory management unit.*

MMX A set of *instruction set* extensions for *Intel's Pentium* microprocessors that enable direct, high-speed execution of multimedia data, including voice, audio, and video. MMX-enabled systems are able to execute multimedia programs up to eight times faster than systems equipped with external multimedia processing circuitry, but programs must be especially designed to take advantage of the MMX instructions.

mnemonic In programming, an abbreviation or word that makes it easier to remember a complex instruction. In *assembly language,* for example, the mnemonic MOV may stand for an instruction that moves data to a storage location.

MNP See *Microcom Networking Protocol.*

MNP-4 The most popular *error-correcting protocol,* which filters out *line noise* and eliminates errors that can occur during the transmission and reception of data via *modem.* For error correcting to function, both modems—the one sending as well as the one receiving the transmission—must have error-checking capabilities conforming to the same error-correcting protocol.

MNP-5 The same *error-correcting protocol* as *MNP-4,* as well as a data-compression protocol for computer *modems* that speeds transmissions by compressing (encoding, actually) data on the sending end and decompressing the data on the reception end. If the data isn't already compressed, gains in effective transmission speeds of up to 200 percent can be realized. See *data-compression protocol*.

MO cartridge   See *magneto-optical (MO) cartridge*.

mode   The operating state in which you place a *program* by choosing among a set of exclusive operating options. Within a given mode, certain commands and *keystrokes* are available, but you may need to change modes to use other commands or keystrokes.

mode indicator   An on-screen message that displays the program's current operating *mode*. In *Lotus 1-2-3*, for example, the mode indicator appears in the upper-right corner of the screen.

model   A simulation of a system that exists in the real world, such as an aircraft fuselage or a business's cash flow. The purpose of constructing a model is to gain a better understanding of the prototype—the system being modeled. By examining or changing the characteristics of the model, you can draw inferences about the prototype's behavior.

modem   A device that converts the digital signals generated by the *serial port* to the modulated analog signals required for transmission over a telephone line and, likewise, transforms incoming analog signals to their digital equivalents. The speed at which a modem (short for modulator/demodulator) transmits data is measured in units called *bits per second,* or *bps* (technically not the same as *baud,* although the terms are often and erroneously used interchangeably). Modems come in various speeds and use various modulation protocols. The most recent standard (at this writing), an addition to the V.34 standard, enables communication at 33.6 Kbps. Several proprietary standards have been offered for 56 Kbps modems, including U.S. Robotics' *x.2* protocol. Two common standards for *error-correcting protocols* eliminate errors attributable to noise and other *glitches* in the telephone system: *MNP-4* and *V.42.* For data-compression, two standards predominate: *V.42bis* and *MNP-5.*

**M
N
O**

moderated   Supervised by a human being rather than a computer. See *moderated newsgroup*.

moderated newsgroup   In a *distributed bulletin board* system (BBS), such as *Usenet,* a topical conference in which one or more moderators screen contributions before the post appears.

The moderator's job, often mistaken for censorship, is to ensure that postings adhere to the group's stated topic. A moderator also may rule out discussion on certain subtopics if postings on such subjects turn out to be *flame bait* (postings likely to cause an unproductive and bitter debate with low information content).

moderator   In *Usenet* and *mailing lists,* a volunteer who takes on the task of screening messages submitted to a *moderated newsgroup* or moderated mailing list.

Modified Frequency Modulation (MFM)   A method of recording digital information on a *magnetic medium,* such as *tapes* and disks, by eliminating redundant or blank areas. Because the MFM *data-encoding scheme* doubles the storage attained under the earlier frequency-modulation (FM) recording technique, MFM recording usually is referred to as *double density.* MFM often is wrongly used to describe *hard disk controllers* conforming to the *ST-506/ST-412* standard. MFM actually refers to the method used to pack data on the disk and isn't synonymous with disk drive *interface standards,* such as ST-506, *Small Computer System Interface (SCSI),* or *Enhanced Small Device Interface (ESDI).* See *Run-Length Limited (RLL).*

MO drive   See *magneto-optical (MO) drive.*

Modula-2   A *high-level programming language* that extends *Pascal* so the language can execute program modules independently. Developed in 1980 by computer wizard and *Pascal* creator Niklaus Wirth, Modula-2 supports the separate compilation of program modules and overcomes many other shortcomings of Pascal. A programmer working as part of a team can write and compile the module he or she has been assigned and then test the module extensively before integrating it with other modules. Although Modula-2 is increasingly popular as a teaching language at colleges and universities, *C++* dominates professional software development. See *modular programming* and *structured programming.*

modular accounting package   A collection of accounting programs—one for each chief accounting function (general ledger, accounts payable, accounts receivable, payroll, and inventory, for example)—designed to work together, even though they aren't integrated into one program. Modular packages require you to follow special procedures to make sure that all the modules work together. These programs haven't found a large market in personal computing for two reasons: They rarely mimic the way small-businesses operators keep their books, and they're often hard to use.

modular jack   Synonymous with RJ-11 jack, the standard receptacle for the connectors on telephone cable, found both in wall sockets and on *modems*. Wall sockets built before 1970 may have an incompatible, four-prong connector that can be connected to a RJ-11 plug with an RJA1X adapter.

modular programming   A *programming* style that breaks down program functions into modules, each of which accomplishes one function and contains all the *source code* and variables needed to accomplish that function. Modular programming is a solution to the problem of very large programs that are difficult to *debug* and maintain. By segmenting the program into modules that perform clearly defined functions, you can determine the source of program errors more easily. *Object-oriented programming (OOP) languages,* such as *SmallTalk* and *HyperTalk,* incorporate modular programming principles.

modulation   The conversion of a *digital* signal to its *analog* equivalent, especially for the purposes of transmitting signals using telephone lines and *modems*. See *demodulation*.

modulation protocol   In *modems,* the standards used to govern the speed at which a modem sends and receives information over the telephone lines. See *Bell 103A, Bell 212A,* and *CCITT protocol.*

module   In a *program,* a unit or section that can function on its own. In an integrated program, for instance, you can use the *word processing* module as though it were a separate, stand-alone program.

moiré effect   An optical illusion, perceived as flickering, that sometimes occurs when you place high-contrast line patterns (such as cross-hatching in *pie graphs*) too close to one another.

monitor   The complete device that produces an on-screen image, including the *display* and all necessary internal support circuitry. A monitor also is called a video display unit (VDU). See *analog monitor, digital monitor, Enhanced Graphics Display, monochrome monitor,* and *multiscanning monitor.*

monitor program   A program that keeps track of and records the behavior of other programs, often for purposes of tracking bugs. Also, an obsolete synonym for *kernel*.

Monochrome Display Adapter (MDA)   A single-color *display adapter* for *IBM PC-compatible* computers that displays text (but not *graphics*) with a resolution of 720 *pixels* horizontally and 350 lines vertically, placing characters in a matrix of 7 by 9. See *Hercules Graphics Adapter*.

Monochrome Display and Parallel Printer Adapter   See *Monochrome Display Adapter (MDA)*.

monochrome monitor   A *monitor* that displays one color against a black or white background. Examples include the IBM monochrome monitor that displays green text against a black background, and paper-white *Video Graphics Array (VGA)* monitors that display black text on a white background. See *paper-white monitor*.

monochrome printer   A printer that can generate output in black, white, and shades of gray, but not color.

monospace   A typeface, such as Courier, in which the width of each character is the same, producing output that looks like typed characters. The following is an example of monospace type:

```
The width of each character in this typeface is exactly the same.
```

Compare to *proportional spacing*.

monospaced font   See *monospace*.

monthly duty cycle   The number of pages a *printer* is designed to print each month. *Personal laser printers* can have monthly duty cycles as low as a few hundred pages, while *departmental laser printers* can have monthly duty cycles in excess of 200,000 pages.

MOO   A type of Multi-User Dungeon *(MUD)* that incorporates a sophisticated, *object-oriented programming language,* which participants can use to construct their own personalized characters and worlds.

Moore's Law   An observation made in 1965, by Intel co-founder Gordon Moore, that chips with approximately twice as much circuit density as their predecessors appear approximately every 2 years. Although Moore's prediction remains true at this writing, chip designers will inevitably run up against physical limitations that prevent further miniaturization of computer circuits.

morphing Short for metamorphosing; a revolutionary animation technique used to "fill in the blanks" between dissimilar figures so that one seems to melt into another, such as changing a man to a werewolf, a bat to a vampire, or a rock singer to a panther. Morphing, a common film industry special-effects technique, is related closely to another, more prosaic animation technique called *tweening* (short for in-betweening), which refers to the computer's capability to calculate and draw frames that are intermediate between the "key" frames hand-drawn by the artist. Morphing is the process of tweening to a different object.

MOS See *metal-oxide semiconductor.*

Mosaic A *Web browser* created by the *National Center for Supercomputing Applications (NCSA)* and placed in the *public domain.* Though Mosaic was one of the earliest Web browsers, it has been superseded by *Netscape Navigator.* See *World Wide Web (WWW).*

most significant bit (MSB) In a *binary number,* the bit representing the position of greatest magnitude (normally, this is the left-most bit). See *least significant bit.*

motherboard A large circuit board that contains the computer's *central processing unit (CPU), microprocessor* support chips, *random-access memory (RAM),* and *expansion slots.* Synonymous with logic board.

Motif A *graphical user interface (GUI)* for *Unix* computers that is based on *X-Windows* and standardized by the *Open Software Foundation (OSF).* See *OpenWindows.*

Motorola A Schaumburg, Illinois-based designer and manufacturer of electronic equipment, notably *semiconductors.* Motorola's *680x0 microprocessors* were used in early *Macintosh* computers, and the company collaborated with IBM and Apple to design the PowerPC series of chips that are found in *Power Macintoshes.* See *PowerPC 601.*

**M
N
O**

Motorola 68000   A *microprocessor* that processes 32 *bits* internally, although it uses a 16-bit *data bus* to communicate with the
rest of the computer. The 68000 can address up to 32 megabytes
of *random-access memory (RAM)*. Running at 8 MHz, the 68000
powers the entry-level Macintosh Classic.

Motorola 68020   A *microprocessor* electronically similar to the
Motorola 68000, except that this microprocessor uses a full 32-
bit architecture and runs at a *clock speed* of 16 *megahertz (MHz)*.
The 68020 powers the original Macintosh II, displaced by newer
models using the *Motorola 68030* chip.

Motorola 68030   A full *32-bit microprocessor* that can run at
substantially higher *clock speeds* (16 to 50 *megahertz [MHz]*) than
the Motorola 68000 and 68020. The 68030 includes special
features for *virtual memory management*. The 68030 incorporates
a chip that controls *page-mode RAM,* so any 68030-equipped
Macintosh can implement the advanced memory management
features of *System 7.5.*

Motorola 68040   A *32-bit microprocessor* in *Motorola's* 680x0
family that represents an evolutionary advance over its immediate predecessor, the *68030.* Analogous to the Intel 80486DX
microprocessor, the 68040 packs more circuitry into its tiny
confines, reducing the need for support chips and improving
performance. For example, the 68040 includes a *numeric coprocessor*, eliminating the need for a coprocessor chip. The 68040
powers the high-end Quadra models of Apple Computer's
Macintosh computers.

Motorola 680x0   Any *microprocessor* in the *Motorola 68000*
family (including the *Motorola 68020, Motorola 68030* and
Motorola 68040).

Motorola 68881   The *numeric coprocessor* used with the
Motorola *68000* and *68020 microprocessors*.

mount   To insert a *floppy disk* into a *floppy disk drive.* Installing
hardware, such as a *motherboard, disk drive,* and *adapters,* is also
referred to as mounting.

mousable interface   A *user interface* that responds to *mouse*
input for such functions as selecting text, choosing commands
from *menus,* and *scrolling* the screen.

mouse   An input device, equipped with one or more control buttons, that is housed in a palm-sized case and designed so that you can roll it about on the table next to your *keyboard*. As the mouse moves, its circuits relay signals that correspondingly move a *pointer* on-screen. A mouse is distinguished by the internal mechanism it uses to generate its signal and by its means of connection with the computer. Two types of internal mechanisms are popular:

- **Mechanical mouse.** This mouse has a rubber-coated ball on the underside of the case. As you move the mouse, the ball rotates and optical sensors detect the motion. You can use a mechanical mouse on virtually any surface, although a smooth mouse pad gives the best results.

- **Optical mouse.** This mouse registers its position by detecting reflections from a light-emitting diode that directs a beam downward. You must have a special metal pad to reflect the beam properly, and you can't move the mouse beyond the pad.

See *built-in pointing device, clip-on pointing device, freestanding pointing device, trackball, Microsoft mouse,* and *snap-on pointing device.*

mouse elbow   A painful *repetitive strain injury (RSI),* similar to tennis elbow, that is produced by lifting one's hand repeatedly to manipulate a *mouse.*

mouse port   Also called a PS/2 mouse port, a mouse port enables you to connect a *mouse* to the computer without tying up a *serial port.* A mouse port is a small, round socket into which you plug a PS/2-compatible mouse.

MOV   See *metal-oxide varistor.*

moving border   See *marquee.*

Moving Picture Experts Group   See *MPEG.*

MP3   Abbreviation for MPEG-I Audio Layer III. An *MPEG audio* format that produces CD-quality audio with a 12:1 compression ratio.

MPC   Acronym for Multimedia Personal Computer. A standard for *multimedia hardware* and software jointly developed by the MPC Consortium, which includes *Microsoft Corporation,*

M
N
O

Philips, Tandy, and Zenith Data Systems. Microsoft Windows 3.1 provides the foundation for MPC. The MPC standard assumes an IBM PS/2 or IBM-compatible hardware platform; Apple Computer, not surprisingly, has offered a competing standard (*QuickTime*) for its *Macintosh* computer. MPC has been replaced by the *MP-3* standard.

MPC-2   Acronym for Multimedia Personal Computer-2. A standard, developed by a consortium of computer-industry companies, that describes the minimum computer configuration needed to run *multimedia* applications. The standard calls for a 486SX–25 *microprocessor,* 8*M* of *random-access memory (RAM),* a *Video Graphics Array (VGA) monitor,* and a *double-speed* CD–ROM *drive*.

MPC-3   Acronym for Multimedia Personal Computer-3. A standard, developed by a consortium of computer-industry companies, that describes the minimum computer configuration needed to run *multimedia* applications. This standard, the current one, calls for a 75 MHz Pentium processor, 8*M* of *random-access memory (RAM)*, *MPEG* video, and a *4X* CD–ROM drive.

MPEG   Acronym for Moving Picture Experts Group (MPEG). A working group of digital video experts who meet regularly under the auspices of the *International Standards Organization (ISO)* and the International Electro-technical Commission (IEC) to develop standards for compressed digital audio. See *MPEG audio* and *MPEG video.*

MPEG audio   A format for the compression of digitized stereo audio that employs a standard developed by the Moving Picture Experts Group *(MPEG).* The MPEG *lossy compression* technique is psychoacoustic; the removed information isn't normally perceived by the ears. Stereo MPEG files can deliver impressive-sounding stereo when played through a good *sound card* and speakers, although the sound is not up to the standards of audio compact discs. The MPEG-I standard calls for near-CD-quality digitized sound (Audio Layer II) or CD-quality sound with 12-1 compression (Audio Layer III).

MPEGPLAY   An MPEG video player for *Microsoft Windows 95,* created by Michael Simmons. This *shareware* program is widely used as a *helper program* for *Web browsers.*

MPEG video   A format for the *lossy compression* of digitized videos and animations that a standard developed by the Moving Picture Experts Group *(MPEG)*. The MPEG-1 standard provides a "postage stamp" video resolution of 352 × 240. The MPEG-2 standard provides video resolutions of 720 × 480 and CD-quality stereo sound. A proposed MPEG-3 standard designed for High-Definition Television (HDTV) has been incorporated into MPEG-2.

MPR I   An old Swedish standard, outmoded by the more stringent *MPR II* and *TCO* standards, for limiting *electromagnetic radiation* from monitors.

MPR II   A standard for monitor radiation developed by Sweden's National Board for Industrial and Technical Development in 1987 and updated in 1990. To meet MPR II standards, a monitor can't emit more than 250 nanoteslas of electromagnetic radiation at a distance of a half-meter.

MPU 401   The standard that governs the design of the *MIDI port,* which is used to connect musical instruments to computer *sound boards.* The MPU 401 standard dictates that the port have some of its own sound-processing circuitry, lessening the load on the rest of the computer.

MR head   See *magneto-resistive (MR) head*.

ms   See *millisecond*.

MSB   See *most significant bit*.

MS-DOS   The standard, single-user *operating system* of IBM and IBM-compatible computers, introduced in 1981. MS-DOS is a command-line operating system that requires you to enter commands, *arguments,* and *syntax.* Although many users are migrating to *Microsoft Windows 95* to use its memory-management capabilities and easier-to-use interface, millions of older IBM-compatible computers exist that can't run Windows well. MS-DOS is unquestionably the world's most widely used operating system and is likely to remain so for years to come. See *application program interface (API), CP/M (Control Program for Microprocessors), Microsoft Windows NT, MS-DOS QBasic, OS/2, PC DOS, protected mode, real mode, terminate-and-stay-resident (TSR) program,* and *Unix*.

M
N
O

MS-DOS QBasic   An improved *BASIC* programming environment, supplied with *MS-DOS* 5.0 and later, that includes extensive online help.

MSIE   See *Microsoft Internet Explorer.*

MTA   See *message transfer agent.*

MTBF   See *mean time between failures.*

MTU   See *maximum transmission unit.*

MUD   Acronym for Multi-User Dungeon. A MUD is a form of virtual reality designed for network use that offers participants an opportunity to interact with other computer users in real time. MUDs, originally developed to support online role-playing games (such as Dungeons & Dragons), have mostly been replaced by more flexible *MOOs.*

Multicast Backbone (Mbone)   An experimental system that can deliver real-time audio and video via the *Internet.* Capable of one-to-many and many-to-many transmission with low consumption of network resources, Mbone requires special software, which is installed on only a small number of the computers currently connected to the Internet. The Rolling Stones broadcast a concert on the Mbone during their 1994 Voodoo Lounge tour. See *multicasting.*

multicasting   In a *network,* the routing of a single message to two or more workstations.

MultiColor Graphics Array   See *MCGA.*

MultiFinder   A *utility program,* included in the *MacOS,* that extends the Finder's capabilities so that the *Macintosh* can run more than one application at a time. With MultiFinder, the Macintosh becomes a multiloading operating system with some limited capabilities to perform tasks in the background, such as downloading information via telecommunications and carrying out *background printing.* Contrary to common belief, MultiFinder isn't a true *multitasking* operating system; when you activate one application, the other application freezes. The lack of true multitasking support is the principle reason that the MacOS has been eclipsed by competing operating systems. Such support may finally appear in the announced *System 8.* See *context switching, Copland, multiple program loading,* and *shell.*

multilaunching   In a *local area network (LAN)*, the opening of an *application program* by more than one user at a time.

multilevel sort   In *database management,* a sort operation that uses two or more data fields to determine the order in which *data records* are arranged. To perform a multilevel sort, you identify two or more *data fields* as sort keys—fields used for ordering records. In a membership database, for example, the primary sort key may be LAST_NAME, so all records are alphabetized by the member's last name. The second sort key, FIRST_NAME, comes into play when two or more records have the same last name. A third sort key, JOIN_DATE, is used when two or more records have the same last name and the same first name. Use a multilevel sort when one sort key can't resolve the order of two or more records in your database.

Multilink Point-to-Point Protocol   An *Internet* standard for *ISDN* connections between an *Internet service provider (ISP)* and an ISDN terminal adapter. MP fragments data packets before transmitting them via ISDN lines, greatly improving efficiency and overall *throughput.*

multimedia   A computer-based method of presenting information by using more than one medium of communication, such as text, *graphics* and sound, and emphasizing interactivity. In *Microsoft Bookshelf,* for example, you can see portraits of William Shakespeare, see a list of his works, and follow *hyperlinks* to related information. Advances in sound and video synchronization enable you to display moving video images within on-screen *windows.* However, because graphics and sound require so much storage space, a minimal configuration for a multimedia system includes a *CD-ROM drive.*

Multimedia Compact Disc   See *MMCD.*

M
N
O

multimedia extensions   Additions to an *operating system* that allow *multimedia* software to synchronize graphics and sound. These extensions—called hooks in *programmers'* slang—enable multimedia software designers to access sound and video capabilities without extensive, nonstandard programming. Apple's *QuickTime* is a multimedia extension to its System 7 software. *Microsoft Windows 95* includes the multimedia extensions (called *Media Control Interface [MCI]*) that were formerly available separately. See *application program interface (API).*

Multimedia Personal Computer　See *MPC*.

Multimedia Personal Computer–2　See *MPC-2*.

Multimedia Personal Computer–3　See *MPC-3*.

multiple document interface (MDI)　In an *application program*, a user interface that allows the user to have more than one *document* or *worksheet* open at once. With its *Microsoft Windows 95 Application Program Interface (API)*, *Microsoft Corporation* discourages the use of MDIs. Instead, Microsoft favors running multiple copies of programs, each with a different document.

multiple program loading　An *operating system* that lets you start more than one program at a time; however, only one of the programs is active at any one time. You press a *key* to switch from one program to another. See *context switching* and *MultiFinder*.

multiple selection　In a *spreadsheet program,* a selection of two or more noncontiguous *ranges*.

multiplex　To combine or interleave messages in a communications channel.

multiplexer (mux)　A device that merges lower speed transmissions into one higher speed channel at one end of the link. Another mux reverses the process at the other end of the link.

multiplexing　In *local area networks (LANs)*, the simultaneous transmission of multiple messages in one channel. A network that can *multiplex* allows more than one computer to access the network simultaneously. Multiplexing increases the cost of a network, however, because multiplexing devices must be included that can mix the signals into a single channel for transmission. See *frequency division multiplexing, local area network (LAN)*, and *time division multiplexing*.

multiple zone recording (MZR)　A way to pack more data onto *hard disks* that use *constant angular velocity (CAV)* recording. MZR drives pack extra data onto their edges, which would otherwise be filled to less than full capacity.

multiprocessing　The simultaneous execution of differing portions of a program by a *multiprocessor,* a computer with more than one *central processing unit (CPU)*. See *parallel processing* and *symmetric multiprocessing (SMP)*.

multiprocessor A computer that contains more than one *central processing unit (CPU)*. In order to make use of the additional processors, the computer must be running an operating system or program capable of *parallel processing*.

Multipurpose Internet Mail Extensions See *MIME*.

multiscan monitor See *multiscanning monitor*.

multiscanning monitor A color monitor that can adjust to a range of input frequencies so that it can work with a variety of *display adapters*. Multiscanning monitors are often called multi-sync monitors, but Multisync is a *proprietary* name of an NEC multiscanning monitor.

multisession PhotoCD A standard for recording *PhotoCD* information onto a *CD-ROM* during several different recording sessions. Unlike standard *CD-ROM drives*, drives that are Multisession PhotoCD-compatible can read information recorded on a disk during several different pressings—an advantage for consumers who don't want to wait until they've taken enough pictures to fill a PhotoCD before having the photos processed, but don't want to waste PhotoCD capacity, either.

Multisync monitor See *multiscanning monitor*.

multitasking The execution of more than one program at a time on a computer system. Multitasking shouldn't be confused with *multiple program loading*, in which two or more programs are present in *random-access memory (RAM)* but only one program executes at a time. When multitasking, the active, or foreground, task responds to the keyboard while the background task continues to run (but without your active control). A complete multitasking solution involves memory protection, in which programs are prevented from invading each other's memory space (see *memory protection*). In addition, the operating system should be able to suspend an unruly program's execution, if necessary (compare *cooperative multitasking* and *preemptive multitasking*). Among the operating systems or shells that provide multitasking are *Operating System/2 (OS/2)*, *Unix*, *Microsoft Windows 95*, and *Microsoft Windows NT*.

M
N
O

multithreaded application A *program* that can run two or more *threads* (independent portions of the program) at the same time. The advantage of dividing a program up into threads is that the operating system can decide which of the threads should get the highest priority for processing. See *preemptive multitasking.*

multithreading An *operating system* architecture for rapid program execution in which programs can be divided into several independent execution paths, called *threads,* which can run simultaneously. Multithreading operating systems include *Microsoft Windows 95* and *Microsoft Windows NT.*

Multi-User Dungeon See *MUD.*

multi-user system A *computer system* that can be used by more than one person to access programs and data at the same time. In a multi-user system, each user is equipped with a terminal. If the system has just one central processing unit, a technique called *time-sharing* allocates access time to several terminals. Personal computers with advanced microprocessors, such as the Intel 80486, are sufficiently powerful to serve as the nucleus of a multi-user system. Such systems typically are equipped with *Unix, OS/2,* or *Microsoft Windows NT.* See *AppleTalk, Ethernet, file server, local area network (LAN), mainframe, minicomputer, Netware,* and *network operating system (NOS).*

multiword DMA mode 1 The method *Enhanced IDE hard disks* use to transfer data to the rest of the computer. Multiword DMA mode 1 enables Enhanced IDE drives to transfer data three to four times faster than *integrated drive electronics (IDE)* hard disks.

Musical Instrument Digital Interface See *MIDI.*

mux See *multiplexer.*

My Computer In *Microsoft Windows 95,* a file- and program-management utility that replaces the Windows 3.1 Program Manager and File Manager, combining the functions of the earlier utilities with a simple, consistent interface. The My Computer window displays files and programs as large *icons,* which can be double-clicked to access the files. In addition, the icons can be dragged and dropped to initiate functions such as printing or deletion (via the *Recycling Bin*).

MZR See *multiple zone recording.*

n Common mathematical variable for expressing an indeterminate number of items.

name server In an *Internet*-connected *local area network (LAN)*, a computer that provides the *Domain Name Service (DNS)*, that is, the translation between alphabetical domain names and numerical *IP addresses*. To establish a connection with an Internet service provider, you need to know the *IP address* of the name server.

nano- A prefix indicating one billionth.

nanosecond (ns) A unit of time equal to one billionth of a second. Far beyond the range of human perception, nanoseconds are relevant to computers. An advertisement for 80 ns RAM chips, for example, means that the RAM chips respond to the central processing unit (CPU) within 80 nanoseconds. See *millisecond (ms)*.

National Center for Supercomputing Applications (NCSA)
A supercomputer research center, affiliated with the University of Illinois at Urbana-Champaign, that specializes in scientific visualization. NCSA most recently achieved fame as the birthplace of *NCSA Mosaic,* the popular *Web browser.*

National Information Infrastructure (NII) A proposed high-speed, high-bandwidth *network* that can deliver voice, data, and video services throughout the United States. NII will be developed by private firms, cable television, and telephone companies, with minimal government funding. See *Asymmetric Digital Subscriber Line (ADSL).*

National Research and Education Network (NREN) A proposed backbone network capable of gigabit-per-second data transfer rates. NREN will link a number of supercomputer research centers and will not be available for public use.

National Science Foundation (NSF) An independent agency of the U.S. government that seeks to promote the public good throughout the development of science and engineering. Until 1995, NSF subsidized and coordinated *NSFnet,* which at one time was the backbone network of the *Internet.*

National Television Standards Committee (NTSC)   A committee that governs physical standards for television broadcasting in the United States and most of Central and South America (but not Europe or Asia). NTSC television uses 525-line frames and displays full frames at 30 frames per second, using two interlaced fields at about 60 frames per second to correspond to the U.S. alternating-current frequency of 60 Hz. Most European and Asian countries use the PAL standard, which is based on their 50 Hz power-line frequencies.

native   Designed for a particular type of computer.

native application   A *software program* designed to work with a particular type of *microprocessor*; in other words, a program that is *binary compatible* with a particular microprocessor. Non-native applications may run on a given microprocessor with the help of an *emulation* program, but native applications are almost always significantly faster than non-native applications.

native code   See *machine code*.

native compiler   In programming, a *compiler* that is designed to execute on the computer for which it is generating code.

native file format   The default *file format* a program uses to store data on disk. The format is often a *proprietary file format*. Many popular programs today can retrieve and save data in several formats. See *ASCII*.

natural language   A naturally occurring language, such as Spanish, French, German, or Tamil, as opposed to an artificial language, such as a *programming language*. Computer scientists are working to improve computers so that they can respond to natural language. Human languages are so complex that no single model of a natural language grammar system has gained widespread acceptance among linguists. The complexity of human languages, coupled with the lack of understanding about what information is needed to decode human sentences, makes it difficult to devise programs that recognize speech. Progress in solving these problems has been slow.

natural language processing   In *artificial intelligence,* using a computer to decipher or analyze human language.

natural recalculation   In a *spreadsheet* program, a *recalculation order* that performs worksheet computations in the manner logically dictated by the formulas you place in cells. If the value of a formula depends on references to other cells that contain formulas, the program calculates the other cells first. See *columnwise recalculation, optimal recalculation,* and *row-wise recalculation.*

navigation In a computer program or network, the process of interacting with the *user interface* in an effort to find resources or files.

navigation button In a Web browser, a tool on the on-screen toolbar that enables the user to display the previously accessed document (Back), return to the document being displayed when the Back button was clicked (Forward), or return to the current default home page (Home). See *Web browser.*

NCSA See *National Center for Supercomputing Applications.*

NCSA Mosaic A graphical *Web browser* created at the *National Center for Supercomputing Applications (NCSA).* Available as *freeware* for noncommercial uses, NCSA Mosaic is available in versions for *Microsoft Windows 95, Unix,* and Macintosh computers. Because NCSA lacks the needed facilities and funding, technical support is unavailable and program bugs may go uncorrected for months. Because of these problems, NCSA has licensed Mosaic to Spyglass, Inc., which in turn licenses a fully supported version of the program to book publishers, computer software firms, and other resellers. Much of the programming team that developed NCSA Mosaic joined Netscape Communications and produced the popular *Netscape Navigator* browser, today in use by an estimated 75 percent of the people roaming the *World Wide Web (WWW).*

near-letter quality (NLQ) A *dot-matrix printer* mode that prints almost typewriter-quality characters. As a result, printing when using this mode is slower than other printing modes.

needle drop In *multimedia,* using a short excerpt from a recorded musical piece instead of creating an original composition. The term stems from the days of vinyl phonograph needles.

negotiation See *handshaking.*

nested structure A structure in which one *control* structure is positioned within another. See *DO/WHILE loop.*

nested subtotal In a *spreadsheet,* a *formula* that adds several *values* and is, in turn, included in a larger formula that adds several subtotals.

M
N
O

net.abuse   In *Usenet*, any action that interferes with peoples' right to use and enjoy Usenet, including flooding newsgroups with unwanted posts (also called *spamming*), conducting an organized forgery campaign, or carrying out an organized effort to prevent the discussion of an issue.

NetBEUI   Acronym for NetBIOS Extended User Interface. A *network transport protocol* that defines the *network layer* of Microsoft and IBM *local area networks (LANs)*

NetBIOS   See *Network Basic Input/Output System.*

net.god(dess)   In *Usenet,* an individual whose lengthy Usenet experience and savvy online demeanor elevates him or her to heroic status. An example of a net.god is James "Kibo" Parry, who is said to have developed a Practical Extraction and Report Language *(perl)* script enabling him to detect when and where his name was mentioned in any article throughout Usenet's thousands of *newsgroups*. His witty responses to these articles and his ubiquity—at one time he claimed to post as many as two dozen articles per day—soon resulted in deification (and the creation of a newsgroup in his honor, called alt.religion.kibology).

netiquette   *Network* etiquette; a set of rules that reflect long-standing experience about getting along harmoniously in the electronic environment (*e-mail* and *newsgroups*). The basics of netiquette are as follows:

- Keep your messages short and to the point, abbreviate whenever possible, and don't include an extravagant *signature* at the bottom of your message that lists your name and electronic mailing address.

- Don't use ALL UPPERCASE LETTERS. This is considered to be "shouting." To emphasize a word, use asterisks as you would quotation marks.

- If you want to criticize, criticize the idea, not the person. Don't criticize a person's spelling or grammatical errors. Today's worldwide networks encompass users willing to learn English and trying to participate; they deserve encouragement, not criticism.

- Don't overreact to something you read online. If you get angry, don't reply right away. Go take a walk or, better yet, sleep on it. Electronic mail is easily forwarded. Don't say anything that you don't want to wind up on your boss's desk.

- Don't ask members of a newsgroup to censor a particular person's contributions, or disallow discussion of a topic that you find offensive; instead, create a *kill file* so those messages don't appear on your screen.

- If you ask a question in a newsgroup, request that replies be sent to you personally, unless you feel that the replies would be of interest to everyone who reads the newsgroup.

- In electronic mail, be cautious in replying to messages that were sent to more than one subscriber. In some systems, your reply will be sent to each person who received the original, which may include every subscriber.

- Don't *cross-post* a message (send it to more than one newsgroup) or reply to a cross-posted message, unless you're genuinely following the discussion in each newsgroup and believe your message would prove of interest to readers of each of them.

- If you're *posting* something that gives away the plot of a movie, novel, or television show, put <*SPOILER*> at the top of your message. That way, people can skip reading it if they don't want to know whodunit.

- If you're posting something that some people may find offensive, such as an erotic story, use the command (available with most networks) that *encrypts* your text so that it looks like garbage characters. (In Usenet, for example, the command *rot-13* shifts each letter 13 characters, so that b becomes o.) To read such a message, use the command that *decrypts* the text. Any reader who is offended will have to take responsibility for having decrypted the message.

M
N
O

Also, use discretion when "getting personal" with other users. Stalking laws are now being interpreted to encompass e-mail messages. See *follow-up post, Internet,* and *net.police.*

net lag   In a *packet-switching network,* the delay in accessing a document that is caused by *latency* and other delivery problems.

netnews   A collective way of referring to the *Usenet newsgroups.*

NETNORTH A Canadian *wide area network (WAN)* fully integrated with *BITNET* that performs the same functions as BITNET.

net.police In *Usenet,* a person or group of persons who take upon themselves the enforcement of Usenet traditions and *netiquette.* For example, the famed *Cancelmoose* applies an automated program (called a *cancelbot*) that seeks out and destroys advertisements that are posted to excessive numbers of *newsgroups.* See *net.abuse* and *spam.*

Netscape Application Programming Interface See *NSAPI.*

Netscape Auto-admin A module included in *Netscape Communicator Pro* that enables *intranet* administrators to control up to 200 configuration settings in distributed copies of the Communicator package.

Netscape Catalog Server An *Internet* server for *Microsoft Windows NT* and *Unix* workstations that enables enterprises to publish complex, hierarchically organized document stores on the World Wide Web. Based on the respected freeware program called Harvest, Catalog Server automatically combs an *intranet* for readable documents of all types, classifies them according to predetermined rules, organizes them into predetermined categories, and makes them available by means of a Web browser. Users can navigate the hierarchical categories or search, much as they access information in *Yahoo.*

Netscape Certificate Server An *Internet* server for *Microsoft Windows NT* and *Unix* workstations that enables organizations to become, in effect, a *certificate authority (CA)* by disseminating *certificates* to valid users. The certificates can be used for *strong authentication* to the network, so it is no longer necessary for the user to supply a different login name and password for every server that is accessed.

Netscape Collabra A module included in *Netscape Communicator* that enables users to access *Usenet* newsgroups. When linked to a *Netscape Collabra* server, the module takes on additional capabilities (see *Netscape Collabra Server*).

Netscape Collabra Server An *NNTP* server, designed to run on *Microsoft Windows NT* systems and *Unix* workstations, that enables enterprises to create private, secure newsgroups.

Advanced features of the Collabra server include *SSL* encryption, strong *authentication* and *non-repudiation* of messages by means of *digital signatures* and *certificates,* access control to selected newsgroups and newsgroup hierarchies, and cross–newsgroup searching. To take advantage of these features, users must have the *Netscape Collabra* client, included in *Netscape Communicator.*

Netscape Commerce Server   A *Web server* for *Microsoft Windows NT* and *Unix* workstations that is designed to enable enterprises to conduct electronic commerce over the Internet. *SSL 3.0* security enables strong authentication by means of digital *certificates* as well as secure, encrypted communication. Compare to *Netscape Enterprise Server* and *Netscape FastTrack Server.*

Netscape Communications Corporation   A publisher of *Web browsers, Web servers,* and related software, based in Menlo Park, CA. The company's *Netscape Navigator* browser, now part of the company's *Netscape Communicator* package, is currently the most popular browser on the Internet, but is facing a spirited challenge from *Microsoft Internet Explorer.* The firm reported 1996 sales of $20.9 million.

Netscape Communicator   A package including the world's most popular *Web browser, Netscape Navigator,* that is available for *Microsoft Windows, Macintosh* computers, and a variety of *Unix* workstations. The Communicator package is intended for general Internet use and includes the following modules in addition to Navigator: *Netscape Collabra* (newsgroups), *Netscape Conference* (Internet telephony), *Netscape Messenger (e-mail), Netscape NetCaster* (push media), and *Netscape Page Composer* (a *WYSIWYG* editor for Web publishing).

Netscape Communicator Pro   A package containing all the applications included in *Netscape Communicator,* plus additional modules designed to make the package appealing for *intranet* use, including *Netscape Calendar, Netscape Host On-Demand,* and *Netscape Auto-Admin.*

Netscape Conference   An Internet telephony module, included with *Netscape Communicator,* that enables users to place voice calls via the Internet. Conference conforms to current *ITU-TSS* standards for teleconferencing and will interoperate with other standards–based telephony programs, such as Intel's Internet Phone.

M
N
O

Netscape Directory Server   A server for *Microsoft Windows NT* and *Unix* workstations that enables enterprises to publish *white pages* directories of employee *e-mail* addresses and telephone numbers. A variety of *access control* and *authentication* options enable administrators to hide sensitive internal information from anonymous external access. Directory Server conforms to the *LDAP* and X.500 protocols, and the white pages databases it creates can be accessed by any LDAP-compatible *e-mail* program.

Netscape Enterprise Server   A *Web server* for *Microsoft Windows NT* and *Unix* workstations that is expressly designed for enterprise computing, and especially for *intranets.* Support is included for *IIOP* object requests via Netscape Communicator, full text searching of all the documents accessible to the server, author-managed access control, and strong authentication by means of *certificates.* Compare with *Netscape Enterprise Server Pro, Netscape Commerce Server* and *Netscape FastTrack Server.*

Netscape Enterprise Server Pro   A version of *Netscape Enterprise Server* for *Microsoft Windows NT* and *Unix* workstations that includes a developmental copy of the Informix OnLine Workgroup Server or Oracle7 Workgroup Server database software, and also includes out-of-the-box solutions that enable organizations to create Web-to-database applications without programming.

Netscape extensions   A set of additions to the *HTML* 2.0 standard that enables Web authors to create documents with tables, frames, and other features not supported by the 2.0 specification. Until competing browsers decided to support Netscape's unilaterally introduced *tags,* these features could be seen only by *Netscape Navigator* users. Most of the extensions have been incorporated into HTML version 3.2, but Netscape (like other browser publishers) has recently introduced new, non-standard tags that other browsers do not support.

Netscape FastTrack Server   A *Web server,* created by Netscape Communications, that is designed to enable companies to establish an Internet presence quickly. Intended for installation and management by end users rather than programmers, the program features wizards that guide users through the most common configuration tasks. FastTrack Server is available for *Microsoft Windows 95, Microsoft Windows NT,* and *Unix* systems.

Netscape Messaging Server   A *e-mail server* for *Microsoft Windows NT* and *Unix* workstations. The program supports *LDAP* services; *SMTP, POP3,* and *IMAP* mail protocols; X.509v3 certificates; and richly formatted e-mail with HTML and MIME.

Netscape Navigator   The leading *Web browser,* now available as part of Netscape's *Netscape Communicator* package. Navigator is much more than a Web browser in that it serves as an interpreter for *Java applets* and *JavaScript.* A *cross-platform* product, Navigator is available in versions for Windows, Macintosh, and Unix systems.

Netscape NetCaster   A *push media* client, included with *Netscape Communicator,* that enables users to subscribe to Web sites so that the most recent version of these sites is automatically displayed, either in a *Netscape Navigator* window or a special, screen-filling window called the Webtop. In addition, users can "tune" to broadcasting "channels" to receive commercial content from providers such as ABC News. NetCaster incorporates Marimba's Castanet client, which enables users to tune to channels that disseminate *Java* programs; updates to these programs are transparent to the user.

Netscape SuiteSpot   A package of *Web server* and related software that includes Netscape Enterprise Server, LiveWire Pro (a development tool for linking to external databases), Catalog Server (utilities for managing and maintaining catalogs of *Internet* and *intranet* resources), Media Server (delivers *streaming audio*), MailServer and Messaging Server (*e-mail* and groupware support), News Server and Collabra Server (internal and external *newsgroups*), Calendar Server (facilitates group scheduling), Directory Server (provides *white pages* support for an organization), Proxy Server (provides intranet users with external Internet access), and Certificate Server (enables organizations to create and manage digital *certificates* for *authentication* purposes). This product competes with *Microsoft BackOffice,* which is intended for Windows-based networks. Netscape SuiteSpot is intended for *cross-platform* networks that include *Unix* systems.

M
N
O

NetWare   A *network operating system (NOS),* manufactured by Novell, for *local area networks (LANs).* NetWare accommodates more than 90 types of *network interface cards,* 30 network architectures, and several *communications protocols.* Versions are available for IBM PC-compatibles and Macintosh computers.

network   A communications and data exchange system created by physically connecting two or more computers with *network interface cards* and cables and running a *network operating system (NOS)*. Personal computer networks differ in their scope. The smallest networks, called *local area networks (LANs),* may connect just two or three computers with an expensive peripheral, such as a *laser printer,* whereas others connect as many as 75 or more computers. Larger networks, called *wide-area networks (WANs),* use telephone lines or other communications media to link together computers separated by tens to thousands of miles. Networks have various topologies (such as bus or star), architectures (such as *client-server* or *peer-to-peer*), and communications standards (such as *AppleTalk, Ethernet,* or IBM's *Token-Ring Network*). See *baseband, broadband, bus network, Internet, intranet, network architecture, network protocol, network topology, star network,* and *token-ring network.*

network administrator   In *local area networks (LANs),* the person responsible for maintaining the network and assisting its users.

network architecture   The complete set of *hardware, software,* and cabling standards for a *local area network (LAN)* design. See *network topology.*

Network Basic Input/Output System (NetBIOS)   An *application program interface (API)* that provides the support applications need to send and receive data on an IBM or Microsoft-based *local area network (LAN).*

network drive   In a *local area network (LAN),* a disk drive made available to you through the network, as distinguished from a drive connected directly to the *workstation* you're using.

Network File System (NFS)   A *network* file-access utility, developed by Sun Microsystems and subsequently released to the public as an *open standard,* that enables users of *Unix* and *Microsoft Windows NT* workstations to access files and directories on other computers as if they were physically present on the user's *workstation.*

Network Information Center (NIC)   A system that contains a repository of *Internet*-related information, including *File Transfer Protocol (FTP)* archives of Requests for Comments (RFCs), Internet Drafts, For Your Information (FYI) papers, and other documents, including handbooks on the use of the

Internet. There are numerous Network Information Centers, but the official repository of network information is the Defense Data Network NIC (DDN NIC). See *InterNIC*.

network interface adapter See *network interface card*.

network interface card An *adapter* that lets you connect a network cable to a microcomputer. The card includes encoding and decoding circuitry and a receptacle for a network cable connection.

network laser printer A *laser printer,* often with a large *monthly duty cycle* and *remote management* features, that is designed to be connected to a *network* and serve the printing needs of several dozen people. See *automatic network switching*.

network layer In the *OSI Reference Model* of computer network architecture, the fifth of seven *layers,* in which packets are addressed so they can be routed to the correct destination. When the packets have been addressed, they are transferred down to the *data link layer,* where they are prepared for transmission on the physical network.

Network Neighborhood In *Microsoft Windows 95,* a desktop *icon* that, when clicked, displays the PCs and other resources within the user's workgroup. With Network Neighborhood, files on other machines can be browsed and accessed just as if they were present on the user's computer.

Network News Transfer Protocol (NNTP) In *Usenet,* the standard that governs the distribution of Usenet newsgroups via the *Internet.* See *news server.*

network operating system (NOS) The system software of a *local area network (LAN)* that integrates the network's *hardware* components, usually adequate for connecting up to 50 workstations. Included, typically, are such features as a menu-driven administration interface, *tape backup* of *file-server* software, *security* restrictions, facilities for sharing *printers,* central storage of *application programs* and *databases,* remote login via *modem,* and support for *diskless workstations.* A network operating system establishes and maintains the connection between the *workstations* and the file server; the physical connections alone aren't sufficient to support networking. The operating system consists of two parts: the file server software and workstation software. See *LAN memory management program,* and *NetWare.*

network operations center (NOC)   An administrative and technical coordination office that is responsible for the day-to-day operation of a local, regional, or national *Internet* backbone service.

network printer   In a *local area network (LAN)*, a printer made available to you through the network, as distinguished from a *local printer* (a printer connected directly to the workstation you're using).

network protocol   The method used to regulate a workstation's access to a computer network to prevent data collisions. Examples include *CSMA/CD (Carrier Sense Multiple Access with Collision Detection)* and *token passing.*

network server   See *file server.*

network termination 1 unit (NT-1)   In an *Integrated Services Digital Network (ISDN)* system, the device in a subscriber's home or office that is connected between ISDN devices (such as *digital modems* and digital telephones) and the telephone company's network. Users must usually buy their own NT-1s.

network topology   The geometric arrangement of nodes and cable links in a *local area network (LAN).* Network topologies fall into two categories: centralized and decentralized. In a centralized topology, such as a *star network,* a central computer controls access to the network. This design ensures data security and central management control over the network's contents and activities. In a decentralized topology, such as a *bus network* or *ring network,* each workstation can access the network independently and establish its own connections with other workstations. See *star network.*

network transport protocol   Any of hundreds of communication standards for transmitting data over a specific type of physical network, such as *fiber-optic* cable.

network virtual terminal (NVT)   A generic *terminal* standard that enables programmers to create applications without having to worry about all the different brands of terminals that are actually in use. The *Internet's* NVT standard is called *Telnet.* See *line mode terminal.*

neural network (NN)   An *artificial intelligence* technique that mimics the way nerve cells are connected in the human brain. Information is supplied to the neural network to train it to recognize patterns. The result is a program that can make predictions, useful in weather forecasting and stock market software.

newbie   In *Usenet,* a new user who nevertheless makes his or her presence known, generally by pleading for information that is readily and easily available in *FAQs.*

news feed   In *Usenet,* a service that enables you to download the day's Usenet articles directly to your computer and to upload all the articles contributed by people using your computer. Not for personal computer users, a news feed dumps as much as 100Mb of Usenet articles per day into your system—far more than one person could fruitfully read. A news feed is for organizations that want to set up a Usenet site, with enough storage space to handle the huge influx of articles. Such a computer also has the multi-user capabilities that enable as many as dozens or even hundreds of people to take advantage of Usenet.

newsgroup   In a *bulletin board system (BBS),* such as The WELL, or a distributed bulletin board system, such as *Usenet,* a discussion group that's devoted to a single topic, such as Star Trek, model aviation, the books of Ayn Rand, or the music of the Grateful Dead. Users *post* messages to the group, and those reading the discussion send reply messages to the author individually or post replies that can be read by the group as a whole. The term newsgroup is a misnomer in that the discussions rarely involve "news"; discussion group would be more accurate, but the term newsgroup has taken root. Synonymous with forum. See *Frequently Asked Questions (FAQ), follow-up post, local Usenet hierarchy, moderated newsgroup, net.god(dess), netiquette,* and *thread unmoderated newsgroup.*

newsgroup reader   See *newsreader.*

newsgroup selector   In a *Usenet newsreader,* a program mode that presents a list of currently subscribed newsgroups, from which you can select one to read.

news hierarchy   In *Usenet,* one of the seven standard newsgroup hierarchies. The news hierarchy is concerned with Usenet itself; the various newsgroups deal with administrative issues, new newsgroups, announcements, and Usenet software. See *local Usenet hierarchy* and *standard newsgroup hierarchy.*

newspaper columns　A page format in which two or more columns of text are printed vertically on the page so the text flows down one column and continues at the top of the next. High-end word processing programs such as *Microsoft Word* and *WordPerfect* do a good job of producing newspaper columns and can even balance the bottom margin of columns (called balanced newspaper columns) for a professional-looking effect.

newsreader　In *Usenet,* a client program that enables you to access a Usenet news server, subscribe to Usenet *newsgroups,* read the articles appearing in these newsgroups, and post your own articles or reply by *e-mail.* Many *Web browsers* (such as *Netscape Navigator*) include newsreader functions.

news server　In *Usenet,* a computer that provides access to *newsgroups.* To read Usenet newsgroups, you must tell your *newsreader* program or *Web browser* the domain name of an *NNTP* server. Your Internet service provider can provide you with the name of this server, if one is available.

Newton　A *personal digital assistant,* driven by a 32-bit, 20 MHz *reduced instruction set computer (RISC)* processor with 640K of random-access memory (RAM), manufactured by *Apple Computer.* The Newton includes a date book, address book, and freeform notebook in which you enter data using a *stylus* or an on-screen "*keyboard.*" The handwriting recognition engine can learn your writing, improving over time, although recognition is slow. More recent models include a keyboard.

NexGen　A *fabless* designer and marketer of *x86 central processing units (CPUs)* that is best known for the *NexGen Nx585,* which the company claims is *binary compatible* with the *Pentium.* Based in San Mateo, CA., the company received a boost from early Pentiums' *floating-point unit (FPU)* troubles and is trying to steal market share from *Intel* by offering its *chips* at relatively low prices.

NexGen Nx585　A *64-bit microprocessor* claimed to be *binary compatible* with the *Pentium* and offered at substantially lower prices by its manufacturer, *NexGen.* The Nx585, available in 70 *megahertz (MHz),* 75 MHz, 84 MHz, and 93 MHz versions, uses *register renaming* to get around the 8-*register* limit that slows the Pentium and uses *0.5-micron* and *CMOS technology* to reduce power consumption. See *AMD K5.*

NeXT   A former computer hardware manufacturer, makers of the discontinued NeXT workstation, that subsequently decided to emphasize the innovative operating system developed for NeXT machines, called *NEXTSTEP*. NeXT has been purchased by *Apple Computer.*

NEXTSTEP   A *graphical user interface* for the *Unix* operating system, developed by NeXT, Inc., for its ill-fated NeXT computer. The program, together with a set of object-oriented developed tools called OpenStep, has been purchased by Apple Computer and will figure in the next-generation Macintosh operating system, called *Rhapsody.*

NFS   See *Network File System.*

nibble   Four *bits,* half of a *byte.* Sometimes cutely spelled "nybble."

NIC   See *Network Information Center.*

NiCad   Abbreviation for nickel-cadmium, a compound used to create rechargeable batteries. Commonly used in *portable computers,* NiCads provide the lowest level of battery quality, judged in terms of output power, recharging time, overall longevity, and output time. Cadmium, one of the materials used in NiCad batteries, is highly toxic and disposal of NiCad batteries poses a serious environment risk. NiCad batteries may demonstrate an undesirable "memory effect," in which batteries lose their capacity to take on a full charge if they are not fully discharged before recharging.

NII   See *National Information Infrastructure.*

NiMH   Abbreviation for nickel-metal hydride, a compound used to create rechargeable batteries that do not include toxic substances, as do *NiCad* batteries. NiMH batteries also offer superior performance, with up to 50 percent longer output time than NiCAD batteries. See *lithium-ion battery.*

NLQ   See *near-letter quality.*

nn   In *Usenet,* a *Unix newsreader* created by Kim F. Storm. A threaded *newsreader* that organizes articles and follow-up articles to show the thread of discussion, nn includes many advanced features but is not particularly easy to use. See *tin* and *trn.*

NNTP   See *Network News Transfer Protocol*.

NNTP server   See *news server*.

NOC   See *network operations center*.

node   In a *local area network (LAN)*, a connection point that can create, receive, or repeat a message. Nodes include *repeaters*, file servers, and shared peripherals. In common usage, however, the term node is synonymous with *workstation*. See *network topology*.

noise   In *data communications*, unwanted or random electrical signals on a communications channel, unlike the signal that carries the information you want. All communications channels have noise, but if the noise is excessive, data loss can occur. Telephone lines are particularly noisy, requiring the use of communications programs that can perform error-checking operations to make sure that the data being received isn't corrupted.

nonadjacent selection   In *spreadsheets*, a selected *range* of cells that is separate from another selected range of cells. Non-adjacent selection is useful in *formatting* operations.

nonbreaking hyphen   In word processing, a special hyphen that prevents a line break, should reformatting push the hyphen to the end of the line. This prevents the program from placing a line break within hyphenated proper nouns (such as A.R. Radcliffe-Brown).

noncontiguous   Nonadjacent; not next to one another. See *nonadjacent selection*.

nondisclosure agreement   A contract designed to keep sensitive information confidential. Software publishers often establish nondisclosure agreements with their *beta test* sites so information about new products is less likely to leak out to the computer press.

non-impact printer   A *printer* that forms a text or graphic image by spraying or fusing ink to the page. Non-impact printers include *inkjet printers, laser printers,* and *thermal printers.* All non-impact printers are considerably quieter than *impact printers,* but non-impact printers can't print multiple copies by using carbon paper.

non-interlaced monitor   A *monitor* that doesn't use the screen refresh technique called *interlacing* and, as a result, can display high-resolution images without flickering or streaking.

non-procedural language   See *declarative language.*

non-repudiation   In a computer network, a desirable quality of network security such that valid users are never denied access to resources to which they are entitled.

non-transactional application   In a *local area network (LAN)*, a program that produces data that you don't need to keep in a shared database for all users to access. Most of the work done with *word processing programs,* for example, is non-transactional.

non-volatile   Not susceptible to memory loss when the power is shut off.

non-volatile memory   The memory specially designed to hold information, even when the power is switched off. *Read-only memory (ROM)* is non-volatile, as are all secondary storage units such as disk drives. See *random-access memory (RAM)* and *volatility.*

non-Windows application   A DOS *application program* that doesn't require *Microsoft Windows* to run. DOS applications can also be run under Windows. Using *Windows 95,* or *Standard* or *386 Enhanced modes* in *Windows 3.1,* you can switch from one non-Windows application to another without closing either program. See *application program interface (API).*

no parity   In *asynchronous communications,* a *communications protocol* that disables *parity checking* and leaves no space for the *parity bit.*

Norton AntiVirus   A leading virus detection and removal program, published by Symantec, and available in both *Microsoft Windows* and *Macintosh* versions. Online updates are available by means of *FTP* or *World Wide Web* connections.

Norton Utilities   The leading system utilities package, published by *Symantec,* and available in both *Microsoft Windows* and *Macintosh* versions. The package includes virus scanning and protection, user interface customization, file recovery, and hard disk maintenance.

NOS   See *network operating system.*

NOT   A *Boolean operator* that can be used to exclude certain documents from a retrieval list. For example, the search expression "sports NOT skiing" retrieves information regarding all sports except skiing.

notebook computer   A *portable computer* that typically weighs less than 7 pounds and measures about 8" × 11" × 1 1/2" inches and easily fits inside a briefcase. Notebook computers, unlike subnotebook computers, usually include a *floppy disk drive.* See *auxiliary battery* and *battery pack.*

Notes   See *Lotus Notes.*

Novell NetWare   A *network operating system* for IBM PCs and compatibles. Current versions of NetWare can use the *IPX/SPX, NetBEUI,* or *TCP/IP* transport protocols.

NREN   See *National Research and Education Network.*

ns   See *nanosecond.*

NSAPI   Acronym for Netscape Application Programming Interface. An *application programming interface (API)* for Netscape *Web servers* that enables programmers to route Web information requests to external programs, such as databases.

NSF   See *National Science Foundation.*

NSFnet   A *wide area network (WAN)* developed by the Office of Advanced Scientific Computing at the *National Science Foundation (NSF).* NSFnet was developed to take over the civilian functions of the U.S. Defense Department's *ARPANET,* which, for security reasons, has been closed to public access. NSFnet, until its abandonment in mid-1995, provided the communications hardware for the *Internet,* which is fast emerging as the world's *e-mail* system.

NT   See *Microsoft Windows NT.*

NT-1   See *network termination 1 unit.*

NTSC   See *National Television Standards Committee.*

NuBus   The high-speed *expansion bus* of Macintosh II computers. NuBus requires adapters specifically designed for its 96-pin receptacles.

nuke   To erase an entire *directory* or disk.

null modem cable   A specially configured serial cable that enables you to connect two computers directly, without mediation by a modem.

null value   In an accounting or *database management* program, a blank *field* in which you've never typed a value, as distinguished from a value of zero that you enter deliberately. In some applications, you need to distinguish between a null value and a deliberately entered zero; a null value doesn't affect computations, but a zero does.

number crunching   A slang term for calculating, especially large amounts of data.

numeric coprocessor   A *microprocessor* support chip that performs mathematical computations at speeds up to 100 times faster than the microprocessor alone.

numeric coprocessor socket   A push-down socket on the *motherboard* of many personal computers into which you or a dealer can mount a *numeric coprocessor,* such as the Intel 80387. See *numeric coprocessor.*

numeric format   In a *spreadsheet* program, the way in which the program displays numbers in a *cell*. With most spreadsheet programs, you can choose among the following numeric formatting options:

- Fixed. Displays values with a fixed number of decimal places, ranging from 0 to 15.

- Scientific. Displays very large or small numbers using scientific notation; for example, 12,460,000,000 appears as 1.25E+11.

- Currency. Displays values with commas and dollar signs and the number of decimal places you specify (0 to 15).

- Comma. Displays numbers larger than 999 with commas separating thousands.

- General. Displays numbers without commas and without trailing zeroes to the right of the decimal point. If the number of digits to the left of the decimal point exceeds the column width, scientific notation is used.

M
N
O

If the number of digits to the right of the decimal point exceeds the column width, the number is rounded.

- +/−. Converts the number to a simple bar graph in the cell, with the number of plus or minus signs equaling the positive or negative whole number value of the entry; for example, 5 appears as +++++.

- Percent. Multiplies the value by 100 and adds a percent sign; for example, 0.485 appears as 48.5 percent. You specify the number of decimal places (0 to 15).

- Date. Converts a number to a date. The number 32734, for example, converts to the date August 14, 1989.

- Text. Displays the formula rather than the value computed by the formula.

- Hidden. Makes the cell entry invisible on-screen. Use the cell definition to see the contents.

numeric keypad   A group of keys arranged like the keys on an adding machine, usually located to the right of the typing area on a *keyboard*. The keypad is designed for the rapid touch-typing entry of numerical data.

Num Lock key   A toggle key that locks the *numeric keypad* into a mode in which you can enter numbers. When the Num Lock key is on, the cursor-movement keys are disabled. On IBM PC-compatible *keyboards,* the keys on the numeric keypad are labeled with arrows and numbers. You can use these keys to move the cursor or to enter numbers. The Num Lock key toggles the keypad back and forth between these two modes.

NVT   See *network virtual terminal.*

n-way set associative cache   See *set-associative cache.*

nybble   See *nibble.*

object 1. In *object-oriented programming (OOP) language,* a self-contained program module that contains data as well as the procedures needed to make the data useful. By following established rules for communicating with the object, other programs can make use of it. 2. In object linking and embedding *(OLE),* a document or portion of a document that has been pasted into another document using the Paste Link, Paste Special, or Embed Object command. See *dynamic object* and *static object.*

object code In *programming,* the machine-readable instructions created by a *compiler* or *interpreter* from *source code.*

Object Database Connectivity See *ODBC.*

object linking and embedding See *OLE.*

Object Management Group An industry consortium that is developing standards for computer networks based on a *distributed object architecture,* in which *objects* can exchange data on a *cross-platform* computer network, even if they were written in differing computer programming languages. See *Common Object Request Broker Architecture (CORBA).*

object-oriented Conforming to the philosophy of *object-oriented programming (OOP),* in which programs are made up of interacting *objects,* which are self-contained, reusable program modules that support a specific function (such as displaying a window on-screen). Every object belongs to a *class* of generalized objects that all share the same function; by means of *inheritance,* objects within the class can automatically take on the class's functions. A programmer can quickly create a new object by taking an existing abstract object of a certain class and filling in specific data and procedures as needed.

object-oriented graphic A *graphic* composed of distinct objects, such as lines, circles, ellipses, and boxes, that you can edit independently. Synonymous with *vector graphic.*

object-oriented programming (OOP) language A non-procedural *programming language* in which program elements are conceptualized as *objects* that can pass messages to each other by following established rules. Object-oriented programming is the ultimate extension of the concept of *modular programming* and is especially suited to *Graphical User Interfaces (GUIs)*. In object-oriented programming, the modules or objects are independent enough to stand on their own, so programmers can copy them into other programs. Rather than create an object again and again, such as the code needed to display a window on-screen, programmers can copy it, add some new features, and then move the new object to another program. Programmers can also move objects around in chunks to compose new programs. The reusability of object-oriented code results in significant efficiency and productivity gains, which explains why object-oriented programming languages (notably *C++*) are in widespread use for professional program development. Other object-oriented languages are *Java* and *SmallTalk*.

Object Packager   In *Microsoft Windows,* an accessory that transforms an object into a package, which you can then insert in a *destination document* as a *linked object* or *embedded object.* The reader of this document sees an *icon,* which he can double-click to start the application that created the object. For example, using Object Packager, you could embed a *spreadsheet* as an icon in a *word processing* document with a note such as "Jan, just double-click this icon to see our Excel worksheet showing the Fall Quarter figures I told you about."

object request broker (ORB)   A standard for requesting services from *objects* in a *distributed object architecture,* a *cross-platform* computer network in which program modules can be written in any computer language but still supply needed functions to other applications. The standard is the work of the *Object Management Group (OMG),* an industry consortium that is developing standards for *middleware* based on distributed object architecture. See *Common Object Request Broker Architecture (CORBA).*

oblique   The italic form of a *sans serif* typeface.

OCR   Abbreviation for optical character recognition, which is machine recognition of printed or typed text. Using OCR software with a *scanner,* a printed page can be scanned and the characters converted into text in a *word processing* document format.

octal   A numbering system that uses a base (radix) of eight. There are eight octal digits: 0, 1, 2, 3, 4, 5, 6, and 7. Because octal notation is more compact than binary notation, it is sometimes used to represent binary numbers. Hexadecimal notation, though, is used even more often for that purpose.

octet   A unit of *data* exactly eight *bits* in length—in other words, a *byte*. Internet people do not like to use the term byte because some of the computers connected to the Internet use data *word* lengths other than eight bits.

OCX   A *control* (an executable *object*) created in conformity to Microsoft's object linking and embedding *(OLE)* standards. OCX controls are now called *ActiveX* controls.

ODBC   Acronym for Object Database Connectivity. A standard that enables applications (including *Web browsers*) to communicate with a variety of *database* applications by means of a standardized set of *SQL* queries.

odd parity   In *asynchronous communications,* an error-checking protocol in which the *parity bit* is set to 1 if the number of 1 digits in a one-byte data item adds up to an odd number. For example, the following byte has five 1s: 01011011. The parity bit therefore would be set to 1 in an odd *parity-checking* scheme. If the parity bit indicates odd but the data transmitted actually contains an even number of 1s, the system will report that a transmission error has occurred. See *communications parameters, communications protocol, even parity,* and *parity checking.*

OEM   See *original equipment manufacturer.*

office suite   A *package* of programs designed to support home and business office computing; typically, office suites include a word processing and spreadsheet program and a collection of tools and utilities (such as clip art). See *Corel WordPerfect Suite, Microsoft Office.*

office automation   The use of computers and *local area networks (LANs)* to integrate traditional office activities such as conferencing, writing, filing, calculating, customer and merchandise tracking, and sending and receiving messages.

offline   1. Not directly connected with a computer; for example, a device that isn't hooked up to your PC is offline or has been switched to offline mode. 2. In *data communications,* not connected with another computer; for example, a workstation you've temporarily or permanently disconnected from a local area network is offline.

off-screen formatting   See *embedded formatting command*.

offset   See *binding offset*.

OK button   A *pushbutton* you can activate in a *dialog box* to confirm the current settings and execute the command. If the OK button is highlighted or surrounded by a thick black line, you can press Enter to choose OK.

OLE   Acronym for object linking and embedding (pronounced olé). A set of standards, developed by Microsoft Corporation and incorporated into *Microsoft Windows* and Apple's *MacOS,* that enables users to create dynamic, automatically updated links between documents and also to embed a document created by one application into a document created by another. These standards, updated for Internet use, are now called *ActiveX.* OLE resembles object-based *middleware* standards, such as *CORBA,* but with an important exception: OLE messages are mediated by means of the *operating system.* As a result, applications developed with OLE components, called *controls,* cannot execute in a *cross-platform* environment unless all the linked computer's operating systems can support OLE. Recognizing this point, Microsoft has released the latest version of OLE, called ActiveX, to an independent, nonprofit standards body, which seeks to extend OLE support to other operating systems (especially *Unix*).

OLE client   See *client application*.

OLE server   See *server application*.

OLTP   See *online transaction processing*.

OMR   See *Object Management Group*.

on-board   Directly contained on a circuit board; contained within.

on-board audio   A circuit on the *motherboard* that simulates a *sound board* and is usually adequate only for *business audio* applications. On-board audio circuits usually use crude *FM synthesis* techniques to produce sounds and can be replaced, in a *desktop computer,* with a sound board of higher quality.

on-board cache   See *internal cache*.

on-board speaker   A small speaker located inside the computer's *case.* Though the on-board speaker can generate crude beeps, buzzes, and honks, it is entirely unsuitable for *multimedia applications*. A *sound board* and *auxiliary speakers* provide much better sound output than the on-board speaker.

one-shot program   A program designed to solve one problem, one time, and never be used again, such as a program designed to compute the trajectory of a test missile. One-shot programs often do not conform to the rules of style and *modular programming* that govern programs meant to be used over and over, which presents a problem if a one-shot program becomes widely popular. See *canonical form*.

one-time password   A password that is generated by a handheld device, a *smart card,* or a computer program and enables a user to gain access to a computer network. The password is known to the authenticating network computer because it is running the same password algorithm as the user's device or program. In contrast to re-used *passwords,* one-time passwords provide superior network security. Even if a one-time password is intercepted while it is being transmitted to the authenticated computer, it cannot be subsequently used to gain *unauthorized access* to the computer network; additionally, it is not possible to derive the underlying password-generating algorithm from an examination of the password itself. Synonymous with *token*. See *authentication* and *security*.

one-way hash function   A mathematical function that transforms a message of any length into a code of fixed length, so that the code is a "fingerprint" of the original message. However, it is impossible to determine the content of the original message by means of an examination of the code. A one-way hash function can be used to determine whether a message has been altered during transmission over a network; the code is transmitted along with an encrypted message, and the receiving computer performs the same hash function on the message after it is decrypted. If the two codes differ, then the message was corrupted or altered en route. See *hash function*.

online   1. Directly connected with and accessible to a computer and ready for use ("The printer is online, finally."). 2. Connected to a network ("You can check your mail when I get online."). 3. Available from a network ("That information is available online.").

online help   A help utility available on-screen while you're using a *network* or an *application program*.

online information service   A for-profit firm that makes current news, stock quotes, and other information available to its subscribers over standard telephone lines. See *America Online (AOL)*.

online transaction processing (OLTP)   In the *Internet,* the capturing and recording of electronic transaction information (including names, addresses, and credit-card numbers) in a database, so that all transactions occurring online can be audited and the resulting data summarized for management purposes.

on-screen formatting   In a *word processing* program, a formatting technique in which formatting commands directly affect the text that's visible on-screen. See *embedded formatting command* and *what-you-see-is-what-you-get (WYSIWYG)*.

on-the-fly data compression   A method by which data to be sent by *modem* is packed into a tighter package during transmission rather than before, thereby increasing apparent transmission speed. Protocols such *V.42bis* and *MNP 5* handle on-the-fly *data compression*.

OOPS   Acronym for object-oriented programming system. See *object-oriented programming (OOP) language*.

op   Common abbreviation for operator, as in "channel op" (a channel operator on *IRC*).

op code   Abbreviation of operation code. In *machine language,* a code that tells the processor to perform a specific operation, such as moving data to a *register*.

open   1. Accessible for user modification. 2. Conforming to well-established, nonproprietary standards or protocols. 3. To read a file into the computer's memory.

open architecture   A system in which all the system specifications are made public so other companies will develop add-on products, such as *adapters* for the system. See *open bus system*.

open bus system   A design in which the computer's *expansion bus* contains receptacles that readily accept *adapters*. An *open-architecture* system generally has an open bus, but not all systems with open buses have open architectures; the Macintosh is an example of the latter.

OpenDoc   A *compound document* architecture similar to Microsoft's object linking and embedding *(OLE)* standard that functions in a *cross-platform* computing environment. Developed by IBM, Apple, and others, OpenDoc enables users to embed features from one or more applications into a single document.

open–loop actuator   An obsolete mechanism for moving the *read/write head* over the *storage medium* of a *hard disk*. Open-loop actuators, unlike *closed-loop actuators,* provide no feedback about the head's position to the *hard disk controller,* therefore reducing the accuracy with which the controller can tightly pack data. Ultimately, open-loop actuators reduce *areal density.*

Open Shortest–Path First Interior Gateway Protocol   See *OSPF.*

Open Software Foundation (OSF)   A consortium of computer companies that promotes standards and publishes specifications for programs operating on computers that run *Unix.* OSF is perhaps best known for designing OSF Motif, a *graphical user interface (GUI)* for Unix that provided much of the design inspiration for *Microsoft Windows 95.* OSF also developed the OSF Distributed Computing Environment (DCE) (a set of programs that supplement a vendor's *operating system* and enable cross-platform network interoperability) and the OSF/1 operating system, a publicly available variant of Unix. See *proprietary.*

open standard   A set of rules and specifications that collectively describes the design or operating characteristics of a program or device and is published and made freely available to the technical community, and (ideally) standardized by an independent international standards body. Open standards may contribute to rapid market growth if they encourage *interoperability* (the ability of a device made by one manufacturer to work with a device made by a different manufacturer) and *cross-platform* computing (use in a network with computers made by several different vendors and running different operating systems). The opposite of an open standard is a *proprietary standard,* which a company pushes in the hope that its standard, and no others, will come to dominate the market. See *de facto standard.*

M
N
O

OpenStep   An *application programming interface (API)* developed by NeXT, Inc., that uses *object-oriented* principles to connect with the computer's operating system. OpenStep enables application developers to sidestep the formerly tedious and inefficient tasks of writing code that communicates directly with the operating system; OpenStep *objects* exist that can perform these tasks, and they can be speedily integrated into applications.

Open System Interconnection (OSI) Reference Model
See *OSI Reference Model.*

Open Systems Interconnection (OSI) Protocol Suite
See *OSI Protocol Suite.*

OpenWindows   A *graphical user interface (GUI),* developed by Sun Microsystems, that is based on the *X Windows* standard for *Unix* computers. See *Motif.*

operand   The *argument* that is appended to an *operator,* such as a spreadsheet program's *built-in function.* For example, in the Excel *expression* AVERAGE(D10..D24), the cell range D10 to D24 is the operand of the AVERAGE function.

operating environment   The total context in which applications function, including the *operating system (OS)* and the *shell.*

operating system (OS)   A master control program that manages the computer's internal functions, such as accepting keyboard input, and provides a means to control the computer's operations and file system. The most popular operating systems for personal computers include *Microsoft Windows 95, Microsoft Windows NT,* and *MacOS.* In *Unix* and most other nonpersonal computer operating systems, the interface to an operating system is called a *shell,* and more than one shell may be available for a given system. *Motif,* for example, is one of several available shells for Unix.

Simple operating systems are designed to run just one program at a time; with *multiple program loading,* more than one program can be run, but only one of them is active. True *multitasking* operating systems enable two or more programs to run simultaneously, while operating systems that support *multithreading* enable two or more functions (called *threads*) within an application to execute simultaneously. In *cooperative multitasking,* found in the MacOS and Windows 3.1, programs take over the CPU until they are ready to give it up (a fact that accounts for these systems' poor recovery rates after an application hangs or crashes). In *preemptive multitasking,* the operating system parcels out CPU time to each application, and can take over if a program stops responding. *Microsoft Windows 95, Microsoft Windows NT,* and *MacOS* System 8 offer preemptive multitasking. In multi-user computer systems, such as *Solaris,* the operating system is also responsible for allocating CPU time to each user and provides security by means of password-based *authentication.*

operating voltage   The electrical voltage at which a *microprocessor* operates. Most microprocessors have operating voltages of 5 volts—a mostly arbitrary specification decided upon when the *transistor* was invented—but some chips run at 3.3 volts to save electricity (a real concern in *portable computers*) and reduce heat output.

operator   In programming, a code name or symbol that is used to describe a command or function, such as multiplying or dividing.

optical character recognition   See *OCR.*

optical disk   A large-capacity data storage medium for computers on which information is stored at extremely high density in the form of tiny pits. The presence or absence of pits is read by a tightly focused laser beam. *CD-ROMs* and CD-ROM drives offer an increasingly economical medium for read-only data and programs. *Write-once, read-many (WORM)* drives enable organizations to create their own huge, in-house databases. Erasable optical disk drives offer more storage than *hard disks,* and the CDs are removable. They are, however, still more expensive and much slower than hard disks. See *interactive videodisk.*

optical fiber   See *fiber optics.*

optical mouse   A *mouse* that does not require cleaning, as a *mechanical mouse* does, but must be used on a special mouse pad. An optical mouse shines a beam of light into a grid in the mouse pad, which conveys the mouse's movements to the computer.

optical resolution   A measure of the sharpness with which a *scanner* can digitize an image without help from software. The more charge-coupled devices (CCDs) in a scanner (300 is about average, 600 is very good), the better its optical resolution. By means of *software interpolation,* output can be improved,

M
N
O

but software interpolation is a poor substitute for high optical resolution.

optical scanner   See *scanner.*

optimal recalculation   In *Lotus 1-2-3* and other advanced *spreadsheet* programs, a method that speeds *automatic recalculation* by recalculating only those cells that have changed since the last recalculation.

optimizing compiler   A *compiler* that translates *source code* into *machine language* optimized to run as efficiently as possible on a particular *microprocessor.* Optimizing compilers are virtually essential when preparing programs to run on any microprocessor equipped with *superscalar architecture.*

option button   See *radio button.*

OR   1. In programming, a *Boolean function* that returns an expression as true if any of its arguments are true. 2. In computer database searching, a *Boolean operator* that retrieves a document if it contains any of the specified search terms.

Oracle Corporation   The leading supplier of *Unix*-based *relational database management systems (RDMS)* for multi-user enterprise computing and the first major database firm to adopt *SQL* as its standard query language.

ORB   See *object request broker.*

ordered list   In *HyperText Markup Language (HMTL),* a numbered list, created with <OL>...</OL> tags.

ordinal number   A number that expresses the numerical rank or position of an item in a hierarchical series (such as first, second, third, and so on).

organization chart   In *presentation graphics,* a text chart you use to diagram the reporting structure of an organization, such as a corporation or a club.

Organizer   See *Lotus Organizer.*

orientation   See *landscape orientation* and *portrait orientation.*

original equipment manufacturer (OEM)   The company that actually manufactures a given piece of *hardware,* unlike the *value-added reseller (VAR)*—the company that changes, configures, repackages, and sells the hardware. For example, only a few companies such as Canon, Toshiba, and Ricoh make the *print engines* used in *laser printers.* These engines are installed in housings with other components and sold by VARs such as Hewlett-Packard.

originate   To make a telephone call, rather than receive one. In computers, the term usually applies to contacting another computer system via *modem.*

originate mode   In *modems,* a mode in which the modem will originate calls but not receive them. See *auto-dial/auto-answer modem.*

orphan   1. In word processing, a formatting flaw in which the first line of a paragraph appears alone at the bottom of a page. Most *word processing* and *page layout programs* suppress *widows* and orphans; the better programs let you switch widow/orphan control on and off and choose the number of lines for which the suppression feature is effective. 2. In *Unix,* a *process* that continues running even though its *parent* has died, consuming CPU time needlessly.

OS   See *operating system.*

OS/2   A *multitasking* operating system for IBM PC-compatible computers that was initially developed jointly by Microsoft Corporation and IBM. A 32-bit operating system, OS/2 was initially seen to be the successor to *Microsoft Windows 3.1,* but Microsoft decided to develop *Microsoft Windows 95* and *Microsoft Windows NT,* leaving IBM as the sole proponent of OS/2. Due to the success of Windows, few application developers find it attractive to develop programs for OS/2. See *OS/2 Warp.*

OS/2 Warp   An *operating system,* designed and marketed by *IBM,* that offers most of the features of *Operating System/2 (OS/2)* and is optimized to run Windows applications as well as OS/2 programs. OS/2 Warp offered many exotic features—notably built-in *Internet* connectivity—several months before the release of *Microsoft Windows 95,* but despite its many merits, OS/2 Warp has been almost totally eclipsed in the marketplace by Windows 95 and Windows NT.

OSF   See *Open Software Foundation.*

M
N
O

OSI Protocol Suite   Abbreviation for Open Systems Interconnect Protocol Suite. A *wide-area network (WAN)* architecture that was developed by the *International Organization for Standardization (ISO),* with heavy support from European state postal and telegraph organizations. The OSI protocol suite has proven to be unwieldy and brittle in practice and would not pose a threat to the global dominance of the competing *TCP/IP* protocol suite were it not for the OSI's strong backing by European nations' postal and telegraph service bureaucracies. See *OSI Reference Model.*

OSI Reference Model   Abbreviation for Open Systems Interconnect (OSI) Reference Model. An international standard for the conceptualizing the *architecture* of computer networks, established by the *International Organization for Standardization (ISO)* and the *Institute of Electrical and Electronic Engineers (IEEE),* that improves network flexibility. The OSI Reference Model employs a divide-and-conquer approach, in which network functions are divided into seven categories, called *layers,* and communication standards are established to handle the transfer of data from one layer to another. Within each layer, *protocols* are developed that focus on that layer's functions, and no others. Within a network-connected computer, outgoing messages move "down" a protocol *stack,* successively undergoing transformations until the data is ready to be sent out via the physical network. At the receiving end, the data moves "up" the stack, undergoing the mirror image of the transformation process, until the data is ready to be displayed by an application. The OSI Reference Model calls for a total of seven layers. From the top of the stack to the bottom, they are: *application layer, presentation layer, session layer, transport layer, network layer, data link layer* and *physical layer.*

OSPF   Acronym for Open Shortest Path First. An improved version of *Internet* protocol (standard) that governs the exchange of data using *TCP/IP* within an internal network (an *autonomous system*). A *router* running OSPF compiles a database of its own current connections, as well as those OSPF-compatible routers to which it is connected, and then uses a routing algorithm to determine the shortest possible path for the data.

outline font   A *printer font* or *screen font* in which a mathematical formula generates each character, producing a graceful and undistorted outline of the character, which the *printer* then fills in. Mathematical formulas, rather than *bitmaps,* produce the arcs and lines of outline characters. The printer can easily change the type size of an outline font without introducing the distortion common with *bit-mapped fonts*. (You may need to reduce the weight of small font sizes by using a process called *hinting*, which prevents the loss of fine detail.)

outline utility   In some full-featured *word processing programs*, a mode that helps you plan and organize a *document* by using outline headings as document headings. The program lets you view the document as an outline or as ordinary text.

output   The process of displaying or printing the results of processing operations. See *input*.

OverDrive   Upgrade *microprocessors* created by *Intel* that fit into special sockets (called an *OverDrive socket*) on *Intel 486DX* and *Intel 486SX motherboards* and improve their performance to the level of *Intel 486DX/2 central processing units (CPUs)*. The performance gain realized by installing an OverDrive chip is only about 20 percent, so installing one is not necessarily the most cost-effective *upgrade* route available. They are also available for some Pentium systems; see *Pentium OverDrive*.

OverDrive socket   A special socket provided on OverDrive-compatible motherboards designed for the *Intel 80486* microprocessor; the chip is designed for *OverDrive* upgrade processors.

overflow   A condition in which a program tries to put more data in a memory area than the area can accommodate, resulting in an error message.

overhead   In a *network,* the additional information that must be added to a message in order to ensure its error-free transmission. In *asynchronous communications,* for example, a *start bit* and *stop bit* must be added to every byte of transmitted data, producing a high, inefficient overhead of roughly 20 percent.

M
N
O

overlaid windows   In a *graphical user interface (GUI),* a display mode in which windows are allowed to overlap each other. If you *maximize* the top window to full size, it completely hides the other windows. See *cascading windows* and *tiled windows*.

overlay   See *program overlay*.

overlay chart   In a business graphics program, a second type of chart that's overlaid on the main chart, such as a line chart on top of a bar chart. Synonymous with combination chart. See *mixed column/line graph.*

overrun error   A *serial port* error in which a *microprocessor* sends data faster than the *Universal Asynchronous Receiver/ Transmitter (UART)* can handle it. An overrun error results in lost data.

overscan   A condition that exists when the image created on a *cathode ray tube (CRT) display* is larger than the visible portion of the display. Users can adjust this to bring the hidden portion into view on most monitors, but some may fail to do so; for this reason, AV professionals try to avoid placing important detail in the outer 10 percent of the image area.

overstrike   Creating a character not found in a printer's character set by placing one character on top of another, such as using O and / to create zeros that can be easily distinguished from an uppercase letter O. Today's graphics-based computer systems eliminate the need for this printing technique; however, users of character-based DOS programs still need it sometimes.

overtype mode   An editing mode in *word processing programs* and other software that lets you enter and edit text. In overtype mode, the characters you type erase existing characters, if any. In *WordPerfect,* the overtype mode is called *typeover mode.* See *insert mode.*

overvoltage   Unusually high voltage, typically in the form of spikes or surges greater than 130 volts from a wall outlet. A surge protector provides overvoltage protection.

overwrite   To write data on a magnetic disk in the same area where other data is stored, thereby destroying the original data.

P100   Abbreviation for *Intel's* 100 MHz version of the *Pentium microprocessor.*

P120   Abbreviation for *Intel's* 120 *MHz* version of the *Pentium microprocessor.*

P133   Abbreviation for *Intel's* 133 *MHz* version of the *Pentium microprocessor.*

P166   Abbreviation for *Intel's* 166 *MHz* version of the *Pentium microprocessor.*

P200   Abbreviation for *Intel's* 200 *MHz* version of the *Pentium microprocessor.*

P24T socket   A receptacle for the *Intel P24T microprocessor* on an *Intel 80486 motherboard.* The P24T boosts the performance of a 486 to near-*Pentium* levels.

P6   Working name for the *Pentium Pro* microprocessor during its development.

P60   Abbreviation for *Intel's* 60 *MHz* version of the *Pentium microprocessor.* Because it has a 5–volt *operating voltage,* the P60 runs very hot and should be avoided in favor of the *P75, P100,* and *P120.*

P66   Abbreviation for Intel's 66 *MHz* version of the *Pentium microprocessor.* Because it has a 5–volt *operating voltage,* the P66 runs very hot and should be avoided in favor of the *P75, P100,* and *P120.*

P75   Abbreviation for *Intel's* 75 *MHz* version of the *Pentium microprocessor.*

P90   Abbreviation for *Intel's* 90 *MHz* version of the *Pentium microprocessor.*

package   In Microsoft Windows 95 and Microsoft Windows 3.1, an *icon,* created by Object Packager, that contains a linked object, *embedded object, file,* or part of a file. See *OLE.*

**P
Q
R**

packaged software   *Application programs* commercially marketed, unlike custom programs privately developed for a specific client. Synonymous with off-the-shelf software.

packet   In a packet-switching unit, a unit of data of a fixed size—not exceeding the network's *maximum transmission unit (MTU)* size—that has been prepared for network transmission. Each packet contains a *header* that indicates its origin and its destination. See *packet-switching network.* Synonymous with *datagram.*

packet driver   In a *local area network (LAN),* a program that divides data into *packets* (transmission units of fixed size) before sending them out on the network.

Packet Internet Groper (PING)   A *diagnostic program* that is commonly used to determine whether a computer is properly connected to the *Internet.*

packet radio   A method of exchanging *TCP/IP* data by means of VHF radio transmissions linking two or more computers. First developed for military applications during the development of *ARPANET,* packet radio is now most widely used among radio hobbyists. Packet radio transmissions are limited by line of sight (approximately 10 to 100 miles, barring obstructions).

packet sniffer   A program designed to search the data *packets* coursing through an *Internet* line for some predetermined pattern, such as a password, social security number, or credit card number; these are often transmitted via the Internet in *cleartext.* The ability of computer criminals to intercept such data is a fundamental security shortcoming of the Internet, and explains why use of the network is inherently insecure unless *encryption* is used.

packet switching   See *packet-switching network.*

packet-switching network   One of two fundamental architectures for the design of a *wide-area network (WAN);* the other is a *circuit switching network.* In a packet-switching network such as the *Internet,* no effort is made to establish a single electrical circuit between two computing devices; for this reason, packet-switching networks are often called *connectionless.* Instead, the sending computer divides a message into a number of efficiently sized units called *packets,* each of which contains the address of the destination computer. These packets are simply dumped onto the network. They are intercepted by devices called *routers,* which read each packet's destination address and, based on that information, send the packets in the appropriate direction. Eventually, the packets arrive at their intended destination, although some may have actually traveled by different physical paths. The receiving computer assembles the packets, puts them in order, and delivers the received message to the appropriate application. Packet-switching networks are highly reliable and efficient, but they are not suited to the delivery of real-time voice and video.

page 1. A fixed-size block of *random-access memory (RAM).* See *paged memory.* 2. In word processing and *desktop publishing,* an on-screen representation of a printed page of text or graphics. 3. A *Web page.* 4. To scroll through a document. 5. To swap a fixed-size block of data into and out of the memory (see *swapping*).

page break In *word processing,* a mark that indicates where the printer will start a new page. Word processing programs insert page breaks automatically when a full page of text has been typed. The automatic page break is called a *soft page break* because the program may adjust its location if you insert or delete text above the break. Users can enter a *hard page break,* also called a forced page break, which forces the program to start a new page at the hard page break's location.

page description language (PDL) A *programming language* that describes *printer* output in device-independent commands. Normally, a program's printer output includes printer control codes that vary from printer to printer. A program that generates output in a PDL, however, can drive any printer containing an interpreter for the PDL. PDLs also transfer the burden of processing the printer output to the printer. See *PostScript.*

paged memory See *paging memory.*

paged memory management unit (PMMU) In *hardware,* a *chip* or circuit that enables *virtual memory.* Virtual memory allows your computer to use space on your *hard disk* to expand the apparent amount of *random-access memory (RAM)* in your system. With virtual memory, a computer with only 4M of RAM can function as though it were equipped with 16M or more of RAM, enabling you to run several programs simultaneously. See *Microsoft Windows* 95 and *System 7.5.*

P
Q
R

page fault   In *virtual memory,* an unsuccessful attempt to retrieve a *page* of data from *random-access memory (RAM).* When a page fault occurs, the *operating system* retrieves the data from the hard disk, which is slower.

page layout program   In *desktop publishing,* an application program that assembles text and *graphics* from various files. You can determine the precise placement, sizing, scaling, and *cropping* of material in accordance with the page design represented on-screen. Page layout programs such as *Adobe PageMaker* and *FrameMaker* display a graphic representation of the page, including nonprinting guides that define areas into which you can insert text and graphics.

page-mode RAM   High-performance *dynamic random-access memory (DRAM)* chips that include a buffer, called a column buffer, that stores data likely to be needed next by the *central processing unit (CPU).* Page-mode RAM chips store data in a matrix of rows and columns. When data is requested from page-mode RAM, the entire column, or page, of data is read into the buffer, since the next piece of data requested likely will be in the same column. If so, the data is read from the buffer, which is faster than accessing the matrix again. Page-mode RAM is not the same as *paging memory* systems. See *FPM.* Faster memory technologies are now available (see *EDO RAM, SDRAM).*

page orientation   See *landscape orientation* and *portrait orientation.*

page printer   A *printer* that develops an image of a printed page in its memory, then transfers that image to paper in one operation. *Laser printers, liquid crystal shutter (LCS) printers,* and *light-emitting diode (LED) printers* are page printers, while *inkjet* and *dot-matrix printers,* which print one line at a time, are not.

pages per minute (ppm)   A measurement of how many pages a *printer* can print in one minute. Manufacturers often inflate their printers' ppm rating, and the ratings are almost always inaccurate for print jobs that involve graphics or fonts other than the printer's *resident fonts.* Like automakers' gas-mileage figures, ppm ratings, although inflated, can serve as a point of comparison between models.

Page Up/Page Down keys   On *IBM PC-compatible computer* keyboards, the keys you press to move the cursor to the preceding screen (Page Up) or the next screen (Page Down).

Because the precise implementation of these keys is up to the programmer, some *word processing* programs use Page Up and Page Down keys to move to the top of the preceding page, rather than to the preceding screen of text.

pagination In *word processing,* the process of dividing a document into pages for printing. Today's advanced word processing programs use background pagination, in which pagination occurs after you stop typing or editing and the microprocessor has nothing else to do. See *page break.*

paging memory A memory system in which the location of data is specified by the intersection of a column and row on the memory *page,* rather than by the actual physical location of the data. This makes it possible to store memory pages wherever memory space of any type becomes available, including disk drives. Paging memory is used to implement *virtual memory,* in which your computer's hard drive functions as an extension of *random-access memory (RAM).* A chip or circuit called a paged memory management unit manages the movement of pages of data in and out of the memory devices. See *paged memory management unit (PMMU).*

paint file format A bit-mapped graphics *file format* found in programs, such as MacPaint and PC Paintbrush. See *paint program.*

paint program A program that enables you to paint the screen by specifying the color of the individual dots or *pixels* that make up a bit-mapped screen display. Although paint programs can produce interesting effects, they are difficult to edit because it is not possible to select objects individually. See *draw program.*

paired bar graph A *bar graph* with two different x-axes (categories axes). A paired bar graph is an excellent way to demonstrate the relationship between two *data series* that share the same y-axis values but require two different *x-axis* categories. Because the bars mirror each other, variations become obvious. See *dual y-axis graph.*

paired pie graph A graphic containing two separate *pie graphs.* For example, a paired pie graph is appropriate for showing the breakdown of product sales in two different time periods. To show the difference in the size of the totals

P
Q
R

represented by each of the two pie graphs, a *proportional pie graph* is useful.

pair kerning   See *kerning.*

palette   In computer video displays, the colors that the system can display. *Video Graphics Array (VGA) displays* offer a palette of 262,144 colors, although each screen can display a maximum of 256 colors simultaneously. In paint and draw programs, an on-screen display of options such as colors and drawing tools. See *draw program* and *paint program.*

pan   1. In *multimedia,* the capability of a synthesizer or *sound board* to alter the left and right channel volumes to create the illusion of movement of the source of the sound. 2. In a video card, a feature than enables the user to zoom in on the desktop and then scroll to view different parts of it.

Pantone Matching System (PMS)   A *device-independent* way of describing and adjusting colors. When using PMS colors, you choose the color you want from a booklet, use that color's code in the *software,* and print to a specially calibrated printer. The output should closely match the color in the PMS book. See *device-dependent color.*

PAP   See *Password Authentication Protocol.*

paperless office   An office in which using paper for traditional purposes—such as sending messages, filling out forms, and maintaining records—has been reduced or eliminated.

paper-white monitor   A *monochrome* monitor that displays black text and graphics on a white background. Paper-white *monitors* are preferred for *word processing* and *desktop publishing* because the display closely resembles the appearance of the printed page. However, some users don't like the glare of a large expanse of white background.

paradigm   An established mode of thinking, consisting of a set of assumptions that, over time, come to be accepted without much reflection or examination. In the *Unix* paradigm, for example, it's assumed that the best programs are small ones that users can combine into useful applications. This assumption may be true for experienced programmers, but not for end users.

Paradox   A *relational database management system (RDBMS)* created by Borland International, and currently licensed to Corel, that provides a powerful system for database development on desktop systems.

parallel interface   See *parallel port*.

parallel port   A connection for the synchronous, high-speed flow of data along parallel lines to a device, usually a *parallel printer*. Parallel ports negotiate with *peripheral* devices to determine whether they're ready to receive data, and report error messages if a device isn't ready. More recent versions of parallel ports enable bi-directional communication between the computer and the printer; see *enhanced parallel port (EPP)* and *extended capabilities port (ECP)*.

parallel printer   A printer designed to be connected to the computer's *parallel port*.

parallel processing   The use of more than one processor in a *multiprocessor* computer to run two or more portions of a problem simultaneously. The task of parceling out portions of the program to each processor may be handled by the operating system or by the application. Although parallel processing can produce significant performance gains under ideal conditions, not all problems are susceptible to solution by processors working in parallel, and *overhead* increases as more processors are added (see *massively parallel processing*). Easiest to implement is *symmetric multiprocessing (SMP)*, in which two or more processors share a single workstation's memory and I/O systems, and communicate via a high-speed bus. The operating system parcels out tasks to each processor. Thanks to *Microsoft Windows NT's* support of SMP, parallel processing is now reaching commercial markets and is expected to accelerate the move away from more expensive *Unix* workstations toward less expensive but comparably-powered *Intel*-based desktop computers running windows.

parameter   A value or option that you add or alter when you give a command so that the command accomplishes its task the way you want. If you don't state a parameter, the program uses a *default setting*. Synonymous with *argument*.

parameter RAM   In the Macintosh environment, a small bank of battery-powered memory that stores your *configuration* choices after you switch off the power.

P
Q
R

parent In a hierarchical organization of data, a superordinate level that may contain one or more subordinate units (each unit is called a *child*). Levels in the hierarchy are named parent or child in relation to each other; for example, a child may be the parent of several children.

parent directory In DOS directories, the *directory* above the current *subdirectory* in the *tree structure*. You can move quickly to the parent directory by typing `CD..` and pressing Enter.

parent process In *Unix,* an executing program that controls one or more subordinate programs (called *child processes*).

parity The quality of oddness or evenness. In comparing two numbers, parity exists if both are odd or both are even; no parity exists if one is even and one is odd.

parity bit In *asynchronous communications* and primary storage, an extra *bit* added to a data word for *parity checking.*

parity checking A technique used to detect memory or *data communication* errors. The computer adds up the number of bits in a one-byte data item, and if the *parity bit* setting disagrees with the sum of the other *bits,* the computer reports an error. Parity-checking schemes work by storing a one-bit digit (0 or 1) that indicates whether the sum of the bits in a data item is odd or even. When the data item is read from memory or received by another computer, a parity check occurs. If the parity check reveals that the parity bit is incorrect, the computer displays an error message. See *even parity* and *odd parity.*

parity error An error that a computer reports when *parity checking* reveals that one or more *parity bits* are incorrect, indicating a probable error in data processing or data transmission.

park To position a *hard drive's* read/write heads over the *landing zone* so the disk isn't damaged by jostling during transport. Most hard drives now do this automatically when they are turned off.

parse To break down into components. *Spreadsheet* programs, for example, often have parsing features that will break *ASCII* data into parts that will fit into *cells.*

parser 1. A program that breaks large units of data into smaller, more easily interpreted pieces. 2. In *SGML,* a program that reads a data file and displays the various marked *elements* according to the *document type definition (DTD)*. A *Web browser* is a parser for *HTML*.

partial-response maximum-likelihood (PRML) read-channel technology   See *PRML read-channel technology*.

partition   A section of the storage area of a *hard disk* created for organizational purposes or to separate different *operating systems*. A partition is created during initial preparation of the hard disk, before the disk is formatted. See *logical drives*.

Pascal   A high-level, *procedural language* that encourages programmers to write well-structured, modular programs that take advantage of modern *control structures* and lack *spaghetti code*. Pascal has gained wide acceptance as a teaching and application-development language, though most professional programmers prefer *C* or *C++*. Pascal is available in interpreted and compiled versions.

passive matrix display   In *notebook computers,* a *liquid-crystal display (LCD)* in which a single transistor controls an entire column or row of the display's tiny electrodes. Passive matrix displays are cheaper than *active matrix displays* (also called *dual-scan displays*) but offer lower *resolution* and contrast.

passive termination   Like *active termination* and *forced-perfect termination,* a way of ending a chain of *Small Computer System Interface (SCSI)* devices. Passive termination is the simplest termination method and works best on *daisy chains* of four or fewer devices.

passphrase   A lengthy *password* of up to 100 characters that is used to encrypt or decrypt secret messages. The use of a lengthy password renders password guessing *computationally infeasible*.

password   An *authentication* tool used to identify authorized users of a *program* or *network* and to define their privileges, such as read-only, reading and writing, or file copying. Passwords are easily guessed or stolen, or acquired through *social engineering,* or intercepted by *packet sniffers* as they are uploaded in *cleartext* to the authenticating network computer, and therefore pose one of the greatest challenges to computer network security. *One-time passwords* and digital signatures provide more secure means of authentication.

P
Q
R

password aging   In a computer network, a feature of the *network operating system (NOS)* that keeps track of the last time you changed your *password*.

Password Authentication Protocol (PAP)   An *Internet* standard providing a simple (and fundamentally insecure) method of *authentication*. The authenticating computer demands the user's *login name* and *password*, and keeps doing so until these are supplied correctly. Computer criminals who possess a known login name can gain *unauthorized access* by running password-guessing programs that supply a variety of known insecure passwords, such as ego–enhancing terms ("genius") or easily–remembered words ("qwerty" or "secret"). A secure network requires some method of *strong authentication*, such as the *Challenge Handshake Authentication Protocol (CHAP), digital signatures,* or *Kerberos*.

password protection   A method of limiting access to a *program, file, computer,* or a *network* by requiring you to enter a *password*. Some programs enable you to password-protect your files so they can't be read or altered by others.

paste   In text editing, inserting at the location of the *cursor* text or *graphics* you've cut or copied from another location. In Windows and Macintosh systems, a temporary storage area called the *Clipboard* stores the cut or copied material while you move to the material's new location. When you paste, the material is copied from the Clipboard to its new location. See *block move*.

patch   1. A quick fix, in the form of one or more program statements, added to a *program* to correct *bugs* or to enhance the program's capabilities. 2. An executable program that repairs a defective program. 3. To fix a program by replacing one or more lines of code.

path   In a *hierarchical file system* such as *Unix* or *MS-DOS,* the route the operating system must follow to find an executable program stored in a *subdirectory*.

path name   In DOS, a statement that indicates the name of a file and precisely where it's located on a *hard disk*. When opening or saving a file with most applications, you must specify the full path name to retrieve or store the file in a *directory* other than the *current directory*. Suppose that you're using WordPerfect, and you want to store the file REPORT9.DOC in the directory C:\DOCS. If C:\DOCS isn't the current directory, you must type C:\DOCS\REPORT9.DOC to name and store the file in the correct location.

path–name separator   The character that is used to differentiate the various *directory* names in a *path name.* In *Unix* and the *World Wide Web (WWW),* the path–name separator is a forward slash (/); in *MS-DOS,* it is a backwards slash (\).

path statement   In DOS, an entry in the *AUTOEXEC.BAT* file that lists the directories in which executable programs are listed. See *path.*

pattern recognition   In *artificial intelligence,* the provision of computers with the ability to identify objects or shapes within the stream of incoming visual data.

PC   1. Abbreviation for *personal computer.* In practice, this abbreviation usually refers to IBM or IBM-compatible personal computers, as opposed to Macintoshes. 2. Abbreviation for printed circuit board.

PC DOS   The version of the *MS-DOS* operating system released by IBM. PC DOS is functionally identical to MS-DOS.

PCI bus   Abbreviation for Peripheral Component Interface (PCI) bus. A 32-bit *expansion bus* specification in wide use today and is used on both PC-compatible and Macintosh computers. *Intel Corporation* released the PCI bus in 1992 to work with its *Pentium* microprocessor, but the design is flexible and works with today's 64-bit microprocessors as well. PCI has displaced the *VESA local bus* standard from the market and will likely soon do the same with the *Industry Standard Architecture (ISA)* expansion bus, although most *motherboards* still include a few ISA slots for *downward compatibility.* PCI *supports Plug and Play,* which likely will help cement its hold on the expansion bus market for the next several years.

PCI slot   A socket for *adapters* in a *motherboard* equipped with a *PCI bus.* 32-bit PCI slots are preferred to *VESA local bus slots* and *ISA slots* because of their superior speed. PCI slots are found most often on motherboards housing the *Pentium, Pentium Pro,* or *Pentium II microprocessor.*

P Q R

PCL   See *Printer Control Language.*

PCL3   The original, now-obsolete version of Hewlett-Packard's *Printer Control Language (PCL)*. PCL3 supports only *cartridge fonts* and restricts users to only one *font* per page.

PCL4   An improved and widely used version of Hewlett-Packard's *Printer Control Language (PCL)* that supports *downloadable fonts* and multiple *fonts* on single pages.

PCL5   A version of Hewlett-Packard's *Printer Control Language (PCL)* that supports *vector graphics* and *scalable fonts*. PCL5 was first used on HP LaserJet III printers.

PCL5e   The latest version of Hewlett-Packard's *Printer Control Language (PCL),* used on HP LaserJet printers. PCL5e is the first version of PCL to support *bi-directional communication* between printer and computer.

PCM   See *pulse code modulation.*

PCMCIA   See *Personal Computer Memory Card Interface Adapter.*

PCMCIA bus   An *expansion bus* specification used to connect a variety of credit-card–sized *peripherals* to computers, typically *portable computers*. PCMCIA (the acronym stands for Personal Computer Memory Card Interface Adapter) bus slots are being found with increasing frequency on *desktop computers*.

PCMCIA card reader   A peripheral device that enables a *desktop computer* to use devices designed to connect to a *PCMCIA bus*. PCMCIA card readers may be useful for computer users who only want to buy one of a particular peripheral, such as a *modem* or *network interface adapter.*

PCMCIA modem   A *modem* designed to connect to a *PCMCIA slot,* usually in a *portable computer.*

PCMCIA slot   A receptacle that's designed to connect devices to a *PCMCIA bus.* These slots can be used to plug in PCMCIA-compatible hardware such as *modems* and *network adapters.*

p-code   Synonymous with *bytecode.*

p-code compiler   A type of *interpreter* that generates *machine language* from the incoming stream of *bytecode,* which is an intermediary between *source code* and complied *object code*. P-code compilers execute faster than source code interpreters, but they do not run as quickly as executable programs that have been compiled using a *native compiler*. See *Java*.

PD   See *public domain program*.

PDA   See *personal digital assistant*.

PDF   See *Portable Document Format*.

PDL   See *page description language*.

PDN   See *private data network* and *public data network*.

PDS   See *portable document software (PDS)*.

Peachtree Accounting   A small-business *accounting package* that critics have lauded for its ease-of-use and power. Designed for companies with 100 employees or fewer, Peachtree Accounting features the ability to manage payroll, keep track of accounts payable and accounts receivable, and manage inventory in a variety of ways (first in, first out; last in, first out, etc.). Peachtree Accounting, available in both Macintosh and *Microsoft Windows* versions, also has several *spreadsheet*-like analysis tools that let business managers develop several *what-if* scenarios.

peer-to-peer file transfer   A file-sharing technique for *local area networks (LANs)* in which each user has access to the public files located on the *workstation* of any other network user. Each user determines which files, if any, he or she wants to make public for network access. See *TOPS*.

peer-to-peer network   A *local area network (LAN)* without a central *file server* and in which all computers in the network have access to the public files located on all other *workstations*. See *client/server* and *peer-to-peer file transfer*.

pel   Abbreviation for *pixel*.

PEM   See *Privacy Enhanced Mail*.

pen computer   A computer equipped with *pattern recognition* circuitry so that it can recognize human handwriting as a form of data input. Some *personal digital assistants (PDAs)* use pen technology, but the high error rate has given handwriting recognition a poor reputation among users.

P
Q
R

Pentium   A *32-bit microprocessor* designed and manufactured by *Intel* and introduced in 1993 that has achieved an overwhelming market share in personal computing. The Pentium, available with *clock speeds* of up to 233 *megahertz (MHz),* uses a speedy version of *complex instruction-set computer (CISC)* technology that borrows many concepts from *reduced instruction set computer (RISC)* processor designs, such as *superscalar architecture* (it has two *pipelines* that employ *branch prediction*). A Pentium running at 200 MHz, and equipped with a 512K L2 cache, achieves a *SPECint95*★ benchmark of 5.10. With more than 3 million transistors, the Pentium employs a 64-bit *internal data bus.* Though early Pentiums had faulty *floating-point units (FPUs),* Intel has corrected the problem and will replace bad parts for free. Recent Pentiums include the *MMX* extensions for rapid processing of multimedia. Unlike the *Pentium Pro,* which is specifically optimized for running *32-bit applications,* the Pentium runs *16-bit applications* as well as *32-bit applications.* Pentium systems are generally equipped with *Microsoft Windows 95,* a hybrid 16-bit/32-bit *operating system.*

Pentium II   A version of the *Pentium Pro* microprocessor that runs *16-bit applications* as well as *32-bit applications* and incorporates the *MMX* extensions for fast execution of multimedia. The successor to the *Pentium,* the Pentium II is currently available in versions running at *clock speeds* of up to 300 MHz. Intended for use in single-user workstations as well as *servers,* the Pentium II does not markedly sacrifice the Pentium Pro's performance: A Pentium II running at 200 MHz, and equipped with a 512K L2 cache, achieves a *SPECint95*★ benchmark of 8.20 (as against a 200 MHz-Pentium Pro's 8.58).

Pentium OverDrive   A *microprocessor* that, as part of an upgrade, plugs into the *OverDrive socket* on the *motherboard* of an *Intel 486DX/2 central processing unit (CPU),* or the processor socket of early Pentium models (60MHz and 66MHz).

Pentium Pro   A *32-bit microprocessor* designed and manufactured by *Intel,* introduced in 1996 that is specifically designed and optimized for executing *32-bit software.* For this reason, Pentium Pro systems are generally equipped with *Microsoft Windows NT,* which does not run *16-bit software.* Code-named P6 during its development, the Pentium Pro incorporates many features of *reduced instruction set computing (RISC)* design philosophy, including *superscalar architecture* and *pipelines.* Important features of the design include a dual independent bus (DIB) architecture (the *L2 cache* and the superpipelined system data bus are separate and independent, enabling up to three times the performance of single-bus designs) and dynamic execution (a combination of *branch prediction* and *speculative execution* that enables the processor to anticipate and schedule the future direction of program flow). A Pentium Pro running at 200 MHz, and equipped with a 512K L2 cache, achieves a *SPECint95*★ benchmark of 8.58 (as against a 200 MHz–Pentium's 5.10). Most Pentium Pro systems are designed to function as high-speed *servers* in *local area networks (LANs)*.

Pentium-ready   Capable of being upgraded to near-*Pentium* performance levels. Pentium-ready 80486 motherboards have a *P24T socket,* into which a *Pentium OverDrive microprocessor* can be inserted.

peripheral   A device, such as a *printer* or disk drive, connected to and controlled by a computer but external to the computer's *central processing unit (CPU).*

Peripheral Component Interface (PCI) expansion bus   See *PCI bus.*

perl   Acronym for Practical Extraction and Report Language. In *Unix,* an interpreted *scripting language* that is specifically designed for scanning text files, extracting information from these files, and preparing reports summarizing this information. Written by Larry Wall, perl is widely used to create *Common Gateway Interface (CGI)* scripts that handle the output of HTML *forms.* See *HTML* and *interpreter.*

permanent font   A Hewlett-Packard term for a *font* that, when downloaded to a *laser printer,* stays in the printer's memory until the printer is shut off. See *downloadable font* and *temporary font.*

permanent swap file   In *Microsoft Windows 3.1,* a disk file composed of contiguous disk sectors that's set aside for the rapid storage and retrieval of program instructions or data in the program's 386 Enhanced mode. This storage space is used in *virtual memory* operations, which use disk space as a seamless extension of *random-access memory (RAM).* The permanent swap file, however, is slower than RAM and consumes a large amount of space on the disk. See *paged memory management unit (PMMU),* and *swap file.*

P
Q
R

persistence   A quality of the *phosphor* that coats the interior of a *cathode ray tube (CRT) display*. Persistence ensures that after being struck by the beam from an *electron gun,* a phosphor will continue to glow until the electron beam strikes it again. Persistence ensures that *displays* appear uniformly bright to human eyes.

persistent connection   In *Microsoft Windows 95,* a network connection that lasts longer than a single working session. A *modem* call to CompuServe is usually not a persistent connection, while an *Ethernet* connection to a *network laser printer* is. Windows 95 tries to establish persistent connections every time it starts.

personal certificate   A digital *certificate* attesting that a given individual who is trying to log on to an authenticated *server* really is the individual he or she claims to be. Personal certificates are issued by *certificate authorities (CA).*

personal computer (PC)   A small computer equipped with all the system, utility, and application software, and the input/output devices and other *peripherals* that an individual needs to perform one or more tasks. The term personal computer, or PC, is used today to refer collectively and individually to stand-alone IBM Personal Computers, *IBM PC-compatible computers,* Macintosh computers, Apple computers, Amiga computers, and others (such as the Commodore) that are no longer manufactured.

Personal Computer Memory Card Interface Adapter (PCMCIA)   An international trade association that has developed standards for devices, such as *modems* and external *hard disk* drives, that can be easily plugged into *notebook computers.* See *Plug and Play (PnP).*

personal digital assistant (PDA)   A small, hand-held computer, capable of accepting input that the user writes on-screen with a stylus, that's designed to provide all the tools an individual would need for day-to-day organization. This would include, for example, an appointment calendar, an address book, a notepad, and a fax modem. See *Newton, pen computer,* and *transceiver.*

personal information manager (PIM)   A program, such as *Lotus Organizer* that stores and retrieves a variety of personal information, including notes, memos, names and addresses, and appointments. Unlike a database management program, a PIM is optimized for the storage and retrieval of a variety of personal information. You can switch among different views of your notes, such as people, to-do items, and expenses. PIMs have been slow to gain acceptance, however, because they're hard to learn and because users often are away from their computers when they need the information.

personal laser printer   A *laser printer* designed to serve the printing needs of only one person, as opposed to a *departmental laser printer* which is designed to serve many people. Personal laser printers have *monthly duty cycles* of a few hundred pages.

PGA   See *Professional Graphics Array* or *pin grid array.*

PGP   See *Pretty Good Privacy.*

PgUp/PgDn keys   See *Page Up/Page Down keys.*

phase   On a monitor, an adjustment that enables the user to stretch or shrink the vertical and horizontal size of the display to minimize or eliminate unused black space around the screen image.

phono plug   A connector with a short stem used to connect home audio devices. In computers, phono plugs are used for audio and composite monitor output ports. Synonymous with RCA plug.

phosphor   An electrofluorescent material used to coat the inside face of a *cathode ray tube (CRT)*. After being energized by the electron beam that's directed to the inside face of the tube, the phosphors glow for a fraction of a second—long enough to make the display appear uniformly bright to human eyes. The beam refreshes the phosphor many times per second to produce a consistent illumination. See *raster.*

PhotoCD   A standard for encoding photographs, taken with ordinary 35-millimeter cameras and film, onto *CD-ROMs*. Though PhotoCD technology has not become a big consumer hit, it is popular among publishers and some photographers.

PhotoGrade   An Apple *resolution enhancement* scheme that improves the appearance of *grayscale* images, such as photographs, when they are printed on a *laser printer.*

P
Q
R

photorealistic   Of photographic quality. *Printer* output is said to be photorealistic when its colors are well-saturated and blend smoothly with one another.

photorealistic output printer   Output that matches the quality of a chemically printed photograph. *Thermal dye sublimation printers* can generate photorealistic output with continuous tones, but they are very expensive and the *cost per page* exceeds $3.00, since they require special *coated paper*.

PhotoShop   See *Adobe PhotoShop*.

phototypesetter   See *imagesetter*.

phrase search   In a database program or Web *search engine,* a keyword search in which the search terms are surrounded by special markers (generally, quotation marks) to show that they form a phrase. The software returns only those items in which these words appear next to each other, and in exactly the same order, as the supplied phrase. For example, an AltaVista search for "pipeline burst cache" returns only those Web pages that contain this exact phrase.

phreaking   An illegal form of recreation that involves using one's knowledge of telephone system technology to make long-distance calls for free.

physical drive   The disk drive actually performing the current read/write operation, as opposed to a logical drive, the existence of which is only apparent to the user of the system. A *hard disk* can be formatted into *partitions,* sections, and directories that have all the characteristics of a separate disk drive, but are *logical drives.* The data, however, is actually encoded either on the surface of a disk in a floppy drive or a hard disk drive, which is referred to as the physical drive. See *floppy disk* and *secondary storage*.

physical format   See *low-level format*.

physical layer   In the *OSI Reference Model* of computer network architecture, the last of seven *layers,* in which the data is transformed into the electrical signals appropriate for the specific type of *physical media* to which the computer is connected.

physical medium   In a computer network, the cabling through which network data travels. See *copper pair, coaxial cable, fiber optics, T1,* and *T3*.

physical memory   The actual *random-access memory (RAM)* circuits in which data is stored, as opposed to *virtual memory*—the "apparent" RAM that results from using the computer's *hard disk* as an extension of physical memory.

physical network   An actual physical *network* such as a *local area network (LAN),* generally constructed using the equipment and software of a single manufacturer, as opposed to a *logical network,* the network that users perceive when they use their *workstations.* At the University of Virginia, for example, there are several physical networks made by a number of different LAN hardware manufacturers. However, the differences among these networks are not apparent, or even discoverable, by the students, faculty, and staff who log on to these networks; so far as they are concerned, there is a single logical network that makes all of the University's computer resources available, and a broader global network (the *Internet*) that makes even more resources available.

pica   1. In *typography,* a unit of measure equal to approximately $1/6$ inch, or 12 *points.* Picas are used to describe horizontal and vertical measurements on the page, with the exception of type sizes, which are expressed in points. 2. In formal typography, one pica is 0.166 of an inch, but many word processing and page layout programs, in the interest of simplification, define one pica as $1/6$ inch. 3. In typewriting and letter-quality printing, pica is a 12-point monospace font that prints at a pitch of 10 *characters per inch (cpi).*

pico-   Prefix for one trillionth (10^{-12}). Abbreviated p.

picosecond   One trillionth (10^{-12}) of a second.

PICT   A Macintosh graphics *file format* originally developed for the MacDraw program. An *object-oriented graphic* format, PICT files consist of separate graphics objects, such as lines, arcs, ovals, or rectangles, each of which you can independently edit, size, move, or color. (PICT files also can store *bit-mapped graphics.*) Some Windows graphics applications can read PICT files.

picture element   See *pixel.*

picture tube   See *cathode ray tube (CRT).*

pie graph   In *presentation graphics,* a graph that displays a *data series* as a circle to emphasize the relative contribution of each

P
Q
R

data item to the whole. Each slice of the pie appears in shades of gray or a distinctive pattern. Patterns can produce moiré distortions if you juxtapose too many patterns. Some programs can produce paired pie graphs that display two data series. For presentations, exploding a slice from the whole is a useful technique to add emphasis. See *exploded pie graph, linked pie/column graph, moiré effect,* and *proportional pie graph.*

PIF   See *program information file.*

PIM   See *personal information manager.*

pin compatible   Able to fit and operate in the same socket as another *chip,* especially one made by another manufacturer. See *zero-insertion force (ZIF) package.*

pincushion   The bowing in of the sides of an image displayed on a computer *monitor* (the opposite effect, in which the sides bow out, is called barreling). Most monitors have a pincushion control that enables the user to correct this distortion.

Pine   An *e-mail* program for *Unix* computer systems. Unlike predecessor programs, such as Elm, the program contains its own easy-to-use full screen editor, thus freeing users from dependence on the not-very-easy-to-use default editors on *Unix* systems (such as *emacs* and *vi*). (The name "Pine" is actually an acronym of the self-referential sort: Pine Is Not Elm.)

pin feed   See *tractor feed.*

PING   See *Packet Internet Groper.*

pingable   Able to respond to *PING;* an *Internet* site that is "alive" and should be able to respond to Internet tools such as *FTP* and *Gopher.*

pin grid array (PGA)   On the bottom side of a *chip,* the collection of protruding pins that enable the chip to connect to a socket or *circuit board.*

pipe   In *MS-DOS* and *Unix,* a symbol that tells the operating system to send the output of one command to another command, rather than display this output. In the following example, the pipe (represented by the | symbol) tells DOS to send the output of the TREE command to the MORE command; the

MORE command then displays the TREE result page by page on-screen:

```
<C:\>TREE C:\ ¦ MORE
```

See *filter* and *input/output (I/O) redirection.*

pipeline In computer design, an "assembly line" in the microprocessor that dramatically speeds the processing of instructions through retrieval, execution, and writing back. Long supported by *Unix,* the pipeline included in the *Intel 80486* allows it to process an instruction every *clock cycle.* The *Intel Pentium* microprocessor features two pipelines, one for data and one for instruction, and can therefore process two instructions (one per pipeline) every clock cycle. A microprocessor with two or more pipelines is said to employ *superscalar architecture.*

pipeline burst cache A *secondary cache* (also known as L2 cache) that enables fast data transfer rates by spreading data fetches from memory over three clock cycles. This results in a slight delay initially, but it enables the cache to place requests in a queue so that subsequent fetches follow in just one clock cycle. Pipeline burst caches require synchronous *SRAM* (chips that can synchronize with the microprocessor's clock). In addition, pipeline burst caches support *burst mode* transfers in which the SRAM chips can deliver an entire line of cache contents when the processor requests just the first word in the line.

pipeline stall An error in a *superscalar architecture*-equipped *microprocessor* that delays the processing of an instruction. In a microprocessor with an *in-order execution* design, such as the *Pentium,* instructions must be processed in a precise order, and a pipeline stall in one *pipeline* will delay processing in the other pipeline as well. In an *out-of-order execution* scheme, a pipeline stall in one pipeline would not hold up the other.

pipelining A *microprocessor* design method that allows a microprocessor to handle more than one instruction at a time. There are typically five sequential steps to a microprocessor's handling of an instruction, and a pipelining scheme allows each of five instructions to be undergoing one of the steps during a *clock cycle.* Microprocessors with *superscalar architecture* have two or more *pipelines,* increasing efficiency further.

P Q R

piracy See *software piracy.*

pitch   A horizontal measurement of the number of characters per linear inch in a *monospace* font, such as those used with type-writers, *dot-matrix printers,* and *daisywheel printers*. By convention, *pica* pitch (not to be confused with the printer's measurement of approximately ¹/₆ inch) is equal to 10 characters per inch, and elite pitch is equal to 12 characters per inch. See *point*.

pixel   Contraction of picture element. The smallest element (a picture element) that a device can display and out of which the displayed image is constructed. See *bit-mapped graphic*.

Plain Old Telephone Service (POTS)   An *analog* communications system, adequate for voice communication and slow data communication with *modems,* but without sufficient *bandwidth* to handle high-speed *digital* communications. Technologies like the *Integrated Services Telecommunications Network (ISDN)* may replace POTS someday and provide higher bandwidth.

plain text document   A document that contains nothing but standard *ASCII* text, number, and punctuation characters.

planar board   See *motherboard*.

planar clock speed   The *clock speed* at which the *motherboard* operates. This speed may differ from the clock speed of the microprocessor, which may be two or more times faster.

plan file   A file in a *Unix* user's home directory that was originally intended to display a colleague's schedule and work plans for the future when accessed with the *finger* utility. It is more often used for compiling humorous quotations or other informal uses.

plasma display   A *display* technology used with *high-end laptop* computers. The display is produced by energizing ionized gas held between two transparent panels. Synonymous with gas plasma display.

platen   In *dot-matrix* and *letter-quality impact printers,* the cylinder that guides paper through the printer and provides a backing surface for the paper when images are impressed onto the page.

platform   See *hardware platform*.

platform-dependent   Not able to function in a cross-platform environment; requiring a specific brand of computer or *operating system* in order to function. *ActiveX controls* are platform-dependent because they cannot run on any computer unless its *operating system* supports Microsoft-originated object linking and embedding *(OLE).*

platform–independent   Capable of functioning in a computing network environment that connects computers made by several different manufacturers and running different *operating systems. Java* is platform-independent because it will execute on any computer system that is capable of running a Java interpreter.

plating   A means of coating a *hard disk* platter with a thin-film magnetic medium. By submerging an electrically charged bare platter in a liquid containing oppositely charged molecules of the recording medium, the platter is evenly coated with the medium. See *sputtering.*

platter   Synonymous with disk.

plot   To construct an image by drawing lines.

plotter   A printer that produces high-quality graphical output by moving ink pens over the surface of the paper. The printer moves the pens under the direction of the computer, so that printing is automatic. Plotters are commonly used for *computer-aided design (CAD)* and presentation graphics.

plotter font   In *Microsoft Windows,* a vector font designed to be used with a plotter. The font composes characters by generating dots connected by lines.

Plug and Play (PnP)   An industry-wide hardware standard for add-in hardware that requires the hardware be able to identify itself, on demand, in a standard fashion. *Microsoft Windows 95* supports Plug and Play, and should help create a market for Plug and Play peripherals, which are expected to overshadow older peripherals in short order. With Plug and Play, you don't need to "install" devices; you don't fuss with *jumper settings* and *dual in-line package (DIP)* switches, or printer drivers for the newest printers. Instead, Plug and Play uses both hardware (a Plug and Play *BIOS*) and software (a Plug and Play-compatible *operating system*) to do its job.

Plug and Play BIOS (PnP BIOS)   A *basic input-output system (BIOS)* compatible with the *Plug and Play (PnP)* standard,

P
Q
R

which, when used in conjunction with a Plug and Play compatible *operating system* (such as *Microsoft Windows 95*) and Plug and Play compatible *adapters,* enables you to install adapters in the *expansion bus* without creating *interrupt request (IRQ) conflicts* or *port conflicts*. Note that a "plug and play" BIOS is not necessarily the same as a "Plug and Play" (capital letters) BIOS, which precisely conforms to the Plug and Play standard.

Plug and Print   A standard designed to improve the way *printers* and computers communicate. Developed by the *Desktop Management Task Force (DMTF),* Plug and Print creates a Management Information Base (MIB) or Management Information File (MIF) that contains details about a printer's operation. Plug and Print, an open standard, competes with *Microsoft at Work,* a standard designed to be used only by systems running Microsoft Windows. Synonymous with MIB/MI.

plug-compatible   See *pin compatible.*

plug-in   A program module that is designed to directly interface with, and give additional capability to, a proprietary application, such as Adobe PhotoShop or Netscape Navigator. After installing the plug-in, the program takes on additional capabilities, which may be reflected in the appearance of new commands in the original application's menu system.

Although plug-ins play a fruitful role in stand-alone applications, they have not proved successful as a means of distributing additional *Web browser* capabilities on the World Wide Web; very few Web users want to take the time needed to download a large plug-in (which may require up to 1 or 2MB of storage space), install the plug-in using a setup program, and restart the system in order to make use of its capabilities. *Java applets* and *ActiveX controls* download more transparently and do not require the user to interrupt the browsing session by restarting the system.

PMJI   In online communications, shorthand for Pardon Me for Jumping In.

PMMU   See *paged memory management unit.*

PMS   See *Pantone Matching System.*

PNG   Acronym for Portable Network Graphics. A bit-mapped graphics format, similar to *GIF,* that does not use patented compression algorithm. A major motivation for developing PNG is

Unisys's actions in collecting licensing fees from software publishers for the use of GIF's *LZW* compression algorithm. The use of PNG graphics is expected to increase rapidly once the major browsers support it.

PnP   See *Plug and Play.*

PnP BIOS   See *Plug and Play BIOS.*

pocket modem   An *external modem* about the size of a pack of cigarettes, designed for use with *portable computers*. Pocket modems have been largely replaced by *PCMCIA* modems.

point   1. To move the mouse pointer on-screen without clicking the button. 2. In *typography*, a fundamental unit of measurement (72 points equal approximately one inch). Computer programs usually ignore this slight discrepancy, making a point exactly equal to $^1/_{72}$ inch. See *pica* and *pitch*.

pointer   1. In a *graphical user interface (GUI)*, an on-screen symbol, usually an arrow, that shows the current position of the *mouse*. 2. In *database management* programs, a record number in an index that stores the actual physical location of the data record. 3. In *programming*, a variable that contains directions to (points to) another variable. Pointers enable programmers to set many variables equal to one another without lots of *assignment statements.*

pointing device   An input device such as a *mouse, trackball,* or *graphics tablet* used to manipulate a pointer on-screen.

pointing stick   A pencil eraser–sized, rubberized device in the center of the *keyboard,* which is moved with the fingertip to relocate the cursor on-screen. Although pointing sticks originated in *portable computers* and are often used in them, pointing sticks appear on some *desktop computers* as well.

point of presence (POP)   In a *wide area network (WAN),* a locality in which it is possible to obtain dialup access to the network by means of a local telephone call. *Internet service providers (ISP)* provide POPs in towns and cities, but many rural areas are without local POPs.

P
Q
R

point-of-sale software   A *program,* such as a *bar code reader,* that automatically makes adjustments to accounting and inventory databases as a business sells merchandise.

Point-to-Point Protocol   See *PPP.*

Point-to-Point Tunneling Protocol   See PPTP.

polarity   1. In electronics, the negative or positive property of a charge. 2. In *graphics,* the tonal relationship between foreground and background elements. Positive polarity is the printing of black or dark characters on a white or light background; negative polarity is the printing of white or light characters on a black or dark background.

polarization   A physical phenomenon, in which light waves vibrate in a single plane, that is part of the foundation of *magneto-optical (MO) disk drive* technology. Along with the *Kerr effect,* polarization is at the core of how MO drives read-and-write data.

Polish notation   See *Reverse Polish Notation (RPN).*

poll   To request status information concerning a peripheral or remote data service in order to determine whether a connection is possible.

polling   In *local area networks (LANs),* a method for controlling channel access in which the central computer continuously asks or polls the workstations to determine whether they have information to send. With polling channel access, you can specify how often, and for how long, the central computer polls the workstations. Unlike CSMA/CD and token-ring channel-access methods, the network manager can give some nodes more access to the network than others. See *Carrier Sense Multiple Access with Collision Detection (CSMA/CD)* and *token-ring network.*

polyline   In *graphics,* a drawing tool used to create a multisided, enclosed shape. To use the tool, draw a straight line to a point, and then continue the line in a different direction to a point. By continuing this operation until you return to the starting point, you can create a complex object of your own design. The result is a *graphics primitive,* which the program treats as a single object. Like the more familiar primitives (squares or circles), the polyline object can be independently edited, sized, moved, or colored. Some programs call this tool a polygon. See *vector graphics.*

polyphony   In *sound boards,* the reproduction of multiple sounds at one time. *High-end* sound boards can put out 20 or more sounds at once.

POP See *point of presence* or *Post Office Protocol*.

POP3 Also spelled POP-3. The current version of the *Post Office Protocol (POP)*, an *Internet* standard for storing *e-mail* on a mail server until you can access it and download it to your computer.

pop-up menu A *menu* that appears when you select a certain on-screen item, such as text, a *scroll bar*, or a *dialog box* option. The name doesn't truly reflect a direction. If a pop-up menu will appear too close to the top of the screen, it pops down. *Microsoft Windows 95* makes extensive use of pop-up menus, both for editing and tutorial tasks. See *pull-down menu*.

port 1. An *interface* that governs and synchronizes the flow of data between the *central processing unit (CPU)* and external devices such as printers and modems. See *parallel port* and *serial port*. 2. On the *Internet*, a *logical* channel through which a certain type of application data is routed in order to decode incoming data and route it to the correct destination. Each type of Internet service, such as *FTP* or *IRC*, has a certain port number associated with it. Port number assignments are controlled by the *Internet Assigned Numbers Authority (IANA)*. 3. To modify or translate a program so that it will run on a different computer.

portability A measure of the ease with which a given program can be made to function in a different computing environment, such as a different brand of computer or *operating system*. Programs written in *C* are said to be highly portable because only a small portion of the code needs to be written with the specifics of a particular computer in mind.

portable Capable of working on a variety of *hardware* platforms or working with differing applications. For example, *Unix* and *Microsoft Windows NT* are examples of portable *operating systems*. Most operating systems are designed around the specific electronic capabilities of a given *central processing unit (CPU)*. Unix and Windows NT, in contrast, are designed with a predetermined, overall structure. Specific machine instructions are embedded within a program module that allows it to function on a given CPU.

portable computer A computer with a screen and keyboard built in and designed to be transported easily from one location to another. The first portable personal computers, such as the

P
Q
R

Osborne I and Compaq II, are best described as "luggables." These computers weighed in at more than 25 pounds and couldn't be carried comfortably for more than a short distance. Today's battery-powered laptop and notebook computers are much smaller and lighter. See *laptop computer, notebook computer,* and *personal digital assistant (PGA).*

portable document   A richly formatted document, which may contain *graphics* as well as text, that can be transferred to another type of computer system without losing the formatting. To create portable documents, you need *portable document software (PDS),* such as *Adobe Acrobat,* that is designed to save the formatting information to a file that can be easily transferred to a different type of computer system. To read the document, you need a file viewer program that is specifically designed to work on the type of computer you are using. For example, you can create an Adobe Acrobat document on a Macintosh, and give the file to somebody using a *Sun* workstation. To read the file, the Sun user needs a copy of the Adobe Acrobat reader program.

Portable Document Format (PDF)   A *portable document* file format created by Adobe Systems that makes extensive use of the *PostScript* printer description language.

portable document software (PDS)   *Application programs* that create *portable documents,* which can be transferred to different types of computer systems without losing their rich formatting and graphics. Two types of software are required: the document publishing program and a file viewer. The document publishing program creates a coded *ASCII* file that retains *fonts,* graphics, and layout information. This file can be distributed electronically by means of online services such as *CompuServe* or the *Internet.* File viewers, which are designed to run on a specific type of computer, enable users to read these files and to see a replica of the original document's fonts, graphics, and layout. The most popular PDS is *Adobe Acrobat,* thanks to the widespread Internet availability of free file viewers for a wide variety of computer systems.

Portable Network Graphics   See *PNG.*

port address   A number that identifies the location of a particular *Internet* application, such as *FTP,* a *World Wide Web (WWW)* server, or *Gopher,* on a computer that is directly connected to the Internet. Regulated by the *Internet Assigned*

Numbers Authority (IANA), port numbers are included in the headers of every Internet packet; the numbers tell the receiving software where to deliver the incoming data. See *well-known port.*

port conflict   An error that occurs when two devices, such as a *mouse* and a *modem,* try to access the same *serial port* at one time. If you can, set your mouse to serial port COM1, your modem to serial port COM2, and disable all other serial ports because using them may cause problems.

portrait font   A *font* oriented toward the short edges of a page. This book is printed with a portrait font.

portrait monitor   See *full-page display.*

portrait orientation   The default printing orientation for a page of text in which the height of the page is greater than the width. Compare to *landscape orientation.*

port replicator   A hardware device, containing standard *parallel ports* and *serial ports,* that is designed to plug into a special receptacle in a *notebook computer.* The purpose of the replicator is to enable notebook users to plug in a printer and monitor quickly and easily.

post   1. In a *newsgroup,* to send a message so that it can be read by everyone who accesses the group. 2. In database management, to add data to a *data record.*

POST   See *Power-On Self-Test.*

postcardware   A type of *freeware,* save that the author requests that those who wish to continue to use the program send the author a postcard.

postfix notation   See *Reverse Polish Notation (RPN).*

postmaster   In a *network,* the human administrator who configures the *e-mail* manager and handles problems that arise.

Post Office Protocol (POP)   An *Internet e-mail* standard that specifies how an Internet-connected computer can function as a mail-handling agent; the current version is called POP3. Messages arrive at a user's electronic mailbox, which is housed on the service provider's computer. From this central storage point, you can access your mail from different computers—

P
Q
R

a networked workstation in the office as well as a PC at home. In either case, a POP—compatible *e-mail* program, which runs on your workstation or PC, establishes a connection with the POP server, and detects that new mail has arrived. You can then download the mail to the workstation or computer, and reply to it, print it, or store it, as you prefer. POP does not send mail; that job is handled by *SMTP*.

postprocessor   A *program* that performs a final, automatic processing operation after you finish working with a file. Post-processing programs include text formatters that prepare a document for printing, and *page description languages (PDL)* that convert an on-screen document into a set of commands that the printer's interpreter can recognize and use to print the document.

PostScript   A sophisticated *page description language (PDL)* that is used for high-quality printing on laser printers and other *high-resolution* printing devices. PostScript is capable of describing the entire appearance of a richly formatted page, including layout, fonts, graphics, and scanned images. Though PostScript is a *programming language* and one can learn to write page descriptions in it, programs generate PostScript code on the fly; the code goes to a display device (such as a printer, slide recorder, *imagesetter,* screen display, or *PostScript printer*), where a PostScript interpreter follows the coded instructions to generate an image of the page precisely according to these instructions. A major benefit of PostScript is its *device independence*; you can print the PostScript code generated by an application on any printer with a PostScript interpreter. You can take PostScript files generated on your PC to a *service bureau,* which can print the document using expensive typesetting machines called *imagesetters* with resolutions of up to 2400 dots per inch (dpi). See *PostScript font* and *PostScript printer.*

PostScript font   A scalable *outline font* that conforms to Adobe Software's specifications for *Type 1 fonts,* which require a *PostScript printer.* Unlike bit-mapped fonts, which often print with crude edges and curves, PostScript's outline font technology produces smooth letters that your printer renders at its maximum possible resolution. A *PostScript* font comes with a *screen font,* which simulates the font's appearance on-screen, and a *printer font,* which must either be built-in to your printer or downloaded to the printer before printing. Note that the type may look jagged on-screen unless you buy Adobe Type Manager, which brings PostScript *scalable font* technology to the display screen.

PostScript Level 2 An improved version of *PostScript* that is faster and supports color printing and file *compression*.

PostScript Level 3 The latest version of *PostScript,* which includes further color optimization as well as support for network and Web publishing.

PostScript printer A *printer,* generally a *laser printer,* that includes the processing circuitry needed to decode and interpret printing instructions phrased in *PostScript,* a *page description language (PDL)* widely used in *desktop publishing.* Because PostScript printers require their own microprocessor circuitry and at least 1M of random-access memory (RAM) to image each page, they're more expensive than non-PostScript printers. However, they can print text or graphics in subtle gradations of gray. They can also use *Encapsulated PostScript (EPS)* graphics and outline fonts, both of which you can size and scale without introducing distortions.

posture The slant of the characters in a *font.* Italic characters slant to the right, but the term italic is reserved by conservative typographers for custom-designed (as opposed to electronically produced) *serif* typefaces.

POTS See *Plain Old Telephone Service.*

pound sign The # character on the standard keyboard. Also called hash.

power down To turn off a device.

power line filter An electrical device that smoothes out the peaks and valleys of the voltage delivered at the wall socket. Every electrical circuit is subject to voltage fluctuations, and if these are extreme, they may cause computer errors and failures. If you're using a computer in a circuit shared by heavy appliances, you may need a power line filter to ensure error-free operation. See *surge protector.*

Power Macintosh The current line of Apple's Macintosh computers that use PowerPC *microprocessors.* Power Macs, introduced in 1994, perform best when using native PowerPC applications; they run software written for previous Macintoshes

P
Q
R

(based on the Motorola 680x0 architecture) only by means of *emulation.*

power management   A *microprocessor* feature that reduces a computer's consumption of electricity by turning off *peripherals* during periods of nonuse. Though power management features are not part of all microprocessors, they are commonly found in chips used in *portable computers,* since energy savings equates to longer battery life in those machines. See *green PC* and *sleep mode.*

Power-On Self-Test (POST)   Internal testing performed when you start or reset your computer. Encoded in *read-only memory (ROM),* the POST program first checks the *microprocessor* by having it perform a few simple operations. Then it reads the *CMOS* ROM, which stores the amount of memory and type of disk drives in your system. Next, the POST writes, then reads, various data patterns to each byte of memory (you can watch the bytes count off on-screen and often end the test with a keystroke). Finally, the POST communicates with every device; you see the keyboard and drive lights flash and the printer resets, for example. The BIOS continues with hardware testing, then looks in drive A for an *operating system*; if drive A isn't found, it looks in drive C. See *BIOS* and *boot sector.*

PowerPC   A *reduced instruction set computer (RISC) microprocessor* developed by *Motorola* that's competitive with the *Pentium.* The PowerPC is being used by *IBM* for its RS/6000 line and by Apple Corporation as the next-generation processor for the Macintosh. The PowerPC will support Windows NT, OS/2, and *Unix,* based on a promise of industry commitment to PowerOpen, a standard for PowerPC operating systems.

PowerPC 601   The first of the *PowerPC microprocessors* jointly developed by *IBM, Apple,* and *Motorola.* The PowerPC 601 is a *32-bit microprocessor* that employs *superscalar architecture* and a portion of *reduced instruction-set computer (RISC)* technology. The PowerPC 601 was used in the first *Power Macintoshes.* The 601 chip runs at 80 MHz.

PowerPC 601v   A version of the *PowerPC 601* that uses *0.5-micron technology* and an increased *clock speed* of 100 *megahertz (MHz)* to improve performance and reduce power consumption.

PowerPC 602   A *32-bit microprocessor* designed for budget-minded computer users. The PowerPC 602 runs at a *clock speed* of 66 *megahertz (MHz),* uses *reduced instruction-set computer (RISC)* technology. See *PowerPC 601.*

PowerPC 603   A *32-bit microprocessor,* similar in performance to the *PowerPC 601,* designed for situations—such as *portable computing*—in which power conservation is key. Available with *clock speeds* of 66 *megahertz (MHz)* and 80 MHz, the PowerPC 603 has a smaller *internal cache* than the PowerPC 601, but uses *0.5-micron technology* to reduce its power demand to only 2 watts. See *PowerPC 601* and *PowerPC 603e.*

PowerPC 603e   A version of the *PowerPC 603* that includes even more *power-management* features. Versions are available with *clock speeds* of up to 300 *MHz.*

PowerPC 604   A *64-bit microprocessor* that incorporates *reduced instruction-set computing (RISC)* technology and *branch prediction* techniques to achieve a *CINT92* score of 160. The PowerPC 604, which runs at a *clock speed* of 100 *megahertz (MHz),* is faster than the *PowerPC 601,* but considerably slower than the *PowerPC 620.* See *PowerPC 601.*

PowerPC 620   Designed for *servers* in *local area networks (LANs),* the PowerPC 620 is twice as fast as the *PowerPC 604* thanks to a *pre-decode* step in the *pipeline,* a large *internal cache,* and excellent *branch prediction* capabilities. A *64-bit microprocessor* that employs *reduced instruction-set computer (RISC)* technology, the PowerPC 620 runs at 133 *megahertz (MHz)* and, due in part to its use of *0.5-micron technology,* draws only 3.3 volts. See *PowerPC 601.*

PowerPoint   See *Microsoft PowerPoint.*

power save mode   In a *portable computer,* an operating mode in which the system automatically switches into a power-conserving state after a specified period of inactivity. Typically, the computer shuts down the display and disk drive. These are automatically reactivated when the user presses a key or moves the pointing device.

power supply   A device that provides the power to electronic equipment. In a computer system, the power supply converts standard AC current to the lower voltage DC current used by the computer.

P
Q
R

power surge   See *surge.*

power up   To turn on a device.

power user   A computer user who has gone beyond the beginning and intermediate stages of computer use. Such a person uses the advanced features of application programs, such as software command languages and macros, and can learn new *application programs* quickly.

PPC   See *PowerPC*.

ppm   See *pages per minute*.

PPP   Acronym for Point-to-Point Protocol. One of the two standards for directly connecting computers to the Internet via dialup telephone connections (the other is SLIP). Unlike the older SLIP protocol, PPP incorporates superior data negotiation, compression, and error correction. However, these features add overhead to data transmission, and are unnecessary when both the sending and receiving modems offer hardware error correction and on-the-fly data compression. See SLIP.

PPTP   Acronym for Point-to-Point Tunneling Protocol. An extension of *PPP* that enables remote users of a corporate *local area network (LAN)* to access the internal network by means of *protocol tunneling,* in which the LAN data is encapsulated within *TCP/IP* and encrypted for secure, confidential transmission via the Internet. In effect, PPTP enables companies to create *virtual private networks (VPNs),* which employ inexpensive Internet connections as a communications medium rather than pricey *private data networks (PDNs).* Developed jointly by Microsoft Corporation and modem makers, the protocol enables companies to extend their LANs securely to remote users without posing a serious security risk. The protocol has been submitted to the *Internet Engineering Task Force (IETF)* for ratification as an Internet standard, but is currently supported only by Microsoft's *Microsoft Windows NT Server.*

Practical Extraction and Report Language   See *perl*.

PRAM   See *parameter RAM*.

precedence   The order in which a *program* performs the operations in a formula. Typically, the program performs exponentiation (such as squaring a number) before multiplication and division and then performs addition and subtraction.

precision   The number of digits past the decimal that are used to express a quantity. See *accuracy*.

pre-decode stage   In *microprocessors* that employ *superscalar architectures,* a step in the processing of instructions in which the microprocessor determines what resources, such as *registers,* will be needed to process a particular instruction. A pre-decode stage allows instructions to move through a *pipeline* faster.

preemptive multitasking   In an *operating system,* a means of running more than one program at a time. In preemptive multitasking, the operating system decides which application should receive the processor's attention. In contrast to *cooperative multitasking,* in which a busy application could monopolize the computer for as much as several minutes, a computer with a preemptive multitasking system seems much more responsive to user commands. *Microsoft Windows 95* employs preemptive applications for *32-bit applications,* but not for *16-bit applications.*

prefix notation   In a programming language, a method of ordering *operators* and *operands* such that the operator precedes all the operands. In prefix notation, the asterisk (★) operator, symbolizing multiplication, precedes the numbers to be multiplied, as in the following example: 2 ★ 4. This operation yields 8. See *infix notation* and *Reverse Polish Notation (RPN).*

presentation graphics   The branch of the graphics profession that's concerned with the preparation of slides, transparencies, and handouts for use in business presentations. Ideally, presentation graphics combines artistry with practical psychology and good taste; color, form, and emphasis are used intelligently to convey the presentation's most significant points to the audience. See *analytical graphics.*

presentation graphics program   An *application* designed to create and enhance charts and graphs so that they're visually appealing and easily understood by an audience. A full-featured presentation graphics package such as Lotus Freelance Graphics or *Microsoft PowerPoint* includes facilities for making a wide variety of charts and graphs and for adding titles, legends, and explanatory text anywhere in the chart or graph. A presentation graphics program also typically includes a library of *clip art,* so you can enliven charts and graphs by adding a picture related to the subject matter—for example, an airplane for a chart of earnings in the aerospace industry. You can print output, direct

P
Q
R

output to a film recorder, or display output on-screen as a computer slide show.

presentation layer   In the *OSI Reference Model* of computer network architecture, the second of seven *layers,* in which data passed "down" the *protocol stack* from the top-most layer (the *application layer*) is reorganized so that it conforms to international standards for the coding of data types. (The term "presentation" is somewhat misleading, in that it implies that the data is being prepared for presentation to the user; that is the function of the application layer.)

Pretty Good Privacy (PGP)   A comprehensive *cryptosystem* for private *e-mail* created by Phil Zimmerman. PGP uses a *public-key encryption algorithm* for initial key exchange and employs the *International Data Encryption Algorithm (IDEA)* to encrypt data after keys have been exchanged. A unique feature of the PGP mail model is the use of circles of trust for authenticating the sender of a message; instead of validating digital signatures by means of a *certificate authority (CA),* PGP instead enables users to digitally sign other peoples' certificates, attesting that they know them personally and can vouch that the signature in question really came from that person and no other.

PRI   See *Primary Rate Interface.*

primary cache   *Cache memory* built into the *microprocessor,* instead of located on the *motherboard* like *secondary cache* memory, which is also called L2 cache. Primary cache is synonymous with *internal cache* and on-board cache.

primary key   In a *database* sort, a *data field* that is selected as the means by which all the data are to be sorted or alphabetized. For example, if a database user wishes to sort a lengthy list of names and addresses by ZIP code, the ZIP code is the primary key. Additional keys (the secondary key, the tertiary key, and so on) are used to order the data at subsequent levels; for example, after all the names and addresses from the ZIP code 22901 have been grouped together, they can be sorted secondarily by street address or name.

Primary Rate Interface (PRI)   A high-capacity *ISDN* service that provides 23 64 Kbps channels and one channel for carrying control information. PRI is designed for business use.

primary storage   The computer's main memory, which consists of the *random-access memory (RAM)* and the *read-only memory (ROM)* that's directly accessible to the *central processing unit (CPU)*.

primitive   A *command* or *operator* that is considered so basic in its utility that it is embedded within the basic functionality of the *operating system* or a programming language; an example is the standard set of arithmetic functions (addition, subtraction, multiplication, and division).

printed circuit board   A thin plastic sheet, coated with a copper sheet, in which the connections between electronic devices has been created by the use of a photo-resist mask and acid etching. Printed circuit boards can be mass-produced at low cost.

print engine   In a *laser printer,* the mechanism that uses a laser to create an electrostatic image of a page and fuses that image to a sheet of paper. You can distinguish print engines by their *resolution,* print quality, longevity, paper-handling features, and speed.

printer   A computer *peripheral* designed to print computer-generated text or graphics on paper or other physical media. Printers vary significantly in their quality, speed, noise, graphics capabilities, *built-in fonts,* and paper usage. The following list provides a brief overview of the types of printers available today:

- **Letter-quality printers** (also called *daisywheel printers*) form an image the same way office typewriters do—by hammering a fully formed image of a character against a ribbon, thus producing an inked image on the paper. Letter-quality printers can't print graphics and are quite slow.

- **Dot-matrix printers** form an image by extruding a pattern (or matrix) of wires against a ribbon, producing an inked image on paper. Dot-matrix printers print rapidly (100 or more characters per second), but printing speeds degrade considerably when you choose high-resolution modes. Some dot-matrix printers come with several fonts and font sizes, and all can print graphics.

- **Inkjet printers** form an image by spraying ink directly on the paper's surface, producing what appears to be a fully formed image. Inkjet printers, which often are rated

P
Q
R

at 4 to 6 *pages per minute (ppm)*, are slower than *laser print-ers*, but they produce text and graphics output that seem comparable to laser printer quality, are less expensive than laser printers, and produce little noise. Like laser printers, most inkjet printers come with a selection of built-in fonts and can use *font cartridges* or *downloadable fonts*.

- **Laser printers** use copy-machine technology to fuse powdered ink to paper, producing high-quality output at relatively high speeds (most are rated at eight or more pages per minute), use cut sheets or letterhead, and operate quietly. Most come with a selection of built-in fonts and can easily accommodate font cartridges or downloadable fonts. Their major drawback was high cost, but laser print-ers are now available for less than $700.

- **LED and LCD printers** closely resemble laser printers, except that these printers don't use lasers to form the image. *LED printers* use an array of light-emitting diodes (LEDs) for this purpose; *LCD printers* use a halogen light, the illumination of which is distributed by means of liquid crystal shutters.

- **Thermal printers** operate quietly, but that's their only advantage. They operate by pushing a matrix of heated pins against special heat-sensitive paper, which means that you must use the right kind of paper. They produce out-put that resembles that of a cheap dot-matrix printer, except that the paper's surface is shiny and smells bad; even worse, they print slowly. Thermal printers are relegated to minor applications in calculators, fax machines, and portable computer systems.

printer control language   A set of commands that tell a *printer* and *printer driver* how to print a document. Printer control languages are usually proprietary—Hewlett-Packard's *Printer Control Language* (note the capital letters) for *laser printers* is a very common example—and are different from *page description languages (PDLs)*, such as PostScript, which are somewhat limited programming languages recognized by many manufacturers. See *PCL3, PCL4, PCL5,* and *PCL5e.*

Printer Control Language (PCL)   The printer control lan-guage used by Hewlett-Packard *laser printers.* See *PCL3, PCL4,* and *PCL5e.*

printer driver   A file that contains the information a *program* needs to print your work with a given brand and model of *printer*. A major difference between the DOS environment and the Macintosh/Windows environments is the way printer drivers are handled. In the *MS-DOS* environment, printer drivers are the responsibility of application programs. Each program must come equipped with its own printer drivers for the many dozens of printers available, and if a program doesn't include a driver for your printer, you may be out of luck. The *Microsoft Windows* and Macintosh operating environments, on the other hand, provide printer drivers for all Windows applications, freeing application software from that responsibility.

printer emulation   The capability of a *printer* to recognize the *printer control language* of a different printer. Widely emulated are Epson and Hewlett-Packard printers.

printer font   A font that doesn't appear on-screen and is available for use only by the *printer*. When using a printer font, you see a generic screen font on-screen; you must wait until printing is complete to see your document's fonts. Ideally, screen and printer fonts should be identical; only then can a computer system claim to offer *what-you-see-is-what-you-get (WYSIWYG)* text processing. Character-based programs, such as WordPerfect 5.1, running under DOS can't display typefaces other than those built into the computer's ROM. With *Microsoft Windows* and Macintosh systems, you can use *TrueType* or Adobe Type Manager (ATM) outline (scalable) fonts, which appear on-screen the way they appear when printed. See *outline font*.

printer maintenance   Regular procedures, such as cleaning, that keep a *printer* operating without problems. *Laser printers* require periodic cleaning of their rollers, *corona wires,* and lenses.

printer port   See *parallel port* and *serial port*.

print head   The mechanism that actually does the printing in a *printer*. There are several kinds of print head technologies, including impact (found in *impact printers*), thermal (found in *thermal printers*), inkjet (found in *inkjet printers*), and electrostatic (found in *laser printers*).

print queue   A list of files that a *print spooler* prints in the *background* while the computer performs other tasks in the foreground.

P
Q
R

Print Screen (PrtScr)   On IBM PC-compatible *keyboards,* a key you can use to print an image of the screen display.

print server   In a *local area network (LAN),* a PC that has been dedicated to receiving and temporarily storing files to be printed, which are then doled out one by one to a *printer.* The print server, accessible to all the workstations in the network, runs *print spooler* software to manage a *print queue.*

print spooler   A *utility program* that temporarily stores files to be printed in a *print queue* and doles them out one by one to the printer. See *background printing,* and *print server.*

privacy   On a *network,* a presumed right that your disk storage area, *e-mail,* and files will not be scrutinized by persons to whom you have not given permission. However, privacy on a computer network does not exist. Although the federal *Electronic Communications Privacy Act (1986)* prohibits federal agencies from accessing your e-mail while it is in transit or temporary storage, no federal law prevents employers or other persons from doing so. Many employers believe that they can read employees' mail with impunity; after all, employees are using the employer's equipment. You can protect your privacy by encrypting your messages. See *encryption* and *Privacy Enhanced Mail (PEM).*

Privacy Enhanced Mail (PEM)   An *Internet* standard that ensures the privacy of *e-mail.* PEM uses *public key encryption* techniques to assure that only the intended recipient of the message will be able to read it. PEM is little used since the *encryption algorithm* PEM employs is patented; the *MIME/S* protocol, implemented in the e-mail utilities of *Microsoft Internet Explorer* and *Netscape Navigator* beginning with version 4.0 of the two products, is the preferred protocol for private e-mail on the Internet.

private data network (PDN)   A highly secure (but expensive) *wide area network (WAN)* composed of *leased lines* that are devoted solely to transmitting one company's data. PDNs are widely used for transmitting sensitive data, such as financial transactions and *Electronic Data Interchange (EDI)* data. Technologies such as *encryption* and *protocol tunneling* are persuading some companies to move such data to the *Internet* and to create *virtual private networks (VPN).*

PRML read-channel technology   Abbreviation for partial-response maximum-likelihood read-channel technology. A new design philosophy for *hard disks* that improves *throughput* and a real density. Typically used with *magneto-resistive heads,* PRML read-channel technology is very expensive and is found only on a few *high-end* hard disks for *network servers.*

problem user In a computer network, a user that violates the network's *acceptable use policies (AUP),* for example, by mailing unsolicited advertising, harassing other users, or attempting to gain unauthorized access to other computer systems.

procedural language A *programming language* such as *BASIC* or *Pascal* that requires the programmer to specify the procedure the computer has to follow to accomplish the task. See *declarative language.*

process In *Unix,* an executing program. A *parent process* may have one or more *child processes* that perform additional tasks.

process color One of the four colors—cyan, magenta, yellow, and black—that are mixed to create other colors. See *CMYK, color model,* and *spot color.*

processing The execution of program instructions by the computer's *central processing unit (CPU)* that in some way transforms data, such as sorting it, selecting some of it according to specified criteria, or performing mathematical computations on it.

processor upgrade A *chip* designed to replace or complement a *microprocessor* and provide improved performance. Intel's *OverDrive* chip is a processor upgrade for the *Intel 80486.* Also, the act of installing such a chip.

Professional Graphics Array (PGA) An early *video adapter* for *IBM* personal computers that was designed for *computer-assisted design (CAD)* applications. The adapter displays 256 colors with a resolution of 640 × 480.

professional workstation A high-performance personal computer optimized for professional applications in fields such as digital circuit design, architecture, and technical drawing. Professional workstations typically offer excellent screen *resolution,* fast and powerful microprocessors, and lots of memory. Examples include the workstations made by Sun Microsystems and NeXT, Inc. Professional workstations are more expensive

P Q R

than personal computers and typically use the *Unix operating system.* The boundary between *high-end personal computers* and professional workstations, however, is eroding as personal computers become more powerful.

program   A list of instructions, written in a *programming language,* that a computer can execute so that the machine acts in a predetermined way. Synonymous with software. The world of computer programs can be divided into system programs, utility programs, and application programs:

- **System programs** include all the programs the computer requires to function effectively, including the operating system, memory management software, and command-line interpreters. The MS-DOS operating system is an example of system software.

- **Utility programs** include all the programs you can use to maintain the computer system. MS-DOS includes several utility programs, such as CHKDSK. Most users equip their systems with utility packages (such as Norton Utilities or PC Tools) that go beyond the basics that MS-DOS provides.

- **Application programs** transform the computer into a tool for performing a specific kind of work, such as word processing, financial analysis (with an electronic spreadsheet), or desktop publishing.

Additional software categories include programming languages, games, educational programs, and a variety of *vertical market programs.* See *executable program, high-level programming language,* and *machine code.*

program generator   A *program* that creates the program code automatically from a description of the application. In *database management programs,* for example, you can use simple program generation techniques to describe the format you want graphically. The program generator then uses your input as a set of *parameters* by which to build the output program code.

program information file (PIF)   A *file* available for non-*Windows application* programs that tells Windows how to run them. *Microsoft Windows 95* can run DOS applications even without a PIF file.

Program Manager   In *Microsoft Windows 3.1,* a utility that enables users to launch applications by double-clicking an icon.

programmable   Capable of being controlled through instructions that can be varied to suit the user's needs.

programmable read-only memory (PROM)   A *read-only memory (ROM)* chip programmed at the factory for use with a given computer. Unlike standard ROM chips, which have their programming included in the internal design of the chip circuits, programmable ROM chips are easy to modify. Though programmable ROM chips can be programmed, or burned, just once, after which the programming becomes permanent, it is easier to change the way the chips are programmed than to change their internal design. See *EPROM.*

programmer   A person who designs, codes, tests, debugs, and documents a computer program. Professional programmers often hold BS or MS degrees in computer science, but a great deal of programming (professional and otherwise) is done by individuals with little or no formal training. More than half the readers of a popular personal computer magazine, for example, stated in a survey that they regularly programmed their personal computers using languages such as *BASIC, Pascal,* and *assembly language.*

programmer/analyst   A person who performs system analysis and design functions as well as *programming* activities. See *programmer.*

programmer's switch   A plastic accessory included with pre-1991 Macintosh computers that, when installed on the side of the computer, enables you to perform a hardware reset and access the computer's built-in debugger.

programming   The process of providing instructions to the computer that tell the *microprocessor* what to do. Stages in programming include design, or making decisions about what the program should accomplish; coding, or using a programming language to express the program's logic in computer-readable form and entering internal documentation for the commands; testing and debugging, in which the program's flaws are discovered and corrected; and documentation, in which an instructional manual for the program is created, either in print or on-screen.

P
Q
R

programming environment   A set of tools for programming that is commonly provided with a computer's *operating system*. Minimally, the tools include a *line editor,* a *debugger,* and an *assembler* to compile *assembly language* programs. These tools usually are not sufficient for professional program development, however, and often are replaced by an *application development system.*

programming language   An artificial language, consisting of a fixed vocabulary and a set of rules (called *syntax*), that you can use to create instructions for a computer to follow. Most programs are written using a text editor or word processing program to create *source code,* which is then interpreted or compiled into the machine language that the computer can actually execute. Programming languages are divided into high-level languages and low-level languages:

- **High-level programming languages**, such as *BASIC, C,* or *Pascal,* enable the programmer to express the program using keywords and syntax that crudely resemble natural human language. These languages are called "high level" because they free the programmer from detailed concerns about just how the computer will physically carry out each instruction. Each statement in a high-level programming language corresponds to several machine language instructions, so you can write programs more quickly than in lower-level languages, such as assembly language. However, the translation is inefficient, so programs written in high-level languages run more slowly than programs written in low-level languages.

- **Low-level programming languages**, such as *assembly language,* enable the programmer to code instructions with the maximum possible efficiency. Using low-level languages requires detailed expertise in the exact capabilities of a given computer system and its microprocessor. Also, assembly language programming requires far more time.

Another way of differentiating programming languages is to distinguish between procedural and declarative languages. In a *procedural language,* such as C, the programmer spells out the procedure the computer will follow to accomplish a given goal. In a *declarative language* (also called a nonprocedural language), such as *COBOL,* the language defines a set of facts and relationships and enables you to query for specific results. See *C++, compiler, expert system, FORTRAN, interpreter, Modula-2, modular programming, object code, object-oriented programming (OOP) language,* and *PROLOG.*

program overlay   A portion of a program kept on disk and called into memory only as required.

project management program   Software that tracks individual tasks that make up an entire job, and enable project managers to discern the critical path—the sequence of activities that must be completed in a timely fashion if the entire project is to be completed on time.

PROLOG   A *high-level programming language* used in *artificial intelligence* research and applications, particularly expert systems. PROLOG, short for PROgramming in LOGic, is a *declarative language;* rather than tell the computer what procedure to follow to solve a problem, the programmer describes the problem to be solved. The language resembles the query language of a *database management system* such as *Standard Query Language (SQL)* in that you can use PROLOG to ask a question such as, "Is Foster City in California?" But an important difference exists between PROLOG and a database management system (DBMS). A database contains information you can retrieve; a PROLOG program, in contrast, contains knowledge, from which the program can draw inferences about what is true or false.

PROM   See *programmable read-only memory.*

prompt   A symbol or phrase that appears on-screen to inform you that the computer is ready to accept input.

property   1. The current settings chosen for a document, a program, or an *object.* 2. In *Microsoft Windows 95,* a characteristic or attribute of an *embedded object.* An object's properties are contained in its *property sheet.*

property sheet   In *Microsoft Windows 95,* a central location in which all of an *embedded object's properties* are recorded.

proportional pie graph   In *presentation graphics,* a paired *pie graph* in which the size of each pie is in proportion to the amount of data the pie represents. Proportional pie graphs are useful for comparing two pies when one is significantly larger than the other.

P
Q
R

proportional spacing In *typefaces,* setting the width of a character in proportion to the character shape, so that a narrow character such as i receives less space than a wide character such as m. The text you're reading now uses proportional spacing. See *kerning* and *monospace.*

proprietary Privately owned; based on trade secrets, privately developed technology, or specifications that the owner refuses to divulge, thus preventing others from duplicating a product or program unless an explicit license is purchased. The Macintosh system architecture, though there are now a few carefully selected makers of Macintosh *clones,* is proprietary. The opposite of proprietary is open (privately developed but publicly published and available for emulation by others). The IBM PC system architecture, with the exception of the *basic input-output system (BIOS),* is open. From the user's perspective, proprietary designs or formats entail risk. If the company prospers and the design or format is widely emulated or accepted, the user benefits. But if the company doesn't prosper or fails, the user could be stuck with a computer system or with data that can't be upgraded or exchanged with others. See *proprietary file format.*

proprietary file format A *file format* developed by a firm for storing data created by its products. In word processing, proprietary file formats are needed to handle formatting choices, which are not represented using the standard ASCII characters. A proprietary file format usually is unreadable by other companies' application programs without the assistance of a file conversion utility. The popular programs typically include the utilities to convert the files of several other file formats.

proprietary local bus A *local bus* standard developed by one company for use on its machines and its machines only. A proprietary bus requires adapter cards specifically designed for use on this bus, and there may be fewer of these than cards developed for open architectures. See *Micro Channel Architecture (MCA).*

proprietary protocol An unpublished and nonpublic communications *protocol* developed by a company to enable its products to communicate with each other. The use of a proprietary communications protocol veils a not-so-subtle strategy to force users of one product to adopt other products made by the same company. The use of an *open protocol,* on the other hand, encourages the connection of the device with products made by other companies. See *connector conspiracy.*

proprietary standard   An unpublished and sometimes secret design or specification for a device or program. The company that owns the standard refuses to permit other firms to emulate it, in the hope that the standard will eclipse all others and become the industry norm. Taken to the extreme, the use of a proprietary standard could force users to buy not just one, but a whole series of the firm's products (since nothing else will work with them). This strategy is often self-defeating in that it retards the development of a market. Users do not like to be forced into buying products from a single manufacturer. *Open standards* promote a growing market, thus benefit all the corporate participants and other users by encouraging competition and *interoperability.*

protected memory   In an *operating system* capable of *preemptive multitasking,* the *random-access memory (RAM)* of the computer, in which programs are allotted memory space in such a way that it is not possible for other programs to invade this space and cause the computer to crash.

protected mode   In *Intel 80286* and later *microprocessors,* one of two operating modes (the other is called *real mode*). In real mode, memory address are directly mapped using the original *IBM PC* memory-addressing scheme. This limits the total amount of system memory, in effect, to 640MB. In protected mode, the real mode's limited memory registers contains pointers to additional registers, effectively breaking the 640K memory limitation. In addition, the pointers contain memory protection information, which enables the processor to protect the referenced memory from invasion by other programs—hence the term "protected mode." With *operating system* support, this enables *preemptive multitasking,* in which programs can safely coexist in the same memory space. In 80386 and later Intel processors, a *page mode memory unit (PMMU)* provides further memory mapping functions, enabling *virtual memory* and faster processing. By default, all Intel processors start in the real mode, and require software to switch them into the protected mode. That's why *MS-DOS,* or some version of it—such as the real-mode startup software in *Microsoft Windows 95*—just won't go away.

P
Q
R

protocol   In data communications and networking, a standard that specifies the format of data as well as the rules to be followed. Networks could not be easily or efficiently designed or maintained without protocols; a protocol specifies how a program should prepare data so that it can be sent on to the next stage in the communication process. For example, *e-mail* programs prepare messages so that they conform to prevailing *Internet* mail standards, which are recognized by every program that is involved in the transmission of mail over the network. See *protocol stack* and *protocol suite.*

protocol stack   In a computer connected to a network, the "vertical stack" of protocols, ranging from the lowest-level protocols (the ones that handle the electrical connection to the network's physical media) to the highest-level protocols (the ones that prepare the data for presentation to the user). The *OSI Reference Model* conceptualizes seven distinct *layers,* each of which is governed by its own *protocol.* At each layer, a protocol provides services to the layers above and below.

protocol suite   In a *network,* a set of related standards that, taken together, define the architecture of the network. For example, the *Internet* is based on the *TCP/IP* protocol suite, a collection of more than 100 standards that are all designed to work smoothly together.

protocol switching   See *automatic network switching.*

protocol tunneling   The encapsulation of data *packets* conforming to one network's *protocols* within the packets of another network's protocols. By means of protocol tunneling, for example, an external workstation that uses *local area network (LAN)* protocols (such as *IPX/SPX* or *NetBEUI*) can employ the Internet (which packages data according to the *TCP/IP* protocols) to exchange data with internal LAN servers. See *PPTP* and *virtual private network (VPN).*

prototype   A demonstration version of a proposed *program* or *hardware* device. In software, a prototype is usually a mock-up of a program's user interface, without much *back-end* code to support it. In hardware, a prototype is usually a cumbersome device with lots of wires and components that, if the prototype is mass produced, will be replaced by *circuit boards* and *integrated circuits.*

proximity operator   In database and Web searching, an operator (such as NEAR or WITH) that tells the search software to retrieve an item only if the words linked by the operator occur within a predetermined number of words of each other (such as five or ten words). The use of a proximity operator is one way to narrow the focus of a search; if the specified words occur close together, it is more likely that the document pertains to the searcher's interests.

proxy   Also called *proxy server*. A program that stands between an internal network and the external Internet, intercepting requests for information. A proxy is generally part of a broader solution to internal network security called a *firewall*. The purpose of a proxy is to prevent external users from directly accessing resources inside the internal network or, indeed, knowing precisely where those resources are located. The proxy intercepts an external request for information, determines whether the request can be fulfilled, and passes on the request to an internal *server,* the address of which is not disclosed to the external client. By disguising the real location of the server that actually houses the requested information, the proxy makes it much more difficult for computer criminals to exploit potential security holes in servers and related applications, which might enable them to gain unauthorized access to the internal network. This protection from outside attack comes at the price of imposing inconveniences (including configuration hassles and slower performance) on internal users who wish to access the external Internet.

proxy gateway   See *proxy.*

proxy server   In an *online service,* such as America Online, a server that has been configured to store Web pages that are frequently accessed by the service's members. When members request these pages, the server provides the copy it has stored rather than requesting the page from the external Internet. Members see Web pages more quickly and the network experiences lighter load, but these benefits come at a price: the displayed page may be out of date. This term is often used synonymously (but incorrectly) with *proxy,* a security program that walls off an internal network from external attack.

PrtScr   See *Print Screen.*

PS/2 mouse   A *mouse* with a special connector that fits into a *mouse port*. PS/2 mice, or mice equipped with PS/2 connectors,

P
Q
R

do not require a *serial port* to operate and are much simpler to install.

PS/2 mouse port A *mouse port* on the back of the computer's case that enables the user to connect any mouse with a *PS/2 mouse* connector. This port enables users to connect a mouse without using a *serial port* or having to deal with the *port conflict* issues that such a connection might cause.

pseudoanonymous remailer In the *Internet,* an *e-mail* forwarding service that enables Internet users to send anonymous e-mail or to post anonymously to *Usenet.* These services maintain records that preserve the sender's true identity, so they are not truly anonymous. Compare *anonymous remailer.*

pseudocode An *algorithm* expressed in English to conceptualize a program before coding it in a *programming language.* Pseudocode cannot be *compiled*; it is for human use only.

PSTN See *public switched telephone network.*

public data network (PDN) A *wide area network (WAN)* that makes long-distance data communication services available to organizations and individuals. PDNs are extensively used by corporations to enable secure communication with branch officers, field agents, and suppliers, as well as to implement *Electronic Data Interchange (EDI)* transaction processing. PDNs set up custom, dedicated connections, called *leased lines,* which are much more secure than the *Internet* because they are not used by anyone other than the network's authorized corporate users. There are two kinds of PDNs: circuit-switched PDNs, which use telephone switching equipment to set up dedicated connections, and packet-switched PDNs, which are *packet-switching* networks based on the *X.25* protocol. In the future, PDNs may face competition from *virtual private networks (VPNs),* which employ the *Internet* and ensure security by means of *encryption* and *protocol tunneling.*

public domain Intellectual property that has been expressly released for unconditional use, including for-profit distribution or modification, by any party under any circumstances whatsoever. According to international copyright law, no work should be considered public domain, even in the absence of an explicit copyright notice, unless the author of the work has clearly stated that the work is intended for the public domain and that all claims to the work are relinquished. By this definition virtually all of the ostensibly "public domain" software that is widely distributed by computer *bulletin board systems (BBS)* and *FTP* sites should not be regarded to be in the public domain, but rather as *freeware,* and should not be modified, sold, or re-used without the author's explicit permission.

public domain program   A program that has been distributed with an explicit notification from the program's author that the work is in the *public domain.* Very few publicly distributed programs meet this criterion. See *freeware, postcardware,* and *shareware.*

public key cryptography   In cryptography, a revolutionary new method of *encryption* that does not require the message's receiver to have received the decoding *key* in a separate transmission. The need to send the key, required to decode the message, is the chief vulnerability of previous encryption techniques. In public key cryptography, there are two keys, a public one and a private one. The public key is used for encryption, and the private key is used for *decryption.* If John wants to receive a private message from Alice, John sends his public key to Alice; Alice then uses the key to encrypt the message. Alice sends the message to John. Anyone trying to intercept the message en route would find that it is mere gibberish. When John receives the message, he uses his private key to decode it. Because John never sends his private key anywhere or gives it to anyone, he can be certain that the message is secure. Public key cryptography places into the hands of individuals a level of security that was formerly available only to the top levels of government security agencies. Also called asymmetric key cryptography. See *symmetric key encryption algorithm.*

public key encryption   The use of *public key cryptography* to encrypt messages for secret transmission. Because public key encryption techniques consume enormous amounts of computer processing *overhead,* they are generally used only for the initial phase of a connection between the sender and receiver of a secret message. In this phase, the users establish their identities by means of *digital signatures,* and exchange the *keys* that will be used for *symmetric key encryption* using an encryption algorithm such as *DES.*

P
Q
R

public switched telephone network (PSTN)   The worldwide network of switched telephone interconnections, enabling hundreds of millions of telephones worldwide to establish direct connections. Originating in 1876 with Alexander Graham Bell's patent, the PSTN began with a number of local, manually switched *analog* networks, which were gradually interconnected as standards emerged. By the 1950s and 1960s, most local switching networks had made the transition from manual switching, which requires a human operator, to electronic switching, which enables direct dialing. In the industrialized nations today, much of the switching network employs *digital* technology, with the exception of the *local loop,* which is still primarily analog due to the antiquated wiring found in older homes. *ISDN* provides an international standard for the extension of digital telephony to homes and offices. Worldwide telephone standards are governed by the *International Telecommunications Union (ITU),* a division of the United Nations.

pull–down menu   In the *Macintosh,* an on-screen *menu* of command options that appears after the user uses the mouse to click on the menu name, and drags down to display the menu. In *Microsoft Windows,* the user need only click the menu name to display the menu; it is not necessary to keep depressing the mouse button or to drag down to display the menu.

pull media   In the *Internet,* the traditional Internet services (such as FTP and the World Wide Web), in which users do not obtain information unless they expressly and deliberately originate a request for it. To attract users (and therefore justify advertising), content providers must "pull" users to the site. See *push media* and *Netscape NetCaster.*

pull quote   In *desktop publishing,* a quotation extracted from the *copy* of a newsletter or magazine article and printed in larger type in the column, often blocked off with ruled lines, and sometimes shaded.

pulse code modulation (PCM)   A technique used to transform an incoming analog signal into a noise-free, digital equivalent. In *multimedia,* PCM is used to sample sounds digitally.

punched card   An obsolete method of data and program *input* in which data is represented by means of holes physically punched through a stiff piece of cardboard. Punched cards originated in the early twentieth century as a means of representing data for processing by means of mechanical tabulating machines.

purge   To remove unwanted or outdated information, usually from the *hard drive,* in a systematic, and ideally automatic, manner. Also, in systems using a form of delete protection, purge refers to deleting protected files so that they no longer can be undeleted. See *undelete utility.*

pushbutton   In industry-standard and *Graphical User Interfaces (GUIs),* a large button in a dialog box that initiates actions after you choose an option. Most dialog boxes contain an *OK button,* which confirms your choices and carries out the command, and a Cancel button, which cancels your choices and closes the dialog box. The button representing the option you're most likely to choose, called the default button, is highlighted.

push media   In the *Internet,* a series of new content delivery mechanisms, in which users subscribe to what amounts to a broadcasting service, which subsequently delivers content to the user's computer without the user having to make further requests for information. In contrast to *pull media,* which must attract the user to the site, push media can guarantee advertisers that subscribers will continue to receive updates and view advertising banners. Among the various push media models that have been developed are applications such as PointCast that deliver news, weather, and sports scores to the user's *screen saver,* and services such as *Castanet,* which employ a radio metaphor: The user "tunes" to a "channel," and content is delivered to the user whenever updates are available. The delivered content may appear in a special window that appears on the user's *desktop.* Castanet can also automatically deliver software and updates to software, and thus creates a new and potentially significant model for software distribution and maintenance. The ultimate push medium is e-mail *spamming,* in which e-mail advertisers send unsolicited e-mail advertisements to as many as millions of e-mail addresses.

P
Q
R

QBasic See *MS-DOS QBasic.*

QBE See *query by example.*

QEMM 386 A *memory-management program* by Quarterdeck Office Systems that moves *network* drivers, disk–cache programs, device drivers, and *terminate-and-stay-resident (TSR) programs* to the *upper memory area,* thus freeing *conventional memory* for DOS programs.

QIC See *quarter-inch cartridge.*

QIC–wide A variation on *quarter-inch cartridge (QIC)* technology that uses tape 0.32 inches wide instead of 0.25 inches wide to increase data capacity.

quad density See *high density.*

quad–issue processor A *microprocessor* with a dual-pipeline *superscalar architecture* that can begin handling four instructions at the same time.

quadrature modulation A *group coding* technique used in *modems* to modulate the *carrier.* Modems that use quadrature modulation can exchange data at 2400 *bits per second (bps).* *trellis-code modulation* enables higher *data transfer rates.*

quad–speed drive A *CD-ROM drive* capable of transferring data at $600K$ per second. Quad-speed drives are, overall, not four times faster than single-speed drives because *access time* acts as a bottleneck that cannot be reduced as easily as data transfer rates can be increased. Quad-speed drives are about 40 percent faster than *double-speed drives.*

quarter-inch cartridge (QIC) A tape cartridge using quarter-inch-wide *magnetic tape* widely used for *backup operations.* Standards for QIC devices are maintained by Quarter-Inch Drives Standards Association, Inc. The following table lists the various QIC data storage formats:

QIC standard	Data storage capacity
QIC–24	60M (full-sized cartridge)
QIC–40	40M (mini cartridge)
QIC–80	80M (mini cartridge)
QIC–100	40M (mini cartridge)
QIC–120	125M (full-sized cartridge)
QIC–128	128M (mini cartridge)
QIC–150	250M (full-sized cartridge)
QIC–380	380M (mini cartridge)
QIC–525	525M (full-sized cartridge)
QIC–1000	1G (full-sized cartridge)
QIC–1350	1.35G (full-sized cartridge)
QIC–3010	340M (mini cartridge)
QIC–3020	680M (mini cartridge)
QIC–4GB	4G (full-sized cartridge)
QIC–5GB	5G (full-sized cartridge)

Quattro Pro   A full-featured *spreadsheet program* (developed by Borland International and currently marketed by Corel as part of Corel's office suites) that is claimed to include more *built-in functions* than *Microsoft Excel* or *Lotus 1-2-3,* including many functions for specialized engineering and financial uses.

query   In *database management,* a search question that tells the program what kind of *data* should be retrieved from the *database.* An effective database management system lets you retrieve only the information you need for a specific purpose. A query specifies the characteristics (criteria) used to guide the computer to the required information. See *data independence, declarative language, query language,* and *SQL.*

query by example (QBE)   In *database management programs,* a query technique (developed by IBM for use in the QBE program) that prompts you to type the search criteria into a template resembling the *data record.*

P
Q
R

query language   In *database management programs,* a retrieval and data-editing language you use to specify what information to retrieve and how to arrange the retrieved information on-screen or when printing. See *query* and *SQL.*

question mark (?)   The *wild-card* symbol that stands for a single character at a specific location, unlike the *asterisk* (*), which can stand for one or more characters. In AB?DE, for example, only file names or character strings that are five characters long, with AB as the first two characters and DE as the last two characters, are selected.

queue   See *job queue* and *print queue.*

QuickBasic   See *MS-DOS QBasic.*

QuickDraw   The *object-oriented graphics* and text-display technology stored in every Macintosh's *read-only memory (ROM).* When creating Macintosh programs, programmers achieve a common look by drawing on the QuickDraw resources to create on-screen windows, *dialog boxes, menus,* and shapes.

QuickTime   An extension to the *Macintosh* System software that allows applications that support QuickTime to display animated or video sequences precisely synchronized with high-quality digital sound. In a training document, for instance, you can click an icon to see a QuickTime video sequence (a "movie") that visually shows a specific technique or procedure.

quit   To exit a *program* properly so that all your configuration choices and data are properly saved.

QWERTY   (Pronounced "kwer-tee.") The standard typewriter keyboard layout, also used for computer keyboards. The keyboard name comes from the six keys on the left end of the top row of letter keys. Alternative keyboard layouts, such as the *Dvorak keyboard,* are said to speed typing by placing the most commonly used letters on the home row.

radio button In a *Graphical User Interface (GUI),* the round option buttons that appear in *dialog boxes.* Unlike *check boxes,* radio buttons are mutually exclusive; you can pick only one radio button option within a group.

radio frequency interference (RFI) The radio noise generated by computers and other electronic and electromechanical devices. Excessive RFI generated by computers can disrupt the reception of radio and television signals. See *FCC certification.*

RAID Acronym for Redundant Array of Independent Disks. A group of *hard disks* under the control of array management *software* that work together to improve performance and decrease the odds of losing data due to mechanical or electronic failure by using such techniques as *data striping.* Because of their complexity and steep cost, RAID implementations are most often used on *network servers.* Several RAID levels exist, each with advantages and disadvantages. RAID arrays are generally used for high-volume *servers.* See *RAID level 0* through *RAID level 53.*

RAID level 0 A *RAID* scheme that includes *data striping* to improve disk performance but offers no protection against data loss due to drive failure.

RAID level 0 & 1 See *RAID level 10.*

RAID level 1 A *RAID* scheme involving an array of two *hard disks* with identical contents. RAID level 1 does not employ *data striping,* so it offers no speed advantage and is not economical.

RAID level 2 A *RAID* scheme that uses *data striping* over an array of as many as a dozen *hard disks.* Several of the drives in the array have copies of data that exist elsewhere, enabling them to catch and fix errors in the outgoing data stream. RAID level 2 is one of the most popular RAID implementations.

RAID level 3 A *RAID* implementation very similar to *RAID level 2,* in which the *hard disks* that contain the copies of data that appears elsewhere can detect but not fix errors in the outgoing data stream. Though RAID level 3 is slightly slower than RAID level 2 when errors occur, modern *hard disks* rarely make errors.

RAID level 4   A *RAID* implementation that distributes copies of *sectors* across an array of *hard disks* and uses one drive to check for, but not correct, errors in the outgoing data stream. RAID level 4's sector-copying technique is a special type of *data striping*.

RAID level 5   The most commonly used *RAID* implementation. RAID level 5 uses a sector-based data striping scheme such as *RAID level 4,* but does not require a special data-checking disk because it distributes that function across the entire array as well.

RAID level 6   A *RAID* implementation that allows two *hard disks* to fail without loss of *data* and boasts very good data-reading performance, but also has poor data-writing performance. RAID level 6 is similar to *RAID level 5,* except that it distributes two copies of the error-checking data across the array.

RAID level 10   A *RAID* implementation that combines the *data striping* of *RAID level 0* with the data-redundancy of *RAID level 1.* RAID level 10 arrays have high performance but are not economical.

RAID level 53   A *RAID* scheme that uses *data striping* on two separate *RAID level 3* arrays. RAID level 53 arrays are very fast and quite *fault-tolerant,* but expensive to implement.

RAM   See *random-access memory*.

RAM cache   See *cache memory*.

RAMDAC   Acronym for random-access memory digital-to-analog converter. A *chip* in the *video adapter* that converts three *digital* signals (one for each primary color) into one *analog* signal that is sent to the monitor. RAMDACs use on-board *random-access memory (RAM)* to store information before processing it.

RAM disk   An area of *random-access memory (RAM)* configured by a *utility program* to emulate a *hard disk drive*. Data stored in a RAM disk can be accessed more quickly than data stored on a disk drive, but this data is erased whenever you turn off or reboot the computer. See *configuration file, device driver,* and *RAMDRIVE.SYS*.

RAMDRIVE.SYS In *MS-DOS*, a *configuration file* provided with the *operating system* that sets aside part of your computer's *random-access memory (RAM)* as a *RAM disk*, which is treated by MS-DOS as though it were a *hard disk drive*. RAMDRIVE.SYS is a *device driver* that must be loaded using a DEVICE or DEVICEHIGH statement in your *CONFIG.SYS file*.

random access An information storage and retrieval technique in which the computer can access information directly, without having to go through a sequence of locations. A better term is direct access, but the term "random" access has become enshrined in the acronym *random-access memory (RAM)*. To understand the distinction between random and *sequential access*, compare a cassette tape (sequential access) with a vinyl record (random access).

random-access memory (RAM) The computer's primary working *memory*, in which *program* instructions and *data* are stored so they can be accessed directly by the *central processing unit (CPU)* via the processor's high-speed *external data bus*. RAM often is called read/write memory to distinguish it from *read-only memory (ROM)*, the other component of a personal computer's *primary storage*. In RAM, the CPU can write and read data. Most programs set aside a portion of RAM as a temporary workspace for your data, so you can modify (rewrite) as needed until the data is ready for printing or storage on *secondary storage* media, such as a *hard* or *floppy disk*. RAM doesn't retain its contents when the power to the computer is switched off, so save your work frequently.

random-access memory digital-to-analog converter See *RAMDAC*.

range In a *spreadsheet program*, a *cell* or a rectangular group of adjacent cells. Valid ranges include a single cell, part of a column, part of a row, and a block spanning several *columns* and several *rows*. Ranges allow you to perform operations, such as *formatting*, on groups of cells. See *range expression* and *range name*.

range expression In a *spreadsheet program*, an expression that describes a *range* by defining the *cells* in opposing corners of a rectangle. In *Lotus 1-2-3*, for example, you write a range expres-

P
Q
R

sion by typing the beginning cell address, two periods, and the ending cell address, A9..B12, for example. *Microsoft Excel* uses a colon in place of the two periods. See *range name.*

range format   In a *spreadsheet program,* a *numeric format* or *label alignment* format that applies only to a *range* of cells and overrides the *global format.*

range name   In a *spreadsheet program,* a title you assign to a *range* of cells. A range name, such as "Total Rainfall," is easier to remember than a *range expression.*

RARP   See *Reverse Address Resolution Protocol.*

raster   On a *monitor* or television screen, the horizontal pattern of lines that forms the image. Within each line are dots, called *pixels,* that can be illuminated individually.

raster font   See *bit-mapped font.*

raster graphics   See *bit-mapped graphic.*

raster image processor (RIP)   A device that converts *object-oriented graphics* into *raster graphics* before printing to output devices. See *vector-to-raster conversion program.*

rave   In *e-mail* and *newsgroups,* to carry on an argument in support of a position beyond all bounds of reason and sensitivity. Raving is annoying but isn't considered to be worthy of a *flame* unless the argument is couched in offensive terms.

raw data   Unprocessed or unformatted *data* that hasn't been arranged, edited, or represented in a form for easy retrieval and analysis.

ray tracing   In computer graphics, a computationally intensive technique for *rendering* three-dimensional objects by introducing variations in color and shading that are produced by specific light rays falling upon the object. To create a ray-traced graphic, the designer begins by specifying the source and intensity of the light source.

RBOC   See *Regional Bell Operating Companies.*

RC4   A widely used *symmetric key encryption algorithm* developed by RSA Data Security, Inc. The algorithm's vulnerability to *cryptanalysis* (code-breaking) is highly dependent on the length of the key; a key of 40 characters or less can be easily broken, even by amateur cryptanalysts. This is the encryption method that is used by the Secure Sockets Layer *(SSL)* standard. U.S. Government export restrictions prevent the use of RC4 keys greater than 40 characters for exported products, which means— essentially—that supposedly "secure" programs based on 40-key RC4 encryption are, in fact, quite insecure and vulnerable to interception and decoding while they are being transmitted via the network.

RCA plug   See *phono plug.*

RDBMS   See *relational database management system.*

read   To retrieve *data* or *program* instructions from a device such as a *hard* or *floppy disk* and place the data into the computer's *random-access memory (RAM).*

read buffering   A method of increasing the apparent speed of disk access by storing frequently accessed program instructions or data in memory chips, which operate more quickly than disks. See *buffer.*

README file   A *text file,* often included on the installation disk of *application programs,* that contains last-minute information not contained in the program's *documentation.* Typical README file names are README.1ST, README.TXT, and READ.ME.

read-only   Capable of being displayed or used, but not deleted. If a display of read-only data can be edited, *formatted,* or otherwise modified, it can't be saved under the same *file name.* See *file attribute, locked file,* and *read/write.*

read-only attribute   In *operating systems* such as *MS-DOS* and *Microsoft Windows,* a file *attribute* stored with a file's *directory* entry that indicates whether the file can be changed or deleted. When the *read-only* attribute is on, you can display the file, but you can't modify or erase it. When the read-only attribute is off, you can modify or delete the file.

read-only memory (ROM)   The portion of a computer's *primary storage* that doesn't lose its contents when you switch off the power. ROM contains essential system programs that neither you nor the computer can erase. Because the computer's internal memory is blank at power-up, the computer can perform no

P
Q
R

functions unless given startup instructions. These instructions are stored in ROM. A growing trend is toward including substantial portions of the *operating system* on ROM chips instead of on disk. See *EPROM* and *programmable read-only memory (PROM)*.

read/write   The capability of a *primary* or *secondary storage* device to record *data* (write) and to play back data previously recorded or saved (read).

read/write file   In *MS-DOS, Microsoft Windows 95,* and *Operating System/2 (OS/2),* a file whose *read-only file attribute* is set so the file can be deleted and modified. See *locked file*.

read/write head   In a *hard disk* or *floppy disk,* the magnetic recording and playback device that travels back and forth across the surface of the disk, storing and retrieving *data*.

read/write memory   See *random-access memory (RAM)*.

Real Audio   A *streaming audio* technology developed by Real Audio, Inc., which enables Internet users to begin hearing an audio file moments after they start downloading the file. Quality is that of an AM radio broadcast, which is sufficient for voice broadcasts.

real mode   In *Intel* microprocessors, an operating mode in which memory locations are directly mapped by a limited set of registers, producing a total maximum memory size of 1M (and, in practice, 640K, due to the allocation of some of the memory for the use of peripheral devices). Processors prior to the 80286 could work only in the real mode; the 80286 and higher processors can be switched into the *protected mode,* which enables them to address much larger amounts of memory and to support the reliable execution of two or more programs simultaneously (see *multitasking*).

real time   The immediate processing of *input,* such as a point-of-sale transaction or a measurement performed by an *analog* laboratory device. The computers used in your car are real-time systems.

real-time clock   A battery-powered clock contained in the computer's internal circuitry. The real-time clock keeps track of the time of day even when the computer is switched off. This clock should be distinguished from the *system clock* that governs the *microprocessor's* cycles.

reboot   To restart. Rebooting is often necessary after a *crash*. In most cases, you can restart the system from the *keyboard*, but especially severe crashes may require you to push the *reset button*, or if no such button exists, turn off the computer and turn it on again. See *programmer's switch*.

recalculation method   In a *spreadsheet program*, the way the program recalculates *cell values* after you change the contents of a cell. See *automatic recalculation*, *manual recalculation*, and *recalculation order*.

recalculation order   In a *spreadsheet program*, the sequence in which calculations are performed when you enter new *values*, *labels*, or *formulas*. Options for recalculation order usually include *column-wise recalculation*, *row-wise recalculation*, and *natural recalculation*. See *optimal recalculation*.

recall   In database searching, a measure of how successfully the search retrieved records that are pertinent to the search subject. In a search with poor recall, many relevant records exist, but they are not retrieved.

rec hierarchy   One of the seven *standard newsgroup hierarchies* in *Usenet*, this category includes newsgroups relating to recreational interests, such as movies, comics, science fiction, or audio systems.

record   See *data record*.

record locking   In a *database program*, a feature than enables users to protect a data record from further alteration.

record-oriented database management program   A *database management program* that displays *data records* as the result of *query* operations, unlike a *relational database management program*, in which the result of all data query operations is a table. See *data retrieval*, *database management system (DBMS)*, and *SQL*.

record pointer   In a *database management program*, an on-screen status message that states the number of the *data record* now visible (or in which the cursor is positioned).

recover   To bring a *computer system* back to a previous stable operating state or to restore erased or misdirected *data*. Recovery is needed after a system or user error occurs, such as telling the

P
Q
R

system to *write* data to a drive that doesn't contain a disk. See *undelete utility*.

recoverable error   An error that doesn't cause the *program* or system to *crash* or to erase *data* irretrievably.

recto   The right-hand (odd-numbered) page in facing pages.In a book or magazine, the recto page is the right-hand, odd-numbered page. See *verso*.

recursion   In *programming,* a *program* instruction that causes a *module* or *subroutine* to call itself. A recursive function may be used to implement search strategies or perform repetitive calculations.

recycle bin   In *Microsoft Windows 95,* an on-screen icon where deleted files are stored. From the recycle bin, you can restore deleted files or discard them permanently.

Red Book   An International Standards Organization (ISO) standard (number 10149) that describes the way in which music is recorded on *Compact Disc-Digital Audio (CD-DA)* disks.

redirection   See *input/output (I/O) redirection*.

redirection operator   In *MS-DOS,* a symbol that routes the results of a command from or to a device other than the *keyboard* and video display (*console*), such as a *file* or a *printer*. See *input/output (I/O) redirection*.

redlining   In *word processing,* a display attribute (such as *reverse video* or double underlining) that marks the text that co-authors have added to a document.The redlined text is highlighted so that other authors or editors know exactly what has been added to or deleted from the document.

reduced instruction set computer   See *RISC*.

Redundant Array of Independent Disks   See *RAID*.

reengineering   Redesigning the way work is done, then choosing computer tools that enhance the redesigned work process. Computerization of a process doesn't automatically make it more efficient.To realize big productivity gains, managers must rethink the way work is done and alter the process to be more efficient. In many companies, for example, after the credit department grants credit, the receiving department receives goods, and the accounting department writes checks. The reengineering strategy for this kind of setting may be to put computers in the receiving department, so that the receiving staff can confirm what's received and then write the checks on the spot.

reflective liquid–crystal display   A *liquid-crystal display (LCD)* with no *edgelighting* or *backlighting* to enhance readability in bright-light conditions. Reflective LCDs are generally unsuitable for outdoor use.

reformat   In *operating systems,* to repeat a *formatting* operation on a *floppy* or *hard disk.* In *word processing* or *page layout programs,* to change the arrangement of text elements on the page.

refresh   To repeat the display or storage of *data* to keep it from fading or becoming lost. The *monitor* and *random-access memory (RAM)* must be refreshed constantly.

refresh rate   See *vertical refresh rate.*

REGEDIT   A *Microsoft Windows 95* utility program that enables knowledgeable users to edit the *Registry* directly. This should not be attempted by novices.

regexp   See *regular expression.*

Regional Bell Operating Companies (RBOC)   The regional telephone companies (Baby Bells) that were created as a result of the 1982 breakup of AT&T, which forced the former telephone monopoly to leave the local and regional telephone business.

register   A *memory* location within a *microprocessor,* used to store values and external memory addresses while the microprocessor performs logical and arithmetic operations on them. A larger number of registers enables a microprocessor to handle more information at one time.

register renaming   A means of enabling *software* designed to run on *x86 microprocessors,* which can recognize only 8 *registers,* to use the 32 or more registers available in more advanced microprocessors with *superscalar architecture.* A microprocessor capable of register renaming differentiates between the registers an x86 program can address and the actual number of registers available, and will divert information sent to an occupied register to one that is not in use.

P
Q
R

Registry   In *Microsoft Windows 95,* a database that provides programs a way to store configuration data, program file locations, and other information that is needed for the programs to execute correctly. The Registry replaces the text-based *.INI files used with Windows 3.1 applications. See *REGEDIT.*

regular expression (regexp)   In *Unix,* the syntax by which users can type *wild-card* expressions.

relational database management   An approach to *database management,* employed by *Microsoft Access* and other *database management programs,* in which data that's stored in two–dimensional data *tables* of *columns* and *rows* can be related if the tables have a common column or field. The term "relational" suggests the ability of this type of database software to relate two tables on the basis of this common field and to construct a new, third table based on this relation. For example, suppose a bookstore's database program stores one table listing customer names and customer numbers, and a second table listing customer numbers and the subjects of the books purchased by the customer with this number. By formulating a *query,* a user could produce a third, new table, which lists the customer name and the subjects of the books purchased by this customer. The customer number provides the common field by which the two original tables can be related.

relational database management system (RDBMS)   A *relational database* management program, especially one that comes with all the necessary support programs, *programming* tools, and *documentation* needed to create, install, and maintain custom *database* applications.

relational operator   A symbol used to specify the relationship between two numeric *values.* The result of a calculation using a relational operator is either true or false. In *query languages,* relational operators often are used in specifying search criteria. For example, a video store manager may want to tell the computer, "Show me all the telephone numbers of customers with overdue tapes that are due on a date less than or equal to May 7, 1995." In *spreadsheets,* relational operators are used, for example, in @IF formulas to perform tests on data so that different values are displayed, depending on whether the result of the test is true or false.

To permit the expression of logical operators in the character-based world of computing, many programs use the following conventions:

=	Equal to
<	Less than
>	Greater than
<=	Less than or equal to
>=	Greater than or equal to
<>	Not equal to

relative addressing   In a *program,* specifying a *random-access memory (RAM)* location using an expression so the address can be calculated instead of using an *absolute address.*

relative cell reference   In a *formula* in a *spreadsheet program,* a reference to the contents of a *cell* that's adjusted by the program when you copy the formula to another cell or *range* of cells. To understand what happens when you copy a relative cell reference, you need to know how a spreadsheet program actually records a cell reference. Suppose that you type the formula @SUM(C6..C8) in cell C10. The program records a code that means, "Add all the values in the cells positioned in the second, third, and fourth rows up from the current cell." When you copy this formula to the next four cells to the right (D10..G10), it still reads, "Add all the values in the cells positioned in the second, third, and fourth rows up from the current cell," and sums each column correctly. See *absolute cell reference* and *mixed cell reference.*

relative path   In MS-DOS and *Unix,* a path–name expression that does not specify the exact location of a directory, but rather its relative position (up or down) from the current directory.

Relative URL (RELURL)   One of two basic kinds of *Uniform Resource Identifiers (URIs),* a string of characters that gives a resource's file name (such as merlot.html), but does not specify its type or exact location. *Parsers* (such as *Web browsers*) will assume that the resource is located in the same directory that contains the RELURL. See *URL.*

release number   See *version.*

relevance feedback   In *Wide Area Information Servers (WAIS),* an innovative search feature that enables you to select a highly

P
Q
R

relevant *document,* which the search *software* subsequently uses in an attempt to discover additional relevant documents. Usually, you provide relevance feedback by *clicking* a *check box* next to a document that contains just the sort of information you are looking for.

reliability   The capability of *hardware* or *software* to perform as the user expects and to do so consistently, without failures or erratic behavior. See *mean time between failures (MTBF).*

reliable connection   See *reliable link.*

reliable link   An error-free connection established via the telephone system (despite its high *line noise* and low *bandwidth*) by two *modems* that use *error-correction protocols.*

RELURL   See *Relative URL.*

remark   In a *batch file, macro,* or *source code,* explanatory text that's ignored when the computer executes the commands.

remote access   In a *local area network (LAN),* a means by which mobile users can gain authenticated access to internal network resources, preferably without posing a security risk to valuable assets within the network. The simplest but most expensive means of remote access is a direct long-distance call to a *modem* within the network, but this method of access is risky without some means of *strong authentication.* Medium- to large-scale corporations provide remote access to branch offices and business allies by means of *private data networks (PDNs);* new developments in this area include *extranets* and *virtual private networks (VPNs),* which make use of *Internet* connections.

remote control program   A *utility program* that lets you link two computers so you can use one to control the other.

remote login   See *remote access.*

remote management   A feature of newer *departmental laser printers* that transmits information about *toner* level, paper supply, and mechanical problems across a network to the person responsible for maintaining the printer.

remote procedure call (RPC)   In *middleware,* a *protocol* that enables one program to request another program, located elsewhere on the network, to execute and supply needed data.

remote system The computer or *network* to which a computer is connected by a *modem* and a telephone line. The computer connected to the remote system is a *remote terminal*.

remote terminal See *terminal*.

removable hard disk A *hard disk* that employs a data cartridge that can be removed for storage and replaced with another.

removable mass storage A high-capacity data storage device (such as a *Bernoulli box* or a *tape drive*) in which the disk or tape is encased in a plastic cartridge or cassette so it can be removed from the drive for safekeeping.

removable storage media See *removable mass storage*.

rendering In *graphics*, the conversion of an outline drawing into a fully formed, three-dimensional image by means of a mathematical model. See *ray tracing*.

repagination See *pagination*.

repeater In *local area networks (LANs)*, a *hardware* device used to extend the length of network cabling by amplifying and passing along the messages traveling through the network. See *bridge* and *router*.

repeating field In *database design*, a *data field* in which the user must type the same few *data* items repeatedly—such as suppliers' names and addresses—thus creating many possibilities for errors due to typos or misspellings. See *data integrity* and *data redundancy*.

repeating label In a *spreadsheet program*, a character preceded by a *label prefix* that causes the character to be repeated across a *cell*. For example, *Lotus 1-2-3* uses \ to repeat one or more characters across a cell. The entry \= would produce a line of equal signs across the cell.

repeat key A *key* that continues to enter the same character as long as you hold it down.

repetitive strain injury (RSI) Also called repetitive stress injury and cumulative trauma disorder (CTD). A serious and potentially debilitating occupational illness caused by prolonged

P
Q
R

repetitive hand and arm movements that can damage, inflame, or kill nerves in the hands, arms, shoulders, or neck. RSI occurs when constantly repeated motions strain tendons and ligaments, resulting in scar tissue that squeezes nerves and eventually may kill them. With the proliferation of computer *keyboards,* RSI is increasingly noted among office workers and poses a genuine threat to personal computer users who work long hours at the keyboard. Specific RSI disorders include *carpal tunnel syndrome (CTS).*

repetitive stress injury (RSI)   See *repetitive strain injury.*

replace   In *word processing programs,* a feature that searches for a *string* and replaces it with another string.

replaceable parameter   In *MS-DOS,* a symbol used in a *batch file* that MS-DOS replaces with information you type. The symbol consists of a percent sign and a number from 1 through 9, such as %1.

replication   In a *spreadsheet program,* the copying of a formula down a column or across a row; the program automatically adjusts the cell references so the formulas function correctly relative to their new location.

report   In *database management,* printed output that usually is formatted with page numbers and headings. With most programs, reports can include *calculated fields,* showing subtotals, totals, averages, and other figures computed from the data. See *band.*

report generator   A *program* or *function* that allows a nonprogrammer to request printed output from a *database.*

Report Program Generator (RPG)   An innovative programming language, created by IBM in 1965, that enabled programmers to write programs capable of generating formatted *reports* (printouts) of transaction data.

Request for Comments (RFC)   An *Internet* publication that constitutes the chief means by which standards are promulgated (although not all RFCs contain new standards). More than 1,000 RFCs are accessible from *network information centers (NIC).* The publication of RFCs is currently controlled by the *Internet Architecture Board (IAB).*

research network   A *wide area network (WAN)*, such as *ARPANET* or *NSFnet*, developed and funded by a governmental agency to improve research productivity in areas of national interest.

ResEdit   A *Macintosh utility program*, available free from *Apple Computer* dealers, that lets you edit (and copy to other programs) many program features, such as *menu* text, *icons*, and *dialog boxes*.

reserved memory   In the original IBM PC memory architecture, the memory locations between the maximum 640K available for user programs, and the 1024K maximum memory that is defined by the *real mode* of *Intel* microprocessors. Within this range, certain portions of the memory are reserved for the *basic input-output system (BIOS)* and video cards. Memory that is not utilized cannot be made available to user programs without the use of a memory management utility. See *upper memory area* and *upper memory block (UMB)*.

reserved word   In a *programming language* or *operating system*, a word—also called a *keyword*—that has a fixed function and can't be used for any other purpose. In *BASIC*, for example, the word REM is reserved to indicate the beginning of a *remark*. You can use a reserved word only for its intended purpose; you can't use the word for naming files, *variables*, or other user–named *objects*.

reset button   A button, usually mounted on the system unit's front panel, that lets you perform a *warm boot* if the *reset key* doesn't work. On older *Macintoshes*, the reset button is part of the *programmer's switch*. Synonymous with *hardware reset*.

reset key   A *key* combination that, when pressed, restarts the computer. This key combination (Ctrl+Alt+Del on IBM-compatible machines) provides an alternative to switching the power off and on after a *crash* so severe that the keyboard doesn't respond. See *hardware reset*, *programmer's switch*, and *warm boot*.

resident font   As opposed to a *downloadable font* or a *cartridge font*, a *font* that is present in a *printer's* memory whenever it is turned on.

resident program   See *terminate-and-stay-resident (TSR) program*.

resolution   The quality of a computer-represented image or sound, especially with respect to its ability to trick the eye (or

P
Q
R

ear) into perceiving it as a convincing duplicate of the original. In *printers,* resolution quality is expressed in linear *dots per inch (dpi).* In *sound boards,* resolution is expressed by means of the number of *bits* used to encode sounds. Resolution determines the number of sound levels with which recorded sounds must be represented. Higher resolutions ensure greater fidelity to the original sound. Though a resolution of 8 bits is minimally acceptable for voice reproduction, 16-bit resolution is required to reproduce the range of sounds in complex pieces of music. In graphics, resolution is measured by means of dots per inch (dpi) and *color depth* (the number of colors that make up the image). In *monitors,* resolution is expressed as the number of *pixels* horizontally and *lines* vertically on-screen. For example, a *color graphics array (CGA)* monitor displays fewer lines than a *video graphics array (VGA)* monitor, and therefore, a CGA image appears more jagged than a VGA image. The following table lists the resolutions of common video adapters for IBM PCs and compatibles:

Resolution Adapter	Pixels × Lines
Monochrome Display Adapter (MDA)	720 × 350
Color Graphics Adapter (CGA)	640 × 200
Enhanced Graphics Adapter (EGA)	640 × 350
MultiColor Graphics Array (MCGA)	640 × 480
Video Graphics Array (VGA)	640 × 480
Super VGA (extended VGA)	800 × 600
Super VGA (VGA Plus)	1,024 × 768

resolution enhancement technology   A way of reducing *aliasing* and smoothing the curves in *laser printer* output. Resolution enhancement technology, which inserts small dots between large ones, increases *effective resolution.*

resource fork   In the *Macintosh* file system, one of two portions of a file (the other is the *data fork*). The resource fork is used to store information about the file, such as the code number of the application that created it and the icon that the Finder should display.

response time   The time a computer needs to carry out a request. Response time is a better measurement of system performance than *access time* because it more fairly states the system's *throughput*.

retrieval   All the procedures involved in finding, summarizing, organizing, displaying, or printing information from a *computer system* in a form useful for the user.

Return   See *Enter/Return.*

return on investment (ROI)   A calculation that considers the projected economic benefits of an investment as a percentage of the investment cost; for example, if a company invests $10,000 in a new computer system and can document $20,000 in future savings due to the installation of the system, the return on investment is 100 percent.

reusable object   In *object-oriented programming (OOP),* an *object* that has been designed with such sufficient generality and customizability that it can be quickly and easily incorporated into new programs. For example, a programmer may develop a single object to support the creation of an on-screen window, and when this is done, the object can be used in any program. The reuse of objects in this way saves enormous amounts of programming time and increases programming efficiency accordingly.

Reverse Address Resolution Protocol (RARP)   An *Internet* standard *(protocol)* that enables *diskless workstations* to obtain an *IP address* so they can fully function as Internet *hosts.* See *BOOTP.*

reverse engineering   The process of systematically taking apart a *chip* or *application program* to discover how it works, with the aim of imitating or duplicating some or all of its functions.

Reverse Polish Notation (RPN)   A means of describing mathematical operations that makes calculations easier for computers. Many *compilers* convert arithmetic expressions into RPN. In RPN, the expression "a b +" adds the variables a and b and would be written as "a + b" in standard notation. Synonymous with Polish notation and postfix notation. See *infix notation, prefix notation.*

reverse video   In *monochrome monitors,* a means of *highlighting* text on the *display* so that normally dark characters are displayed as bright characters on a dark background or normally bright

P
Q
R

characters are displayed as dark characters on a bright background.

rewrite   Synonymous with *overwrite.*

RFC   See *Request for Comments.*

RFI   See *radio frequency interference.*

RGB   Acronym for red–green–blue. A *color model* (a means by which colors can be mathematically described) in which a given color is specified by the relative amounts of the three primary colors. The amount of each color is specified by a number from 0 to 255; 0,0,0 is black, while 255,255,255 is white.

RGB monitor   A color *digital monitor* that accepts separate inputs for red, green, and blue, and produces a much sharper image than *composite color monitors.*

Rhapsody   Code name for the next-generation *Macintosh* operating system, which will be based on technology developed by NeXT, Inc. Rhapsody will sport a user interface closely resembling the current *MacOS* user interface, but there the resemblance ends: Rhapsody is essentially *Unix* with a friendly face, and Rhapsody will be able to run current Macintosh applications only by emulation. While Rhapsody is under development, Apple intends to continue upgrading and supporting the current MacOS (version 8.0 is in the works at this writing) and will do so until the end of the millennium, the company promises.

Rich Text Format (RTF)   A text *formatting* standard developed by *Microsoft Corporation* that allows a *word processing program* to create a file encoded with all the document's formatting instructions, but without using any special *hidden codes.* An RTF-encoded document can be transmitted over *telecommunications* links or read by another RTF-compatible word processing program, without loss of the formatting.

right justification   See *justification.*

ring network   In *local area networks (LANs),* a decentralized *network topology* in which a number of *nodes* (including workstations, shared *peripherals,* and *file servers*) are arranged around a closed loop cable. Like a *bus network,* a ring network's workstations can send messages to all other workstations. Each node in the ring has a unique address, and its reception circuitry constantly monitors the bus to determine whether a message is being sent. The failure of a single node can disrupt the entire network; however, *fault-tolerance* schemes have been devised that allow ring networks to continue to function even if one or more nodes fail. See *token-ring network.*

RIP See *raster image processor* or *Router Information Protocol (RIP).*

ripple-through effect In a *spreadsheet program,* the sudden appearance of ERR values throughout the cells after you make a change that breaks a link among *formulas.* If this happens, you may think that you've ruined the entire spreadsheet, but after you locate and repair the problem, all the affected formulas are restored.

RISC Acronym for reduced instruction set computer. A *central processing unit (CPU)* architecture in which the number of instructions the *microprocessor* can execute is reduced to a minimum to increase processing speed. The idea of RISC architecture is to reduce the instruction set to the bare minimum, emphasizing the instructions used most of the time and optimizing them for the fastest possible execution. A RISC processor ostensibly runs faster than its *CISC* counterpart, but CISC manufacturers—such as *Intel*—have substantially narrowed the performance gap by including many of the design features found in *CISC* architectures.

river In *desktop publishing (DTP),* a formatting flaw that results in the accidental alignment of *white space* between words in sequential lines of text, encouraging the eye to follow the flow down three or more lines. Rivers injure what typographers refer to as the *color* of the page.

RJ-11 Standardized name for the four-wire modular connector used for telephone and *modem* connections. See *modular jack.*

RJ-45 Standardized name for the eight-pin connector used in *10 Base-T* network connections.

RLE See *Run-Length Encoding.*

RLL See *Run-Length Limited.*

P
Q
R

rlogin   A *Unix* utility that enables users of one machine to connect to other Unix systems via the Internet and gain full control over the other machine's operation. This utility is rarely implemented due to its obvious security perils.

rn   In *Usenet,* a non-threaded *newsreader* for *Unix* systems. Written by Larry Wall in the mid-1980s, rn has been replaced by *threaded newsreaders* such as *trn, tin,* and *nn.*

robust   Able to survive exceptional conditions and unpredicted errors; relatively free from bugs and fault-tolerant.

ROI   See *return on investment.*

ROM   See *read-only memory.*

Roman   In *typography,* an upright *serif typeface* of medium *weight.* In proofreading, characters without emphasis.

root   In *Unix,* an administrative account that enables the account holder to override file permissions and to browse freely through the computer's file directories. A fundamental objective of system intruders is to gain root user status, which enables the user to obtain the encrypted password file; this file can be analyzed by password guessing programs, which may succeed in decrypting user passwords and destroying the system's security.

root directory   On a *hard* or *floppy disk,* the top-level *directory* that *MS-DOS* and *Microsoft Windows 95* creates when you format the disk. See *parent directory* and *subdirectory.*

root name   The first, mandatory part of an *MS-DOS file name,* using from one to eight characters. See *file extension.*

rot-13   In *Usenet newsgroups,* a simple *encryption* technique that offsets each character by 13 places (so that an e becomes an r, for example). Rot-13 encryption is used for any message that may spoil someone's fun (such as the solution to a game) or offend some readers (such as erotic poetry). If the reader chooses to decrypt the message by issuing the appropriate command, then the reader—not the author of the message—bears the responsibility for any discomfort that may be caused by reading the message. Lately, rot-13 has fallen into disuse. See *netiquette* and *spoiler.*

rotated type   In a *graphics, word processing,* or *desktop publishing (DTP)* program, text that has been turned vertically from its normal, horizontal position on the page. The best graphics programs, such as CorelDRAW!, allow you to edit the type even after you rotate it.

rotation tool   In a *graphics* or *desktop publishing (DTP)* program, a command option (represented by an *icon*) you can use to rotate type from its normal, horizontal position. See *rotated type.*

roughs   In *desktop publishing (DTP),* the preliminary page *layouts* that the designer creates using rough sketches to represent page design ideas. Synonymous with thumbnails.

router   In a *packet-switching network* such as the *Internet,* one of two basic devices (the other is a *host*). A router is an electronic device that examines each packet of data it receives and then decides which way to send it onward toward its destination.

Router Information Protocol (RIP)   An *Internet* protocol that routes data within an internal TCP/IP-based network based on a table of distances. A more recent and sophisticated version of this protocol is the *OSPF* Interior Gateway Protocol.

routine   A program module that carries out a well-defined task. Synonymous with *subroutine.*

row   In a *spreadsheet program,* a block of *cells* running horizontally across the spreadsheet. In most programs, rows are numbered sequentially from the top. In a *database,* a row is the same as a record or *data record.*

row-wise recalculation   In *spreadsheet programs,* a *recalculation order* that calculates all the values in row 1 before moving to row 2, and so on. See *column-wise recalculation* and *optimal recalculation.*

RPC   See *remote procedure call.*

RPG   See *Report Program Generator.*

RPN   See *Reverse Polish Notation.*

RS-232C   A standard recommended by the Electronic Industries Association (EIA) concerning the transmission of *data* between computers using *serial ports.* Most *personal computers* are equipped with an RS-232-compatible serial port, which you can use for external *modems, printers, scanners,* and other *peripheral* devices.

P
Q
R

RS-232C port   See *serial port*.

RS-422   A standard recommended by the Electronic Industries Association (EIA) and used as the *serial port* standard for *Macintosh* computers. RS-422 governs the asynchronous transmission of computer data at speeds of up to 920,000 bits per second.

RSA Data Security, Inc.   The leading cryptography software publisher. The company holds patents on a number of widely used encryption algorithms, including the *RSA public key encryption algorithm,* the de facto world standard, and several *symmetric key encryption algorithms,* including *RC4,* which is part of the Secure Sockets Layer *(SSL)* standard.

RSA public key encryption algorithm   The most popular algorithm for *public key encryption* and a de facto world standard. RSA Data Security, Inc., holds a patent on this algorithm, which is confidential; nevertheless, the algorithm has been incorporated in a number of major *protocols,* including *S/MIME* and Secure Sockets Layer *(SSL).* See *Diffie-Hellman public key encryption algorithm.*

RSI   See *repetitive strain injury.*

RTF   See *Rich Text Format.*

RTFM   Acronym for Read the "Frigging" Manual.

rule   In *graphics* and *desktop publishing (DTP),* a thin horizontal or vertical line.

ruler   In many *word processing* and *desktop publishing (DTP)* programs, an on-screen bar that measures the page horizontally, showing the current margins, *tab stops,* and paragraph *indents.*

run   To *execute* a *program.*

Run-Length Encoding (RLE)   A *data compression* algorithm that looks for commonly occurring sequences of data and *replaces* them with a much shorter code. RLE is a *lossless* compression technique because the original data can be totally restored by reversing the encoding process.

Run-Length Limited (RLL)   A method of storing and retrieving information on a *hard disk* that, compared to *double-density* techniques, increases by at least 50 percent the amount of *data* a hard disk can store. The improvement in storage density is achieved by translating the data into a digital format that can be written more compactly to the disk. See *Advanced Run-Length Limited (ARLL)* and *Modified Frequency Modulation (MFM).*

running head   See *header.*

runtime version   A limited version of a supporting *program* that's bundled with an *application program.* For example, early versions of *Microsoft Excel* were sold with run-time versions of Microsoft Windows for users who didn't yet own Windows.

r/w   A common abbreviation for *read/write,* indicating that the *file* or device is configured so you can write *data* to it as well as read data from it. See *read/write file.*

P
Q
R

SAA   See *Systems Application Architecture.*

safe format   A disk *formatting* method that doesn't destroy the data on the disk so you can recover it if necessary. To format safely with *MS-DOS,* use the FORMAT command without the /u switch.

safe mode   In *Microsoft Windows 95,* a start mode in which the *operating system* initializes without user-added extensions. This mode enables the user to determine which of the recently added programs are causing problems.

sampling rate   The frequency with which a recording device, such as a *sound board,* takes readings of the sound it is recording. High-quality sound boards, such as the equipment used to record audio compact discs, have sampling rates of 44.1 *kilohertz (KHz)* or higher. Although sound boards with lower sampling rates may be adequate for recording simple noises or even voice clips, they are not adequate for recording music.

sandbox   In *Java,* a safe area for the execution of *applets,* created by the *Java virtual machine,* in which applets cannot get access to the computer's file system.

sans serif   A *typeface* that lacks *serifs,* the ornamental straight or curved lines across the ends of the main strokes of a character. *Helvetica* and Arial are two readily available sans serif fonts. Sans serif typefaces are preferable for *display type* but, when used for *body type,* are harder to read than serif typefaces such as Times Roman.

SASI   See *Shugart Associates Standard Interface.*

SATAN   A network security diagnostic tool that exhaustively examines a network and reveals security holes. SATAN is a two-edged sword: in the hands of network administrators, it is a valuable tool for detecting and closing security loopholes. In the hands of intruders, it is an equally valuable tool for exposing remaining loopholes and gaining *unauthorized access* to a network.

satellite   1. In a *multi-user system,* a *terminal* or *workstation* linked to a centralized *host* computer. 2. In the output of *inkjet* and *laser* *printers,* an extraneous spot of ink in the area around characters in which no ink should be present.

S
T
U

saturation   1. In a *charge-coupled device (CCD),* the degree to which *pixels* can hold a charge, and therefore sustain the appearance of even color in the display. 2. In monitors, the degree to which the display can differentiate between colors and display each color accurately, throughout the screen area.

save   To transfer *data* from the computer's *random-access memory (RAM),* where the data is vulnerable to erasure, to a storage medium such as a *disk drive.*

sawtooth distortion   See *aliasing.*

scalability   The capability of hardware or software to accommodate increasing numbers of users. A *server* that can accommodate a dozen users may fail catastrophically when the number of users expands to 1,000. A scalable system includes an upgrade path that enables administrators to add extra capacity as needed so that overall system performance is not degraded in the slightest.

scalable font   A *screen font* or *printer font* that you can enlarge or reduce to any size, within a specified range, without introducing unattractive distortions. *Outline font* technology is most commonly used to provide scalable fonts, but other technologies—including stroke fonts, which form characters from a matrix of lines—are sometimes used. The most popular scalable fonts for *Macintosh* and *Microsoft Windows 95* systems are *PostScript* and *TrueType* fonts. See *bit-mapped font.*

scalar architecture   The design of a *microprocessor* with only one *pipeline.* Microprocessors with multiple pipelines have *superscalar architecture.*

scale-up problem   In a *network,* a technical problem caused by the system expanding far beyond its projected maximum size. For example, every computer connected to the *Internet* must have its own unique address, called an *IP address.* However, the Internet's designers, never guessing how popular the Internet would become, did not allow for a sufficient number of IP addresses. The network will have to be redesigned from the ground up—that is, with a new *IP protocol* (called *IPv6)* in order to cope with the problem.

scale well   To handle very large increases in size or scope of usage without *scale-up problems*.

scaling   1. In graphics, the resizing of an image. 2. In *presentation graphics,* the adjustment of the *y-axis* (values), chosen arbitrarily by the program, to make differences in the data more apparent. Most *presentation graphics* programs scale the y-axis, but the programs' scaling choice can be unsatisfactory. Manually adjusting the scaling often produces better results.

scanner   A *peripheral* device that digitizes artwork or photographs and stores the image as a *file* that you can merge with text in many *word processing* and *page layout programs.*

scanning pass   A trip made by a scanner's *charge-coupled devices (CCDs)* over the material being scanned. Although more popular than *triple-pass scanners, single-pass scanners* are not always faster than their triple-pass counterparts.

scan rate   See *vertical refresh rate.*

scatter diagram   An analytical *graphic* that plots *data* items as points on two numeric axes; also called a scattergram. Scatter diagrams show clustering relationships in numeric data. Computer magazines often use a scatter diagram to compare similarly configured computer systems, with price on one axis and the result of performance testing on the other axis to draw your attention to slow, expensive computers and fast, inexpensive computers.

scatter plot   See *scatter diagram.*

scientific notation   A method for expressing very large or very small numbers as powers of 10, such as 7.24×10^{23}. *Spreadsheet* programs usually express scientific notation with the symbol E, which stands for exponent, as in the following example: 7.24E23.

sci hierarchy   In *Usenet's standard newsgroup hierarchy,* a category of *newsgroups* devoted to topics in the sciences. The category includes newsgroups that cover astronomy, biology, engineering, geology, mathematics, psychology, and statistics.

scissoring   In *graphics,* an editing technique in which you crop an image to a size determined by a frame that you place over the image.

Scrapbook On the *Macintosh,* a *desk accessory (DA)* that can hold frequently used *graphic* images, such as company letterhead, which you can then insert into new *documents* as required.

screen blanking An obsolete electricity-conservation scheme, far inferior to *display power management signaling (DPMS).* Screen blanking-capable *monitors* go blank when they recognize that a *screen-saver* utility has begun to operate, saving some electricity but not nearly as much as a DPMS monitor and *video adapter* save.

screen capture A copy of a screen display that is saved as a text or graphics file on disk. Screen captures can then be printed in books or reports to show how a computer screen looks at a certain point in a program.

screen dump A printout of the screen's current contents, with little or no attempt made to format the printed data aesthetically. See *Print Screen (PrtScr).* Also, sometimes used (inaccurately) to refer to *screen captures,* in which a screen capture program processes the saved image for attractive printing.

screen element In *Microsoft Windows 95,* a component of the displayed image, such as a *dialog box,* border, *pushbutton, check box,* or *scroll bar.*

screen flicker See *flicker.*

screen font A *bit-mapped font* designed to mimic the appearance of *printer fonts* when displayed on medium-resolution monitors. Modern *laser printers* can print text with a *resolution* of 300 *dots per inch (dpi)* or more, but video displays, except for the most expensive professional units, lack such high resolution and can't display *typefaces* with such precision. What you see on screen usually isn't as good as what you get from the printer. Adobe International's Adobe Type Manager (ATM) and the *TrueType* standard developed by *Apple Computer* and *Microsoft Corporation* provide screen fonts that closely mimic printer fonts. See *outline font.*

screen memory See *video memory.*

screen pitch See *dot pitch.*

screen saver A *utility program* that changes the screen display—to an aquarium scene, or a variable pattern of lines—while you are away from your computer. In the past, screen savers were needed to prevent "burn-in," which could damage a monitor by recording a permanent "ghost" image of a frequently viewed screen display in the screen's phosphors. Today's advanced phosphors are not as susceptible to burn-in, so the use of screen savers is not required for system maintenance. Some screen savers come with password utilities, so they become very useful for disguising screen contents when users are away from their desks.

script   A series of instructions, similar to a *macro* and typed in plain text, that tells a program how to perform a specific procedure, such as logging on to an *e-mail* system. Some programs have built-in script capabilities. You must learn how to write the script using a rather limited *programming language*. Some programs write the script automatically by recording your keystrokes and command choices as you perform the procedure. See *HyperTalk* and *scripting language*.

scripting language   A simple *programming language* designed to enable computer users to write useful programs quickly. Examples of scripting languages are *HyperTalk* (the scripting language for the *Macintosh HyperCard* application) and *perl,* which is widely used to write *Common Gateway Interface (CGI)* scripts for *World Wide Web (WWW)* forms processing.

scroll   To move a *window* horizontally or vertically so its position over a *document* or *worksheet* changes. In some programs, scrolling is clearly distinguished from *cursor* movement; when you scroll, the cursor stays put. In other programs, however, scrolling the screen also moves the cursor.

scroll arrow   In a *Graphical User Interface (GUI),* an arrow (pointing up, down, left, or right) that you can click to scroll the screen in the desired direction. The scroll arrows are located at the ends of *scroll bars.*

scroll bar/scroll box   A *Graphical User Interface (GUI)* feature that enables the user to scroll horizontally and vertically using rectangular scrolling areas on the right and bottom borders of the window. You scroll the *document* horizontally or vertically by clicking the scroll bars (or *scroll arrows*) or by dragging the scroll boxes.

Scroll Lock key   On *IBM PC-compatible keyboards,* a *toggle key* that, in some programs, switches the *cursor-movement keys* between two different modes. The exact function of this key varies among programs.

SCSI See *Small Computer System Interface.*

SCSI-1 Commonly used name for the original *Small Computer System Interface (SCSI),* which enables *data transfer rates* of up to 5MB per second using an 8-bit bus.

SCSI-2 The current version of the *Small Computer System Interface (SCSI)* standard. SCSI-2 reduces the number of conflicts among devices in a *daisy chain* and includes a common command set to enable different types of devices (such as scanners, CD-ROM drives, and tape backup drives) to work together smoothly. SCSI-2 defines a *Fast SCSI* mode (with a *data transfer rate* of up to 10M per second) as well as an *Ultra SCSI* mode with data transfer rates of up to 20M per second). Both standards call for an 8-bit bus. More recent versions of these standards use a 16-bit bus: *Fast Wide SCSI* transfers data at 20M per second, while *Ultra Wide SCSI* transfers data at speeds up to 40M per second. To distinguish the earlier 8-bit standards from the newer 16-bit ("wide") standards, Fast SCSI (8-bit) is sometimes called Fast/Narrow SCSI, while Ultra SCSI (8-bit) is sometimes called Ultra/Narrow SCSI.

SDH Acronym for *Synchronous Digital Hierarchy,* the international name for *SONET.*

SDRAM Acronym for synchronous dynamic random–access memory. A high-speed *random-access memory (RAM)* technology that can synchronize itself with the *clock speed* of the *microprocessor's* data bus (up to 66 MHz in today's fastest systems). Faster than *EDO RAM,* SDRAM is the memory technology of choice for *high-end systems.*

search and replace See *replace.*

search engine Any *program* that locates needed information in a *database,* but especially an *Internet*-accessible search service that enables you to search for information on the Internet. To use a search engine, you type one or more key words; the result is a list of *documents* or *files* that contain one or more of these words in their titles, descriptions, or text. The databases of most Internet search engines contain *World Wide Web (WWW)* documents; some also contain items found in *Gopher* menus and *File Transfer Protocol (FTP)* file *archives.* Compiling the database requires an automated search routine called a *spider* (forms filled out by Web authors) or a search of other databases of Internet documents. See *AltaVista, HotBot, InfoSeek, Lycos,* and *WebCrawler.*

secondary cache   *Cache memory* that is on the *motherboard* rather than inside a *microprocessor.* Also called L2 cache memory, secondary cache memory dramatically improves system performance and is essential to every *computer system.* Several kinds of secondary cache memory are available, ranging from the slow but inexpensive *direct-map cache* to fast and expensive *four-way set-associative cache. Write-back* secondary cache memory is better than *write-through* secondary cache memory. See *full-associative cache.*

secondary key   In a sorting operation performed on a *database,* the second key that is used to order the data within subgroupings, after an initial grouping has been performed by the *primary key.* For example, a user may want to sort a mailing list by ZIP code (the primary key); within a given ZIP code, a secondary sort organizes the records by last name.

secondary storage   A nonvolatile storage medium, such as a *disk drive,* that stores program instructions and data even after you switch off the power. Synonymous with *auxiliary storage.* See *primary storage.*

second-generation computer   An early type of computer, built during the 1950s and early 1960s, which was constructed out of hand-wired transistors rather than vacuum tubes.

second-generation programming language   The first programming language, called *assembly language,* that enabled programmers to work at one level of abstraction higher than *machine language.*

second-person virtual reality   A *virtual reality (VR)* system that presents the user with a high-definition video screen and a cockpit with navigation controls, as in a flight simulator program. This type of virtual reality is less engaging than computer-generated worlds that can be explored through the use of goggles and *sensor gloves* (hence the term "second person").

sector   A segment of one of the concentric tracks encoded on a *floppy* or *hard disk* during a *low-level format.* In *IBM*

PC-compatible computing, a sector usually contains 512 *bytes* of information. See *cluster.*

sector interleave   See *interleaving.*

sector interleave factor   See *interleave factor.*

Secure Sockets Layer   See *SSL.*

security   The protection of valuable assets stored on computer systems or transmitted via computer networks. Computer security involves the following conceptually differentiated areas:

- **Authentication** (ensuring that users are indeed the persons they claim to be).

- **Access control** (ensuring that users access only those resources and services that they are entitled to access).

- **Confidentiality** (ensuring that transmitted or stored data is not examined by unauthorized persons).

- **Integrity** (ensuring that transmitted or stored data is not altered by unauthorized persons in a way that is not detectable by authorized users).

- **Nonrepudiation** (ensuring that qualified users are not denied access to services that they legitimately expect to receive, and that originators of messages cannot deny that they in fact sent a given message).

seek   In a *disk drive,* to locate a specific region of a disk and to position the *read/write head* so that the computer can retrieve *data* or *program* instructions.

seek time   In a *secondary storage* device, the time that it takes the *read/write head* to reach the correct location on the disk. See *access time.*

segmented memory architecture   A computer memory design in which the *addresses* of specific locations in the *random-access memory (RAM)* are specified by means of segments (base addresses) and offsets (the number of data elements away from the base address). The use of segments and offsets enables computer system designers to use more system memory than would be permitted by the width of the *address bus.*

select To *highlight* part of a *document* so the *program* can identify the material on which you want to perform the next operation. In addition to selecting text, you can highlight or select
an item from a *list box* or select a *check box* item to *toggle* it on
or off.

selection 1. A portion of a document's text or graphics that
has been highlighted in *reverse video* for formatting or editing
purposes. 2. In programming, a branch or conditional control
structure. 3. In *database management programs,* the retrieval of
records by using a *query.* See *branch control structure.*

self-extracting archive A compressed file that contains the
software needed to decompress itself. Double-clicking a self-
extracting archive launches the decompression portion of the
program and decompresses the files.

semantic net In *hypertext* theory, a set of connections
among the ideas in a *document.* To create a hypertext document,
you first "chunk" the document—breaking the document into
"chunks" or units of meaning. For example, a hypertext document on California wines might break the subject down into
the following categories: wineries, wine varietals, history of
California wine, climate of wine-growing areas, and scientific
research on wine growing. A separate document would cover
each of these topics. *Hyperlinks* within the document exploit
every possible connection with every other document in the
series of linked documents, which is called a semantic net (this
term is synonymous with *web,* spelled with a small *w*).

semiconductor A material, such as silicon or germanium, that
is less electrically conductive than excellent electrical conductors, such as copper, and insulating materials. Semiconductor
wafers or *chips* of varying resistance can be assembled to create a
variety of electronic devices. In *personal computers,* semiconductor
materials are used for *microprocessors, memory,* and other circuits.
See *integrated circuit (IC).*

sendmail A *Unix* utility that sends *e-mail* over the *Internet* in
accordance with the *SMTP* protocol. To create the message, you
use an *e-mail client* such as *Eudora* or *Netscape Messenger.* Mail is
received and stored by the programs conforming to the *Post
Office Protocol (POP).*

send statement In a *SLIP* or *PPP* dialer program's *script
language,* a statement that tells the program to send certain

characters. Send statements follow *expect statements,* which tell the program to wait until the service provider's computer sends certain characters to your computer.

sensor glove   In *virtual reality (VR)* systems, an interface that is worn on a hand and enables the user to manipulate and move *virtual* objects in a virtual reality environment. See *head-mounted display (HMD).*

sequence control structure   A *control structure* that tells the computer to execute program statements in the order in which the statements were written. One of three fundamental *control structures* that govern the order in which *program* statements are executed, the sequence control structure is the default in all *programming languages.* You can use loops and *branch control structures* to alter the sequence.

sequential access   An *information* storage and retrieval technique in which the computer must move through a sequence of stored data items to reach the desired one. Sequential access media, such as cassette tapes, are much slower than *random-access* media, such as *hard disk drives.*

serial   See *asynchronous communication, multitasking, parallel port, serial communication,* and *serial port.*

serial communication   A type of electronic communication that, unlike *parallel communication,* requires that *data bits* be sent one after the other rather than several at once. *Modems* rely on serial communication to send data over telephone lines. See *serial port.*

Serial Line Internet Protocol   See *SLIP.*

serial mouse   A *mouse* designed to be connected directly to one of the computer's *serial ports.* See *bus mouse.*

serial port   A *port* that synchronizes and manages *asynchronous communication* between the computer and devices such as *serial printers, modems,* and other computers. The serial port not only sends and receives asynchronous data in a one-bit-after-the-other stream, but it also negotiates with the receiving device to ensure that no data is lost when it is sent or received. The negotiation occurs through *hardware* or *software handshaking.* See *FireWire, RS-232C* and *Universal Asynchronous Receiver/Transmitter (UART).*

serial printer   A *printer* designed to be connected to a computer's *serial port*. Due to the inherent difficulty of configuring serial printers, most printers are now designed to use the computer's *parallel port*.

serif   The fine, ornamental cross strokes across the ends of the main strokes of a character. Serif fonts are easier to read for *body type,* but most designers prefer to use *sans serif* typefaces for *display type.*

server   1. In a *client/server network,* a computer or program that is dedicated to providing information in response to external requests. See *file server, print server.* 2. On the *Internet,* a program that supplies information when it receives external requests via Internet connections. See *Web server.*

server application   In object linking and embedding *(OLE),* the *program* that creates a *source document.* Data from a source document is linked or embedded in one or more *destination documents* created by *client applications.*

server-based application   A *network* version of a *program* stored on a network's *file server* and available to more than one user at a time. See *client application.*

service bureau   A business that provides a variety of publication services such as *graphics file format* conversion, optical scanning of graphics, and typesetting on high-resolution *imagesetters* such as Linotronics and Varitypes.

service provider   See *Internet service provider (ISP)* and *Internet access provider (IAP).*

servo-controlled DC motor   An electric motor used to turn the *spindle* of a *hard disk.* Unlike *synchronous motors,* servo-controlled DC motors are inexpensive and can operate at whatever speed the disk's designers want, because the motor's rotation speed is independent of the frequency of the wall outlet's current.

servo-voice coil actuator   The most popular kind of *head actuator* used in modern *hard disks.* Servo-voice coil actuators are *closed-loop actuators* that operate by using an electromagnet to pull the *read/write head* against tension created by a spring.

session layer   In the *OSI Reference Model* of computer network architecture, the third of seven *layers,* in which a virtual connection is established with a corresponding service at the same layer on another computer. (The connection is virtual because the link to the destination computer at this level is only apparent; the actual connection requires passing the data "down" the *protocol stack* all the way to the *physical layer*, where the data is sent out over the network.) Protocols at the session layer govern this virtual connection.

set–associative cache A *cache* design used in the fastest *random-access memory (RAM)* caches and in the *internal caches* included on 486–class and *Pentium* chips. This design divides the cache into two to eight sets, or areas. Data stored in the cache is distributed in bits to each set in sequence. In most instances, data from each set in the cache is read sequentially. Therefore, the set just read or written to can prepare to be read or written to again while data is being read from or written to the next set. The *set-associative cache* design enables the *microprocessor* to complete an instruction in one *clock cycle*. A *four-way set-associative cache* provides the best compromise between cost and performance.

setup parameters Information about a *computer system* encoded as part of the *basic input-output system (BIOS)*. Setup parameters include the amount of *random-access memory (RAM)* in the computer, the type of *keyboard* used, and the hard disk's *geometry*. To change the setup parameters, use the *setup program*.

setup program A program, recorded as part of the *basic input-output system (BIOS)*, that changes the setup options. To run the setup program, you press a special *key* combination (usually shown on-screen) as the computer *boots* up.

setup string A series of characters that a *program* conveys to a *printer* so the printer operates in a specified mode.

setup switches *Dual in-line package (DIP) switches* in older *modems* that enabled you to set certain options, such as whether to answer incoming calls. Modern modems have no setup switches; instead, the *communications program* handles the setup.

SGML Acronym for Standard Generalized Markup Language. A means of describing markup languages, such as the HyperText Markup Language *(HTML)*, which is widely used on the *World Wide Web (WWW)*. SGML can be used to define a *document type definition (DTD)*, which defines the *elements* of a specific type of document and the *tags* that can be used to display these elements with distinctive formats. A program called a *parser* is needed to read the tags and display the text appropriately. SGML is an open, international standard defined by the International Standards Organization (ISO).

SGRAM   Acronym for Synchronous Graphics Random-Access Memory. A type of *dynamic random-access memory (DRAM)* chip that can synchronize with the computer's *clock speed,* enabling significantly higher data transfer rates than earlier DRAM technologies. SGRAM chips are used on high-end *video adapters.*

shadowing   Copying the contents of *read-only memory (ROM)* into *random-access memory (RAM)* to enable the microprocessor to access them more quickly. See *shadow RAM.*

shadow mask   A metal screen located just inside a *cathode ray tube's (CRT's)* display that prevents electron beams from striking *phosphors* that glow in the incorrect color. The shadow mask, which is very carefully aligned with the *electron guns* and the phosphors on the inside of the display, causes the red electron gun to strike only red phosphors and the blue electron gun to strike only blue phosphors, for example.

shadow RAM   In *Intel*-based PCs, a portion of the *upper memory area* between 640K and 1M set aside for programs ordinarily retrieved from *read-only memory (ROM)*. *Random-access memory (RAM)* is faster than ROM, so shadow RAM increases performance.

shareware   Copyrighted *programs* made available free of charge on a trial basis. If you like a shareware program and decide to use it, you are expected to pay a fee to the program's author. See *public domain program.*

sheet-fed scanner   A *flatbed scanner* that can automatically load a series of documents for scanning. Sheet-fed scanners are useful for optical character recognition *(OCR)* work.

sheet feeder   See *cut-sheet feeder.*

shell   A *program* that puts an easy-to-use *user interface* between the user and an *operating system.* Though *COMMAND.COM* is technically a shell (it works between the user and the inner workings of *MS-DOS*), the term usually applies to a program that replaces a *command line* with a set of *menus*.

shell account   An inexpensive but limited type of *Internet dialup access*. A shell account does not directly connect your computer to the Internet. Instead, you use a *communications program* to access a computer, usually a *Unix* computer, on which you have established an account. After logging on to this computer, you get text-only access to this Unix computer's operating system (its *shell*). From the shell, you can run the Internet tools that are available on the *service provider's* computer, such as a text-only *Usenet* newsreaders or the text-only *Web browser* called Lynx.

shell script   A *script*, written in a *scripting language* such as *perl*, that enables programmers to automate certain functions of an *operating system*. The first *server* for *Usenet* was a *Unix* shell script.

shielded speaker   An *auxiliary speaker* designed to protect the *monitor* and other computer components from the magnetic field that generates sounds. Magnetic fields, if unshielded, can distort a monitor's image or even erase data on disks.

Shift+click   A *mouse* maneuver accomplished by holding down the Shift key while you click the mouse. Applications implement Shift+clicking differently, but in most applications, the action extends a selection.

Shift key   The key you press to enter uppercase letters or punctuation marks. Early IBM *keyboards* labeled the Shift key only with an up-pointing arrow. More modern keyboards label this key with the word *Shift*. See *Caps Lock key*.

shopping basket   In *Internet* shopping, a method of implementing an online store in which users can select items and add them to a virtual "shopping basket"; when shopping is done, users then see all the items they have selected on an order page. Shopping baskets require *cookies* in order to function.

shortcut   In *Microsoft Windows 95*, an icon that provides fast access to a program. After you create the shortcut, you see the program's icon on the desktop, where you can start it quickly by double-clicking the icon.

shortcut key   A *key* combination that provides one-stroke access directly to a command or *dialog box*, bypassing any intermediate *menus*. See *hot key*.

S-HTTP   Acronym for Secure HyperText Transport Protocol. An extension of the *World Wide Web's (WWW) HyperText Transport Protocol (HTTP)* that supports secure commercial transactions on the Web. Secure HTTP provides this support in two ways: by assuring vendors that the customers attempting to buy the vendors' wares are who they say they are (authentication) and by encrypting sensitive information (such as credit-card numbers) so that it cannot be intercepted while en route. Secure HTTP was developed by Enterprise Integration Technology (EIT) and the *National Center for Supercomputer Applications (NCSA),* with subsequent commercial development by Terisa Systems. *Netscape Communications* developed a competing security technology, the Secure Sockets Layer *(SSL)* protocol. Although S-HTTP is still used by some *Web servers,* SSL has emerged as the clear de facto stand—and for good reason. S-HTTP is an application-layer protocol, which means that it cannot support secure, encrypted exchange of other types of data, including *FTP* or *NNTP* resources.

Shugart Associates Standard Interface (SASI)   An early-1980s standard for connecting *hard disks* to personal computers. SASI later became the *Small Computer System Interface (SCSI)* standard.

sig   Common abbreviation for *signature.*

SIG   See *special interest group.*

signal   The portion of a transmission that coherently represents information, unlike the random and meaningless *line noise* that occurs in the transmission channel.

signal–to–noise ratio   In *Usenet,* the ratio between meaningful content and noise (ranting, raving, and *flaming*). A good *newsgroup* has a high signal-to-noise ratio; a poor newsgroup has a low one. A major advantage of *moderated newsgroups* is to ensure a high signal-to-noise ratio. The term was originally used in electrical engineering to describe the ratio of information to background noise in an electronic circuit.

signature   1. In *e-mail* and *Usenet newsgroups,* a brief file (of approximately three or four lines) that contains the message sender's name, organization, address, e-mail address, and (optionally) telephone numbers. You can configure most systems to add this file automatically at the end of each message you send. *Netiquette* advises against long, complicated signatures, especially when posting to Usenet. See *ASCII art.* 2. In virus-protection utilities, program code identifiable as belonging to a known *virus.*

silicon chip　See *chip.*

Silicon Valley　An area in California's Santa Clara Valley with one of the largest concentrations of high-technology businesses in the world. The word silicon suggests the area's prominence in *chip* design and manufacturing.

SIM　See *Society for Information Management.*

SIMM　See *single in-line memory module.*

simple list text chart　In *presentation graphics,* a text chart used to display items in no particular order, with each item given equal emphasis.

Simple Mail Transport Protocol (SMTP)　An *Internet* protocol that governs the transmission of *e-mail* over computer networks. SMTP is simple indeed; it does not provide any support for the transmission of data other than plain text. For this reason, the Multipurpose Internet Mail Extensions *(MIME)* provide support for *binary files* of many types, and *S/MIME* provides support for *encrypted* e-mail.

Simple Network Management Protocol (SNMP)　A method for keeping track of various *hardware* devices, such as *printers,* connected to a *network.* SNMP can tell network administrators when printers are low on paper or *toner,* or when a paper jam has occurred. SNMP seems destined to be replaced by the *Microsoft at Work* standard or *the Desktop Management Interface (DMI)* standard.

simulation　An analytical technique in which an analyst investigates an item's properties by creating a *model* of the item and exploring the model's behavior. Aeronautical engineers, for example, use computer simulation techniques to design and test thousands of alternative aircraft models quickly, pushing the wind tunnel toward obsolescence in modern aerospace firms. Simulation is also applied in education (to perform virtual science experiments) and in business (to perform financial *what-if analyses*). As with any model, however, a simulation is only as good as its underlying assumptions. If these assumptions aren't correct, the model doesn't accurately mimic the behavior of the real-world system being simulated.

single density   A magnetic recording scheme for digital data that uses a technique called *frequency modulation (FM) recording.* Single-density disks, common in early personal computing, use large-grained magnetic particles. Such disks have low storage capacity, such as 90K per disk, and are rarely used today. They have been superseded by *double-density* disks with finer grained partitions, and high-density disks with even finer partitions. See *Modified Frequency Modulation (MFM).*

single in-line memory module *(SIMM)*   A plug-in memory unit that contains all the chips required add 256K, 1M, 2M, or more of *random-access memory (RAM)* to a computer.

single in-line package (SIP)   A set of *random-access memory (RAM)* chips encased in hard plastic and attached to the *motherboard* with pins. Modern computers have replaced SIPs with *single in-line memory modules (SIMMs).*

single in-line pinned packages (SIPPs*)   Synonymous with *single in-line package (SIP).*

single-pass scanner   Any *scanner* that scans a document in one *scanning pass,* but especially a *color scanner* that does so. Single-pass color scanners collect data about all three primary colors on a single trip, unlike *triple-pass scanners,* which require three trips. Single-pass scanners are not necessarily faster than triple-pass scanners, however.

single-sided disk   A *floppy disk* designed so that only one side of the disk can be used for read/write operations. See *single density.*

SIP   See *single in-line package.*

SIPP   See *single in-line package.*

site license   An agreement between a software publisher and a buyer that permits the buyer to make copies of specific software for internal use. Often a company using a *local area network (LAN)* buys a site license for a program so that all the users on the LAN can access the program. Most site licenses limit the number of copies that the purchasing organization can make. The cost per copy is much less than that of individually purchased copies.

sixteen-bit   See *16-bit computer.*

skip factor   In a *presentation graphics program,* an increment that specifies how many *data* items the program should skip when it labels a chart or graph. Use a skip factor when the category axis is too crowded with headings. If you are labeling an axis with months, for example, a skip factor of three displays the name of every third month.

Skipjack   A *public key encryption algorithm,* reportedly closely related to the *Diffie-Hellman public key encryption algorithm,* that the U.S. National Security Agency wants American citizens and others to use when they encrypt their Internet transactions. The algorithm contains a *key recover* scheme that would enable government investigators to obtain the decoding key from a (supposedly) independent authority, and only when "public safety" or "national security" was at stake. The algorithm has been ignored by the cryptographic industry because the government has refused to enable cryptographers to examine the algorithm, which some suspect to contain deliberate built-in weaknesses that would aid government surveillance of encrypted communications.

slave   The second *hard disk* in a series of two connected to an *Integrated Drive Electronics (IDE) host adapter.* The first disk in the series, the *master* disk, does not control the disk, but decodes instructions from the host adapter before sending them to the slave.

sleep mode   In computers equipped with *power-management* features, a state in which the *microprocessor* shuts down nonessential components during periods of disuse. Often, computers in sleep mode write the contents of their *random-access memory (RAM)* to a *hard disk* to save the energy required to refresh memory chips. See *Display Power Management Signaling (DPMS)* and *green PC.*

slider   See *write-protect tab.*

slide show   In *presentation graphics,* a predetermined list of charts and graphs displayed one after the other.

SLIP   Acronym for Serial Line Internet Protocol. The earliest of two *Internet* standards specifying how a *workstation* or *personal computer* can link to the *Internet* by means of a *dialup connection* (the other standard is *PPP*). SLIP defines the transport of data *packets* through an *asynchronous* telephone line. Therefore, SLIP enables computers not directly connected to *local area networks (LANs)* to be fully connected to the Internet. This mode of connectivity is far superior to a *shell account* (a dialup, text-only account on a Unix computer) because it enables you to use the Internet tools of your choice (such as a graphical *Web browser*) to run more than one Internet application at a time and to download data directly to your computer, with no intermediate storage required.

SLIP/PPP   A commonly used abbreviation for the two types of dialup Internet access that directly integrate your computer with the Internet: *SLIP* and *PPP*. See *shell account*.

slot   See *expansion slot*.

slot pitch   The distance between the wires of a *Trinitron*-type *monitor's aperture grille*. Although slot pitch is an important specification for Trinitron-type monitors, *screen pitch* is even more important.

slow mail   A "polite" term for the postal service. See *snail mail*.

slug   In *word processing* and *desktop publishing (DTP)*, a code inserted in headers or footers to generate page numbers when the document is printed.

Small Computer System Interface (SCSI)   An interface amounting to a complete *expansion bus* in which you can plug devices such as *hard disk drives, CD-ROM drives, scanners,* and *laser printers*. The most common SCSI device in use is the SCSI hard disk, which contains most of the controller circuitry, leaving the SCSI interface free to communicate with other peripherals. You can *daisy chain* as many as seven SCSI devices to a single SCSI port. See *Enhanced System Device Interface (ESDI)* and *ST-506/ST-412*.

Small Scale Integration (SSI)   The first generation of *semiconductor* technology, developed during the 1950s, in which it is possible to fabricate devices with between 2 and 100 on each individual flake of silicon.

SmallTalk   A *high-level, declarative programming language* and *programming environment* that treats computations as *objects* that send messages to one another. SmallTalk encourages the *programmer* to define objects in terms relevant to the intended application. The language is highly extensible because it enables you to create objects, which can be reused, quite easily. SmallTalk inspired *HyperTalk,* the *software command language* of *HyperCard,* an application provided with every *Macintosh* produced since 1987. In this new guise, SmallTalk fulfills its goal of making programming more accessible; tens of thousands of Macintosh users have learned how to program in HyperTalk. See *object-oriented programming (OOP) language.*

smart card   A credit–card sized *token* that contains a microprocessor and memory circuits used for authenticating a user of computer, banking, or transportation services. When used for authentication purposes, a smart card is often paired with a *personal identification number (PIN)*; the combination between what you have (the token) and what you know (the PIN) is considered to establish *strong authentication.*

SMARTDRV   In *MS-DOS* and *Microsoft Windows,* a *disk cache* program that substantially speeds apparent disk access times by caching frequently accessed program code.

smart machine   Any device containing *microprocessor*-based electronics that enables the device either to branch to alternative operating sequences depending on external conditions, to repeat operations until a condition is fulfilled, or to execute a series of instructions repetitively. Microprocessors are so inexpensive that they can be embedded in even the most prosaic of everyday devices, such as toasters, coffeemakers, and ovens.

smart terminal   In a *multi-user system,* a *terminal* that contains its own processing circuitry so that it not only retrieves data from the *host* computer, but also carries out additional processing operations and runs host–delivered programs.

smiley   See *emoticon.*

S/MIME   Abbreviation for Secure Multipurpose Internet Mail Extensions. An addition to the *MIME* protocol that supports the exchange of encrypted *e-mail* via the *Internet.* S/MIME uses RSA's *public-key encryption algorithm* for the initial authentication (which makes use of *certificates*); after the secure connection is established, an exchange of *symmetric encryption algorithm* keys occurs.

SMIS See *Society for Information Management.*

SMP See *symmetric multiprocessing.*

SMTP See *Simple Mail Transport Protocol.*

SNA See *Systems Network Architecture.*

snaf The messy strips of waste paper that litter the office after you remove the perforated edge from continuous, *tractor-fed printer* paper. The term *snaf* was the winning entry in a contest sponsored by National Public Radio's *All Things Considered.* The runner-up, *perfory,* is worthy of mention.

snail mail A derogatory term for the postal service. In an *e-mail* message, you might say "I'm sending the article to you by snail mail."

snaking columns See *newspaper columns.*

snap-on pointing device In *portable computers,* a *pointing device* that snaps on to the side of the computer's *case* in a special port. No *serial port* or *mouse* port cable is required. Snap-on pointing devices are convenient because they save you from having to connect the serial or mouse port cable every time that you want to use the computer. Instead, you simply snap the *trackball* into its receptacle. See *built-in pointing device* and *clip-on pointing device.*

snapshot See *Print Screen (PrtScr)* and *screen capture.*

sneakernet A *network architecture* in which a person physically carries a data-laden *floppy disk* or *tape* from one computer to another. Although sneakernets usually are small, they sometimes involve transcontinental air travel.

sniffer Synonymous with packet sniffer. A program that intercepts routed *Internet* data and examines each packet in search of specified information, such as passwords transmitted in *cleartext.*

SNOBOL A *high-level programming language* designed for text-processing applications. SNOBOL (String-Oriented Symbolic Language), which has particularly strong text pattern-matching capabilities, has been used for research work in fields such as language translation, the generation of indexes or concordances to literary works, and text reformatting. However, SNOBOL tends to generate inefficient, hard-to-read *source code,* and thus is rarely used. See *BASIC* and *FORTRAN.*

snow   See *video noise.*

soc hierarchy   In *Usenet,* one of the *standard newsgroup hierar-chies.* The soc newsgroups deal with social issues, social groups, and world cultures.

social engineering   A method used by computer intruders to obtain passwords for *unauthorized access.* Typically, this involves calling an authorized user of a computer system, and posing as a network administrator. The caller says, "We've run into a serious problem and we can't access your mailbox. If you give me your password, there's a chance we can save your mail."

Society for Information Management (SIM)   A professional society for executives in information-systems fields that has branches in many cities. The SIM was formerly called the Society for Management Information Systems (SMIS).

Society for Management Information Systems (SMIS)   See *Society for Information Management.*

socket   In the *Internet* and *Unix,* a virtual *port* that enables *client* applications to connect to the appropriate *server.* To achieve a connection, a client needs to specify both the *IP address* and the *port number* of the server application.

soft   Temporary or changeable, as opposed to *hard* (perma-nently wired, physically fixed, or inflexible). Compare *software, soft return,* and a page break inserted by a *word processing program* and subject to change if you add or delete text, to *hardware,* a *hard return,* and a page break that you insert manually and that remains fixed in place despite further editing.

soft boot   A system restart that does not involve switching the power off and on (a *hard boot*).

soft cell boundary   In a *spreadsheet program,* a feature of *cells* that enable you to enter labels that are longer than the cell's width (unless the adjacent cells are occupied).

soft font   See *downloadable font.*

soft hyphen   A hyphen formatted so that it doesn't take effect unless the word that contains the hyphen otherwise *word wraps* to the next line. In that event, the word is hyphenated to improve the *kerning* of the line. Synonymous with optional hyphen. See *hard hyphen.*

soft page break In a *word processing program,* a page break that the program inserts based on the current format of the text. This page break could move up or down if you insert or delete text or change margins, page size, or fonts. See *forced page break.*

soft return In a *word processing program,* a line break that the program inserts to maintain the margins. The location of soft returns changes automatically if you change the margins or insert or delete text. See *hard page break* and *word wrap.*

soft-sectored disk A disk that, when new, contains no fixed magnetic patterns of tracks or sectors. *Tracks* and *sectors* are created during *formatting.*

soft start See *warm boot.*

software A computer program or programs, in contrast to the physical equipment on which programs run *(hardware).* Simultaneously singular and plural, the word compels some speakers to add the redundant "software program" or "software programs" in an attempt to clarify the noun's number. Software is conventionally divided into two categories, system software (programs needed to operate the computer) and application programs (programs that enable users to perform tasks using the computer). See *firmware* and *hardware.*

software cache A large area of *random-access memory (RAM)* that a program, such as SMARTDRV.EXE, sets aside to store frequently accessed data and program instructions. A 1*M* to 2M software cache can speed up disk-intensive applications such as *database management programs.*

software compatibility The capability of a computer system to run a specific type of software. The Commodore 64, for example, isn't software-compatible with software written for the Apple II, even though both computers use the MOS Technology 6502 microprocessor.

software engineering An applied science devoted to improving and optimizing the production of *software.*

software error control An *error-correction protocol* that resides partly or entirely in a *communications program* rather than in *modem* hardware. Software error control makes modems cheaper, but also taxes the rest of the *computer system* and is supported by very few communications programs. For these reasons, you should avoid software error control.

software handshaking A method of *flow control* that ensures that the data that a *modem* sends does not overwhelm the modem with which it is communicating. In a software hand-shaking scheme, such as *XON/XOFF handshaking,* modems exchange special codes when they are ready to send and receive data.

software interpolation In *scanners,* a method of improving the scanner's true optical resolution by using computer algorithms to guess how the image would appear at a higher *resolution.*

software license A legal agreement included with commercial programs that specifies the rights and obligations of the program's purchaser and limits the liability of the software publisher. See *site license.*

software package A *program* delivered to the user in a complete and ready-to-run form, including all necessary *utility programs* and *documentation.* See *application software.*

software patent A patent, sometimes granted by the U.S. patent office but not often recognized by other nations, on a computer algorithm or programming technique. A software patent is a contradiction in terms; formal descriptions of mathematical truths cannot be granted patents by any civilization that hopes to witness continued technological progress.

software piracy The illegal duplication of copyrighted software without the permission of the software publisher.

software protection See *copy protection.*

software suite A collection of programs, which are generally also for sale individually, that taken together provide what is intended to be a comprehensive solution for the customer. For example, Netscape's SuiteSpot server suite contains servers for a variety of applications, including Web publishing, e-mail, news-groups, and more.

SoHo Abbreviation for Small Office/Home Office, a growing and important market for computers and computer software.

Solaris A *flavor* of the *Unix* operating system developed by Sun Microsystems. Solaris includes *OpenWindows,* an *X-windows*-based *Graphical User Interface (GUI).*

SONET Acronym for Synchronous Optical Network. An emerging standard for high-speed networks based on *fiber-optic cable.* The basic data transfer rate is 51.8 megabits per second, which is more than 50 times the data capacity (*bandwidth*) of the *T1* lines that carry much of the data traffic in industrialized nations. Bandwidth can be increased in multiples of 51.8 megabits per second, up to a maximum of 48 gigabits per second. Synonymous with Synchronous Digital Hierarchy (SDH), the non-U.S. name for this standard.

sort An operation that rearranges data so it is in a specified ascending or descending order, usually alphabetical or numerical.

sort key In *sort* operations, the data that determines the order in which the operation arranges data records. See *primary key* and *secondary key.* A *database* sort key is the *data field* by which to sort; in a *spreadsheet,* the sort key is the column or row used to arrange the data in alphabetical or numerical order. In a word processing program, the sort key is a word, but the word can be in any position.

sort order The order, such as ascending and descending, in which a program arranges data when performing a *sort.* Most programs also sort data in the standard order of ASCII characters. Synonymous with *collating sequence.* See *ASCII sort order* and *dictionary sort.*

sound board An *adapter* that adds digital sound reproduction capabilities to an *IBM PC-compatible personal computer,* making it more competitive with *Macintosh* computers and better suited to *multimedia applications.*

sound card See *sound board.*

soundex An algorithm for retrieving records from a *data base* that can retrieve items that are homonyms of the search terms. A soundex search will retrieve "Woulthers" as well as "Walters."

Sound Recorder A *Microsoft Windows 95* accessory that you use to record and play back sounds. To operate Sound Recorder, your system must have a Multimedia Personal Computer

(MPC)-compatible *sound board* with recording capabilities, including a microphone. Sound Recorder serves as a control device, turning your computer into a digital tape recorder and saving recordings in .WAV files that other MPC-compatible programs can access.

source   The record, *file, document,* or disk from which information is taken or moved, as opposed to the *destination.*

source code   In a *high-level programming language,* the typed program instructions that *programmers* write before the program is *compiled* or *interpreted* into *machine language* instructions the computer can execute.

source document   In *dynamic data exchange (DDE)* and Object Linking and Embedding *(OLE),* the *document* that contains data linked to copies of that data in other documents, called *destination documents.*

source file   In many *MS-DOS* commands, the file from which data or program instructions are copied. See *destination file.*

source worksheet   In *Microsoft Excel,* a *worksheet* containing a *cell* or *range* linked to one or more *dependent worksheets.* The dependent worksheets reflect the changes that you make to the source worksheet.

SPA   See *Association for Systems Management (ASM).*

spaghetti code   A poorly organized *program* that results from excessive use of GOTO statements, making the program almost impossible to read and debug. The cure is to use a well-structured programming language (such as *QuickBASIC, C,* or *Pascal)* that offers a full set of control structures. See *structured programming.*

spam   Unsolicited advertising in a *Usenet* newsgroup or *e-mail.* The term is apparently derived from a Monty Python skit, in which patrons of a restaurant are unable to converse due to the constant repetition of "Spam, spam, eggs and spam, spam, spam, [etc.]" by a group of Vikings in the scene's background.

SPARC   Acronym for Scalable Processor Architecture. An open standard for a *RISC* microprocessor. Sun Microsystems manufactures a series of workstations based on the SPARC architecture called SPARCstations.

SPARCstation   See *SPARC.*

spawn   In *Unix,* to initiate a *child process* for accomplishing further processing tasks. Early versions of *Netscape Navigator* for Windows and Macintosh once displayed the message "spawning external process" when starting a *helper program,* betraying the program's Unix roots.

SPEC   See *Standard Performance Evaluation Corporation.*

SPEC 95   A pair of *benchmarks,* established by the *Standard Performance Evaluation Corporation (SPEC),* that establishes a new numerical system for evaluating the performance of microprocessors. The new standard was needed due to significant increases in the processing throughput of microprocessors, the growing complexity of applications, and the availability of more accurate measurement tools. The two benchmarks are *SPECint95* and *SPECfp95.*

SPECfp95   A *benchmark* that evaluates the performance of *microprocessors* based on the speed with which they execute *floating-point* operations.

SPECint95   A *benchmark* that evaluates the performance of *microprocessors* based on the speed with which they execute integer (whole number) operations.

**special interest group (SIG*)*   A subgroup of an organization or *network,* consisting of members who share a common interest. Common SIG topics include software, hobbies, sports, and literary genres such as mystery or science fiction. See *user group.*

speculative execution   A method of analyzing instructions entering a *microprocessor* with *superscalar architecture* and determining how to route the instructions through the *pipelines* as efficiently as possible. Speculative execution, supposedly employed on Intel's *P6* microprocessor, greatly increases a microprocessor's *throughput.*

speech recognition   The decoding of human speech into transcribed text by means of a computer program. To recognize spoken words, the program must transcribe the incoming sound signal into a digitized representation, which must then be compared to an enormous database of digitized representations of spoken words. To transcribe speech with any tolerable degree of accuracy, users must speak each word independently, with a pause between each word (see *discrete speech recognition*). This substantially slows down the speed of speech recognition systems and calls their utility into question, save in the case of physical disabilities that would prevent input by other means. Dragon Software, a leader in the speech recognition field, has announced a new speech recognition technology that the company claims is capable of recognizing continuous speech. This and other improvements in speech recognition algorithms, coupled with impressive increases in computing horsepower, will eventually relegate the keyboard and mouse—and the *repetitive strain injuries (RSI)* that they cause—to the technological dustbin.

speech synthesis   Computer production of audio output that resembles human speech. Such output is particularly useful to visually impaired computer users. Unlike *speech recognition,* speech synthesis technology is well developed. Existing speech synthesis boards are inexpensive and can do an impressive job of reading virtually any file containing English sentences in ASCII script—although, to some listeners, the English sounds as though it's being spoken with a Czech accent.

spell checker   A *program,* often a feature of *word processing* programs, that checks for the correct spelling of words in a *document* by comparing each word against a file of correctly spelled words. A good spell checker displays suggestions for the correct spelling of a word and enables you to replace the misspelled word with the correct one. You usually can add words to the spell checker's dictionary.

spider   A program that prowls the *Internet,* attempting to locate new, publicly accessible resources such as *World Wide Web (WWW)* documents, files available in public *File Transfer Protocol (FTP) archives,* and *Gopher* documents. Also called wanderers or robots, spiders contribute their discoveries to a *database,* which Internet users can search by using an Internet-accessible *search engine* (such as *Lycos* or *WebCrawler*). Spiders are necessary because the rate at which people are creating new Internet documents greatly exceeds manual indexing capacity.

spike   See *surge.*

spindle   The "axle" on which a *hard* or *floppy disk* turns. The spindle, which is turned by a *spindle motor,* is not permanently attached to floppy disks but is permanently attached at the center of *hard disk* platters.

spindle motor   The electric motor—either a *synchronous motor* or a *servo-controlled DC motor*—that turns *hard* and *floppy disks.* Floppy-disk spindle motors turn only when you are writing data to a disk in your drive, but hard disk spindle motors turn whenever your computer is on.

split bar   In a *Graphical User Interface (GUI)* such as *Microsoft Windows 95* or the *Macintosh Finder,* a bar that you can drag to split the *window* horizontally or vertically.

split screen   A display technique that divides the screen into two or more *windows.* In *word processing programs* that have split-screen capabilities, you can usually display two parts of the same document independently or display more than one document. Splitting the screen is useful when you want to refer to one document, or part of a document, while writing in another. The technique also facilitates cut-and-paste editing.

spoiler   In a *Usenet newsgroup,* a message that contains the ending of a novel, movie, or television program, or the solution to a computer or video game. Network etiquette (or *netiquette*) requires that you encrypt such messages so that users can't read them unless they choose to do so. In *Usenet* newsgroups, the *encryption* technique is called *rot-13.*

spoofing   1. A method of increasing the apparent speed of a network by configuring routers so that they send faked conformation signals in response to a workstation's *polling* signals, which attempt to confirm that a distant server is still connected. Polling signals consume a great deal of network bandwidth, but this is unnecessary in today's more reliable network environment. Spoofing enables network administrators to cut down on network *overhead* while still retaining an acceptable level of service. 2. A method of falsifying the *IP address* of an Internet *server* by altering the IP address recorded in the transmitted *packets.* The fact that spoofing is possible reflects an underlying security hole of prodigious magnitude in the current Internet *protocol suite*: The *headers* of data packets are transmitted in *cleartext* with no network-level support for *authenticating* their true origin.

spooler   A *utility program,* often included with an *operating system,* that routes *printer* commands to a file on disk or in *random-access memory (RAM)* rather than to the printer, and then doles out the printer commands when the *central processing unit (CPU)* is idle. A print spooler provides *background printing;* your program thinks that it's printing to a super-fast printer, but the spooler is actually directing the printer output to RAM or a disk file. You can continue working with your program, and the spooler guides the printer data to the printer whenever the CPU isn't busy handling your work.

spot color   A color defined by the *Pantone Matching System (PMS)*. Spot color is a form of *device-independent color.*

spreadsheet   In a *spreadsheet program,* a graphic representation of an accountant's worksheet, replete with rows and columns for recording *labels* (headings and subheadings) and values. A spreadsheet is a matrix of rows (usually numbered) and columns (usually assigned alphabetical letters) that form individual *cells.* Each cell has a distinct *cell address,* such as B4 or D19. Into each cell, you can place a value, which is a number or a hidden formula that performs a calculation, or a *label,* which is a heading or explanatory text. A formula can contain constants, such as 2+2, but the most useful formulas contain cell references, such as D9+D10. By placing formulas in a spreadsheet's cells, you can create a complex network of links among the parts of a spreadsheet. After embedding formulas, you can adjust constants—such as the tax rate or acceleration due to gravity—to see how the bottom line changes.

spreadsheet program   A *program* that simulates an accountant's *worksheet* on-screen and lets you embed hidden *formulas* that perform calculations on the visible data. Many spreadsheet programs also include powerful *graphics* and presentation capabilities to create attractive products.

sputtering   Like *plating,* a means of coating *hard disk substrate* with *thin-film magnetic media.* Sputtering uses heat and the attraction of oppositely charged particles to coat the platters evenly.

SQL   Acronym for Structured Query Language. (Pronounced "sequel.") In *database management systems,* an IBM-developed *query language* that has become the de facto standard for querying databases in a *client/server network.* The four basic commands (SELECT, UPDATE, DELETE, and INSERT) correspond to the four basic functions of *data manipulation* (*data retrieval, data modification, data deletion,* and *data insertion,* respectively). SQL queries approximate the structure of an English *natural-language* query. A data table consisting of columns (corresponding to data fields) and rows (corresponding to data records) displays a query's results. See *ODBC.*

squelch In a *network,* to suspend or cancel a *problem user's* access privileges. A network might squelch such privileges after a user repeatedly violates the terms under which the *account* was created.

SRAM Acronym for static random access memory. A type of *random-access memory (RAM) chip* that holds its contents without constant *refreshing* from the *central processing unit (CPU).* Although as *volatile* as *dynamic random-access memory (DRAM)* chips, SRAM doesn't require the CPU to refresh its contents several hundred times per second. These chips are substantially faster but also are significantly more expensive than DRAM chips and are, there-fore, most often used for RAM *caches.* Two types of SRAM are available: asynchronous and synchronous. Unlike asynchronous SRAM, synchronous SRAM is significantly faster because it is able to synchronize with the microprocessor's *clock speed,* enabling it to perform operations that are timed by the *system clock;* synchronous SRAM is needed for today's fast micro-processors. See *cache memory* and *pipeline burst cache.*

S register A special unit of memory inside a *modem* that con-tains alterations to the *AT command set,* such as the number of rings to wait before answering a call or the time to wait for the *carrier* to be established.

SSL Acronym for Secure Sockets Layer. An *Internet* security standard proposed by *Netscape Communications* and incorpo-rated into its *Netscape Navigator* browser and *Netscape Commerce Server* software. Unlike its chief competition, *S-HTTP,* SSL is application-independent—it works with all Internet tools, not just the *World Wide Web (WWW).* This is because SSL functions at the *network layer* rather than the *application layer,* and is thus available to any SSL-ready Internet application, including *news-readers.* (Netscape has developed a secure SSL newsreader for private organizational newsgroups, called *Collabra.*) Applications that use SSL use *RSA public key encryption* and RSA *certificates* and *digital signatures* to establish the identities of parties to the transaction; after the link is established, a key exchange takes place, and RSA's *RC4* encryption technology (a *symmetric key encryption algorithm*) is used to secure the transaction. With the 128-bit *keys* used for SSL communication within the U.S., the encrypted transaction would be *computationally infeasible* to decode, so it is safe from snoopers and criminals. (The 40-bit version used in export versions of *Netscape Navigator,* however, is not secure, and should not be avoided for commercial transactions.)

ST-506/ST-412 A hard disk *interface standard* once widely used in IBM and IBM-compatible computers. These drives, virtually unavailable today, are slower and cheaper than drives that use more recent interface standards, such as *Enhanced System Device Interface (ESDI), Integrated Drive Electronics (IDE),* and *Small Computer System Interface (SCSI).* The ST-506/ST-412 interface uses the *Modified Frequency Modulation (MFM)* and *Run-Length Limited (RLL)* standards.

stack In *programming,* a *data structure* in which the first items inserted are the last ones removed. Programs that use *control structures* use the Last In First Out (LIFO) data structure. A stack enables the computer to track what it was doing when it branched or jumped to a procedure. In *HyperCard,* the term *stack* refers to a file that contains one or more cards that share a common background.

stacked column graph A column graph that displays two or more data series on top of one another. See *histogram.*

STACKS In *MS-DOS,* an area set aside to store information about the current task when an interrupt instruction is issued. After processing the interrupt, DOS uses the information in the stack to resume the original task. If you are running an *application program* that requires stacks, include a STACKS command in the *CONFIG.SYS* file to specify the size and number of stacks that you want set aside.

staggered windows See *cascading windows.*

stale Out of date; no longer accurate.

stale link In the *World Wide Web (WWW),* a *hyperlink* to a document that has been erased or moved. Synonymous with black hole.

stand-alone Self-sufficient; not requiring any additional component or service.

stand-alone computer A *computer system* dedicated to meeting all the computing needs of an individual user. The user chooses just the *software* needed for his or her daily tasks. Links with other computers, if any, are incidental to the system's chief purpose. See *distributed processing system, multi-user system,* and *professional workstation.*

stand–alone server   In a *client/server* network, a *server* that maintains its own *authentication* and user accounting services. Although this is convenient for a small network, it quickly becomes a liability in a larger network, in which users may have to access several servers to get the data they need. If each of these servers is a stand-alone server, users will have to supply multiple login names and passwords. An additional liability: Each server represents a different point of vulnerability to intrusion by unauthorized users. In networks with several servers, a better solution is to move authentication and user accounting to the network level (see *DCE* and *Kerberos*).

standard   In computing, a set of rules or specifications which, taken together, define the architecture of a hardware device, program, or operating system. Standards are often maintained by an independent standard body such as the *American National Standards Association (ANSI).* See *de facto standard, open standard,* and *proprietary standard.*

Standard Generalized Markup Language   See *SGML.*

standard newsgroup hierarchy   In *Usenet,* a collection of categories that every Usenet site is expected to carry, if sufficient storage room exists. The standard *newsgroup hierarchy* includes the following newsgroup categories: *comp.*★, *misc.*★, *news.*★, *rec.*★, *sci.*★, *soc.*★, and *talk*★. A voting process creates new newsgroups within the standard newsgroup hierarchies. See *alt hierarchy* and *Call for Votes (CFV).*

standard parallel port   A *parallel port* that transfers *data,* in one direction only, at about 200K per second. Used since the days of the first IBM personal computers, standard parallel ports connect computers to *peripherals* such as *printers.* However, *bidirectional parallel ports* such as the *enhanced parallel port (EPP)* and the *extended capabilities port (ECP)* have made the standard parallel port obsolete.

Standard Performance Evaluation Corporation (SPEC)
A consortium of computer-industry companies, founded in 1988, that works to establish fair *benchmark* tests for evaluating

computers. SPEC has developed several tests thus far: the CINT92 test, which measures integer calculations, and the CFP92 test, which tests *floating-point* computations.

standby UPS   An *uninterruptible power supply (UPS)* that protects against complete power failure but does not protect against reductions in line voltage (brownouts). Standby units are less expensive than *line interactive UPS* devices, but their inability to protect against brownouts might render them generally useless. See *surge protector.*

star network   In *local area networks (LANs),* a centralized *network topology* with a physical layout that resembles a star. At the center is a central network processor or wiring concentrator; the nodes are arranged around and connected directly to the central point. A star network's wiring costs are considerably higher than those of other network topologies because each *workstation* requires a cable that links the workstation directly to the central processor.

start bit   In *serial communications,* a *bit* inserted into the data stream to inform the receiving computer that a byte of data is to follow. See *asynchronous communication* and *stop bit.*

starting point   In the *World Wide Web (WWW),* a Web document that contains useful starting points for Web navigation, such as introductions to the *Internet* and to the Web, *subject trees, search engines,* and interesting Web sites.

start page   In a *Web browser,* the page that appears when the user launches the program (or clicks the Home button on the toolbar). By default, this is generally the browser publisher's home page; both *Netscape Navigator* and *Microsoft Internet Explorer* enable users to customize the start page.

startup disk   The disk that you normally use to boot your computer. The disk—often a *hard disk*—contains portions of the *operating system.* Synonymous with boot disk and system disk.

startup screen   A text or *graphics* display at the beginning of a program. Usually, the startup screen includes the program name and version and often contains a distinctive program logo.

statement   In a *high-level programming language,* an expression that can generate *machine language instructions* when the program is interpreted or compiled.

state-of-the-art   Technically sophisticated, representing the highest level of technical achievement.

static object   A *document* or portion of a document pasted into a *destination document* using standard copy-and-paste techniques. The object doesn't change if you make changes to the *source document*. To update the information in the object, you make changes to the source document and copy from it again. See *embedded object, linked object,* and *OLE.*

static random-access memory   See *SRAM.*

station   See *workstation.*

statistical software   An *application program* that makes conducting statistical tests and measurements easier.

status bar   In a *Graphical User Interface (GUI),* a bar across the bottom of the window that displays information about the program.

status line   A line of an *application program's* display screen, usually at the bottom, that describes the state of the program. The information presented in the status line often includes the name of the *file* that you are modifying, the cursor location, and the name of any toggle keys that you have pressed, such as *Num Lock* or *Caps Lock.*

stem   In *typography,* the main vertical stroke of a character.

stepper motor   A motor that makes a precise fraction of a turn each time that it receives an electrical impulse. Stepping motors are used as part of *head actuator* mechanisms in *hard* and *floppy disk drives.*

stepping motor   See *stepper motor.*

stereoscopy   A technology that presents two pictures taken from slightly different perspectives that, when viewed together using a stereoscope, creates a profound illusion of three-dimensional space. Stereoscopic viewers were popular in the last century, and the technology lives on today as one of the foundations of *virtual reality (VR).* See *head-mounted display (HMD).*

stickup initial   See *initial.*

S
T
U

stop bit   In *serial communications,* a *bit* inserted into the data stream to inform the receiving computer that the transmission of a *byte* of data is complete. See *asynchronous communication* and *start bit.*

storage   The retention of program instructions and data within the computer so that this information is available for processing purposes. See *primary storage* and *secondary storage.*

storage device   Any optical or magnetic device capable of information storage functions in a computer system. See *secondary storage.*

storage medium   In a *storage device,* the material that retains the stored information (such as the magnetic material on the surface of a floppy disk).

store–and–forward network   A *wide area network (WAN)* created by means of the telephone system. Each computer in the network stores messages received during the day. At night, when telephone rates are low, the computer's automatic software dials a central distribution site. The computer uploads those messages addressed to other computers on the system and downloads messages from other computers. Store-and-forward technology is the basis of the *Unix-to-Unix Copy Program (UUCP),* a Unix network, and *FidoNet,* one of several wide area networks that link computer *bulletin board systems (BBS).*

stored program concept   The idea, which underlies the *architecture* of all modern computers, that programs should be stored in *memory* with *data.* This concept suggests that a program can jump back and forth through instructions instead of executing them sequentially. This insight launched virtually the entire world of modern computing, but it also introduced a known limitation; see *von Neumann bottleneck* and *parallel processing.*

storefront   In the *World Wide Web (WWW),* a Web document that establishes a commercial enterprise's presence on the Web. Typically, a storefront does not attempt to provide a complete catalog, but instead illustrates a few items or services that typify what the firm has to offer. Web marketing experience demonstrates that the most successful storefronts are those that offer some interesting "freebies," such as information or downloadable *software.* As security protocols become more widely used, customers will be able to use their credit cards safely to place orders. See *S-HTTP* and *SSL.*

stream   A continuous flow of data through a channel, in contrast to data delivery by means of *packets* (fixed, numbered, and addressed units of data that may arrive out of order).

streaming audio   An *Internet* sound delivery technology that sends audio data as a continuous, compressed stream that is played back on the fly. In contrast to downloaded sounds, which may not begin playing for several minutes, streaming audio begins almost immediately. To get acceptable sound quality, the user needs a fast modem connection (preferably 28 MHz or better). At best, though, the sound is that of a good AM radio—acceptable for voice, but only marginal for music. There is no universally-supported streaming audio standard; the de facto standard is *Real Audio.*

streaming tape drive   A *secondary storage device* that uses continuous tape, contained in a cartridge, for *backup* purposes.

streaming video   An *Internet* video delivery technology that sends video data as a continuous, compressed stream that is played back on the fly. Like *streaming audio,* streaming videos begin playing almost immediately. A high-speed modem is required. Quality is marginal; the video appears in a small, on-screen window, and motion is jerky.

stress test   An *alpha test* procedure in which the manufacturer tries to determine how a program will behave under heavy demands. By pushing lots of data into a program, a manufacturer can determine whether, when, and how the program will fail under real-life conditions.

strikeout   See *strikethrough.*

strikethrough   A font attribute where text is struck through with a hyphen, as in the following example:

~~This text has strikethrough formatting~~.

Strikethrough is often used to mark text to be deleted from a co-authored document so that the other author can see changes easily. Also called strikeout. See *redlining.*

string 1. In programming, a series of alphanumeric characters or a unit of data other than a numeric value. 2. A *keyword* in a *database* search.

string formula In a *spreadsheet program,* a *formula* that performs a *string operation* such as changing a label to upper- or lowercase.

string operation A computation performed on alphanumeric characters. Computers can't understand the meaning of words, and therefore can't process them like people do; however, computers can perform simple processing operations on textual data, such as comparing two *strings* to see whether they're the same, calculating the number of characters in a string, and arranging strings in *ASCII order.*

String-Oriented Symbolic Language See *SNOBOL.*

stroke weight The width of the lines that make up a character. "Light," "medium," and "bold" are designators of stroke weight for *fonts.*

strong authentication In computer security, the use of *authentication* measures that go beyond supplying a reusable password. Strong authentication techniques include the use of *digital signatures* and *certificates, tokens,* and *smart cards.*

structured programming A set of quality standards that make *programs* more verbose but more readable, reliable, and easily maintained. The goal of structured programming is to avoid *spaghetti code* caused by over-reliance on GOTO statements, a problem often found in *BASIC* and *FORTRAN* programs. Structured programming—such as that promoted by *C, Pascal, Modula-2,* and the *dBase* software command language—insists that the overall program structure reflect what the program is supposed to do, beginning with the first task and proceeding logically. Indentations help make the logic clear, and the *programmer* is encouraged to use *loops* and *branch control structures* and named procedures rather than GOTO statements.

Structured Query Language See *SQL.*

style 1. In *fonts,* a defining characteristic such as italics, underlining, or boldface. 2. In *word processing,* a saved definition consisting of formatting commands that you regularly apply to specific kinds of text, such as main headings. Styles can include alignment, font, line spacing, and any other text-formatting features. After creating and saving a style, you can quickly apply it to the text by using one or two keystrokes. See *style sheet.*

style sheet   In some *word processing* and *page layout programs,* a collection of styles frequently used in a specific type of *document,* such as newsletters, that are saved together. Synonymous with style library.

stylus   A pen–shaped instrument used to select menu options on a monitor screen or to draw *line art* on a *graphics tablet.*

subdirectory   In *MS-DOS* and *Unix,* a *directory* structure created in another directory. A subdirectory can contain files and additional subdirectories. When a *hard disk* is formatted, a fixed-size *root directory* area is created that's only large enough to contain the information for 512 files. To add more files to the hard drive, you create subdirectories in which you can store other files. By using subdirectories, you can create a treelike, hierarchical structure of nested directories so you can group programs and files, and organize your data to suit your needs. You can create subdirectories within subdirectories, up to a maximum of nine levels.

subdomain   In the *Internet's domain name system (DNS),* a domain that is subordinate to a domain name; for example, in the Web address http://www.virginia.edu/tcc, www.virginia.edu is the domain and tcc is the subdomain.

subject drift   In *Usenet newsgroups,* the tendency of the subject lines of follow-up posts to become increasingly irrelevant to the articles' contents. Subject drift is an unintended consequence of *newsreader* software, which automatically echoes the original article's subject (a brief one-line description) when you write a follow-up post. As the discussion progresses into new territory, newsreaders keep echoing the same subject line, even though it soon becomes irrelevant to the subject actually being discussed.

subject selector   In a *Usenet newsreader,* a program mode in which you have a list of articles, sorted by subject. Note that sorting by subject is not the same thing as sorting by threads; a *threaded newsreader* shows the precise relationship among articles and *follow-up posts,* while a subject-sorted newsreader merely alphabetizes the subjects (thus obscuring some of the relationships among articles in a thread). See *thread selector.*

subject tree   In the *World Wide Web (WWW),* a guide to the Web that organizes Web sites by subject. The term originates from many of the subject classifications (such as Environment or Music) having "branches," or subcategories. At the lowest level of the tree, you find *hyperlinks,* which you can click to display the cited Web document. See *Yahoo.*

submenu   A subordinate *menu* that may appear when you choose a command from a pull-down menu. The submenu lists further choices. Not all menu commands display submenus. Some carry out an action directly; others display *dialog boxes* (these options are shown with ellipses [...]).

subnet   In the *Internet,* a segment of an Internet-connected *local area network (LAN)* that is differentiated from other segments by using an operation (called a *subnet mask*) that is performed on the networks *IP address.* Subnets share a common *IP address* with the rest of the network of which they are a part, but they can function autonomously. A subnet is a virtual unit, identified conceptually by using the addressing methodology, and is generally created to reflect valid organizational distinctions—even if the members of an organizational unit are in fact using two or more physically dissimilar portions of the network. For example, in a university, a single academic department can be assigned a subnet, even though some of the faculty connect to the Internet by using a high-speed Ethernet, and others by using an AppleTalk network.

subnet mask   A transformation performed on an organization's *IP address* that enables the network administrators to create *subnets,* which are virtual subunits of the organization's physical network.

subroutine   A section of a computer program that is designed to perform a specific task. Set aside from the rest of the code, the subroutine can be used *(called)* from one or more sections of the main part of the program, as needed.

subscribe   In *Usenet,* to add a *newsgroup* to the list of groups that you're reading regularly. Subscribed newsgroups appear in the *newsgroup selector,* enabling you to choose them easily. If you stop reading a newsgroup, you can *unsubscribe* to remove the newsgroup name from your subscription list.

subscript   In *word processing,* a number or letter printed slightly below the typing line, as in the following example: n_1. See *superscript.*

substrate   The material to which the recording medium of a *hard* or *floppy disk* is affixed. Floppy disks usually have plastic substrates, which are coated with a mixture of recording medium and *binder,* and hard disks have aluminum or glass substrates that, by *plating* or *sputtering,* are coated with *thin-film magnetic media.*

suitcase   In the *Macintosh* environment, an icon containing a *screen font* or *desk accessory (DA)* not yet installed in the *System Folder.*

suite   A group of *applications programs,* sold in a single package, that are designed to work well together. Suites (such as *Microsoft Office Standard* and Corel WordPerfect Suite*)* usually include a *word processing* program, a *spreadsheet,* and an *e-mail* program. High-end suites (such *Corel Office Suite, Microsoft Office Professional,* and *Lotus SmartSuite)* include *database management programs.* Suites cost less than the individual applications would if you purchased them separately.

Sun Microsystems   The world's leading manufacturer of *Unix*-based workstations, with an estimated one-third of the market. Based in Mountain View, CA, the company's products include the *Solaris* operating system, as well as workstations (SPARCstation) and servers (SPARCserver) based on the high-performance SPARC and UltraSPARC microprocessors, which are based on reduced instruction set computer *(RISC)* principles. A major new Sun initiative is the *Java* programming language, which is capable of producing computer programs that can run on any computer.

supercomputer   A sophisticated, expensive computer designed to execute complex calculations at the maximum speed permitted by state-of-the-art technology. Supercomputers are used for scientific research, especially for modeling complex, dynamic systems, such as the world's weather, the U.S. economy, or the motions of a galaxy's spiral arms. The Cray-MP is an example of a supercomputer.

SuperDrive   An innovative *3¹/₂-inch floppy disk drive* now standard on *Macintosh* computers. SuperDrives can read all

S
T
U

Macintosh formats (400K, 800K, and 1.4M). With the aid
of Apple's Apple File Exchange software, included with all
Macintosh system software, the drive also can read and write to
720K and 1.44M *MS-DOS* disks. SuperDrives also can format
disks in the MS-DOS format.

superpipelining   A method of extending *pipelining,* in which
the *microprocessor* begins executing a new instruction before the
previous instruction's execution is complete, so that as many as
four or five instructions are being executed simultaneously. Intel's
Pentium Pro microprocessor employs superpipelining.

superscalar architecture   A design that enables the *microprocessor* to take a sequential instruction and send several instructions at a time to separate execution units so that the processor
can execute multiple instructions per *clock cycle.* The *architecture*
includes a built-in scheduler, which looks ahead in the instruction queue, identifies a group of instructions that do not conflict
with one another or require simultaneous use of a particular service, and passes the group along for execution. The two *pipelines*
available in the *Pentium* chip enable the processor to execute two
instructions per clock cycle. The *PowerPC,* with three execution
units, can handle three instructions simultaneously.

superscript   A number or letter printed slightly above the typing line, as in the following example: a^2. See *subscript.*

Super VGA   An enhancement of the *Video Graphics Array
(VGA)* display standard. Super VGA can display at least 800 pixels horizontally and 600 lines vertically, and up to 1280 pixels
by 768 lines with 16 colors, 256 colors, or 16.7 million colors
simultaneously displayed. The amount of *video memory* required
to display 16 colors is nominal, but as much as 3.9M of video
memory is required to display 16.7 million colors.

support   1. To be able to work with a device, file format, or
program. For example, *Netscape Navigator* supports a variety of
plug-ins. 2. To provide human assistance with computer problems
(see *technical support*).

surf   To explore the *World Wide Web (WWW)* serendipitously
by following *hyperlinks* that seem interesting.

surfing   Exploring the Web by following interesting links—to
some, a monumental waste of time; to others, a joy.

surge   A momentary and sometimes destructive increase in the amount of voltage delivered through a power line. A surge is caused by a brief and often very large increase in line voltage resulting from appliances being turned off, lightning striking, or power being reestablished after a power outage. See *power line filter* and *surge protector.*

surge protector   An inexpensive electrical device that prevents high-voltage *surges* from reaching a computer and damaging its circuitry. See *power line filter.*

SVID   See *System V Interface Definition.*

S-Video   A standard specifying a video cable with a 4-pin mini-plug connector. Video boards (as well as all A/V Macintoshes) have S-Video inputs, which accept data from VCRs and camcorders.

swap file   In *Microsoft Windows 3.1* and *Microsoft Windows 95,* a large, hidden system file that stores *program* instructions and *data* that don't fit in the computer's *random-access memory (RAM).* See *virtual memory.*

swash   A character that sweeps over or under adjacent characters with a curvilinear flourish.

switch   An addition to an *MS-DOS* command that modifies the way that the command performs its function. The switch symbol is a forward slash (/), which is followed by a letter. For example, the command DIR /p displays a directory listing one page at a time.

switchable power supply   A *power supply* that lets you use both U.S. and European electrical power to run the computer. Unlike cheap "travel converters," which can ruin a PC's electronics, switchable power supplies enable a computer to use either 115-volt 60-Hertz U.S. electricity, or 230-volt 50-Hertz European electricity.

Sybase, Inc.   A major publisher of *Unix*-based *relational database management systems (RDMS)* for *client/server* computing in multi-user enterprise contexts. Based in Emeryville, CA, Sybase offers extensive consulting and system integration services to corporations who need sophisticated database management systems.

Symantec   The leading publisher of *utility software* for Macintosh and Microsoft Windows computers, including the well-known *Norton AntiVirus* and *Norton Utilities*. Based in Cupertino, CA, the company also publishes a number of popular application programs, including *Act!* (a contact management program), *WinFax* (a fax program for Microsoft Windows), and pcANYWHERE (a remote control program).

symbolic coding   Expressing an *algorithm* in coded form by using symbols and numbers that people can understand (rather than the *binary* numbers that computers use). All modern *programming languages* use symbolic coding.

symmetric key encryption algorithm   An *encryption algorithm* that uses the same key to encode and decode messages. Symmetric key algorithms have many advantages: They require relatively small amounts of computer *overhead,* and when used with *keys* of sufficient length, they produce virtually uncrackable *ciphertext*. However, it is necessary to convey the key to the message's receiver by some secure means. In *Internet* security services, this is typically done by means of *public key encryption algorithms,* which are used initially to authenticate the two parties to the transaction and to manage the initial exchange of symmetric keys; subsequent communication between the two parties uses the symmetric key algorithm. See *SSL*.

symmetric multiprocessing (SMP)   In a computer with more than one *central processing unit (CPU),* a type of *multiprocessing* architecture in which each processor has equal access to the system's memory and *I/O devices*. The processors are connected by a high-speed *bus*. Processing tasks are parceled out by the *operating system (OS),* usually in fairly straightforward ways, such as assigning printing or communication tasks to one processor while assigning data processing tasks to another. Alternatively, the processor can parcel out a single application's *threads* among the available processors. *Microsoft Windows NT* supports multiprocessing. See *parallel processing*.

synchronous   Occurring together thanks to regular pulses received by some type of timing device. See *asynchronous*.

synchronous communication   Sending *data* at very high speeds by using circuits in which electronic clock signals synchronize the data transfer. Computers in high-speed *mainframe* computer networks use synchronous communication. See *asynchronous communication.*

Synchronous Digital Hierarchy (SDH)　See *SONET.*

Synchronous Dynamic Random–Access Memory　See *SDRAM.*

Synchronous Graphics Random–Access Memory　See *SGRAM.*

synchronous motor　An obsolete kind of electric motor that some *hard disks* once used as a *spindle motor.* Now replaced by the *servo-controlled DC motor,* synchronous motors ran on high-voltage alternating current and could not be designed to run at different speeds.

Synchronous Optical Network　See *SONET.*

syntax　The rules that govern the structure of commands, statements, or instructions.

syntax error　An error resulting from stating a command in a way that violates a program's *syntax* rules.

SyQuest drive　A type of *removable hard disk* that is compatible with the *Small Computer System Interface (SCSI)* standard and very popular among both *Macintosh* and IBM *PC-compatible* computer users. In addition to the traditional 44M and 88M cartridges, new storage formats include 135, 230, and 270M cartridges, but these are not *backwards-compatible* with previous SyQuest drives.

SyQuest Technology, Inc.　A leading manufacturer of *removable hard disks* for data backup purposes. The company faces very stiff competition from *Iomega Corporation,* which markets the very popular *Zip* drives.

sysop　Abbreviation for *system operator.* A person who runs a *bulletin board system (BBS).*

system　1. An organized collection of components that have been optimized to work together in a functional whole. 2. The entire computer system, including peripheral devices (see *computer system*).

System 7.5　An *operating system* for *Power Macintosh* computers equipped with *PowerPC* microprocessors. Not capable of *preemptive multitasking,* this operating system lags behind *Microsoft Windows 95* and *Microsoft Windows NT.* Apple now calls its operating systems *MacOS;* the latest version, MacOS 7.6, still does not offer features that Microsoft has made available for more than two years. MacOS 8, still in development at this writing, should finally bring Apple's operating system technology up to prevailing industry standards.

System 8   See *MacOS.*

system administrator   The human being responsible for running and maintaining a *computer system,* especially a *mainframe, minicomputer,* or *local area network (LAN).* System administrators, sometimes called *network* administrators, issue *login names,* maintain *security,* fix failures, and advise management about *hardware* and *software* purchases.

system board   IBM's term for *motherboard.*

system call   An application's request for services from the computer's *operating system,* such as a request to open a file. The syntax for writing system calls is specified by the operating system's *application programming interface (API).*

system clock   A timer circuit on the *motherboard* that emits a synchronizing pulse at a regular interval, such as 33,000,000 times per second on a 33 *megahertz* (MHz) motherboard. The pulses of the system clock help synchronize processing operations. See *clock cycle.*

system date   The calendar date that a computer system maintains even when the power is switched off, thanks to a battery inside the computer's case.

system disk   A disk that contains the *operating system (OS)* files necessary to start the computer. *Hard disk* users normally configure a hard disk to serve as the system disk.

system file   A *program* or *data file* that contains information that the *operating system* needs; distinguished from the program or data files that the *application programs* use.

System Folder   A *folder* in the *Macintosh* desktop environment that contains the *System* and *Finder* files, the two components of the Mac's *operating system (OS).* In addition to the System and Finder files, the System Folder also contains all the *desk accessories*

(DAs), INITs, control panel devices (CDEVs), screen fonts, downloadable printer fonts, and *printer drivers* available during an operating session. See *blessed folder* and *downloadable font.*

system integrator   An individual or company that provides
value-added reseller (VAR) services by combining various components and programs into a functioning system, customized for a
particular customer's needs.

System Management Mode (SMM)   In *Intel* microprocessors, a low power-consumption state that can be switched on to
conserve battery power. All recent Intel microprocessors are
equipped with SMM circuitry and are, therefore, suitable for use
in notebook computers.

system prompt   In a *command-line operating system,* the text
that indicates that the *operating system (OS)* is available for tasks
such as copying files, formatting disks, and loading programs. In
MS-DOS, the system prompt (a letter designating the disk drive,
followed by a greater-than symbol) shows the current drive.
When you see the prompt C>, for example, drive C is the current drive, and DOS is ready to accept instructions. You can customize the system prompt by using the PROMPT command.

systems analysis   A professional specialty that involves determining an organization's computing needs and designing *computer systems* to fit those needs. Systems analysis is less structured
than *programming* or other aspects of computer science, because it
is often difficult to determine whether the analyst has found the
best system for an organization, or even whether the analyst has
completely solved an organization's computing problems.

Systems and Procedures Association (SPA)   See *Association
for Systems Management (ASM).*

Systems Application Architecture (SAA)   A set of standards for communication among various types of IBM computers, from *personal computers* to *mainframes.* Announced in 1987,
SAA was IBM's response to criticisms that its products didn't
work well together, and to the competitive pressure exerted by
Digital Electronic Corporation (DEC), which claimed that it
had optimized its products for easy interconnection. SAA calls
for a consistent *user interface* and consistent system terminology
across all environments. The standard influenced the design of

Presentation Manager, the windowing environment jointly developed by Microsoft and IBM for *Operating System/2 (OS/2)*. See *windowing environment*.

Systems Network Architecture (SNA) A proprietary suite of protocols, developed by IBM, for linking mainframe computers to smaller computers throughout an organization.

system software All the software used to operate and maintain a computer system, including the *operating system (OS)* and *utility program;* distinguished from *application programs.*

system time The time of day maintained by the computer system even when the power is off, thanks to a battery inside the computer's case.

system unit The *case* that houses the computer's internal processing circuitry, including the *power supply, motherboard, disk drives, plug-in boards,* and a speaker. The case often is called the *central processing unit (CPU),* but this usage is inaccurate. Properly, the CPU consists of the computer's *microprocessor* and memory (usually housed on the motherboard) but not *peripherals* such as disk drives.

System V Interface Definition (SVID) A standard for *Unix operating systems,* established by AT&T Bell Laboratories and demanded by corporate buyers, and based on Unix version 5. See *Berkeley Unix.*

T1   A high-bandwidth telephone trunk line that is capable of transferring 1.544 *megabits per second (Mbps)* of data. See *physical medium* and *T3.*

T3   A very-high-bandwidth telephone trunk line that is capable of transferring 44.7 *megabits per second (Mbps)* of computer data. See *physical medium* and *T1.*

TA   See *terminal adapter.*

tab–delimited file   A *data file,* usually an *ASCII file,* in which the data items are separated by tab keystrokes. See *comma-delimited file.*

Tab key   A *key* used to move a fixed number of spaces or to the next *tab stop* in a document. The Tab key often is used to guide the cursor in on-screen command menus.

table   1. In a *relational database management system,* the fundamental structure of data storage and the display in which data items are linked by the relations formed by placing the items in rows and columns. The rows correspond to the *data records* of record-oriented database management programs, and the columns correspond to *data fields.* 2. In a *word processing program,* a matrix of columns and rows, usually created using a *table utility.* 3. In *HTML,* a matrix of rows and columns that appears on a Web page, if the user is browsing with a table-capable browser (such *as Netscape Navigator*).

table of authorities   A table of legal citations generated by a *word processing program* from references that have been marked in a *document.*

table utility   In a *word processing program,* a utility that makes the typing of tables easier by creating a spreadsheet-like matrix of rows and columns, into which you can insert text without forcing word wrapping.

tabloid printer   See *B-size printer.*

tab stop   The place where the *cursor* stops after you press the *Tab key.* Most *word processing programs* set default tab stops every

$^1/_2$ inch, but you can set tabs individually anywhere you want, or you can redefine the default tab width.

tactile feedback   Any information gained through the sense of touch. Typically, tactile feedback applies to the way a *keyboard's* keys feel to a typist, but the term also applies to *mouse* and *joystick* design and a variety of *virtual reality* applications.

tag   In *HTML*, a code that identifies an element (a certain part of a document, such as a heading or list) so that a *Web browser* can tell how to display it. Tags are enclosed by beginning and ending delimiters (angle brackets). Most tags begin with a start tag (delimited with <>), followed by the content and an end tag (delimited with </>), as in the following example:

```
<H1>Welcome to my home page</H1>
```

Tagged Image File Format (TIFF)   A *bit-mapped graphics* format for scanned images with resolutions of up to 300 *dots per inch (dpi)*. TIFF simulates *grayscale* shading.

talk   A *Unix* utility that enables users to engage in a typed, real-time conversation while they are online.

talk hierarchy   In *Usenet,* one of the seven *standard newsgroup hierarchies.* The talk newsgroups are expressly devoted to controversial topics and are often characterized by acrimonious debate. Topics covered include abortion, drugs, and gun control.

Tandem Computers, Inc.   A major manufacturer of *Unix*-based *servers* for enterprise computing. Based in Cupertino, CA., the company specializes in *online transaction processing (OLTP)*.

tape   A strip of thin plastic, coated with a magnetically sensitive recording medium. In *mainframe* computing and minicomputing, tape is widely used as a *backup* medium. Thanks to a dramatic price drop in cartridge *tape backup units,* tape has become increasingly common in personal computing for backing up entire *hard drives*. See *backup procedure, backup utility, quarter-inch cartridge (QIC), random access, sequential access,* and *tape backup unit.*

tape backup unit   A device that reads and writes data on a magnetically sensitive *tape.* Tape backup units are useful for performing *backups* on *hard disks*—thus protecting data from loss by accidental erasure—and for storing important but rarely needed data that would otherwise take up space on a hard disk. *Quarter-inch cartridge (QIC)* tape drives are the most common tape backup units for personal computers.

tape drive   See *tape backup unit.*

tar   A *Unix file archive* utility that does not offer compression services. After they are created, tar archives are generally compressed using the Unix *compress* (.Z extension) or *gzip* (.GZ extension) utilities, resulting in compound extensions such as TAR.Z or TAR.GZ.

targa   A graphics *file format* developed by Truevision for Targa and Vista graphics products and now widely used as a standard file format for high-end graphics output (such as *rendering* and *ray tracing*). Targa files, with the extension .TGA, can have a *color depth* of up to 32 bits for certain purposes, although the most common color depth is 24 bits, providing more than 16 million colors.

taskbar   In *Microsoft Windows 95,* an application launcher and task switcher that (by default) remains visible at the bottom of the screen. After launching a program with the Start menu, the program's *task button* appears on the taskbar, allowing the user to switch to it by clicking the button.

task button   In *Microsoft Windows 95,* a button that appears on the taskbar after an *application program* is launched. The user can switch to the application by clicking the task button.

TCM   See *trellis-code modulation.*

TCO   Acronym for Tjänstemännens Centralorganisation, the Swedish Confederation of Professional Employees (Sweden's largest white-collar labor union). In *monitors,* TCO is known for its very stringent regulations regarding *electromagnetic radiation*— even stricter than *MPR II* rules. Not many TCO-certified monitors are available in the U.S., but the TCO standards are the toughest in the world.

TCP   See *Transmission Control Protocol.*

TCP/IP   Abbreviation for Transmission Control Protocol/ Internet Protocol (TCP/IP) and a commonly used phrase to refer to the entire Internet *protocol suite.*

TCP/IP network   A network that uses the *TCP/IP* protocols, whether or not it is connected to the external *Internet*. See *extranet* and *intranet*.

techie   An often derogatory term for a *programmer* or other computer expert. Like "bit twiddler," "computer jock," and "computer nerd," the term sometimes connotes a lack of interpersonal skills but does not convey the maliciousness of "*hacker*."

technical support   Providing technical advice and problem-solving expertise to registered users of a *hardware* device or *program*.

technocentrism   An overidentification with computer technology, often associated with a preference for factual thinking, denial of emotions, a lack of empathy for other people, and a low tolerance for human ambiguity. First noted by the psychotherapist Craig Brod, technocentrism stems from the stress that individuals encounter as they try to adapt to a computer-driven society.

telecommunications   The transmission of information, whether expressed by voice or computer signals, via the telephone system. See *asynchronous communication* and *modem*.

telecommuting   Performing work at home while linked to the office by means of a telecommunications-equipped *computer system*.

telemedicine   The provision of high-quality, up-to-date medical information to medical practitioners. In rural areas and community health centers, doctors who are out of touch with the latest knowledge may make faulty diagnoses or prescribe an out-of-date therapy. A telemedicine system that can provide these practitioners with high-quality information could indeed save lives.

Telenet   A commercial *public data network (PDN)* with thousands of local *dialup* numbers. Telenet provides logon services to various commercial *online information services,* such as Dialog Information Services and *CompuServe*.

telepresence   A psychological sensation of being immersed in a *virtual reality* that's persuasive and convincing enough to pass for the real world.

teletype (TTY) display   A method of displaying characters on a *monitor* in which characters are generated and sent, one-by-one, to the video display; as the characters are received, the screen fills, line-by-line. When full, the screen scrolls up to accommodate the new lines of characters appearing at the bottom of the screen. Teletype display mode should be familiar to *DOS* users. DOS uses a teletype display for accepting commands and displaying messages. See *character-mapped display.*

Telnet   An *Internet* protocol that enables Internet users to log on to another computer linked to the Internet, including those that cannot directly communicate with the Internet's *TCP/IP* protocols. Telnet establishes a "plain vanilla" computer terminal called a *network virtual terminal.* This capability is frequently used to enable communications with bulletin board systems *(BBSs)* and *mainframe* computers. For example, you will often see *hyperlinks* to Telnet sessions while browsing the *World Wide Web (WWW).* If you click such a hyperlink, your browser starts a Telnet *helper program,* and you see a text-only command window. In this window, you type commands and see the remote system's responses.

template   In a *program,* a *document* or *worksheet* that includes the text or formulas needed to create standardized documents. The template can be used to automate the creation of these documents in the future. In *word processing,* templates frequently are used for letterheads; the template version of the file contains the corporate logo, the company's address, and all the formats necessary to write the letter, but no text. You use the template by opening it, adding text to it, and printing. In *spreadsheet* programs, templates are available for repetitive tasks such as calculating and printing a mortgage amortization schedule.

temporary font   A Hewlett-Packard term for a *font* that, when downloaded to a *laser printer,* stays in the printer's memory only until the printer is reset. See *downloadable font* and *permanent font.*

tensioning wire   A very thin wire that stretches across an *aperture grille,* perpendicular to the other wires, to keep them steady. Sometimes, tensioning wires cast shadows on the *display.* The shadows are most visible in solid white images.

tera-   Prefix indicating one trillion (10^{12}).

terabyte   A unit of *memory* measurement equal to approximately 1 trillion *bytes* (actually, 1,099,511,627,776 bytes). One terabyte is equal to 1000 *gigabytes,* or 1 million *megabytes.* See *gigabyte (G)* and *kilobyte (K).*

terminal   An input/output device, consisting of a *keyboard* and *monitor,* commonly used with *multi-user systems.*

terminal adapter (TA)   A device, functionally equivalent to a *modem,* that connects a computer or *fax* machine to an *Integrated Services Digital Network (ISDN)* system. TAs typically plug into the *expansion bus* like other *adapters,* though external versions exist. A terminal lacking its own *central processing unit (CPU)* and disk drives is called a *dumb terminal* and is restricted to interacting with a distant multi-user computer. A *smart terminal,* on the other hand, has some processing circuitry and, in some cases, a disk drive so you can download information and display it later. A *personal computer* is a terminal when it is connected to a *network,* either by a cable or a *modem.* See *terminal emulation.*

terminal emulation   The use of a *communications program* to transform a computer into a *terminal* for the purpose of *data communication.*

terminal mode   A state of a *communications program* in which the computer on which it is running becomes a *remote terminal* of another computer, to which it is linked by a *modem.*

terminate–and–stay–resident (TSR) program   An accessory or *utility program* designed to remain in *random-access memory (RAM)* at all times so you can activate it quickly, even if another program also is in memory.

test driver   A program that tests another program, often as part of an *alpha test.* Test drivers typically send every conceivable input to a program and monitor the results.

test message   In *Usenet,* a message that is posted just to see whether one's *newsreader* software and Usenet connection are really working.

TeX   A *page description language (PDL)* for professional typesetting created by noted computer scientist and programming expert Donald Knuth. It is often used in the computer science community—in part out of homage to Knuth, and in part because TeX contains a number of interesting programming features that are in themselves illustrative of the didactic points that Knuth makes in his multivolume *Art of Computer Programming.* TeX is not widely used outside computer science circles.

Texas Instruments Graphics Architecture (TIGA*)*   A *high-resolution* graphics standard for *IBM PC-compatible* personal computers. TIGA boards and monitors display 1024 *pixels* horizontally by 786 lines vertically with 256 simultaneous colors. See *Super VGA.*

text   Data composed only of standard *ASCII* characters, without any *formatting codes.*

text chart   In *presentation graphics,* a slide, transparency, or handout that contains text, such as a bulleted list. See *bulleted list chart, column text chart, free-form text chart, organization chart,* and *simple list text chart.*

text editor   A program designed for writing and editing text, but without the features of a full-fledged *word processing program.* Text editors are used for writing *source code* as well as creating basic text documents.

text file   A file consisting of nothing but standard *ASCII* characters (with no *control codes* or characters from the *extended character set*).

text mode   An operating mode of *IBM PC-compatible video boards* in which the computer displays images constructed using the built-in 256-character *ASCII character set.* Text mode is synonymous with character mode and the opposite of *graphics mode.* Because the character set includes several graphics characters, text mode can display graphic images such as boxes and lines. Also, text can be displayed in *bold* and *reverse video.* Text mode is much faster than graphics mode.

TFT   Acronym for Thin Film Transistor. See *active matrix display.*

TGA   See *targa.*

thermal dye sublimation printer   A *high-end color printer* capable of generating *photorealistic output*—but at a very high price. By focusing a precisely controllable heat source on a special ribbon containing dyes, the dyes can be transferred to the special coated paper that thermal dye-sublimation printers require. Thermal dye-sublimation printers have very good color *saturation,* but can cost more than $15,000, plus a *cost per page* of $3 or more.

thermal fusion printer A *printer* that melts dye from a special ribbon onto plain paper to form sharp text. Thermal fusion printers are often designed to be portable.

thermal printer A *non-impact printer* that forms an image by moving heated styluses over specially treated paper. Although quiet and fast, thermal printers have one disadvantage: Most of them require specially treated paper that smells odd and has an unpleasant, waxy feel.

thermal wax-transfer printer A *printer* that heats wax-based dyes and deposits them on the page in a very dense pattern. Though thermal wax-transfer printers cannot generate *photorealistic output,* as *thermal dye-sublimation printers* can, they produce excellent *saturation* and output that is nearly photorealistic. Thermal wax-transfer printers are much less expensive than thermal dye-sublimation printers (they can be had for less than $1,000), and the *cost per page* is lower, too—about fifty cents.

thin client In a *client/server* network, a client that occupies relatively little memory or disk storage space and leaves most of the processing to the server. Advocates of thin clients point to the exceptionally high cost of training employees to use *fat clients,* which are full-featured application programs running on the user's desktop systems; to access needed external data, users would typically have to learn how to use several fat clients, each with its own proprietary commands and menu structure. The thin client par excellence is the Web browser, such as *Netscape Navigator,* which can access Web pages configured to display data from virtually any service an enterprise can make available.

thin-film magnetic medium A recording medium used in *hard disks* that is not composed of tiny bits of metal oxide, but instead is made up of thin layers of special metal alloys. Thin-film magnetic media, applied to disk *substrates* by *plating* or *sputtering,* allow higher *areal densities* and increased *coercivities* than oxide-based media.

thin-film transistor (TFT) See *active matrix display.*

third-generation computer   A mid-1960s-era computer based on small-scale integrated circuits and, generally, the use of *semiconductors* for main memory. This period in the computer's development saw the rise of *multi-user systems* and *minicomputers*. See *first generation computer, second-generation computer,* and *fourth-generation computer.*

third-generation programming language   A *high-level programming language* that enables programmers to write programs in a language that is easier for humans to understand than *second-generation programming languages* (that is, *assembly language*) or *first-generation programming languages* (*machine code*).

third-party vendor   A firm that markets an accessory *hardware* product for a given brand of computer equipment. Many companies act as third-party vendors of *Macintosh* accessories.

thirty-two bit computer   See *32-bit computer.*

thread   1. In a *Usenet* newsgroup, a chain of postings on a single subject. Most *newsreaders* include a command that lets you follow the thread (that is, jump to the next message on the topic rather than display each message in sequence). 2. A portion of a *program* that can operate independently. In a *multithreaded application,* a running program may have two or more threads running at the same time. The operating system decides which of these threads should receive the processor's attention. In this way, an operation such as printing or downloading a file can occur in the background, without tying up other threads or other applications. This is called *preemptive multitasking.* See *cooperative multitasking.*

threaded newsreader   A *Usenet newsreader* program that can group articles by topic of discussion and then show where a given article stands in the chain of discussion. Often, this is done using indentation. See *thread selector.*

thread selector   In a *Usenet newsreader,* a program mode in which you see articles sorted by *threads.* Many newsreaders use indentation to indicate that the indented article is a response to the one positioned above it. See *subject selector* and *threaded newsreader.*

three-dimensional graph   A business or scientific chart that depicts information using three axes: width (*x-axis*), height (*y-axis*), and depth (*z-axis*). In *Microsoft Excel,* the vertical axis—the one that measures the data items is called the value (y) axis, and the horizontal axis is called the category (x) axis. The axis that shows depth—the one that seems to go "back" into the page—is the series (z) axis. Three-dimensional graphs are very useful when you're showing more than one *data series*.

three–dimensional spreadsheet   A *spreadsheet program* that can create a *workbook* file made up of multiple stacked pages, each page resembling a separate worksheet.

three-gun tube   A color *cathode ray tube (CRT)*. Each of the three *electron guns* emits electrons that paint one of the primary colors on the *display*. So-called one-gun tubes in color *monitors* really have three guns, but the three guns are assembled into one unit. A *monochrome* monitor truly has only one gun.

throughput   1. A measure of a computer's overall performance, as measured by its capability to send data through all components of the system, including data storage devices such as disk drives. Throughput is a much more meaningful indication of system performance than some of the *benchmark* speeds commonly reported in computer advertising. 2. In *modems,* the rate at which data moves from one modem to another, including the effects of *data-compression* and *error-correction protocols.*

thumbnail   A small version of a graphic, large enough to show what's in the full-sized version but small enough to be opened, or transmitted via a network, without making inordinate demands on the system. On a Web page, users can click on a thumbnail to see a larger version of the graphic.

thunking   The means by which a *32-bit operating system,* such as *Microsoft Windows 95* or *Operating System/2 (OS/2),* communicates with a *16-bit application program.* A computer system slows significantly when it must pause to perform this communication, which is why 32-bit application programs will soon become the norm.

TIF   The *extension* usually attached to a file containing *graphics* in *Tagged Image File Format (TIFF).* TIF files often are used to hold scanned photographic images.

TIFF   See *Tagged Image File Format.*

tiled windows   In a *graphical user interface (GUI),* a display mode in which all windows occupy an equal portion of screen space. If you open additional windows, the others are automatically sized so that you still see all of them. See *cascading windows* and *overlaid windows.*

time bomb   A *program,* either existing independently or built into a larger program, that waits until a specific day and time to come out of hiding and be disruptive. The famous Michelangelo *virus* activated itself on the birthday of the artist Michelangelo. See *Trojan horse.*

timed backup   A desirable *application program* feature that saves your work at a specified interval, such as every five minutes. Synonymous with AutoSave. If a power outage or system *crash* occurs and a timed backup of your work has been performed, you'll be notified when you next start the program that a timed backup is available and asked whether you want to keep it. The best word processing programs include timed backup features that let you specify the interval.

time division multiplexing   In *local area networks (LANs),* a technique for transmitting two or more signals over the same cable by alternating them, one after the other. Time division is used in *baseband* (digital) networks. See *frequency division multiplexing.*

time out   An interruption, resulting in a frozen *keyboard,* that occurs while the computer tries to access a device (or a remote computer) that isn't responding as it should. The computer keeps trying for a predetermined time and then gives up, returning control to you.

time–sharing   A technique for sharing a *multi-user system's* resources in which each user has the illusion that he or she is the only person using the system. In the largest *mainframe* systems, hundreds or even thousands of people can use the system simultaneously without realizing that others are doing so. At times of peak usage, however, system response time tends to decline noticeably.

tin   A *Usenet newsreader program* for *Unix* computers. Developed by Iain Lee, this *threaded newsreader* offers powerful features like its other Unix newsreader counterparts, but is much easier to use. See *nn* and *trn.*

title bar   In *graphical user interfaces (GUIs)* such as *Operating System/2 (OS/2),* a bar that stretches across the top of a *window,* indicating the name of the document displayed in that window. The color of the title bar indicates whether the window is active.

toggle   To switch back and forth between two modes or states. On the *IBM PC-compatible keyboard,* for example, the Caps Lock key is a toggle key. When you press the key the first time, you switch the keyboard into a capitals-only mode. When you press the key the second time, you switch the keyboard back to the normal mode, in which you must press the Shift key to type capital letters.

toggle key   A *key* that switches back and forth between two modes. See *Caps Lock key, Num Lock key, Scroll Lock key,* and *toggle.*

token   1. In *authentication* systems, some type of physical device (such as a card impregnated with a magnetic stripe, a *smart card,* or a calculator-like device that generates a password) that must be in the individual's possession in order to access a network. The token itself is not sufficient; the user must also be able to supply something memorized, such as a *personal identification number (PIN).* Combining "something you have" with "something you know," tokens provide *strong authentication.* 2. In *token-ring networks,* a bit configuration that is circulated among workstations; workstations cannot broadcast data to the network unless they possess the token.

token passing   In *local area networks (LANs),* a *network protocol* in which a special *bit* configuration, called a token, is circulated among the *workstations.* A *node* can send information across the network only if the node can obtain an available token, in which case the node converts the token into a data frame containing a network message. Nodes constantly monitor the network to catch tokens addressed to them. Because token-passing rules out the data collisions that occur when two devices begin transmitting at the same time, this channel access method is preferred for large, high-volume networks. See *Carrier Sense Multiple Access with Collision Detection (CSMA/CD), contention, local area network (LAN),* and *polling.*

token-ring network   A *local area network (LAN)* architecture that combines *token passing* with a hybrid star/ring topology. Developed by *IBM* and announced in 1986, the IBM Token-Ring Network uses a Multistation Access Unit at its hub.

This unit is wired with *twisted-pair* cable in a star configuration with up to 255 workstations, but the resulting network is actually a decentralized ring network.

toner   The electrically charged ink used in *laser printers* and photocopying machines. To form the image, toner is applied to an electrostatically charged drum and fused to the paper by a heating element. See *toner cartridge*.

toner cartridge   In *laser printers,* a cartridge containing the *toner* that the printer fuses to the page.

toolbar   A bar across the top of a *window* containing buttons, each with a distinctive *icon* and, sometimes, some explanatory text. These icons represent frequently accessed commands. Synonymous with icon bar.

toolbox   1. A set of *programs* that helps *programmers* develop *software* without having to create basic *routines* from scratch. Some software publishers call these sets developer's toolkits. 2. In programs such as drawing and *presentation graphics* applications, the on-screen *icon* bar of drawing tools is called the toolbox.

toolkit   See *toolbox*.

top-down programming   A method of *program* design and development in which the design process begins with a statement (in English) of the program's fundamental purpose. This purpose is broken into a set of subcategories that describe aspects of the program's anticipated functions. Each subcategory corresponds to a specific program module that can be coded independently. *Structured programming* languages (such as *Pascal, C,* and Modula-2) and object-oriented programming languages (such as *C++*) are especially amenable to the top-down approach.

topic drift   See *subject drift*.

topology   See *network topology*.

TOPS   A file-serving program for *local area networks (LANs)* that allows *IBM PC-compatible* and *Macintosh* computers to be linked in an *AppleTalk* or *Ethernet network*. TOPS allows Macintosh and PC users to share *files* more or less seamlessly. File-serving software provides peer-to-peer file transfer in which each user has access to the public files located on the workstations of all other users in the network. When a TOPS user decides to make a file public, he or she publishes the file on the network. Every *node* on the network, therefore, is potentially a *file server.*

touch screen   See *touch-sensitive display.*

touch-sensitive display   A *display* designed with a pressure-sensitive panel mounted in front of the screen; synonymous with touch screen. You select options by pressing the screen at the appropriate place. Hewlett-Packard championed the touch-sensitive display concept in the mid 1980s, but users disliked it because the screen quickly became smudged and unreadable. Touch-sensitive displays are now used for public-access information purposes in such settings as museums, supermarkets, and airports.

tower case   A *system* unit case designed to stand vertically on the floor rather than sit horizontally on a desk. Tower cases usually have much more room for accessories than *desktop* cases and permit you to move noisy components, including cooling fans and hard disks, away from the immediate work area.

tpi   See *tracks per inch.*

track   On a *floppy* or *hard disk,* one of many concentric rings that are encoded on the disk during the low-level format and that define distinct areas of data storage on the disk. See *cluster* and *sector.*

trackball   An input device, designed to replace the *mouse,* that moves the mouse pointer on-screen as you use your thumb or fingers to rotate a ball embedded in the *keyboard* or in a case near the keyboard. Unlike a mouse, a trackball doesn't require a flat, clean surface to operate; as a result, trackballs are often used with portable or notebook computers. See *built-in pointing device, clip-on pointing device, freestanding pointing device,* and *snap-on pointing device.*

track buffering   A *hard disk* design feature in which the entire contents of a hard disk *track* are read into a memory area, regardless of how much of the information on the track is requested by the *hard disk controller* and *host adapter.* Track buffering eliminates the need for *interleaving,* so all track-buffered disks (all modern hard disks and most *Enhanced Small Device Interface*

[*EDSI*] drives are track-buffered) should have *interleave factors* of 1.

trackpad   A pointing device that allows you to move the mouse pointer by sliding a finger around on a touch-sensitive surface. To click, you tap your finger on the surface or press a button.

tracks per inch (tpi)   A measurement of the data-storage density of magnetic disks, such as *floppy disks*. The greater the tpi, the more data the disk can hold. In *DOS, double-density 5¹/₄-inch floppy disks* are formatted with 48 tpi, and *high-density* 5¹/₄-inch disks are formatted with 96 tpi. High-density *3¹/₂-inch floppy disks* are formatted with 135 tpi.

track–to–track seek time   The time a hard or floppy disk drive requires to move the *read/write head* from one *track* to the next. Track-to-track seek time is much less important than *access time* in comparing disk drives.

tractor feed   A *printer* paper-feed mechanism in which *continuous paper* is pulled (or pushed) into and through the printer with a sprocket wheel. The sprockets fit into prepunched holes on the left and right edges of the paper. *Dot-matrix printers* normally come with tractor-feed mechanisms. Tractor-feed printers require you spend time carefully separating the pages after printing.

traffic   The volume of messages sent over a *network*.

transactional application   In a *local area network (LAN),* a program that creates and maintains a master record of all the transactions in which *network* participants engage, such as filling out invoices or time-billing forms. If a system *crash* results in the loss of data, this record can be used to restore data files to an earlier state. See *nontransactional application*.

transceiver   Concatenation of transmitter and receiver. 1. In *local area networks (LANs),* an adapter that enables a workstation to connect to the network cabling. 2. In wireless *wide area networks (WANs),* a *modem* that can send and receive data via radio frequencies. See *personal digital assistant (PDA)*.

transducer   A device that converts a detectable physical phenomenon, such as sound, pressure, or light, into electronic signals that can be processed by a computer.

transfer rate   The number of *bytes* of data that can be transferred per second from a disk to the *microprocessor,* after the *read/write head* reaches the data. The maximum transfer rate is limited by how fast the disk rotates and the *areal density* of the data on the disk (or how fast data passes under the drive head). These inflexible hardware limitations can be overcome by caching disk information. See *access time, Enhanced System Device Interface (ESDI), hardware cache,* and *Small Computer System Interface (SCSI).*

transient   See *surge.*

transient command   See *external command.*

transistor   An electronic device, with three connectors, that can be used for switching or amplification. Invented at Bell Laboratories in 1947, transistors are simple *semiconductor* devices that provide an inexpensive, low-power replacement for the bulky, power-consuming, and unreliable vacuum tubes that were used previously for amplification and switching purposes in electronic circuits.

transistor-transistor logic (TTL) monitor   An obsolete type of *monochrome monitor* that accepts *digital video signals.* TTL monitors work only with *Hercules* and *MDA video adapters,* and have been replaced by monitors that conform to *Video Graphics Array (VGA)* and *Super VGA* display standards.

translate   To convert a *data file* from one *file format* to another, or to convert a *program* from one *programming language* or *operating system* to another.

Transmission Control Protocol (TCP)   On the *Internet,* the protocol (standard) that permits two Internet-connected computers to establish a reliable connection. TCP ensures reliable data delivery with a method known as Positive Acknowledgment with Re-Transmission (PAR). The computer that sends the data continues to do so until it receives a confirmation from the receiving computer that the data has been received intact. See *Internet Protocol* and *TCP/IP.*

Transmission Control Protocol/Internet Protocol   See *TCP/IP.*

transmitter   In *push media,* a program that sends updated information to subscribers. An example is Castanet's Transmitter, which automatically downloads updates to *Java* programs installed on subscribers' computers.

transparency   A see-through piece of acetate that can be displayed during presentations by overhead projection. *Laser* and *inkjet printers* can both print transparencies, but be sure to get the right kind of transparency material—inkjet transparency material will melt inside a laser printer.

transparency adapter   A *scanner* attachment that lets you scan slides and *transparencies*.

transparent   A computer operation or entity that programmers have made invisible so you don't have to deal with it. A transparent computer function is present, but you can't see it; a *virtual* computer function isn't present, but you can see it. *Microsoft Word,* for example, inserts formatting codes in your document, but they're transparent—you see only your formatted text. A *random-access memory (RAM)* disk drive, in contrast, isn't a disk drive at all; it's just part of your computer's memory, set aside to act like a disk drive.

transport layer   In the *OSI Reference Model* of computer network architecture, the fourth of seven *layers,* in which the data is broken up into discrete units, called *packets,* each of which is addressed to the destination computer and numbered so the destination computer can reassemble them on receipt. The protocols on this level govern the precise format for the data packets as well as the procedures to be followed for dividing the data packets on transmission and reassembling them on reception.

transpose   To change the order in which characters, words, or sentences are displayed. Some *word processing programs* include commands that transpose text.

trap   In programming, an exception to program execution that enables the program to recover from an unanticipated or unusual situation. See *error trapping.*

trap door   1. In computer networks, a built-in entry point that enables an employee or ex-employee to gain access to the network without *authentication.* 2. In programming, a *function* that takes input values and produces a series of output values with very little computational effort; however, it is impossible (or impossible in practice) to derive the original input values from an examination of the output values. Trap doors have important applications in *strong authentication* and *cryptography;* see *hash function.*

trapping   See *error trapping.*

trash can   In the *MacOS,* an icon that can be used to dispose of unwanted files. The files are not actually erased unless the user chooses Empty Trash from the Special menu.

tree   A conceptual or graphic representation of data organized into a *tree structure.*

tree structure   A way of organizing *information* into a hierarchical structure with one root and several branches, much like a family tree or genealogy chart. There is only one possible route between any two data items in a tree structure. See *directory* and *subdirectory.*

trellis–code modulation (TCM*)*   A *group coding modulation* technique employed by *high-speed modems.* By enabling a modem to alter the *carrier* in a variety of ways, TCM enables modems to communicate at *data transfer rates* of 9600 *bits per second (bps)* or faster.

trigger   In a computer program, an event—such as a mouse click—that automatically initiates a procedure.

Trinitron   A *cathode ray tube (CRT)* design that, instead of a *shadow mask,* has an *aperture grill* to ensure that electrons from the *electron guns* hit the proper *pixels* on the *display.* An invention of Sony, Trinitron monitors are uniformly bright all over the display, unlike other monitor designs that are less bright around the edges. On the down side, Trinitron monitors have *tensioning wires* that sometimes cast shadows on the display.

Triple DES   In *cryptography,* an encryption method that involves encrypting the same data three times with the *DES* encryption algorithm. The result is a form of very strong encryption that is *computationally infeasible* to decode without possessing the *key.*

triple–pass scanner   A *color scanner* that gathers data about one of the primary colors on each of three *scanning passes.* Triple-pass scanners are not necessarily slower than *single-pass scanners,* but the extra scanning passes can put extra wear on the scanning mechanism.

Triton   A *chip set* for IBM and IBM-compatible *Pentium*-based computers that (in the most recent versions) provides support for *EDO RAM* and *SDRAM* memory chips, *Plug and Play (PnP)* adapters, *ECC* bi-directional printer ports, and high-speed *IDE* hard disk interfaces.

trn   A *Usenet newsreader* for *Unix computer systems*. A *threaded newsreader* that can show the chain of discussion in a newsgroup, trn is a successor to the widely used *rn*. Somewhat difficult to learn and use, trn is a powerful program that offers many advanced features (such as the ability to decode binary postings).

troff   In *Unix,* a text formatting program that, in the days prior to *PostScript, TeX,* and *desktop publishing software,* was extensively used to prepare programming documentation for output to typesetting devices.

Trojan horse   A *program* that appears to perform a valid function but contains, hidden in its code, instructions that cause damage (sometimes severe) to the systems on which it runs. Trojan horses, unlike computer *viruses,* can't replicate themselves, but that may be small consolation indeed to someone who has just lost days or weeks of work.

trolling   In *Usenet,* posting a facetious message containing an obvious exaggeration or factual error. The troller hopes to trick a gullible person into posting a follow-up post pointing out the error.

troubleshooting   The process of determining why a *computer system* or specific *hardware* device is malfunctioning. When a computer fails, most people panic and assume that a huge bill is on the way. Most likely, however, the problem is a minor one, such as a loose connection. Turn off the power and carefully inspect all the cables and connections. Remove the *case* lid and press down on the *adapters* to make sure that they're well seated in the *expansion slots.* You also should check connections at *peripheral* devices.

True BASIC   A modern, structured version of the *BASIC programming language* developed by its originators, John Kemeny and Thomas Kurtz, in response to criticism of earlier versions of BASIC. With modern control structures and optional line numbers, True BASIC is a well-structured language used to teach the principles of *structured programming.* The language, which is interpreted rather than compiled, isn't frequently used for professional programming purposes.

TrueType   A *font* technology, included with *MacOS* and *Microsoft Windows 95,* that brings *scalable fonts* to the screens and *printers* of *Macintosh* and Windows systems. Jointly developed by Apple Computer and Microsoft Corporation, TrueType offers a cost-effective alternative to *PostScript* font technology. TrueType doesn't require an add-on *utility program* or an expensive, *microprocessor*-driven *interpreter.* The TrueType fonts you see on-screen are exactly the same as the ones you see when you print your document.

truncate   To cut off part of a number or character string.

truncation error   A rounding error that occurs when part of a number is omitted from storage because it exceeds the capacity of the *memory* set aside for number storage. See *floating-point unit.*

truth table   In logic, a table that is formed to show all the possible permutations when two propositions are connected by a *Boolean operator.* For example, consider two propositions, P and Q. Either could be true or false. If the two propositions are joined by the AND operator, the resulting compound proposition is true only if both P and Q are true. The resulting truth table lists four options: P is true and Q is true (therefore P AND Q is true); P is true and Q is false (therefore P AND Q is false); P is false and Q is true (therefore P AND Q is false); and P is false and Q is false (therefore P AND Q is false). Truth tables are extensively used in programming and computer system design.

TSR   See *terminate-and-stay-resident (TSR) program.*

TTL monitor   See *transistor-transistor logic (TTL) monitor.*

TTY   See *teletype (TTY) display.*

Turbo Pascal   A high-performance *compiler* developed by Borland International for *Pascal.* The compiler comes with a full-screen *text editor* and creates executable programs (*object code*). Outperforming compilers that cost 10 times as much, Turbo Pascal took the world of DOS programming by storm when released in 1984 and is now one of the most popular compilers ever written. Turbo Pascal is used in hobby and academic environments, and some professional *programmers* use Turbo

Pascal to prepare short- to medium-sized programs. See *interpreter.*

turnkey system A *computer system* developed for a specific application, such as a point-of-sale terminal, and delivered ready to run, with all the necessary *application programs* and *peripherals.*

tutorial A form of instruction in which the student is guided step-by-step through the application of a program to a specific task, such as developing a budget or writing a business letter. Some *programs* come with on-screen tutorials.

tweak To adjust a program or computer system slightly to improve performance. For example, an unethical researcher might alter an underlying variable slightly so *program* output is more in line with what is expected.

twisted-pair An improved physical medium for *local area networks (LANs)* and telephone service to homes and offices. Twisted-pair wiring consists of two insulated copper cables that are twisted together like a braid, thus randomizing interference from other electrical circuits. Unlike the plain copper cable used in pre-1970 telephone installations, twisted-pair can handle computer data and is sufficient for *Basic Rate Interface (BRI).* See *ISDN.*

two-way set-associative cache A *secondary cache* memory design that is faster than the *direct-map cache* design, but less expensive than the *four-way set-associative cache,* which is the fastest of the three.

TXT The *MS-DOS file extension* usually attached to a file containing *ASCII* text.

Type 1 font A *PostScript*-compatible font that includes Adobe Systems' proprietary font-scaling technology, which improves type legibility at low resolutions and small type sizes. See *PostScript font.*

typeface The distinctive design of a set of type, distinguished from its weight (such as *bold*), posture (such as *italic*), and *type size.* Many *laser printers* come with as many as a dozen or more typefaces available in the printer's *read-only memory (ROM),* and literally hundreds more can be downloaded. Notice that professional graphic artists rarely use more than two typefaces in one document. They choose one typeface for *display type* and a second for *body type*. See *font* and *font family*.

typeover   See *overtype mode*.

typeover mode   See *overtype mode*.

typesetter   See *imagesetter*.

typesetting   The production of *camera-ready copy* on a high-end *imagesetter*—such as a Linotronic or Varityper. The current crop of office-quality *PostScript laser printers* can produce 1200-*dots-per-inch (dpi)* output, which is considered crude by professional typesetting standards, but which may be acceptable for applications such as newsletters, textbooks, instructional manuals, brochures, and proposals. See *resolution*.

type size   The size of a *font,* measured in *points* (approximately $^1/_{72}$ inch) from the top of the tallest *ascender* to the bottom of the lowest *descender*. See *pitch*.

type style   The weight (such as bold) or posture (such as italic) of a font distinguished from a font's typeface design and type size. See *attribute* and *emphasis*.

typography   The science and art of designing aesthetically pleasing and readable *typefaces*.

UART   See *Universal Asynchronous Receiver / Transmitter.*

UDP   See *User Datagram Protocol.*

ultra–large scale integration (ULSI)   In *integrated circuit* technology, the fabrication of a chip containing more than one million transistors. The *Pentium* chip, for example, includes more than three million transistors.

Ultra SCSI   A *SCSI* standard that employs an 8-bit data bus to provide data transfer rates of up to 20 Mbps.

Ultra Wide SCSI   A *SCSI* standard that employs a 16-bit data bus to provide data transfer rates of up to 40 MBps.

unauthorized access   A computer break-in, done by a computer *cracker* for criminal or ego-boosting purposes. Unauthorized access is a crime in most states.

undelete utility   A *utility program* that can restore a file that was accidentally deleted from a disk.

Undernet   One of several international *Internet Relay Chat (IRC)* networks, independent of other IRC networks.

underscore   The underline character on the standard keyboard, which is often used to connect the words in a phrase when a program cannot tolerate spaces in a *string* ("This_is_a_phrase").

undo   A command that restores a *program* and your data to the stage they were in just before the last command was given or the last action was initiated. Undo commands let you reverse the often catastrophic effects of giving the wrong command.

undocumented feature   A program feature that is present in the software but not discussed in the user documentation and not accessible by means of program menus because testing revealed that the feature's behavior was unsatisfactory or erratic for some reason.

unformat utility   A *utility program* that can restore the data on an inadvertently formatted disk.

unformatted text file   See *plain text document*.

Unicode   A 16-bit *character set* that is capable of representing all of the world's languages, including non-Roman characters such as Chinese, Japanese, and Hindi.

Uniform Resource Identifier (URI)   In the *HyperText Transfer Protocol (HTTP)*, a string of characters that identifies an Internet resource, including the type of resource and its location. There are two types of URIs: *Uniform Resource Locators (URLs)* and *Relative URLs*.

Uniform Resource Locator   See *URL*.

uninterruptible power supply (UPS)   A battery that can supply continuous power to a *computer system* in the event of a power failure. The battery, charged while your computer is switched on, kicks in if the power fails and provides power for 10 minutes or more, during which time you can save files and shut down the computer to preserve the integrity of crucial data.

Universal Asynchronous Receiver/Transmitter (UART) An integrated circuit that transforms the parallel data stream within the computer to the serial, one-after-the-other data stream used in *asynchronous communications*. Serial communication requires, in addition to the UART, a serial port and modem. See *modem, motherboard,* and *serial port*.

Universal Serial Bus   See *USB port*.

Unix   An *operating system* used on a wide variety of computers, from *mainframes* to *personal computers,* that supports multitasking and is ideally suited to multi-user applications. The term Unix is not an acronym (and thus is not capitalized like an acronym), but is instead a pun on the name of an earlier, complex operating system called Multics. Unix is a very flexible operating system, well-suited to the needs of advanced computer users. However, with more than 200 commands, inadequate error messages, and a cryptic command *syntax,* Unix imposes heavy burdens on occasional users and the technically unsophisticated. With the development of Unix *shells* such as NeXTStep, the operating system may play a much wider role in computing. Because Bell Laboratories was prohibited from marketing Unix by the antitrust regulations governing AT&T before the 1980s, Unix was provided without charge to colleges and universities throughout North America, beginning in 1976. In 1979, the University of California at Berkeley developed a popular version of Unix for VAX computers. In the early 1980s, AT&T gained the right to market the system and released System V in 1983. See *Berkeley Unix, Linux, System V Interface Definition (SVID), Rhapsody,* and *Wide Area Information Server (WAIS).*

Unix-to-Unix Copy Program (UUCP)   A *network,* based on long-distance telephone *uploads* and *downloads.* UUCP allows *Unix* users to exchange files, *e-mail,* and *Usenet* articles. In the 1980s, when *Internet* connectivity was hard to come by, UUCP played an important role in providing support for the Unix *operating system.*

unmoderated newsgroup   In a distributed *bulletin board system (BBS)* such as EchoMail (*FidoNet*) or *Usenet* (Internet), a topical discussion group in which postings aren't subject to review before distribution. Unmoderated newsgroups are characterized by spontaneity, but some postings may be inflammatory or inconsiderate, and *flame wars* may erupt. See *moderated newsgroup* and *newsgroup.*

unordered list   In *HTML,* a bulleted list created with <UL>_</UL> tags. Text tagged as an unordered list often appears bulleted.

unsubscribe   In *Usenet,* to remove a *newsgroup* from your subscription list, so it does not appear on the list of newsgroups you are actively following. You can also unsubscribe from a mailing list. See *subscribe.*

update   In *database management,* a fundamental data manipulation that involves adding, modifying, or deleting data records so data is brought up-to-date.

upgrade   To buy a new release or version of a *program,* or a more recent or more powerful version of a *microprocessor* or *peripheral.*

upload   To send a file by *telecommunications* to another computer user or a *bulletin board system (BBS).*

upper memory area (UMA)   In an *IBM PC-compatible* computer running *MS-DOS,* the memory between the 640K limit of *conventional memory* and 1024K. In the original PC system design, some of the memory in this area was reserved for system use, but most was actually unused. Memory management programs, as well as *HIMEM.SYS,* available with MS-DOS 6.2, can configure the upper memory area so it's available for system utilities and application programs. The upper memory area is distinguished from the *high memory area (HMA),* which is the first 64K of extended memory. See *Microsoft Windows 95.*

upper memory block (UMB) A collection of noncontiguous memory locations in the *upper memory area (UMA)* that can be combined to provide *MS-DOS* programs with additional memory. The portions of this memory that cannot be assigned to user programs have been reserved for system functions.

UPS See *uninterruptible power supply.*

upward compatibility Software that functions, without modification, on later or more powerful versions of a *computer system.*

URL Acronym for Uniform Resource Locator. In the World Wide Web *(WWW),* one of two basic kinds of *Universal Resource Identifiers (URI),* a string of characters that precisely identifies an *Internet* resource's type and location. For example, the following fictitious URL identifies a *World Wide Web (WWW)* document (http://), indicates the domain name of the computer on which it is stored (www.wolverine.virginia.edu), fully describes the document's location within the directory structure (~toros/winerefs/), and includes the document's name and extension (merlot.html).

```
http://www.wolverine.virginia.edu/~toros/winerefs/merlot.html
```

See *Relative URL (RELURL).*

USB port Abbreviation for Universal Serial Bus (USB) port. A newly developed external bus for connecting peripherals that is capable of transferring data at 12 Mbps.

Usenet A worldwide computer-based discussion system that uses the Internet and other networks for transmission media. Discussion is channeled into more than 30,000 topically named *newsgroups,* which contain original contributions called *articles,* as well as commentaries on these articles called *follow-up posts.* As follow-up posts continue to appear on a given subject, a *thread* of discussion emerges; a *threaded newsreader* collates these articles together so readers can see the flow of the discussion. *Unix* Usenet is accessed daily by more than 15 million people in more than 100 countries. See *Network News Transfer Protocol (NNTP)*.

Usenet site A *computer system*—one with lots of disk storage— that receives a news feed and enables dozens or hundreds of people to participate in Usenet. Currently, approximately 120,000 Usenet sites exist, providing an estimated four million people with access to Usenet newsgroups.

user See *end user.*

user agent (UA) In the terminology established by the *OSI Reference Model,* a client program that runs on the user's machine and assists in contacting a server. You may run across this term in references to e-mail clients (such as Eudora or Pegasus Mail).

User Datagram Protocol (UDP) One of the fundamental *Internet* protocols. UDP operates at the same level as the Transmission Control Protocol *(TCP),* but has much lower *overhead* and is less reliable. Unlike TCP, it does not attempt to establish a connection with the remote computer, but simply hands the data down to the connectionless *IP* protocol. UDP comes into play when network *bandwidth* could be preserved by not making a connection (for example, when responding to a *ping* request).

user default A user-defined program operating preference, such as the default margins for every new *document* that a *word processing program* creates. Also called preferences, options, or setup in various applications.

user-defined Selected or chosen by the user of the *computer system.*

user-friendly A *program* or *computer system* designed so individuals who lack extensive computer experience or training can use the system without becoming confused or frustrated.

user group A voluntary association of users of a specific *computer system* or *program* who meet regularly to exchange tips and techniques, hear presentations by computer experts, and obtain *public domain software* and *shareware.*

user interface All the features of a program or computer that govern the way people interact with the computer. See *command-driven program* and *Graphical User Interface (GUI).*

utility program A *program* that assists you in maintaining and improving the efficiency of a *computer system*.

UUCP See *Unix-to-Unix Copy Program*.

uudecode A *Unix utility program* that decodes a *uuencoded ASCII file,* restoring the original *binary file* (such as a program or *graphic*). A uudecode utility is needed to decode the binary files posted to *Usenet*. Programs with uudecoding capabilities are available for *Macintosh* and *Microsoft Windows 95* systems, and are often built into Usenet *newsreaders*.

uuencode A *Unix utility program* that transforms a *binary file,* such as a program or *graphic,* into coded *ASCII text.* This text can be transferred by using the *Internet* or it can be posted to a *Usenet newsgroup.* At the receiving end, the *uudecode* utility decodes the message and restores the binary file. Programs with uuencoding capabilities are available for *Macintosh* and *Microsoft Windows 95* systems and are often built into Usenet *newsreaders*.

V.17   An *ITU-TSS modulation protocol* for transmitting and receiving *faxes* at speeds up to 14,400 *bits per second (bps)*.

V.21   An *ITU-TSS modulation protocol* for *modems* transmitting and receiving data at 300 *bits per second (bps)*. V.21 conflicts with the *Bell 103A* standard once widely used in the U.S. and Canada.

V.22   An *ITU-TSS modulation protocol* for *modems* transmitting and receiving data at 1200 *bits per second (bps)*. V.22 conflicts with the *Bell 212A* standard once widely used in the U.S. and Canada.

V.22bis   An *ITU-TSS modulation protocol* for *modems* transmitting and receiving data at 2400 *bits per second (bps)*. V.22bis modems can *fall back* to slower data transfer rates if necessary, but they are obsolete—replaced by the *V.32bis* standard that costs little, if at all, extra.

V.27ter   An *ITU-TSS modulation protocol* for *fax modems* and *fax* machines transmitting and receiving fax information at 4800 *bits per second (bps)*. V.27ter *modems* can *fall back* to 2400 bps if necessary.

V.29   An *ITU-TSS modulation protocol* for *fax modems* and *fax* machines transmitting and receiving data at 9600 *bits per second (bps)*. V.29 modems can *fall back* to 7200 bps if *line noise* dictates such a switch.

V.32   An *ITU-TSS modulation protocol* for *modems* transmitting and receiving data at 9600 *bits per second (bps)*. Modems compliant with the V.32 standard can *fall back* to 4800 bps if needed, but use *trellis-code modulation* only at 9600 bps.

V.32bis   An *ITU-TSS modulation protocol* for *modems* transmitting and receiving data at 14,400 *bits per second (bps)*. Modems that use the V.32bis standard are very common and can transfer data at 12,000 bps, 9600 bps, 7200 bps, and 4800 bps if needed.

V.32terbo   A *proprietary* modulation protocol developed by AT&T to regulate *modems* transmitting and receiving data at 19,200 *bits per second (bps)* and to *fall back,* if needed, to the

data transfer rates supported by the *V.32bis* standard. Despite its
sneaky name, V.32terbo is not recognized by the *ITU-TSS*. The
V.34 standard has replaced V.32terbo.

V.34   An *ITU-TSS modulation protocol* for *modems* transmitting
and receiving data at 28,800 *bits per second (bps)*. V.34 modems
adjust to changing line conditions to achieve the highest possible
data transfer rate. A recent addition to the protocol enables transmission rates of up to 33.6 Kbps.

V.42   An *ITU-TSS error-correction protocol* designed to counter
the effects of *line noise*. A pair of V.42–compliant *modems* will
check each transmitted piece of data to make sure it arrives
error-free, and will retransmit any faulty data. The V.42 standard
uses *the Link Access Protocol for Modems (LAPM)* as its default
error-correction method, but will switch to *MNP4* if needed.

V.42bis   An *ITU-TSS compression protocol* that increases the
throughput of *modems*. V.42bis is an *on-the-fly compression* technique
that reduces the amount of data a modem needs to transmit.

vaccine   A *program* designed to offer protection against *viruses*.
By adding a small amount of code to files, an alert sounds when
a virus tries to change the file. Vaccines are also called immuniz-
ing programs.

validation   In *programming*, proving that a program does its job.
Many programmers prefer the term "validation" to "testing" or
"debugging," since it has a more positive ring.

value   In a *spreadsheet* program, a numeric cell entry. Two kinds
of values exist. The first kind, called a constant, is a value you
type directly into a *cell*. The second kind of value looks like a
constant but is produced by a *formula* placed into a cell. Be careful not to confuse the two and type a constant over a formula.
See *cell protection* and *label*.

value-added network (VAN)   A *public data network (PDN)*
that provides value-added services for corporate customers,
including end-to-end dedicated lines with guaranteed security.

value-added reseller (VAR)   A business that repackages and
improves *hardware* manufactured by an *original equipment manufacturer (OEM)*. A value-added reseller typically improves the original equipment by adding superior *documentation*, packaging,

system integration, and exterior finish. Some VARs, however, do little more than put their name on a device.

vanilla   Plain and unadorned, without bells, whistles, or advanced *features,* as in, "I'm using a plain vanilla 486." See *bells and whistles.*

vaporware   A *program* that's heavily marketed even though it's still under development, and no one knows whether its development problems will be solved.

variable   In *programming,* a named area in *memory* that stores a value or string assigned to that variable.

VBA   See *Visual BASIC for Applications.*

VDT   Acronym for video display terminal. Synonymous with *monitor.*

VDT radiation   See *cathode ray tube (CRT)* and *extremely low-frequency (ELF) emission.*

VDU   Abbreviation for video display unit. Synonymous with *monitor.*

vector font   See *outline font.*

vector graphics   The formation of an image made of independent objects, each of which can be individually selected, sized, moved, and otherwise manipulated. Vector graphics are much easier to edit than *bitmapped graphics* and are preferred for professional illustration purposes.

vector-to-raster conversion program   A *utility program* available with many professional illustration programs, such as CorelDRAW!, that transforms object-oriented (vector) graphics into *bit-mapped (raster) graphic* images. See *object-oriented graphic.*

vendor   A seller or supplier of *computers systems,* peripherals, or computer-related services.

Vendor Independent Messaging (VIM*)*   In *e-mail* programs, an *application program interface (API)* that lets e-mail programs from different manufacturers exchange mail with one another. The consortium of developers that designed VIM did not include *Microsoft Corporation,* which uses the *Messaging Application Program Interface (MAPI).* A VIM-to-MAPI *dynamic link library*

(DLL) file makes it possible for the two interfaces to exchange messages.

verify   To determine the accuracy and completion of a computer operation.

Veronica   In *Gopher,* a search service that scans a database of Gopher directory titles and resources (such as *documents, graphics,* movies, and sounds), and generates a new Gopher menu containing the results of the search. See *Jughead.*

version   A specific release of a *software* or *hardware* product. A larger version number indicates a more recent product release. For example, MS-DOS 6.22 is a more recent product than MS-DOS 5.0. In many cases, version numbers are skipped, such as 3.4 to 3.9 in the MS-DOS example. Revisions that repair minor bugs, called bug fixes or *maintenance releases,* often have small intermediate numbers such as 1.02 or 1.2a.

verso   In printing, the left-side, even-numbered page in a two-page spread. See *recto.*

vertical application   An *application program* created for a narrowly defined market, such as the members of a profession or a specific type of retail store. A vertical application is usually designed to provide complete management functions such as scheduling, billing, inventory control, and purchasing.

vertical centering   The automatic centering of graphics or text vertically on the page. *WordPerfect,* for example, includes a Center Top to Bottom command that centers text vertically.

vertical frequency   See *vertical refresh rate.*

vertical justification   The alignment of *newspaper columns* by means of *feathering* (adding vertical space) so all columns end evenly at the bottom margin. A *page layout program* capable of vertical justification inserts white space between frame borders and text, between paragraphs, and between lines to even the columns at the bottom margin.

vertically flat   A *monitor* design, used in *Trinitron*–type and other monitors, that somewhat reduces image distortion. Vertically flat displays are curved like cylinders, instead of like spheres, as most *cathode ray tubes (CRTs)* are. See *flat-square monitor* and *flat tension-mask monitor.*

V
W

vertical market program   See *vertical application*.

vertical refresh rate   The rate at which a *monitor* and *video adapter* pass the *electron guns* of a *cathode ray tube (CRT)* from the top of the display to the bottom. Measured in *Hertz (Hz)*, refresh rate determines whether a display appears to *flicker*. At a *resolution* of 1280 *pixels* by 1024 lines, a refresh rate of 72 Hz or more will eliminate visible flicker.

vertical retrace   The process of the electron beam in a *cathode ray tube (CRT)* being directed by the *yoke* from the end of one vertical scan to the beginning of the next. *Video adapters* must allow time for vertical retrace in preparing the video signal. During vertical retrace, blanking is in effect.

very high–level language (VHL)   A *declarative language* that is used to solve a particular kind of problem. VHLs, nearly all of which are *proprietary,* are used to generate *reports* in *spreadsheets* and *database management programs*.

very large scale integration (VLSI)   A level of technological sophistication in the manufacturing of semiconductor *chips* that allows the equivalent of more than 100,000—and up to 1 million—transistors to be placed on one chip.

VESA   Acronym for Video Electronics Standards Association. See *video standard* and *VL-Bus*.

VESA bus   See *local bus* and *VL-Bus*.

VESA local bus   A *local bus* design designed to work with the *Intel 80486* and provide a standard to compete with incompatible *proprietary local buses*. VESA local bus *adapters* typically are used to connect *video adapters* and *network adapters* to the *expansion bus*.

VESA local bus slot   A socket for *adapters* found on *expansion buses* compatible with the *VESA local bus* standard. VESA local bus slots provide 32-bit communication between the *microprocessor* and *adapters,* and were common in computers based on various versions of the 486-class microprocessor. However, *PCI* slots are much more flexible than VESA local bus slots and are expected to be the standard used for the next several years. See *Industry Standard Architecture (ISA)* and *ISA slot*.

V.Fast Class (V.FC) A *proprietary* modulation protocol used by several *modem* manufacturers before the *V.34* standard was published. Most V.FC modems can be upgraded to comply fully with V.34.

V.FC See *V.Fast Class*.

VGA See *Video Graphics Array*.

VHL See *very high-level language*.

vi A text editor that is configured to be the *default editor* on many *Unix* systems. Notoriously difficult to learn, vi has little in common with *Macintosh* and *Microsoft Windows 95* word processing programs. To avoid vi, many Unix users prefer to use applications that have their own built-in text editors, such as the *e-mail* program *pine*. See *emacs*.

video accelerator See *graphics accelerator board*.

video adapter The *adapter* that generates the output required to display text and *graphics* on a *monitor*.

video amplifier Part of the *monitor* circuitry that increases the weak signal received from the *video adapter* to a level high enough to drive the *electron guns*. *Monochrome* monitors have one video amplifier while color monitors have three, carefully tuned to work together.

video board See *video adapter*.

video capture camera A video camera device that records data in the form of digitized images. The images are saved as *files* that later can be retrieved using appropriate *software*, making it possible to run the movies on-screen.

video capture card An *adapter* that plugs into the computer's *expansion bus* and enables you to control a video camera or videocassette recorder (VCR) and manipulate its output. Video capture cards usually *compress* the video input to a manageable size and are useful for developing *multimedia* presentations.

video card See *graphics accelerator board*.

video controller A *microprocessor* on the *video adapter* that reads the information in *video memory*, arranges it into a continuous stream, and sends it to the *monitor*.

videodisk   See *interactive videodisk.*

video driver   A *program* that tells other programs how to work with a particular *video adapter* and *monitor.* Video drivers often have user-accessible controls that determine *resolution, refresh rate,* and *color depth.*

Video Graphics Array (VGA)   A color *bit-mapped graphics* display standard, introduced by IBM in 1987 with its PS/2 computers. VGA *video adapters* and *analog monitors* display as many as 256 continuously variable colors simultaneously, with a resolution of 640 *pixels* horizontally by 480 lines vertically. VGA circuitry is downwardly compatible with all previous display standards, including *Color Graphics Adapter (CGA), monochrome display adapter (MDA),* and *Enhanced Graphics Adapter (EGA).*

video memory   A set of memory *chips* to which the *central processing unit (CPU)* writes display information, and from which the *video controller* reads data prior to sending it to the *monitor.* Video memory often uses inexpensive *dynamic random-access memory (DRAM)* chips, but *high-end* video adapters use much faster *video RAM (*VRAM*).*

video monitor   See *monitor.*

video noise   Random dots of interference on a *display.* Synonymous with "snow." Video noise is rarely a problem in modern displays, but it caused problems for users of *Color Graphics Array (CGA) video adapters* and *monitors.*

video RAM (VRAM)   Specially designed *dynamic random-access memory (DRAM)* chips that maximize the performance of video adapters. The central processing unit (CPU) loads display information into VRAM, which is then read by the video system. *High-end* VRAM, called dual-ported VRAM, allows simultaneous reading and writing of data. *See random-access memory (RAM)* and *video adapter.*

video standard   A standard for *displays* developed so *software* developers can anticipate how their *programs* will appear on-screen. Video standards, such as *color graphics adapter (CGA), enhanced graphics adapter (EGA),* and *video graphics array (VGA),* are defined by industry groups and include specifications on, among other things, screen resolution and color capability. The VGA standard, for example, allows for resolution of 640 *pixels* by

480 lines, and 256 simultaneous colors. See *eXtended Graphics Array (XGA), Hercules Graphics Adapter, MCGA,* and *Super VGA.*

videotext   The transmission of information (such as news headlines, stock quotes, and movie reviews) through a cable television system. See *online information service.*

view   In *database management programs,* an on-screen display of the information in a *database* that meets the criteria specified in a *query.* With most database management programs, you can save views; the best programs update each view every time you add or edit *data records.* Also, to display an image on-screen from a different perspective, particularly with three-dimensional *computer-aided design (CAD)* drawings.

VIM   See *Vendor Independent Messaging.*

virtual   Not real; a computer representation of something that is real.

Virtual 8086 mode   A mode available with 80386 and higher *microprocessors,* in which the *chip* simulates an almost unlimited number of *Intel 8086* machines.

virtual community   A group of people who, although they may have never met, share interests and concerns and communicate with each other via *e-mail* and *newsgroups.* The people who see themselves as members of such communities feel a sense of belonging and develop deep emotional ties with other participants, even though the relationships that develop are mediated by the computer and may never involve face-to-face interaction.

virtual corporation   A means of organizing a business in which the various units are geographically dispersed, but actively and fruitfully linked by the *Internet* or some other *wide area network (WAN).*

virtual device   The simulation of a computer device or *peripheral,* such as a *hard disk drive* or *printer,* that doesn't exist—at least not nearby. In a *local area network (LAN),* a computer may appear to have an additional, enormous hard disk, but it is really located on the *file server.*

Virtual Device Driver (VxD)   In *Microsoft Windows 95,* a 32-bit program that manages a specific system resource, such as a sound card or printer. Unlike the device drivers used in

Windows 3.1, Virtual Device Drivers run in the processor's *protected mode,* where they are less likely to conflict with other applications and cause system crashes. The abbreviation "VxD" covers a range of devices, including virtual printer devices (VPD), virtual display devices (VDD), and virtual timing devices (VTD).

Virtual Library In the *World Wide Web (WWW),* a subject tree in which volunteers take on the responsibility of maintaining the portion of the tree that is devoted to a specific subject, such as astronomy or zoology. The Virtual Library is a good place to look for academically oriented information on the Web. See *subject tree.*

virtual machine 1. In 80386 and higher *microprocessors,* a protected memory space created by the microprocessor's *hardware* capabilities. Each virtual machine can run its own *programs,* completely isolated from other machines. The virtual machines can also access the *keyboard, printer,* and other devices without conflicts. Virtual machines are made possible by a computer with the necessary processing circuitry and a lot of *random-access memory (RAM).* See *Virtual 8086 mode.* 2. In *Java,* a protected memory space in which a Java *applet* can execute safely, without any access to the computer's file system. Synonymous with *sandbox.*

virtual memory A method of extending the apparent size of *random-access memory (RAM)* by using part of the *hard disk* as an extension of RAM. Many application programs, such as *Microsoft Word,* routinely use the disk instead of memory to store some data or program instructions while you're running the program. See *virtual memory management.*

virtual memory management The management of *virtual memory* operations at the *operating system* level rather than the *application program* level. An advantage to implementing virtual memory at the operating system level rather than the application level is that any program can take advantage of the virtual memory, with the result that memory extends seamlessly from random-access memory (RAM) to the computer's secondary storage. *Microsoft Windows 95* can take full advantage of the virtual memory capabilities of virtual memory. In the *Macintosh* world, *Apple's System* 7.5 makes virtual memory management available for users of 68030-based Macintoshes.

virtual private network (VPN) A highly secure network for transmitting sensitive data (including electronic commerce transactions) that uses the public *Internet* as its transmission medium. To ensure data confidentiality and integrity, VPNs use *encryption* and *protocol tunneling*. See *PPTP*.

virtual reality (VR) A *computer system* that can immerse the user in the illusion of a computer-generated world and permit the user to navigate through this world at will. Typically, the user wears a *head-mounted display (HMD)* that shows a stereoscopic image, and wears a *sensor glove,* which permits the user to manipulate "objects" in the virtual environment. See *cyberspace, electrocutaneous feedback, second-person virtual reality, sensor glove,* and *stereoscopy.*

virus A *program,* designed as a prank or as sabotage, that replicates itself by attaching to other programs and carrying out unwanted and sometimes damaging operations. When viruses appear, the effects vary, ranging from prank messages to erratic system software performance or catastrophic erasure of all the information on a *hard disk.* Don't ever assume that a prank message means that's all the virus will do. See *antivirus program, Trojan horse,* and *vaccine.*

Visio A popular business graphics program, created by Visio, that creates business diagrams such as flowcharts, organization charts, block diagrams, and project timelines. Professional versions include support for external database access and technical symbols.

Visual BASIC A *high-level programming language* for developing applications designed to run in *Microsoft Windows 95*. Using Visual BASIC, the *programmer* uses a screen designer to set up the contents of a window, selecting control objects (*pushbuttons,* list boxes, and so on) from an on-screen *toolbox* and placing them in your design. The programmer then writes procedures for the objects using a modern version of *BASIC.*

Visual BASIC for Applications (VBA) A version of the *Visual BASIC* programming language included with *Microsoft Windows 95* applications, such as *Microsoft Excel*; also called Visual BASIC Programming System, Applications Edition. Visual BASIC for Applications is used to create procedures as simple as basic *macros* and as complex as custom *application programs,* complete with *dialog boxes, menus, pushbuttons,* and unique commands. See *event-driven environment.*

Visual Café   A *programming environment* for developing applications in Java, created by *Symantec.* Advanced features of the package include a class editor for editing general versions of objects (classes), visual drag-and-drop application development that enables programmers to quickly build user interfaces, a real-time interpreter and debugger, and a compiler that builds stand-alone Java applications that execute up to 25 times faster than previous Java code.

VL–Bus   See *VESA local bus.*

VLSI   See *very large scale integration.*

voice actuation   Computer recognition and acceptance of spoken commands as instructions to be processed. See *speech recognition.*

voice–capable modem   A *modem* that, like a *fax switch,* can distinguish between *fax* transmissions, *data* transmissions, and voice telephone calls, and then route each to the proper device. Voice-capable modems can serve as *voice-mail* systems for small offices.

voice coil actuator   See *servo-voice coil actuator.*

voice mail   In *office automation,* a communications system in which voice messages are transformed into digital form and stored on a *network.* When the person to whom the message is directed logs on to the system and discovers that a message is waiting, the system plays the message. Synonymous with voice store and forward.

voice recognition   See *speech recognition.*

voice store and forward   See *voice mail.*

voice synthesis   The audible output of computer-based text in the form of synthesized speech that people can recognize and understand. Voice synthesis is much easier to achieve than voice recognition; you can equip virtually any personal computer to read *ASCII text* aloud with few errors. This capability has helped blind people gain increased access to written works not recorded on cassette tape. See *speech recognition.*

volatility   The susceptibility of a computer's *random-access memory (RAM)* to the complete loss of stored information if power is interrupted.

volume   In *MS-DOS,* a unit of storage that is normally the same as a disk (floppy or hard); however, it is possible to map volumes to more than one disk, and a disk can likewise contain two or more volumes.

volume label   In *MS-DOS,* an identifying name assigned to a disk and displayed on the first line of a *directory.* The name can be no longer than 11 characters and is assigned when you *format* the disk.

V
W

von Neumann bottleneck   The limitation on processing speed imposed by computer architectures linking a single *microprocessor* with *memory.* John von Neumann discovered that a program will spend more time retrieving data from memory than it spends actually processing it. One proposed solution to the von Neumann bottleneck is *parallel processing,* in which a program's tasks are divided among two or more microprocessors. Existing *programming languages* and techniques, however, can't handle parallel processing very well. The *Pentium* microprocessor minimizes the von Neumann bottleneck by incorporating separate *caches* for data and instructions. See *stored program concept.*

VR   See *virtual reality.*

VRAM   See *video RAM.*

W3   See *World Wide Web (WWW)*.

W3C   See *World Wide Web Consortium*.

WAIS   See *Wide Area Information Server*.

wait state   A *microprocessor clock cycle* in which nothing occurs. A wait state is programmed into a *computer system* to allow other components, such as *random-access memory (RAM)*, to catch up with the *central processing unit (CPU)*. The number of wait states depends on the speed of the processor in relation to the speed of memory. Wait states can be eliminated—resulting in a "zero wait state" machine—by using fast (but expensive) *cache memory, interleaved memory*, page-mode RAM, or static RAM chips.

wallpaper   See *desktop pattern*.

warm boot   A system restart performed after the system has been powered and operating. A warm boot is performed by using a special key combination or by pressing a *reset button*, while a *cold boot* involves actually turning the big red *switch* off and on. See *programmer's switch*.

warm link   In Object Linking and Embedding *(OLE)* and dynamic data exchange (DDE), a dynamic link that's updated only when you explicitly request the update by choosing an update link command. Warm links have also been available in *Lotus 1-2-3* since Release 2.2 and in *Quattro Pro* since version 1.0. See *hot link*.

WAV   A sound file format jointly developed by *Microsoft* and *IBM*, and prominently featured in *Microsoft Windows 95's* accessories for storing wave sounds. The format's specification calls for both 8-bit and 16-bit storage formats, in both monaural and stereo, but most of the WAV sounds you'll encounter on the *Internet* are 8-bit mono sounds.

waveform audio   See *waveform sound*.

waveform sound   Like *MIDI sound*, a type of digitized audio information. Waveform sound, especially when recorded with 16-bit *resolution*, can produce startlingly good fidelity, but it takes up monstrous amounts of storage space. Each minute of sound recorded in the *Microsoft Windows 95* WAV format, for example, takes up 27*MB*.

wave sound   One of the two types of sounds recorded in computer-readable files; contains a digitized recording of an actual sound. Wave sound files tend to be voluminous; in the Windows *.WAV format, for example, as many as 5*M* of storage may be required to store a four-minute popular tune. Popular *Internet* WAV file formats include *AU, AIFF,* and *MPEG* sounds. See *MIDI sound.*

wave table synthesis   A method, far superior to *FM synthesis,* of generating and reproducing music in a *sound board.* Wave table synthesis uses a prerecorded sample of dozens of orchestral instruments to determine how particular notes played on those instruments should sound.

web   In the *World Wide Web (WWW)* or any *hypertext* system, a set of related documents that together make up a hypertext presentation. The documents do not have to be stored on the same *computer system,* but they are explicitly interlinked, generally by providing internal *navigation buttons.* A web generally includes a *welcome page* that serves as the top-level document *(home page)* of the web. Synonymous (in practical usage) with site.

Web browser   A program that runs on an *Internet*-connected computer and provides access to the riches of the *World Wide Web (WWW).* Web browsers are of two kinds: text-only browsers and graphical Web browsers. The two most popular graphical browsers are *Microsoft Internet Explorer* and *Netscape Navigator,* the browser component of *Netscape Communicator.* Graphical browsers are preferable because you can see *in-line images,* fonts, and document layouts.

WebCrawler   A *search engine* for locating *World Wide Web (WWW)* documents that is based at the University of Washington and supported by DealerNet, Starwave Corporation, and Satchel Sports. Relying on an automated search routine (called a *spider)* that indexes all the words in the documents it finds, WebCrawler is slow to compile its database (which contains only 300,000 documents at this writing). However, the fact that it retrieves and indexes all the words in the document makes it unusually accurate when you're searching for words that may not appear in document titles or headings.

V
W

Web server In the *World Wide Web (WWW)*, a *program* that accepts requests for information framed according to the *HyperText Transfer Protocol (HTTP)*. The server processes these requests and sends the requested document. Web servers have been developed for most computer systems, including *Unix* workstations, *Microsoft Windows 95* and *Microsoft Windows NT* systems, and *Macintoshes*. See *HyperText Transfer Protocol Daemon (httpd), MacHTTP, Netscape Commerce Server* and *Netscape Messaging Server*.

Web site In the *World Wide Web (WWW)*, a *computer system* that runs a *Web server* and has been set up for publishing documents on the Web.

weight The overall lightness or darkness of a *typeface* design, or the gradations of lightness to darkness within a font family. A type style can be light or dark, and within a type style, you can see several gradations of weight: extra light, light, semi–light, regular, medium, semi–bold, bold, extra bold, and ultra–bold. See *book weight*.

Weitek coprocessors Numeric coprocessors Created for computers that use *Intel 80386* or *80486* microprocessors. These coprocessors offer faster performance than the *Intel 80387* and 80487SX and are widely used for professional *computer-aided design (CAD)* applications. The Weitek 4167 can perform floating-point math three to five times faster than a 486 alone, but programs often require special modifications to use Weitek coprocessors.

welcome page In the *World Wide Web (WWW)*, a Web-accessible document that is meant to be the point of entry to a series of related documents, called a *web*. For example, a company's welcome page typically includes the company's logo, a brief description of the web's purpose, and links to the additional documents available at that site. Welcome pages are also called *home pages* because they are the home page (the top-level document) of the series of related documents that makes up the web.

well-known port An *Internet* port address that has been permanently linked with a certain application by the *Internet Assigned Numbers Authority (IANA)*. A *port address* enables the *TCP/IP* software to direct incoming data to a certain application. The port address 80, for example, directs the incoming data to a Web server. Because IANA fixes port numbers for frequently used Internet applications (such as *Telnet, File Transfer Protocol [FTP],* and the *World Wide Web [WWW]*), it is not generally necessary to include port addresses when you are trying to locate data; the *domain name* is sufficient.

well-structured programming language A *programming language* that encourages programmers to create logically organized programs that are easy to read, debug, and update. Poorly structured programming languages allow *programmers* to create illogically organized programs, based on *spaghetti code,* that are almost impossible to debug or alter. *Modular programming* languages encourage *structured programming:* clear, logical code by allowing the programmer to break down the program into separate modules, each of which accomplishes just one function. More recently, *object-oriented programming (OOP) languages* (such as SmallTalk and *C++)* have introduced another approach to modularity. The languages are structured by a hierarchy of objects, such as option buttons, *dialog boxes,* and *windows.*

what-if analysis In *spreadsheet* programs, an important form of data exploration in which you change key variables to see the effect on the results of the computation. What-if analysis provides businesspeople and professionals with an effective vehicle for exploring the effect of alternative strategies.

what-you-see-is-what-you-get (WYSIWYG) A design philosophy for word processing programs in which formatting commands directly affect the text on-screen, so the screen shows the appearance of the printed text. See *embedded formatting command.*

white pages A computer version of the white pages section of a telephone book. White pages services are set up by organizations (such as corporations or universities) to provide computer assistance to people looking for a person's phone number or e-mail address. Many white pages services are accessible via the *Internet.* See *X.500.*

white space The portion of the page not printed. Good page design involves the use of white space to balance the areas that receive text and graphics, and also to improve the readability of the document.

white-write technique See *print engine.*

whois A *Unix* utility, run by a *whois server,* that enables users to locate the *e-mail* address, and often the telephone number and other information, of people who have an account on the same computer system. In Novell *networks,* a command that displays a list of all users logged on the network.

whois server An *Internet* program that accepts incoming requests for *e-mail* addresses and telephone numbers, and tries to provide this information by searching a database of account holders. See *whois.*

Wide Area Information Server (WAIS) A *Unix*-based system linked to the *Internet;* also, a program that permits the user to search worldwide archives for resources based on a series of *keywords.* Users familiar with personal computer *database* programs are likely to find WAIS a less-than-satisfactory search tool because WAIS generates a list of documents that's sure to contain many "false drops" (irrelevant documents that don't really pertain to the search subject). See *anonymous FTP.*

wide area network (WAN) A *network* that uses high-speed, long-distance communications networks or satellites to connect computers over distances greater than those traversed by local area networks (LANs)—about two miles. See *ARPANET, Fidonet,* and *Internet.*

wide SCSI An *SCSI-2* specification that enables the use of a 16-bit data bus, doubling the *data transfer rate* of SCSI drives and devices.

widow A formatting flaw in which the last line of a paragraph appears alone at the top of a new column or page. Most word processing and page layout programs suppress widows and *orphans;* better programs let you switch widow/orphan control on and off and to choose the number of lines at the beginning or end of the paragraph that you want kept together.

wild card Characters (such as asterisks and question marks) that stand for any other character that may appear in the same place. *DOS* and *Microsoft Windows* use two wild cards: the asterisk (*), which stands for any character or characters, and the question mark (?), which stands for any single character.

Win32 The 32-bit Windows *application programming interface (API).* Programs that are written following the Win32 API guidelines will run only on *Microsoft Windows 95* and *Microsoft Windows NT.*

Win32s A *freeware* utility, developed by *Microsoft Corporation,* that upgrades Microsoft Windows 3.1 and Microsoft Windows for Workgroups 3.11 so they can run *32-bit applications.*

Winchester drive See *hard disk.*

window A rectangular, on-screen frame through which you can view a *document,* worksheet, *database,* drawing, or *application program.* In most programs, only one window is displayed. This window functions as a frame through which you can see your document, database, or worksheet. A windowing environment carries multiple windowing even further by enabling you to run two or more applications concurrently, each in its own window. See *application program interface (API), Graphical User Interface (GUI),* and *Microsoft Windows 95.*

windowing environment An *application program interface (API)* that provides the features commonly associated with a graphical user interface (GUI) (such as windows, pull-down menus, on-screen fonts, and scroll bars or scroll boxes). A windowing environment makes these features available to programmers of application packages. See *Graphical User Interface (GUI)* and *Microsoft Windows.*

window menu In *Microsoft Windows 95,* a synonym for *control menu.*

Windows See *Microsoft Windows 3.1, Microsoft Windows 95,* and *Microsoft Windows NT.*

Windows 3.1 See *Microsoft Windows 3.1.*

Windows 95 See *Microsoft Windows 95.*

Windows 95 keyboard A keyboard that contains special keys that activate certain menus and commands in Windows 95, in addition to all the normal computer keyboard keys.

Windows accelerator See *graphics accelerator board.*

Windows application An application that can run only within the Microsoft Windows windowing environment, taking full advantage of Windows' *application program interface (API),* its capability to display *fonts* and *graphics* on-screen, and its capability to exchange data dynamically between applications. See *non-Windows application*.

Windows Explorer   In *Microsoft Windows 95,* a file management program that replaces the Windows 3.1 File Manager. Most users will find it easier to manage files and programs by clicking the *My Computer* icon.

Windows Metafile Format (WMF)   An object-oriented (vector) graphics *file format* for *Microsoft Windows 95* applications. All Windows applications that support *object-oriented graphics* can read graphics files saved with the WMF format.

Windows NT   See *Microsoft Windows NT.*

Windows printer   See *Graphical Device Interface (GDI) printer.*

WinFax Pro   A popular fax program, created by Delrina and now marketed by *Symantec,* that enables Windows users to send and receive faxes from Windows applications.

Winsock   An open standard that specifies how a dynamic link library (DLL) should be written to provide *TCP/IP* support for *Microsoft Windows 95* systems. An outgrowth of a "birds of a feather" session at a *Unix* conference, the Winsock standard—currently in Version 2.0—is actively supported by *Microsoft Corporation.*

Winstone   A *benchmark* test developed by Ziff-Davis Publishing's PC Labs that attempts to simulate real-world conditions and test all aspects of a system's performance. By making a computer system execute *scripts* in more than a dozen popular *application programs,* the Winstone gives an idea of how well a system performs.

WinVN   A respected, public domain *Usenet newsreader* for *Microsoft Windows 95* and earlier Windows versions. Originally developed by Mark Riordan, this *threaded newsreader* is now developed and supported by programmers at NASA's Kennedy Space Center.

wireless wide area network   A radio network for computers equipped with *transceivers* that are used to receive (or, in two-way systems, to send and receive) *e-mail* messages, news broadcasts, and *files.* Coverage is now limited to a few large metropolitan areas, but future satellite-based systems, which offer saturation coverage, may make wireless data communications more common.

wizard An interactive help utility, originally developed by Microsoft for its Windows applications (and now widely imitated). The wizard guides the user through each step of a multistep operation, offering helpful information and explaining options along the way.

WMF A file-name extension indicating that the file contains a graphic saved in the Windows Metafile Format (WMF).

word A unit of information, composed of characters, *bits* or *bytes,* that's treated as an entity and can be stored in one location. In *word processing programs,* a word is defined as including the space, if any, at the end of the characters.

Word See *Microsoft Word.*

WordPad In *Microsoft Windows 95,* a small *word processing program* that can directly read the files created by *Microsoft Word* and Microsoft Write. The program replaces the Notepad and Write accessories included with Windows 3.1.

WordPerfect A full-featured *word processor* published by Corel and featured in that firm's *Corel WordPerfect Suite. MS-DOS* versions of WordPerfect once dominated the word processing marketplace but the program was very late to make an effective transition to Microsoft Windows, leaving the market wide open for *Microsoft Word.* The program still prevails in certain niche markets, such as law offices, due to its provision of special-purpose word processing functions.

word processing Using the computer to create, edit, proofread, format, and print documents. By a wide margin, word processing is the most popular computer application and is probably responsible for the dramatic growth of the personal computer industry. Unlike typewriters, computer word processing programs allow users to change text before printing it and provide powerful editing tools. The most popular word processing programs include WordPerfect and Microsoft Word.

word processing program A program that transforms a computer into a tool for creating, editing, proofreading, formatting, and printing documents, such as *Lotus Word Pro, Microsoft*

Word, or *WordPerfect. Word processing* programs top the best-seller lists, and for a simple reason: Of all computer applications, people have found word processing the most useful. Modern word processors include many features to make writers' and editors' jobs easier. Search-and-replace features help ease revising documents, while spell-checkers and thesauruses ensure clean, readable output. Various formatting tools make words graphically appealing. With the rise of *graphical user interface (GUI)* systems such as the *Macintosh* and IBM PC-compatible computers running *Microsoft Windows 95,* programs acquired the capability to display fonts and font size choices on-screen. Today's word processing software can take on light desktop publishing duties, such as newsletter production. See *what-you-see-is-what-you-get (WYSIWYG).*

word wrap　A feature of *word processing programs,* and other programs that include text-editing features, that wraps words down to the beginning of the next line if they go beyond the right margin.

workaround　A way of circumventing a *bug* without actually fixing it. Workarounds may be desirable when time is short or *programmers* are unavailable.

workbook　In a *spreadsheet* program, a collection of related *worksheets* kept in a single *file.* Workbooks make it easy to create *hot links* among worksheets.

workgroup　A small group of employees assigned to work together on a specific project. Much of the work accomplished in large businesses is done in workgroups. If this work is to be done well and quickly, the workgroup needs to communicate effectively and share resources. *Personal computer* technology, especially when linked in a *local area network (LAN),* is thought to enhance workgroup productivity by giving the group additional communication channels (in the form of *e-mail*), facilities for the group editing of *documents* (such as *redlining* and *strikethrough*), and shared access to a common *database.*

working model　See *crippled version.*

worksheet　In *spreadsheet programs,* the two-dimensional matrix of rows and columns within which you enter headings, *values,* and formulas. The worksheet resembles the ledger sheet used in accounting. Synonymous with spreadsheet.

worksheet window   In spreadsheet programs, the portion of the worksheet visible on-screen. With up to 8,192 rows and 256 columns, modern electronic spreadsheets are larger than a two-car garage in size. The worksheet window displays only a small portion of the total area potentially available.

workstation   In a *local area network (LAN),* a desktop computer that runs *application programs* and serves as an access point to the network. See *file server, personal computer (PC),* and *professional workstation.*

World Wide Web (WWW)   A global *hypertext* system that uses the *Internet* as its transport mechanism. In a hypertext system, you navigate by clicking hyperlinks, which display another document (which also contains hyperlinks). Most Web documents are created using the *HTML,* a markup language that is easy to learn and will soon be supplanted by automated tools. Incorporating *hypermedia* (graphics, sounds, animations, and video), the Web has become the ideal medium for publishing information on the Internet. See *Web browser.*

World Wide Web Consortium (W3C)   An independent standards body, composed of university researchers and industry practitioners, that is devoted to setting effective standards to promote the orderly growth of the World Wide Web. Housed at the Massachusetts Institute of Technology (MIT), W3C sets standards for *HTML* and many other aspects of Web usage.

worm   A *virus* that's designed to find all *data* in memory or on disk and alter any data it encounters. The alteration may be to change certain characters to numbers or to swap bytes of stored memory. A few programs may still run, but usually data is irretrievably corrupted.

WORM   See *write-once, read-many.*

wrap-around type   Type contoured so it surrounds a *graphic.* Because wrap-around type is harder to read than noncontoured type, use wrap-around type sparingly.

write   A fundamental processing operation in which the *central processing unit (CPU)* records information in the computer's *random-access memory (RAM)* or the computer's *secondary storage* media, such as disk drives. In personal computing, the term most often refers to storing information on disks.

write-back cache   A type of *cache memory* that stores information written to memory as well as information read from memory. Write-back caches, particularly those used in *secondary caches,* are considered to be technically superior to *write-through caches.*

write-black engine   See *print engine.*

write head   See *read/write head.*

write-once, read-many (WORM)   An optical disk drive with storage capacities of up to 1 *terabyte.* After you write data to the disk, it becomes a read-only storage medium. WORM drives can store huge amounts of information and have been touted as an excellent technology for organizations that need to publish large *databases* internally (such as collections of engineering drawings or technical documentation). The advent of fully read/write-capable optical disk drives, however, has greatly diminished the appeal of WORM technology. See *CD-ROM* and *erasable optical disk drive.*

write precompensation   A *hard disk's* upward adjustment of the magnetic field that the *read/write head* uses to record data near the *spindle,* where data must be closely packed. The disk *geometry* includes the *cylinder* at which write precompensation begins.

write-protect   To modify a *file* or disk so no one can edit or erase its data.

write-protect notch   On a *5¼-inch floppy disk,* a small notch cut out of the disk's protective jacket that, when covered by a piece of tape, prevents the disk drive from performing erasures or write operations to the disk.

write-protect tab   On a *3½-inch floppy disk,* a tab located in the disk's upper-left corner as you hold the disk with the label facing away from you. When you slide the tab up to open the hole, you've write-protected the disk.

write-through cache   A *cache memory* scheme in which memory read operations are cached, but not memory write operations. Write operations are cached in *random-access memory (RAM),* which is much slower than cache memory. Experts consider write-through caches to be inferior to *write-back* caches, which record both read-and-write operations.

write–white engine   See *print engine*.

WWW   See *World Wide Web*.

WYSIWYG   Acronym for *what-you-see-is-what-you-get* (pronounced "wiz–zee–wig").

V
W

x2 An unratified *modulation protocol* for *modems* transferring data at 56.6 Kbps. At this writing there is a competing but incompatible protocol called *K56Plus*.

X.25 An international standard for a *packet-switching network* that is widely used in *public data networks (PDNs)*.

X.400 An international standard, maintained by the *ITU-TSS*, for *e-mail* and fax transmissions.

X.500 An international standard for *e-mail* directories, maintained by *ITU-TSS*, that can be maintained by organizations to facilitate looking up users' e-mail addresses. See *white pages*.

X.509 An international standard for digital *certificates*, maintained by *ITU-TSS*, that can be used for *strong authentication*. The latest version, X.509V3, helps to assure interoperability among software employing certificates.

x86 The *microprocessor* architecture, developed by *Intel Corporation*, that is *binary compatible* with *MS-DOS* and *Microsoft Windows 95* programs.

x-axis In a graph, the categories axis, which usually is the horizontal axis. See *bar graph, column graph, y-axis,* and *z-axis*.

Xbase A generic term denoting any of the *programming* environments derived from the original *dBase programming language* created by Ashton–Tate, Inc. Because the word dBase is a registered trademark, the term Xbase has come to be used as a description for any programming language based on the dBase programming language. Examples of the Xbase language would include FoxPro, dBase, Clipper, Arago, and Force.

XCFN See *external function*.

XCMD See *eXternal CoMmanD*.

XENIX An *operating system* developed by *Microsoft Corporation* that conforms to the Unix System V Interface Definition (SVID) and runs on *IBM PC-compatible* computers.

XGA See *eXtended Graphics Array*.

x-height   In *typography,* the height of a *font's* lowercase letters, measured from the *baseline* up. Because many fonts have unusually long or short *ascenders* and *descenders,* the x-height is a better measurement of the actual size of a font than the type size, measured in points.

XMODEM   An asynchronous *File Transfer Protocol (FTP)* for *personal computers* that makes the error-free transmission of files through the telephone system easier. Developed by Ward Christiansen for 8-bit computers running *Control Program for Microprocessors (CP/M)* and placed in the public domain, the XMODEM protocol is included in most personal computer *communications programs* and commonly is used to download files from *bulletin board systems (BBSs).*

XMODEM-1K   A *data transmission protocol* that retains *XMODEM/CRC's* error-checking capabilities but has higher *throughput.* By performing a *cyclic redundancy check (CRC)* only on 1024-*byte blocks* of data, transmission overhead is reduced. See *YMODEM* and *ZMODEM.*

XMODEM/CRC   A version of the *XMODEM data transmission protocol* that reduces *throughput* but also reduces errors. XMODEM/CRC performs a *cyclic redundancy check (CRC)* on every two *bytes* transmitted—a more reliable scheme than the *checksum* technique employed by *XMODEM.* See *XMODEM-1K, YMODEM,* and *ZMODEM.*

XMS   See *eXtended Memory Specification.*

XON/XOFF handshaking   See *handshaking.*

X Windows   A *network windowing environment* commonly used on *Unix*-based *workstations.* X Windows is a *device-independent application program interface (API)* that can run under *operating systems* ranging from disk operating systems to a *mainframe* operating system. It's used most frequently on Unix machines. Unlike *Microsoft Windows 95* and other PC-based windowing environments, X Windows is designed for use on a *minicomputer*-based network.

x-y graph   See *scatter diagram.*

Yahoo In the *World Wide Web (WWW)*, a popular subject tree created by David Filo and Jerry Yang of the Department of Computer Science at Stanford University. With a keen eye for the popular as well as the useful, Filo and Yang have created a directory of Web resources that currently includes nearly 35,000 Web documents. In 1995, Yahoo moved out of Stanford to www.yahoo.com, where it is supported by advertising. Yahoo reportedly performs 10 million searches each week.

y-axis In a graph, the values axis, which normally is vertical. See *bar graph, column graph, x-axis,* and *z-axis.*

Yellow Book An *International Standards Organization (ISO)* standard that describes the way data is encoded on CD-ROMs. The Yellow Book standard includes CD-XA specifications.

YMCK See *CMYK.*

YMODEM A *file transfer protocol (ftp)* that is an improved version of *XMODEM-1K.* YMODEM transfers data in 1024-*byte blocks* and performs a *cyclic redundancy check (CRC)* on each *frame.* Also, YMODEM supports sending more than one file in sequence. See *YMODEM-g* and *ZMODEM.*

YMODEM-g A *file transfer protocol (ftp)* that leaves error-checking to protocols encoded on modem hardware, such as *V.42* and *MNP4,* and is best used with *high-speed modems* in low *line noise* conditions. *ZMODEM* is usually a better choice than YMODEM-g.

yoke The collection of electromagnets precisely arrayed around the outside of a *cathode ray tube (CRT).* The yoke, controlled by the *monitor* circuitry and *video adapter,* steers electrons from the *electron guns* to the proper *pixels* on the *display.* If the yoke gets out of alignment, the monitor is useless. Make sure any monitor you buy has a 30-day guarantee, especially if you purchase by mail.

Z39.50 A protocol for the *network* retrieval of bibliographic data that was developed by the National Information Standards Organization (NISO), a unit of the *American National Standards Institute (ANSI)*. Using a Z39.50-compatible application, a user can frame a query that can be processed on any other computer attached to a *network,* even if it is made by a different manufacturer. The protocol precisely specifies the format of the query in a way that is ideal for searching bibliographic databases, such as library card catalogues. Z39.50 applications are being developed to allow Internet applications to retrieve data from databases stored on IBM *mainframe* computers, which house most of the online library catalogues currently in existence.

Zapf Dingbats A set of decorative symbols developed by Herman Zapf, a German typeface designer. Dingbats originally were ornamental symbols used between columns or, more commonly, between paragraphs, to provide separation.

z-axis In a three-dimensional graphic image, the third dimension, usually depth. See *three-dimensional graph, x-axis,* and *y-axis.*

zero-insertion force (ZIF) package A socket for large *chips,* such as *microprocessors,* that makes it easy to remove and install *parts* without bending pins. By raising a lever at the side of the ZIF package, the pins are released and the chip may be easily removed. When another chip is installed, the lever may be moved back to clamp the pins in place again.

zero-slot LAN A *local area network (LAN)* designed to use a computer's *serial port* rather than require the user to buy a *network interface card.*

zero wait state computer An *IBM PC-compatible* computer with memory speed optimized by using a scheme such as *cache memory, interleaved memory, page-mode random-access memory* (RAM), or static random access memory *(SRAM)* chips, so the microprocessor doesn't have to wait—enter a *wait state*—for the memory to catch up with processing operations.

ZIF See *zero-insertion force (ZIF) package.*

ZIF socket   See *zero-insertion force (ZIF) package.*

ZIP   The *MS-DOS file extension* usually attached to a file, generated by PKZIP, that contains several compressed files. ZIP files often are found on *bulletin board systems (BBSs).*

Zip drive   A popular *removable storage* medium, created by *Iomega Corporation,* that provides 100M of storage on relatively inexpensive, portable disks. Not much larger than floppy disks, Zip cartridges are easily transported, mailed, or stored. Currently, Zip drives are emerging as a de facto standard for backup storage devices on personal computers, and conceivably could replace the $3^1/_2$-inch *floppy disk,* which does not offer sufficient storage to be useful in today's computing environment.

ZMODEM   An asynchronous *file transfer protocol (ftp)* for personal computers that makes the error-free transmission of computer files with a *modem* easier. ZMODEM is a very fast protocol that lets you use wild-card file names for transfers. It's also well liked because you can resume the transfer of a file if the first attempt is interrupted before completion. Next to *XMODEM,* ZMODEM is the most popular file transfer protocol and is included in most communications applications.

zone   In a *local area network (LAN),* a subgroup of networked computers set aside and named by the network administrator so these computers can be treated as a group. If an administrator sets up zones called Marketing, Design, and Manufacturing, for example, someone in manufacturing can address an *e-mail* message to everyone in marketing by sending the message to the marketing zone.

zone–bit recording   A *multiple zone recording (MZR),* in Seagate Technologies parlance.

Zoned Constant Angular Velocity (ZCAV)   See *multiple zone recording (MZR).*

zoom   To enlarge a *window* or part of a document or image so it fills the screen.

zoom box   In a *graphical user interface (GUI),* a box—usually positioned on the window border—that you click to zoom the window to full size or restore the window to normal size. Synonymous with *maximize button.*